BEYOND BLACK & WHITE

SAGE was founded in 1965 by Sara Miller McCune to support the dissemination of usable knowledge by publishing innovative and high-quality research and teaching content. Today, we publish over 900 journals, including those of more than 400 learned societies, more than 800 new books per year, and a growing range of library products including archives, data, case studies, reports, and video. SAGE remains majority-owned by our founder, and after Sara's lifetime will become owned by a charitable trust that secures our continued independence.

Los Angeles | London | New Delhi | Singapore | Washington DC | Melbourne

BEYOND BLACK & WHITE

A READER ON CONTEMPORARY RACE RELATIONS

Edited by

ZULEMA VALDEZ

University of California, Merced

Los Angeles | London | New Delhi
Singapore | Washington DC | Melbourne

FOR INFORMATION:

SAGE Publications, Inc.
2455 Teller Road
Thousand Oaks, California 91320
E-mail: order@sagepub.com

SAGE Publications Ltd.
1 Oliver's Yard
55 City Road
London EC1Y 1SP
United Kingdom

SAGE Publications India Pvt. Ltd.
B 1/I 1 Mohan Cooperative Industrial Area
Mathura Road, New Delhi 110 044
India

SAGE Publications Asia-Pacific Pte. Ltd.
3 Church Street
#10-04 Samsung Hub
Singapore 049483

Acquisitions Editor: Jeff Lasser
Editorial Assistant: Alexandra Croell
eLearning Editor: Gabrielle Piccininni
Production Editor: Tracy Buyan
Copy Editor: Erin Livingston
Typesetter: Hurix Systems Pvt. Ltd.
Proofreader: Pam Suwinsky
Cover Designer: Scott Van Atta
Marketing Manager: Kara Kindstrom

Printed in the United States of America

Library of Congress Cataloging-in-Publication Data

Names: Valdez, Zulema, editor.

Title: Beyond black and white : a reader on contemporary race relations / [edited by] Zulema Valdez, University of California, Merced.

Description: Thousand Oaks, California : SAGE, 2017. | Includes bibliographical references.

Identifiers: LCCN 2016013696 | ISBN 9781506306940 (pbk. : alk. paper)

Subjects: LCSH: United States—Race relations—21st century. | Minorities—United States—History—21st century.

Classification: LCC E184.A1 B46 2017 | DDC 305.800973—dc23 LC record available at https://lccn.loc.gov/2016013696

This book is printed on acid-free paper.

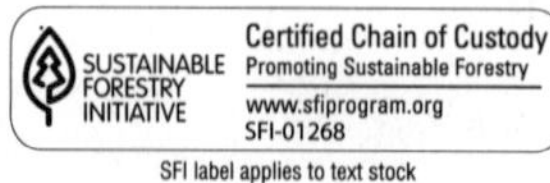

16 17 18 19 20 10 9 8 7 6 5 4 3 2 1

Contents

Preface ix

Acknowledgments xiii

About the Editor xiv

About the Contributors xv

PART I. THEORIES OF RACE AND ETHNICITY

1. **A Critical and Comprehensive Sociological Theory of Race and Racism** 1
   Reading by Tanya Golash-Boza
2. **The Theory of Racial Formation** 15
   Reading by Michael Omi and Howard Winant
3. **Rethinking Racism: Toward a Structural Interpretation** 27
   Reading by Eduardo Bonilla-Silva

PART II. THEORIES OF ASSIMILATION

4. **Rethinking Assimilation Theory for a New Era of Immigration** 44
   Reading by Richard Alba and Victor Nee
5. **Segmented Assimilation and Minority Cultures of Mobility** 71
   Reading by Kathryn M. Neckerman, Prudence Carter, and Jennifer Lee

PART III. RACE AND BIOLOGY REVISITED

6. **Race as Biology Is Fiction, Racism as a Social Problem Is Real: Anthropological and Historical Perspectives on the Social Construction of Race** 85
   Reading by Audrey Smedley and Brian D. Smedley

7. **Back to the Future? The Emergence of a Geneticized Conceptualization of Race in Sociology** 99
   Reading by Reanne Frank

PART IV. COLOR-BLIND AND OTHER RACISMS

8. **Unmasking Racism: Halloween Costuming and Engagement of the Racial Other** 111
   Reading by Jennifer C. Mueller, Danielle Dirks, and Leslie H. Picca

9. **Invisibility in the Color-Blind Era: Examining Legitimized Racism against Indigenous Peoples** 128
   Reading by Dwanna L. Robertson

PART V. BOUNDARY MAKING AND BELONGING

10. **Who Are We? Producing Group Identity through Everyday Practices of Conflict and Discourse** 142
    Reading by Jennifer A. Jones

11. **Illegality as a Source of Solidarity and Tension in Latino Families** 156
    Reading by Leisy J. Abrego

12. **Are Second-Generation Filipinos "Becoming" Asian American or Latino? Historical Colonialism, Culture and Panethnicity** 171
    Reading by Anthony C. Ocampo

PART VI. COLORISM

13. **The Persistent Problem of Colorism: Skin Tone, Status, and Inequality** 186
    Reading by Margaret Hunter

14. **The Case for Taking White Racism *and* White Colorism More Seriously** 199
    Reading by Lance Hannon, Anna DalCortivo, and Kirstin Mohammed

PART VII. EDUCATION AND SCHOOLING

15. "I'm Watching Your Group": Academic Profiling and Regulating Students Unequally 208

Reading by Gilda L. Ochoa

16. Race, Age, and Identity Transformations in the Transition from High School to College for Black and First-Generation White Men 223

Reading by Amy C. Wilkins

PART VIII. POLITICAL PARTICIPATION AND COOPERATION

17. Out of the Shadows and Out of the Closet: Intersectional Mobilization and the DREAM Movement 239

Reading by Veronica Terriquez

18. Racial Inclusion or Accommodation? Expanding Community Boundaries among Asian American Organizations 254

Reading by Dina G. Okamoto and Melanie Jones Gast

19. The Place of Race in Conservative and Far-Right Movements 269

Reading by Kathleen M. Blee and Elizabeth A. Yates

PART IX. SOCIOECONOMIC STATUS AND WORK

20. Negotiating "The Welfare Queen" and "The Strong Black Woman": African American Middle-Class Mothers' Work and Family Perspectives 282

Reading by Dawn Marie Dow

21. Nailing Race and Labor Relations: Vietnamese Nail Salons in Majority–Minority Neighborhoods 297

Reading by Kimberly Kay Hoang

22. Becoming a (Pan)ethnic Attorney: How Asian American and Latino Law Students Manage Dual Identities 311

Reading by Yung-Yi Diana Pan

PART X. HEALTH AND MENTAL HEALTH DISPARITIES

23. Miles to Go before We Sleep: Racial Inequities in Health 326

Reading by David R. Williams

24. **Identity and Mental Health Status among American Indian Adolescents** 339
Reading by Whitney N. Laster Pirtle and Tony N. Brown

25. **Assimilation and Emerging Health Disparities among New Generations of U.S. Children** 357
Reading by Erin R. Hamilton, Jodi Berger Cardoso, Robert A. Hummer, and Yolanda C. Padilla

PART XI. CRIMINALIZATION, DEPORTATION, AND POLICING

26. **The Racialization of Crime and Punishment: Criminal Justice, Color-Blind Racism, and the Political Economy of the Prison Industrial Complex** 371
Reading by Rose M. Brewer and Nancy A. Heitzeg

27. **Mass Deportation at the Turn of the Twenty-First Century** 387
Reading by Tanya Golash-Boza

28. **The Hyper-Criminalization of Black and Latino Male Youth in the Era of Mass Incarceration** 396
Reading by Victor M. Rios

PART XII. INTERRACIAL RELATIONSHIPS AND MULTIRACIALITY

29. **"Nomas Cásate"/"Just Get Married": How a Legalization Pathway Shapes Mixed-Status Relationships** 410
Reading by Laura E. Enriquez

30. **I Wouldn't, but You Can: Attitudes toward Interracial Relationships** 420
Reading by Melissa R. Herman and Mary E. Campbell

31. **Love Is (Color)Blind: Asian Americans and White Institutional Space at the Elite University** 436
Reading by Rosalind S. Chou, Kristen Lee, and Simon Ho

32. **A Postracial Society or a Diversity Paradox? Race, Immigration, and Multiraciality in the Twenty-First Century** 450
Reading by Jennifer Lee and Frank D. Bean

Glossary 464

Preface

The population of the United States is large, diverse, and growing. The U.S. Census Bureau projects that from 2014 to 2060, the American population will reflect an increase of almost 100 million people, from 319 million to 417 million (Colby & Ortman, 2015, p. 1). The racial and ethnic composition of the population, including U.S.-born and foreign born, is also on the rise. The Census Bureau projects that by 2044, the non-Hispanic White population will fall below 50%—what some have described as the moment the United States becomes a "majority–minority" nation—and by 2060, one in five will be foreign born (Colby & Ortman, 2015, p. 9).

Perhaps surprisingly, given the overwhelming national focus on the twelve million undocumented Mexican immigrants that currently reside in the United States, the fastest-growing racial group in the United States is not Latina/o, nor can it be identified by one racial category only. Instead, it falls under the category of *two or more races*, a relatively new racial classification first introduced in Census 2000, associated with those individuals who identify as *biracial* or *multiracial.* Asians make up the second-fastest-growing racial group, followed by Latina/os in third place. In contrast, the Black American population is expected to grow more modestly from now until 2060, increasing the total population by only 1% (from 13% to 14%).

These numbers demonstrate that the mixed-race, Asian, and Latina/o populations in America are on a projected path of phenomenal growth. And yet, social scientists concerned with racial and ethnic relations—and in particular, racial and ethnic inequality or stratification—continue to concentrate their attention on racial differences between non-Hispanic Whites and Blacks, or what has been coined *the Black/White binary.* Classical theory and empirical research has tended to focus on the Black/White binary because of the unique history and legacy of slavery and White racism against Blacks (Perea, 1997) and also because, prior to 1965, the American racial landscape was much less diverse than it is today, due in large part to racist immigration laws that excluded the migration of nonwhites to the United States in significant numbers (Valdez, 2015). Classic works thus focused on racial inequality and disparities between Blacks and Whites or the process of assimilation experienced by White ethnics, such as Italians, Jews, and Germans, when compared to their native-born White counterparts (Gans, 1962; Gordon, 1964). Historically, *scientific racism*, or the belief that Whites were biologically superior to Blacks (Steinberg, 2007), provided the rational to maintain White racial dominance throughout the preindustrial and industrial eras in the United States (Wilson, 1978).

Following World War II, however, a changing economy, polity, and civil society coalesced against the dogma of essential racial difference, ushering in a new conception of race. What was once understood to be fixed, primordial, and rooted in biology was now understood as fluid, ancillary, and embedded in notions of shared culture and history (Omi & Winant, 1994). Thus the meaning of race was redefined from a distinctly biological classification to a cultural or ethnic one. This process, the way in which the meaning of race can change over time, is illustrative of the idea that race is a social construct or the product of a dynamic historical and social context, albeit one that remains stubbornly associated with physical traits and features.

This shift, from "race thinking" to "ethnicity thinking" (Omi & Winant, 1994, p. 96) set the stage for the 1960s civil rights movement (CRM), a political, legal, and social struggle for racial equality that sought to dismantle *de facto* and *de jure* racism in America by targeting its racist and discriminatory laws and policies. Toward this end, the CRM was effective in driving the passage of major legislation that outlawed racial segregation in employment, public places, and housing and terminated antimiscegenation laws. This sociohistorical moment of progressive race politics was reflected in greater racial tolerance and equality of opportunity than in the antebellum or Jim Crow past. Coupled with civil rights legislation was a lifting of restrictive immigration policy. In particular, the Immigration and Naturalization Act of 1965 has been characterized as representing a historical shift in America's race relations toward a more liberal racial democracy. The Act clearly represented a softening from overtly "racially restrictive" policies such as the Chinese Exclusion Act of 1882 and the 1924 Immigration Act, the latter of which implemented a national origins quota system that favored migration from Northern Europe and discriminated against Jewish and Catholic migrants from Southern and Central Europe. The 1965 Act, which, for the most part, remains how U.S. immigration policy is conducted today, was based largely on a race-neutral system that sought to reunite American citizens and permanent legal residents with their families, grant asylum to refugees, and prioritize the entry of highly skilled labor. Following its passage, over 18 million legal immigrants entered the United States, triple the number that preceded the Act, mostly from Latin America, Asia, Africa, and the Caribbean.

In the post–civil rights era, two separate research programs emerged that sought to capture the changes taking place in American racial and ethnic relations. First, race scholars renewed their interest in Black/White inequalities as progressive laws and policies increased social and economic opportunities for Black Americans. For some, this period marked the start of what they believed was the declining significance of race (Wilson, 1978). For example, the earning and income gaps narrowed considerably between Whites and Blacks in this period (Blau & Beller, 1992; Brown, 1984; Shapiro, 2004, p. 7). Accordingly, Black men and women increased their representation in middle-class occupations. In 1960, less than one million Black Americans held middle-class occupations, but by 1980, that number increased to over three million (Shapiro, 2004, pp. 7–8). Nevertheless, persistent and even widening disparities between Blacks and Whites were also observed. Scholars sought to understand why Black Americans failed to make socioeconomic progress relative to Whites, publishing a spate of books on this topic, including *The Truly Disadvantaged* (Wilson, 1987), *Black Wealth/White Wealth* (Oliver & Shapiro, 1997), and *American Apartheid* (Massey & Denton, 1993). These works capitalized on enduring social and economic differences between these two groups that underscored a "linear story of the Black struggle for civil rights" (Perea, 1997, p. 1213). Other, more insidious works sought to rekindle notions of scientific racism and biological inferiority to explain continued disparities (see Herrnstein & Murray, 1996).

Separately, a second set of researchers concerned with the "second wave" of immigrants of color to the United States sought to explain the process of immigrant incorporation and assimilation. Whereas classic assimilation theory detailed a gradual process of integration into the American mainstream—that is, Southern, Central, and European immigrants and their descendants becoming culturally and economically similar to middle-class White Anglo-Saxon Protestants—scholars reconsidered this *straight-line* trajectory for immigrants of color. Alejandro Portes and Min Zhou (1993) have been at the forefront of this paradigm shift in our understanding of how assimilation applies to contemporary (post-1965) immigrants. They argue that today's immigrants face greater challenges to Anglo conformity than those in the past because they are nonwhite and the economy has changed. They introduce segmented assimilation theory to capture this process. In addition to mainstream assimilation, this approach predicts two additional patterns of socioeconomic integration: *ethnic cohesion* (Zhou & Bankston, 1998), a delayed process of assimilation whereby some groups foster and maintain their own coethnic communities within the host society for ease of entry and settlement, which gives way eventually to mainstream assimilation, and *downward assimilation*, which predicts that disadvantaged groups will integrate into "permanent poverty and assimilation into the underclass" (Portes & Zhou, 1993, p. 82). Although the segmented assimilation framework can apply to and account for a variety of trajectories of assimilation in progress for a diverse group of ethnic groups, especially Latina/os and Asians, this approach maintains that an Anglo-conformity trajectory of assimilation remains the gold standard while downplaying the distinct consideration of race in the process of assimilation, especially for Black immigrants and Black Americans. This approach has fallen short of considering seriously how American race relations affect assimilation among racial minorities.

Much contemporary research continues in this vein, asking questions that examine the Black/White binary or the process of incorporation among nonblack people of color. Nevertheless, the growing diversity reflected in the demographic landscape of the United States calls into question this bifurcation of scholarship and is beginning to make an impact on social science research. As undergraduate, graduate, and faculty from diverse backgrounds enter the academy, newer scholarship has begun to focus on the relationships across, between, and within ethnic, racial, and biracial/multiracial groups and how these groups are incorporated into America's highly stratified economy and society. Traditional social science texts and readers have not kept abreast of this newer research, failing to capture the experiences of their diverse student populations in traditional colleges and universities in urban areas, let alone those students attending Hispanic Serving Institutions (HSIs) or Historically Black Colleges and Universities (HBCUs). Instead, teaching materials and resources in the study of race and ethnicity continue to emphasize a narrow examination of ethnic and racial disparities or inequalities from a White/Black or a White/nonwhite perspective—an approach that limits the conversation of racial and ethnic dynamics in the United States. Consequently, students enrolled in courses on racial and ethnic relations, stratification, and inequality tend to understand racial relations as a majority/minority issue only. This notion obfuscates and diminishes inter- and intragroup racial and ethnic minority dynamics and the questions, concerns, and issues surrounding nonwhite relationships—whether racial and ethnic minority groups can be racist or prejudiced against each other; whether power is relegated to Whites only; or whether collaborative or cooperative multiethnic and multiracial projects can effect change, and if so, how.

Beyond Black and White showcases cutting-edge research from eminent and up-and-coming social science scholars who are engaged in the study of racial and ethnic relations from new perspectives and paradigms. The essays in this text consist of theory-driven, empirical research that situates the study of race relations beyond the White/Black binary or White/nonwhite concerns. Some essays have been lightly edited from the original for length. For the sake of readability, I did not demarcate within the essays where such text was omitted. Instead, a note with a reading's original source information will indicate if such edits were made. The text includes twelve sections that each focus on one major area, from theories of race and ethnicity to criminalization, deportation, and policing. Each section includes two to four essays for a total of thirty-two works from innovative scholars in the field. These essays explore a contemporary aspect of inter-/intraracial or ethnic minority relations, reflecting the diverse and changing demographic landscape of today's undergraduate population across American colleges and universities. It is my hope that *Beyond Black and White* introduces students to up-and-coming scholars engaged in innovative research in an effort to engage a new generation of students and inspire them to pursue new directions in racial and ethnic relations research.

References

Blau, F., & Beller, A. (1992). Black–White earnings over the 1970s and 1980s: Gender differences in trends. *Review of Economics and Statistics, 5*(1), 276–286.

Brown, C. (1984). Black–White earnings ratios since the Civil Rights Act of 1964: The importance of labor market dropouts. *Quarterly Journal of Economics, 99*, 31–44.

Colby, S. L., & Ortman, J. M. (2015). *Projections of the size and composition of the U.S. population: 2014–2060.* U.S. Census Bureau, Report Number P25-1143. Washington, DC: U.S. Department of Commerce.

Gans, H. J. (1962). *The urban villagers.* New York, NY: Free Press of Glencoe.

Gordon, M. (1964). *Assimilation in American life: The role of race, religion and national origins.* Oxford, England: Oxford University Press.

Herrnstein, R., & Murray, C. (1996). *The bell curve: Intelligence and class structure in American life.* New York, NY: Free Press.

Massey, D. S., & Denton, N. A. (1993). *American apartheid: Segregation and the making of the underclass.* Cambridge, MA: Harvard University Press.

Oliver, M., & Shapiro, T. (1997). *Black wealth/White wealth: A new perspective on racial inequality.* New York, NY: Routledge.

Omi, M., & Winant, H. (1994). *Racial formations in the United States: From the 1960s to the 1990s.* New York, NY: Routledge.

Portes, A., & Zhou, M. (1993). The new second generation: Segmented assimilation and its variants. *Annals of the American Academy of Political and Social Science, 5*(30), 74–96.

Perea, J. F. (1997). The Black/White binary paradigm of race: The normal science of American racial thought. *California Law Review, 85*(1), 1213–1258.

Shapiro, T. M. (2004). *The hidden cost of being African American: How wealth perpetuates inequality.* Oxford, England: Oxford University Press.

Steinberg, S. (2007). *Race relations: A critique.* Stanford, CA: Stanford University Press.

Valdez, Z. (2015). The abandoned promise of civil rights. *Sociological Forum, 30*(S1), 612–626.

Wilson, W. J. (1978). *The declining significance of race: Blacks and changing American institutions.* Chicago, IL: University of Chicago Press.

Wilson, W. J. (1987). *The truly disadvantaged: The inner city, the underclass, and public policy.* Chicago, IL: University of Chicago Press.

Zhou, M., & Bankston, C. L., III. (1998). *Growing up American: The adaptation of Vietnamese children to American society.* New York, NY: Russell Sage Foundation.

Acknowledgments

I am grateful to have taught at two institutions of higher learning with very different undergraduate populations. The first, Texas A&M University, is often described as a Historically White College/Predominately White Institution (HWC/PWI), whereas the second, my current institution, is designated as a Hispanic-Serving Institution (HIS). The University of California at Merced, like other universities and colleges in California and urban areas more generally, is made up of a diverse student population, including a significant proportion of traditionally underrepresented minority groups, undocumented students, and first-generation college students. My experience in transitioning back to California, and to a campus with such a diverse student population, informed my desire to develop this reader. *Beyond Black and White* attempts to fill what I see as a critical gap in existing readers and anthologies—to identify and showcase compelling and exciting cutting-edge research that moves beyond the Black/White binary in an attempt to better reflect the experiences of students living in and around diverse populations. I am grateful to Jeff Lasser, my publisher at SAGE, for believing in this project, and Alexandra Croell, the editorial assistant for sociology at SAGE, for helping me through the production process.

I am also grateful to the contributors—some who are eminent scholars in the field and others who are just starting out. What they share in common is an eye for uncovering racial and ethnic relations that are often overlooked or understudied. These scholars are committed to developing new empirical and theoretical directions in race research and offer a comparative and relational understanding of racial and ethnic dynamics in the United States. I am thankful for the opportunity to bring together the work of these scholars in this manuscript, which I believe strengthens the value of these separate works and encourages a new, more comprehensive approach to the study of American racial and ethnic relations.

Finally, I thank my family, friends, and colleagues for their support, especially Andrew Yinger and Tanya Golash-Boza; Write-on-Site colleagues Susana Ramirez, Dalia Magaña, and Irenee Beattie; my colleagues at Texas A&M University and UC Merced; and my daily accountability group members, Neha Vora and Vanita Reddy.

~ ~ ~ ~ ~ ~ ~ ~ ~ ~ ~ ~

SAGE acknowledges the following reviewers:

Katherine Everhart, Northern Arizona University

Tomás R. Jiménez, Stanford University

Jose Prado, Sociology Department, California State University, Dominguez Hills

About the Editor

Zulema Valdez is an associate professor of sociology at the University of California, Merced. She is the author of two books on entrepreneurship, *The New Entrepreneurs: How Race, Class and Gender Shape American Enterprise* (Stanford, 2011) and *Entrepreneurs and the Search for the American Dream* (Routledge, 2016). She has published peer-reviewed articles focusing on American race relations, entrepreneurship, intersectionality, social and economic inequality, and health disparities. She has been awarded grants and fellowships from the Ford Foundation, the National Science Foundation, and the Social Science Research Council. Zulema Valdez earned her PhD in sociology from the University of California, Los Angeles. She lives in Mariposa, California, with her husband, two dogs, two cats, and a handful of chickens.

About the Contributors

Leisy J. Abrego is an associate professor in the César E. Chávez Department of Chicana and Chicano Studies at the University of California—Los Angeles. Her expertise is in the areas of families, Central American migration, and lived experiences of immigration policies. She is the author of *Sacrificing Families: Navigating Laws, Labor, and Love across Borders.*

Richard Alba is a distinguished professor at the Graduate Center, CUNY. His books include *Blurring the Color Line* and *Remaking the American Mainstream.*

Frank D. Bean is a Chancellor's Professor of Sociology and the director at the Center for Research on Immigration, Population and Public Policy at the University of California, Irvine. His interests include international migration, demography, racial and ethnic relations, economic sociology, and family. He is the author of *Parents without Papers: The Progress and Pitfalls of Mexican American Integration* (with Susan K. Brown and James D. Bachmeier).

Kathleen M. Blee is a distinguished professor of sociology in the department of sociology at the University of Pittsburgh. Her areas of interest include gender, race and racism, social movements, and sociology of space and place. She is the author of *Democracy in the Making: How Activist Groups Form.*

Eduardo Bonilla-Silva is a professor and chair of the sociology department at Duke University. His areas of interest include racial stratification in the United States. He is the author of *Racism without Racists.*

Tanya Golash-Boza is an associate professor of sociology at the University of California, Merced. Her latest book is *Deported: Immigrant Policing, Disposable Labor and Global Capitalism.*

Rose M. Brewer is the Morse Alumni Distinguished Teaching Professor of African American & African Studies at the University of Minnesota at Twin Cities. She has written extensively on Black families; race, class, and gender; and public policy and social change. She is the author of *Black Radical Theory and Practice: Gender, Race, and Class.*

Tony N. Brown is an associate professor of sociology and the associate director of the Center for Research on Health Disparities at Vanderbilt University. His research and teaching interests include race and racism, social psychology, and the sociology of mental health.

Mary E. Campbell is an associate professor of sociology at Texas A&M University. Her interests include racial and ethnic relations and identity, social inequality, and social demography.

Jodi Berger Cardoso is an assistant professor in the Graduate College of Social Work at the University of Houston. Her research interests include cultural stressors in Latina/o immigrants and their children.

Prudence Carter is the dean of the Graduate School of Education at the University of California, Berkeley. She is the author of *Stubborn Roots: Race, Culture, and Inequality in U.S. and South African Schools.*

Rosalind S. Chou is an assistant professor of sociology at Georgia State University. She is the author of *The Myth of the Model Minority: Asian Americans Facing Racism* (with Joe R. Feagin) and *Asian Americans on Campus.*

Anna DalCortivo is a graduate student in the department of criminology at Villanova University.

Danielle Dirks is the author of *Confronting Campus Rape: Legal Landscapes, New Media, and Networked Activism.* Her research interests include racial and ethnic relations and criminal justice issues related to incarceration and the death penalty.

Dawn Marie Dow is an assistant professor in the sociology department of the Maxwell School of Citizenship and Public Affairs at Syracuse University and is also a faculty fellow in the Institute for the Study of the Judiciary, Politics, and the Media. Her research focuses on the intersection of gender, race, and class within the context of the family, the workplace, and the law.

Laura E. Enriquez is an assistant professor of Chicano/Latino studies at the University of California, Irvine. Her research interests include the undocumented population, 1.5-generation young adults, international migration, citizenship, and Latino families.

Reanne Frank is an associate professor of sociology at the Ohio State University. Her research focuses on the sociology of immigration and race/ethnic inequality with an emphasis on health and mortality.

Melanie J. Gast is an assistant professor of sociology at DePaul University. Her interests include race/ethnicity, social class, and processes related to social mobility.

Erin R. Hamilton is an assistant professor of sociology at the University of California, Davis. Her research interests include international migration, health, and social demography.

Lance Hannon is a professor of sociology at Villanova University. His research and teaching interests include White colorism, intersectionality, and the criminal justice system.

Nancy A. Heitzeg is an associate professor of sociology and a codirector of the Critical Studies of Race/Ethnicity program at the College of St. Catherine, St. Paul, Minnesota. She has written and presented widely on race, class, gender, and social control; formal, medical, and extralegal color-blind racism; and social movements/social change.

Melissa R. Herman is a lecturer in writing on the topic of multiracial identity development at Dartmouth.

Simon Ho is an MD candidate at the University of Central Florida School of Medicine.

Kimberly Kay Hoang is an assistant professor of sociology at the College of the University of Chicago. Dr. Hoang is the author of *Dealing in Desire: Asian Ascendancy, Western Decline, and the Hidden Currencies of Global Sex Work.*

Robert A. Hummer is a Howard Odum Professor in the department of sociology at University of North Carolina, Chapel Hill. His research interests include demography, population health, aging, and the life course.

Margaret Hunter is an assistant professor in the department of sociology and anthropology at Mills College in Oakland, California. Her research areas include comparative racial and ethnic relations, skin-color politics, feminist theory, and the sociology of gender.

Jennifer A. Jones is an assistant professor of sociology at the University of Notre Dame and faculty fellow at the Institute for Latino Studies. Her research uses qualitative methods to explore increasing migration, the growing multiracial population, and shifting social relations between and within racial groups.

Jennifer Lee is a professor of sociology at University of California, Irvine. Her research interests include immigration, race/ethnicity, social inequality, culture, education, and Asian American studies. She is the author of *The Asian American Achievement Paradox* (with Min Zhou).

Kristen Lee graduated from Duke University with a degree in sociology.

Kirstin Mohammed is an undergraduate student in the department of sociology at Villanova University.

Jennifer C. Mueller is an assistant professor of sociology at Skidmore College. Her research interests include racial and ethnic relations, social inequality and intersectionality, everyday culture, and teaching social justice pedagogy.

Kathryn M. Neckerman is an associate professor of the Institute for Social and Economic Research and Policy at Columbia University and an affiliate of the Robert Wood Johnson Foundation's Health and Society Scholars Program and the Institute's Center for the Study of Wealth and Inequality.

Victor Nee is a sociologist, the Frank and Rosa Rhodes Professor, and director of the Center for the Study of Economy and Society at Cornell University.

Anthony C. Ocampo is an assistant professor of sociology at Cal Poly Pomona. His research interests include immigration, race and ethnicity, and gender and sexuality. He is the author of *The Latinos of Asia: How Filipino Americans Break the Rules of Race.*

Gilda L. Ochoa is a professor of sociology and Chicana/o Latina/o Studies at Pomona College. Her research focuses on education, inequalities in schools, and community partnerships. She is the author of *Academic Profiling: Latinos, Asian Americans, and the Achievement Gap.*

Dina G. Okamoto is an associate professor of sociology at Indiana University. Her research focuses on understanding how group boundaries and identities shift and change with respect to the civic and political incorporation of immigrants in the United States. She is the author of *Redefining Race: Asian American Panethnicity and Shifting Ethnic Boundaries.*

Michael Omi is an associate professor of Asian American and Asian diaspora studies in the department of ethnic studies at the University of California, Berkeley. His research interests include racial theory and politics, racial/ethnic classification and identity, and comparative racialization.

Yolanda C. Padilla is a professor of social work and women's studies at the University of Texas at Austin and is director of the Center for Diversity and Social & Economic Justice.

Yung-Yi Diana Pan is an assistant professor of sociology at Brooklyn College. Her work examines the socialization of Asian American and Latino law students as racialized immigrants entering an elite profession.

Whitney N. Laster Pirtle is an assistant professor of sociology at the University of California, Merced. Her research interests include race, identity, and mental health. Her research is primarily informed by social psychological framework and explores how social structures, like racial hierarchies, affect individuals' lived experiences, well-being, and identities.

Leslie H. Picca is an assistant professor of sociology at the University of Dayton. Her areas of interest include racial/ethnic relations, sexualities, symbolic interactionism, and structures of privilege, especially Whiteness.

Victor Rios is a professor of sociology at the University of California, Santa Barbara. His research interests include juvenile justice, law and society, and inequality. He is the author of *Punished: Policing the Lives of Black and Latino Boys.*

Dwanna L. Robertson is an assistant professor at Kansas State University. Her research focuses on the reproduction of social inequality within the structure of policy, particularly for American Indians.

Audrey Smedley is professor emeritus of anthropology at the School of World Studies and African American Studies at Virginia Commonwealth University.

Brian D. Smedley is the vice president and director of the Health Policy Institute Joint Center for Political and Economic Studies in Washington, D.C.

Veronica Terriquez is an associate professor of sociology at the University of California, Santa Cruz. Her interests include immigrant incorporation, civic engagement, social inequality, Latinos in the United States, and youth transitions to adulthood.

Amy C. Wilkins is an associate professor of sociology at the University of Colorado–Boulder. Her research focuses on identity transformations in the transition to college for first-generation, Black, and LGBQ young adults.

David R. Williams is the Florence and Laura Norman Professor of Public Health and a professor of African and African American studies and of sociology at Harvard University. His research interests are focused on socioeconomic and racial disparities in health and the effects of stress, racism, and religious involvement on health.

Howard Winant is a professor of sociology at the University of California, Santa Barbara. His research interests focus on racial theory and social theory, comparative historical sociology, political sociology, and cultural sociology of race in the United States and globally. He is the author of *The New Politics of Race: Globalism, Difference, Justice.*

Elizabeth A. Yates is a PhD student in the department of sociology at the University of Pittsburgh.

CHAPTER 1

A Critical and Comprehensive Sociological Theory of Race and Racism

Tanya Golash-Boza

In this article, Tanya Golash-Boza challenges the claim that sociology lacks a sound theoretical approach to the study of **race** *and* **racism**. *Instead, she argues that a comprehensive and critical sociological theory of race and racism exists. Her essay outlines this theory, drawing from the work of key scholars in and around the field. This consideration of the state of race theory in sociology leads to four contentions regarding what a critical and comprehensive theory of race and racism should do: (1) bring race and racism together into the same analytical framework, (2) articulate the connections between racist ideologies and racist structures, (3) lead us toward the elimination of racial oppression, and (4) include an intersectional analysis.*

Questions to Consider

What is the relationship between race and racism? Can a society that organizes individuals and groups into different races ever be free of racism?

Source: Adapted from Tanya Golash-Boza, "A Critical and Comprehensive Sociological Theory of Race and Racism," *The Sociology of Race and Ethnicity Journal*, SAGE Publications, Inc., 2016.

Three of the most prominent sociologists of race in the United States agree on one thing: sociology lacks a sound theoretical approach to the study of race and racism. In his 1997 *American Sociological Review* article, sociologist Eduardo Bonilla-Silva stated, "The area of race and ethnic studies lacks a sound theoretical apparatus" (p. 465). Shortly thereafter, another prominent sociologist of race, Howard Winant (2000:178) agreed, when he stated in his *Annual Review* article on race and race theory, "The inadequacy of the range of theoretical approaches to race available in sociology at the turn of the twenty-first century is striking." One year later, sociologist Joe Feagin (2001:5), in *Racist America*, posited "in the case of racist oppression, . . . we do not as yet have as strongly agreed-upon concepts and well-developed theoretical traditions as we have for class and gender oppression." Notably, that line stayed intact in the 2014 edition of *Racist America*. And, in the third edition of *Racial Formation*, Michael Omi and Howard Winant (2015:4) wrote, "Despite the enormous legacy and volume of racial theory, the concept of race remains poorly understood and inadequately explained."

In this essay, I contest this assertion that theories in the sociology of race and racism are underdeveloped. Instead, I argue we can bring together the work of the scholars cited above along with other critical work on race and racism, . . . [to outline] a comprehensive and critical sociological theory of race and racism. This essay thus contests the bold claim made by Mustafa Emirbayer and Matthew Desmond (2015:1) that "there has never been a comprehensive and systematic theory of race."

The purpose of a critical theory of race and racism is to move forward our understanding of racial and racist dynamics in ways that bring us closer to the eradication of racial oppression. Legal scholar Dorothy Roberts (2012:5) explains that race is a "political category" and a "political system," which means we "must use political means to end its harmful impact on our society." Roberts cautions that this does not mean we should discard the idea of race; instead she posits we should use a politicized lens to understand the pernicious impacts of race as a political system. Roberts' position stands in contrast to Emirbayer and Desmond's (2015:42) distinction between political and intellectual motivations for scholarship and their preference for the latter. Nevertheless, in the spirit of Emirbayer and Desmond (2015:43), I agree that "reflexivity requires not only exposing one's intellectual biases but also being honest about how one's political allegiances and moral convictions influence one's scientific pursuits" and thus contend that the study of race *must* be political and politicized because there is no good reason to study race other than working toward the elimination of racial oppression.

Furthermore, in the spirit of reflexivity, it is also crucial to consider one's positionality when doing race scholarship. I write this piece as a tenured professor and a white woman. My position as a tenured professor provides me with the academic freedom to write what I think without the fear of losing my job. As a white woman, I can be critical of racism without being labeled "angry" in the same way that people of color may be. I also write as a committed antiracist. I work to end racial oppression even though I reap the material and psychological benefits of white privilege for two main reasons: (1) the system of white supremacy materially and psychologically damages people I love more than I love myself, and (2) racial oppression suppresses human potential by holding back amazing people of color while pushing forward mediocre white people. In this sense, racism has pernicious societal effects for all.

Defining Race

The idea of "race" includes the socially constructed belief that the human race can be divided into biologically discrete and exclusive groups based on physical and cultural traits (Morning 2011). This idea of race is inextricably linked to notions of white or European superiority that became concretized during the colonization of the Americas and the concomitant enslavement of Africans. Race is a modern concept and a product of colonial encounters (Mills 1997). The way we understand the idea of race today is distinct from previous ways of thinking about human difference. Before the conquest of the Americas, there was no worldview that separated all of humanity into distinct races (Montagu 1997; Quijano 2000; Smedley 1999). The idea that some people are white and others are black, for example, emerged in the seventeenth century when European settlers in North America gradually transitioned from referring to themselves as Christians to calling themselves whites and enslaved Africans, Negroes (Jordan 1968).

In the current context of globalization, every corner of the earth has been affected by "global white supremacy" (Mills 1997:3). However, that does not mean that every form of social differentiation is necessarily connected to race or racism. For example, the skin color distinctions between Chinese people that Desmond and Emirbayer (2009) reference are not racial distinctions but another form of social classification that predates colonialism. Moreover, colorism prior to colonialism did not involve the biological conceptualization of race that emerged after European colonial domination of non-European populations. . . . These precolonial modes of social differentiation involve evaluations of skin color but do not constitute a racial hierarchy insofar as they are unrelated to the history of the idea of race, do not derive from a biological theory of superior and inferior groups with innate differences, and are not part of a racial worldview.

It is imperative to trace the genealogy of the idea of race as it helps us to perceive what is "race" and what is not. Racial categories and ideologies change over time, but race as a worldview can be traced back to ideas European scientists promulgated in the eighteenth century. One of the earliest examples of racial pseudoscience is the work of Swedish botanist Carolus Linnaeus (Eze 1997). In 1735, Linnaeus proposed that all human beings could be divided into four groups. These four groups are consistent with the modern idea of race in two ways: the four categories continue to be meaningful today; and Linnaeus connected physical traits, such as skin color, with cultural and moral traits, such as "indolent." Carolus Linnaeus described these four groups, which correspond to four of the continents, in *Systemae Naturae* in 1735:

> *Americanus*: reddish, choleric, and erect; . . . obstinate, merry, free; . . . regulated by customs.
>
> *Asiaticus*: sallow, melancholy, . . . black hair, dark eyes, . . . haughty, . . . ruled by opinions.
>
> *Africanus*: black, phlegmatic, relaxed; women without shame, . . . crafty, indolent, negligent; governed by caprice.
>
> *Europaenus*: white, sanguine, muscular; inventive; governed by laws. (cited in Golash-Boza 2015b:24)

These racial categories were invented by Europeans in the context of European colonization, slavery, and genocide, and they form the basis for racial thinking today. Any theory of race and racism must take into account this brutal history.

A Sociological Theory of Race and Racism

Sociological scholarship tends to focus primarily on race (Cornell and Hartmann 2007; Omi and Winant 2015) or on racism (Feagin 2014; Bonilla-Silva 1997, 2014), thereby separating out these dialectically related concepts. Whereas Omi and Winant (2015) argue we need a more refined understanding of the concept of race, Bonilla-Silva (1997) contends we need a better understanding of the structures of racial oppression, and Feagin (2014) maintains that racial formation theory does not adequately account for the deep entrenchment of systemic racism as a core function of U.S. society. A comprehensive theory of race and racism should bring race and racism together into the same analytical framework because we cannot separate the construction of race from the reproduction of racism. This framework further needs to articulate the connections between racist ideologies and racist structures. *Racism* refers to both (1) the *ideology* that races are populations of people whose physical differences are linked to significant cultural and social differences and that these innate hierarchical differences can be measured and judged and (2) the micro- and macrolevel *practices* that subordinate those races believed to be inferior (Golash-Boza 2015a).

Individual, Institutional, and Structural Racism

Although it is evident that racial categories were created using pseudoscience, we continue to use these categories today. Moreover, these categories are used in ways that are psychologically and materially harmful. For example, individual acts of bigotry, such as using racial slurs or committing hate crimes, continue to be prevalent in the United States (Feagin 2014). In addition, microaggressions—daily, commonplace insults and racial slights that cumulatively affect the psychological well-being of people of color—abound (Solorzano, Ceja, and Yosso 2000). Studies consistently find that individual acts of bigotry are commonplace, even in places such as college campuses, which one might presume to be more accepting than most other places (Chou, Lee, and Ho 2015; Harper and Hurtado 2007).

Individual acts of bigotry sustain racism and are harmful to people of color. However, race-neutral acts can also serve the same function. For example, my white colleagues have told me that they give hiring preference to people with whom they get along. These same colleagues often have social circles that are almost exclusively white. Although they may be unaware of these biases, it is harder for them to imagine "getting along" with nonwhites. Psychologists have labeled this phenomenon "aversive racism," understood as "a subtle, often unintentional, form of bias that characterizes many White Americans who possess strong egalitarian values and who believe that they are nonprejudiced" (Dovidio et al. 2002). Similarly, admissions committees that take into account biased tests, such as the SAT or the Graduate Record Examinations (GRE), limit access to higher education through this allegedly race-neutral act. A recent article in *Nature* reported that the practice of relying on GRE scores is a poor method of "selecting the most capable students and severely restricts the flow of women and minorities into the sciences" (Miller and Stassun 2014:303). This practice is so widespread, however, that it has become part of institutional racism, to which I will now turn.

In the late 1960s and 1970s, sociological thinking on racism moved away from a focus solely on prejudice and individual acts of racism toward an institutional or structural approach. Carmichael and Hamilton (1967) introduced the idea of institutional racism in their book, *Black Power*, when they explained that the high rates of black infant mortality in Birmingham and the prevalence of black families in slums are best understood through an analytic of institutional racism. Two years later, Samuel Robert Friedman (1969:20) defined "structural racism" as a "pattern of action in which one or more of the institutions of society has the power to throw on more burdens and give less benefits to the members of one race than another on an on-going basis."

In an essay published in 1979, Carol Camp Yeakey posited that research on institutional racism in the late 1960s and throughout the 1970s represented a marked departure from previous research, which had not focused on "the attributes of the majority group and the institutional mechanisms by which majority and minority relations are created, sustained, and changed" (Yeakey 1979:200). Yeakey then argued that racism operates on both a covert and an overt level and takes two related forms: "The first is on an individual level. The second is on an institutional level where racism as a normative, societal ideology operates within and among the organizations, institutions, and processes of the larger society. And the overt acts of individual racism and the more covert acts of institutional racism have a mutually reinforcing effect" (Yeakey 1979:200).

The arguments and concepts Yeakey (1979) laid out in her essay continue to be relevant today. She wrote about . . . the way racism works in "social systems," and explained,

> The resource allocation of city schools; residential segregation and housing quality; the location, structure, and placement of transport systems; hiring and promotion practices; academic underachievement of racial and ethnic minority youth; availability of decent health care; behavior of policemen and judges . . . these and a myriad of other forms of social, political, and economic discrimination concurrently interlock to determine the status, welfare, and income of the racial and ethnic minorities of color. (Yeakey 1979:203)

Unfortunately, nearly 40 years later, we can make the same assessment with regard to systemic racism. Fortunately, scholars of race and racism continue to refine these theories and approaches. The work of Joe Feagin and Eduardo Bonilla-Silva has been at the center of macrolevel theories of racism in sociology. Joe Feagin (2001:16) builds on the concept of "systemic racism," which he defines as "a diverse assortment of racist practices; the unjustly gained economic and political power of whites, the continuing resource inequalities; and the white-racist ideologies, attitudes, and institutions created to preserve white advantage and power."

Eduardo Bonilla-Silva (1997:469) builds upon the concept of "racialized social systems," which he defines as "societies in which economic, political, social, and ideological levels are partially structured by the placement of actors in racial categories." Bonilla-Silva places particular emphasis on racial hierarchies and points to how these hierarchies influence all social relations. Societies that have racialized social systems differentially allocate "economic, political, social, and even psychological rewards to groups along racial lines" (Bonilla-Silva 1997:442).

In *Beneath the Surface of White Supremacy*, sociologist Moon-Kie Jung (2015) contends that Bonilla-Silva's structural theory of racism is one of the "most compelling and influential reconceptualizations" of racism insofar as it moves racial theories beyond the realm of ideology. However, Jung contends that race theory requires a more complex understanding of structure and a clearer articulation of how dominant racial ideology articulates with structures of racial inequality. To address this concern, Jung redefines racism as "structures of inequality and domination based on race" and argues that the structure of racism refers to the "reiterative articulation of schemas and resources through practice" (Jung 2015:49). In this way, Jung's redefinition helps us to see how racist ideologies and racist structures are mutually constitutive of one another.

Racist Ideologies

In his 1997 article, Bonilla-Silva explains how racialized social systems develop racial ideologies and contends that racial ideologies have a structural foundation. A racial ideology is a set of principles and ideas that (1) divides people into different racial groups and (2) serves the interests of one group. Ideologies are created by the dominant group and reflect the interests of that group. Racial ideologies change over time because the needs and interests of the elite change. As Karl Marx and Frederick Engels ([1848] 1970:64) wrote in *The German Ideology*, "The ideas of the ruling class are in every epoch the ruling ideas." Both historically and today, the dominant racial group in the United States is white (Feagin 2014).

Eduardo Bonilla-Silva (2014:25) elaborates on this notion that white supremacy in the United States has changed since the 1960s yet continues to produce racial inequality. Bonilla-Silva lays out the elements of the "new racial structure," which he defines as "*the totality of social relations and practices that reinforce white privilege* [italics in original]" (Bonilla-Silva 2014:9). These elements include "the increasingly *covert* [italics in original] nature of racial discourse and racial practices; the avoidance of racial terminology" (Bonilla-Silva 2014:27) and other practices that make racism more discrete yet nonetheless potent. He further posits that "much as Jim Crow racism served as the glue for defending a brutal and overt system of racial oppression in the pre–civil rights era, color-blind racism serves today as the ideological armor for a covert and institutionalized system in the post–civil rights era" (Bonilla-Silva 2014:3).

Eduardo Bonilla-Silva's work on color-blind racism has been critical in efforts to understand how racial ideologies work on the ground. Color-blind racism is a racial ideology that explains contemporary racial inequality as the outcome of nonracial factors, such as market dynamics, naturally occurring phenomena, and nonwhites' supposed cultural limitations. However, color-blind ideology is not the only racial ideology that operates today. Moon-Kie Jung (2015:44) explains that "schemas of 'colorblindness' operate at rather 'shallow' depths—as ideology." Jung contends that if we dig just a bit deeper, we find widespread and persistent antiblack schemas and discourses. Jung gives an example of hiring practices: employers do not use just colorblind discourses when they decide not to hire black men; they often use antiblack discourses, such as that black men are unmotivated and have bad attitudes.

There are many excellent examples of how the understanding of racial ideologies is constantly advancing. For example, sociologist Amanda Lewis (2004:632) proffers the notion of "hegemonic whiteness" as an example of a discourse that undergirds racial ideologies and justifies racial inequalities. Lewis explains,

> For an ideology to gain hegemony, . . . it must successfully naturalize the status quo. . . . Racial ideologies in particular provide ways of understanding the world that make sense of racial gaps in earnings, wealth, and health such that whites do not see any connection between their gain and others' loss. (Lewis 2004:632–33)

The work of Patricia Hill Collins (2004:96) is also useful here as she explains, "When ideologies that defend racism become taken-for-granted and appear to be natural and inevitable, they become hegemonic. Few question them and the social hierarchies they defend." Two important consequences of racist ideologies today are the prevalence of racialized identities and the proliferation of racial stereotypes. An examination of these facets of white supremacy renders it evident that an understanding of racial ideology must be clearly articulated with other structures of domination, such as capitalism and patriarchy.

Controlling Images

Although the concept of "hegemonic whiteness" that Lewis proposes is useful, the work of Collins (2004) helps us perceive that an understanding of how racial ideologies are promulgated must be intersectional. Hegemonic whiteness is not only racialized; it is also classed and gendered. One of the most compelling sociological discussions of racial discourses can be found in the work of sociologist Patricia Hill Collins (2004:187), who explains that "hegemonic masculinity" is the social idea of what "real men" are and is shaped by ideologies of gender, age, class, sexuality, and race. Collins contends that "controlling images" (Collins 2004:165)—gendered depictions of African Americans in the media—define hegemonic masculinity in opposition, by showing what it is not. Controlling images define what marginalized masculinity and subordinated femininity are, thereby defining what hegemonic masculinity is not.

In *Race and Racisms* (Golash-Boza 2015b), I brought together a broad range of scholarship on media stereotypes and used Patricia Hill Collins' concept of controlling images to develop a characterization of prevalent gendered stereotypes of nonwhites in contemporary U.S. media. For example, when someone says "terrorist" in the United States, the image of an Arab man comes to mind for many Americans. Likewise, the stereotypical "welfare queen" is a black woman.

These stereotypical representations not only shape how people in the United States view one another; they also work to justify rampant inequalities. Representations of Latinos as drug kingpins, gangbangers, and petty criminals work to justify the disproportionate rates of imprisonment for Latinos. Shoba Sharad Rajgopal (2010:145) argues that representations of Arab women as veiled, traditional, and oppressed work to reinforce the stereotype that Western culture is "dynamic, progressive, and egalitarian," whereas Arab cultures are "backward, barbaric, and patriarchal." A consideration of these stereotypes helps us to see how ideologies articulate with structures: the "controlling image" of the black man as a thug has been critical to the expansion of the criminal justice system. Racialized and gendered fears of crime have justified the development of the prison industrial complex.

Because media depictions shape our perceptions, and portray white characters with more depth and redeeming qualities, they work to justify the fact that whites tend to do better on nearly any social measure. In a similar fashion, the depiction of Americans as the (white) saviors of the world helps to shape our perception of the United States as the beacon of democracy, even as the military wreaks havoc on the Middle East. These gendered and racialized discourses reinforce prevalent stereotypes about people of color in the United States and also work to define whites as morally superior. These ideologies articulate with structures that reproduce inequality as explained in the work of Bonilla-Silva, Feagin, Collins, and Mills.

Racialized Identities

Although racial categories were created during the time of slavery, genocide, and colonialism, they have taken on their own meaning over time. We still use categories, such as white, black, Asian, and Native American, to make meaning of our social world. In the United States, Arab and Latino/Latina have emerged as meaningful racial categories. In Latin America, *mestizo* (white/Indian) and *mulato* (white/black) as well as other racialized categories continue to shape social life. One key aspect of racial categories is that they are flexible and can accommodate distinct social realities. The emergence of Arab and Latino as racialized categories in the United States is an example of how racial ideologies can evolve and change the racial structure itself.

Insofar as racialized categories have taken on deep meaning for many marginalized groups, it may seem problematic to trace all racialized identities to racist ideologies. However, if we think about the root of these unity struggles, it becomes clear that these calls for unity come about because of racist ideologies and structures. A recent example of this is the emergence of #blacklivesmatter in response to police killings of black people.

Many scholars of race would agree with this line of argument. Charles Mills (1997:63) posits that the racial contract creates not only "racial exploitation, *but race itself* as a group identity." Amanda Lewis (2004:625) contends that "*race* as a set of identities, discursive practices, cultural forms, and ideological manifestations would not exist without racism." Michael Omi and Howard Winant (2015:138) sum up the thinking on this succinctly: "We make our racial identities, both individually and collectively, but not under conditions of our own choosing." Omi and Winant further contend: "The forging of new collective racial identities during the 1950s and 1960s has been the single most enduring contribution of the anti-racist movement" (Omi and Winant 2015:153).

The work of Omi and Winant on "racial formation" is particularly useful for an understanding of racial identities. Omi and Winant (1994:56) define racial formation as "the sociohistorical process by which racial categories are created, inhabited, transformed, and destroyed," and as a "process or historically situated project." They argue that the state (national government) is the primary site where race is constructed and contested. Omi and Winant explore "how concepts of race are created and changed" and argue that "concepts of race structure both state and civil society" (Omi and Winant 1994: vii). They also say that "race" is the symbolic representation of social conflict expressed through physical characteristics. And it is variable over time.

The concept of racial formation blends an understanding of social structures with cultural representations. Omi and Winant (1994:56) use the concept of a racial project, which they define as being "simultaneously an interpretation, representation, or explanation of racial dynamics, and an effort to reorganize and redistribute resources along particular racial lines." Racial projects give meaning to racial categories through cultural representations while also organizing our social world on the basis of race through social structures. Cultural ideas and social structures work together in racial formation projects.

Racial Formation (Omi and Winant 2015) has served as the basis for a substantial body of scholarly work on racial identities and meanings. It is useful for thinking about how race is "a template for the processes of marginalization that continue to shape social structures as well as collective and individual psyches" (Omi and Winant 2015:107). It is worthwhile to think about this concept of racial meanings alongside scholarship that deals specifically with identity as a concept. A useful starting point is Brubaker and Cooper's (2000) clarification on the difference between identification and identity (notwithstanding the fact that they reject the concept of identity). A person can be identified as a member of a racial group by the state, by himself or herself, or by other members of society. The state has the "material and symbolic resources to impose the categories, classificatory schemes, and modes of social counting and accounting with which bureaucrats, judges, teachers, and doctors must work and to which nonstate actors must refer" (Brubaker and Cooper 2000:16).

The (racial) state has produced racial categories, and Clara Rodriguez's (2000) work sheds important light on how this happened and is a useful starting point for thinking about how people can "ignore, resist, or accept . . . the state-defined categories and the popular conventions concerning race" (p. 18). "Hispanic" is a state-produced ethnic category that many people with roots in Latin America resist, preferring instead to identify with their national origin (Rodriguez 2000). Nevertheless, about half of the self-identified Latino respondents to the 2002 National Latino Survey reported their race as Latino. Moreover, those with darker skin and who had experienced discrimination were more likely to self-identify as Latino (Golash-Boza and Darity 2008). It can be difficult for African Americans (or other people identified as black) to reject a black identity given that it is harder for many people of African descent to escape racialization as black. However, embracing a black identity has positive outcomes insofar as African Americans who identify closely with other blacks tend to have higher self-esteem and fewer depressive symptoms (Hughes et al. 2015). In sum, although racial categories are produced by the state and through daily interactions, and emerge from a brutal history of oppression, people have embraced these racial identities and transformed them into positive group-based identities. In addition, people have also contested these categories and made claims to the state for distinctive forms of recognition—for example, the calls for the addition of "multiracial" and "Middle Eastern" as racial categories to the Census.

Racist Ideologies and Structures

Racist ideologies lead to controlling images, discourses of hegemonic whiteness, and racialized identities, which in turn lead to racist practices on the micro- and macrolevel, which themselves reinforce racial identities and discourses. These structures and ideologies thus reproduce one another in a dialectical manner. One clear empirical example of the articulation between ideology and structure comes from the work of Wendy Leo Moore (2008), who argues that ideologies of white supremacy and a history of racial oppression work together to produce "white institutional spaces" in elite white schools (p. 27). For Moore, law schools are white institutional spaces both because of the fact that the upper administration is (and has always been) primarily white and because of how discourses about whiteness and the law are disseminated within the law school.

I will use another example from my work on deportations to explore how these ideologies articulate with structures. In 1996, president Bill Clinton signed into law two pieces of legislation that expanded the grounds on which a person could be deported, narrowed the grounds on which they could appeal, and dedicated increased funding to immigration law enforcement. These laws led to the deportation of 5 million people between 1997 and 2015 (Golash-Boza 2015a). Politicians advocated for and implemented these extremely punitive laws because of racialized and gendered ideologies that painted Latino men as criminal and Latina women as breeders (Golash-Boza and Hondagneu-Sotelo 2013). The racial ideologies that lead many Americans to see Mexican immigrants as unfit to be citizens or as undesirable residents have led to the implementation of a state apparatus designed to remove Latino immigrants. In turn, this state apparatus, which criminalizes Latinos as "illegal aliens," reinforces ideologies of Latino criminality. This is one example among many possible examples of a clear articulation between racial ideologies and racial structures and allows us to see the material consequences of racial ideologies as well as the dialectical relationship between ideologies and structures.

This example, however, also makes it clear that racial ideologies alone do not account for mass deportation. To understand the implementation of mass deportation, we need to consider gendered, raced, and anti-immigrant discourses. We also need to consider these discourses in light of broader structures of patriarchy, white supremacy, and global capitalism. This brings me back to a consideration of intersectionality.

Intersectionality

At a certain level of abstraction, we can talk about racist ideologies and structures without mentioning class or gender. As Barbara Risman (2004:444) argues, "Each structure of inequality exists on its own yet coexists with every other structure of inequality." This is similar to arguments made by Omi and Winant (2015:106) that "race is a master category" and that race, class, and gender oppression are produced in tandem. Nevertheless, once we move beyond abstractions and begin to think about lived experiences, an intersectional framework becomes necessary. The racist discourses that circulate about black men and black women are distinct and therefore lead to distinct acts of individual and institutional racism. For example, the discourse of black men as dangerous leads to white women crossing the street when they see a black man approaching and also leads to police officers shooting black boys, like Tamir Rice, for holding a toy gun. The typical white reaction to black women is not marked by the same kind or level of fear. Similarly, the barriers that black women and black men face in employment are not the same, and an examination of these barriers requires an intersectional framework (Wingfield 2012).

Kimberle Crenshaw (1991) developed the concept of intersectionality, using the example of black and Latina women in a battered women's shelter to make her point. She contends we have to consider race, class, and gender oppression to understand how they ended up in the shelter. The women faced abuse because of gender oppression, but their economically vulnerable situation and racism also play a role. If they had the economic resources, they likely would have gone elsewhere—not to a shelter. If they were white, they would not face racial discrimination in employment, meaning they may have had more resources.

In a similar vein, Priya Kandaswamy (2012) contends that an intersectional perspective helps us understand welfare policies better. She argues that the perspectives of race scholars, Marxists, and feminists often look past one another. In contrast, she takes an intersectional perspective to shed light on the 1996 welfare reforms. Ideas of gender, sexuality, race, and class work together to create public understandings of who deserves state assistance and who does not. The subtext of the "welfare queen" in the successful passage of the 1996 welfare reform is due to the raced, class-based, gendered, and heteronormative ideas surrounding the welfare queen. The 1996 law explicitly embraced marriage, was based on a public discussion of family values and personal responsibility, and was designed to reform the "welfare queen," a stereotype often imagined as a black woman. Priya Kandaswamy explains how the idea that race is historically produced and constantly changing can complicate our understanding of intersectionality, as it forces us to look at how race and gender "are constituted in and through each other" (Kandaswamy 2012:26). Kandaswamy's and Crenshaw's work are both exemplary of how empirical analyses can question existing theoretical frameworks and move them forward in exciting ways.

Returning to the example of mass deportation, it is also clear that a comprehensive understanding of mass deportation requires looking not only at race/class/gender as many intersectionality scholars do but also at white supremacy/global capitalism/patriarchy as the structures that maintain and are justified by racist, sexist, and classist discourses. An understanding of mass deportation requires a consideration of the political economy of racialized and gendered state repression. Mass deportation is a form of state repression based on stereotypes of "criminal aliens" that disproportionately target Latino and Caribbean men. "Controlling images" (Collins 2004) of black, Latino, and Arab men as threatening have served as discursive fodder for the implementation of state repression. Moreover, we have to consider deportation as part of a system of global apartheid—where (mostly white) affluent citizens of the world are free to travel to where they like whereas the (mostly nonwhite) poor are forced to make do in places where there are fewer resources. Global apartheid depends on the possibility and reality of deportation. Finally, 98 percent of people deported are sent to Latin America and the Caribbean, and 90 percent of them are men even though there is no raced or gendered language in the Immigration and Nationality Act, which governs immigration policy enforcement (Golash-Boza 2015a). We need more work in this line of thinking that grapples with race, class, and gender not just as discourses or ideologies but also as structures or systems of oppression.

Discussion and Conclusion

This essay pulls theories of race and racism together into one theoretical framework by articulating the connection between racist ideologies and racist structures. This analysis began with a discussion of the genealogies of the idea of race and the sociological understanding of racism in order to highlight the points of agreement among race scholars. I use a few key empirical examples to show how empirical research has helped to move theories of race and racism forward. These examples, however, reveal the need for an intersectional framework in most areas of race scholarship. These and other examples of empirical work constantly push the boundaries of race theory and render it clear which direction the field should move in.

Now that it has become clear that we do have a sociological theory of race and racism, where do we go from here? Moving forward, I suggest we (1) design empirical studies that help move our field forward, (2) develop projects that draw from existing frameworks to delve deeper into these understandings of how race and racism work on the ground, (3) imagine ways that theories of race and racism can become more conversant with feminist theory and world systems theory, and (4) get involved in movements to dismantle racism as the best ideas often come through struggle.

The first two are relatively self-explanatory, so I will use the remainder of this conclusion to specify what I mean by the third point, which references intersectionality, and the fourth, which involves activism. In a recent essay, feminist scholar Kathy Davis (2008:68) wrote, "[I]t is unimaginable that a women's studies programme would only focus on gender." As race scholars we should hold ourselves to the same standard and incorporate political economy and feminist theory into our analyses of race on a consistent basis. It is impossible to study black identity, for example, and separate out the gender, sexuality, class, (dis)ability, and other aspects of people who embody blackness. As for activism, race is not a topic that one should study only for its intellectual interest. It should be studied to the end of eradicating racial oppression. Knowledge is most useful when it is produced in community and through struggle. An understanding of racial oppression cannot be an armchair exercise. Instead, race scholars have to start with empirical questions about why things are the way they are and push forward theoretical understandings that help us to explicate and end racial oppression. Working toward dismantling racism both helps us to understand it better and moves us toward its demise. In a conversation about this essay, Sam Friedman reminded me that "struggles against racism tend to lead to creative and more systemic thinking." I could not agree more.

References

Bonilla-Silva, Eduardo. 1997. "Rethinking Racism: Toward a Structural Interpretation." *American Sociological Review* 62(3):465–80.

Bonilla-Silva, Eduardo. 2014. *Racism without Racists: Color-blind Racism and the Persistence of Racial Inequality in the United States.* Lanham, MD: Rowman & Littlefield.

Brubaker, Rogers, and Frederick Cooper. 2000. "Beyond 'Identity.'" *Theory and Society* 29(1):1–47.

Carmichael, Stokely, and Charles V. Hamilton, 1967. *Black Power: The Politics of Liberation in America.* New York: Vintage Books.

Chou, Rosalind S., Kristen Lee, and Simon Ho. 2015. "Love Is (Color) Blind: Asian Americans and White Institutional Space at the Elite University." *Sociology of Race and Ethnicity* 1(2):302–16.

Collins, Patricia Hill. 2004. *Black Sexual Politics: African Americans, Gender, and the New Racism.* New York: Routledge.

Cornell, Stephen, and Douglas Hartmann. 2007. *Ethnicity and Race: Making Identities in a Changing World.* Thousand Oaks, CA: Pine Forge Press.

Crenshaw, Kimberle. 1991. "Mapping the Margins: Intersectionality, Identity Politics, and Violence against Women of Color." *Stanford Law Review* 43(6):1241–99.

Davis, Kathy. 2008. "Intersectionality as Buzzword: A Sociology of Science Perspective on What Makes a Feminist Theory Successful." *Feminist Theory* 9(1):67–85.

Desmond, Matthew, and Mustafa Emirbayer. 2009. "What Is Racial Domination?" *Du Bois Review: Social Science Research on Race* 6(2):335–55.

Dovidio, John F., Gaertner Samuel E., Kerry Kawakami, and Gordon Hodson. 2002. "Why Can't We Just Get Along? Interpersonal Biases and Interracial Distrust." *Cultural Diversity and Ethnic Minority Psychology* 8(2):88–102.

Emirbayer, Mustafa, and Matthew Desmond. 2015. *The Racial Order.* Chicago: University of Chicago Press.

Eze, Emannuel C. 1997. *Race and the Enlightenment: A Reader.* New York: Wiley-Blackwell.

Feagin, Joe. R. 2014. *Racist America: Roots, Current Realities, and Future Reparations.* New York: Routledge.

Friedman, Samuel. R. 1969. "How Is Racism Maintained?" *Et Al* 2:18–21.

Golash-Boza, Tanya. 2015a. *Deported: Immigrant Policing, Disposable Labor, and Global Capitalism.* New York: New York University Press.

Golash-Boza, Tanya. 2015b. *Race and Racisms: A Critical Approach.* New York: Oxford University Press.

Golash-Boza, Tanya, and William Darity Jr. 2008. "Latino Racial Choices: The Effects of Skin Colour and Discrimination on Latinos' and Latinas' Racial Self-identifications." *Ethnic and Racial Studies* 31(5):899–934.

Harper, Shaun R., and Sylvia Hurtado. 2007. "Nine Themes in Campus Racial Climates and Implications for Institutional Transformation." *New Directions for Student Services* 2007(120):7–24.

Hughes, Michael, K. Jill Kiecolt, Verna M. Keith, and David H. Demo. 2015. "Racial Identity and Well-being among African Americans." *Social Psychology Quarterly* 78(1):25–48.

Hughey, Matthew W. 2010. "The (Dis)similarities of White Racial Identities: The Conceptual Framework of "Hegemonic Whiteness." *Ethnic and Racial Studies* 33(8):1289–1309.

Jenkins, Richard. 1994. "Rethinking Ethnicity: Identity, Categorization and Power." *Ethnic and Racial Studies* 17(2):197–223.

Jordan, Winthrop. 1968. *White over Black: American Attitudes toward the Negro, 1550–1812.* Chapel Hill: University of North Carolina Press.

Jung, Moon K. 2015. *Beneath the Surface of White Supremacy: Denaturalizing US Racisms Past and Present.* Palo Alto, CA: Stanford University Press.

Kandaswamy, Priya. 2012. "Gendering Racial Formation." Pp. 23–43 in *Racial Formation in the Twenty-first Century*, edited by D. M. HoSang, O. La Bennett, and L. Pulido. Berkeley: University of California Press.

Lewis, Amanda E. 2004. "'What Group?' Studying Whites and Whiteness in the Era of 'Colorblindness.'" *Sociological Theory* 22(4):623–46.

Marx, Karl, and Friedrich Engels. [1848] 1947. *The German Ideology.* New York: International.

Miller, Casey, and Keivn Stassun. 2014. "A Test That Fails." *Nature* 510(7504):303–304. Retrieved February 2016 (http://www.nature.com/naturejobs/science/articles/10.1038/nj7504-303a).

Mills, Charles W. 1997. *The Racial Contract.* Ithaca, NY: Cornell University Press.

Montagu, Ashley. 1997. *Man's Most Dangerous Myth: The Fallacy of Race.* Lanham, MD: Rowman & Littlefield.

Moore, Wendy L. 2008. *Reproducing Racism: White Space, Elite Law Schools, and Racial Inequality.* Lanham, MD: Rowman & Littlefield.

Morning, Ann. 2011. *The Nature of Race.* Berkeley: University of California Press.

Omi, Michael, and Howard Winant. 2015. *Racial Formation in the United States.* New York: Routledge.

Phinney, Jean. S., Cindy L. Cantu, and Dawn A. Kurtz. 1997. "Ethnic and American Identity as Predictors of Self-esteem among African American, Latino and White Adolescents." *Journal of Youth and Adolescence* 26(2):165–85.

Quijano, Aníbal. 2000. "Coloniality of Power and Eurocentrism in Latin America." *International Sociology* 15(2):215–32.

Rajgopal, Shoba S. 2010. "The Daughter of Fu Manchu": The Pedagogy of Deconstructing the Representation of Asian Women in Film and Fiction." *Meridians* 10(2):141–62.

Risman, Barbara J. 2004. "Gender as a Social Structure: Theory Wrestling with Activism." *Gender and Society* 18(4):429–50.

Roberts, Dorothy. 2012. *Fatal Invention: How Science, Politics, and Big Business Re-create Race in the Twenty-first Century.* New York: New Press.

Rodriguez, Clara E. 2000. *Changing Race: Latinos, The Census, and the History of Ethnicity in the United States.* New York: New York University Press.

Rondilla, Joanne L., and Paul Spickard. 2007. *Is Lighter Better? Skin-tone Discrimination among Asian Americans.* Lanham, MD: Rowman & Littlefield.

Saraswati, L. Ayu. 2010. "Cosmopolitan Whiteness: The Effects and Affects of Skin-whitening Advertisements in a Transnational Women's Magazine in Indonesia." *Meridians: Feminism, Race, Transnationalism* 10(2):15–41.

Saraswati, L. Ayu. 2012. *Seeing Beauty, Sensing Race in Transnational Indonesia.* Honolulu: University of Hawai'i Press.

Smedley, Audrey. 1999. *Race in North America: Origin of a Worldview.* Boulder, CO: Westview Press.

Solorzano, Daniel, Miguel Ceja, and Tara Yosso. 2000. "Critical Race Theory, Racial Microaggressions, and Campus Racial Climate: The Experiences of African American College Students." *Journal of Negro Education,* 69(Winter/Spring 2000):60–73.

Sue, Derald W., Jennifer Bucceri, Annie Lin, Kevin Nadal, and Gina C. Torino. 2007. "Racial Microaggressions and the Asian American Experience." *Cultural Diversity & Ethnic Minority Psychology* 13(1):72–81.

Winant, Howard. 2000. "Race and Race Theory." *Annual Review of Sociology* 26(2000):169–85.

Wingfield, Adia Harvey. 2012. *No More Invisible Man: Race and Gender in Men's Work.* Philadelphia: Temple University Press.

Yeakey, Carol. 1979. "Ethnicity as a Dimension of Human Diversity." In *Human Diversity and Pedagogy* (pp. 5.1–5.49). Princeton, NJ: Educational Testing Services.

CHAPTER 2

The Theory of Racial Formation*

Michael Omi and Howard Winant

Omi and Winant's Racial Formation in the United States *sparked a new and enduring conversation in social science research on the meaning of race in society. In this excerpt from their groundbreaking book, they introduce the concept of* **racial formation***. They (2015, p. 56) speak of racial formation as "the sociohistorical process by which racial categories are created, inhabited, transformed, and destroyed." They argue that the racial formation process, which takes place at the level of the state and society, shapes what race means, how it is reproduced, and how it can change over time.*

Questions to Consider

Michael Omi and Howard Winant contend that the concepts of race and racism should not be used interchangeably. How do they define each concept, and what do they mean when they say the concept of race can change over time?

In 1982–1983, Susie Guillory Phipps unsuccessfully sued the Louisiana Bureau of Vital Records to change her racial classification from black to white. The descendant of an 18th-century white planter and a black slave, Phipps was designated *black* in her birth certificate in accordance with a 1970 state law which declared anyone with at least 1/32nd "Negro blood" to be black.

Source: Adapted from Michael Omi and Howard Winant, "Racial Formation," *Racial Formation in the United States: From the 1960s to the 1990s*, Second Edition, 53–56; 69–76, Routledge, 2015.

*Some text and accompanying endnotes have been omitted. Please consult the original source.

The Phipps case raised intriguing questions about the concept of race, its meaning in contemporary society, and its use (and abuse) in public policy. Assistant Attorney General Ron Davis defended the law by pointing out that some type of racial classification was necessary to comply with federal record-keeping requirements and to facilitate programs for the prevention of genetic diseases. Phipps's attorney, Brian Begue, argued that the assignment of racial categories on birth certificates was unconstitutional and that the 1/32nd designation was inaccurate. He called on a retired Tulane University professor who cited research indicating that most Louisiana whites have at least 1/20th "Negro" ancestry. In the end, Phipps lost. The court upheld the state's right to classify and quantify racial identity.[1]

Phipps's problematic racial identity, and her effort to resolve it through state action, is in many ways a parable of America's unsolved racial dilemma. It illustrates the difficulties of defining race and assigning individuals or groups to racial categories. It shows how the racial legacies of the past—slavery and bigotry—continue to shape the present. It reveals both the deep involvement of the state in the organization and interpretation of race, and the inadequacy of state institutions to carry out these functions. It demonstrates how deeply Americans both as individuals and as a civilization are shaped, and indeed haunted, by race.

Having lived her whole life thinking that she was white, Phipps suddenly discovers that by legal definition she is not. In U.S. society, such an event is indeed catastrophic.[2] But if she is not white, of what race is she? The state claims that she is black, based on its rules of classification,[3] and another state agency, the court, upholds this judgment. But despite these classificatory standards which have imposed an either/or logic on racial identity, Phipps will not in fact change color. Unlike what would have happened during slavery times if one's claim to whiteness was successfully challenged, we can assume that despite the outcome of her legal challenge, Phipps will remain in most of the social relationships she had occupied before the trial. Her socialization, her familial and friendship networks, her cultural orientation, will not change. She will simply have to wrestle with her newly acquired hybridized condition. She will have to confront the Other within.

The designation of racial categories and the determination of racial identity is no simple task. For centuries, this question has precipitated intense debates and conflicts, particularly in the U.S.—disputes over natural and legal rights, over the distribution of resources, and indeed, over who shall live and who shall die.

A crucial dimension of the Phipps case is that it illustrates the inadequacy of claims that race is a mere matter of variations in human physiognomy, that it is simply a matter of skin color. But if race cannot be understood in this manner, how *can* it be understood? We cannot fully hope to address this topic—no less than the meaning of race, its role in society, and the forces which shape it—in one chapter, nor indeed in one book. Our goal in this chapter, however, is far from modest: we wish to offer at least the outlines of a theory of race and racism.

What Is Race?

There is a continuous temptation to think of race as an essence, as something fixed, concrete, and objective. And there is also an opposite temptation: to imagine race as a mere *illusion*, a purely ideological construct which some ideal non-racist social order would eliminate. It is necessary to challenge both these positions, to disrupt and reframe the rigid and bipolar manner in which they are posed and debated, and to transcend the presumably irreconcilable relationship between them.

The effort must be made to understand race as an unstable and decentered complex of social meanings constantly being transformed by political struggle. With this in mind, let us propose a definition: *Race is a concept which signifies and symbolizes social conflicts and interests by referring to different types of human bodies.* Although the concept of race invokes biologically based human characteristics (so-called phenotypes), selection of these particular human features for purposes of racial signification is always and necessarily a social and historical process. In contrast to the other major distinction of this type, that of gender, there is no biological basis for distinguishing among human groups along the lines of race.[4] Indeed, the categories employed to differentiate among human groups along racial lines reveal themselves, upon serious examination, to be at best imprecise, and at worst completely arbitrary.

If the concept of race is so nebulous, can we not dispense with it? Can we not do without race, at least in the enlightened present? This question has been posed often, and with greater frequency in recent years.[5] An affirmative answer would of course present obvious practical difficulties: it is rather difficult to jettison widely held beliefs, beliefs which moreover are central to everyone's identity and understanding of the social world. So the attempt to banish the concept as an archaism is at best counterintuitive. But a deeper difficulty, we believe, is inherent in the very formulation of this schema, in its way of posing race as a *problem*, a misconception left over from the past, and suitable now only for the dustbin of history.

A more effective starting point is the recognition that despite its uncertainties and contradictions, the concept of race continues to play a fundamental role in structuring and representing the social world. The task for theory is to explain this situation. It is to avoid both the utopian framework which sees race as an illusion we can somehow get beyond, and also the essentialist formulation which sees race as something objective and fixed, a biological datum.[6] Thus we should think of race as an element of social structure rather than as an irregularity within it; we should see race as a dimension of human representation rather than an illusion. These perspectives inform the theoretical approach we call racial formation.

Racial Formation

We define *racial formation* as the sociohistorical process by which racial categories are created, inhabited, transformed, and destroyed. Our attempt to elaborate a theory of racial formation will proceed in two steps. First, we argue that racial formation is a process of historically situated *projects* in which human bodies and social structures are represented and organized. Next we link racial formation to the evolution of hegemony, the way in which society is organized and ruled. Such an approach, we believe, can facilitate understanding of a whole range of contemporary controversies and dilemmas involving race, including the nature of racism, the relationship of race to other forms of differences, inequalities, and oppression such as sexism and nationalism, and the dilemmas of racial identity today. From a racial formation perspective, race is a matter of both social structure and cultural representation. Too often, the attempt is made to understand race simply or primarily in terms of only one of these two analytical dimensions.[7] For example, efforts to explain racial inequality as a purely social structural phenomenon are unable to account for the origins, patterning, and transformation of racial difference.

Conversely, many examinations of racial difference—understood as a matter of cultural attributes *a la* ethnicity theory, or as a society-wide signification system, *a la* some poststructuralist accounts—cannot comprehend such structural phenomena as racial stratification in the labor market or patterns of residential segregation.

An alternative approach is to think of racial formation processes as occurring through a linkage between structure and representation. Racial projects do the ideological "work" of making these links. *A racial project is simultaneously an interpretation, representation, or explanation of racial dynamics, and an effort to reorganize and redistribute resources along particular racial lines.* Racial projects connect what race *means* in a particular discursive practice and the ways in which both social structures and everyday experiences are racially *organized*, based upon that meaning.

What Is Racism?

Since the ambiguous triumph of the civil rights movement in the mid 1960s, clarity about what racism means has been eroding. The concept entered the lexicon of "common sense" only in the 1960s. Before that, although the term had surfaced occasionally,[46] the problem of racial injustice and inequality was generally understood in a more limited fashion, as a matter of prejudiced attitudes or bigotry on the one hand,[47] and discriminatory practices on the other.[48] Solutions, it was believed, would therefore involve the overcoming of such attitudes, the achievement of tolerance, the acceptance of brotherhood, etc., and the passage of laws which prohibited discrimination with respect to access to public accommodations, jobs, education, etc. The early civil rights movement explicitly reflected such views. In its espousal of integration and its quest for a beloved community it sought to overcome racial prejudice. In its litigation activities and agitation for civil rights legislation it sought to challenge discriminatory practices.

The later 1960s, however, signaled a sharp break with this vision. The emergence of the slogan *black power* (and soon after, of *brown power*, *red power*, and *yellow power*), the wave of riots that swept the urban ghettos from 1964 to 1968, and the founding of radical movement organizations of nationalist and Marxist orientation, coincided with the recognition that racial inequality and injustice had much deeper roots. They were not simply the product of prejudice, nor was discrimination only a matter of intentionally informed action. Rather, prejudice was an almost unavoidable outcome of patterns of socialization which were "bred in the bone," affecting not only whites but even minorities themselves.[49] Discrimination, far from manifesting itself only (or even principally) through individual actions or conscious policies, was a structural feature of U.S. society, the product of centuries of systematic exclusion, exploitation, and disregard of racially defined minorities.[50] It was this combination of relationships—prejudice, discrimination, and institutional inequality—which defined the concept of racism at the end of the 1960s.

Such a synthesis was better able to confront the political realities of the period. Its emphasis on the structural dimensions of racism allowed it to address the intransigence which racial injustice and inequality continued to exhibit, even after discrimination had supposedly been outlawed[51] and bigoted expression stigmatized. But such an approach also had clear limitations. As Robert Miles has argued, it tended to inflate the concept of racism to a point at which it lost precision.[52] If the institutional component of racism were so pervasive and deeply rooted, it became difficult to see how the democratization of U.S. society could be achieved, and difficult to explain what progress had been made. The result was a leveling critique which denied any distinction between the Jim Crow era (or even the whole longue durée of racial dictatorship since the conquest) and the present. Similarly, if the prejudice component of racism were so deeply inbred, it became difficult to account for the evident hybridity and interpenetration that characterizes civil society in the U.S., as evidenced by the shaping of popular culture, language, and style, for example. The result of the inflation of the concept of racism was thus a deep pessimism about any efforts to overcome racial barriers, in the workplace, the community, or any other sphere of lived experience. An overly comprehensive view of racism, then, potentially served as a self-fulfilling prophecy.

Yet the alternative view—which surfaced with a vengeance in the 1970s—urging a return to the conception of racism held before the movement's radical turn, was equally inadequate. This was the neoconservative perspective, which deliberately restricted its attention to injury done to the individual as opposed to the group, and to advocacy of a color-blind racial policy.[53] Such an approach reduced race to ethnicity,[54] and almost entirely neglected the continuing organization of social inequality and oppression along racial lines. Worse yet, it tended to rationalize racial injustice as a supposedly natural outcome of group attributes in cornpetition.[55]

The distinct, and contested, meanings of racism which have been advanced over the past three decades have contributed to an overall crisis of meaning for the concept today. Today, the absence of a clear common-sense understanding of what racism means has become a significant obstacle to efforts aimed at challenging it. Bob Blauner has noted that in classroom discussions of racism, white and nonwhite students tend to talk past one another. Whites tend to locate racism in color consciousness and find its absence color-blindness. In so doing, they see the affirmation of difference and racial identity among racially defined minority students as racist. Nonwhite students, by contrast, see racism as a system of power, and correspondingly argue that blacks, for example, cannot be racist because they lack power. Blauner concludes that there are two "languages" of race, one in which members of racial minorities, especially blacks, see the centrality of race in history and everyday experience, and another in which whites see race as "a peripheral, nonessential reality."[56]

Given this crisis of meaning, and in the absence of any common-sense understanding, does the concept of racism retain any validity? If so, what view of racism should we adopt? Is a more coherent theoretical approach possible? We believe it is.

We employ racial formation theory to reformulate the concept of racism. Our approach recognizes that racism, like race, has changed over time. It is obvious that the attitudes, practices, and institutions of the epochs of slavery, say, or of Jim Crow, no longer exist today. Employing a similar logic, it is reasonable to question whether concepts of racism which developed in the early days of the post–civil rights era, when the limitations of both moderate reform and militant racial radicalism of various types had not yet been encountered, remain adequate to explain circumstances and conflicts a quarter century later.

Racial formation theory allows us to differentiate between race and racism. The two concepts should not be used interchangeably. We have argued that race has no fixed meaning, but is constructed and transformed sociohistorically through competing political projects, through the necessary and ineluctable link between the structural and cultural dimensions of race in the U.S. This emphasis on projects allows us to refocus our understanding of racism as well, for racism can now be seen as characterizing some, but not all, racial projects.

A racial project can be defined as *racist* if and only if it *creates or reproduces structures of domination based on essentialist*[57] *categories of race.* Such a definition recognizes the importance of locating racism within a fluid and contested history of racially based social structures and discourses. Thus there can be no timeless and absolute standard for what constitutes racism, for social structures change and discourses are subject to rearticulation. Our definition therefore focuses instead on the work essentialism does for domination, and the need domination displays to essentialize the subordinated.

Further, it is important to distinguish racial awareness from racial essentialism. To attribute merits, allocate values or resources to, and/or represent individuals or groups on the basis of racial identity should not be considered racist in and of itself. Such projects may in fact be quite benign. Consider the following examples: first, the statement, "Many Asian Americans are highly entrepreneurial"; second, the organization of an association of, say, black accountants.

The first racial project, in our view, signifies or represents a racial category (Asian Americans) and locates that representation within the social structure of the contemporary U.S. (in regard to business, class issues, socialization, etc.). The second racial project is organizational or social structural, and therefore must engage in racial signification. Black accountants, the organizers might maintain, have certain common experiences, can offer each other certain support, etc. Neither of these racial projects is essentialist, and neither can fairly be labeled racist. Of course, racial representations may be biased or misinterpret their subjects, just as racially based organizational efforts may be unfair or unjustifiably exclusive. If such were the case, if for instance in our first example the statement in question were "Asian Americans are naturally entrepreneurial," this would by our criterion be racist. Similarly, if the effort to organize black accountants had as its rationale the raiding of clients from white accountants, it would by our criterion be racist as well.

Similarly, to allocate values or resources—let us say, academic scholarships—on the basis of racial categories is not racist. Scholarships are awarded on a preferential basis to Rotarians, children of insurance company employees, and residents of the Pittsburgh metropolitan area. Why then should they not also be offered, in particular cases, to Chicanos or Native Americans?

In order to identify a social project as racist, one must in our view demonstrate a link between essentialist representations of race and social structures of domination. Such a link might be revealed in efforts to protect dominant interests, framed in racial terms, from democratizing racial initiatives.[58] But it might also consist of efforts simply to reverse the roles of racially dominant and racially subordinate.[59] There is nothing inherently white about racism.[60]

Obviously a key problem with essentialism is its denial, or flattening, of differences within a particular racially defined group. Members of subordinate racial groups, when faced with racist practices such as exclusion or discrimination, are frequently forced to band together in order to defend their interests (if not, in some instances, their very lives). Such "strategic essentialism" should not, however, be simply equated with the essentialism practiced by dominant groups, nor should it prevent the interrogation of internal group differences.[61]

Without question, any abstract concept of racism is severely put to the test by the untidy world of reality. To illustrate our discussion, we analyze the following examples, chosen from current racial issues because of their complexity and the rancorous debates they have engendered:

- Is the allocation of employment opportunities through programs restricted to racially defined minorities, so-called preferential treatment or affirmative action policies, racist? Do such policies practice racism in reverse? We think not, with certain qualifications. Although such programs necessarily employ racial criteria in assessing eligibility, they do not generally essentialize race, because they seek to overcome specific socially and historically constructed inequalities.[62] Criteria of effectiveness and feasibility, therefore, must be considered in evaluating such programs. They must balance egalitarian and context-specific objectives, such as academic potential or job-related qualifications. It should be acknowledged that such programs often do have deleterious consequences for whites who are not personally the source of the discriminatory practices the programs seek to overcome. In this case, compensatory measures should be enacted to vitiate the charge of "reverse discrimination."[63]
- Is all racism the same, or is there a distinction between white and nonwhite versions of racism? We have little patience with the argument that racism is solely a white problem, or even a "white disease."[64] The idea that nonwhites cannot act in a racist manner, since they do not possess "power," is another variant of this formulation.[65]

For many years now, racism has operated in a more complex fashion than this, sometimes taking such forms as self-hatred or self-aggrandizement at the expense of more vulnerable members of racially subordinate groups.[66] Whites can at times be the victims of racism—by other whites or nonwhites—as is the case with anti-Jewish and anti-Arab prejudice. Furthermore, unless one is prepared to argue that there has been no transformation of the U.S. racial order over the years, and that racism consequently has remained unchanged—an essentialist position *par excellence*—it is difficult to contend that racially defined minorities have attained no power or influence, especially in recent years.

Having said this, we still do not consider that all racism is the same. This is because of the crucial importance we place in situating various racisms within the dominant hegemonic discourse about race. We have little doubt that the rantings of a Louis Farrakhan or Leonard Jeffries—to pick two currently demonized black ideologues—meet the criteria we have set out for judging a discourse to be racist. Bur if we compare Jeffries, for example, with a white racist such as Tom Metzger of the White Aryan Resistance, we find the latter's racial project to be far more menacing than the former's. Metzger's views are far more easily associated with an essentializing (and once very powerful) legacy: that of white supremacy and racial dictatorship in the U.S., and fascism in the world at large. Jeffries's project has far fewer examples with which to associate: no more than some ancient African empires and the (usually far less bigoted) radical phase of the black power movement.[67] Thus black supremacy may be an instance of racism, just as its advocacy may be offensive, but it can hardly constitute the threat that white supremacy has represented in the U.S., nor can it be so easily absorbed and rearticulated in the dominant hegemonic discourse on race as white supremacy can. All racisms, all racist political projects, are not the same.

- Is the redrawing—or gerrymandering—of adjacent electoral districts to incorporate large numbers of racially defined minority voters in one, and largely white voters in the other, racist? Do such policies amount to segregation of the electorate? Certainly this alternative is preferable to the pre–Voting Rights Act practice of simply denying racial minorities the franchise. But does it achieve the Act's purpose of fostering electoral equality across and within racial lines? In our view such practices, in which the post-1990 redistricting process engaged rather widely, are vulnerable to charges of essentialism. They often operate through "racial lumping," tend to freeze rather than overcome racial inequalities, and frequently subvert or defuse political processes through which racially defined groups could otherwise negotiate their differences and interests. They worsen rather than ameliorate the denial of effective representation to those whom they could not effectively redistrict—since no redrawing of electoral boundaries is perfect, those who get stuck on the "wrong side" of the line are particularly disempowered. Thus we think such policies merit the designation of "tokenism"—a relatively mild form of racism—which they have received.[68]

Parallel to the debates on the concept of race, recent academic and political controversies about the nature of racism have centered on whether it is primarily an ideological or structural phenomenon. Proponents of the former position argue that racism is first and foremost a matter of beliefs and attitudes, doctrines and discourse, which only then give rise to unequal and unjust practices and structures.[69] Advocates of the latter view see racism as primarily a matter of economic stratification, residential segregation, and other institutionalized forms of inequality which then give rise to ideologies of privilege.[70]

From the standpoint of racial formation, these debates are fundamentally misguided. They frame the problem of racism in a rigid either/or manner. We believe it is crucial to disrupt the fixity of these positions by simultaneously arguing that ideological beliefs have structural consequences, and that social structures give rise to beliefs. Racial ideology and social structure, therefore, mutually shape the nature of racism in a complex, dialectical, and overdetermined manner.

Even those racist projects which at first glance appear chiefly ideological turn out upon closer examination to have significant institutional and social structural dimensions. For example, what we have called *far right* projects appear at first glance to be centrally ideological. They are rooted in biologistic doctrine, after all. The same seems to hold for certain conservative black nationalist projects which have deep commitments to biologism.[71] But the unending stream of racist assaults initiated by the far right, the apparently increasing presence of skinheads in high schools, the proliferation of neo-Nazi computer bulletin boards, and the appearance of racist talk shows on cable access channels, all suggest that the organizational manifestations of the far right racial projects exist and will endure.[72] Perhaps less threatening but still quite worrisome is the diffusion of doctrines of black superiority through some (though by no means all) university based African American Studies departments and student organizations, surely a serious institutional or structural development.

By contrast, even those racisms which at first glance appear to be chiefly structural upon closer examination reveal a deeply ideological component. For example, since the racial right abandoned its explicit advocacy of segregation, it has not seemed to uphold—in the main—an ideologically racist project, bur more primarily a structurally racist one. Yet this very transformation required tremendous efforts of ideological production. It demanded the rearticulation of civil rights doctrines of equality in suitably conservative form, and indeed the defense of continuing large-scale racial inequality as an outcome preferable to (what its advocates have seen as) the threat to democracy that affirmative action, busing, and large-scale race-specific social spending would entail.[73] Even more tellingly, this project took shape through a deeply manipulative coding of subtextual appeals to white racism, notably in a series of political campaigns for high office which have occurred over recent decades. The retreat of social policy from any practical commitment to racial justice, and the relentless reproduction and divulgation of this theme at the level of everyday life—where whites are now fed up with all the "special treatment" received by nonwhites, etc.—constitutes the hegemonic racial project at this time. It therefore exhibits an unabashed structural racism all the more brazen because on the ideological or signification level, it adheres to a principle of treating everyone alike.

In summary, the racism of today is no longer a virtual monolith, as was the racism of yore. Today, racial hegemony is messy. The complexity of the present situation is the product of a vast historical legacy of structural inequality and invidious racial representation, which has been confronted during the post–World War II period with an opposition more serious and effective than any it had faced before. As we will survey in the chapters to follow, the result is a deeply ambiguous and contradictory spectrum of racial projects, unremittingly conflictual racial politics, and confused and ambivalent racial identities of all sorts. We begin this discussion by addressing racial politics and the state.

Notes

1. *San Francisco Chronicle*, 14 September 1982, 19 May 1983. Ironically, the 1970 Louisiana law was enacted to supersede an old Jim Crow statute which relied on the idea of "common report" in determining an infant's race. Following Phipps' unsuccessful attempt to change her classification and have the law declared unconstitutional, a legislative effort arose which culminated in the repeal of the law. See *San Francisco Chronicle*, 23 June 1983.

2. Compare the Phipps case to Andrew Hacker's well-known "parable" in which a white person is informed by a mysterious official that "the organization he represents has made a mistake" and that ". . . [a]ccording to their records . . ., you were to have been born black: to another set of parents, far from where you were raised." How much compensation, Hacker's official asks, would "you" require to undo the damage of this unfortunate error? See Hacker, *Two Nations: Black and White, Separate, Hostile, Unequal* (New York: Charles Scribner's Sons, 1992) pp. 11–12.

3. On the evolution of Louisiana's racial classification system, see Virginia Dominguez, *White by Definition: Social Classification in Creole Louisiana* (New Brunswick: Rutgers University Press, 1986).

4. This is not to suggest that gender is a biological category while race is not. Gender, like race, is a social construct. However, the biological division of humans into sexes—two at least, and possibly intermediate ones as well—is not in dispute. This provides a basis for argument over gender divisions—how "natural," etc.—which does not exist with regard to race. To ground an argument for the "natural" existence of race, one must resort to philosophical anthropology.

5. "The truth is that there are no races, there is nothing in the world that can do all we ask race to do for us. . . . The evil that is done is done by the concept, and by easy—yet impossible—assumptions as to its application." (Kwame Anthony Appiah, *In My Father's House: Africa in the Philosophy of Culture* [New York: Oxford University Press, 1992].) Appiah's eloquent and learned book fails, in our view, to dispense with the race concept, despite its anguished attempt to do so; this indeed is the source of its author's anguish. We agree with him as to the nonobjective character of race, but fail to see how this recognition justifies its abandonment. This argument is developed below.

6. We understand essentialism as belief in real, true human essences, existing outside or impervious to social and historical context. We draw this definition, with some small modifications, from Diana Fuss, *Essentially Speaking: Feminism, Nature, & Difference* (New York: Routledge, 1989) p. xi.

7. Michael Omi and Howard Winant, "On the Theoretical Status of the Concept of Race" in Warren Crichlow and Cameron McCarthy, eds., *Race, Identity, and Representation in Education* (New York: Routledge, 1993).

46. For example, in Magnus Hirschfeld's prescient book, *Racism* (London: Victor Gollancz, 1938).

47. This was the framework, employed in the crucial study of Myrdal and his associates; see Gunnar Myrdal, *An American Dilemma: The Negro Problem and Modern Democracy*, 20th Anniversary Edition (New York: Harper and Row, 1962[1944]). See also the articles by Thomas F. Pettigrew and George Fredrickson in Pettigrew et al., *Prejudice: Selections from the Harvard Encyclopedia of American Ethnic Groups* (Cambridge, MA: The Belknap Press of Harvard University, 1982).

48. On discrimination, see Frederickson in ibid. In an early essay which explicitly sought to modify the framework of the Myrdal study, Robert K. Merton recognized that prejudice and discrimination need not coincide, and indeed could combine in a variety of ways. See Merton, "Discrimination and the American Creed," in R. M. MacIver, ed., *Discrimination and National Welfare* (New York: Harper and Row, 1949).

49. Gordon W. Allport, *The Nature of Prejudice* (Cambridge, MA: Addison-Wesley, 1954) remains a classic work in the field; see also Philomena Essed, *Understanding Everyday Racism: An Interdisciplinary Theory* (Newbury Park, CA: Sage, 1991). A good overview of black attitudes toward black identities is provided in William E. Cross, Jr., *Shades of Black: Diversity in African-American Identity* (Philadelphia: Temple University Press, 1991).

50. Stokely Carmichael and Charles V. Hamilton first popularized the notion of "institutional" forms of discrimination in *Black Power: The Politics of Liberation in America* (New York: Vintage, 1967), although the basic concept certainly predated that work. Indeed, President Lyndon Johnson made a similar argument in his 1965 speech at Howard University:

    But freedom is not enough. You do not wipe away the scars of centuries by saying: Now you are free to go where you want, do as you desire, and choose the leaders you please.

    You do not take a person who, for years, has been hobbled by chains and liberate him [*sic*], bring him up to the starting line of a race and then say, "You are free to compete with all the others," and still justly believe that you have been completely fair.

    Thus it is not enough just to open the gates of opportunity. All our citizens must have the opportunity to walk through those gates.

    This is the next and more profound stage of the battle for civil rights. We seek not just freedom but opportunity—not just legal equity but human ability—not just equality as a right but equality as a fact and as a result. (Lyndon B. Johnson, "To Fulfill These Rights," reprinted in Lee Rainwater and William L. Yancey, *The Moynihan Report and the Politics of Controversy* [Cambridge, MA: MIT Press, 1967, p. 125].)

    This speech, delivered at Howard University on June 4, 1965, was written in part by Daniel Patrick Moynihan. A more systematic treatment of the institutional racism approach is David T. Wellman, *Portraits of White Racism* (New York: Cambridge University Press, 1977).

51. From the vantage point of the 1990s, it is possible to question whether discrimination was ever effectively outlawed. The federal retreat from the agenda of integration began almost immediately after the passage of civil rights legislation, and has culminated today in a series of Supreme Court decisions making violation of these laws almost impossible to prove. See Ezorsky, *Racism*

and Justice; Kairys, *With Liberty and Justice (or Some)*. As we write, the Supreme Court has further restricted antidiscrimination laws in the case of *St. Mary's Honor Center v. Flicks*. See Linda Greenhouse, "Justices Increase Workers' Burden in Job-Bias Cases," *The New York Times*, 26 June 1993, p. 1.

52. Robert Miles, *Racism* (New York and London: Routledge, 1989), esp. chap. 2.

53. The *locus clasicus* of this position is Nathan Glazer, *Affirmative Discrimination: Ethnic Inequality and Public Policy*, 2nd ed. (New York: Basic Books, 1978); for more recent formulations, see Murray, *Losing Ground*; Arthur M. Schlesinger, *The Disuniting of America: Reflections on a Multicultural Society* (New York: W. W. Norton, 1992).

54. See Chapter 1.

55. Thomas Sowell, for example, has argued that one's "human capital" is to a large extent culturally determined. Therefore, the state cannot create a false equality which runs counter to the magnitude and persistence of cultural differences. Such attempts at social engineering are likely to produce negative and unintended results: "If social processes are transmitting real differences—in productivity, reliability, cleanliness, sobriety, peacefulness (!)—then attempts to impose politically a very different set of beliefs will necessarily backfire. . . ." (Thomas Sowell, *The Economics and Politics of Race: An International Perspective* (New York: Quill, 1983) p. 252).

56. Bob Blauner, "Racism, Race, and Ethnicity: Some Reflections on the Language of Race" (unpublished manuscript, 1991).

57. Essentialism, it will be recalled, is understood as belief in real, true human essences, existing outside or impervious to social and historical context.

58. An example would be the "singling out" of members of racially defined minority groups for harsh treatment by authorities, as when police harass and beat randomly chosen ghetto youth, a practice they do not pursue with white suburban youth.

59. For example, the biologistic theories found in Michael Anderson Bradley, *The Iceman Inheritance: Prehistoric Sources of Western Man's Racism, Sexism and Aggression* (Toronto: Dorset, 1978), and in Frances Cress Welsing, *The Isis (Yssis) Papers* (Chicago: Third World Press, 1991).

60. "These remarks should not be interpreted as simply an effort to move the gaze of African-American studies to a different site. I do not want to alter one hierarchy in order to institute another. It is true that I do not want to encourage those totalizing approaches to African-American scholarship which have no drive other than the exchange of dominations-dominant Eurocentric scholarship replaced by dominant Afrocentric scholarship. More interesting is what makes intellectual domination possible; how knowledge is transformed from invasion and conquest to revelation and choice; what ignites and informs the literary imagination, and what forces help establish the parameters of criticism." (Toni Morrison, *Playing in the Dark*, p. 8; emphasis in original)

61. Lisa Lowe states: "The concept of 'strategic essentialism' suggests that it is possible to utilize specific signifiers of ethnic identity, such as Asian American, for the purpose of contesting and disrupting the discourses that exclude Asian Americans, while simultaneously revealing the internal contradictions and slippages of Asian Americans so as to insure that such essentialisms will not be reproduced and proliferated by the very apparatuses we seek to disempower." Lisa Lowe, "Heterogeneity, Hybridity, Multiplicity: Marking Asian American Differences," *Diaspora*, Vol. 1, no. 1 (Spring 1991) p. 39.

62. This view supports Supreme Court decisions taken in the late 1960s and early 1970s, for example in *Griggs v. Duke Power*, 401 U.S. 424 (1971). We agree with Kairys that only ". . . [F]or that

brief period in our history, it could accurately be said that governmental discrimination was prohibited by law" (Kairys, *With Liberty and Justice for Some,* p. 144).

63. This analysis draws on Ezorsky, *Racism and Justice.*

64. See for example, Judy H. Katz, *White Awareness: Handbook (or Anti-Racism Training* (Norman: University of Oklahoma Press, 1978).

65. The formula "racism equals prejudice plus power" is frequently invoked by our students to argue that only whites can be racist. We have been able to uncover little written analysis to support this view (apart from Karz, ibid., p. 10), but consider that it is itself an example of the essentializing approach we have identified as central to racism. In the modern world, "power" cannot be reified as a thing which some possess and others don't, but instead constitutes a relational field. The minority student who boldly asserts in class that minorities cannot be racist is surely not entirely powerless. In all but the most absolutist of regimes, resistance to rule itself implies power.

66. To pick but one example among many: writing before the successes of the civil rights movement, E. Franklin Frazier bitterly castigated the collaboration of black elites with white supremacy. See Frazier, *Black Bourgeoisie: The Rise of a New Middle Class in the United States* (New York: The Free Press, 1957).

67. Interestingly, what they share most centrally seems to be their antisemitism.

68. Having made a similar argument, Lani Guinier, Clinton's nominee to head the Justice Department's Civil Rights Division was savagely attacked and her nomination ultimately blocked. See Guinier, "The Triumph of Tokenism: The Voting Rights Act and the Theory of Black Electoral Success," *Michigan Law Review* (March 1991).

69. See Miles, *Racism,* p. 77. Much of the current debate over the advisability and legality of banning racist hate speech seems to us to adopt the dubious position that racism is primarily an ideological phenomenon. See Mari J. Matsuda et al., *Words that Wound: Critical Race Theory, Assaultive Speech, and the First Amendment* (Boulder, CO: Westview Press, 1993).

70. Or ideologies which mask privilege by falsely claiming that inequality and injustice have been eliminated. See Wellman, *Portraits of White Racism.*

71. Racial teachings of the Nation of Islam, for example, maintain that whites are the product of a failed experiment by a mad scientist.

72. Elinor Langer, "The American Neo-Nazi Movement Today," *The Nation,* July 16/23, 1990.

73. Such arguments can be found in Nathan Glazer, *Affirmative Discrimination,* Charles Murray, *Losing Ground,* and Arthur M. Schlesinger, Jr., *The Disuniting of America,* among others.

CHAPTER 3

Rethinking Racism*

Toward a Structural Interpretation

Eduardo Bonilla-Silva

In this essay, Eduardo Bonilla-Silva develops a structural theory of racism. He argues that the study of racial and ethnic relations tends to focus on individual psychology to explain racism as a set of beliefs that lead to persistent racial inequality and conflict. Instead, he contends that a new approach is needed, one that focuses explicitly on the study of racism from a structural perspective. Here, he advances a structural approach to racism based on the concept of ***racialized social systems.***

Questions to Consider

According to Bonilla-Silva, what is the advantage of understanding racism as rooted in structural forces rather than thinking about it as a set of beliefs or ideas held by individuals? This theory of racism seems to suggest that racism is embedded in the American social structure. From this perspective, what types of individuals or actions might be labeled as *racist*?

Source: Adapted from Eduardo Bonilla-Silva, "Rethinking Racism: Toward a Structural Interpretation," *American Sociological Review*, Volume 62, Number 3, pages 465–480. American Sociological Association—SAGE Publications, Inc., 1997.

*Endnotes have been omitted. Please consult the original source.

"The habit of considering racism as a mental quirk, as a psychological flaw, must be abandoned."

—Frantz Fanon (1967:77)

The area of race and ethnic studies lacks a sound theoretical apparatus. To complicate matters, many analysts of racial matters have abandoned the serious theorization and reconceptualization of their central topic: racism. Too many social analysts researching racism assume that the phenomenon is self-evident, and therefore either do not provide a definition or provide an elementary definition (Schuman, Steeh, and Bobo 1985; Sniderman and Piazza 1993). Nevertheless, whether implicitly or explicitly, most analysts regard racism as a purely ideological phenomenon.

Although the concept of racism has become the central analytical category in most contemporary social scientific discourse on racial phenomena, the concept is of recent origin (Banton 1970; Miles 1989, 1993). It was not employed at all in the classic works of Thomas and Znaniecki (1918), Edward Reuter (1934), Gunnar Myrdal (1944), and Robert Park (1950). Benedict (1945) was one of the first scholars to use the notion of racism in her book, Race and Racism. She defined racism as "the dogma that one ethnic group is condemned by nature to congenital inferiority and another group is destined to congenital superiority" (p. 87). Despite some refinements, current use of the concept of racism in the social sciences is similar to Benedict's. Thus van den Berghe (1967) states that racism is "any set of beliefs that organic, genetically transmitted differences (whether real or imagined) between human groups are intrinsically associated with the presence or the absence of certain socially relevant abilities or characteristics, hence that such differences are a legitimate basis of invidious distinctions between groups socially defined as races" (p. 11, emphasis added). Schaefer (1990) provides a more concise definition of racism: ". . . a doctrine of racial supremacy, that one race is superior" (p. 16).

This idealist view is still held widely among social scientists. Its narrow focus on ideas has reduced the study of racism mostly to social psychology, and this perspective has produced a schematic view of the way racism operates in society. First, racism is defined as a set of ideas or beliefs. Second, those beliefs are regarded as having the potential to lead individuals to develop prejudice, defined as "negative attitudes towards an entire group of people" (Schaefer 1990:53). Finally, these prejudicial attitudes may induce individuals to real actions or discrimination against racial minorities. This conceptual framework, with minor modifications, prevails in the social sciences.

Some alternative perspectives on racism have closely followed the prevailing ideological conceptualization in the social sciences. For example, orthodox Marxists (Cox 1948; Perlo 1975; Szymanski 1981, 1983), who regard class and class struggle as the central explanatory variables of social life, reduce racism to a legitimating ideology used by the bourgeoisie to divide the working class. Even neo-Marxists (Bonacich 1980a, 1980b; Carchedi 1987; Cohen 1989; Hall 1980; Miles 1989, 1993; Miles and Phizacklea 1984; Solomos 1986, 1989; Wolpe 1986, 1988) share to various degrees the limitations of the orthodox Marxist view: the primacy of class, racism viewed as an ideology, and class dynamics as the real engine of racial dynamics. For example, although Bonacich's work provides an interesting twist by regarding race relations and racism as products of a split labor market, giving theoretical primacy to divisions within the working class, racial antagonisms are still regarded as byproducts of class dynamics. Other scholars have advanced nonideological interpretations of racism but have stopped short of developing a structural conceptualization of racial matters. From the institutionalist perspective (Alvarez et al. 1979; Carmichael 1971; Carmichael and Hamilton 1967; Chesler 1976; Knowles and Prewitt 1969; Wellman 1977), racism is defined as a combination of prejudice and power that allows the dominant race to institutionalize its dominance at all levels in a society. Similarly, from the internal colonialism perspective (Barrera 1979; Blauner 1972; Moore 1970), racism is viewed as an institutional matter based on a system in which the White majority "raises its social position by exploiting, controlling, and keeping down others who are categorized in racial or ethnic terms" (Blauner 1972:22). The main difference between these two perspectives is that the latter regards racial minorities as colonial subjects in the United States; this view leads unequivocally to nationalist solutions. Both perspectives contribute greatly to our understanding of racial phenomena by stressing the social and systemic nature of racism and the structured nature of White advantages. Furthermore, the effort of the institutionalist perspective to uncover contemporary mechanisms and practices that reproduce White advantages is still empirically useful (e.g., Knowles and Prewitt 1969). Yet neither of these perspectives provides a rigorous conceptual framework that allows analysts to study the operation of racially stratified societies. The racial formation perspective (Omi and Winant 1986, 1994; Winant 1994) is the most recent theoretical alternative to mainstream idealist approaches. Omi and Winant (1994) define racial formation as "the sociohistorical process by which racial categories are created, inhabited, transformed, and destroyed" (p. 55). In their view, race should be regarded as an organizing principle of social relationships that shapes the identity of individual actors at the micro level and shapes all spheres of social life at the macro level. Although this perspective represents a breakthrough, it still gives undue attention to ideological/cultural processes, does not regard races as truly social collectivities, and overemphasizes the racial projects (Omi and Winant 1994; Winant 1994) of certain actors (neoconservatives, members of the far right, liberals), thus obscuring the social and general character of racialized societies.

In this paper I point out the limitations of most contemporary frameworks used to analyze racial issues and suggest an alternative structural theory built on some of the ideas and concepts elaborated by the institutionalist, the internal colonial, and the racial formation perspectives. Although "racism" has a definite ideological component, reducing racial phenomena to ideas limits the possibility of understanding how it shapes a race's life chances. Rather than viewing racism as an all-powerful ideology that explains all racial phenomena in a society, I use the term *racism* only to describe the racial ideology of a racialized social system. That is, racism is only part of a larger racial system.

Limitations of Mainstream Idealist Views and of Some Alternative Frameworks

I describe below some of the main limitations of the idealist conception of racism. Because not all limitations apply to the institutionalist, the internal colonialist, and the racial formation perspectives, I point out the ones that do apply, and to what extent.

Racism is excluded from the foundation or structure of the social system. When racism is regarded as a baseless ideology ultimately dependent on other, "real" forces in society, the structure of the society itself is not classified as racist. The Marxist perspective is particularly guilty of this shortcoming. Although Marxists have addressed the question of the historical origin of racism, they explain its reproduction in an idealist fashion. Racism, in their accounts, is an ideology that emerged with chattel slavery and other forms of class oppression to justify the exploitation of people of color and survives as a residue of the past. Although some Marxists have attempted to distance their analysis from this purely ideological view (Solomos 1986; Wolpe 1988) and to ground racial phenomena in social relations, they do so by ultimately subordinating racial matters to class matters.

Even though the institutionalist, internal colonialism, and racial formation perspectives regard racism as a structural phenomenon and provide some useful ideas and concepts, they do not develop the theoretical apparatus necessary to describe how this structure operates.

Racism is ultimately viewed as a psychological phenomenon to be examined at the individual level. The research agenda that follows from this conceptualization is the examination of individuals' attitudes to determine levels of racism in society (Schuman et al. 1985; Sears 1988; Sniderman and Piazza 1993). Given that the constructs used to measure racism are static—that is, that there are a number of standard questions which do not change significantly over time—this research usually finds that racism is declining in society. Those analysts who find that racist attitudes are still with us usually leave unexplained why this is so (Sniderman and Piazza 1993).

This psychological understanding of racism is related to the limitation I cited above. If racism is not part of a society but is a characteristic of individuals who are "racist" or "prejudiced"—that is, racism is a phenomenon operating at the individual level—then (1) social institutions cannot be racist and (2) studying racism is simply a matter of surveying the proportion of people in a society who hold "racist" beliefs.

Orthodox Marxists (Cox 1948; Perlo 1975; Szymanski 1983) and many neo-Marxists (Miles 1993; Miles and Phizaclea 1984; Solomos 1986) conceive of racism as an ideology that may affect members of the working class. Although the authors associated with the institutionalist, internal colonialist, and racial formation perspectives focus on the ideological character of racism, they all emphasize how this ideology becomes enmeshed or institutionalized in organizations and social practices.

Racism is treated as a static phenomenon. The phenomenon is viewed as unchanging; that is, racism yesterday is like racism today. Thus, when a society's racial structure and its customary racial practices are rearticulated, this rearticulation is characterized as a decline in racism (Wilson 1978), a natural process in a cycle (Park 1950), an example of increased assimilation (Rex 1973, 1986), or effective "norm changes" (Schuman et al. 1985). This limitation, which applies particularly to social psychologists and Marxist scholars, derives from not conceiving of racism as possessing an independent structural foundation. If racism is merely a matter of ideas that has no material basis in contemporary society, then those ideas should be similar to their original configuration, whatever that was. The ideas may be articulated in a different context, but most analysts essentially believe that racist ideas remain the same. For this reason, with notable exceptions (Kinder and Sears 1981; Sears 1988), their attitudinal research is still based on responses to questions developed in the 1940s, 1950s, and 1960s.

Analysts defining racism in an idealist manner view racism as "incorrect" or "irrational thinking"; thus they label "racists" as irrational and rigid. Because racism is conceived of as a belief with no real social basis, it follows that those who hold racist views must be irrational or stupid (Adorno 1950; Allport 1958; Santa Cruz 1977; Sniderman and Piazza 1993; for a critique see Blauner 1972 and Wellman 1977). This view allows for a tactical distinction between individuals with the "pathology" and social actors who are "rational" and racism-free. The problem with this rationalistic view is twofold. First, it misses the rational elements on which racialized systems originally were built. Second, and more important, it neglects the possibility that contemporary racism still has a rational foundation. In this account, contemporary racists are perceived as Archie Bunker–type individuals (Wellman 1977).

Racism is understood as overt behavior. Because the idealist approach regards racism as "irrational" and "rigid," its manifestations should be quite evident, usually involving some degree of hostility. This does not present serious analytical problems for the study of certain periods in racialized societies when racial practices were overt (e.g., slavery and apartheid), but problems in the analysis of racism arise in situations where racial practices are subtle, indirect, or fluid. For instance, many analysts have suggested that in contemporary America racial practices are manifested covertly (Bonilla-Silva and Lewis 1997; Wellman 1977) and racial attitudes tend to be symbolic (Pettigrew 1994; Sears 1988). Therefore it is a waste of time to attempt to detect "racism" by asking questions such as, "How strongly would you object if a member of your family wanted to bring a Black friend home to dinner?" Also, many such questions were developed to measure the extent of racist attitudes in the population during the Jim Crow era of race relations; they are not suitable for the post-1960s period.

Contemporary racism is viewed as an expression of "original sin"—as a remnant of past historical racial situations. In the case of the United States, some analysts argue that racism preceded slavery and/or capitalism (Jordan 1968; Marable 1983; Robinson 1983). Others regard racism in the United States as the result of slavery (Glazer and Moynihan 1970). Even in promising new avenues of research, such as that presented by Roediger (1991) in *The Wages of Whiteness,* contemporary racism is viewed as one of the "legacies of white workerism" (p. 176). By considering racism as a legacy, all these analysts downplay the significance of its contemporary materiality or structure.

Racism is analyzed in a circular manner. "If racism is defined as the behavior that results from the belief, its discovery becomes ensnared in a circularity—racism is a belief that produces behavior, which is itself racism" (Webster 1992:84). Racism is established by racist behavior, which itself is proved by the existence of racism. This circularity results from not grounding racism in social relations among the races. If racism, viewed as an ideology, were seen as possessing a structural foundation, its examination could be associated with racial practices rather than with mere ideas and the problem of circularity would be avoided.

Racialized Social Systems: An Alternative Framework for Understanding Racial Phenomena

Because all kinds of racial matters have been explained as a product of racism, I propose the more general concept of *racialized social systems* as the starting point for an alternative framework. This term refers to societies in which economic, political, social, and ideological levels are partially structured by the placement of actors in racial categories or races. Races typically are identified by their phenotype, but (as we see later) the selection of certain human traits to designate a racial group is always socially rather than biologically based.

These systems are structured partially by race because modern social systems articulate two or more forms of hierarchical patterns (Hall 1980; Williams 1990; Winant 1994). Although processes of racialization are always embedded in other structurations (Balibar and Wallerstein 1991), they acquire autonomy and have "pertinent effects" (Poulantzas 1982) in the social system. This implies that the phenomenon which is coded as racism and is regarded as a free-floating ideology in fact has a structural foundation.

In all racialized social systems the placement of people in racial categories involves some form of hierarchy that produces definite social relations between the races. The race placed in the superior position tends to receive greater economic remuneration and access to better occupations and/or prospects in the labor market, occupies a primary position in the political system, is granted higher social estimation (e.g., is viewed as "smarter" or "better looking"), often has the license to draw physical (segregation) as well as social (racial etiquette) boundaries between itself and other races, and receives what DuBois (1939) calls a "psychological wage" (Marable 1983; Roediger 1991). The totality of these racialized social relations and practices constitutes the racial structure of a society.

Although all racialized social systems are hierarchical, the particular character of the hierarchy, and thus of the racial structure, is variable. For example, domination of Blacks in the United States was achieved through dictatorial means during slavery, but in the post–civil rights period this domination has been hegemonic (Omi and Winant 1994; Winant 1994). Similarly, the racial practices and mechanisms that have kept Blacks subordinated changed from overt and eminently racist to covert and indirectly racist (Bonilla-Silva and Lewis 1997). The unchanging element throughout these stages is that Blacks' life chances are significantly lower than those of Whites, and ultimately a racialized social order is distinguished by this difference in life chances. Generally, the more dissimilar the races' life chances, the more racialized the social system, and vice versa.

Insofar as the races receive different social rewards at all levels, they develop dissimilar objective interests, which can be detected in their struggles to either transform or maintain a particular racial order. These interests are collective rather than individual, are based on relations between races rather than on particular group needs, and are not structural but practical; that is, they are related to concrete struggles rather than derived from the location of the races in the racial structure. In other words, although the races' interests can be detected from their practices, they are not subjective and individual but collective and shaped by the field of real practical alternatives, which is itself rooted in the power struggles between the races. Although the objective general interests of races may ultimately lie in the complete elimination of a society's racial structure, its array of alternatives may not include that possibility. For instance, the historical struggle against chattel slavery led not to the development of race-free societies but to the establishment of social systems with a different kind of racialization. Race-free societies were not among the available alternatives because the nonslave populations had the capacity to preserve some type of racial privilege. The historical "exceptions" occurred in racialized societies in which the nonslaves' power was almost completely superseded by that of the slave population.

A simple criticism of the argument advanced so far would be that it ignores the internal divisions of the races along class and gender lines. Such criticism, however, does not deal squarely with the issue at hand. The fact that not all members of the superordinate race receive the same level of rewards and (conversely) that not all members of the subordinate race or races are at the bottom of the social order does not negate the fact that races, as social groups, are in either a superordinate or a subordinate position in a social system. Historically the racialization of social systems did not imply the exclusion of other forms of oppression. In fact, racialization occurred in social formations also structured by class and gender. Hence, in these societies, the racial structuration of subjects is fragmented along class and gender lines. The important question—which interests move actors to struggle?—is historically contingent and cannot be ascertained a priori (Anthias and Yuval-Davis 1992; Wolpe 1988). Depending on the character of racialization in a social order, class interests may take precedence over racial interests as they do in contemporary Brazil, Cuba, and Puerto Rico. In other situations, racial interests may take precedence over class interests as in the case of Blacks throughout U.S. history. In general, the systemic salience of class in relation to race increases when the economic, political, and social distance between races decreases substantially. Yet this broad argument generates at least one warning: The narrowing of within-class differences between racial actors usually causes more rather than less racial conflict, at least in the short run, as the competition for resources increases (Blalock 1967; Olzak 1992). More significantly, even when class-based conflict becomes more salient in a social order, the racial component survives until the races' life chances are equalized and the mechanisms and social practices that produce those differences are eliminated. Hence societies in which race has declined in significance, such as Brazil, Cuba, and Mexico, still have a racial problem insofar as the racial groups have different life chances. Because racial actors are also classed and gendered, analysts must control for class and for gender to ascertain the material advantages enjoyed by a dominant race. In a racialized society such as ours, the independent effects of race are assessed by analysts who (1) compare data between Whites and non-Whites in the same class and gender positions, (2) evaluate the proportion as well as the general character of the races' participation in some domain of life, and (3) examine racial data at all levels—social, political, economic, and ideological—to ascertain the general position of racial groups in a social system. The first of these procedures has become standard practice in sociology. No serious sociologist would present racial statistics without controlling for gender and class (or at least the class of persons' family of origin). By doing this, analysts assume they can measure the unadulterated effects of "discrimination" manifested in unexplained "residuals" (Farley 1984, 1993; Farley and Allen 1987). Despite its usefulness, however, this technique provides only a partial account of the "race effect" because (1) a significant amount of racial data cannot be retrieved through surveys and (2) the technique of "controlling for" a variable neglects the obvious—why a group is over- or underrepresented in certain categories of the control variables in the first place (Whatley and Wright 1994). Moreover, these analysts presume that it is possible to analyze the amount of discrimination in one domain (e.g., income, occupational status) "without analyzing the extent to which discrimination also affects the factors they hold constant" (Reich 1978:383). Hence to evaluate "race effects" in any domain, analysts must attempt to make sense of their findings in relation to a race's standing on other domains.

But what is the nature of races or, more properly, of racialized social groups? Omi and Winant (1986; also see Miles 1989) state that races are the outcome of the racialization process, which they define as "the extension of racial meaning to a previously racially unclassified relationship, social practice or group" (p. 64). Historically the classification of a people in racial terms has been a highly political act associated with practices such as conquest and colonization, enslavement, peonage, indentured servitude, and, more recently, colonial and neocolonial labor immigration. Categories such as "Indians" and "Negroes" were invented (Allen 1994; Berkhoffer 1978; Jordan 1968) in the sixteenth and seventeenth centuries to justify the conquest and exploitation of various peoples. The invention of such categories entails a dialectical process of construction; that is, the creation of a category of "other" involves the creation of a category of "same." If "Indians" are depicted as "savages," Europeans are characterized as "civilized"; if "Blacks" are defined as natural candidates for slavery, "Whites" are defined as free subjects (Gossett 1963; Roediger 1991, 1994; Todorov 1984). Yet although the racialization of peoples was socially invented and did not override previous forms of social distinction based on class or gender, it did not lead to imaginary relations but generated new forms of human association with definite status differences. After the process of attaching meaning to a "people" is instituted, race becomes a real category of group association and identity.

Because racial classifications partially organize and limit actors' life chances, racial practices of opposition emerge. Regardless of the form of racial interaction (overt, covert, or inert), races can be recognized in the realm of racial relations and positions. Viewed in this light, races are the effect of racial practices of opposition ("we" versus "them") at the economic, political, social, and ideological levels.

Races, as most social scientists acknowledge, are not biologically but socially determined categories of identity and group association. In this regard, they are analogous to class and gender (Amott and Matthaei 1991). Actors in racial positions do not occupy those positions because they are of X or Y race, but because X or Y has been socially defined as a race. Actors' phenotypical (i.e., biologically inherited) characteristics, such as skin tone and hair color and texture, are usually, although not always (Barth 1969; Miles 1993), used to denote racial distinctions. For example, Jews in many European nations (Miles 1989, 1993) and the Irish in England have been treated as racial groups (Allen 1994). Also, Indians in the United States have been viewed as one race despite the tremendous phenotypical and cultural variation among tribes. Because races are socially constructed, both the meaning and the position assigned to races in the racial structure are always contested (Gilroy 1991). What and who is to be Black or White or Indian reflects and affects the social, political, ideological, and economic struggles between the races. The global effects of these struggles can change the meaning of the racial categories as well as the position of a racialized group in a social formation.

This latter point is illustrated clearly by the historical struggles of several "White ethnic" groups in the United States in their efforts to become accepted as legitimate Whites or "Americans" (Litwack 1961; Roediger 1991; Saxton 1990; Williams 1990). Neither light-skinned—nor, for that matter, dark-skinned—immigrants necessarily came to this country as members of race X or race Y. Light-skinned Europeans, after brief periods of being "not-yet White" (Roediger 1994), became "White," but they did not lose their "ethnic" character. Their struggle for inclusion had specific implications: racial inclusion as members of the White community allowed Americanization and class mobility. On the other hand, among dark-skinned immigrants from Africa, Latin America, and the

Caribbean, the struggle was to avoid classification as "Black." These immigrants challenged the reclassification of their identity for a simple reason: In the United States "Black" signified a subordinate status in society. Hence many of these groups struggled to keep their own ethnic or cultural identity, as denoted in expressions such as "I am not Black; I am Jamaican," or "I am not Black; I am Senegalese" (Kasinitz and Freidenberg-Herbstein 1987; Rodriguez 1991; Sutton and Makiesky-Barrow 1987). Yet eventually many of these groups resolved this contradictory situation by accepting the duality of their social classification as Black in the United States while retaining and nourishing their own cultural or ethnic heritage—a heritage deeply influenced by African traditions. Although the content of racial categories changes over time through manifold processes and struggles, race is not a secondary category of group association. The meaning of Black and White, the "racial formation" (Omi and Winant 1986), changes within the larger racial structure. This does not mean that the racial structure is immutable and completely independent of the action of racialized actors. It means only that the social relations between the races become institutionalized (forming a structure as well as a culture) and affect their social life whether individual members of the races want it or not. In Barth's words (1969), "Ethnic identity implies a series of constraints on the kinds of roles an individual is allowed to play [and] is similar to sex and rank, in that it constrains the incumbent in all his activities" (p. 17). For instance, free Blacks during the slavery period struggled to change the meaning of "blackness," and specifically to dissociate it from slavery. Yet they could not escape the larger racial structure that restricted their life chances and their freedom (Berlin 1975; Franklin 1974; Meir and Rudwick 1970).

The placement of groups of people in racial categories stemmed initially from the interests of powerful actors in the social system (e.g., the capitalist class, the planter class, colonizers). After racial categories were used to organize social relations in a society, however, race became an independent element of the operation of the social system (Stone 1985).

Here I depart from analysts such as Jordan (1968), Robinson (1983), and Miles (1989, 1993), who take the mere existence of a racial discourse as manifesting the presence of a racial order. Such a position allows them to speak of racism in medieval times (Jordan) and to classify the antipeasant views of French urbanites (Miles) or the prejudices of the aristocracy against peasants in the Middle Ages (Robinson) as expressions of racism. In my view, we can speak of racialized orders only when a racial discourse is accompanied by social relations of subordination and superordination between the races. The available evidence suggests that racialized social orders emerged after the imperialist expansion of Europe to the New World and Africa (Boggs 1970; Cox 1948; Furnivall 1948; Magubane 1990; E. Williams [1944] 1961; R. Williams 1990).

What are the dynamics of racial issues in racialized systems? Most important, after a social formation is racialized, its "normal" dynamics always include a racial component. Societal struggles based on class or gender contain a racial component because both of these social categories are also racialized; that is, both class and gender are constructed along racial lines. In 1922, for example, White South African workers in the middle of a strike inspired by the Russian revolution rallied under the slogan "Workers of the world unite for a White South Africa." One of the state's "concessions" to this "class" struggle was the passage of the Apprenticeship Act of 1922, "which prevented Black workers acquiring apprenticeships" (Ticktin 1991:26). In another example, the struggle of women in the

United States to attain their civil and human rights has always been plagued by deep racial tensions (Caraway 1991; Giddings 1984).

Nonetheless, some of the strife that exists in a racialized social formation has a distinct racial character; I call such strife "racial contestation"—the struggle of racial groups for systemic changes regarding their position at one or more levels. Such a struggle may be social (Who belongs here?), political (Who can vote? Should they be citizens?), economic (Who should work? They are taking our jobs!), or ideological (Black is beautiful!).

Although much of this contestation is expressed at the individual level and is disjointed, sometimes it becomes collective and general, and can effect meaningful systemic changes in a society's racial organization. The form of contestation may be relatively passive and subtle (e.g., in situations of fundamental overt racial domination, such as slavery and apartheid) or more active and more overt (e.g., in quasi-democratic situations such as the contemporary United States). As a rule, however, fundamental changes in racialized social systems are accompanied by struggles that reach the point of overt protest. This does not mean that a violent racially based revolution is the only way of accomplishing effective changes in the relative position of racial groups. It is a simple extension of the argument that social systems and their supporters must be "shaken" if fundamental transformations are to take place. On this structural foundation rests the phenomenon labeled racism by social scientists.

I reserve the term *racism* (racial ideology) for the segment of the ideological structure of a social system that crystallizes racial notions and stereotypes. Racism provides the rationalizations for social, political, and economic interactions between the races (Bobo 1988). Depending on the particular character of a racialized social system and on the struggles of the subordinated races, racial ideology may be developed highly (as in apartheid), or loosely (as in slavery), and its content can be expressed in overt or covert terms (Bobo and Smith forthcoming; Jackman 1994; Kinder and Sears 1981; Pettigrew 1994; Sears 1988).

Although racism or racial ideology originates in race relations, it acquires relative autonomy in the social system and performs practical functions. In Gilroy's (1991) words, racial ideology "mediates the world of agents and the structures which are created by their social praxis" (p. 17; also see Omi and Winant 1994; van Dijk 1984, 1987, 1993). Racism crystallizes the changing "dogma" on which actors in the social system operate (Gilroy 1991), and becomes "common sense" (Omi and Winant 1994); it provides the rules for perceiving and dealing with the "other" in a racialized society. In the United States, for instance, because racial notions about what Blacks and Whites are or ought to be pervade their encounters, Whites still have difficulty in dealing with Black bankers, lawyers, professors, and doctors (Cose 1993; Graham 1995). Thus, although racist ideology is ultimately false, it fulfills a practical role in racialized societies.

At this point it is possible to sketch the elements of the alternative framework presented here. First, racialized social systems are societies that allocate differential economic, political, social, and even psychological rewards to groups along racial lines; lines that are socially constructed. After a society becomes racialized, a set of social relations and practices based on racial distinctions develops at all societal levels. I designate the aggregate of those relations and practices as the racial structure of a society. Second, races historically are constituted according to the process of racialization; they become the effect of relations of opposition between racialized groups at all levels of a social formation. Third, on the basis of this structure, there develops a racial ideology (what analysts have coded as racism). This ideology is not simply a "superstructural" phenomenon (a mere reflection of the racialized system), but becomes the organizational map that guides actions of racial actors in society. It becomes as real as the racial relations it organizes. Fourth, most struggles in a racialized social system contain a racial component, but sometimes they acquire and/or exhibit a distinct racial character. Racial contestation is the logical outcome of a society with a racial hierarchy. A social formation that includes some form of racialization will always exhibit some form of racial contestation. Finally, the process of racial contestation reveals the different objective interests of the races in a racialized system.

Conclusion

My central argument is that racism, as defined by mainstream social scientists to consist only of ideas, does not provide adequate theoretical foundation for understanding racial phenomena. I suggest that until a structural framework is developed, analysts will be entangled in ungrounded ideological views of racism. Lacking a structural view, they will reduce racial phenomena to a derivation of the class structure (as do Marxist interpreters) or will view these phenomena as the result of an irrational ideology (as do mainstream social scientists). Although others have attempted to develop a structural understanding of racial matters (such as authors associated with the institutionalist, internal colonial, and racial formation perspectives) and/or to write about racial matters as structural (Bobo and Smith forthcoming; Cose 1993; Essed 1991; Feagin and Feagin 1993; Page 1996; van Dijk 1993), they have failed to elaborate a framework that extends beyond their critique of mainstream views. In the alternative framework developed here, I suggest that racism should be studied from the viewpoint of racialization. I contend that after a society becomes racialized, racialization develops a life of its own. Although it interacts with class and gender structurations in the social system, it becomes an organizing principle of social relations in itself (Essed 1991; Omi and Winant 1986; Robinson 1983; van Dijk 1987). Race, as most analysts suggest, is a social construct, but that construct, like class and gender, has independent effects in social life. After racial stratification is established, race becomes an independent criterion for vertical hierarchy in society. Therefore different races experience positions of subordination and superordination in society and develop different interests.

The alternative framework for studying racial orders presented here has the following advantages over traditional views of racism:

Racial phenomena are regarded as the "normal" outcome of the racial structure of a society. Thus we can account for all racial manifestations. Instead of explaining racial phenomena as deriving from other structures or from racism (conceived of as a free-floating ideology), we can trace cultural, political, economic, social, and even psychological racial phenomena to the racial organization of that society.

The changing nature of what analysts label "racism" is explained as the normal outcome of racial contestation in a racialized social system. In this framework, changes in racism are explained rather than described. Changes are due to specific struggles at different levels among the races, resulting from differences in interests. Such changes may transform the nature of racialization and the global character of racial relations in the system (the racial structure). Therefore, change is viewed as a normal component of the racialized system.

The framework of racialization allows analysts to explain overt as well as covert racial behavior. The covert or overt nature of racial contacts depends on how the process of racialization is manifested; this in turns depends on how race originally was articulated in a social formation and on the process of racial contestation. This point implies that rather than conceiving of racism as a universal and uniformly orchestrated phenomenon, analysts should study "historically-specific racisms" (Hall 1980:336). This insight is not new; Robert Park (1950) and Oliver Cox (1948) and Marvin Harris (1964) described varieties of "situations of race relations" with distinct forms of racial interaction.

Racially motivated behavior, whether or not the actors are conscious of it, is regarded as "rational"—that is, as based on the races' different interests. This framework accounts for Archie Bunker–type racial behavior as well as for more "sophisticated" varieties of racial conduct. Racial phenomena are viewed as systemic; therefore all actors in the system participate in racial affairs. Some members of the dominant racial group tend to exhibit less virulence toward members of the subordinated races because they have greater control over the form and the outcome of their racial interactions. When they cannot control that interaction—as in the case of revolts, general threats to Whites, Blacks moving into "their" neighborhood—they behave much like other members of the dominant race.

The reproduction of racial phenomena in contemporary societies is explained in this framework, not by reference to a long-distant past, but in relation to its contemporary structure. Because racism is viewed as systemic (possessing a racial structure) and as organized around the races' different interests, racial aspects of social systems today are viewed as fundamentally related to hierarchical relations between the races in those systems. Elimination of the racialized character of a social system entails the end of racialization, and hence of races altogether. This argument clashes with social scientists' most popular policy prescription for "curing" racism, namely education. This "solution" is the logical outcome of defining racism as a belief. Most analysts regard racism as a matter of individuals subscribing to an irrational view, thus the cure is educating them to realize that racism is wrong. Education is also the choice "pill" prescribed by Marxists for healing workers from racism. The alternative theorization offered here implies that because the phenomenon has structural consequences for the races, the only way to "cure" society of racism is by eliminating its systemic roots. Whether this can be accomplished democratically or only through revolutionary means is an open question, and one that depends on the particular racial structure of the society in question.

A racialization framework accounts for the ways in which racial/ethnic stereotypes emerge, are transformed, and disappear. Racial stereotypes are crystallized at the ideological level of a social system. These images ultimately indicate (although in distorted ways) and justify the stereotyped group's position in a society. Stereotypes may originate out of (1) material realities or conditions endured by the group, (2) genuine ignorance about the group, or (3) rigid, distorted views on the group's physical, cultural, or moral nature. Once they emerge, however, stereotypes must relate—although not necessarily fit perfectly—to the group's true social position in the racialized system if they are to perform their ideological function. Stereotypes that do not tend to reflect a group's situation do not work and are bound to disappear: For example, notions of the Irish as stupid or of Jews as athletically talented have all but vanished since the 1940s, as the Irish moved up the educational ladder and Jews gained access to multiple routes to social mobility. Generally, then, stereotypes are reproduced because they reflect the group's distinct position and status in society. As a corollary, racial or ethnic notions about a group disappear only when the group's status mirrors that of the dominant racial or ethnic group in the society.

The framework developed here is not a universal theory explaining racial phenomena in societies. It is intended to trigger a serious discussion of how race shapes social systems.

To test the usefulness of racialization as a theoretical basis for research, we must perform comparative work on racialization in various societies. One of the main objectives of this comparative work should be to determine whether societies have specific mechanisms, practices, and social relations that produce and reproduce racial inequality at all levels—that is, whether they possess a racial structure. I believe, for example, that the persistent inequality experienced by Blacks and other racial minorities in the United States today is due to the continued existence of a racial structure (Bonilla-Silva and Lewis 1997). In contrast to race relations in the Jim Crow period, however, racial practices that reproduce racial inequality in contemporary America (1) are increasingly covert, (2) are embedded in normal operations of institutions, (3) avoid direct racial terminology, and (4) are invisible to most Whites. By examining whether other countries have practices and mechanisms that account for the persistent inequality experienced by their racial minorities, analysts could assess the usefulness of the framework I have introduced.

References

Adorno, Theodore W. 1950. *The Authoritarian Personality.* New York: Harper and Row.

Allen, Theodore W. 1994. *The Invention of the White Race. Vol. I, Racial Oppression and Social Control.* London, England: Verso.

Allport, Gordon W. 1958. *The Nature of Prejudice.* New York: Doubleday Anchor Books.

Alvarez, Rodolfo, Kenneth G. Lutterman, and Associates. 1979. *Discrimination in Organizations: Using Social Indicators to Manage Social Change.* San Francisco, CA: Jossey-Bass.

Anthias, Floya and Nira Yuval-Davis. 1992. *Racialized Boundaries: Race, Nation, Gender, Colour and Class and the Anti-Racist Struggle.* London, England: Routledge.

Amott, Theresa and Julie A. Matthaei. 1991. *Race, Gender, and Work: A Multicultural Economic History of Women in the United States.* Boston, MA: South End Press.

Balibar, Ettienne and Immanuel Wallerstein. 1991. *Race, Nation, Class: Ambiguous Identities.* New York: Verso.

Banton, Michael. 1970. "The Concept of Racism." Pp. 17–34 in *Race and Racialism,* edited by S. Zubaida. London, England: Tavistock.

Barrera, Mario. 1979. *Race and Class in the Southwest: A Theory of Racial Inequality.* Notre Dame, IN: University of Notre Dame Press.

Barth, Fredrik. 1969. "Introduction." Pp. 9–38 in *Ethnic Groups and Boundaries: The Social Organization of Culture Difference,* edited by F. Barth. Bergen, Norway: Universitetsforlaget.

Benedict, Ruth F. 1945. *Race and Racism.* London, England: Routledge and Kegan Paul.

Berkhoffer, Robert E. 1978. *The White Man's Indian: Images of the American Indian from Columbus to the Present.* New York: Vintage.

Blalock, Hubert M., Jr. 1967. *Toward a Theory of Minority-Group Relations.* New York: John Wiley and Sons.

Blauner, Robert. 1972. *Racial Oppression in America.* New York: Harper and Row.

Bobo, Lawrence. 1988. "Group Conflict, Prejudice and the Paradox of Contemporary Racial Attitudes." Pp. 85–114 in *Eliminating Racism: Profiles in Controversy,* edited by P. A. Katz and D. A. Taylor. New York: Plenum.

Bobo, Lawrence and Ryan Smith. Forthcoming. "From Jim Crow Racism to Laissez-Faire Racism: An Essay on the Transformation of Racial Attitudes in America." In *Beyond Pluralism,* edited by W. Katchin and A. Tyree. Urbana, IL: University of Illinois Press.

Boggs, James. 1970. *Racism and the Class Struggle: Further Pages from a Black Worker's Notebook.* New York: Monthly Review Press.

Bonacich, Edna. 1980a. "Advanced Capitalism and Black/White Relations in the United States: A Split Labor Market Interpretation." Pp. 341–62 in *The Sociology of Race Relations: Reflection and Reform,* edited by T. Pettigrew. New York: Free Press.

———. 1980b. "A Theory of Ethnic Antagonism: The Split Labor Market." *American Sociological Review* 37:547–59.

Bonilla-Silva, Eduardo and Amanda Lewis. 1997. "The 'New Racism': Toward an Analysis of the U.S. Racial Structure, 1960s–1990s." Department of Sociology, University of Michigan, Ann Arbor, MI. Unpublished manuscript.

Caraway, Nancy. 1991. *Segregated Sisterhood: Racism and the Politics of American Feminism.* Knoxville, TN: The University of Tennessee Press.

Carchedi, Guglielmo. 1987. *Class Analysis and Social Research.* Oxford, England: Basil Blackwell.

Carmichael, Stokely. 1971. *Stokely Speaks: Black Power Back to Pan-Africanism.* New York: Vintage Books.

Carmichael, Stokely and Charles Hamilton. 1967. *Black Power: The Politics of Liberation in America.* New York: Vintage Books.

Chesler, Mark. 1976. "Contemporary Sociological Theories of Racism." Pp. 21–71 in *Towards the Elimination of Racism,* edited by P. A. Katz. New York: Pergamon.

Cohen, Gerry A. 1989. "Reconsidering Historical Materialism." Pp. 88–104 in *Marxist Theory,* edited by A. Gallinicos. Oxford, England: Oxford University Press.

Cose, Ellis. 1993. *The Rage of a Privileged Class: Why Are Middle Class Blacks Angry? Why Should America Care?* New York: Harper Collins.

Cox, Oliver C. 1948. *Caste, Class, and Race.* New York: Doubleday.

Dubois, William E. B. 1939. *Black Folk, Then and Now: An Essay in the History and Sociology of the Negro Race.* New York: Henry Holt.

Essed, Philomena. 1991. *Understanding Everyday Racism: An Interdisciplinary Approach.* London, England: Sage.

Fanon, Frantz. 1967. *Black Skin, White Masks.* New York: Grove.

Farley, Reynolds. 1984. *Blacks and Whites: Narrowing the Gap?* Cambridge, MA: Harvard University Press.

———. 1993. "The Common Destiny of Blacks and Whites: Observations about the Social and Economic Status of the Races." Pp. 197–233 in *Race in America: The Struggle for Equality,* edited by H. Hill and J. E. Jones, Jr. Madison, WI: University of Wisconsin Press.

Farley, Reynolds and Walter R. Allen. 1987. *The Color Line and the Quality of Life in America.* New York: Russell Sage.

Feagin, Joe R. and Clarence Booher Feagin. 1993. *Racial and Ethnic Relations.* Upper Saddle River, NJ: Prentice Hall.

Franklin, John Hope. 1974. *From Slavery to Freedom: A History of Negro Americans.* New York: Alfred A. Knopf.

Furnivall, J. S. 1948. *Colonial Policy and Practice: A Comparative Study of Burma and Netherlands India.* Cambridge, England: Cambridge University Press.

Giddings, Paula. 1984. *When and Where I Enter: The Impact of Black Women on Race and Sex in America.* New York: Bantam.

Gilroy, Paul. 1991. *"There Ain't No Black in the Union Jack": The Cultural Politics of Race and Nation.* Chicago, IL: The University of Chicago Press.

Glazer, Nathan and Daniel P. Moynihan. 1970. *Beyond the Melting Pot: The Negroes, Puerto Ricans, Jews, Italians, and Irish of New York City.* Cambridge, MA: MIT Press.

Gossett, Thomas. 1963. *Race: The History of an Idea in America.* Dallas, TX: Southern Methodist University Press.

Graham, Otis Lawrence. 1995. *Member of the Club: Reflections on Life in a Racially Polarized World.* New York: Harper Collins.

Hall, Stuart. 1980. "Race Articulation and Societies Structured in Dominance." Pp. 305–45, in *Sociological Theories: Race and Colonialism,* edited by UNESCO. Paris, France: UNESCO.

Harris, Marvin. 1964. *Patterns of Race in the Americas.* New York: Walker.

Jackman, Mary R. 1994. *Velvet Glove: Paternalism and Conflict in Gender, Class, and Race Relations.* Berkeley, CA: University of California Press.

Jordan, Winthrop. 1968. *White Over Black: American Attitudes toward the Negro, 1550–1812.* New York: W. W. Norton.

Kasinitz, Philip and Judith Freidenberg-Herbstein. 1987. "The Puerto Rican Parade and West Indian Carnival: Public Celebrations in New York City." Pp. 305–25 in *Caribbean Life in New York City: Sociocultural Dimensions,* edited by C. R. Sutton and E. M. Channey. New York: Center for Migration Studies of New York.

Kinder, Donald R. and David O. Sears. 1981. "Prejudiced and Politics: Symbolic Racism versus Racial Threats to the Good Life." *Journal of Personality and Social Psychology* 40: 414–31.

Knowles, Louis L. and Kenneth Prewitt. 1969. *Institutional Racism in America.* Patterson, NJ: Prentice Hall.

Litwack, Lenn F. 1961. *North of Slavery: The Negro in the Free States.* Chicago, IL: University of Chicago Press.

Magubane, Bernard M. 1990. *The Political Economy of Race and Class in South Africa.* New York: Monthly Review Press.

Marable, Manning. 1983. *How Capitalism Underdeveloped Black America.* Boston, MA: South End.

Meir, August and Elliot Rudwick. 1970. *From Plantation to Ghetto.* New York: Hill and Wang.

Miles, Robert. 1989. *Racism.* London, England: Routledge.

———. 1993. *Racism after "Race Relations."* London, England: Routledge.

Miles, Robert and Annie Phizacklea. 1984. *White Man's Country.* London, England: Pluto.

Moore, Joan W. 1970. "Colonialism: The Case of the Mexican-Americans." *Social Problems* 17:463–72.

Myrdal, Gunnar. 1944. *An American Dilemma: The Negro Problem and Modern Democracy.* New York: Harper and Brothers.

Olzak, Susan. 1992. *The Dynamics of Ethnic Competition and Conflict.* Stanford, CA: Stanford University Press.

Omi, Michael and Howard Winant. 1986. *Racial Formation in the United States: From the 1960s to the 1980s.* New York: Routledge and Kegan Paul.

———. 1994. *Racial Formation in the United States: From 1960s to the 1980s.* 2d ed. New York: Routledge.

Page, Clarence. 1996. *Showing My Color: Impolite Essays on Race and Identity.* New York: Harper Collins.

Park, Robert Ezra. 1950. *Race and Culture.* Glencoe, IL: Free Press.

Perlo, Victor. 1975. *Economics of Racism U.S.A.: Roots of Black Inequality.* New York: International Publishers.

Pettigrew, Thomas. 1994. "New Patterns of Prejudice: The Different Worlds of 1984 and 1964." Pp. 53–59 in *Race and Ethnic Conflict,* edited by F. L. Pincus and H. J. Erlich. Boulder, CO: Westview.

Poulantzas, Nicos. 1982. *Political Power and Social Classes.* London, England: Verso.

Reich, Michael. 1978. "The Economics of Racism." Pp. 381–88 in *The Capitalist System: A Radical Analysis of American Society,* edited by R. Edwards, M. Reich, and T. Weisskopf. Englewood Cliffs, NJ: Prentice Hall.

Reuter, Edward B. 1934. "Introduction: Race and Culture Contacts." Pp. 1–12 in *Race and Culture Contacts,* edited by E. B. Reuter. New York: McGraw Hill.

Rex, John. 1973. *Race, Colonialism and the City.* London, England: Routledge and Kegan Paul.

———. 1983. *Race Relations in Sociological Theory.* London, England: Weidenfeld and Nicolson.

———. 1986. *Race and Ethnicity.* Philadelphia, PA: Open University Press.

Robinson, Cedric J. 1983. *Black Marxism: The Making of the Black Radical Tradition.* London, England: Zed.

Rodriguez, Clara. 1991. *Puerto Ricans: Born in the U.S.A.* Boulder, CO: Westview.

Roediger, David. 1991. *The Wages of Whiteness: Race and the Making of the American Working Class.* London, England: Verso.

———. 1994. *Towards the Abolition of Whiteness: Essays on Race, Politics, and Working Class History.* London, England: Verso.

Santa Cruz, Hernán. 1977. *Racial Discrimination: Special Rapporteur of the Sub-Commission on Prevention of Discrimination and Protection of Minorities.* New York: United Nations.

Saxton, Alexander. 1990. *The Rise and Fall of the White Republic: Class Politics and Mass Culture in Nineteenth-Century America.* London, England: Verso.

Schaefer, Richard T. 1990. *Racial and Ethnic Groups.* 4th ed. Glenview, IL: Scott Foresman/Little Brown Higher Education.

Schuman, Howard, Charlotte Steeh, and Lawrence Bobo. 1985. *Racial Attitudes in America: Trends and Interpretations.* Cambridge, MA: Harvard University Press.

Sears, David O. 1988. "Symbolic Racism." Pp. 53–84 in *Eliminating Racism: Profiles in Controversy,* edited by P. A. Katz and D. A. Taylor. New York: Plenum.

Sniderman, Paul M. and Thomas Piazza. 1993. *The Scar of Race.* Cambridge, MA: Harvard University Press.

Solomos, John. 1986. "Varieties of Marxist Conceptions of 'Race,' Class and the State: A Critical Analysis." Pp. 84–109 in *Theories of Race and Ethnic Relations,* edited by J. Rex and D. Mason. Cambridge, England: Cambridge University Press.

———. 1989. *Race and Racism in Contemporary Britain.* London, England: MacMillan.

Stone, John. 1985. *Racial Conflict in Contemporary Society.* Cambridge, England: Cambridge University Press.

Sutton, Constance R. and Susan R. Makiesky-Barrow. 1987. "Migration and West Indian Racial and Ethnic Consciousness." Pp. 86–107 in *Caribbean Life in New York City: Sociocultural Dimensions,* edited by C. R. Sutton and E. M. Channey. New York: Center for Migration Studies of New York.

Szymanski, Albert. 1981. "The Political Economy of Racism." Pp. 321–46 in *Political Economy: A Critique of American Society,* edited by S. G. McNall. Dallas, TX: Scott Foresman.

———. 1983. *Class Structure: A Critical Perspective.* New York: Praeger Publishers.

Thomas, William I. and Florian Znaniecki. 1918. *The Polish Peasant in Europe and America.* Vol. I. New York: Knopf.

Ticktin, Hillel. 1991. *The Politics of Race: Discrimination in South Africa.* London, England: Pluto.

Todorov, Tzevetan. 1984. *The Conquest of America: The Question of the Other.* New York: Harper Colophon.

van den Berghe, Pierre. 1967. *Race and Racism: A Comparative Perspective.* New York: John Wiley and Sons.

van Dijk, Teun A. 1984. *Prejudice in Discourse: An Analysis of Ethnic Prejudice in Cognition and Conversation.* Amsterdam, The Netherlands: John Benjamins.

———. 1987. *Communicating Racism: Ethnic Prejudice in Thought and Talk.* Newbury Park, CA: Sage.

———. 1993. *Elite Discourse and Racism.* Newbury Park, CA: Sage.

Webster, Yehudi O. 1992. *The Racialization of America.* New York: St. Martin's.

Wellman, David. 1977. *Portraits of White Racism.* Cambridge, England: Cambridge University Press.

Whatley, Warren and Gavin Wright. 1994. *Race, Human Capital, and Labour Markets in American History.* Working Paper #7, Center for Afroamerican and African Studies, University of Michigan, Ann Arbor, Ml.

Williams, Eric. [1944] 1961. *Capitalism and Slavery.* New York: Russell and Russell.

Williams, Richard. 1990. *Hierarchical Structures and Social Value: The Creation of Black and Irish Identities in the United States.* Cambridge, England: Cambridge University Press.

Wilson, William J. 1978. *The Declining Significance of Race: Blacks and Changing American Institutions.* Chicago, IL: The University of Chicago Press.

Winant, Howard. 1994. *Racial Conditions: Politics, Theory, Comparisons.* Minneapolis, MN: University of Minnesota Press.

Wolpe, Harold. 1986. "Class Concepts, Class Struggle and Racism." Pp. 1 10–30 in *Theories of Race Relations,* edited by J. Rex and D. Mason. Cambridge, England: Cambridge University Press.

———. 1988. *Race, Class and the Apartheid State.* Paris, France: UNESCO Press.

CHAPTER 4

Rethinking Assimilation Theory for a New Era of Immigration[1]

Richard Alba and Victor Nee

In this canonic work, Richard Alba and Victor Nee present the classic account of ***assimilation*** *theory. They make the case that although contemporary research on patterns of immigrant incorporation tend to question the utility of this traditional approach—especially as it pertains to today's immigrant, ethnic, and racial minority groups—there is evidence in support of retaining this perspective.*

Questions to Consider

The authors contend that assimilation theory is often challenged by contemporary scholars of race and ethnicity; yet, they argue assimilation theory is "not dead yet." What are some of the reasons they give for its continued use? Are you convinced by their reasoning?

Assimilation has fallen into disrepute. In an essay tellingly entitled "Is Assimilation Dead?" Nathan Glazer (1993:122) summarizes pithily the contemporary view: "Assimilation today is not a popular term." Glazer writes that he asked some Harvard students what they thought of the term and discovered that "the large majority had a

Source: Adapted from Richard Alba and Victor Nee, "Rethinking Assimilation Theory for a New Era of Immigration," *The International Migration Review*, Volume 31, Issue 4, pages 826–849, 862–874, John Wiley and Sons Inc., 2007.

negative reaction to it." The rejection of assimilation is not limited to students. While it was once the unquestioned organizing concept in sociological studies of ethnic relations, in recent decades assimilation has come to be viewed by social scientists as a worn-out theory which imposes ethnocentric and patronizing demands on minority peoples struggling to retain their cultural and ethnic integrity.

Without question, earlier social scientists in this field committed what are now regarded as intellectual sins. For instance, Warner and Srole (1945:285 ff.), in their classic account of assimilation among ethnic groups in New Haven, describe ethnic groups as "unlearning" their "inferior" cultural traits (inferior, that is, from the standpoint of the host society) in order to "successfully learn the new way of life necessary for full acceptance." Warner and Stole also correlated the potential for assimilation with a hierarchy of racial and cultural acceptability, ranging from English-speaking Protestants at the top to "Negroes and all Negroid mixtures" at the bottom. The depiction of the ethnocentric tendency in classical American assimilation could hardly be clearer.

Yet, whatever the deficiencies of earlier formulations and applications of assimilation, we hold that this social science concept offers the best way to understand and describe the integration into the mainstream experienced across generations by many individuals and ethnic groups, even if it cannot be regarded as a universal outcome of American life. In this essay, we attempt to redefine assimilation in order to render it useful in the study of the new immigration. (We are not alone in this attempt; see, for instance, Barkan, 1995; Kazal, 1995; Morawska, 1994.) Our reformulation of assimilation emphasizes its utility for understanding the social dynamics of ethnicity in American society, as opposed to its past normative or ideological applications. As a state-imposed normative program aimed at eradicating minority cultures, assimilation has been justifiably repudiated. But as a social process that occurs spontaneously and often unintendedly in the course of interaction between majority and minority groups, assimilation remains a key concept for the study of intergroup relations. In what follows, we review the sociological literature on assimilation, with an eye to assessing its strengths and weaknesses; assay the validity of arguments for rejecting assimilation in understanding the new immigration; and sift through recent studies for clues concerning assimilation's course among the new immigrant groups.

The Canonical Account

Whatever the precise words, conceptions of assimilation have been central to understanding the American experience at least since colonial times. The centrality of assimilation for the scientific understanding of immigration is more recent, traceable to the Chicago School of the early twentieth century and especially to the work of Robert E. Park, W. I. Thomas, and their collaborators and students (McKee, 1993). The social science use of assimilation thus emerged at the highpoint of a previous era of immigration and by means of observations in a city where the first and second generations then constituted the great majority of residents.

In 1921, Park and E.W. Burgess (1969:735) provided an early definition of assimilation: "a process of interpenetration and fusion in which persons and groups acquire the memories, sentiments, and attitudes of other persons and groups and, by sharing their experience and history, are incorporated with them in a common cultural life." When read closely, this definition does not appear to require what many critics assume assimilation must—namely, the erasure of all signs of ethnic origins. Instead, it equates assimilation with the social processes that bring ethnic minorities into the mainstream of American life. The limited extent of the assimilation Park envisioned was made even more clear by another definition that he later created for the *Encyclopedia of the Social Sciences*, where "social" assimilation was "the name given to the process or processes by which peoples of diverse racial origins and different cultural heritages, occupying a common territory, achieve a cultural solidarity sufficient at least to sustain a national existence" (Park, 1930:281).

Park's legacy is closely identified with the notion of assimilation as the end-stage of a "race-relations cycle" of "contact, competition, accommodation, and eventual assimilation," a sequence that, in the most famous statement of it, was viewed as "apparently progressive and irreversible" (Park, 1950:138; see Barkan, 1995:39–40; Lal, 1990:41–45). In depicting the race-relations cycle, Park was rather deliberately painting with broad brush strokes on a large canvas, for the cycle refers obliquely to the processes in the modern world, including long-distance labor migration, that are bringing once separated peoples into closer contact. Competition is the initial, unstable consequence of contact as groups struggle to gain advantages over one another, and it eventuates in the more stable stage of accommodation, where a social structure of typically unequal relations among groups and a settled understanding of group position have come into being (Shibutani and Kwan, 1965; Lal, 1990:41–45). But no matter how stable, accommodation will eventually be undermined by the personal relationships that cross group boundaries, according to Park, who wrote that "in our estimates of race relations we have not reckoned with the effects of personal intercourse and the friendships that grow up out of them" (Park, 1950:150).

Park has been faulted by many later writers for appearing to portray assimilation as an inevitable outcome in multiethnic societies (e.g., Lyman, 1973; Stone, 1985). This is implied in Park's conception of stages. However, recent scholarship, as by Lal (1990), argues that the race-relations cycle played but a minor role in Park's sociology and that its fame rests more on his students' writings than on his own (see also McKee, 1993:109–111). Park's students and associates did, in fact, make seminal contributions to the formulation of assimilation (e.g., Burgess, 1925; Wirth, 1956; Warner and Srole, 1945).

Assimilation Concepts: Milton Gordon's Framework

The confusion among various formulations of assimilation in the early sociological literature has often been noted (e.g., Barkan, 1995; Gordon, 1964; for other general reviews of assimilation concepts, see Abramson, 1980; Gleason, 1980; Hirschman, 1983). This problem was not solved until Milton Gordon's *Assimilation in American Life* (1964) provided a systematic dissection of the concept. His multidimensional formulation has proven attractive in part because it readily lends itself to operationalization and hypothesis formulation suitable for middle-range research. Although Gordon conceived of seven dimensions in all, the critical distinction in his conceptual scheme lay between acculturation and what he termed "structural" assimilation, by which he meant the entry of members of an ethnic minority into primary-group relationships with the majority group. This distinction, and its emphasis in particular on the character of an individual's primary-group affiliations, suggests one of the limitations of Gordon's scheme, namely, that it is oriented to a microsociological account of assimilation not conceptually integrated to larger social processes (e.g., the dynamics of ethnic boundaries, Barth, 1956). Nevertheless, Gordon's conceptual scheme proved to be useful to many students of ethnicity and has profoundly influenced scholarship on assimilation and ethnic change.

Acculturation, the minority group's adoption of the "cultural patterns" of the host society, typically comes first and is inevitable, Gordon argued. His discussion makes clear that these patterns extend beyond the acquisition of the English language, to dress and outward emotional expression, and to personal values (Gordon, 1964:79). He distinguished intrinsic cultural traits, those that are "vital ingredients of the group's cultural heritage," exemplified by religion and musical tastes, from extrinsic traits, which "tend to be products of the historical vicissitudes of the group's adjustment to the local environment" and thus are deemed less central to group identity (Gordon, 1964:79). The distinction would seem to imply that extrinsic traits are readily surrendered by the group in making more or less necessary accommodations to the host society, but its implications are less clear about intrinsic ones. Certainly, Gordon had no expectation that fundamental religious identities are given up as a result of acculturation.

Gordon defined a cultural standard that represented the direction and eventual outcome of acculturation—the "middle-class cultural patterns of, largely, white Protestant, Anglo-Saxon origins," which he also described with Joshua Fishman's term as the "core culture" (Gordon, 1964:72). In his view, acculturation was a largely one-way process; except in the domain of institutional religion, the minority group adopted the core culture, which remained in Gordon's view basically unchanged by this absorption. Gordon acknowledged only the possibility of change at the margins—"minor modifications in cuisine, recreational patterns, place names, speech, residential architecture, sources of artistic inspiration, and perhaps few other areas" (Gordon, 1964:100).

In Gordon's account, acculturation could occur without being accompanied by other forms of assimilation, and the stage of acculturation only could last indefinitely. The catalyst for more complete assimilation instead is structural assimilation, which Gordon defined as "entrance of the minority group into the social cliques, clubs, and institutions of the core society at the primary group level." He hypothesized that "*once structural assimilation has occurred, . . . all of the other types of assimilation will naturally follow*" (Gordon, 1964:80–81, italics in original). This means in particular that prejudice and discrimination will decline (if not disappear), intermarriage will be common, and the minority's separate identity will wane.

On closer examination, Gordon's hypothesis is ambiguous as to whether it is meant to apply to individuals or groups. Even though the measurement of assimilation was put at the individual level, the hypothesis has been interpreted as applying literally to groups—a reading that becomes obvious when one recognizes that the hypothesized relationships among the different dimensions of assimilation need not hold in fact at the level of individuals. For example, individuals may be structurally assimilated, but prejudice and discrimination can still be widespread, as Gordon clearly understood. This ambiguity is important because of the desirability of formulating a concept of assimilation in which some independence between the individual and group levels is explicitly preserved (Barkan, 1995). We will return to this point subsequently.

Another limitation of Gordon's account was that it conceived of assimilation within a two-group framework of analysis (the "Sylvanians" and "Mundovians") and thus did not take account of the multigroup nature of American society. The language used by Gordon's definition ("social cliques, clubs, and institutions of the core society") implies that structural assimilation is to be equated with minority-group relationships to members of the majority group. The problem has been accentuated as American society has become more heterogeneous and the majority group smaller relative to the number of minority groups. Strictly speaking, Gordon's account does not extend to relationships between members of different ethnic minorities. Yet, such situations are increasingly common. A broad rather than a narrow two-group conception should be entertained if assimilation is to be faithful to the level of ethnic intermixing in American society (especially evident in terms of intermarriage and embodied in the Triple Melting Pot idea of Kennedy, 1944).

Perhaps Gordon's structural-assimilation hypothesis should not be given the causal inflection his language implies. The strength of Gordon's conceptual scheme lies in its lucid articulation of some of the key dimensions of assimilation viewed as a composite concept. This leads to the recognition that, to some extent, the dimensions of assimilation can be arranged in terms of stages (Barkan, 1995). When his hypothesis is read in this spirit, the core of the assertion is seen to be that structural assimilation signals the maturity of the assimilation process. Indeed, this has been the main use of the concept in the literature, as indicated by the frequent use of intermarriage data to measure assimilation's progress (e.g., Alba and Golden, 1986; Lieberson and Waters, 1988).

Identificational assimilation, which represents a third dimension of Gordon's schema, has taken on importance in contemporary discussion of assimilation with respect to both the descendants of European immigrants and the new immigrant groups. Gordon (1964:71) defined this as the "development of [a] sense of peoplehood based exclusively on [the] host society." He recognized, too, that ethnic identity was not an undifferentiated concept and distinguished between "historical identification," which derived from a sense of the "interdependence of fate" in Kurt Lewin's phrase and typically extended to the ethnic group as a whole, and "participational identity," whose locus was the segment of the group most socially similar to the individual (the "ethclass" in Gordon's terminology, 1964:53). With the benefit of hindsight, Gordon's concept of identificational assimilation appears overly demanding, requiring the extinction of any form of ethnic identity in favor of an exclusively national, American identity. Consequently, it would seem to imply even the loss of family memories of extra-American origins, which seems not only an extraordinary expectation, but one that flies in the face of the data demonstrating that the overwhelming majority of Americans still acknowledge some non-American ethnic ancestry (Lieberson, 1985; Lieberson and Waters, 1993). However, the knowledge many individuals possess about their family histories should not be conflated with an ethnic identity that has practical consequences (Alba, 1990; Gans, 1979; Waters, 1990).

An important part of Gordon's legacy is his delineation of alternative conceptions of the process and outcome of assimilation in the United States. Gordon described these as Anglo-Conformity and the Melting Pot. (He also identified a third model, Cultural Pluralism, which is less relevant to the canonical account.) These alternative conceptions are appropriately viewed as expressions of popular beliefs or ideologies about the constitution of civil society in America. The model of Anglo-Conformity, which corresponds in spirit with the campaign for rapid, "pressure-cooker" Americanization during and after World War I, equated assimilation with acculturation in the Anglo-American mold and ignored other assimilation dimensions, being therefore indifferent to the occurrence or nonoccurrence of structural assimilation. The model of the Melting Pot has enjoyed several periods of popularity in American discussions of ethnicity, most recently in the immediate aftermath of World War II. It offered an idealistic vision of American society and identity as arising from the biological and cultural fusion of different peoples; and while its exponents usually emphasized the contributions of Europeans to the mixture, it allowed for a recognition of those of non-European groups as well. In terms of Gordon's scheme, the model operated along the dimensions of cultural and structural assimilation. This latter was invoked by the forecast of widespread intermarriage (Gordon, 1964:125; Herberg, 1960; Kennedy, 1944, 1952). The cultural assimilation portion of the Melting Pot idea was rather ambiguous, however. Many early exponents spoke in ways that suggested a truly syncretic American culture blending elements from many different groups, but later commentators were more consistent with Gordon's own conception, that acculturation is a mostly one-directional acceptance of Anglo-American patterns (Gordon, 1964:127–128).

Gordon was an adherent of neither model. This may come as a surprise to many who know Gordon's views only in the context of the contemporary discussion of assimilation, for he has often been identified with a school that portrays assimilation as an almost inevitable outcome for immigrant groups. But this is not, in fact, a fair characterization. Although Gordon left little doubt that, in his view, acculturation was inevitable to a large degree, he did not see structural assimilation as similarly foreordained. His analysis of American society led to the conclusion that structural pluralism rather than cultural pluralism was the more accurate description. He envisioned the United States as constituted from ethnic subsocieties, in whose institutions and social networks most individuals spend the major portions of their social lives, literally from cradle to grave in many cases (Gordon, 1964:159).

Straight-Line Assimilation

Another major piece of the canon is the notion of "straight-line assimilation," a phrase popularized by Gans (1973) and Sandberg (1973) to describe an idea stemming from Warner and Srole (1945). The straight-line notion adds a dynamic dimension to Gordon's somewhat static formulation in that it envisions a process unfolding in a sequence of generational steps; each new generation represents on average a new stage of adjustment to the host society, i.e., a further step away from ethnic "ground zero," the community and culture established by the immigrants, and a step closer to more complete assimilation (Lieberson, 1973). Implied is the idea that generations are the motor for ethnic change, not just the time frame within which assimilation takes place. Each generation faces a distinctive set of issues in its relationship to the larger society and to the ethnic group, and their resolution brings about a distinctive pattern of accommodation. The idea of the generational inevitability of assimilation has been criticized, however, for assuming that all ethnic content is imported by immigrants and not recognizing that it can be created in response to conditions and out of cultural materials in the host society. Critics of the straight-line notion have argued that, instead, ethnicity may go through periods of recreation, if not renaissance (Glazer and Moynihan, 1970; Yancey, Ericksen and Juliani, 1976; Greeley, 1977; Conzen et al., 1992). In recognition of this criticism, Gans (1992) has modified his description to the "bumpy-line theory of ethnicity," while still adhering to the core of the original concept—namely, that there is a generational dynamic behind ethnic change and that it moves, perhaps with tangents, in the general direction of assimilation.

The generational time frame assumes a view of ethnic change that is decidedly endogenous and that, perhaps ironically, tends to be ahistorical. By casting assimilation in terms of a dynamic internal to the group, the straight-line notion overlooks the impact of historically specific changes, as, for example, the shifts in residential patterns resulting from the rapid expansion of suburbs in the post-World War II era. This, in combination with the hiatus of mass immigration in the 1920s, led to ethnic changes that corresponded closely with generational status—in, for example, mother tongue competence (Stevens, 1985). Such generational effects may not be as pronounced in the current immigration where births in an ethnic group may be scattered across decades. Consequently, a common set of historical experiences is not likely to coincide with generational status, as was the case in the earlier mass immigration from Europe (and also Japan).

Extensions of the Conceptual Canon

Assimilation has been criticized over the decades, both from outside by those who reject it as a valid approach and by others who, operating within its conceptual frame, point out gaps or identify features that seem idiosyncratic to the experiences of some groups. Our concern here is to address criticism internal to the framework, leading us to consider some extensions of Gordon's contribution to the canon.

Gordon's concept of culture has been criticized for being static and overly homogeneous. As already noted, Gordon assumed that acculturation involved change on the part of an ethnic group in the direction of middle-class Anglo-American culture, which itself remained largely unaffected, except possibly for "minor modifications." An obvious problem with Gordon's view is that American culture varies greatly by locale and social class; acculturation hardly takes place in the shadow of a single, middle-class cultural standard. What is lacking in Gordon is a more differentiated and syncretic conception of culture and a recognition that American culture was and is more mixed, much more an amalgam of diverse influences, and that it continues to evolve.

It does not require a radical shift in perspective to recognize that assimilation and its expression in the form of acculturation are, at bottom, no more than the attenuation of an ethnic or racial distinction and the cultural and social differences that are associated with it. Such processes can occur by changes in one group that make it more like another or by changes in two (or more) groups that shrink the differences and distance between them—group convergence, in other words. Moreover, acculturation need not be defined simply as the substitution of one cultural expression for its equivalent, whether the replacement comes from the majority or minority cultures, though such substitution certainly takes place. This narrow conception of acculturation is at the root of the frequently encountered view that one group "adopts" the cultural traits of another. The influence of minority ethnic cultures can occur also by an expansion of the range of what is considered normative behavior within the mainstream; thus elements of minority cultures are absorbed alongside their Anglo-American equivalents or are fused with mainstream elements to create a hybrid cultural mix.

We suspect that ethnic influences on the mainstream American culture happen continuously—as the recent literature on the invention of ethnic and national traditions suggests (Conzen et al., 1992; Hobsbawm and Ranger, 1983; Sollors, 1989)—and that their occurrence is not limited to the domains where expansion and hybridization are most apparent, such as food and music. An obvious question is how one can recognize the incorporation into American culture of ethnic influences. The hallmark, we think, is that a cultural trait gradually loses its association with an ethnic group. In part, this happens because nongroup members take it on, so that the empirical correlation between the trait and group membership is weakened. In part, it occurs as the trait is no longer labeled in an ethnic way. Over a longer time frame, the ethnic origins of a new element may be forgotten, and it becomes part of the mainstream repertoire, like the currently archetypal American recreational practices which, as Thomas Sowell (1996) notes, are derived from those brought by German immigrants. Similarly, the more intense family contacts that Greeley (1977) has documented for some groups, such as Irish and Italians, may have gradually influenced American conceptions of family life.

As noted earlier, Gordon's scheme did not recognize the distinction between individual and group levels of ethnic change. Thereby, it inadvertently sidestepped some of the most important lines of investigation within the assimilation framework—the reciprocal effects between group processes and individual attainment. The insight that a theory of assimilation must take the interaction between micro (individual) and mezzo (group or community) levels into account dates at least as far back as Breton's (1964) hypothesis that an ethnic community's "institutional completeness" influences its members' propensities to assimilate. In other words, the supply-side of ethnicity, the group and community context, may be decisive to the outcome at the individual level (Portes and Rumbaut, 1996). If at the community level the opportunities to express ethnicity are meager or socially inappropriate, the intent to maintain ethnicity, assuming it exists, may be thwarted or transformed. The desire to find ethnic modes of behavior and expression, then, is likely to succeed where the supply-side of ethnicity is fairly rich in possibility. Where individuals assimilate in large numbers and are not replaced by a continuing immigration stream, a pattern characterizing many European-ancestry groups, the supply-side of ethnicity is diminished as a whole as well as narrowed in specific respects. Organizations dwindle in membership or find that their members belong to early generations or those with a more parochial outlook. Neighborhoods fail to retain the socially mobile sons and daughters of their residents, and their class character does not change to match the expanding class distribution of the group.

Some gaps in Gordon's account lend themselves to natural extensions by the addition of further dimensions of assimilation. (Odd though it seems, his multidimensional formulation overlooked important forms of assimilation.) Occupational mobility and economic assimilation, the key dimensions of socioeconomic assimilation, are not addressed in his discussion of assimilation. Yet this kind of assimilation is of paramount significance, both in itself, because parity of life chances with natives is a critical indicator of the decline of ethnic boundaries, and for the reason that entry into the occupational and economic mainstream has undoubtedly provided many ethnics with a motive for social (i.e., structural, in Gordon's sense) assimilation. Furthermore, socioeconomic mobility creates the social conditions conducive to other forms of assimilation since it likely results in equal status contact across ethnic lines in workplaces and neighborhoods.

Yet the concept of socioeconomic assimilation is not unambiguous, and two different usages need to be distinguished. In one, by far the more common in the literature on ethnicity and assimilation, socioeconomic assimilation is equated with attainment of average or above average socioeconomic standing, as measured by indicators such as education, occupation, and income (e.g., Neidert and Farley, 1985), a usage that can be traced to Warner and Srole (1945). Since many immigrant groups have entered the American social structure on its lower rungs, this meaning of socioeconomic assimilation is usually conflated with social mobility, leading to the frequently expressed expectation that assimilation and social mobility are inextricably linked. In the second usage, socioeconomic assimilation can be defined as minority participation in institutions such as the labor market and education on the basis of parity with native groups of similar backgrounds. If the emphasis in the first version falls on equality of attainment or position, the emphasis in the second is on equality of treatment; members of the immigrant minority and similarly situated members of native groups (which could be other minorities) have the same life chances in the pursuit of such scarce values as high-status jobs and higher education. The key question for the second version is: To what extent has an ethnic distinction lost its relevance for processes of socioeconomic attainment, except for initial conditions?

The distinction between the two types of socioeconomic assimilation is important because it pertains to whether the relationship between socioeconomic and other forms of assimilation is historically contingent. The descendants of European immigrants of the nineteenth and early twentieth centuries experienced a close link between social mobility and other forms of assimilation. But this may have reflected the opportunity structure available during a particular era in American history (Gans, 1992; Portes and Zhou, 1993). The question of whether the possible narrowing of opportunities in the contemporary United States will limit the prospects for socioeconomic assimilation of new immigrant groups or, instead, lead to a different pattern of assimilation must be kept open for the time being. The second kind of socioeconomic assimilation allows for "segmented" assimilation (Portes and Zhou, 1993). According to this view, many labor migrants, with Mexicans as the preeminent example, may end up in the lower rungs of the stratification order, while human capital immigrants, common among Asian groups and Russian Jews in the current mass immigration, experience rapid social mobility.

Another dimension of assimilation that has received attention in recent years is residential or, following Massey (1985), spatial assimilation. Massey's formulation is the most systematic and has been used as a standard to assess the residential segregation of major racial/ethnic populations in the United States (Massey and Denton, 1987, 1993). Spatial assimilation as a concept is linked to a model of incorporation that continues the Chicago School's ecological tradition and that views the spatial distribution of groups as a reflection of their human capital and the state of their assimilation, broadly construed. The basic tenets of the ecological model are that residential mobility follows from the acculturation and social mobility of individuals and that residential mobility is an intermediate step on the way to structural assimilation. As members of minority groups acculturate and establish themselves in American labor markets, they attempt to leave behind less successful members of their groups and to convert occupational mobility and economic assimilation into residential gain, by "purchasing" residence in places with greater advantages and amenities. This process entails a tendency toward dispersion of minority group members, opening the way for increased contact with members of the ethnic majority and thus desegregation. According to the model, entry into relatively advantaged suburban communities that contain many whites is a key stage in the process (Massey and Denton, 1988).

Like socioeconomic assimilation, residential assimilation has been given related but distinguishable interpretations in past discussion. Analogously, one is that the residential distribution of the minority approximates that of the majority—in other words, that the group is found in the same locations and in similar concentrations as the majority. This is the condition of no segregation and is applicable only on the group level. A second meaning is that the residential opportunities of minority group members are equivalent to those of majority group members with similar resources. "Opportunities" here should be given a broad interpretation to include not just location (e.g., access to desirable suburbs) but also housing (e.g., home ownership, quality of dwelling). The question of whether minority group members can achieve residential situations as desirable as those of others with similar qualifications is one that can be posed at the individual level. A third and final meaning of residential assimilation refers to the existence of ethnic neighborhoods, which are generally viewed as housing social structures and cultural milieux supportive of ethnic distinctiveness (e.g., LaRuffa, 1988; Alba, Logan and Crowder, 1997).

Creating Assimilation Theory: Shibutani and Kwan's Ecological Analysis

Even when extended as above, Gordon's analysis, the touchstone for all subsequent studies of assimilation, remains limited. Most important, it lacks a specification of the causal mechanisms giving rise to assimilation. Despite Gordon's reference to theories of assimilation, he did not formulate a theory in this sense. His contribution was to define a multidimensional framework whose descriptive concepts have proven highly useful, allowing analysts to measure the extent of the assimilation of racial and ethnic groups along various empirical dimensions. His linchpin hypothesis asserts that incorporation into primary groups of the dominant group precedes and stimulates other forms of assimilation. Yet the direction of causality could well be the opposite of what was claimed by the structural assimilation hypothesis, a question that cannot be resolved within Gordon's framework because there is no causal theory of assimilation.

At least one attempt to formulate a more complete theory of ethnic stratification and assimilation exists; although it is not now a part of the assimilation canon, we include it in our discussion to suggest a direction in which the canon might fruitfully be expanded. The attempt we have in mind is that of Tomatsu Shibutani and Kian Kwan in *Ethnic Stratification* (1965). Whereas Gordon focused his study on assimilation in American society, Shibutani and Kwan elaborated a theory that expanded upon Park's race-relations cycle, to focus broadly on explaining the dynamics of ethnic stratification around the globe. Despite this reach, their underlying aim was to gain new insights on the American experience of race relations through comparative historical analysis of systems of ethnic domination in diverse historical and societal settings, ranging widely to include Manchu rule over Han Chinese and ethnic stratification in the Roman empire.

As Chicago School sociologists, Shibutani and Kwan employed Mead's symbolic interactionism as a core building block of their theory. Following Mead, they argued that how a person is treated in society depends "not on what he is," but on the "manner in which he is defined." Out of necessity, humans place people into categories, each associated with expected behavior and treatment, in order to deal in a routine and predictable manner with strangers and acquaintances outside of their primary groups. Differences giving rise to social distances are created and sustained symbolically through the practice of classifying and ranking. The social distances that arise thereby are the fundament of the color line that segregates minorities and impedes assimilation.

By social distance, Shibutani and Kwan (1965:263–271) mean the subjective state of nearness felt to certain individuals, not physical distance between groups. In their account, change in subjective states—reduction of social distance—precedes and stimulates structural assimilation, and not the reverse as implied in Gordon's hypothesis. When social distance is low, there is a feeling of common identity, closeness, and shared experiences. But when social distance is high, people perceive and treat the other as belonging to a different category; and even after long acquaintance, there are still feelings of apprehension and reserve. Social distance may be institutionalized, as it is in the case of the color line, where stereotypes, customs, social norms, and formal institutional arrangements maintain a system of stratification that employs ethnic markers to determine differential access to opportunity structures (Merton, 1968). In Shibutani and Kwan's view of the American experience, social mobility through economic advancement, though not as common as it is perceived to be, allows for upward movement in class standing. But the system of ethnic stratification is more rigid. Ethnic identity for nonwhites is especially resilient to change. Although a member of a racial minority can improve his or her position in the opportunity structure, "ethnic identity, in those areas in which it makes a difference, places a ceiling upon the extent to which he can rise" (Shibutani and Kwan, 1965:33).

Shibutani and Kwan intended their theory as an extension of Park's natural history of the race-relations cycle. Through a comparative historical approach, they examined case studies of contact, competition, accommodation, and assimilation stemming from migration. Their analysis uncovered many apparent exceptions to Parks optimistic conception of assimilation, for ethnic stratification orders tend to be long-lasting once established and institutionalized. Domination is initially gained through competitive advantages accruing to the group whose culture is best adapted to exploit the resources of the environment. Competition and natural selection push minorities into the least desirable residential locations and economic niches. A stable system of ethnic stratification is rooted in part in a moral order in which the dominant group is convinced that its advantages derive from natural differences and minorities come to believe in their inferiority and accept their lot at the bottom. But the dominant group also upholds its position and privileges through institutionalized power and outright coercion. Individual minority group members may achieve social mobility and gain economic parity, but as exceptions to the rule. Such upwardly mobile individuals, often of mixed race, acquire a marginal status that gives them a modicum of privilege and respect, but they are fully accepted neither by the dominant group nor by their own ethnic community. In a stable ethnic stratification order, individual assimilation can occur even while the system maintaining dominance remains intact.

Nevertheless, Shibutani and Kwan agree with Park that even stable ethnic stratification orders ultimately tend to become undone and that assimilation occurs at the final stage of the natural history of the race-relations cycle. Their use of ecological theory, which informs their analysis of ethnic stratification, plays a central role here, too, contributing a dynamic, macrosociological dimension that is vital to their theoretical framework. It provides the crucial causal links between the microsociological part of the theory and much larger structures and processes.

The causal mechanisms that bring about the reduction of social distance stem from changes in "life conditions" that occur at the ecological level. In the absence of such changes, ethnic stratification orders tend towards stable equilibrium. In explaining the transformation of such orders, Shibutani and Kwan emphasize particularly the importance of technological innovation, which in turn induces alterations in the mode of production. As an illustration, they cite the invention of the automatic cotton picker, which diminished the demand for cheap labor in the south and sparked the migration of poor blacks and whites to the industrial north, altering the pattern of racial stratification throughout the United States. Changes in the economic system associated with technological shifts often introduce opportunities for minority groups to acquire new competitive advantages that make them indispensable to employers. These in turn lead employers to seek institutional changes favorable to the interests of minority groups—changes that, in a capitalist system, are relatively easy to institute when organizations and individuals pursuing profits find it in their economic interest to do so. As a contemporary example, one could point to the role of employers in supporting the immigration of workers, both skilled and unskilled, legal and undocumented, despite the public clamor for greater limits on legal immigration and a curtailing of illegal immigration. At one end of the economic spectrum, the interest of employers stems from the growing labor market demand for highly skilled workers (e.g., computer programmers) because of the postindustrial transformation of the American economy; at the other end, there is a continuing need for elastic sources of low-wage labor in the agricultural sector, in "degraded" manufacturing sectors such as the garment industry, and in personal service such as childcare (Sassen, 1988).

Another ecological source of change stems from shifts in the often unstable demographic balance between majority and minority groups. As the relative size of minority groups increases, shifts in power become likely. For example, the increasing percentage of nonwhites in the United States contributes to the pressure on employers and schools to institute changes, such as policies promoting the value of diversity, to accommodate a more heterogeneous population; similar changes can also be observed in other countries with large immigrant populations, such as Germany, where multiculturalist pressures have also arisen as an accommodative response to growing population diversity (Cohn-Bendit and Schmid, 1992). Likewise, increases in population density, mainly in cities, alter ethnic relations by increasing the probability of chance meetings and, eventually, of stable relationships between members of different ethnic groups.

The effects of ecological changes notwithstanding, Shibutani and Kwan assert that the most immediate source of a decline in social distance occurs when other changes stimulate the introduction of new ideas that challenge values and cultural beliefs previously taken for granted, as in the discrediting of white supremacist ideologies in the postcolonial world, and a "transformation of values" ensues.

> Systems of ethnic stratification begin to break down when minority peoples develop new self-conceptions and refuse to accept subordinate roles. As they become more aware of their worth in comparison to members of the dominant group, what they had once accepted as natural becomes unbearable. (Shibutani and Kwan, 1965:350)

In Shibutani and Kwan's account, the context giving rise to higher rates of assimilation often follows the outbreak of protests and opposition. Social movements are the engine that sparks interest among dominant elites in instituting changes and reforms to alter the relationship between majority and minority in a manner that promotes assimilation.

We intend our brief discussion of Shibutani and Kwan's theory of ethnic stratification to sketch the outline of a missing component in the canon of assimilation, but not necessarily to provide the exact blueprint. Without a dynamic of the sort provided by this theory, Gordon's analysis of assimilation remains static, allowing for individual-level assimilation but not for more wholesale shifts in ethnic and racial boundaries. (As we noted earlier, Gordon remained a structural pluralist in his view of American society.) The link between microsociological changes in social distance, and thus interethnic relations and structural assimilation, and macrosociological shifts points in the direction in which a theory of assimilation must move. Although the causal mechanisms that the Shibutani-Kwan theory posits may be revised in light of new research, clearly any analysis of the potential for assimilation in the United States, or anywhere else for that matter, cannot rely solely on confidence in processes of individual-level assimilation alone, but must pay attention to macroscopic processes rooted in population ecology, and how these impinge on prospects for assimilation.

How Relevant Are the Differences between Past and Present "Eras of Immigration"?

There is abundant evidence that assimilation has been the master trend among the descendants of the immigrants of the previous era of mass immigration, who mainly came from Europe in the period before 1930. This assimilation can be equated, above all, with long-term processes that have eroded the social foundations for ethnic distinctions and ultimately the distinctions themselves. These processes have brought about a rough parity of opportunities (among groups, not individuals) to obtain the desirable social goods of the society, such as prestigious and remunerative jobs, and loosened the ties between ethnicity and specific economic niches (Greeley, 1976; Lieberson, 1980; Lieberson and Waters, 1988; Neidert and Farley, 1985). Parity here refers to a broad convergence toward the life chances of the "average" white American, which has particularly affected the descendants of immigrants from peasant backgrounds (e.g., southern Italians) and does not exclude the exceptional achievements of a few small groups, such as Eastern European Jews. Assimilation has diminished cultural differences that once served to signal ethnic membership to others and to sustain ethnic solidarity; one result has been an implosion of European mother tongues (Alba, 1988; Stevens, 1992; Veltman, 1983). Assimilation is also associated with a massive shift in residence during the postwar era—away from urban ethnic neighborhoods towards ethnically intermixed suburbs (Alba, Logan and Crowder, 1997; Gans, 1967; Guest, 1980)—and with relatively easy social intermixing across ethnic lines which has resulted in high rates of ethnic intermarriage and ethnically mixed ancestry (Alba, 1995; Alba and Golden, 1986; Lieberson and Waters, 1988). Finally, assimilation finds expression in the ethnic identities of many whites, which are "symbolic" in the sense defined by Herbert Gans and involve few commitments in everyday social life (Gans, 1979; Alba, 1990; Waters, 1990).

Admittedly, the causes of this assimilation of European ancestry ethnic groups are much less well understood than is the result. But, at a minimum, the fact that this assimilation has involved groups with very different characteristics at time of immigration and varied histories in the United States suggests that the forces promoting it have been, and perhaps still are, deeply embedded in American society. Yet many scholars of contemporary immigration reject assimilation as a likely outcome on a mass scale for contemporary immigrant groups. One of the most compelling arguments they raise is that assimilation, as represented by the canonical account, is specific to a set of historical circumstances that characterized mass immigration from Europe but does not, and will not, apply to contemporary non-European immigrant groups (see Massey, 1994; Portes and Rumbaut, 1996).

The Absence of a Foreseeable Hiatus in the Immigration Stream

The decisive halt in the stream of mass immigration from Europe in the late 1920s, induced by restrictive immigration legislation followed by the Great Depression, is widely thought to have been fateful for ethnic groups. The ensuing, four-decade interruption in steady, large-scale immigration virtually guaranteed that ethnic communities and cultures would be steadily weakened over time. The social mobility of individuals and families drained these communities, especially of native-born ethnics, and undermined the cultures they supported. There were few newcomers available as replacements. Over time, the modal generation shifted from the immigrant to the second and then from the second to the third.

Many students of post-1965 immigration believe that a similar hiatus in the contemporary immigration stream is unlikely. One reason is the apparent disinclination of the federal government to ratchet down the level of immigration, though this may be changing as the political climate generated by immigration issues heats up (see Brimelow, 1995). The legislation that has set the main parameters for immigration during the 1990s, the Immigration Act of 1990, appears to have raised the level of legal immigration above the nearly record-setting pace of the 1980s (Heer, 1996; Reimers, 1992:262). Moreover, recent attempts to control the immigration flow, such as the 1986 IRCA law, have generally had unanticipated and even counterproductive consequences in the end, perhaps, many suggest, because the immigration-generating forces in the United States and in sending societies are so powerful that they thwart or bypass the attempts of the U.S. government to harness them (Donato, Durand and Massey, 1992; Heer, 1996).

Movement across national borders appears to be an endemic feature of the contemporary international system, and this adds to the difficulty of substantially limiting contemporary immigration. United Nations projections of the world population suggest very large population increases in the near future (by 2025), which will occur mostly outside the highly developed nations and thus add to the huge reservoir of people available to move (Heer, 1996:137–145). Needless to say, emigration from less developed countries is not just a product of population pressure but of the curve of economic development, which instills in broad segments of the population consumption tastes that cannot be satisfied by their native economies, and of the historical linkages that exists between less and more developed nations in the international system (Sassen, 1988; Portes and Rumbaut, 1996). Further, it is more difficult for national governments to control emigration than was the case a century ago. Such forces seem likely to engender large, difficult-to-control population movements far into the future, as exemplified by the large legal and illegal flows from Mexico to the United States.

If immigration to the United States continues indefinitely at its current level, then population projections show that many of the ethnic groups arising from it will be dominated by the first and second generations well into the next century (Edmonston and Passel, 1994). This will create a fundamentally different ethnic context from that faced by the descendants of European immigrants, for the new ethnic communities are highly likely to remain large, culturally vibrant, and institutionally rich. Ethnic community life in combination with ethnic economies, according to this scenario, are likely to provide particularistic channels of mobility. In sum, there are likely to be strong incentives to keep ethnic affiliations alive even for the third generation, as long as the distance between the generations does not grow so great as to alienate them from one another.

Yet, if there is any proven rule in population projections, it is that the patterns of the present cannot be projected indefinitely into the future, for they will change in unforeseeable ways. The level of immigration could go up, to be sure, but it could also go down—as a result of restrictive legislation backed up by tougher enforcement, a decline in the attractiveness of the United States to one or more of the main sources of current immigration, a weakening of the forces generating emigration from these countries, or some combination of these changes. Despite the current pessimism about efforts to control immigration flows to the United States, especially the undocumented immigration, control is not impossible, as is shown by the example of Germany, which has lengthy land borders with Eastern Europe, a potential source of many immigrants, but only a small residential population of undocumented immigrants in comparison with that of the United States.

Moreover, a decline in the attractiveness of the United States to potential immigrants could happen for any of a number of reasons—such as changes in the labor market that eliminate some of the niches exploited by immigrants, declines in the relative quality of life in the metropolitan areas that are the main receiving areas, or a rise in the relative attractiveness and accessibility of other countries as immigrant destinations.

Raising the prospect of a future decline in the general level of immigration is admittedly speculative. We are on firmer ground, we believe, in predicting that the immigration of some groups will decline and will not live up to the assumption of continued inflow far into the future. The assumption, in other words, will hold selectively, not uniformly. One reason for suspecting such declines is that the level of economic development of some sending nations may approach or even catch up to that of the United States, undermining a principal motive for immigration. This has happened in the case of Japan, which sent many immigrants around the turn of the century, but currently is the source for few immigrants, other than managers in Japanese companies who are doing a tour of duty at U.S. branches. It could well happen in the cases of Korea and Taiwan. Indeed, there are signs of an incipient decline in Korean immigration; between 1990 and 1994, the number of immigrant visas allocated to Koreans fell by 60 percent while the number returning home surged (Belluck, 1995; Min, 1996). For groups whose immigration abates, the prediction of ethnic communities continually revitalized by new immigration will prove inaccurate.

Finally, it perhaps should not be assumed that the cessation of mass immigration was essential to opening the way for assimilation for the descendants of late European immigration. We do not know whether and to what extent assimilation would have taken place in any case. It is certainly a plausible hypothesis that assimilation would have proceeded, albeit at a slower pace. Similarly, in the new era of mass immigration, even if immigration continues at present levels, there is no reason to assume that the second and third generation will be locked into the same communal life and economic niches of the first generation. With the possible exception of Mexican immigration, which might be compared to the French-Canadian situation, the numbers of immigrants from each of the many immigrant streams are small relative to the overall U.S. population. Far from the closed ethnic boundaries common to situations of stable ethnic stratification often involving only a few ethnic groups, such heterogeneity increases the likelihood of chance meeting and associations across groups. Moreover, as long as ethnic economies are populated by small businesses with limited opportunities for advancement, the direction of job changes over time, even for the first generation, will be to secure jobs with better conditions of employment and returns to human capital in the mainstream economy (Nee, Sanders and Sernau, 1994).

The Racial Distinctiveness of Many New Immigrant Groups

A common argument holds that the descendants of earlier European immigrations, even those composed of peasants from economically backward parts of Europe, could eventually assimilate because their European origins made them culturally and racially similar to American ethnic core groups—those from the British Isles and some northern and western European countries. The option of assimilation will be less available to the second and later generations of most new immigrant groups because their non-European origins mean that they are more distinctive, with their distinctiveness of skin color especially fateful.

While we wish to avoid at all cost a Panglossian optimism about American racism, we find this argument less compelling than many do because we think that it treats perceptions of racial difference as more rigid than they have proven themselves historically. We grant that American treatment of non-Europeans has generally been characterized by racist discrimination of a more extreme cast than anything experienced by even the most disparaged of the European groups, as the well-known examples of the Chinese Exclusion Act of the late nineteenth century and the internment of Japanese Americans during World War II testify. Nevertheless, the view that the pathway to assimilation was smoothed for the descendants of European immigrants by their racial identification is an anachronism, inappropriately imposing contemporary racial perceptions on the past. There is ample evidence that native-born whites perceived some of the major European immigrant groups, such as the Irish, Jews, and Italians, as racially distinct from themselves and that such perceptions flowered into full-blown racist theorizing during the high-water period of mass immigration in the early decades of this century (Higham, 1970). This is not just a matter of a language usage in which "race" was treated as a synonym for "nation" or "ethnic group." Many Americans believed that they could identify the members of some groups by their characteristic appearance (e.g., "Jewish" facial features), and nineteenth-century caricatures of the Irish frequently gave them a distinctly simian cast.

Over time, racial perceptions of the most disparaged European groups shifted. The Irish, and perhaps other groups, initially struggled to put some racial and social distance between themselves and African Americans (Ignatiev, 1995; Roediger, 1991). But as these groups climbed the socioeconomic ladder and mixed residentially with other whites, their perceived distinctiveness from the majority faded. (World War II, a watershed in many ways for ethnic relations among whites, also had a powerful impact on attitudes towards European ethnics.) Intermarriage both marked this shift and accelerated it. We see no a priori reason why a similar shift could not take place for some contemporary immigrant groups and some segments of other groups. We think here particularly of Asians and light-skinned Latinos. In the case of some Asian groups, the relatively high intermarriage rates of their U.S.-born members suggest their acceptability to many whites, the most frequent partners in intermarriage, and the absence of a deep racial divide (Lee and Yamanaka, 1990; Qian, 1997). Loewen's (1971) study of Chinese immigrants who migrated from the Western states to the South in the 1870's documents a transformation of racial attitudes that parallels that for the Irish. When Chinese laborers first arrived in the Mississippi Delta they joined free blacks as part of the "colored" agricultural labor force in a race-segregated society. Chinese immigrants and their descendants gradually "crossed-over" to gain acceptance in the white community by distancing themselves socially from blacks and acculturating to southern white culture. The post-1965 immigration of Asians to the United States takes place in a substantially different historical context of the post–Civil Rights Movement and a new era of mass immigration. Although Loewen's case study of the Mississippi Chinese may not be applicable to the current immigration, it nonetheless shows that ethnic identity and boundaries are socially constructed and malleable.

The most intractable racial boundary remains that separating those deemed phenotypically black from whites. This boundary is likely to exert a powerful influence on the adaptation possibilities of immigrant groups, depending on where they are situated with respect to it. The evidence of this influence is already apparent; it is registered in the research observations about the identificational dilemmas confronted by the children of black Caribbean parentage (Waters, 1994; Woldemikael, 1989) and recognized in the concept of "segmented assimilation" (Portes and Zhou, 1993). But despite such evidence, there is also the countervailing experience of South Asian immigrants. Although South Asians have dark skin color, they are the highest income group in the United States and are predominantly suburban in their residence (Portes and Rumbaut, 1996). Their experience suggests that not dark skin color per se, but the appearance of connection to the African-American group raises the most impassable racist barriers in the United States.

The Impact of Economic Restructuring on Immigrant Opportunity

The assimilation of European-ancestry Americans is linked to opportunities for social mobility that, within a brief historical period, brought about a rough parity of life chances across many ethnic groups (though not within them, as life chances remained structured by social class origins) (Greeley, 1976; Lieberson, 1980). These opportunities were in turn linked to historically contingent, broad avenues of intergenerational movement that allowed immigrants of peasant origins with few work skills of relevance in an urban industrial economy nevertheless to gain a foothold through steady employment, often beginning in manufacturing sectors (Bodnar, 1985). According to a common view, similar openings are not to be found with the same frequency in the contemporary economy because of economic restructuring, which has led to the elimination of many manufacturing jobs and the degradation of others and to their replacement in the spectrum of jobs open to immigrant workers with low-level service jobs that do not offer comparable wages, stability of employment, or mobility ladders (Sassen, 1988). This result of economic restructuring is described by Portes and Zhou (1993) as an "hourglass economy," with a narrowed band of middle-level jobs and bulging strata at the bottom and the top. The presumption is that it will be more difficult for the descendants of contemporary immigrants, many of whom enter the labor force at or near the bottom, to make the gradual intergenerational transition upwards, because footholds in the middle of the occupational structure are relatively scarce (Portes and Zhou, 1993). Movement into the top strata requires substantial human capital, particularly higher educational credentials, that is not likely to be within reach of all members of the second generation. A conclusion drawn by a number of scholars is that, to a degree not true of European ethnics, the current second generation is at risk of experiencing no, or even downward, mobility, unless the American economy becomes more dynamic than it has been since the early 1970s (Gans, 1992).

Without question, economic opportunities are critical to the assimilation prospects of new immigrant groups. But the restructuring of the economy does not have an equally negative impact on the opportunities of all groups, because of the enormous variety among groups in the forms of capital—economic, cultural and social—they bring with them and in degree of support provided by the community contexts they enter (Light, 1984; Portes and Rumbaut, 1996; Waldinger, 1986/87, 1996). Some groups, like the Cubans of Miami, have distinguished themselves by the development of ethnic subeconomies that are likely to afford the second generation better-than-average chances to succeed in the educational system and enter professional occupations. Others—several Asian groups spring readily to mind—enjoy, whether because of the professional occupations of their immigrant parents or the cultural capital they possess, high levels of educational attainment in the United States (Gibson, 1988; Hirschman and Wong, 1986; Model, 1988; Nee and Sanders, 1985; Light and Bonacich, 1988). Moreover, the 1980s economic restructuring has stimulated economic growth in the 1990s, and this has brought about a sharp reduction of unemployment. As a result of tighter labor markets, even low-skilled manual laborers have experienced increases in hourly earnings.

The significance of economic restructuring for the second and subsequent generations would appear to be greatest for those groups described by Portes and Rumbaut (1996) as "labor migrant" groups, like the Mexicans. Even here, we caution that the distinction from the experiences of comparable European groups (e.g., southern Italians) can be overdrawn, for they too did not enter an economy that was continuously generating a bountiful supply of opportunities for secure employment and upward mobility. A large portion of the second generation of the southern and eastern European groups came of age in the teeth of the Depression. Like the children of some contemporary immigrants, many in the earlier second generation responded to their perceived lack of opportunity and to their rejection at the hands of nativist whites by constructing what are now called "reactive identities," identities premised upon value schemes that invert those of the mainstream in important ways. We know for instance that, during the 1930s and perhaps afterwards, the children of southern Italian immigrants were widely perceived as posing problems in the educational system—they had high rates of dropout, truancy, and delinquency (Covello, 1972), all signs that they were rejecting the conventions and values of a system that they perceived as rejecting them.

Yet the analyses of Lieberson (1980) demonstrate that the U.S.-born members of these groups experienced a fairly steady upgrading of educational and occupational attainment, even in the cohorts whose life chances would have been most affected by the Depression. This suggests to us that the emphasis on economic restructuring in the discussion of assimilation chances for contemporary immigrant groups may produce a too pessimistic reading of their prospects. Our additional remarks can only be suggestive at this point. But, since there is as yet no fully satisfactory explanation for the assimilation of the once disparaged southern and eastern European groups, it seems premature to judge the assimilation chances of contemporary immigrant groups as diminished because the socioeconomic structure of the United States has changed in the interim. As Perlmann and Waldinger (1997) note, to insist that assimilation is likely only if the situation of contemporary groups parallels that of earlier ones in precise ways seems to require something that history almost never does—repeat itself exactly. With respect to mobility, such an insistence loses sight of the ability of individuals and groups to adjust their strategies to the economic structures they find. We note in particular that the focus of the economic restructuring argument as applied to immigrants has been almost entirely on the labor market, and it has therefore ignored the educational system. However, not only has the association between social origins and educational attainment weakened over time (Hout et al., 1993), but postsecondary education is more available in some of the states where immigrants have concentrated (California and New York, especially) than elsewhere in the nation. Perhaps the pathways followed by earlier groups have been narrowed over time, but other pathways are likely to have opened up.

We are not denying that there are differences, and important ones, between the immigrations of the past and present and in the circumstances facing immigrant groups after arrival, nor are we claiming that the parallels between the situations faced by the descendants of contemporary immigrants and those of earlier ones are so strong that patterns of assimilation among European Americans can be inferred as a likely outcome for new immigrant groups. But the distinctions between these situations are not as clearcut as they are usually made out to be. None of them is, in our judgment, sufficiently compelling to rule out a priori the possibility of assimilation as a widespread outcome for some, or even most, contemporary immigrant groups. It is therefore imperative to examine with an open mind the cultural, residential, educational and other patterns established by the new immigrants and their children for clues about the potential importance of assimilation.

Conclusion

Assimilation as a concept and as a theory has been subjected to withering criticism in recent decades. Much of this criticism rejects assimilation out of hand as hopelessly burdened with ethnocentric, ideological biases and as out of touch with contemporary multicultural realities. It has been common in this critique to portray assimilation as reliant upon simplistic conceptions of a static homogeneous American culture and to target the normative or ideological expression of assimilation—Anglo-conformity. While we think this criticism is frequently unfair in that it fails to consider, and properly discount, the intellectual and social context in which the canonical statements of assimilation were written, we recognize that it often enough hits the mark. But there is danger in the view of many critics that they have provided a strong rationale for rejecting assimilation, rather than for amending it. We believe that the latter is the appropriate course, for assimilation still has great power for an understanding of the contemporary ethnic scene in the United States. It must, in our view, remain part of the theoretical tool kit of students of ethnicity and race, especially those who are concerned with the new immigration.

One challenge that must be faced is whether the language of assimilation can bear this refashioning. If the terminology of assimilation is so freighted with bias and ambiguity, as many critics believe, then perhaps it must be abandoned and a new vocabulary invented, even if this merely redeploys some of assimilation's conceptual arsenal. We think a change in language would be unwise. Assimilation has had a central place in the American experience, and the issue of the continuity between the experiences of European Americans and those of new immigrant groups lies at the very heart of the doubts about the relevance of assimilation for the contemporary United States. To invent a new vocabulary is, in effect, to foreclose the examination of this issue with a terminological solution, separating contemporary realities from past ones with new words. The question of continuity must be left open.

In the most general terms, assimilation can be defined as the decline, and at its endpoint the disappearance, of an ethnic/racial distinction and the cultural and social differences that express it. This definition does not assume that one of these groups must be the ethnic majority; assimilation can involve minority groups only, in which case the ethnic boundary between the majority and the merged minority groups presumably remains intact. Assimilation of this sort is not a mere theoretical possibility, as the assimilation of many descendants of earlier Caribbean black immigration into the native African-American group indicates. Nevertheless, the type of assimilation that is of greatest interest does involve the majority group. The definition stated above avoids a pitfall frequently stumbled upon by conventional definitions, which focus exclusively on the minority ethnic group, assuming implicitly that only it changes. By intent, our definition is agnostic about whether the changes wrought by assimilation are one-sided or more mutual. Indeed, there should be no definitional prescription on this point, for it is likely that the unilaterality of the changes depends upon the minority group, the era, and the aspect of group difference under consideration. Language acculturation in the United States appears to be overwhelmingly one-sided, even if American English contains many borrowings from other tongues, indigenous and immigrant; we still understand the English of the British and they ours, indicating that our language has not strayed very far from its roots. Acculturation in some other areas—cuisine the most obvious, perhaps—is more mutual.

The above definition of assimilation is formulated at the group level, and the next question is how it is to be translated to the individual plane. Here there may be no alternative to defining assimilation in a more one-sided manner. It seems impossible to meaningfully discuss assimilation at the individual level as other than changes that make the individuals in one ethnic group more like, and more socially integrated with, the members of another. When assimilation implicates both majority and minority groups, the assimilation of individuals of minority origins involves changes that enable them to function in the mainstream society. From their point of view, acculturation, say, takes place in the direction of the mainstream culture, even if on another plane that culture is itself changing through the ingestion of elements from minority cultures. Over time, then, the cultural and social distance that minority-group individuals traverse while assimilating may narrow.

Though its definition of assimilation requires modification, the canonical account, especially as extended in the direction of manner suggested by Shibutani and Kwan (1965), has much to offer to the analysis of contemporary immigrant groups. Assimilation as a social process is in progress along a variety of indicators, as our review of the evidence indicates. The socioeconomic mobility of the new immigrants shows a distinct bimodal pattern. Human capital immigrants in particular appear to be experiencing substantial economic and residential mobility. By contrast, labor migrants have made slower progress, a finding that Borjas has attributed to the very low educational attainment of migrants from Central

America and other underdeveloped regions of the world. Analyses of spatial assimilation show a mixed pattern of ethnic concentration and residential mobility. Labor migrants appear to concentrate in ethnic communities, while human capital immigrants show rapid transition to suburban residence and are less likely to congregate in dense settlement patterns. Not only does the early evidence attest to assimilation as a social process being experienced to greater or lesser extent by new immigrants, but it is difficult even to discuss the new immigration without encountering the need to refer to the very substantial literature on assimilation. Only by contrasting differences and similarities between the old and new immigration will scholars gain a deeper understanding of the meaning of ethnicity in this new era of immigration.

Note

1. Revised version of paper presented at the conference "Becoming American/America Becoming: International Migration to the United States," sponsored by the Social Science Research Council, Sanibel Island, Florida, January 18–21, 1996. We are grateful to the Social Science Research Council and to Josh DeWind for providing us the opportunity and encouragement to work on this project. The participants at the conference gave us numerous helpful comments and suggestions, as well as the encouragement to see the project as worthy of continuing. In both respects, the comments of Phil Kasinitz, Ruben Rumbaut, and Joel Perlmann and Roger Waldinger deserve special acknowledgement. Victor Nee also acknowledges fellowship support from NSF grant No. SBR-9022192 as a Fellow of the Center for Advanced Study in the Behavioral Sciences.

References

Abramson, H. 1980 "Assimilation and Pluralism." In *Harvard Encyclopedia of American Ethnic Groups*. Ed. S. Thernstrom, A. Orlov, and O. Handlin. Cambridge, MA: Harvard University Press.

Alba, R. 1995 "Assimilation's Quiet Tide," *The Public Interest*, 119:1–18.

———. 1990 *Ethnic Identity: The Transformation of White America*. New Haven, CT: Yale University Press.

———. 1988 "Cohorts and the Dynamics of Ethnic Change." In *Social Structures and Human Lives*. Ed. M. W. Riley, B. Huber, and B. Hess. Newbury Park, CA: Sage.

Alba, R. and J. Logan. 1993 "Minority Proximity to Whites in Suburbs: An Individual-Level Analysis of Segregation," *American Journal of Sociology*, 98:1388–1427.

———. 1991 "Variations on Two Themes: Racial and Ethnic Patterns in the Attainment of Suburban Residence," *Demography*, 28:431–453.

Alba, R., J. Logan and K. Crowder. 1997 "White Ethnic Neighborhoods and Assimilation: The Greater New York Region, 1980–1990," *Social Forces*, 75:883–912.

Alba, R., J. Logan, G. Marzan, B. Stults and W. Zhang. 1997 "Immigrant Groups and Suburbs: A Test of Spatial Assimilation Theory." State University of New York–Albany. Unpublished paper.

Alba, R., J. Logan and B. Stults. 1997 "Making a Place in the Immigrant Metropolis: The Neighborhoods of Racial and Ethnic Groups, 1990." State University of New York–Albany. Unpublished paper.

Aldrich, H. and R. Waldinger. 1990 "Ethnicity and Entrepreneurship," *Annual Review of Sociology*, 16:111–135.

Barkan, E. 1995 "Race, Religion, and Nationality in American Society: A Model of Ethnicity—From Contact to Assimilation," *Journal of American Ethnic History*, 14:38–101.

Barth, F. 1956 "Ecologic Relationships of Ethnic Groups in Swat, North Pakistan," *American Anthropologist*, 58:1079–1089.

Bean, F. and M. Tienda. 1987 *The Hispanic Population of the United States*. New York: Russell Sage Foundation.

Belluck, P. 1995 "Healthy Korean Economy Draws Immigrants Home," *The New York Times*, August 22. Pp. A1, B4.

Bodnar, J. 1985 *The Transplanted: The History of Immigrants in Urban America*. Bloomington: Indiana University Press.

Bonacich, E. and J. Modell. 1980 *The Economic Basis of Ethnic Solidarity: Small Business in the Japanese-American Community*. Berkeley: University of California Press.

Borjas, G. 1994 "The Economics of Immigration," *Journal of Economic Literature*, 32:1667–1717.

———. 1990 *Friends or Strangers, the Impact of Immigrants in the U.S. Economy*. New York: Basic Books.

———. 1987 "Self-selection and the Earnings of Immigrants," *American Economic Review*, 77:531–553.

———. 1986 "The Self-employment Experience of Immigrants," *The Journal of Human Resources*, 21:485–506.

———. 1985 "Assimilation, Changes in Cohort Quality, and the Earnings of Immigrants," *Journal of Labor Economics*, 3:463–489.

Borjas, G. and R. Freeman. 1992 "Introduction and Summary." In *Economic Consequences for the U.S. and Source Areas*. Ed. G. Borjas and R. Freeman. Chicago: University of Chicago.

Breton, R. 1964 "Institutional Completeness of Ethnic Communities and the Personal Relations of Immigrants," *American Journal of Sociology*, 70:193–205.

Brimelow, P. 1995 *Alien Nation: Common Sense about America's Immigration Disaster*. New York: Random House.

Burgess, E. 1925 "The Growth of the City: An Introduction to a Research Project." In *The City*. Ed. R. Park, E. Burgess, and R. McKenzie. Chicago: University of Chicago.

Child, I. 1943 *Italian or American? The Second Generation in Conflict*. New Haven, CT: Yale University Press.

Chiswick, B. 1986 "Is the New Immigration Less Skilled Than the Old?" *Journal of Labor Economics*, 4:168–192.

———. 1978 "The Effect of Americanization on the Earnings of Foreign-Born Men," *Journal of Political Economy*, 86:897–921.

———. 1977 "Sons of Immigrants: Are They at an Earnings Disadvantage?" *American Economic Review*, 67:376–380.

Cohn-Bendit, D. and T. Schmid. 1992 *Heimat Babylon: Das Waghis der multikulturellen Demokratie*. Hamburg: Hoffmann und Campe.

Conzen, K., D. Gerber, E. Morawska, G. Pozzetta and R. Vecoli. 1992 "The Invention of Ethnicity: A Perspective from the U.S.A.," *Journal of American Ethnic History*, 12:3–41.

Covello, L. 1972 *The Social Background of the Italo-American School Child*. Totowa, NJ: Rowman & Littlefield.

Denton, N. and D. Massey. 1989 "Racial Identity among Caribbean Hispanics: The Effect of Double Minority Status on Residential Segregation," *American Sociological Review*, 54:790–808.

Donato, K., J. Durand and D. Massey. 1992 "Stemming the Tide? Assessing the Deterrent Effects of the Immigration Reform and Control Act," *Demography*, 29:139–157.

Edmonston, B. and J. Passel. 1994 "The Future Immigrant Population of the United States." In *Immigration and Ethnicity: The Integration of America's Newest Arrivals*. Ed. B. Edmonston and J. Passel. Washington, DC: The Urban Institute Press.

Farley, R. 1996 *The New American Reality: Who We Are, How We Got Here, Where We Are Going.* New York: Russell Sage.

Farley, R. and W. Frey. 1994 "Changes in the Segregation of Whites from Blacks during the 1980s: Small Steps towards a More Integrated Society," *American Sociological Review*, 59:23–45.

Fix, M. and J. Passel. 1994 *Immigration and Immigrants: Setting the Record Straight.* Washington, DC: The Urban Institute.

Frey, W. 1995 "Immigration and Internal Migration 'Flight' from U.S. Metropolitan Areas: Toward a Demographic Balkanization," *Urban Studies*, 32:733–757.

Gans, H. 1992 "Second Generation Decline: Scenarios for the Economic and Ethnic Futures of Post-1965 American Immigrants," *Ethnic and Racial Studies*, 15:173–192.

———. 1982 *The Urban Villagers: Group and Class in the Life of Italian-Americans.* 1962. Reprint. New York: The Free Press.

———. 1979 "Symbolic Ethnicity: The Future of Ethnic Groups and Cultures in America," *Ethnic and Racial Studies*, 2:1–20.

———. 1973 "Introduction." In *Ethnic Identity and Assimilation: The Polish Community.* Ed. N. Sandberg. New York: Praeger.

———. 1967 *The Levittowners: Ways of Lie and Politics in a New Suburban Community.* New York: Pantheon.

Gibson, M. 1988 *Accommodation without Assimilation: Sikh Immigrants in an American High School.* Ithaca, NY: Cornell University Press.

Glazer, N. 1993 "Is Assimilation Dead?" *The Annals of the American Academy of Social and Political Sciences*, 530:122–136.

Glazer, N. and D. P. Moynihan. 1970 *Beyond the Melting Pot: The Negroes, Puerto Ricans, Jews, Italians, and Irish of New York City.* 1963. Reprint. Cambridge, MA: MIT Press.

Gleason, P. 1980 "American Identity and Americanization." In *Harvard Encyclopedia of American Ethnic Groups.* Ed. S. Thernstrom, A. Orlov, and O. Handlin. Cambridge, MA: Harvard University Press.

Gold, S. 1992 *Refugee Communities: A Comparative Field Study.* Newbury Park, CA: Sage.

Gordon, M. 1964 *Assimilation in American Life.* New York: Oxford University Press.

Greeley, A. 1977 *The American Catholic: A Social Portrait.* New York: Basic Books.

———. 1976 *Ethnicity, Denomination, and Inequality.* Beverly Hills, CA: Sage.

Greenwood, M. J. 1983 "The Economics of Mass Migration from Poor to Rich Countries: Leading Issues of Fact and Theory," *American Economic Review*, 73:173–177.

Guest, A. 1980 "The Suburbanization of Ethnic Groups," *Sociology and Social Research*, 64:497–513.

Heer, D. 1996 *Immigration in America's Future: Social Science Findings and the Policy Debate.* Boulder, CO: Westview.

Herberg, W. 1960 *Protestant-Catholic-Jew.* New York: Anchor.

Higham, J. 1970 *Strangers in the Land: Patterns of American Nativism, 1860–1925.* New York: Atheneum.

Hirschman, C. 1983 "America's Melting Pot Reconsidered," *Annual Review of Sociology*, 9:397–423.

Hirschman, C. and M. Wong. 1986 "The Extraordinary Educational Attainment of Asian Americans: A Search for Historical Evidence and Explanations," *Social Forces*, 65:1–27.

Hobsbawm, E. and T. Ranger. 1983 *The Invention of Tradition.* Cambridge: Cambridge University.

Horton, J. 1995 *The Politics of Diversity: Immigration, Resistance, and Change in Monterey Park, California.* Philadelphia, PA: Temple University Press.

Hout, M., A. Raftery and E. Bell. 1993 "Making the Grade: Educational Stratification in the United States, 1925–1989." In *Persistent Inequality: Changing Educational Attainment in Thirteen Countries.* Ed. Y. Shavit and H. P. Blossfeld. Boulder, CO: Westview.

Ignatiev, N. 1995 *How the Irish Became White.* New York: Routledge.

Jasso, G. and M. Rosenzweig. 1990 *The New Chosen People: Immigrants in the United States.* New York: Russell Sage Foundation.

Kanjanapan, W. 1994 "The Immigration of Asian Professionals to the United States: 1988–1990," *International Migration Review*, 29:7–32.

Katz, L. 1994 "Labor's Past and Future," *Challenge*, 24:18–25.

Kasinitz, P. 1992 *Caribbean New York: Black Immigrants and the Politics of Race.* Ithaca, NY: Cornell University Press.

Kazal, R. 1995 "Revisiting Assimilation: The Rise, Fall, and Reappraisal of a Concept in American Ethnic History," *American Historical Review*, 100:437–472.

Kennedy, R. J. R. 1952 "Single or Triple Melting Pot? Intermarriage in New Haven, 1870–1950," *American Journal of Sociology*, 58:56–59.

———. 1944 "Single or Triple Melting Pot? Intermarriage Trends in New Haven, 1870–1940," *American Journal of Sociology*, 49:331–339.

Kibria, N. 1993 *Family Tightrope: The Changing Lives of Vietnamese Americans.* Princeton: Princeton University Press.

Kim, I. 1981 *New Urban Immigrants: The Korean Community in New York.* Princeton, NJ: Princeton University Press.

Kim, K. C. 1985 "Ethnic Resources Utilization of Korean Immigrant Entrepreneurs in the Chicago Minority Area," *International Migration Review*, 19:82–111.

Kossoudji, S. 1988 "English Language Ability and the Labor Market Opportunities of Hispanic and East Asian Immigrant Men," *Journal of Labor Economics*, 6:205–228.

Lal, B. B. 1990 *The Romance of Culture in an Urban Civilization: Robert E. Park on Race and Ethnic Relations in Cities.* London: Routledge.

LaLonde, R. and R. Topel. 1991 "Labor Market Adjustments to Increased Immigration." In *Immigration, Trade, and the Labor Market.* Ed. J. Abowd and R. Freeman. Chicago: University of Chicago Press.

LaRuffa, A. 1988 *Monte Carmelo: An Italian-American Community in the Bronx.* New York: Gordon and Breach.

Lee, S. and K. Yamanaka. 1990 "Patterns of Asian American Intermarriage and Marital Assimilation," *Journal of Comparative Family Studies*, 21:287–305.

Lieberson, S. 1985 "Unhyphenated Whites in the United States," *Ethnic and Racial Studies*, 8:159–180.

———. 1980 *A Piece of the Pie: Blacks and White Immigrants since 1880.* Berkeley: University of California Press.

———. 1973 "Generational Differences among Blacks in the North," *American Journal of Sociology*, 79:550–565.

Lieberson, S. and M. Waters. 1993 "The Ethnic Responses of Whites: What Causes Their Instability, Simplification, and Inconsistency?" *Social Forces*, 72:421–450.

———. 1988 *From Many Strands: Ethnic and Racial Groups in Contemporary America.* New York: Russell Sage Foundation.

Liebman, L. 1992 "Immigration Status and American Law: The Several Versions of Antidiscrimination Doctrine." In *Immigrants in Two Democracies: French and American Experience.* Ed. D. L. Horowitz and G. Noiriel. New York: New York University Press.

Light, I. 1984 "Immigrant and Ethnic Enterprise in North America," *Ethnic and Racial Studies*, 7:195–216.

———. 1972 *Ethnic Enterprise in America: Business and Welfare among Chinese, Japanese, and Black.* Berkeley: University of California.

Light, I. and E. Bonacich. 1988 *Immigrant Entrepreneurs: Koreans in Los Angeles, 1965–1982.* Berkeley: University of California.

Light, I. and S. Karageorgis. 1994 "The Ethnic Economy." In *Handbook of Economic Sociology.* Ed. N. Smelser and R. Swedberg. Princeton, NJ: Princeton University Press.

Light, I., G. Sabagh, M. Bozorgmehr and C. Der-Martirosian. 1994 "Beyond the Ethnic Enclave Economy," *Social Problems*, 41:65–79.

Lind, M. 1995 *The Next American Nation: The New Nationalism and the Fourth American Revolution.* New York: Basic.

Loewen, J. 1971 *The Mississippi Chinese: Between Black and White.* Cambridge, MA: Harvard University.

Logan, J. and R. Alba. 1993 "Locational Returns to Human Capital: Minority Access to Suburban Community Resources," *Demography*, 30:243–268.

Logan, J., R. Alba and S. Y. Leung. 1996 "Minority Access to White Suburbs: A Multi-region Comparison," *Social Forces*, 74:851–881.

Logan, J., R. Alba and T. McNulty. 1994 "Ethnic Economies in Metropolitan Regions: Miami and Beyond," *Social Forces*, 72:691–724.

Logan, J., R. Alba, T. McNulty and B. Fisher. 1996 "Making a Place in the Metropolis: Locational Attainment in City and Suburb," *Demography*, 33:443–453.

Lyman, S. 1973 *The Black American in Sociological Thought: A Failure of Perspective.* New York: Capricorn.

Mar, D. 1991 "Another Look at the Enclave Economy Thesis: Chinese Immigrants in the Ethnic Labor Market," *Amerasia*, 17:5–21.

Massey, D. 1994 "The New Immigration and the Meaning of Ethnicity in the United States." Paper presented at the Albany Conference on American Diversity.

———. 1987 "Understanding Mexican Migration to the United States," *American Journal of Sociology*, 92:1372–1403.

———. 1985 "Ethnic Residential Segregation: A Theoretical Synthesis and Empirical Review," *Sociology and Social Research*, 69:315–350.

Massey, D. and N. Denton. 1993 *American Apartheid: Segregation and the Making of the Underclass.* Cambridge, MA: Harvard University Press.

———. 1988 "Suburbanization and Segregation in U.S. Metropolitan Areas," *American Journal of Sociology*, 94:592–626.

———. 1987 "Trends in Residential Segregation of Blacks, Hispanics, and Asians: 1970–1980," *American Sociological Review*, 52:802–825.

McKee, J. 1993 *Sociology and the Race Problem: The Failure of a Perspective.* Urbana: University of Illinois.

Mencken, H. L. 1963 *The American Language.* Abridg. ed. New York: Knopf.

Merton, R. 1968 *Social Theory and Social Structure.* Glencoe: The Free Press.

Min, P. G. 1996 *Caught in the Middle: Korean Communities in New York and Los Angeles.* Berkeley: University of California.

———. 1984 "From White-collar Occupations to Small Business: Korean Immigrants' Occupational Adjustment," *Sociological Quarterly*, 25:333–352.

Model, S. 1988 "The Economic Progress of European and East Asian Americans," *Annual Review of Sociology*, 14:363–380.

Morawska, E. 1994 "In Defense of the Assimilation Model," *Journal of American Ethnic History*, 13:76–87.

Nee, V. and B. Nee. *1973 Longtime Californ': A Documentary Study of an American Chinatown.* Boston: Houghton Mifflin.

Nee, V. and J. Sanders. 1985 "The Road to Parity: Determinants of the Socioeconomic Attainments of Asian Americans," *Ethnic and Racial Studies*, 8:75–93.

Nee, V., J. Sanders and S. Sernau. 1994 "Job Transitions in an Immigrant Metropolis: Ethnic Boundaries and the Mixed Economy," *American Sociological Review*, 59:849–872.

Neidert, L. and R. Farley. 1985 "Assimilation in the United States: An Analysis of Ethnic and Generation Differences in Status and Achievement," *American Sociological Review*, 50:840–850.

Park, R. E. 1950 *Race and Culture.* Glencoe: The Free Press.

————. 1930 "Assimilation, Social." In *Encyclopedia of the Social Sciences.* Ed. E. Seligman and A. Johnson. New York: Macmillan.

Park, R. E. and E. Burgess. 1969 *Introduction to the Science of Sociology*. 1921. Reprint. Chicago: University of Chicago Press.

Perlmann, J. and R. Waldinger. 1997 "Second Generation Decline? Children of Immigrants, Past and Present—A Reconsideration," *International Migration Review*, 31(4).

Portes, A. and R. Bach. 1985 *Latin Journey: Cuban and Mexican Immigrants in the United States*. Berkeley: University of California Press.

Portes, A. and R. Rumhaut. 1996 *Immigrant America: A Portrait*, 2nd ed. Berkeley: University of California Press.

Portes, A. and M. Zhou. 1996 "Self-employment and the Earnings of Immigrants," *American Sociological Review*, 61:219–230.

———. 1993 "The New Second Generation: Segmented Assimilation and Its Variants," *The Annals of the American Academy of Political and Social Sciences*, 530:74–96.

———. 1992 "Gaining the Upper Hand: Economic Mobility among Immigrant and Domestic Minorities," *Racial and Ethnic Studies*, 15:491–522.

Qian, Z. 1997 "Breaking the Racial Barriers: Variations in Interracial Marriages between 1980 and 1990," *Demography*, 34:263–276.

Reimers, D. 1992 *Still the Golden Door: The Third World Comes to America*. New York: Columbia University Press.

Roediger, D. 1991 *The Wages of Whiteness: Race and the Making of the American Working Class*. New York: Verso.

Rumbaut, R. 1994 "The Crucible Within: Ethnic Identity, Self-esteem and Segmented Assimilation among Children of Immigrants," *International Migration Review*, 18:748–794.

Sanders, J. and V. Nee. 1996 "Immigrant Self-employment: The Family as Social Capital and the Value of Human Capital," *American Sociological Review*, 61:231–249.

———. 1987 "The Limits of Ethnic Solidarity in the Enclave Economy," *American Sociological Review*, 52:745–773.

Sandberg, N. 1973 *Ethnic Identity and Assimilation: The Polish Community*. New York: Praeger.

Sassen, S. 1988 *The Mobility of Capital and Labor*. Cambridge: Cambridge University Press.

Shibutani, T. and K. Kwan. 1965 *Ethnic Stratification*. New York: Macmillan.

Smith, J. and B. Edmonston. 1997 *The New Americans: Economic, Demographic, and Fiscal Effects of Immigration*. Washington, DC: National Research Council.

Sollors, W. 1989 *The Invention of Ethnicity*. New York: Oxford University.

Sowell, T. 1996 *Migrations and Cultures: A World View*. New York: Basic Books.

Steinberg, S. 1981 *The Ethnic Myth*. Boston: Beacon.

Stevens, G. 1992 "The Social and Demographic Context of Language Use in the United States," *American Sociological Review*, 57:171–185.

———. 1985 "Nativity, Intermarriage, and Mother-tongue Shift," *American Sociological Review*, 50:74–83.

Stone, J. 1985 *Racial Conflict in Contemporary Society*. London: Fontana Press/Collins.

Suarez-Orozco, M. 1989 *Central American Refugees and U.S. High Schools: A Psychological Study of Motivation and Achievement*. Stanford, CA: Stanford University Press.

Tienda, M. and Z. Liang. 1994 "Poverty and Immigration in Policy Perspective." In *Confronting Poverty: Prescriptions for Change*. Ed. S. H. Danzinger, G. D. Sandefur, and D. H. Weinberg. New York: Russell Sage Foundation. Pp. 331–364.

Tienda, M. and A. Singer. 1994 "Wage Mobility of Undocumented Workers in the United States," *International Migration Review*, 29:112–138.

Veltman, C. 1983 *Language Shift in the United States*. Berlin: Mouton.

Waldinger, R. 1996 *Still the Promised City? African-Americans and New Immigrants in Post-Industrial New York*. Cambridge, MA: Harvard University.

———. 1989 "Immigration and Urban Change," *Annual Review of Sociology*, 15:211–232.

———. 1986/87 "Changing Ladders and Musical Chairs: Ethnicity and Opportunity in Post-industrial New York," *Politics and Society*, 15.

Waldinger, R. and M. Bozorgmehr. 1996 "The Making of a Multicultural Metropolis." In *Ethnic Los Angeles*. Ed. R. Waldinger and M. Bozorgmehr. New York: Russell Sage.

Warner, W. L. and L. Srole. 1945 *The Social Systems of American Ethnic Groups*. New Haven, CT: Yale University Press.

Waters, M. 1994 "Ethnic and Racial Identities of Second-generation Black Immigrants in New York City," *International Migration Review*, 28:795–820.

———. 1990 *Ethnic Options: Choosing Identities in America*. Berkeley: University of California Press.

White, M., A. Biddlecom and S. Guo. 1993 "Immigration, Naturalization, and Residential Assimilation among Asian Americans," *Social Forces*, 72:93–118.

Whyte, W. E 1955 *Street Corner Society: The Social Structure of an Italian Slum*. 1943. Reprint. Chicago: University of Chicago Press.

Wilson, K. and A. Portes. 1980 "Immigrant Enclaves: An Analysis of the Labor Market Experiences of Cubans in Miami," *American Journal of Sociology*, 86:296–319.

Wirth, L. 1956 *The Ghetto*, 1928. Reprint. Chicago: University of Chicago.

Woldemikael, T. 1989 *Becoming Black American: Haitians and American Institutions in Evanston, Illinois*. New York: AMS Press.

Yancey, W., E. Ericksen and R. Juliani. 1976 "Emergent Ethnicity: A Review and a Reformulation." *American Sociological Review*, 41:391–403.

Yoon, I. J. 1996 *On My Own: Korean Immigration, Entrepreneurship, and Korean-Black Relations in Chicago and Los Angeles*. Chicago: University of Chicago Press.

———. 1991 "The Changing Significance of Ethnic and Class Resources in Immigrant Businesses: The Case of Korean Immigrant Businesses in Chicago," *International Migration Review*, 25:303–332.

Zhou, M. 1992 *Chinatown: The Socioeconomic Potential of an Urban Enclave*. Philadelphia, PA: Temple University Press.

CHAPTER 5

Segmented Assimilation and Minority Cultures of Mobility

Kathryn M. Neckerman, Prudence Carter, and Jennifer Lee

Recent work on the new ***second generation*** *posits that racial discrimination and a restructuring economy are likely to create different paths of assimilation for post-1965 nonwhite immigrants than earlier European immigrants experienced and may even decouple* ***acculturation*** *from economic mobility. But while these discussions have considered the minority lower class as a possible destination for assimilation, middle-class minorities have been largely ignored. In this essay, Kathryn Neckerman, Prudence Carter, and Jennifer Lee consider how the experiences of middle-class minorities might alter our models of second-generation incorporation, or* ***segmented assimilation****. They propose that the minority middle classes share a* ***minority culture of mobility****, a set of cultural elements responsive to distinctive problems that usually accompany minority middle-class status, including problems of interracial encounters in public settings and interclass relations within the minority community. They illustrate this minority culture of mobility with a brief case study of the African American middle class and discuss its implications for immigrants.*

Source: Adapted from Kathryn M. Neckerman, Prudence Carter, and Jennifer Lee, "Segmented Assimilation and Minority Cultures of Mobility," *Ethnic and Racial Studies*, Volume 22, Issue 6, pages 945–965. Taylor and Francis, 1999.

Questions to Consider

Can you think of another middle-class minority group besides African Americans that might employ a "minority culture of mobility"? What cultural elements do group members share that help them to incorporate into America's economy and society? Are these elements the same or different from those of the African American middle class?

Introduction

Recent discussions of the 'new second generation'—the children of the post-1965 wave of immigrants—have challenged the conventional idea that acculturation and economic mobility are necessarily linked (Gans 1992; Portes and Zhou 1993; Rumbaut 1994). Because the non-white immigrants who have predominated after 1965 face racial discrimination and a less favorable labor market than did European immigrants several generations ago, it may be unrealistic for them to try to follow the same path. Indeed, it may even be counterproductive, if, in a premature effort to enter the American social and economic mainstream, immigrants relinquish ethnic resources and raise expectations in their children that cannot immediately be satisfied.

Portes and Zhou (1993) have formalized this idea in influential writing about 'segmented assimilation'. For today's non-white immigrants, they outline several alternative paths of adaptation: incorporation into the white middle-class mainstream, incorporation into a largely minority underclass, and a kind of delayed or selective assimilation in which immigrants continue to draw on the moral and material resources of the immigrant community. Immersion in the immigrant community, Portes and Zhou write, slows acculturation to American material standards of living, buffers children from prejudice, and gives parents material resources to aid mobility, perhaps allowing their improving status to keep pace with their children's expectations.

In this menu of paths of adaptation, there is a curious omission: the minority middle class. Portes and Zhou do not suggest that middle-class African Americans, for instance, might provide immigrants with a cultural framework or even a destination for assimilation. Rather, they state that immigrants who assimilate face a stark choice between the mainstream culture of the white middle class and the oppositional culture of the minority underclass. Here Portes and Zhou are themselves in the mainstream of research on immigration, assimilation, and racial and ethnic stratification, in which the minority middle class has been largely invisible.

Portes and Zhou are right to raise concerns about racial barriers that non-white immigrants face. It is because the minority middle class has long coped with such barriers that its experiences might be relevant. Just as immigrants might borrow oppositional culture from poor inner-city minorities, we suggest, they might also borrow cultural elements from the minority middle class. To understand this borrowing, we need a conception of minority middle-class culture that, like our conceptions of minority oppositional culture, is general and rooted in social structural situation. This article takes a step towards such a conception.

We propose that the middle classes of American minority groups share in common a category of cultural elements that we call the *minority culture of mobility.* These cultural elements provide strategies for economic mobility in the context of discrimination and group disadvantage, and respond to distinctive problems that usually accompany minority middle-class status. Here, we highlight two classes of problems, one arising from contact with the white majority, the other from interclass contacts within the minority community. The minority culture of mobility provides interpretations of and strategies for managing these problems.

This minority culture of mobility may not have immediate relevance for immigrants. If immigrants are very poor, for instance, oppositional culture may indeed seem a more compelling account of their condition. And if they remain immersed in and oriented to the immigrant community, employing the strategies of delayed or selective assimilation that Portes and Zhou and others (Gans 1992) describe, relations with whites may be limited and problems of inter-class relations defused by a 'bounded solidarity' that foregrounds ethnic identity and involves dense ties of economic interdependence (Portes and Zhou 1992; Zhou 1992; Portes and Sensenbrenner 1993). But eventually immigrants are likely to seek jobs outside the ethnic enclave and particularly in the corporate and government sectors that dominate big-city labor markets. It is at this point, as immigrants begin to move into the mainstream economy, and even more as they experience some economic success, that the minority culture of mobility might become salient to them.

Our primary purpose in this study is to outline our conception of the minority culture of mobility and to argue its value in research on contemporary non-white immigrants. Section 1 presents a theoretical argument for the existence of distinctive minority cultures of mobility. Section 2 provides a sketch of the African-American culture of mobility; while this description is necessarily brief and tentative, it illustrates our argument and, we hope, further establishes its plausibility. Section 3 considers the implications for immigrants; we consider the extent to which immigrants are likely to adopt a minority culture of mobility, again using the African-American case for illustration.

The Minority Culture of Mobility

We propose that the minority middle classes possess distinctive cultural elements which we call the 'minority culture of mobility', and that this culture has implications for the assimilation trajectory of non-white immigrants. By the minority culture of mobility, we mean a set of cultural elements that is associated with a minority group, and that provides strategies for managing economic mobility in the context of discrimination and group disadvantage. The minority culture of mobility draws on available symbols, idioms and practices to respond to distinctive problems of being middle class and minority. It includes knowledge and behavioral strategies that help to negotiate the competing demands of the white mainstream and the minority community. But it also includes symbolic elements, particularly those relevant to problems of ambiguous identity and affiliation—will one identify (or be identified) in terms of class, ethnic group, or both?—that often accompany minority middle-class status.

This culture of mobility is not a complete culture, but a set of cultural elements within the larger framework of a given minority culture. As Swidler (1986) writes, a culture can contain diverse and even contradictory elements; within a given minority culture, this culture of mobility might coexist with oppositional elements. Like oppositional culture, the culture of mobility is a response to conditions in the host country on the part of longtime minority groups; it is not likely to be a culture of newcomers. Oppositional culture might seem antithetical to the minority culture of mobility, but in fact the two may emerge in tandem, as alternative responses to conditions of racism and discrimination. Existing within the larger framework of a minority culture, the culture of mobility may be accessible to the poor or working class as well as the middle class, with its influence dependent on social environment and personal biography.

The minority culture of mobility may seem to have much in common with a more generic version of the 'American dream', differing only in trivial ways from white middle-class culture. Indeed, this is exactly how some scholars have described black middle-class culture. Gordon (1964), for instance, characterized the black middle class as acculturated to the American mainstream, in contrast to the black lower class which retained its southern folk culture. But we argue that this minority culture of mobility differs from the cultures both of the white middle class and of the black lower or working classes: it emerges in response to distinctive problems that middle-class and upwardly mobile minorities face. Here we identify two categories of such problems, stemming from contacts with whites and from inter-class relations within minority communities.

Contacts with whites are usually more extensive for middle-class than lower-class minorities. Although discrimination in housing markets constrains minority residential choices, higher-income minorities are more likely than their lower-income counterparts to live among whites (Alba and Logan 1993; Massey and Denton 1993, p. 152). In addition, as minority workers climb the economic ladder, they reach work settings in which whites are disproportionately represented and co-ethnics are few or absent. Middle-class status also implies tastes and buying power that cannot be satisfied within the minority community, whose merchants often cater to a downscale market; if they are not barred by discrimination, middle-class minorities are likely to purchase goods and services from merchants who serve a predominantly white clientele (Lee 1998). The predominantly middle-class youth who go to college often do so in racially-integrated settings.

These contacts with whites mean distinctive problems. One is the demand for conformity to white middle-class speech patterns and interactional styles in school, work and other public settings (Kirschenman and Neckerman 1991; Zweigenhaft and Domhoff 1991; Moss and Tilly 1996; Gould forthcoming). In addition, because they move more in white-dominant arenas, middle-class minorities encounter prejudice and discrimination more often than poorer co-ethnics, who may work and meet their daily needs within the confines of the ethnic community. Minorities can also face distinctive forms of prejudice and discrimination in middle-class settings. Finally, being the only minority, or one of few minorities, in a white-dominated setting can mean a psychological burden of loneliness and isolation, as well as social disadvantages such as exclusion from information networks and the exaggerated visibility of the token, as well as economic loss (Kluegel 1978; Cose 1993; Feagin and Sikes 1994).

Of course, poorer minorities also experience white prejudice and discrimination. But there are distinctive aspects of the problems that middle-class minorities face. For instance, the 'glass ceiling' refers to a set of subtle biases and mechanisms of exclusion that are specific to fairly high levels of the occupational structure. The 'glass ceiling' is not a problem with much relevance for the minority poor, whose immediate problem is joblessness or low wages, nor even for the working class, whose economic status is governed by other kinds of structures, such as unions. But for middle class, with their knowledge of the white-collar workplace, the idea of the 'glass ceiling' is intelligible. While middle-class and working-class minorities can understand each other's situation in general, certain kinds of discrimination are particularly salient to the middle class.

A second category of problems concerns inter-class relations. Middle-class minorities are generally more likely than their white counterparts to come into contact with poor co-ethnics. Minority middle-class families must often live near poor co-ethnics (Massey and Denton 1993). In addition, the small size of many minority communities may limit the class differentiation of voluntary associations, leading to class-heterogeneous churches, clubs and civic organizations. The kin networks of middle-class minorities are often more class-heterogeneous than the kin networks of middle-class whites. More than middle-class whites, then, middle-class minorities must manage their relations with poorer co-ethnics who might make claims for assistance, resent their good fortune, or feel intimidated by their success.

These inter-class interactions can also confront middle-class minorities with lower-class oppositional culture, with its claims that an authentic minority identity is one that eschews all that is associated with the dominant white majority. Fordham and Ogbu (1986) write that minority oppositional culture racially codes behavior and styles, defining Standard English, for example, as inappropriate for minorities. Such judgments fall heavily on middle-class minorities, who in order to be successful must adopt behaviors and styles coded as 'acting white'. Minority oppositional culture is reflected in peer pressure not to adopt these behaviors and styles; it can also lead to deep ambivalence about identity.

We have argued that middle-class minorities share in common specific problems of inter-racial and inter-class relations; shared interpretations of and responses to these problems constitute the minority culture of mobility, some version of which is found in all minority groups. But that does not mean minority cultures of mobility are identical across groups. While some elements may diffuse across groups—the idea of the 'glass ceiling' may resonate with a range of minority groups, for instance—the minority culture of mobility is assembled from ethnically distinctive cultural idioms, practice and institutions. Ethnic segregation reinforces this tendency towards ethnically distinct variants of the minority culture of mobility.

In addition, there are ethnic differences in the problems that middle-class minorities face. In their relations with whites, some ethnic groups face more severe prejudice and discrimination than others (Bobo and Hutchings 1996). The character of stereotypes also varies. For some minorities, such as African Americans and Puerto Ricans, racial stereotypes are closely tied to perceptions of the underclass; as Franklin (1991, p. 118) writes, 'the overrepresentation of blacks in the lower class casts shadows that stigmatize working- and middle-class blacks for reasons of race alone'. On the other hand, stereotypes of Asian Americans reflect attributions of foreignness (Alba and Nee 1996). And finally, some minority groups, and some minority individuals, are more clearly identifiable than others. In Miami, for instance, some light-skinned Haitians 'passed' as white or Cuban and thus evaded the prejudice that darker-skinned Haitians encountered (Portes and Stepick 1993).

We expect ethnic variation in problems of inter-class relations as well. If the minority community is very poor, the success of middle-class members becomes more conspicuous. Problems of inter-class relations are also heightened, we expect, when ethnic segregation restricts most social contacts to within the ethnic community. A third consideration is the degree of ethnic solidarity. Members of more solidary ethnic groups are likely to feel a keener sense of identification with and obligation to poorer co-ethnics (Portes and Sensenbrenner 1993). This solidarity may derive from compelling and shared historical experience, and from outsiders' ascription of ethnic identity (Nagel 1994).

The African-American Culture of Mobility

To illustrate our concept of the minority culture of mobility, we draw on recent writing about the black middle class. Racially-segregated and class-differentiated black communities provided the social niche for the emergence of a distinctive black middle-class culture within the context of a distinctive African-American culture (Gates 1984; Banner-Haley 1994). The culture of mobility accommodates the demands of the white mainstream and provides resources for managing the psychological strain and practical difficulties of performance in this mainstream; it also provides an interpretation of inter-class relations within the black community.

Over the last few decades, middle-class African Americans' contacts with whites have increased. The passage of the Civil Rights Act opened economic opportunities for the black middle class in white-dominant workplaces (Landry 1987). There have also been modest reductions in the level of racial segregation in school, and more significant reductions in discrimination in public accommodations (Jaynes and Williams 1989). Increased contact between middle-class blacks and whites, however, is largely confined to work, school and public settings. Few in the black middle class socialize with white colleagues outside of the workplace (Landry 1987; Benjamin 1991). Neighborhoods continue to be highly segregated by race, and marriage between blacks and whites remains uncommon (Kalmijn 1993; Massey and Denton 1993).

At school and at work, middle-class African Americans continue to fight discrimination through the NAACP and other advocacy groups as well as agencies such as the Equal Employment Opportunity Commission. But while these organizations helped middle-class African Americans to gain access to white-dominant settings, they are not well-suited to ease problems of interracial contact that can arise. These problems include new, more subtle kinds of bias, such as the resegregation of racially-mixed schools through academic tracking, and the relegation of black professionals to jobs in community relations and other staff positions with poor promotion prospects (Oakes 1985; Collins 1997). Sophistication about this kind of bias is itself an element of the African American culture of mobility. In addition, as middle-class blacks encounter white strangers in public spaces, they face a different set of problems: whites tend to assume that all black strangers are lower-class and respond accordingly, with fear, insult, or threat. Ellis Cose (1993, p. 41) calls this the 'permanent vulnerability of one's status'. Examples are familiar (Anderson 1990; Carter 1993; West 1993; Feagin and Sikes 1994): black men unable to get taxicabs; black shoppers tailed by store detectives; white pedestrians crossing the street to avoid black youth.

In response, when African Americans have entered a specific niche in sufficient numbers, they often form 'caucus' groups (Jaynes and Williams 1989, pp. 188–89). In addition, the parallel organizations formed decades ago in response to black exclusion from the mainstream professional organizations continue to thrive today—the black National Medical

Association, for instance, continues to attract members even though black physicians readily become members of the American Medical Association—because they, like the caucus groups, respond to this felt need for moral and instrumental support. At racially-integrated high schools and universities, there are usually organizations of black students.

But middle-class African Americans must also manage problems of inter-racial encounters. Here they work hard to signal their class status to whites. Anderson (1990) notes a keen concern with 'propriety and decorum' among black middle-class residents of a race- and class-heterogeneous neighborhood. Display of expensive clothing and accessories and pointed use of Standard English are also ways that middle-class blacks try to manage these encounters (Anderson 1990; Cose 1993; Feagin and Sikes 1994; Lee 1999). Middle-class blacks may use conversational ploys, assume interests or demeanor to put white acquaintances or co-workers at ease (Cose 1993; Zweigenhaft and Domhoff 1998; Hildebrandt 1999).

While middle-class blacks' arsenal of organizational and interactional tactics helps them to accommodate day-to-day the problems of interracial contact, over the long term these problems can exhaust and embitter. For relief from the strains of public interactions with whites, middle-class blacks take refuge in black-dominant social spaces where, after a day's work in white-dominant workplaces, they can return to the comfort of their private lives and 'de-robe', in a sense, switching to ethnic African-American symbolic and interactional styles. The informal circles of family and friends are, of course, important parts of this refuge. So are black-dominant voluntary associations such as the black fraternities and sororities, the family-oriented Jack and Jill, and recreational groups such as the National Brotherhood of Skiers and Ebony Funseekers International, Inc. (a group of black travellers). In these settings, middle-class African Americans share 'combat stories' about personal experiences with isolation, racist encounters and discrimination in the workplace, and exchange strategies for managing within white-dominant environments.

Middle-class African-American culture expresses and validates the practice of straddling two worlds. Themes of dualism—power/impotence, security/uncertainty, insider/outsider—often mark African-American literature and other cultural products (Benjamin 1991; Cose 1993; Lightfoot 1994).

While these cultural expressions convey ambivalence, they also validate black middle-class accommodation of demands of white-dominant arenas, portraying this accommodation as an expedient that need not jeopardize one's private, ethnic identity. In a parallel to the 'accommodation without assimilation' that Gibson (1989) describes among Sikh immigrants, middle-class blacks conform to white linguistic and interactional styles while remaining grounded in a separate social sphere and cultural framework. For immigrants, according to Gibson, this accommodation can be sustained because the immigrants believe discrimination will be transient, fading quickly once they learn the language and customs of the host society. Middle-class African Americans do not have such hope, and instead accommodate white demands with the bitter knowledge that race relations will improve only gradually and with struggle; in that context, retaining a separate, private sense of identity may be the only way to make such accommodation tenable.

In addition to relations with whites, middle-class African Americans must also manage their relations with poorer co-ethnics. The social structural context of these cross-class relations has altered over the past few decades, as the black middle class has increasingly moved away from poor inner-city neighborhoods and schools (Wilson 1987, 1996; Anderson 1990).

The day-to-day experiences of the black middle and lower class have also diverged: the black middle class continues to be engaged in regular employment in the mainstream economy, while the black poor increasingly work informally or not at all (Wilson 1980, 1996).

But despite the increased social separation between middle and lower-class blacks, the social networks of many middle-class blacks continue to be class-heterogeneous. Kin ties cross class lines. Middle-class blacks who have moved out of the inner city return to visit friends and relatives, attend church, or experience a black social and cultural milieu (Patillo 1997). More than their white counterparts, middle-class blacks live in mixed-class neighborhoods (Massey and Denton 1993). These social contacts both reflect and reinforce the solidarity forged by a shared history of racial subordination and resistance, a solidarity so vital that Fordham (1996) describes it as 'fictive kinship'. The history of African Americans remains integral to the way middle-class blacks think about their identity and group interests (Dawson 1994; Hochschild 1995). Anderson, for instance, writes that black professionals moving out of the inner city are sometimes chided by their peers 'about remembering where they came from' (1990, p. 65). In high schools with large black student populations, an oppositional student culture may define mainstream success and educational ambition as inconsistent with an authentic black identity (Fordham 1996). In school and other settings, epithets such as 'race traitor' and 'white-washed' express community disapproval of upwardly mobile members who appear to have rejected an affiliation with the African-American community.

To manage these inter-class relations, middle-class or upwardly mobile African Americans may 'switch' to lower-class linguistic and interactional styles (Neckerman, Marchena, and Powell 1999). Anderson (1990) writes about 'streetwise' middle-class blacks who use their familiarity with black street culture to manage encounters with lower-class blacks. Such switching can allow middle-class blacks to maintain dual lives and identities; students may do this particularly when they can use magnet schools or upper-track classes to segregate their academic and street or neighborhood identities (for example, Hemmings 1996; also see Mehan et al. 1994).

Problems of class relations are also reflected in an on-going conversation about cross-class obligation that has little or no echo among whites. For instance, Stephen Carter (1993, p. 78) writes:

> Many [affluent African Americans] will not feel comfortable unless they are actively involved in assisting the worst-off members of their communities. Others will make choices about where to live, whom to love, how to vacation. Some will reach down the ladder to pull others along. Some will spend their days redesigning the ladder. But even one who spends her career simply being the best she can be at what she does can, if fired by love, insist that she, too, has made a claim [of membership in the African-American community]—and so I would say she has. Moreover, she has even carried her burden of working and helping, for each of us who shatters stereotypes advances the cause.

The taken-for-granted premise of Carter's litany is the tug of obligation, the 'burden of working and helping', that affluent African Americans feel, or should feel, towards poorer co-ethnics. Even when it is not reflected in action, this ongoing conversation about ways to 'give back' is a response to implied questions about loyalty to the ethnic group.

Stephen Carter's insistence that professional accomplishment can be a way of discharging one's obligation to the group, resonating with the old notions of 'race man' and 'race woman' (Drake and Cayton 1945), may represent another element of the African-American culture of mobility. Drawing on the very idioms of shared fate that underlie the oppositional perspective, middle-class African Americans may respond to that perspective with a claim that their achievement may help to advance the race by dispelling racial stereotypes, providing role models, and using the power of high position to help others advance.

Immigrants and the Minority Culture of Mobility

The African-American culture of mobility is deeply rooted in specific historical and contemporary conditions, and one can question whether immigrants would find it a compelling representation of their own situation. After all, despite some parallels among the histories of different minority groups (Okihiro 1994), there are also substantial differences in the ways various minority groups were incorporated into the United States. Contemporary situations also vary; for instance, by very simple indicators of social assimilation, such as residential segregation and intermarriage, Asian Americans and Latinos are more integrated with whites than are African Americans (Kalmijn 1993; Massey and Denton 1993). Indeed, Smith (1997) suggests that rather than identifying with American minorities such as African Americans, immigrants will often seek to distinguish themselves from these minorities in order to gain what DuBois long ago called the 'public and psychological wage' of whiteness.

But the minority culture of mobility may become more salient over time for immigrants and their descendants, as three processes occur: racialization of identity, movement into the mainstream economy, and class formation within the ethnic community. When these processes occur, immigrants begin to share the problems with which the minority culture of mobility is engaged: discrimination and isolation in predominantly white contexts, and problems of inter-class relations with disadvantaged co-ethnics. Most middle-class nonwhite immigrants face these problems to some degree, but demographic and economic conditions make these problems more intense and pervasive for some than for others.

Race, Pan-Ethnicity and the Diffusion of Minority Cultures of Mobility

When middle-class immigrants share the kinds of problems faced by American middle-class minorities, they may begin to develop a minority culture of mobility. The symbols and practices of this culture of mobility may be assembled from the traditions and experiences of the immigrant group itself, or 'borrowed' from others. If immigrants adopt cultural elements from other groups, this diffusion is most likely to be structured along racial or pan-ethnic lines, that is, Asian immigrants will borrow from more established Asian-American communities, Latin American immigrants from American Latino communities, Afro-Caribbean immigrants from African Americans.

This pattern of diffusion is likely because of the effect of racial or pan-ethnic category on patterns of social interaction and identity formation. Take, for example, the patterns of contact and identification between African Americans and immigrants. Because of racial segregation in housing, it is primarily black immigrants who live among African Americans

(Buchanan 1979; Foner 1985, 1987; Stafford 1987). In New York City, the index of dissimilarity for native- and foreign-born blacks is only .43, compared to indices of .83 to .89 for African Americans with white ethnic and Asian ethnic groups (Logan 1996). And because West Indian immigrants fare better economically than do African Americans (Foner 1985; Model 1995; Waldinger 1996), they often live in middle-class African-American neighborhoods. Residential proximity leads to other forms of contact, with black immigrants often meeting African Americans at school, church and the workplace (Foner 1985).

Not only are West Indians more likely to live among African Americans, they are also more likely to work with African Americans than any other minority group. West Indians have moved into the niches that African Americans have dominated, such as health care and government employment (Model 1995; Waldinger 1996). West Indians have also benefited from African-American schools and colleges, with many obtaining professional training from Howard University (Foner 1985). As race structures contact between immigrant and native groups, it also patterns the cultural influences that are diffused through face-to-face interaction.

In addition, race and pan-ethnicity shape identification. As Nagel (1994, p. 154) notes, ethnic identity formation is not a one-sided, internal process, but a 'dialectical process involving internal and external opinions and processes, as well as the individual's self-identification and outsiders' ethnic designations—i.e. what *you* think your ethnicity is, versus what *they* think your ethnicity is'. When outsiders perceive racial similarity between minority groups, their ascription of identity is consequential (Cornell 1988; Lopez and Espiritu 1990).

This outsider ascription often occurs despite the intentions and perceived interests of the immigrants themselves. Studies of West Indian immigrants, for instance, show that regardless of social class or neighborhood of settlement, first-generation immigrants cling to their ethnicity and distance themselves from American blacks (Waters 1994).

But asserting one's ethnic identity for non-white immigrants is difficult, particularly for later generations, in a society that places race above ethnicity. Bashi writes that 'children of West Indian immigrants do not so much choose between membership in an ethnic group (West Indian) and a race (black), as they try to navigate a system which recognizes blackness on sight, and recognizes ethnicity for black native born people rarely, if at all' (1996, p. 30). Although language, accent, culture and clothing distinguish first-generation black immigrants from black Americans, for the second generation these cultural markers fade, making it more difficult for second-generation West Indians to communicate their ethnic identity to others. For second-generation West Indians, ethnic identity plays a less significant role than it did for the first generation (Stafford 1987), and many identify with African Americans (Rumbaut 1994, Waters 1994).

Although cultural diffusion is most likely to take place along racial or pan-ethnic lines, we note two possible means of diffusion across these broad categories. First, some schools (magnet schools, many colleges and universities) have racially and ethnically diverse enrolments, and may serve as sites of cultural diffusion. Non-white immigrants may form relationships with African-American classmates that can serve as a conduit for the minority culture of mobility. Second, immigrants may encounter the African-American culture of mobility indirectly, through literary expression and popular culture. These channels—schools and the popular media—cross-cut racial and pan-ethnic category, potentially disseminating the African-American culture of mobility beyond West Indian immigrants.

Conclusion

We have conceptualized the 'minority culture of mobility' as a set of cultural elements that provide strategies for mobility within the context of racial discrimination coupled with socio-economic disadvantage. This mobility-oriented culture, we suggest, is an interpretation of and response to distinctive problems that middle-class or upwardly mobile minorities experience: interracial relations in white mainstream contexts, and inter-class relations within the minority community. Middle-class minorities are likely to have relatively extensive contacts with whites as a result of their occupational positions as well as in other roles such as consumers, and so must manage the practical problems of prejudice and discrimination they encounter in these settings. Middle-class minorities also have more extensive cross-class contact than white counterparts do, and so encounter within-ethnic class tensions, claims for support, and accusations of racial disloyalty.

Portes and Zhou's (1993) model of segmented assimilation is elaborated, not contradicted, by our discussion of the minority culture of mobility. The practices of selective or delayed assimilation that they write about are most pertinent for immigrants in the early stages of incorporation into the United States, while the minority culture of mobility is likely to become more relevant over time, with the processes of racialization, class formation and entry into the economic mainstream. Indeed, selective or delayed assimilation followed by adoption of a minority culture of mobility together define a likely trajectory for some non-white immigrants. The same racial barriers to full assimilation that make selective or delayed assimilation an advantageous strategy for early-generation non-white immigrants also make the minority culture of mobility salient later on.

We expect diffusion of the minority culture of mobility from one group to another to occur mainly within racial or pan-ethnic category, because of the strong influence of race and pan-ethnicity on social contact and identity formation. Among immigrant groups, for instance, black West Indians are most likely to adopt the African-American culture of mobility, because racial discrimination concentrates them in African-American neighborhoods, schools and workplaces, and outsiders often attribute an African-American identity to West Indians, especially those of the second and later generations.

We do not mean to elide differences among 'non-white' minority groups, whose problems of discrimination and structural disadvantage are certainly not identical. Cross-group variation in idioms of traditional ethnic culture is also likely to be reflected in distinctive cultures of mobility. The differences among minority cultures of mobility, and the patterns of diffusion among them, deserve further research.

References

ALBA, RICHARD D. and LOGAN, JOHN R. 1993 'Minority proximity to whites in suburbs: an individual-level analysis of segregation', *American Journal of Sociology*, vol. 98, no. 6, pp. 1388–1427.

ALBA, RICHARD D. and NEE, VICTOR 1996 'The Assimilation of Immigrant Groups: Concept, Theory and Evidence', paper presented at the Social Science Research Council Conference 'Becoming American/America Becoming: International Migration to the United States', Sanibel, Florida.

ANDERSON, ELIJAH 1990 *Streetwise: Race, Class and Change in an Urban Community*, Chicago, IL: University of Chicago Press.

BANNER-HALEY, CHARLES 1994 *The Fruits of Integration: Black Middle-class Ideology and Culture, 1960–1990*, Oxford, MS: University of Mississippi Press.

BASHI, VILNA 1996 '"We Don't Have That Back Home": Race, Racism, and the Social Networks of West Indian Immigrants', paper presented at the 91st annual meeting of the American Sociological Association, New York.

BENJAMIN, LOIS 1991 *The Black Elite*, Chicago, IL: Nelson-Hall.

BOBO, LAWRENCE and HUTCHINGS, V. L. 1996 'Perceptions of racial group composition: extending Blumer's theory of group position to a multiracial social context', *American Sociological Review*, vol. 61, no. 6, pp. 951–72.

BUCHANAN, SUSAN HUELSENBUSCH 1979 'Language and identity: Haitians in New York City', *International Migration Review*, vol. 19, no. 2, pp. 298–313.

CARTER, PRUDENCE 1999 'Balancing "Acts": Issues of Identity, Resistance, and Opportunity among Low-Income Minority Adolescents', PhD dissertation in progress, Columbia University.

CARTER, STEPHEN 1993 'The black table, the empty seat, and the tie', in Gerald Early (ed.), *Lure and Loathing: Essays on Race, Identity, and the Ambivalence of Assimilation*, New York: Penguin Books, pp. 55–79.

COLLINS, SHARON M. 1997 *Black Corporate Executives: The Making and Breaking of a Black Middle Class*, Philadelphia, PA: Temple University Press.

CORNELL, STEPHEN 1988 'The transformations of tribe: organization and self-concept in Native American ethnicities', *Ethnic and Racial Studies*, vol. 11, no. 1, pp. 368–88.

COSE, ELLIS 1993 *The Rage of a Privileged Class*, New York: HarperCollins.

DAWSON, MICHAEL 1994 *Behind the Mule: Race and Class in African-American Politics*, Princeton, NJ: Princeton University Press.

DRAKE, ST. CLAIR and CAYTON, HORACE. [1945] 1962 *Black Metropolis: A Study of Negro Life in a Northern City*, New York: Harper and Row.

FEAGIN, JOE R. and SIKES, MELVIN P. 1994 *Living with Racism: The Black Middle-Class Experience*, Boston, MA: Beacon Press.

FONER, NANCY 1985 'Race and color: Jamaican migrants in London and New York City', *International Migration Review*, vol. 19, no. 4, pp. 708–27.

FORDHAM, SIGNITHIA 1996 *Blacked Out: Dilemmas of Race, Identity, and Success at Capital High*, Chicago, IL: University of Chicago Press.

FORDHAM, SIGNITHIA and OGBU, JOHN U. 1986 'Black students' school success: coping with the burden of acting white', *The Urban Review*, vol. 58, no. 3, pp. 54–84.

FRANKLIN, RAYMOND S. 1991 *Shadows of Race and Class*, Minneapolis, MN: University of Minnesota Press.

GANS, HERBERT J. 1992 'Second generation decline: scenarios for the economic and ethnic futures of the post-1965 American immigrants', *Ethnic and Racial Studies*, vol. 15, no. 2, pp. 173–92.

GATES, HENRY LOUIS, JR. 1984 'Criticism in the jungle', in Henry Louis Gates, Jr. (ed.), *Black Literature and Literary Theory*, New York: Methuen, pp. 1–24.

GIBSON, MARGARET 1989 *Accommodation without Assimilation: Sikh Immigrants in an American High School*, Ithaca, NY: Cornell University Press.

GORDON, MILTON M. 1964 *Assimilation in American Life: The Role of Race, Religion, and National Origins*, New York: Oxford University Press.

GOULD, MARK (forthcoming) 'Race and theory: culture, poverty and adaptation to discrimination in Wilson and Ogbu', *Sociological Theory.*

HEMMINGS, ANNETTE 1996 'Conflicting images? Being black and a model high school student', *Anthropology and Education Quarterly*, vol. 27, no. 1, pp. 20–50.

HILDEBRANDT, MELANIE 1999 'The Construction of Racial Identity: A Comparison of African Americans and Caribbean Americans and their White Spouses', PhD dissertation in progress, Columbia University.

HOCHSCHILD, JENNIFER L. 1995 *Facing Up to the American Dream: Race, Class, and the Soul of the Nation*, Princeton, NJ: Princeton University Press.

JAYNES, GERALD DAVID and WILLIAMS, ROBIN M., JR. (eds) 1989 *A Common Destiny: Blacks and America Society*, Washington, DC: National Academy Press

KALMIJN, MATTHIJS 1993 'Trends in black/white intermarriage', *Social Forces*, vol. 72, no. 1, pp. 119–46.

KIRSCHENMAN, JOLEEN and NECKERMAN, KATHRYN M. 1991 '"We'd love to hire them but . . .": the meaning of race to employers', in Christopher Jencks and Paul E. Peterson (eds), *The Urban Underclass*, Washington, DC: Brookings, pp. 203–32.

KLUEGEL, JAMES R. 1978 'The causes and cost of racial exclusion from job authority', *American Sociological Review*, vol. 43, no. 3, pp. 285–301.

LANDRY, BART 1987 *The New Black Middle Class*, Berkeley, CA: University of California Press.

LEE, JENNIFER 1998 'Immigrant Entrepreneurs: Opportunity Structure and Intergroup Relations', PhD dissertation, Columbia University.

——— 1999 'What Class You Wear: African-American Customers' Shopping Experiences in Black and White Neighborhoods', manuscript.

LIGHTFOOT, SARA LAWRENCE 1994 *I've Known Rivers: Lives of Loss and Liberation*, New York: Penguin Books.

LOGAN, JOHN R. 1996 'STILL a Global City: The Racial and Ethnic Segmentation of New York', manuscript.

LOPEZ, DAVID and ESPIRITU, YEN 1990 'Pan-ethnicity in the United States: a theoretical framework', *Ethnic and Racial Studies*, vol. 13, no. 2, pp. 198–223.

MASSEY, DOUGLAS and DENTON, NANCY 1993 *American Apartheid: Segregation and the Making of the Underclass*, Cambridge, MA: Harvard University Press.

MEHAN, HUGH, HUBBARD, LEA, and VILLANUEVA, IRENE 1994 'Forming academic identities: accommodation without assimilation among involuntary minorities', *Anthropology and Education Quarterly*, vol. 25, no. 2, pp. 91–117.

MODEL, SUZANNE 1995 'West Indian prosperity: fact or fiction?' *Social Problems*, vol. 42, no. 4, pp. 535–53.

MOSS, PHILIP and TILLY, CHRIS 1996 '"Soft" skills and race: an investigation of black men's employment problems', *Work and Occupations*, vol. 23, no. 3, pp. 252–76.

NAGEL, JOANE 1994 'Constructing ethnicity: creating and recreating ethnic identity and culture', *Social Problems*, vol. 41, no. 1, pp. 152–76.

NECKERMAN, KATHRYN M., MARCHENA, ELAINE, and POWELL, CARLEN 1999 'White Collar, White Talk: Oppositional Culture and the Dilemmas of Standard English', manuscript.

OAKES, JEANNIE 1985 *Keeping Track*, New Haven, CT: Yale University Press.

OKIHIRO, GARY Y. 1994 *Margins and Mainstreams: Asians in American History and Culture*, Seattle, WA: University of Washington Press.

PATILLO, MARY E. 1997 'Adolescence in a Middle Class Black Neighborhood', paper presented at the 92nd Annual Meeting of the American Sociological Association, Toronto, Canada.

PORTES, ALEJANDRO and SENSENBRENNER, JULIA 1993 'Embeddedness and immigration: notes on the social determinants of economic action', *American Journal of Sociology*, vol. 98, no. 6, pp. 1320–50.

PORTES, ALEJANDRO and STEPICK, ALEX 1993 *City on the Edge: The Transformation of Miami*, Berkeley, CA: University of California Press.

PORTES, ALEJANDRO and ZHOU, MIN 1992 'Gaining the upper hand: economic mobility among immigrant and domestic minorities', *Ethnic and Racial Studies*, vol. 15, no. 4, pp. 491–522.

——— 1993 'The new second generation: segmented assimilation and its variants', *Annals of the American Political and Social Sciences*, vol. 530, pp. 74–96.

RUMBAUT, RUBEN G. 1994 'The crucible within: ethnic identity, self-esteem, and segmented assimilation among children of immigrants', *International Migration Review*, vol. 28, no. 4, pp. 748–94.

SMITH, ROBERT C. 1997 'Public Wages and Social Locations: Race and the Concept of Segmented Assimilation in the Incorporation of Immigrants', paper presented at the annual meetings of the Eastern Sociological Society, Baltimore, MD.

STAFFORD, SUSAN BUCHANAN 1987 'The Haitians: the cultural meaning of race and ethnicity', in Nancy Foner (ed.), *New Immigrants in New York*, New York: Columbia University Press, pp. 131–58.

SWIDLER, ANN 1986 'Culture in action: symbols and strategies', *American Sociological Review*, vol. 51, no. 2, pp. 273–86.

WALDINGER, ROGER 1996 *Still the Promised City? African-Americans and New Immigrants in Postindustrial New York*, Cambridge, MA: Harvard University Press.

WATERS, MARY C. 1994 'Ethnic and racial identities of second-generation black immigrants in New York City', *International Migration Review*, vol. 28, no. 4, pp. 795–820.

WEST, CORNEL 1993 *Race Matters*, New York: Vintage Books.

WILSON, WILLIAM JULIUS 1980 *The Declining Significance of Race: Blacks and Changing American Institutions*, 2nd edn, Chicago, IL: University of Chicago Press.

——— 1987 *The Truly Disadvantaged: The Inner City, the Underclass, and Public Policy*, Chicago, IL: University of Chicago Press.

——— 1996 *When Work Disappears: The World of the New Urban Poor*, New York: Knopf.

ZHOU, MIN 1992 *Chinatown: The Socioeconomic Potential of an Urban Enclave*, Philadelphia, PA: Temple University Press.

ZWEIGENHAFT, RICHARD L. and DOMHOFF, G. WILLIAM 1991 *Blacks in the White Establishment? A Study of Race and Class in America*, New Haven, CT: Yale University Press.

——— 1998 *Diversity in the Power Elite: Have Women and Minorities Reached the Top?*, New Haven, CT: Yale University Press.

CHAPTER 6

Race as Biology Is Fiction, Racism as a Social Problem Is Real*

Anthropological and Historical Perspectives on the Social Construction of Race

Audrey Smedley and Brian D. Smedley

Racialized science, also known as scientific racism, seeks to explain human population differences in health, intelligence, education, and wealth as the consequence of immutable, biologically based differences between racial groups. Recent advances in the sequencing of the human genome and in an understanding of biological correlates of behavior have fueled racialized science, despite evidence that racial groups are not genetically discrete, reliably measured, or scientifically meaningful. Yet even these counterarguments often fail to take into account the origin and history of the idea of race. Audrey Smedley and Brian Smedley review the origins of the concept of race, placing the contemporary discussion of racial differences in an anthropological and historical context.

Source: Adapted from Audrey Smedley and Brian D. Smedley, "Race as Biology Is Fiction, Racism as a Social Problem Is Real," *American Psychologist*, Volume 60, Number 1, pages 16–26, American Psychological Association, 2005.

*Endnotes have been omitted. Please consult the original source.

Questions to Consider

The idea that the concept of race captures real biological differences between racial groups continues to persist in American mainstream thought despite a wealth of evidence to the contrary. How does a social science understanding of race help explain this false, yet enduring, notion of race? How can public policy help overcome the idea that race is biological or alleviate racial disparities?

Psychological science has a long and controversial history of involvement in efforts to measure and explain human variation and population differences. Psychologists such as Jensen (1974), Herrnstein (Herrnstein & Murray, 1996), and more recently, Rushton (1995) and Rowe (Rowe, 2002; Rowe & Cleveland, 1996) have advanced the argument that racial group variation on measures such as intelligence tests reflects genetically determined differences in group ability that cannot be explained by differences in environmental living conditions or socioeconomic differences. These psychologists have generally concluded that Africans and African descendants are intellectually inferior to Europeans and European descendants, who in turn are assigned (in more recent work) to a lower intellectual status than Asian populations and their descendants (Rushton, 1995). Although these arguments have been vigorously debated and the influence of "racial" science has been stronger at some times than at others, some scholars interested in racial distinctions have found new grist for the racial differences mill, as geneticists have made important advances in sequencing the human genome (Crow, 2002).

Less prominent in this debate has been a discussion of what is meant by racial groups and whether such groups are, in fact, discrete, measurable, and scientifically meaningful. The consensus among most scholars in fields such as evolutionary biology, anthropology, and other disciplines is that racial distinctions fail on all three counts—that is, they are not genetically discrete, are not reliably measured, and are not scientifically meaningful. Yet even these counterarguments often fail to take into account the origin and history of the idea of "race." This history is significant because it demonstrates that race is a fairly recent construct, one that emerged well after population groups from different continents came into contact with one another. In this article we examine the origins of the concept of race, placing the contemporary discussion of racial differences in an anthropological and historical context. Our aim is not to review the psychological literature regarding the construction of race but to bring anthropological and historical perspectives to the study of race.

In many multiracial nations such as the United States, there are profound and stubbornly persistent racial and ethnic differences in socioeconomic status, educational and occupational status, wealth, political power, and the like. Whether and how governments respond to these disparities should rest on the best available interdisciplinary scientific information. Racialized science—with its conclusion that immutable differences between racial groups underlie social and economic racial hegemony—requires a very different response from government than scientific perspectives that place race in a social and historical context. We therefore conclude this article with a discussion of the public policy implications of racialized science.

Anthropological and Historical Perspectives on Ethnicity, Culture, and Race

Ethnicity and Culture

What is common to most anthropological conceptions of culture is the contention that culture is external, acquired, and transmissible to others. They do not treat culture as a part of the innate biological equipment of humans (Harris, 1999). It is studied as extrasomatic, socially acquired traditions of thought and behavior and includes patterned, repetitive ways of thinking, acting, and feeling, as well as all arenas of creativity and invention (Harris, 1999). Humans, as individuals or groups, are not born with propensities for any particular culture, culture traits, or language, only with the *capacity* to acquire and to create culture (Harris, 1999; Marks, 1995). It is largely the human capacity for language that enables individuals to transmit culture traits from one person or group to another (see, e.g., Boas, 1940; Harris, 1999; Lewontin, 1995). But as both psychologists and anthropologist understand, language is not the only way by which an individual acquires or achieves cultural information.

Thus, for heuristic purposes, anthropologists do not operate with the assumption of innate biological causes for any social (or economic, religious, political, etc.) behavior. They argue that culture traits—that is, human behavior—can best be understood in terms of other culture phenomena, not as products of some variable biogenetic reality as yet unproved. The evidence from history and the study of thousands of diverse cultures around the world are testament to the overwhelming and coercive power of culture to mold who we are and what we believe (Harris, 1999; Kaplan & Manners, 1972; Rapport & Overing, 2000).

Ethnicity and culture are related phenomena and bear no intrinsic connection to human biological variations or race. Ethnicity refers to clusters of people who have common culture traits that they distinguish from those of other people. People who share a common language, geographic locale or place of origin, religion, sense of history, traditions, values, beliefs, food habits, and so forth, are perceived, and view themselves as constituting, an ethnic group (see, e.g., Jones, 1997; Parrillo, 1997; A. Smedley, 1999b; Steinberg, 1989; Takaki, 1993). But ethnic groups and ethnicity are not fixed, bounded entities; they are open, flexible, and subject to change, and they are usually self-defined (Barth, 1998). Because culture traits are learned, ethnicity or ethnic traits are transmissible to other people—sometimes easily so, such as the widespread adoption of western dress (jeans and tee shirts) found all over the world, and the contemporary manifestation of industrial culture globally. History shows that people can and do learn another language and/or move into another ethnic group and become participants in that ethnicity (A. Smedley, 1999a; Takaki, 1993).

Ethnic differences also constitute an arena of diverse interests that can lead to conflict, but this should not be confused with what in contemporary times is referred to as "racial" conflict. Ethnocentrism (belief in the superiority of one's own culture and lifestyle) and ethnic conflict are widespread and often have deep historical roots, but this is not to say that they are universal or inevitable. Ethnocentric beliefs and attitudes, because they are cultural phenomena, can and do change, sometimes rapidly (Omi & Winant, 1994; A. Smedley, 1999a). Some of the ethnocentrism seen today is mild, such as the enmity between the French and the English, or Canadians and the United States, or even sports teams from different nations.

However, the kind of ethnocentrism that most attracts attention, and which scholars have long studied, has often been vehement and malignant, leading to enduring conflicts. In circumstances of extreme conflict, such as warfare, ethnic groups have demonized one another, creating hate-filled images of "the Other," even to the point of posing the argument that the other ethnic group is less than human (Fredrickson, 2002; Jones, 1997; Omi & Winant, 1994; A. Smedley 1999a, 1999b).

The most significant thing about interethnic conflict is that the vast majority of such conflicts has been, and still are, with neighboring groups—people who inhabit the same general environment and who virtually always share physical similarities, as, for example, the English and the Irish, Serbians and Croatians, Indians and Pakistanis, Armenians and Turks, Japanese and Koreans. Until recently such conflict has not been perceived as being racial. Numerous wars, historical and contemporary, around the globe, including both world wars, attest to the reality of ethnic conflict as primarily a local phenomenon (Barth, 1998; A. Smedley, 1999b). Thus, most human conflicts have not been racial, and there is no reason for antagonism to exist or persist simply because protagonists are identified as racially different.

Historical Perspectives on Human Variation

With the rise of empires, language and other cultural features were expanded territorially to encompass populations in more remote geographical areas. With the addition of distance, conquering armies encountered peoples who were physically as well as culturally different. Ancient empires tended to incorporate these peoples into their polities, regardless of their physical variations. The empires of the ancient world—the Egyptian, Greek, and Roman empires, and later the Muslim empire, with its center at Baghdad—encompassed peoples whose skin colors, hair textures, and facial features were highly varied, representing the same range of physical diversity that is seen in the "Old World" today—Africans, Europeans, Middle Easterners, and Asians (see Blakely, 1993; Boardman, Griffin, & Murray, 1986; Cavalli-Sforza, 1995; Fryer, 1984; Godolphin, 1942; Hitti, 1953; Hourani, 1991; Snowden, 1983). History shows that Africans in Europe were assimilated into those societies wherever they were found, and no significant social meanings were attached to their physical differences. Throughout the Middle Ages and up until the 17th century, religion and language were the most important criteria of identity (Hannaford, 1996).

It follows from this brief account of historical facts that physical characteristics should never be included in a *definition* of ethnic identity. It is inaccurate to associate physical features with any specific cultural identity. This is particularly true in modern times, when individuals may have physical traits associated with one region of the world but may manifest very different cultures or ethnic identities. Immigration, intermating, intermarriage, and reproduction have led to increasing physical heterogeneity of peoples in many areas of the world. Africans and East Indians in England learn the English of the British Broadcasting Company and participate fully in English culture. Five hundred years ago, Africans, natives of South and Central America, and Spanish or Portuguese people in the New World began to merge or assimilate (both biologically and culturally) and create new ethnic identities. Their descendants today, whether they are called Latinos or Hispanics, represent intricate and complex new mixtures of biogenetic or physical features, but they also have many cultural similarities in language and religion (Degler, 1971; Morner, 1967). As we discuss later, the concept of race that characterizes North American society carries with it the notion that each race has its own forms of social or cultural behavior. This is not borne out by anthropological and historical studies but is part of the myths connected to the ideology of race.

Many historians and sociologists have recognized that race and racism are not "mere ethnocentric dislike and distrust of the Other" (Fredrickson, 2002, p. 5). Steinberg (1989) made a clear distinction between racism and ethnocentrism. In speaking of the differences in America between European immigrant minorities early in the 20th century and racial groups, he pointed out that immigrants were "disparaged for their cultural peculiarities," and they were discriminated against, but the message conveyed by the nation to them was, "You will become like us whether you want to or not." Assimilation was necessary and expected. With the low-status racial groups, the message was, "No matter how much like us you are, you will remain apart" (Steinberg, 1989, p. 42). Ethnicity was recognized as plastic and transmissible, but race conveyed the notion of differences that could not be transcended.

Scientific Conceptions of Race

From the 19th century on, races have been seen in science as subdivisions of the human species that differ from one another phenotypically, on the basis of ancestral geographic origins, or that differ in the frequency of certain genes (Lewontin, 1995; Marks, 1995; A. Smedley, 1999b). The genetic conception of race appeared in the mid-20th century and remains today as a definition or working hypothesis for many scholars (A. Smedley, 1999b; Spencer, 1982). However, other scholars have recognized that there are no neutral conceptualizations of race in science, nor have any of the definitions ever satisfactorily fully explained the phenomenon of race (Brace, 1969; A. Smedley, 1999a, 1999b). When geneticists appeared who emphasized the similarities among races (humans are 99.9% alike), the small amount of real genetic differences among them (0.01%), and the difficulties of recognizing the racial identity of individuals through their genes, doubts about the biological reality of race appeared (see Littlefield, Lieberman, & Reynolds, 1982).

Thus, in the 20th century two conceptions of race existed: one that focused on human biogenetic variation exclusively and was the province of science, and a popular one that dominated all thinking about human differences and fused together both physical features and behavior. This popular conception, essentially a cultural invention, was and still is the original meaning of *race* that scholars in many fields turned their attention to in the latter part of the 20th century and the early 21st century (A. Smedley, 1999a, 1999b, 2002a, 2002b). It is important to explore its origins, examine how it has evolved, and analyze its meaning and significance in those cultures where race became important.

A History of Race and the Ideology of Race

Historians have now shown that between the 16th and the 18th centuries, *race* was a folk idea in the English language; it was a general categorizing term, similar to and interchangeable with such terms as *type, kind, sort, breed,* and even *species* (Allen, 1994, 1997; Hannaford, 1996; A. Smedley, 1999a, 1999b). Toward the end of the 17th century, *race* gradually emerged as a term referring to those populations then interacting in North America—Europeans, Africans, and Native Americans (Indians).

In the early 18th century, usage of the term increased in the written record, and it began to become standardized and uniform (Poliakov, 1982). By the Revolutionary era, *race* was widely used, and its meaning had solidified as a reference for *social* categories of Indians, Blacks, and Whites (Allen, 1994, 1997; A. Smedley, 1999b). More than that, *race* signified a new ideology about human differences and a new way of structuring society that had not existed before in human history. The fabrication of a new type of categorization for humanity was needed because the leaders of the American colonies at the turn of the 18th century had deliberately selected Africans to be permanent slaves (Allen, 1994, 1997; Fredrickson, 1988, 2002; Morgan, 1975; A. Smedley, 1999b). In an era when the dominant political philosophy was equality, civil rights, democracy, justice, and freedom for all human beings, the only way Christians could justify slavery was to demote Africans to nonhuman status (Haller, 1971; A. Smedley, 1999b). The humanity of the Africans was debated throughout the 19th century, with many holding the view that Africans were created separately from other, more human, beings.

The Components of Racial Ideology in United States Society

Eighteenth and 19th-century beliefs about human races have endured into the 20th and 21st centuries. Those societies in which racial categories are critical to the social structure have certain ideological features—that is, beliefs about human differences—in common. Race therefore can be seen as an ideology or worldview, and its components have often been spelled out explicitly in social policy. The ideological ingredients can be analytically derived from ethnographic reality (i.e., from descriptions of racist behavior, and especially from the hundreds of historical publications that document the existence of race and racism in North America). This material has been analyzed and these ingredients identified as diagnostic social characteristics of race in North America (see A. Smedley, 1999b, chap. 1). There is widespread agreement in historical and sociological studies about the following characteristics:

1. Race-based societies perceive designated racial groups as biologically discrete and exclusive groups, and certain physical characteristics (e.g., skin color, hair texture, eye shape, and other facial features) become markers of race status.
2. They hold that races are naturally unequal and therefore must be ranked hierarchically (inequality is fundamental to all racial systems). In the United States and South Africa, Africans and their descendants occupy the lowest level of the hierarchy.
3. They assume that each race has distinctive cultural behaviors linked to their biology. The idea of inherited forms of behavior is fundamental to the concept of race and is one basis for the belief in the separation of races (as, e.g., Black music, Black language, etc.).
4. They assume that both physical features and behavior are innate and inherited.
5. They assume that the differences among races are therefore profound and unalterable. This justifies segregation of the races in schools, neighborhoods, churches, recreational

centers, health centers, and so forth, and proscriptions against intermarriage or intermating.

6. They have racial classifications stipulated in the legal and social system (racial identity by law). (This obtained until recently in the United States and South Africa.)

Skin color, hair texture, nose width, and lip thickness have remained major markers of racial identity in the United States (A. Smedley, 2002a), although the use of these criteria continues to be arbitrary, given the ranges of physical variations in U.S. racial populations. However, physical features and differences connoted by them are not the effective or direct causes of racism and discrimination (see, e.g., Barnes, 2000; Correspondents of the New York Times, 2001; Mathis, 2002). It is the culturally invented ideas and beliefs about these differences that constitute the meaning of race (A. Smedley, 1999b).

The History of Race Ideology

In the United States, race ideology began developing during the late 17th century, in conjunction with the legal establishment of slavery for Africans, and in the 18th century it eventuated in three major groups that were roughly defined and ranked (European Whites, Native Americans [Indians], and "Negroes" from Africa; Allen, 1994; A. Smedley, 1999b). In the mid-19th century, Asian people—first the Chinese and later the Japanese—began to arrive in the United States, and they were fitted into the racial ranking system, somewhere between Whites and Blacks (A. Smedley, 1999b; Takaki, 1993). Also in the mid-19th century, the Irish began to immigrate, followed toward the end of the century by peoples from southern and eastern Europe who were both physically and culturally different from the original English and northern Europeans (Ignatiev, 1995; Takaki, 1993). They, too, were initially seen as separate races and were ranked lower than other Europeans (Chase, 1980; Steinberg, 1989; Takaki, 1993). However, they were eventually assimilated into the "White" category. The single most important criterion of status was, and remains, the racial distinction between Black and White (Massey, 2001; A. Smedley, 1999b).

Despite legal and social attempts to prohibit intermarriage or intermating, some genetic mixture still occurred. In response, the United States had to resort to a fiction to help preserve the distinctiveness of the White/Black racial (and social) dichotomy. North Americans define as Black anyone who has known African ancestors, a phenomenon known and introduced by historians over half a century ago as the "one drop rule" (see, e.g., Degler, 1971). There is no socially sanctioned in-between classification, even though the last census of 2000 permitted individuals to identify two or more racial ancestries. In South Africa in the 1940s, for historical reasons a large middle category was created, the Colored, so that essentially three more or less exclusive races were established in law (Fredrickson, 1981). And each year, a government board functioned to review racial identities and reassign individuals according to certain subjective appraisals. In none of the states in the United States has there developed a legal mechanism for changing one's race (Fredrickson, 1981).

There is mounting historical evidence that this modern ideology of race took on a life of its own in the latter half of the 19th century (Hannaford, 1996; A. Smedley, 1999b). As a paradigm for portraying the social reality of permanent inequality as something that was natural, this ideology, often but not necessarily connected to human biophysical differences, has been perceived as useful by many other societies. It has led to the exacerbation of already existing interethnic animosities. In Europe, Nazi Germany took the ideology to its greatest extreme, ultimately resulting in the Holocaust of World War II. In Asia, elements of the Western ideology of race were imported to Japan, China, India, and Malaysia (Channa, 2002, 2003; Dikotter, 1997; Katayama, 2002; Kurokawa, 2003; Robb, 1997; Sakamoto, 2002; Tomiyama, 2002).

The Beginnings of Scientific Classifications of Human Groups

While colonists were creating the folk idea of race, naturalists in Europe were engaged in efforts to establish classifications of human groups in the 18th century. They had to rely on colonists' descriptions of indigenous peoples for the most part, and their categories were replete with subjective comments about their appearances and behaviors. Ethnic chauvinism and a well-developed notion of the "savage" or "primitives" dictated that they classify native peoples as inferior forms of humans. Although there were earlier attempts to categorize all human groups then known, Linnaeus and Blumenbach introduced classifications of the varieties of humankind that later became the established names for the races of the world (Slotkin, 1965).

But it was the influence of Thomas Jefferson that may have had greater impact in bringing science to the support of race ideology. Jefferson was the first American to speculate and write publicly about the character of the "Negro," whom he knew only in the role of slaves on his plantations. He was the first to suggest the natural inferiority of the Negro as a new rationalization for slavery in the only book he wrote, *Notes on the State of Virginia* (Jefferson, 1785/1955), published first in Paris and later in the United States. More than that, he revealed his uncertainty about the position he was taking and called on science to ultimately prove the truth of this speculation (see Jefferson, 1785/1955; for a discussion, see also A. Smedley, 1999b). Since the 1790s and well into the 20th century, the role of science has been to confirm and authenticate the folk beliefs about human differences expressed in the idea of race by examining the bodies of the different peoples in each racial category.

The rise of scientific and scholarly input into the character of races began during the latter part of the 18th century with the writings of the philosopher Voltaire, the planter and jurist Edward Long, and a physician, Dr. Charles White of Manchester, England, among others (A. Smedley, 1999b). In the 19th century, some scholarly men initiated attempts to quantify the differences among races by measuring heads, and later other parts of the human body, with the stated purpose of documenting race inequality (A. Smedley, 1999b; Haller, 1971; Marks, 1995). By the end of the 19th century, more refinements in measuring heads and greater attention to the size and contents of the brain case led scientists to the final critical criterion by which they thought race differences could be measured: the development of tests to measure the functions of the brain. In the early 20th century, intelligence tests became the dominant interest of scientists who were seeking ways of documenting significant differences, especially between Blacks and Whites. As Haller (1971) has pointed out, no one doubted that the races were unequal or that each race had distinctive behaviors that were unique: "The subject of race inferiority was beyond critical reach in the late 19th century" (p. 132).

Recent developments in the fields of genetics and evolutionary biology have prompted a renewed focus on identifying the biological basis of human behavior as well as ascertaining the historical relationships among different populations (Graves, 2004; Olson, 2002). With studies of the human genome and discoveries of the role of DNA in disease, it has become possible to speculate on specific genes as sources of human behavior. Population variations in the genes linked to the making of serotonin, testosterone, and dopamine have already led some race scientists to speculate about race differences in behavior (Oubre, 2004; Rushton, 1995). Some anticipate that they will eventually be able to actually prove race differences in violence, temperament, sexuality, intelligence, and many other mental characteristics. More important, developments in the structuring of an International HapMap, which maps clusters of genes, have revealed variations in strings of DNA that correlate with geographic differences in phenotypes among humans around the world (Olson, 2002). Such findings may well be used by race scientists to argue that geographic variations in DNA confirm the existence of biological human races.

From its inception, race was a folk idea, a culturally invented conception about human differences. It became an important mechanism for limiting and restricting access to privilege, power, and wealth. The ideology arose as a rationalization and justification for human slavery at a time when Western European societies were embracing philosophies promoting individual and human rights, liberty, democracy, justice, brotherhood, and equality. The idea of race distorts, exaggerates, and maximizes human differences; it is the most extreme form of difference that humans can assert about another human being or group, as one of its components is the belief that differences are permanent and cannot be overcome.

Race essentializes and stereotypes people, their social statuses, their social behaviors, and their social ranking. In the United States and South Africa, one cannot escape the process of racialization; it is a basic element of the social system and customs of the United States and is deeply embedded in the consciousness of its people. Physical traits have been transformed into markers or signifiers of social race identity. But the flexibility of racial ideology is such that distinctive physical traits need no longer be present for humans to racialize others (Katayama, 2002; Saitou, 2002).

Racialized Science and Public Policy

Given that racialized science is based on an imprecise and distorted understanding of human differences, should the term *race* be abandoned as a matter of social policy? Stated differently, if race is not a biological or anthropological reality, should race play a role in policy discussions? From a policy perspective, although the term *race* is not useful as a biological construct, policymakers cannot avoid the fact that social race remains a significant predictor of which groups have greater access to societal goods and resources and which groups face barriers—both historically and in the contemporary context—to full inclusion. The fact of inequality renders race an important social policy concern. At its core, the concept of race depends fundamentally on the existence of social hegemony. As Michael Omi noted, "the idea of race and its persistence as a social category is only given meaning in a social order structured by forms of inequality—economic, political, and cultural—that are organized, to a significant degree, by race" (Omi, 2001, p. 254).

How are resources allocated differentially on the basis of race? The sources of racial inequality remain controversial. Discrimination, the differential and negative treatment of individuals on the basis of their race, ethnicity, gender, or other group membership, has been the source of significant policy debate over the past several decades. Federal and state laws adapted since the landmark 1964 Civil Rights Act outlaw most forms of discrimination in public accommodations, access to resources and services, and other areas. Although this legislation appears to have spurred significant change in some segments of American society, such as in the overt behavior of lenders and real estate agents, debate continues regarding whether and how discrimination persists today. Conservative legal scholars and social scientists argue that discrimination has largely been eliminated from the American landscape (D'Souza, 1996; Thernstrom & Thernstrom, 1999), whereas others argue that discrimination has simply taken on subtler forms that make it difficult to define and identify. Complicating this assessment is the fact that whereas individual discrimination is often easier to identify, *institutional discrimination*—the uneven access by group membership to resources, status, and power that stems from facially neutral policies and practices of organizations and institutions—is harder to identify. Further, it is difficult to distinguish the extent to which many racial and ethnic disparities are the result of discrimination or other social and economic forces.

There is little doubt among researchers who study discrimination, however, that the history of racial discrimination in the United States has left a lasting residue, even in a society that overtly abhors discrimination. "Deliberate discrimination by many institutions in American society in the past has left a legacy of [social and] economic inequality between Whites and minorities that exists today" (Turner & Skidmore, 1999, p. 5), preserving the economic and educational gap between population groups. But discrimination persists today. Racial and ethnic discrimination and disadvantage have been consistently documented in studies of home mortgage lending (U.S. Department of Housing and Urban Development, 1999), housing discrimination and residential segregation (Massey, 2001), employment and housing practices (Fix, Galster, & Struyk, 1993), [and racial and ethnic disparities in health care] (B. D. Smedley, Stith, & Nelson, 2003; Physicians for Human Rights, 2003).

Public Policy Cannot Ignore Race

Contrary to the optimistic assessments of conservative thinkers (D'Souza, 1996; Thernstrom & Thernstrom, 1999) and, more generally, the American public, race continues to play an important role in determining how individuals are treated, where they live, their employment opportunities, the quality of their health care, and whether individuals can fully participate in the social, political, and economic mainstream of American life. The studies cited previously demonstrate that race continues to matter in important ways. Race is a means of creating and enforcing social order, a lens through which differential opportunity and inequality are structured. Racialized science, with its emphasis on identifying immutable differences between racial groups, can be expected only to maintain and reinforce existing racial inequality, in that its adherents indirectly argue that no degree of government intervention or social change will alter the skills and abilities of different racial groups. The disproportionate representation of some "racial" groups (e.g., African Americans, American Indians) among lower socioeconomic tiers can therefore be explained as an unavoidable byproduct of human evolution. Yet reinforcing this widely held social stereotype of racial inferiority risks limiting individual human potential, in that individuals' abilities and opportunities would likely be assessed in relation to their racial group.

California businessman Ward Connerly and his allies have proposed that government should not be involved in the collection or analysis of information related to the race or ethnicity of its citizens. They argued (unsuccessfully in California's recent voter referendum, Proposition 54) that data disaggregated by race or ethnicity merely serves to create more social divisions and schisms and that the racial and ethnic disparities observed are generally the product of socioeconomic differences between the racial and ethnic groups. Implicit in this argument is that socioeconomic differences are acceptable—that is, race is increasingly irrelevant in determining one's life opportunities and barriers, but the poor will always be among us. An abundance of evidence, however, demonstrates that race continues to matter in meaningful ways. As long as governments fail to assess racial and ethnic inequality, racialized science will likely attempt to find explanations for racial hegemony in the biology and genetics of the "racial" group rather than in the social attitudes and institutions that perpetuate the idea of race.

References

Allen, T. W. (1994). *The invention of the White race* (Vol. 1). London and New York: Verso.

Allen, T. W. (1997). *The invention of the White race* (Vol. 2). London and New York: Verso.

Barnes, A. S. (2000). *Everyday racism: A book for all Americans.* Naperville, IL: Sourcebooks.

Barth, F. (1998). *Ethnic groups and boundaries: The social organization of culture difference.* Boston: Little, Brown.

Blakely, A. (1993). *Blacks in the Dutch world.* Bloomington: Indiana University Press.

Boardman, J., Griffin, J., & Murray, O. (Eds.). (1986). *The Oxford history of the classical world.* Oxford, England: Oxford University Press.

Boas, F. (1940). *Race, language, and culture.* New York: Free Press.

Brace, C. L. (1969). A nonracial approach towards the understanding of human diversity. In A. Montagu (Ed.), *The concept of race* (pp. 103–152). New York: Collier.

Brace, C. L. (1982). The roots of the race concept in physical anthropology. In F. Spencer (Ed.), *A history of American physical anthropology, 1930–1980* (pp. 11–29). New York: Academic Press.

Brace, C. L. (2003). Social construct vs. biological reality. In Y. Takezawa (Ed.), *Is race a universal idea? Colonialism, nation-states, and a myth invented.* Kyoto, Japan: Kyoto University, Institute for Research in Humanities.

Cavalli-Sforza, L. L. (1995). *The great human diasporas: The history of diversity and evolution.* Reading, MA: Perseus Books.

Channa, S. M. (2002, September). The crafting of human bodies and the racialization of caste in India. In A. Smedley & Y. Takezawa (Chairs), *Racializing the human body: A cross-cultural perspective.* Symposium conducted at the meeting of the Inter-Congress of the International Union of Anthropological and Ethnological Sciences, Tokyo, Japan.

Channa, S. M. (2003). Colonialism, caste, and the myth of race: A historical perspective on the interaction of Indian beliefs and Western science. In Y. Takezawa (Ed.), *Is race a universal idea? Colonialism, nation-states, and a myth invented.* Kyoto, Japan: Kyoto University, Institute for Research in Humanities.

Chase, A. (1980). *The legacy of Malthus.* Urbana: University of Illinois Press.

Correspondents of the New York Times. (2001). *How race is lived in America: Pulling together, pulling apart.* New York: Times Books.

Crow, J. F. (2002). Unequal by nature: A geneticist's perspective on human differences. *Daedalus, 131*(1), 81–88.

Degler, C. N. (1971). *Neither Black nor White.* New York: Macmillan.

Dikotter, F. (Ed.). (1997). *The construction of racial identities in China and Japan: Historical and contemporary perspectives.* Honolulu: University of Hawai'i Press.

D'Souza, D. (1996). *The end of racism: Principles for a multiracial society.* New York: Free Press.

Fish, J. M. (Ed.). (2002). *Race and intelligence: Separating science from myth.* London and Mahwah, NJ: Erlbaum.

Fix, M., Galster, G., & Struyk, R. (1993). An overview of auditing for discrimination. In M. Fix & R. Struyk (Eds.), *Clear and convincing evidence: Measurement of discrimination in America* (pp. 1–68). Washington, DC: Urban Institute Press.

Fredrickson, G. M. (1981). *White supremacy: A comparative study in American and South African history.* New York & Oxford, England: Oxford University Press.

Fredrickson, G. M. (1987). *The Black image in the White mind.* Middletown, CT: Wesleyan University Press.

Fredrickson, G. M. (1988). *The arrogance of race.* Middletown, CT: Wesleyan University Press.

Fredrickson, G. M. (2002). *Racism: A short history.* Princeton, NJ: Princeton University Press.

Fryer, P. (1984). *Staying power: The history of Black people in Britain.* London: Pluto Press.

Godolphin, F. R. B. (Ed.). (1942). *The Greek historians* (Vols. 1–2). New York: Random House.

Graves, J. L., Jr. (2004). *The race myth: Why we pretend race exists in America.* New York: Dutton.

Haller, J. S., Jr. (1971). *Outcasts from evolution: Scientific attitudes of racial inferiority, 1859–1900.* Urbana: University of Illinois Press.

Hannaford, I. (1996). *Race: The history of an idea in the West.* Baltimore: Johns Hopkins University Press and the Woodrow Wilson Center.

Harris, M. (1999). *Theories of culture in postmodern times.* Walnut Creek, CA: AltaMira Press.

Hitti, P. K. (1953). *History of the Arabs.* London: Macmillan.

Hourani, A. (1991). *A history of the Arab peoples.* Cambridge, MA: Harvard University Press.

Ignatiev, N. (1995). *How the Irish became White.* New York and London: Routledge.

Jefferson, T. (1955). *Notes on the state of Virginia.* Chapel Hill: University of North Carolina Press. (Original work published 1785)

Jensen, A. R. (1974). Ethnicity and scholastic achievement. *Psychological Reports, 34,* 659–668.

Jones, J. M. (1997). *Prejudice and racism.* New York: McGraw-Hill.

Kaplan, D., & Manners, R. A. (1972). *Culture theory.* Englewood Cliffs, NJ: Prentice Hall.

Katayama, K. (2002, September). What is the "race" concept for Japanese biological anthropologists? In A. Smedley & Y. Takezawa (Chairs), *Racializing the human body: A cross-cultural perspective.* Symposium conducted at the meeting of the Inter-Congress of the International Union of Anthropological and Ethnological Sciences, Tokyo, Japan.

Kurokawa, M. (2003). Racism and Buraku discrimination. In Y. Takezawa (Ed.), *Is race a universal idea? Colonialism, nation-states, and a myth invented.* Kyoto, Japan: Kyoto University, Institute for Research in Humanities.

Lewontin, R. (1995). *Human diversity.* New York: Scientific American Library.

Littlefield, A., Lieberman, L., & Reynolds, L. (1982). Redefining race: The potential demise of a concept in physical anthropology. *Current Anthropology, 23,* 641–656.

Marks, J. (1995). *Human biodiversity: Genes, race, and history.* New York: Aldine de Gruyter.

Massey, D. G. (2001). Residential segregation and neighborhood conditions in U.S. metropolitan areas. In N. J. Smelser, W. J. Wilson, & F. Mitchell (Eds.), *America becoming: Racial trends and their consequences* (Vol. 1, pp. 391–434). Washington, DC: National Academies Press.

Mathis, D. (2002). *Yet a stranger: Why Black Americans still don't feel at home.* New York: AOL Time Warner Books.

Morgan, E. S. (1975). *American slavery, American freedom.* New York: Norton.

Morner, M. (1967). *Race mixture in the history of Latin America.* Boston: Little, Brown.

Olson, S. (2002). *Mapping human history: Discovering the past through our genes.* Boston & New York: Houghton Mifflin.

Omi, M. A. (2001). The changing meaning of race. In N. J. Smelser, W. J. Wilson, & F. Mitchell (Eds.), *America becoming: Racial trends and their consequences* (Vol. 1, pp. 243–263). Washington, DC: National Academies Press.

Omi, M. A., & Winant, H. (1994). *Racial formation in the United States* (2nd ed.). New York: Routledge.

Oubre, A. (2004). *Race, genes, and ability: Rethinking ethnic differences.* Unpublished manuscript.

Parrillo, V. N. (1997). *Strangers to these shores* (5th ed.). Boston: Allyn & Bacon.

Peoples, J., & Garrick, B. (2000). *Humanity: An introduction to cultural anthropology* (5th ed.). Belmont, CA: Wadsworth/Thomson Learning.

Physicians for Human Rights. (2003). *The right to equal treatment.* Boston: Author.

Poliakov, L. (1982). Racism from the enlightenment to the age of imperialism. In R. Ross (Ed.), *Racism and colonialism: Essays on ideology and social structure* (pp. 55–64). The Hague, the Netherlands: Martinus Nijhoff.

Rapport, N., & Overing, J. (2000). *Social and cultural anthropology: The key concepts.* London: Routledge.

Robb, P. (Ed.). (1997). *The concept of race in South Asia.* New Delhi, India: Oxford University Press.

Rowe, D. C. (2002). IQ, birth weight, and number of sexual partners in White, African American, and mixed-race adolescents. *Population and Environment, 23,* 513–534.

Rowe, D. C., & Cleveland, H. H. (1996). Academic achievement in Blacks and Whites: Are the developmental processes similar? *Intelligence, 23,* 205–228.

Rushton, P. (1995). *Race, evolution, and behavior: A life history perspective.* New Brunswick, NJ: Transaction Publishers.

Saitou, N. (2002, September). *Farewell to race.* Paper presented at the meeting of the Inter-Congress of the International Union of Anthropological and Ethnological Sciences, Tokyo, Japan.

Sakamoto, H. (2002, September). *Historical view of Chinese concept of race.* Paper presented at the meeting of the Inter-Congress of the International Union of Anthropological and Ethnological Science, Tokyo, Japan.

Slotkin, J. S. (Ed.). (1965). *Readings in early anthropology.* London: Methuen.

Smedley, A. (1999a). Race and the construction of human identity. *American Anthropologist, 100,* 690–702.

Smedley, A. (1999b). *Race in North America: Origin and evolution of a worldview* (2nd ed.). Boulder, CO: Westview Press.

Smedley, A. (2002a, September). *Racializing the human body: Example of the United States.* Paper presented at the meeting of the Inter-Congress of the International Union of Anthropological and Ethnological Sciences, Tokyo, Japan.

Smedley, A. (2002b). Science and the idea of race: A brief history. In J. Fish (Ed.), *Race and intelligence: Separating science from myth* (pp. 145–176). Mahwah, NJ: Erlbaum.

Smedley, B. D., Stith, A. Y., & Nelson, A. R. (Eds.). (2003). *Unequal treatment: Confronting racial and ethnic disparities in health care* (Committee on Understanding and Eliminating Racial and Ethnic Disparities in Health Care, Institute of Medicine). Washington, DC: National Academies Press.

Snowden, F. (1983). *Before color prejudice* (Rev. ed.). Cambridge, MA: Harvard University Press.

Spencer, F. (1982). *A history of American physical anthropology.* New York: Academic Press.

Steinberg, S. (1989). *The ethnic myth: Race, ethnicity, and class in America.* Boston: Beacon Press.

Takaki, R. (1993). *A different mirror: A history of multicultural America.* Boston: Little, Brown.

Thernstrom, S., & Thernstrom, A. (1999). *America in Black and White: One nation indivisible.* New York: Simon & Schuster.

Tomiyama, I. (2002, September). The diffusion of the idea of race and its application in Japan. In Y. Takezawa (Ed.), *Is race a universal idea? Colonialism, nation-states, and a myth invented.* Kyoto, Japan: Kyoto University, Institute for Research in Humanities.

Turner, M. A., & Skidmore, F. (1999, September). *Mortgage lending discrimination: A review of existing evidence.* Retrieved October 14, 2003, from Urban Institute Web site: www.urban.org/housing/mortgage_lending.html

U.S. Department of Housing and Urban Development. (1999). *What we know about mortgage lending discrimination in America.* Retrieved May 21, 2003, from www.hud.gov/library/bookshelf18/pressrel/newsconf/menu.html

CHAPTER 7

Back to the Future?*

The Emergence of a Geneticized Conceptualization of Race in Sociology

Reanne Frank

Discoveries in human molecular genetics have reanimated unresolved debates over the nature of human difference. In this context, the idea that race has a discrete and measurable genetic basis is currently enjoying a resurgence. The return of a biologized construction of race is somewhat surprising because one of the primary pronouncements to come out of the Human Genome Project was one of human genetic similarity (i.e., humans are over 99.9% similar at the molecular level). Perhaps even more surprising is that genetically based notions of race have not been restricted to the biomedical sciences but have recently emerged within the social sciences, specifically sociology, to explicitly challenge a socially constructed understanding of race. Drawing on existing critiques, Reanne Frank describes problems in recent sociological scholarship and the potential role of social scientists in future work occurring at the intersection of race and genetics. She argues that recent scholarly work meant to challenge the notion of ***race as a social construction*** *actually makes a powerful case for its continued utility.*

Source: Adapted from Reanne Frank, "Back to the Future? The Emergence of a Geneticized Conceptualization of Race in Sociology," *The ANNALS of the American Academy of Political and Social Science*, 661, pages 51–64. SAGE Publications, Inc., September 2015.

*Endnotes have been omitted. Please consult the original source.

Questions to Consider

Why does the idea that race is rooted in biology or genetics continue to persist? Is it possible to imagine a future American society that thinks differently about race?

The Human Genome Project and Race

Initially, one of the great promises of the first map of the human genome was that it would finally dispel the notion of biologically discrete racial groups. Once humans were broken down into our smallest building blocks, it was expected that our commonalities would be revealed and the long entrenched belief in essentialized racial differences would be finally laid to rest. As cited by Phelan, Link, and Feldman (2013, 169–70), at the unveiling of a draft of the human genome map in 2000, Bill Clinton announced that "one of the great truths to emerge from this triumphant expedition is that in genetic terms, all human beings, regardless of race, are more than 99.9 percent the same. What that means is that modern science has confirmed the most important fact of life on this Earth is our common humanity." But almost immediately, attention turned to the small amount of variation that was not shared across population groups. Aided by such initiatives as the International HapMap Project and the Human Genome Diversity Project (HGDP) that focused on genetic diversity, headlines emphasizing commonalities turned into ones proclaiming that "Under the Skin, We're All Alike, *Except Medically, Science Says*" (Schmickle 2002, emphasis added).

A racialized understanding of human genetic population structure has not reverberated equally throughout the sciences. It has been most evident in the realms of health and forensic science and reflected in direct-to-consumer companies that estimate individual-level "bio-ancestry" and calculate individual risk profiles for a growing number of diseases and traits. Until recently, the idea that race has a discrete and measurable genetic component has been entirely absent from the contemporary mainstream sociological literature. This is perhaps unsurprising, given that the theory of race as socially constructed, that is, an idea produced by human thought and interaction and without a biological basis, has been most extensively developed within the discipline of sociology. In 2003, the American Sociological Association (ASA) reinforced its commitment to conceiving of race as a purely social construct, warning that "although racial categories are legitimate subjects of empirical sociological investigation, it is important to recognize the danger of contributing to the popular conception of race as biological" (ASA 2003). It is precisely ASA's contention that "race as biology" is dangerous and, by implication, not a legitimate subject of empirical sociological investigation, that recently has been challenged in the pages of the discipline's leading journals (i.e., Shiao et al. 2012; Guo et al. 2014b) and warrants further comment here.

"Biogeographical Ancestry Estimates": The Genetic Component of Race?

As Shiao et al. (2012) argue in their *Sociological Theory* article, recent research on the human genome has shown "the existence of genetic clusters consistent with certain racial classifications" (p. 68), thus challenging "the basic assumption that human races have no biological basis" (p. 67). The research to which they refer encompasses two broad categories. The first involves efforts to distinguish population groups on the basis of individual genotypes, that is, clustering individuals by genotype until a certain number of genetically distinct groups are defined (Rosenberg et al. 2002). This work has received considerable attention in the popular press and is often taken as "proving" the existence of biological racial groups (Leroi 2005). Another area of research involves inferring "biogeographical ancestries" (BGA) of individuals based on a set of predetermined genetic markers, referred to as "ancestry informative markers" (AIMs) (Shriver and Kittles 2004). BGA estimates are produced by comparisons made between an individual's DNA and a set of AIMS that are derived from existing genetic databases of individuals sampled from present-day populations in different geographic regions (i.e., data from the HapMap Project and the HGDP).

It is this latter approach that Guo et al. (2014b) utilize in their *Demography* article, titled "Genetic Bio-Ancestry and Social Construction in Social Surveys in the Contemporary United States." In it, the authors argue that racial self-identity "could be analyzed and examined against a measurable continental and biological ancestry" (p. 169). Using saliva DNA from respondents from two different U.S. surveys, the authors employed a panel of 186 AIMs to estimate each respondent's BGA. After parsing out the "amount" of each ancestry represented in the different race/ethnic groups, the authors conclude that they "replicate the match between genetic bio-ancestry and self-reported race" (p. 142); and as a result, their analysis "establishes geographic genetic bio-ancestry as a component of racial classification" (p. 141). In doing so, they reflect the idea that has been commonly touted by the direct-to-consumer ancestry testing companies, namely that BGA estimates capture the biological or genetic component of race (Gannett 2014).

As noted by Morning (2014a), neither Shiao et al. (2012) nor Guo et al. (2014b) subscribe to a genomic articulation of race in its most extreme form. In the case of Guo et al. (2014b), they argued that BGA estimates capture but one component (the biological one) of racial/ethnic categories. One of their main objectives was to empirically model the social inputs that influence racial categorization, above and beyond what they conceive of as its biological basis (via BGA). In doing so they avoid simplistic claims that race is strictly or even primarily a genetic construct. And yet their insistence that BGA estimates are able to capture the biogenetic component of race relies on the (mis)understanding that among human groups there are objective and genetically distinct clusters that can be impartially measured and that form the basis of our socially constructed racial/ethnic identification categories (Morning 2014a).

Not acknowledged in any depth by either article is the existing set of critiques targeting this technology (Bolnick et al. 2007, 2008; Fullwiley 2008; Morning 2014b; Paradies, Montoya, and Fullerton 2007; Royal et al. 2010). These critiques are no less applicable to social scientists who are using BGA analysis to question the continued relevance of a social construction of race. One of the primary issues of BGA is that, currently, in all existing genome databases there is incomplete representation of human genetic diversity, which creates systematic bias that is difficult to quantify statistically (Braun and Hammonds 2012; Royal et al. 2010). The populations that are used as references rely on the problematic assumption that contemporary groups are accurate substitutes for ancestral populations. Doing so ignores the diffuse and changing nature of the populations sampled, and converts them into fixed and unchanging databases (Duster 2011). Furthermore, AIMs analysis often relies on a model that stipulates the existence of three genetically distinct parental populations for which there is little evidence at any point in the evolutionary history of our species (Bolnick et al. 2007, 2008). Although there are currently statistical programs that allow the number of hypothesized ancestral populations to be varied, the problematic premise of a small discrete number of genetically distinct parental populations remains. As does the practice of naming these parental populations with descriptors that match up to modern-day racial/ethnic groups, which even supporters of genetic ancestry testing acknowledge "might lead to misinterpretations" (Frudakis 2008, 1039). Guo et al. (2014b) illustrated this slippage themselves in the discussion of their results. Figure 1 in their paper purports to show each individual's composite biogeographical makeup as consisting of up to three ancestral populations: European, African, and East Asian. But in discussing the figure, the authors mistakenly referred to the continental ancestries as "European, *black* and Asian (p. 154, emphasis added), conflating the supposed "ancestral" African population with the contemporary racial term of "black."

Attempts to infer ancestry at the individual level depend on how the existing human genetic diversity is surveyed, including who was sampled and the number and type of genetic markers used, which populations were used as referents, the levels of ancestry examined, and the statistical methods used for interpreting the patterns of variation (Royal et al. 2010). Ultimately, ancestry estimates are the product of a chain of decisions made by individual researchers. In this sense, BGA estimates are no more "logical" or "objective" than the socially constructed categories against which they are being compared.

One of the results of the genetic reinscription of race is that it enables previously established findings to be recast as new but now with the imprimatur of genetic authority that comes with the addition of recent advances in human molecular genetics. In the case of the Guo et al. paper (2014b), for instance, the core of their analysis was to demonstrate that race has a genetic component and that this can be leveraged to illuminate how racial self-identity is constructed in ways not previously known. The authors went so far as to say that in the case of the one-drop rule of hypodescent, "in the absence of bio-ancestry, the 'one drop' rule cannot be measured, and thus the rule cannot be tested directly and generally" (p. 143). Race scholars who work strictly within a social construction of race framework would likely be hard pressed to acknowledge that the "one-drop" rule has never been measured or tested. What is new, and what makes the authors claim that their findings are the first-ever test of the one-drop rule, is the use of genetic material that gives the imprimatur of biological legitimacy to the findings.

Racialized Genetics as a Means of Explanation

There are two main types of research occurring at the nexus of race and genetics that are actively incorporating genetic data. The first, illustrated by Guo et al. (2014b), and the only instance so far in the mainstream sociological literature, is occurring at the level of identification and classification, that is, using BGA estimates at the individual-level to "objectively" partition individual DNA into different "ancestral" groupings. Another type uses the conceptualization of race as having a genetic component as a means of explanation, that is, to explain racial difference as a function of genetic variation (Goodman 2000). The two are not entirely separate enterprises because the latter (as a means of explanation) requires the former (as a means of identification and classification). Only by first operationalizing genetic differences across racial groups can causal models incorporate these effects. It is here that most concerns of combining race with genotype data lie. This is also the direction that Shiao et al. (2012) encouraged sociologists to move, at least theoretically, saying, "In brief, we recommend that sociologists theoretically embed the genetic effects of ancestry in causal processes that include but extend beyond persons" (p. 77).

Before heeding this advice, however, a closer look at the existing empirical research in this vein is warranted. An emerging subset of research within genetic epidemiology takes as its starting point the idea that a racialized understanding of population genetic structure potentially holds the promise of identifying medically important genotypes that vary in frequency across populations and that, relatedly, may also help to explain racial disparities in health (Burchard et al. 2003; Risch 2006). For the most part, the promise of identifying susceptibility variants via these techniques has not been realized. Instead, much of this work has been reduced to simplistic attributions of between-group differences to racialized genetics (Paradies, Montoya, and Fullerton 2007).

Rarely mentioned in these studies is the instability of ancestry estimates, the absence of established relationships between genetic variants and phenotype, the strong correlations between ancestry estimates and unmeasured environmental exposures, and omitted variable bias. Instead, BGA estimates are entered into the equation as decontextualized measures that are interpreted as the biogenetic component of race, when, in fact, in the presence of considerable confounding, they are actually a catch-all for a large amount of nongenetically determined variation. Typically these studies illustrate what Kahn (2006) calls "slippage," namely, a process whereby the race/ethnic categories become further and further separated from the hypothesized genetic correlates in the analysis at the same time that they remain tightly connected conceptually.

One can imagine that the risk of slippage becomes greater and the stakes considerably higher when the focus turns from trying to identify a genetic basis of disease toward one of the central endeavors of social science—understanding human behavior. It is for this reason that Duster (2006) forewarned that "these new molecular techniques are poised to usher in a whole new era of scientific justification for theories of racial and ethnic differences in social behavior" (p. 8). Whether this scenario comes to pass is inextricably tied to how social science, and sociology in particular, addresses the present challenge to the theory of race as a social construct.

Reaffirming a Social Constructionist Approach

One of the most consistent messages surrounding AIMs technology and BGA analysis is that, even despite the recognized methodological and conceptual problems, its ability to discern individual ancestry with a certain degree of confidence largely invalidates the conceptualization of race as a "purely" social construction. This messaging is evident in both the biomedical and social science literatures (Frudakis 2008; Hochschild, Weaver, and Burch 2012; Shiao 2014; Shiao et al. 2012). In this characterization, race as a social construction is set up as existing on the other end of a continuum from race as a strictly genetic construct, with the actual reality supposedly located somewhere in between. Shiao (2014, 253) labeled this the "binary of essentialism and constructionism," and Shiao et al. (2012) advised that "sociology set aside the claim of biological nonreality and adopt an approach more consistent with recent genetics research" (p. 83). This "approach" is evident in the Guo et al. (2014b) article, which examines BGA estimates alongside racial self-identification to help understand the social construction of race. Both endeavors encourage sociologists and other social scientists to seek a middle ground and come, "to acknowledge both the identifiability of a biological basis for race/ethnicity and the complexity of its social construction" (Shiao et al. 2012, 84).

These pleas rely on a straw man that characterizes proponents of "race as a social construction" as deniers of any sort of population-level genetic variation while at the same time misconstruing the developments in genetic research as demonstrating the biological realities of race. To argue that BGA accurately captures a biogenetic component of race is to ignore a weight of evidence suggesting otherwise (Royal et al. 2010). It misidentifies human genetic variation as being racially patterned and inaccurately claims that racial/ethnic groupings have a discrete genetic component. To assert that race is a purely social construction in no way denies that there is some imprecise correlation between self-identified race and patterns of genetic variation (Fujimura et al. 2014). Many who refute the claim that BGA captures the biogenetic component of race acknowledge that "worldwide patterns of human genetic diversity are weakly correlated with racial and ethnic categories because both are partially correlated with geography" (Bolnick et al. 2007, 400). What social constructionists do challenge is the causal ordering between social categorization schemes and human genetic variation. True to their label, social constructionists argue that racial groups are social categories first upon which humans attempt to impose biological meaning. According to Morning (2014a), "To presume that races are biological categories that get mistranslated in the social sphere is to get the direction completely backwards. Racial groupings are rooted in political and social rumination—they are not the product of laboratory discoveries that only later get caught up in power relations" (p. 1679).

Fullwiley (2008) illustrates just this premise in her ethnographic account of how a group of physician-researchers in two interconnected laboratories came to rely on "a tautological product of genetic racial admixture" (i.e., BGA estimates) in pursuing questions of asthma severity and racial differences therein. Through her fieldwork Fullwiley deconstructs the labs' attempts to bracket the social in favor of the biological and in doing so demonstrates that, far from departing from preconceived notions of race, new genetic technologies that link geography and ancestry are inextricably informed by them. Fullwiley's account, as well as those of others (e.g., Montoya 2007; Gannett 2014), provides a glimpse behind the curtain of BGA technology and admixture mapping in practice and in doing so reveals the heavy hand of the social in creating, informing, and interpreting supposedly value-neutral genetic facts about the nature of human variation. In light of this work, the recent sociological scholarship advancing the idea that BGA estimates capture a discrete genetic component of race reflects a surprising naiveté. It relies on a concreteness in demarcating the social from the scientific when none actually exists (Reardon 2008).

The Stakes

As the idea that race has a biogenetic component is becoming "ever more entrenched in medicine, law, science, and personal identity" (Fullwiley 2014, 814), at stake is nothing less than the perpetuation of racism and racial inequality. In lieu of the initial claims made at the onset of the HGP regarding the power of human genetics to eradicate the basis of racial prejudices, attention has increasingly turned to the realization that it will likely reinforce them. As Duster (1990/2003) argues in *Backdoor to Eugenics*, the molecular reinscription of race has the potential to reinforce one of the core tenets of modern racism, namely, the belief in essentialized differences between racial groups. Even seemingly innocuous efforts to discern a genetic basis to disease can exacerbate racism to the extent that they rely on a biologized conceptualization of race and, in doing so, reify race.

A 2013 study that appeared in the *American Sociological Review* tested this precise possibility via a survey experiment (Phelan, Link, and Feldman 2013). The researchers randomly assigned 559 participants to read one of three different mock newspaper articles, each reflecting a different message about race and genetics, drawn from contemporary scientific research and the public discourse.

The vignette of interest, labeled "the backdoor vignette," was designed to explicitly test Duster's idea that genetics has the potential to increase belief in essentialized differences between racial groups, even if it makes no explicit mention of them. Titled "Genes May Cause Racial Difference in Heart Attacks," the fake article described how a group of geneticists identified a version of a specific gene that was more strongly associated with heart attacks in African Americans than in Caucasians. Following the reading, each respondent was asked a series of questions to measure her or his belief in essential racial differences. The authors found that respondents assigned to "the backdoor vignette" had beliefs in essential racial differences that were similar to participants who read a vignette emphasizing "race-as-genetic-reality," and that these beliefs did not vary significantly by participants' preexisting levels of racial bias. The researchers argue that their findings provide empirical support for Duster's original prediction that genomic research, even with a decidedly nonracist agenda, such as investigating the differential distribution of genes related to disease across racial groups, results in the belief that racial groups differ genetically in much broader terms. Their finding that the process was not limited to people who were highly racially biased suggests that, likely because of their noncontroversial presentation, this type of scientific research will have a wide-ranging impact; it reinscribes taxonomies of race and essentializing racial groups as immutable categories in nature.

Those described by the "backdoor" scenario are frequently adamant that their work is not reifying race. In the health sciences, research has shown that the clinician scientists often spearheading efforts to conceptualize genetic variation as racialized are themselves committed to eliminating racial disparities in health (Fullwiley 2008). Similarly, in the social sciences, Guo et al. (2014a) appear to be concerned that social scientists do not get left behind in the "genetic revolution," arguing that "work using bio-ancestry markers continues to forge ahead in biology and medicine. It is important that demographers and other social scientists are part of this growing area of research to ensure that the sociocultural nature of race is understood" (pp. 2341–42). What they fail to accept is that a headlong rush toward a biologized conceptualization of race has the potential, as proposed by Duster (1990/2003) and empirically demonstrated by Phelan, Link, and Feldman (2013), to reanimate old racial thinking and reinvigorate previously discredited beliefs in essential racial differences. As summed up by Fullwiley (2014), "In the present, the potential for racism is often embedded in good intentions" (p. 812).

The Public Discourse

While the "back door" scenario characterizes the recent spate of scientific research occurring at the intersection of race and genetics, the "front door" approach (i.e., racist ideas that are propped up by genetic arguments) continues to be part of the landscape. This is particularly the case in nonscholarly work, as exemplified by the recent publication of *A Troubled Inheritance: Genes, Race and Human History* (Wade 2014). In it, the author, Nicholas Wade, previously a science writer for the *New York Times*, argues that genetic differences between races are the reason for present-day differences in levels of national prosperity.

Phelan, Link, and Feldman (2013) have argued that this type of racial essentializing through "the front door," that is, through a thinly veiled racist agenda, is "less concerning" than the "backdoor" efforts" because "the message of essential racial differences is clear to see, and scholars are already aware of these messages' possibly harmful effects" (p. 186). While the latter is certainly true, Phelan, Link, and Feldman (2013) likely overestimate the power of scientists committed to a "race as social construction" perspective to limit the consequences of "front door" messaging with scholarly work. What is largely at stake with books such as Wade's is their reception by the public (Morning 2015). But the ability of scholars to equip the public to be critical consumers of this type of work is severally compromised by a reoccurring narrative that accompanies products of "front door" racial essentializing (and oftentimes "back door" work, too). Labeled in prior work as "the forbidden knowledge" narrative, such a narrative references instances when a genetic explanation is depicted as forbidden, that is, unwanted knowledge that is perceived as too dangerous or politically unpalatable to be accepted (Frank 2012). This messaging is evident throughout Wade's writings; for example, he writes, "The subject of human race soon became too daunting for all but the most courageous and academically secure of researchers to touch" (pp. 120–21) or "Most scholars will not enter this territory from lively fear of being demonized by their fellow academics" (p. 201). At its core, a forbidden knowledge argument characterizes a racialized understanding of human genetic variation as an objective truth, while portraying critiques as originating from a place of fear (Frank 2012). Fee (2006) has pointed out that those who invoke a forbidden knowledge narrative often are represented (and represent themselves) as "brave scientific martyr-pioneers" who are struggling against the repression of political correctness to reveal knowledge that other scientists consider off limits (Fee 2006).

What is really at stake in research that promotes a biologized conceptualization of race is not the politically correct silencing of brave journalists and researchers but the integrity of the scientific process itself. References to forbidden knowledge, fear, and political correctness relegate those who argue alternative perspectives to the sidelines. Invoking a forbidden knowledge argument creates rhetorical battle lines and curtails the potential for meaningful scientific debate. A necessary first step for a productive dialogue over how sociologists would be best positioned to engage genetics when it comes to advancing our understandings of race and racism is to eschew a forbidden knowledge argument.

Conclusion

In the context of the ongoing "genomic revolution," what is the role for sociologists and other social scientists who study race? To answer, it is perhaps useful to return to the broader movement currently under way in sociology toward "genetics-informed sociology." In a review essay on genetics and social inquiry, Freese and Shostak (2009) categorize social scientists at the forefront of engagement with genetics into two categories. In the first are those who are actually incorporating techniques from quantitative and molecular genetics into their own work. In the second fall those who are focused on understanding aspects of genetic science as a social phenomenon, that is, they concentrate on trying to identify the consequences of genetic science for society. At the intersection of race and genetics, I have described early forays by sociologists into the first category. As evidenced by Guo et al. (2014b), incorporating genetic information in the form of BGA estimates into the study of racial identification represents an explicit effort to bring techniques from human molecular genetics into the sociological study of race. Theirs followed a separate effort by Shiao et al. (2012) to use genetics to question the utility of the "race as social construction" perspective in sociology. Both efforts represent a turn toward the scientific reductionism that Duster warned of in his 2005 ASA presidential address. The fact that these forays appeared in two of the leading journals of sociology, within whose bounds a social construction of race was forged, underscores their consequence.

Whether this type of research remains an outlier or becomes a sustained trend in the field is closely tied to the extent that the discipline engages in research occurring in the second category, that is, that which focuses on genetic science as a social phenomenon. In the context of the sociological study of race, this work will involve mobilizing a social construction of race to interrogate the ways in which genetics and race collide. Only by using their analytic tools to complicate and challenge reductionist genetic explanations for racial difference will sociologists be able to stem increasing attempts to embrace them at face value. This work will involve using the discipline's analytic and methodological tools at the site of "reductionist knowledge production" to reveal the social forces shaping its claims. It will also involve the continued monitoring of biologized conceptualizations of race in both the academic literature and the public sphere, because, as Morning (2014a) notes, "the (re)-biologization of race is proceeding apace outside the ivory tower" (p. 1682). In both arenas, vigilance against forbidden knowledge arguments will be a necessity. At its core, this emerging body of scholarship will rest on the understanding that "genomics might, indeed, bring new levels of refinement to these efforts to order and know human beings, but that process of refinement cannot gain meaning apart from its ties to the social order" (Reardon 2008, 317). The results of these efforts will determine whether we emerge from this tumultuous period of racialized genetics with Sociology's fundamental contributions to the understanding of race, racism, and racial inequality intact.

References

American Sociological Association. 2003. *The importance of collecting data and doing social scientific research on race.* Washington, DC: American Sociological Association.

Bolnick, Deborah A., Duana Fullwiley, Troy Duster, Richard S. Cooper, Joan H. Fujimura, Jonathan Kahn, Jay S. Kaufman, Jonathan Marks, Ann Morning, and Alondra Nelson, et al. 2007. The science and business of genetic ancestry testing. *Science* 318 (5849): 399–400.

Bolnick, Deborah A., Duana Fullwiley, Jonathan Marks, Susan M. Reverby, Jonathan Kahn, Kimberly Tallbear, Jenny Reardon, Richard S. Cooper, Troy Duster, and Joan H. Fujimura, et al. 2008. The legitimacy of genetic ancestry tests: A response. *Science* 319:1039–40.

Braun, Lundy, and Evelynn Hammonds. 2012. The dilemma of classification: The past in the present. In *Genetics and the unsettled past: The collision of DNA, race, and history*, eds. Keith Wailoo, Alondra Nelson, and Catherine Lee, 67–80. New Brunswick, NJ: Rutgers University Press.

Burchard, Esteban Gonzalez, Elad Ziv, Natasha Coyle, Scarlett Lin Gomez, Hua Tang, Andrew J. Karter, Joanna L. Mountain, Eliseo J. Perez-Stable, Dean Sheppard, and Neil Risch. 2003. The importance of race and ethnic background in biomedical research and clinical practice. *New England Journal of Medicine* 348 (12): 1170–75.

Duster, Troy. 1990/2003. *Backdoor to eugenics.* New York, NY: Routledge.

Duster, Troy. 2006. Comparative perspectives and competing explanations: Taking on the newly configured reductionist challenge to sociology. *American Sociological Review* 71 (1): 1–15.

Duster, Troy. 2011. Ancestry testing and DNA: Uses, limits and caveat emptor. In *Race and the genetic revolution: Science, myth and culture*, eds. Sheldon Krimsky and Kathleen Sloan, 99–115. New York, NY: Columbia University Press.

Fee, Margery. 2006. Racializing narratives: Obesity, diabetes and the aboriginal thrifty genotype. *Social Science & Medicine* 62 (12): 2988–97.

Frank, Reanne. 2012. Forbidden or forsaken?: The (mis)use of a forbidden knowledge argument in research on race, DNA, and disease. In *Genetics and the unsettled past: The collision of DNA, race, and history*, eds. Keith Wailoo, Alondra Nelson, and Catherine Lee, 315–24. New Brunswick, NJ: Rutgers University Press.

Freese, Jeremy, and Sara Shostak. 2009. Genetics and social inquiry. *Annual Review of Sociology* 35: 107–28.

Frudakis, Tony. 2008. Letters. The legitimacy of genetic ancestry tests. *Science* 319:1039–40.

Fujimura, Joan H., Deborah A. Bolnick, Ramya Rajagopalan, Jay S. Kaufman, Richard C. Lewontin, Troy Duster, Pilar Ossorio, and Jonathan Marks. 2014. Clines without classes: How to make sense of human variation. *Sociological Theory* 32 (3): 208–27.

Fullwiley, Duana. 2008. The biologistical construction of race: "Admixture" technology and the new genetic medicine. *Social Studies of Science* 38 (5): 695–735.

Fullwiley, Duana. 2014. The "contemporary synthesis": When politically inclusive genomic science relies on biological notions of race. *Isis* 105:803–14.

Gannett, Lisa. 2014. Biogeographical ancestry and race. *Studies in History and Philosophy of Biological and Biomedical Sciences* 47:173–84.

Goodman, Alan H. 2000. Why genes don't count (for racial differences in health). *American Journal of Public Health* 90 (11): 1699–1702.

Guo, Guang, Yilan Fu, Hedwig Lee, Tianji Cai, Yi Li, and Kathleen Harris. 2014a. Recognizing a small amount of superficial genetic differences across African, European and Asian Americans helps understand social construction of race. *Demography* 51 (6): 2337–42.

Guo, Guang, Yilan Fu, Hedwig Lee, Tianji Cai, Kathleen Mullan Harris, and Yi Li. 2014b. Genetic bio-ancestry and social construction of racial classification in social surveys in the contemporary United States. *Demography* 51 (1): 141–72.

Guo, Guang, Yuying Tong, and Tianji Cai. 2008. Gene by social context interactions for number of sexual partners among white male youths: Genetics-informed sociology. *American Journal of Sociology* 114:S36–S66.

Hochschild, Jennifer, Vesla M. Weaver, and Traci R. Burch. 2012. *Creating a new racial order: How immigration, multiracialism, genomics, and the young can remake race in America.* Princeton, NJ: Princeton University Press.

Kahn, Jonathan. 2004. How a drug becomes "ethnic": Law, commerce, and the production of racial categories in medicine. *Journal of Health Policy, Law, and Ethnics* IV (1): 1–46.

Kahn, Jonathan. 2006. Genes, race, and population: Avoiding collision of categories. *American Journal of Public Health* 96 (11): 6–11.

Leroi, Armand Marie. 14 March 2005. Op-ed. A family tree in every gene. *New York Times.*

Montoya, Michael J. 2007. Bioethnic conscription: Genes, race, and Mexicana/o ethnicity in diabetes research. *Cultural Anthropology* 22 (1): 94–128.

Morning, Ann. 2014a. And you thought we had moved beyond all that: Biological race returns to the social sciences. *Ethnic and Racial Studies* 37 (10): 1676–85.

Morning, Ann. 2014b. Does genomics challenge the social construction of race? *Sociological Theory* 32 (3): 189–207.

Morning, Ann. 2015. Scientific racism redux? The many lives of a troublesome idea. *Du Bois Review* 21 (1): 187–211.

Ossorio, Pilar, and Troy Duster. 2005. Race and genetics: Controversies in biomedical, behavioral, and forensic sciences. *American Psychologist* 60 (1): 115–28.

Paradies, Yin C., Michael J. Montoya, and Stephanie M. Fullerton. 2007. Racialized genetics and the study of complex diseases. *Perspectives in Biology & Medicine* 50 (2): 203–27.

Phelan, Jo C., Bruce G. Link, and Naumi M. Feldman. 2013. The genomic revolution and beliefs about essential racial differences: A backdoor to eugenics? *American Sociological Review* 78 (2): 167–91.

Reardon, Jenny. 2005. *Race to the finish: Identity and governance in an age of genomics, information series.* Princeton, NJ: Princeton University Press.

Reardon, Jenny. 2008. Race without salvation: Beyond the science/society divide in genomic studies of human diversity. In *Revisiting race in a genomic age*, eds. Barbara A. Koenig, Sandra Soo-Jin Lee, and Sarah S. Richardson, 304–19. New Brunswick, NJ: Rutgers University Press.

Risch, Neil. 2006. Dissecting racial and ethnic differences. *New England Journal of Medicine* 354 (4): 408–11.

Rosenberg, Noah A., Jonathan K. Pritchard, James L. Weber, Howard M. Cann, Kenneth K. Kidd, Lev A. Zhivotovsky, and Marcus W. Feldman. 2002. Genetic structure of human populations. *Science* 298 (5602): 2381–85.

Royal, Charmaine D., John Novembre, Stephanie M. Fullerton, David B. Goldstein, Jeffrey C. Long, Michael J. Bamshad, and Andrew G. Clark. 2010. Inferring genetic ancestry: Opportunities, challenges, and implications. *American Journal of Human Genetics* 86 (5): 661–73.

Schmickle, Sharon. 26 March 2002. Under the skin, we're all alike, except medically, science says. *Star Tribune.*

Shiao, Jiannbin Lee. 2014. Response to Hosang; Fujimura, Bolnick, Rajagopalan, Kaufman, Lewontin, Duster, Ossorio, and Marks, and Morning. *Sociological Theory* 32 (3): 244–58.

Shiao, Jiannbin Lee, Thomas Bode, Amber Beyer, and Daniel Selvig. 2012. The genomic challenge to the social construction of race. *Sociological Theory* 30 (2): 67–88.

Shriver, Mark D., and Rick A. Kittles. 2004. Genetic ancestry and the search for personalized genetic histories. *Nature Reviews Genetics* 5:611–18.

TallBear, Kimberly. 2013. Genomic articulations of indigeneity. *Social Studies of Science* 43 (4): 509–33.

Wade, Nicholas. 2014. *A troublesome inheritance: Genes, race and human history*. New York, NY: Penguin Press.

Wailoo, Keith, Alondra Nelson, and Catherine Lee, eds. 2012. *Genetics and the unsettled past: The collision of DNA, race, and history*: New Brunswick, NJ: Rutgers University Press.

CHAPTER 8

Unmasking Racism*

Halloween Costuming and Engagement of the Racial Other

Jennifer C. Mueller, Danielle Dirks, and Leslie H. Picca

In this essay, Mueller and colleagues draw on data collected using journals from college students to explore Halloween as a uniquely constructive space for engaging racial concepts and identities, particularly through ritual costuming. During Halloween, many individuals actively engage the racial other in costuming across racial/ethnic lines. Although some recognize the significance of racial ***stereotyping*** *in costuming, it is often dismissed as being part of the holiday's social context. They explore how cross-racial costuming and making light of racialized concepts in the safe context of Halloween allows students to trivialize and reproduce racial* ***stereotypes*** *while supporting the* ***racial hierarchy****. They argue that Whites contemporarily engage Halloween as a sort of ritual of rebellion in response to the seemingly restrictive social context of the post–civil rights era and in a way that ultimately reinforces White dominance.*

Source: Adapted from Jennifer C. Mueller, Danielle Dirks, and Leslie Houts Picca, "Unmasking Racism: Halloween Costuming and Engagement of the Racial Other," *Qualitative Sociology*, Volume 30, Number 3, pages 315–335, Springer, 2007.

*Endnotes have been omitted. Please consult the original source.

Questions to Consider

When does a Halloween costume cross the line from a fun, playful act of rebellion to racial stereotyping? Is this line always clear? How does an individual's choice of costume connect to larger issues of power and dominance? Do individuals who engage in cross-racial costuming have the right to do so, and does their choice contribute to reproducing the U.S. racial hierarchy?

In 2003, Louisiana State District Judge Timothy Ellender arrived at a Halloween party costumed in blackface makeup, afro wig, and prison jumpsuit, complete with wrist and ankle shackles. When confronted with his actions, he noted wearing the costume was "a harmless joke" (Simpson, 2003). In 2002, Massachusetts-based Fright Catalog marketed and sold the Halloween mask "Vato Loco," a stereotyped caricature of a bandana-clad, tattooed Latino gang thug, while retail giants Wal-Mart, Party City, and Spencer Gifts began sales for "Kung Fool," a Halloween ensemble complete with Japanese kimono and a buck-toothed, slant-eyed mask with headband bearing the Chinese character for "loser" (Hua, 2002; Unmasking Hate, 2002). Additionally, there have been several Halloween party-related blackface incidents documented at universities across the United States over the past several years. White college students have donned blackface and reenacted images of police brutality, cotton picking, and lynching at such parties, invoking degrading stereotypes and some of the darkest themes in our nation's racial past and present.

Collectively, these incidents indicate that Halloween may provide a unique opportunity to understand contemporary racial relations and racial thinking in the U.S. Although the gendered implications of Halloween costuming have been examined (Martin, 1998; Nelson, 2000; Ogletree, Denton, & Williams, 1993), to our knowledge, there has not been any empirical investigation into the ways in which race is engaged during this holiday. Given the relevance of a sociological study of holidays (Etzioni, 2000) and what very little work has critically addressed Halloween as a social phenomenon reflective of the broader society, the current research uses empirical data to address how racial concepts are employed during Halloween.

Halloween Ritual Costuming: Role-Taking, Role-Making

Donning costumes has become a ritual component of the Halloween tradition in North America (Nelson, 2000; Santino, 1994). Over half of all U.S. consumers celebrate Halloween in some way, with sixty percent reporting that they will costume for the holiday (The Macerich Company, 2005). Several studies suggest that most college students participate in some form of costuming—whether donning store-bought or homemade costumes (McDowell, 1985; Miller, Jasper, & Hill, 1991, 1993). Indeed, "dressing up" according to one's "fantasy" is very much a part of the release afforded by the holiday and consumers spend millions of dollars each year on Halloween costumes (Belk, 1994; Rogers, 2002).

Halloween allows masqueraders to step out of their everyday roles, opening up a wide range of personas for adoption, if only temporarily. Indeed, even when costumes do not disguise their actual identity, playing different roles remains a major part of the appeal of Halloween among college students (Miller et al., 1991). Significantly, adopting new roles through costume is not merely about *playing* different roles, but may also involve *constructing* and defining those roles. As McDowell (1985) suggests, costuming is about creating inhabitable representations of the "Other"—that is, "metaphors that can be carried about on the mobile human frame" (p. 1). If one adopts this definition, it becomes clear how powerful the experience of costuming across racial or ethnic lines can be in creating, resurrecting and communicating generic and negative ideas about a "racial other"—those persons of color, particularly African Americans, defined in negative contrast to white normativity.

Significance of the Social Context

Goffman's (1959) frontstage/backstage dramaturgical analysis provides a useful framework for considering the way in which Halloween costuming rituals operate as social performances between actors and their audiences. Indeed, McDowell (1985) found that college students in his sample "thrived" on the reactions provoked by the "prop" of their costumes. Stone (1962), too, stresses the social requirement in playing the role of the other while costuming. He argues that while one must first *dress out* of his or her own role and into the other, the significance and meaning of such a performance is acquired only through the collusive interplay between the costumer and her or his audience. Halloween's social license permits and endorses a blending of the inherent contradictions of frontstage and backstage performances. In addition, it creates a unique collusion between actor and audience in which typically hidden backstage behaviors are celebrated in the frontstage through the use of humor and play.

Significantly, the goal of Halloween humor and play is often achieved at the expense of a target, for example, an individual or group that is mocked. While a costume may represent an ultimately aggressive judgment about its target, the joking nature of this practice makes acceptable the sharing of information, which in its unadulterated form might be considered unacceptable (Freud, 1960). Because both masquerader and his or her audience identify the humor as the principal feature of the costume, they are able to circumvent any judicious assessment of the negative images of the racial other being shared. It is for precisely these reasons that humor is such an effective tool in communicating racist thoughts, particularly in the contemporary post–Civil Rights era where open, frontstage expression of such ideas is considered socially taboo (Bonilla-Silva, 2003; Dundes, 1987; Feagin, 2006; Picca & Feagin, forthcoming). Collectively, individuals' behavior in the social setting is reinforced, encouraging both the continued reproduction of racially prejudiced ideas, as well as an uncritical appraisal of them.

Racial Relations and Halloween

Examining both Halloween and racial relations in the U.S. requires a historical lens that considers the unquestionable relationship between the two. Children's antique Halloween costumes remain some of the most popularly collected items from the Jim Crow era (Pilgrim, 2001). For example, Sears' 1912 "Negro make-up outfit" allowed children to "play at being a 'Negro'" and was described as "the funniest and most laughable outfit ever sold" (Wilkinson, 1974, p. 105). To be sure, today's popular caricatures extend a long history of blackface minstrelsy and racist iconography, reconstructing deep-seated ideas of white superiority against the clear contrast of black inferiority (Feagin, 2000, 2006). This history is replete with numerous empirical examples to support Stone's (1962) general assertion that acting out the role of the other allows individuals to develop and enhance conceptions regarding their own attitudes and roles as differentiated from the adopted role. Although occasionally less explicit, today it would appear that cross-racial costuming often serves the same purpose in accenting the goodness of whiteness through the relational devaluation of the racial other as did the minstrel shows of old. Caricatured imitations of people of color, as in costuming, are written off as harmless joking, but the method of parody seems to be nothing less than an updated version of the same old show.

It is important to entertain the argument offered by some researchers, who suggest that rather than simply reifying prevailing societal beliefs, Halloween presents the opportunity to advance new beliefs and stimulate change (Etzioni, 2000; Grider, 1996; Yinger, 1977). In some respects this premise may ring true; Rogers (2002), for instance, suggests that much of contemporary Halloween celebration has oriented itself toward reaffirming the values of feminist and gay cultures. However, given the long legacy of racism in the U.S. and the ways in which it continues to structure "the rhythms of everyday life" today, it is important to discover how American holidays—particularly Halloween—remain sites where racial concepts and images are passed down and racist actions occur (Feagin, 2000, p. 2; Litwicki, 2000; Pilgrim, 2001; Rogers, 2002; Skal, 2002). In light of the notable examples described above, an examination of the current relationship between the Halloween costuming ritual and the social reproduction of racism is a critical undertaking.

Participant Observation Journals

The current study uses data collected from two samples of college students, [mostly from the Southeastern United States] who contributed a total of 663 individually-written participant observation journals on racial events.

Halloween License: Setting the Stage for Engagement with Racial Concepts

One of our primary arguments is that Halloween provides a uniquely constructive space for engaging race, in part because of the holiday's intuitive license, such that revelers assume the right to do, say, and be whatever they want. Indeed, college students in our sample consistently described Halloween as a holiday affording them freedom and a license to "take a break from" or even "defy" social norms. As one student observed of her friend's enjoyment of holidays like Halloween, "He calls them 'breaks from reality where he can just go wild'" (white female). In addition, for many college students, the freeing experience of Halloween costuming is intimately tied to breaking from their everyday roles as one student shared: "Halloween is a way for people to see themselves as something different and uninhibited, if only for a day. Instead of being tied by how they expect others to interact with them" (Hispanic/Latino male). Such comments suggest that being "tied" to a certain identity in everyday life creates limits and inhibitions that one feels compelled to abide by, and for which Halloween provides an appropriate release.

For students, costuming also represents a liberty to experiment with new personas. One male student, who identified himself as a routine female impersonator, noted his own intrigue regarding the way which cross-dressing "becomes socially acceptable on this one holiday." For him, performing as a "character" is "fun and exciting," similar, in his estimation, to what Halloween must be for "non-gay, non-transsexual, non-transvestites who get to play and explore that within themselves, JUST THIS ONCE, of course" (white male). Somewhat ironically, while students describe Halloween as an opportunity to step outside and disregard societal norms, this defiance is made possible only because the norm for Halloween is to do just that. In this way, Halloween creates a figurative "disguise" that allows revelers freedom:

> Halloween is a very social and freedom-eliciting moment in the year. Those who are even the most consistent in their style and attitudes can become different. I guess it is the excuse of dressing up in wild and crazy things and playing a role you normally wouldn't which appeals to people's imaginative freedom. Everyone's being weird and having fun and no one will think it is too out of context if I'm being strange myself. (Asian American/Pacific Islander male)

It would seem that this release is an experience that students not only enjoy, but perhaps feel they need in order to deal with the inhibitions of everyday life, as the above student added this final statement to his thoughts, "We should have more holidays like Halloween."

Within the "safe" space formed by Halloween license, college students often take up the opportunity to engage race through the costuming ritual. Many students documented incidents where they or someone they knew considered, observed, participated in and/or discussed costuming across racial or ethnic lines. For one student, failing to take advantage of the holiday in this way represented an opportunity missed: "I saw my friend John who dressed up as a Buddha. I found it a bit silly he chose to dress up as something Asian when he was already Asian" (Asian American/Pacific Islander male). The remainder of our findings details what emerges when students engage race through costume.

Stereotyping as the Predominant Guide in Cross-Racial Costuming

While students discussed and employed cross-racial costuming in a variety of ways, our analysis of journals reveals the near universal guide of racial stereotype in directing their efforts. Student commentary suggests that capturing race, both "physically" and "behaviorally," is the core criterion for determining cross-racial costuming success and as a result, most portrayals play to stereotypical ideas about the racial other. Our analysis of this phenomenon within the journals led to an emergent typology, such that the cross-racial costuming discussed, described and engaged in by our participants tended to fall within three categories: celebrity portrayals, "role" portrayals, and generic/essentialist portrayals. In some respects, these "discrete" types capture overlapping concepts. Most critically, all three types rely on stereotype to guide their portrayals. As such, it is useful to conceptualize these categories as something of a continuum in this regard.

Celebrity Portrayals

In some cases, cross-racial/ethnic dressing occurred as a function of students masquerading as celebrities, television/movie personalities, and otherwise notorious individuals. For instance, one Asian American woman recorded seeing a black man dressed as the white rapper, Eminem. Another white woman found two white male friends "covered in black paint from head to toe" in preparation for their costuming as Venus and Serena Williams, describing the scene as "the funniest thing [she] had seen in a long time." Yet another student wrote of dressing with two friends as "Charlie's Angels." She, a white woman, dressed as Asian American actress Lucy Liu's character; Stacy, her African American roommate, dressed as white actress Cameron Diaz's character; and, another friend, Tina, who is white, dressed as white actress Drew Barrymore's character.

While in these instances dressing across racial lines would appear to be required solely as a function of the chosen personality, the attention devoted to properly capturing the celebrity's race was in most cases intentional and elaborate. Notably, this respondent recorded that while Tina's costume would be "easy" because she was white (like her character), Stacy would have to borrow a long-sleeved upper body leotard "to hide her skin color." Additionally, she detailed the need for further makeup, "We are going to put makeup on her [Stacy's] hands and face to try and make her look Caucasian. For my costume the girls are going to do my makeup, particularly my eyes to try and make me look Oriental." From this detailed narrative, matching one's skin color appears to be more important than wearing a similar outfit or portraying an Angel's demeanor.

Interestingly, even among students attempting to portray famous people or personalities, students suggest that the "success" of the costume is principally determined by how well the race of the individual is captured. Students frequently evaluated cross-racial costuming on this basis of how convincing masqueraders were in portraying their "new" race, to the exclusion of other evaluations regarding believability. For example, one student wrote that an Asian man who had dressed as one of the Blues Brothers happily reported to her that "at the party he went to several people thought he was white and did not recognize him" (white female). Following her own Halloween celebrating, this same student recorded the following:

> An Oriental male . . . was dressed as President Bush. One of the really good costumes was this black male, also in his twenties, who dressed as Osama bin Laden. He really looked like he was Middle Eastern. (white female)

Addition of the singular remark regarding what she considered a "really good" costume stands in contrast to the lack of such validation for the Asian male's impersonation of President Bush.

While cross-racial celebrity costumes tend toward the seemingly more "innocuous" end of the range—focused primarily on embodying the physical attributes of real "characters" while attempting to capture race as the most important or salient feature—it is important to remark on celebrity portrayals that involve distinctly more behavioral and stereotypical prescriptions. Consider the following student's recollections regarding a dinner conversation he had with friends over their ideas for Halloween costumes:

> My friend, who is white, well educated, and comes from a prominent upper-class family, immediately told us his plans. He planned on being 'The Black Girl from [the movie] Coyote Ugly.' He then elaborated, 'All I'll have to do is paint my skin and smell bad, oh and it'll help if I act like I don't know how to swim.' Everyone got a good laugh out of it. (white male)

It is not clear whether this young man's comments are solely meant to communicate a joke rather than his actual plans for costuming; yet what is distinctive about this disclosure is that the young man draws on a celebrity identity ("The Black Girl from Coyote Ugly" being African American actress/model Tyra Banks), but reaffirms strictly raced conceptions of that identity, essentially negating her personhood. In other words, it would appear that it is fundamentally critical to capture race in cross-racial costuming not only in the most obvious "physical" way, through skin color, but also through behaviorally prescribed ways such as smelling "bad" and acting like one cannot swim, two degrading stereotypes of African Americans.

"Role" Portrayals

One student responded to a friend's use of blackface paint, saying, "[His] outfit would be perfect if he went out and stole something before we left" (white male). Costumes such as this are indicative of racial "role" portrayals, and highlight attempts to embody race through the use of demeaning stereotypical notions about people of color. Unlike celebrity portrayals however, "role" portrayals have no person-specific or "real" reference, leaving much room for white imagineering of racial others.

Mass marketing of items such as "Vato Loco," "Kung Fool," and numerous pimp, thug and American Indian-themed costumes suggest the prevalence of racial caricatures in the larger culture. Rather than purchasing ready-made costumes, however, most journals documented students employing their own creativity in fashioning stereotypical cross-racial/ethnic identities, a finding that echoes McDowell (1985). Particularly plentiful were descriptions of "gangstas," "thugs," pimps, and Mafiosos. While some might contend that such representations are not fixed to one particular race or ethnicity, in reality they are typically connected to stereotypical racial caricatures, a finding supported by the students' journals.

As such, when whites costume in "ghetto" dress (with low-slung baggy pants and thick gold chains) or as pimps (complete with gold teeth, afro-like wigs, and velvet suits) they are arguably attempting to parody stereotypical images of blacks, even if they do not make use of blackface. Many students were clear about this in their responses: "one of my white friends, Eric, wanted to be a ghetto pimp. He defined ghetto as acting or being black" (black female). Another student's journal echoes this theme in more detail:

> The theme (of the fraternity party) was 'thug holiday' . . . my friends and I were wondering what we were supposed to wear. . . . I was the first to admit that the image that popped into my mind when I thought about a 'thug' was a modern-day rapper wearing baggy jeans, big gold chains around his neck, and a football jersey. . . . Missy was laughing when I was describing what I thought we should all wear. She said, 'so basically we should dress like black rappers.' We were all laughing at the thought of us, three preppy white girls, dressing as what we had just described. (white female)

According to her later journaling, this young woman, her friends, and by her account "everybody (at the party), without any exceptions" costumed as they had discussed. Although she does not report the use of blackface, the party's theme invoked images that in her own words "thoroughly involved race," and in particular made reference to blackness. These examples illustrate that whether individuals are explicit about their targets or not, such costumed caricatures intend to convey racially stereotypical, degraded ideas. Students seek out and fulfill the generic requirements of these imagined images of racial and ethnic groups with relative ease, and with a disturbing level of unthinking.

Generic/Essentialist Portrayals

While stereotypical cross-racial costuming most often drew on caricatured images of the racial other, a number of students described costumes that represented completely generic representations, such that simply portraying "race," usually blackness, was considered a costume.

Consider two non-celebrity examples: one young woman recalled a discussion over costumes prior to Halloween, "We were all getting dressed up and one person said that they wanted to paint themselves black and wear a diaper and be a black baby" (white female). Another young woman recalled her and her boyfriend's interest in simply costuming "as a black couple" (Native American/white female). While it is not known whether these individuals actually decided to cross-racially costume, what is significant is the non-descript nature of the costumes suggested. We might imagine that individuals actually choosing to costume as the nonspecific "black person" would actively engage in some type of stereotypical behavior in assuming the role of their costume. In any case, it would appear that such generic ideas represent whites' most fundamental attempts to strip all unique identity from people of color, to reveal race as the only relevant marker of those they claim to represent in costume. It is also significant that all generic representations in our sample referred to blackness. Arguably, generic and essentialist portrayals such as these tap into the most debased of representations, invoking the historical and archetypal consideration of the racial other in the white mind—that of the inferior black (Feagin, 2000, 2006).

Collectively considered, each cross-racial costume type helps us understand how such costumes serve as vehicles for transmitting racial judgments about people of color, particularly in light of the fact that stereotype guides each to a greater or lesser degree. From the relatively "innocuous" celebrity portrayal, to the "role" portrayal, to the fundamentally degrading generic/essentialist portrayal, cross-racial costuming represents the effort to create inhabitable representations (McDowell, 1985) of the racial other and to indeed, engage costume as a metaphor for those depictions.

Responses in the Halloween Context

The journal writing opportunity provided a regular way for students to reflect on the cross-racial costuming and other racialized Halloween rituals ongoing during this time. Students' compelling reflections serve as some of the most interesting points for analysis. For example, one student, observing the tendency of "ethnic costumes" to reflect stereotypes, posed the rhetorical question, "are these stereotypical costumes offensive, or merely observing that there are differences between people that can be parodied?" (white female). This was a concern addressed both explicitly and implicitly by other students, and indeed, how they responded formed a basis for thematically organizing students' reflections.

Active Participation/Unquestioning Support

Moving beyond rhetorical theorizing about the potential to offend on Halloween, several students' reflections reveal a great deal of decidedness about cross-racial costuming. For most students, notions of sensitivity or social or political correctness should be put aside for the holiday, as cross-racial costuming is afforded by the Halloween license for fun. Students adhering to this rationale unsurprisingly invoked the racial other in their own costuming, or provided minimal critique of those who did. As such, this line of thinking served as a justification for cross-racial dressing. Dressing up for a day, "as anything . . . or anyone you want" is entitled by the holiday: "Consciously, I can't think of a time when I have placed a limitation on Halloween costumes or decorations based on race/ethnicity, gender, sexuality, social class or even age" (white female). Similarly, another white woman wrote, "Halloween is a holiday in which people like to believe that the lines of race and gender are blurred, with no one truly caring exactly where they lie." She appears confident that her belief is universal, and as such, concerns about choosing a gendered or racially offensive costume need not be entertained.

Indeed, other journals echo that while not necessarily universal, for most Halloween license is a "given," and extends to cross-racial costuming, such that invoking ethnicity and race has "no bounds" (black female). Unlike other days of the year, Halloween affords individuals the right to reveal one's "true self" through "disguise" as another (in many cases, as our data show, a racial other). Ironically, this freedom from self-correction takes form in interesting ways. For example, in writing of a white friend who dressed as a Rastafarian, Josh recognized that while his friend may have "broken norms," he had not gone too far:

> . . . because this is Halloween and anything goes. Normally dressing up as people from other cultures, such as the Rastafari, would be considered some sort of racism or people might be offended . . . This is the great thing about Halloween, people can go all out and be whoever they want to be, without having to worry about what people will think or who will be offended. (white male)

This excerpt highlights that students understand the potentially invidious nature of this type of costuming, but feel comfortable "playing" with racial ideas and roles on Halloween because they can get away with it within the holiday context. Clearly, students carry these caricatured ideas in their consciousness, but withhold them from public frontstage expression, having learned, as a result of political correctness or other means, to do so.

Among students who uncritically embrace cross-racial costuming, a belief in the "fun factor" of dressing across racial/ethnic lines emerges. Frequently, students who emphasize the fun of costumes translate that impression into an equation where humor "trumps" offensiveness—in other words, as long as a costume is perceived as funny, onlookers should take no offense, as this student's recollection demonstrates:

> Tonight I went to a costume party and the whitest kid I know was dressed up as a rapper. Baggy jeans, backwards hat, gold chain, whole deal. He did such a good job overplaying it that no one was offended, they just found it comical. It was hilarious to see him greet the black kids at the party. (white male)

Like other students, this individual understands the potentially offending nature of cross-racial costuming (although he does not explicitly say that his friend went as a "black" rapper, it becomes implicit in his racialized account); however, he assumes it will be negated as long as individuals "play up" the humor potential of the costume and convey the experience as merely a joke. The alleged hilarity of the "whitest kid" greeting the "black kids at the party" averts a potentially offensive situation according to the narrative. Seen through the eyes of this young white writer, the description of this interaction overemphasizes the social requirement of racial joking—that both sides appear to receive it as a joke. Conveniently, objections that may have been entertained by the "black kids," or anyone else for that matter, are effectively erased with the conclusion that "no one was offended" because of the successful ways in which the costumer was able to so humorously appropriate notions of blackness and rap. Even without invoking the use of blackface makeup, this narrative highlights the ways in which racialized images are constructed in the white imagination, speaking to the various boundary negotiations that occur during the holiday. We are left with the easy sense that racial harmony is restored—injustice and offense are averted—all thanks to the cleverness of the "whitest kid" and his ability to make stereotyping comical. One must ask if this event was not so comical, would this respondent's writing be any more critical?

Dubious Curiosity/Questioning Support

Similar to the student who pondered whether the stereotypes evoked on Halloween were offensive or realistic, a number of students expressed dubious curiosity and questioning support for cross-racial costuming. Responses in this group reflect a sense of ambivalence, with students appearing less confident about the social permissibility of cross-racial dressing. However, critical thinking about doing so is often coupled with statements that invalidate the offensiveness of the practice, as the following quote demonstrates:

> We were all talking about what we should dress up as for Halloween. My boyfriend's friend Mike (22-year-old white male) is having a huge costume party and my boyfriend thought it would be fun to go as a black couple. I think it would be really fun and funny to do that but I'm afraid that black people would be offended. I don't get offended when people dress up as "Indians" for Halloween and I don't see why black people would care if we dress as black people. I asked my mom what she thought and she said we choose another costume because even though it's silly, black people probably would be offended and we shouldn't do things that could hurt someone's feelings intentionally. (Native American/white female)

Notably, as discussed in reference to generic/essentialist portrayals, this young woman and her boyfriend entertain no other defining feature to their costume, other than they go as a "black couple." While she recognizes such costumes might offend black people, she discredits their potential "silly" objections, particularly given her estimation that masquerading in this way would be both "really fun and funny," a clear return to the theme of the "fun factor" litmus test. Interestingly, we also note that relying on her identity as a racial minority, in one sense, led her to give pause in contemplating the issue, but in another sense served as validation for cross-racially dressing as a generic "black couple."

Collectively, the dubious curiosity of such responses reflects not a fundamental concern with the racism of cross-racial costuming, but rather a concern over whether the practice can pass the censors of political correctness in the Halloween context. They do not object to cross-racial costuming; it is a problem of others, and deciding whether to consider that becomes the primary focus, and the basis for the rhetorical questions posed.

Firm Objection—Antiracism Versus White Supremacy

Finally, we reach the other end of the pole—those responses grouped as firm objections to cross-racial costuming. For one student who posed a similar rhetorical question regarding cross-racial costuming offensiveness (albeit in a biracial frame) the answer was clear: blacks and whites dressing as the "other race" represented a way to "mock each other" (multiracial male). While his analysis represents a form of "equal opportunity racism" and neglects the stereotypical and highly degrading ways in which people of color are often portrayed by whites, it does represent a firm belief that the practice is offensive.

Given the disturbing abundance of negatively racialized incidents in our sample, it is important to acknowledge those students who expressed their own or detailed others' antiracist thinking regarding cross-racial costuming. Typically these students chose not to cross-racially costume, or to critically evaluate this practice based on beliefs that it is offensive and degrading to people of color. One of the most hard-lined excerpts was the following:

> I saw the most disturbing thing tonight. I went with a group of friends to a Halloween party. As we were leaving, I saw two white people, a male and a female, standing outside the other party who were dressed in blackface, as what I can only assume was their rendition of Jamaicans. I could do nothing but stand there with my mouth, literally, open. I was so shocked. I have never seen anything in person as horrifically blatantly racist and offensive as I found that to be. Who comes up with an idea like that? I don't know if they were doing it as a joke or what their costume purpose was, but I don't find that funny at all. (white female)

This student's objections are unequivocal, and while circumstances did not really allow for her to take antiracist action based on her beliefs, we might imagine that she would attempt to interrupt what is to her clearly racist, for instance, if a friend of hers were to consider cross-racially costuming. Unfortunately, while a number of white students expressed antiracist concerns about cross-racial costuming, only a few shared that they had verbally challenged others about offensive costumes. Because many of the writers were recounting incidents with friends, they often seemed compelled to excuse their comments and actions, and engage in diffuse, light challenges, which may or may not have been perceptible to those they were directed at, as the following quote illuminates:

> While my friend Greg was putting on black face paint for his costume, Luke made the comment that he looked like a 'scummy nigg' and that people are going to think he's trying to rob them . . . I didn't comment on it at the time . . . I couldn't forget about it all night, partly because I had this assignment on my mind when it occurred . . . I know that the reasoning behind his making such a comment was in trying to get a laugh out of the people who were present. Most of the people just gave him a dirty look and stared at him in silence . . . and I am sure that Luke realized how racist and stereotypical his statements were upon seeing the reactions of those who heard them. (white male)

This student has no difficulty recognizing these statements for what they were—"racist and stereotypical"—and indeed, it appears that the journal-writing project encouraged a deeper reflection on this incident than might ordinarily have occurred. However, rather than challenging his friend in a direct way, he remains concerned but verbally non-sanctioning. Criticism here is offered via dirty looks, stares, and silence—forms of challenge that may or may not actually reach the target and mark the comment or action as problematic. The social setting, which could have facilitated an antiracist deconstruction of what occurred, was instead transformed into a space where this group of white students, reluctant to lead any firmer confrontation, ended up avoiding any explicit challenge of the racist reproduction of stereotypes and white supremacy.

While expressed antiracism was the exception and not the rule among white students, students of color were more universal in their critique of cross-racial costuming, as well as in their willingness to challenge others, particularly when they observed highly stereotypical portrayals. It is important to give voice to the frustration and hurt they expressed, as well. One Latina woman skeptically attended a "ghetto party" with a black friend. As she detailed:

> When we arrived at the party we were shocked at what we saw. First, we did not see one black or Hispanic person. Blonde hair, blue-eyed kids were walking around with aluminum foil on their teeth, bandanas on their head, fur coats, big huge earrings, and shirts that said 'Project Chick' or 'Ghetto Fabulous.' . . . when I was younger my family was pretty poor and our living situation was very bad. We lived in what people refer to as the 'ghetto,' and it wasn't fun and it sure wasn't what those kids were portraying it to be. They were glamorizing it and at the same time almost making fun of it. My friend was insulted because this is how a lot of white people view black people and it is sad that this is true. (Hispanic/Latina female)

Another black woman wrote that after an initial amusement with the cross-racial costumes of white students she witnessed wore off, "something felt not right with me. I don't think it was the fact that white people were impersonating African Americans, but it was more of how they were impersonating them" (black female). Sadly, as has been documented, costumes portraying people of color rarely, if ever, deviate from the principle guide of stereotype, and as such, it is hard to imagine this woman ever experiencing a costume portrayal of her race that "felt right."

Collectively, these narratives reveal the boundary negotiations over deciding what is offensive and what is not. When stereotyping and race talk remain in the safe and slippery terrain of color-blind "now you see it now you don't" ideology, cross-racial costuming appears more acceptable. However, when events that have been more definitively deemed racist occur (e.g., dressing in blackface, using the "n-word"), a seeming contemporary racial relations line is crossed, and we find more frequent attempts at antiracist thinking and action by white students.

Conclusion

While Skal (2002) suggests that "tasteless" Halloween costumes might simply represent an extension of Halloween's historical pranking tradition, it is perhaps more fitting to draw on a different relic from Halloween's historical tradition—that of departed spirits returning to wreak mischief and even harm. As Bonilla-Silva (2003) documents, the societal norms of the post–Civil Rights era have disallowed the open expression of racial views. In this way, for many, Halloween has become a culturally tolerated, contemporary space for the racist "ghost" to be let out of the box. Indeed, our findings support the thesis that Halloween's combination of social license, ritual costuming and social setting make the holiday a uniquely constructive context for negative engagement of racial concepts and identities.

While our respondents reflect an oversampling and concomitant overrepresentation of data from the Southeast region of the U.S., nationwide marketing of racist costumes like "Vato Loco" and "Kung Fool," and local news stories and editorials documenting similar occurrences at universities around the nation suggest that we should not simply dismiss this as a "southern phenomenon." Additionally, even if this trend is ultimately revealed as uniquely "southern," that does not discount the need to analyze how it reinforces the racial order. We thus urge future research to investigate if and how such practices vary nationwide, and what such a variance might mean.

With respect to theorizing what activates the cross-racial costuming behavior of our respondents, it is useful to further draw upon the "rituals of rebellion" concept. Interestingly, although the Gluckman [1963] and Bakhtinian [Bakhtin 1981] frameworks should predict the ample use of cross-racial costuming among people of color, it is not immediately apparent that students of color use Halloween as an opportunity to create costume performances that subvert the racial and/or social hierarchy. Even in the very few cases where cross-racial costuming among respondents of color did occur, costumes were most frequently celebrity portrayals, and none appeared to pose an indictment of whiteness *per se* (as particularly opposed to the clear degradation of blackness revealed). Only one, the African American student said to be costuming as a Haitian refugee, attempted an explicit challenge, offering a quite critical commentary regarding the racial politics of immigration policy. We must recall, too, the more vocal antiracist critiques of students of color toward white cross-racial costuming. To be sure, the relatively small proportion of students of color in our sample limits our ability to fully explore this theme, and future research is needed to examine this phenomenon in greater depth.

In contrast, there does appear to be a unique, ritually rebellious form of performance that occurs among many white students. In the "colorblind" post–Civil Rights era, it has become commonplace for whites to express frustration and resentment toward color-conscious racial remediation programs, such as affirmative action (Feagin, 2000, 2006; Wellman, 1997). Both Bonilla-Silva (2003) and Wellman (1997) document the regularity with which whites employ anecdotal storylines regarding antiwhite discrimination and "reverse racism," despite the relative infrequency of credible, substantive, and supporting evidence. Similarly, many whites complain of the threat to free speech and censorship imposed by political and social correctness.

Although in truth white students occupy the dominant racial social identity group, we posit that many may entertain if not a sense of "oppression," at minimum a sense of normative restriction by a social code which prescribes "nonracist" frontstage presentations, and for which racialized Halloween "rituals of rebellion" afford some release. Recall, for example, one white student's praise of Halloween as "great" because it eliminates the need to worry about racial offense. For those whites who actively endorse the idea that whites are now victimized by the preferencing of people of color (e.g., in employment, admissions, etc.), Halloween may ironically signify a suspension of this imagined "hierarchy." Considered within the American socio-historical racial context, however, this white "ritual of rebellion" seems almost a harkening back to the Jim Crow period of more overt, often celebrated expressions of racism and white supremacy.

While some, like Skal (2002), may reduce the holiday engagement of racial concepts to a matter of simple Halloween "fun," this practice must be viewed within a greater framework.

Seemingly playful and innocuous cultural practices, such as cross-racial costuming, should be considered within the sociohistorical and ideological context of the society, as a reflection of dominant group values and doctrines (Wilkinson, 1974). We must put aside the "fun" of costumes, which can distract from the subtle and not-so-subtle messages conveyed about people of color, and recognize that costumes provide a format for engaging commentary on personal and social values (McDowell, 1985). Indeed, to render people into character pieces, they must already exist as characters in one's mind, and there are many social forces that drive our constructions of race and people of different racial groups toward such ends.

In revealing the ideological role that such costuming can play, and in light of our findings, particularly with respect to cross-racial costuming responses, we must also examine the needs left unfulfilled by contemporary approaches to multiculturalism and political correctness, some of which have become dogmatic. The confused critiques of many students reflect the ways in which we have become a society reproducing what Bonilla-Silva (2003) refers to as "racism without racists." He suggests that research on racism in this color-blind era may lead us away from the idea that mere education will lead to racial tolerance, to question rather what education actually does and does not do and for whom, as well as to the other conditions that may be required for true impact.

Indeed, as Johnson (1997) points out, the social reproduction of racism does not require people explicitly acting in racially hostile ways, but simply those who will uncritically acquiesce in the larger cultural order. While our data indeed reveal the explicit intentions of some students to degrade blackness through costume, the majority of white respondents actively suspended their criticisms or behaved in wholly uncritical ways. It is highly significant that regardless of intention, each of these response "types" share the outcome of reproducing stereotypical racist images, thereby supporting the racial social structure. Even among the minority of white students who journaled firm antiracist objections, few extended their internalized criticisms of cross-racial costuming to offer explicit challenges within their social groups, a social silence that, too, empowers the structure of racial dominance.

Rogers (2002) notes that while "Halloween is unquestionably a night of inversion," the holiday's context probably provides little substantial opportunity to actually challenge how society operates in a determined or sustained way—"At its best, Halloween functions as a transient form of social commentary or 'deep play'" (p. 137). With respect to race, we would argue that the holiday provides a context ripe for reinforcing existing racialist concepts. In particular, it provides an implicitly approved space for maintaining the privilege that whites have historically enjoyed, to define and caricature African Americans and other people of color in degraded and essentialist ways. At its worst, contemporary cross-racial costuming bores a track deep into history, intimately connecting itself to the ugly practice of American blackface minstrelsy. Ultimately, the white privilege to racially differentiate supports both material and ideological benefits and disadvantages built into the systemic racial structure. In the United States this system has deep historical roots and is well-formulated and ingrained into the everyday rhythms of life. As such, Halloween social commentary which engages race can hardly be described as transient, and actually reflects the dominant racist ideology, coupling contemporary imaging with racist conceptualizations as old as the country itself.

References

Bakhtin, M. (1981). *The dialogic imagination: Four essays.* Austin, TX: University of Texas Press.

Belk, R. W. (1994). Carnival, control and corporate culture in Halloween celebrations. In P. Santino (Ed.), *Halloween and other festivals of death and life* (pp. 105–132). Knoxville, TN: University of Tennessee Press.

Bonilla-Silva, E. (2003). *Racism without racists: Color-blind racism and the persistence of racial inequality in the United States.* Lanham, MD: Rowman and Littlefield.

Dundes, A. (1987). *Cracking jokes: Studies of sick humor cycles and stereotypes.* Berkeley, CA: Ten Speed Press.

Etzioni, A. (2000). Toward a theory of public ritual. *Sociological Theory, 18,* 44–59.

Feagin, J. (2000). *Racist America: Roots, current realities and future reparations.* New York: Routledge.

Feagin, J. R. (2006). *Systemic racism: A theory of oppression.* New York: Routledge.

Freud, S. (1960). *Jokes and their relations to the unconscious.* New York: W. W. Norton & Company, Inc.

Gluckman, M. (1963). *Order and rebellion in tribal Africa: Collected essays with an autobiographical introduction.* London: Cohen and West.

Goffman, E. (1959). *The presentation of self in everyday life.* New York: Anchor Books.

Grider, S. A. (1996). Conservatism and dynamism in the contemporary celebration of Halloween: Institutionalization, commercialization, gentrification. *Southern Folklore, 53,* 3–15.

Hua, V. (2002). Bucktoothed Halloween mask bites the dust. *The San Francisco Chronicle,* October 17. Retrieved June 1, 2005 (http://sfgate.com/cgi-bin/article.cgi?file=/chronicle/archive/2002/10/17/BU168521.DTL).

Johnson, A. G. (1997). *Power, privilege and difference.* New York: McGraw Hill.

Litwicki, E. M. (2000). *America's public holidays: 1865–1920.* Washington, DC: Smithsonian Institution Press.

The Macerich Company. (2005, September). *Shopping in America Halloween 2005: Shopper survey analysis.* Santa Monica, CA: August Partners, Inc.

Martin, K. A. (1998). Becoming a gendered body: Practices of preschools. *American Sociological Review, 63,* 494–511.

McDowell, J. (1985). Halloween costuming among young adults in Bloomington, Indiana: A local exotic. *Indiana Folklore and Oral History, 14,* 1–18.

Miller, K. A., Jasper, C. R., & Hill, D. R. (1991). Costume and the perception of identity and role. *Perceptual and Motor Skills, 72,* 807–813.

Miller, K. A., Jasper, C. R., & Hill, D. R. (1993). Dressing in costume and the use of alcohol, marijuana, and other drugs by college students. *Adolescence, 28,* 189–198.

Nelson, A. (2000). The pink dragon is female: Halloween costumes and gender markers. *Psychology of Women Quarterly, 24,* 137–144.

Ogletree, S. M., Denton, L., & Williams, S. W. (1993). Age and gender differences in children's Halloween costumes. *The Journal of Psychology, 127,* 633–637.

Picca, L. H., & Feagin, J. R. (forthcoming, expected April 2007). *Two-faced racism: Whites in the backstage and the frontstage.* New York: Routledge.

Pilgrim, D. (2001). New racist forms: Jim Crow in the 21st century. Retrieved August 28, 2004 (http://www.ferris.edu/jimcrow/newforms/).

Rogers, N. (2002). *Halloween: From pagan ritual to party night.* New York: Oxford University Press.

Santino, P. (1994). *Halloween and other festivals of death and life.* Knoxville, TN: University of Tennessee Press.

Simpson, D. (2003). White La. judge draws fire for costume." *The Associated Press,* November 10, Dateline: New Orleans, Domestic News. Retrieved June 5,2005. Available: LEXIS-NEXIS Academic Universe, News Wires.

Skal, D. J. (2002). *Death makes a holiday: A cultural history of Halloween.* New York: Bloomsbury.

Stone, G. P. (1962). Appearance and the self. In A. M. Rose (Ed.), *Human behavior and social processes: An interactionist approach* (pp. 86–118). Boston, MA: Houghton Mifflin Company.

Wellman, D. (1997). Minstrel shows, affirmative action talk and angry white men: Marking racial otherness in the 1990s. In R. Frankenberg (Ed.), *Displacing whiteness: Essays in social and cultural criticism* (pp. 311–331). Durham, NC: Duke University Press.

Wilkinson, D. (1974). Racial socialization through children's toys: A sociohistorical examination. *Journal of Black Studies, 5,* 96–109.

Yinger, J. M. (1977). Presidential address: Countercultures and social change. *American Sociological Review, 42,* 833–853.

CHAPTER 9

Invisibility in the Color-Blind Era*

Examining Legitimized Racism against Indigenous Peoples

Dwanna L. Robertson

In this essay, Dwanna L. Robertson argues that Native people have not experienced ***color-blind racism****, the form of racism that is more emblematic of the contemporary period. Instead, she contends that* ***indigenous people*** *have been and continue to be subjected to an overt form of racism that is more consistent with an earlier era of American history. Using interviews with forty-five Native people from twenty-nine tribes to illustrate her argument, she introduces a theory of* ***legitimized racism****.*

Questions to Consider

Most contemporary scholars of racial and ethnic relations tend to understand today's racism as color-blind. How does the experience of indigenous peoples challenge this conclusion? Is legitimized racism becoming more common in the contemporary period, or does color-blind racism continue to persist as the dominant form?

Source: Dwanna L. Robertson, "Invisibility in the Color-Blind Era: Examining Legitimized Racism against Indigenous Peoples," *The American Indian Quarterly*, Volume 39, Number 2, pages 113–153, University of Nebraska Press, 2015.

*Some text and accompanying endnotes have been omitted. Please consult the original source.

A few of the whites that I'm around make Indian jokes. . . . I've been called a basket weaver, blanket Indian, blanket ass, skin, breed, which I don't let bother me, you know. 'Cause I just look at the person that's doing the talking and the so-called name calling, and a lot of that shows ignorance, the way I look at it. I laugh at it and go on and try not to let it deter me.

—Will (Chickasaw)

Beginning in the mid-1990s, scholarship on the ideology of color-blind racism gained acceptance within the mainstream of the sociology of race in the United States. Scholars contend that after the US civil rights era, overtly racist acts generally gave way to color-blind (covert) racism in the maintenance of white privilege.[1] It became socially unacceptable to express blatant antagonism toward people of color.[2] Eduardo Bonilla-Silva explains that this shift allows whites to refute all culpability for the current racial oppression of minorities.[3] Indeed, color-blind racism enables whites to justify the current gaps in educational attainment, wages, chronic health disorders, and wealth, between them and everyone else, through the ideologies of individualism and culture without thought to historical context. Thus, the political and economic inequality of people of color becomes their own fault. Marginalized groups still experience inequality, but Bonilla-Silva argues that it is increasingly covert, institutionalized, and "void of direct racial terminology."[4]

Yet, this does not hold true for Indigenous Peoples in the United States.[5] Like other marginalized groups, Natives certainly experience the same covert mechanisms of color-blind racism that limit life opportunities. However, Natives still routinely experience *overt* racism in the form of racial epithets like "redskin," "injun," and "squaw" and horribly distorted depictions of Natives as mascots, reminiscent of the propaganda used against black, Irish, and Jewish people in the nineteenth and twentieth centuries. And this overt racism is *not* confined to hate groups but is visible in everyday discourse and throughout the media. Historically, Native Peoples were portrayed as savages, Native women as sexually permissive, and Native culture as engendering laziness.[6] Contemporary American Indians still live under the prevalence of Native misrepresentations in the media, archaic notions of Indianness, and the federal government's appropriation of "Indian" names and words as code for military purposes. Their oppression also becomes invisible in the very visible mechanism often used to reproduce racial inequality—through informal communication—with statements like being an "Indian-giver," sitting "Indian-style," learning to count through the "one little, two little, three little Indians" song, or getting together to "pow wow" over a business idea. This racialization goes beyond words and pictures.

While minstrel shows have long been castigated as racist, American children are socialized into *playing* Indian. Columbus Day celebrations, Halloween costumes, and Thanksgiving reenactments stereotype Indigenous Peoples as a much-distorted, monolithic culture. That is, other groups assert racial power over Indigenous Peoples by relegating indigeneity (complex understandings and representations of Indigenous identity) to racist archetypes and cultural caricatures. Playing Indian is actually an American tradition with its roots in colonial times.[7] During the Boston Tea Party, when colonists rebelled against British rule by boarding English ships and throwing the tea into the harbor, they were dressed up in blankets and feathers and had black soot and grease on their faces, pretending to be Indians.[8] Playing Indian is racist—in no way different from wearing blackface or participating in minstrel shows—because it collapses distinct cultures into one stereotypical racialized group. Even worse, because playing Indian is deemed socially acceptable, any other racial or ethnic group may now participate—*without recognizing the inherent racism in doing so.*

Historians, philosophers, and Indigenous media document that Indigenous Americans cope daily with overtly racist language, images, and behaviors without social recourse. I argue that racism against American Indians has been normalized and institutionally legitimized, thereby rendering it invisible. To legitimize is to make legitimate, that is, to justify, reason, or rationalize in accordance with established or accepted patterns and standards.[9] In other words, the institutions that shape social norms—those seen as social authorities—reproduce symbolic racial violence against American Indians through legal structures, public education locations, consumer products, sports associations, and so on. More than 235 years of federal Indian policy have systematically racialized Indians as inferior, incapable, and uncivilized. Indeed, anti-Indian terminology, imagery, and behavior have become legitimated to such a degree that other marginalized people accept them as nonracist and readily maintain and participate in them.[10]

This work is guided by two questions: With such blatant racist acts, what accounts for the lack of attention by contemporary race theory to anti-Indian rhetoric and overt racism against Indigenous Peoples in the United States? How do Native people negotiate these persistent racist stereotypes and cultural appropriation in their daily lives? Using an Indigenous epistemology and a qualitative approach, I examine what I call the phenomenon of "legitimized racism." I analyze its impact and provide narratives of confrontations of legitimized racism through conversations with forty-five Indigenous people.

Methodology

My research sample consisted of forty-five Native people over the age of eighteen from twenty-nine distinct tribes. I recruited participants between June 2009 and May 2013. Purposive sampling was necessary because the participants needed to identify *ethnically* as Indigenous. Snowballing (a method of expanding the sample by asking one participant to recommend others for interviewing) helped maintain a relational quality. It is protocol to be introduced by established community members into a new community. I recruited Natives who wanted the opportunity to speak directly to contemporary issues of racism. Conversations that included reflection, sharing stories, and dialogue that lasted between one and two hours were the primary methods of the research. I asked participants about their general demographic and tribal information, and then we discussed American Indian identity issues concerning stereotyping and cultural appropriation. I used open-ended questions and occasional prompts to keep the conversations flowing, once established. Conversations included relating experiences of racism and reactions to visual media and images. I also followed up with additional questions and clarifications with each individual.

The Phenomenon of Legitimized Racism

Over 500 years of Western dominance and 235 years of federal Indian policy have shaped public perception of Indigenous Peoples. Because American Indians are framed within the mainstream media as simply a racialized group—one without cultural ethnicity or political autonomy—society remains unaware of our multiple identity statuses.[86] Historical racist discourses directly link to the contemporary racism experienced by Natives in the United States and the current invisibility of Indigenous Peoples in academic literature. Overt racism against Indians has become legitimized through centuries of racist discourse created and perpetuated by hegemonic power structures. Indeed, American institutions—the government, economy, education, media, and family—legitimize a stereotypical and racialized understanding of Indigenous Peoples. But legitimized racism is not just about the production of racial images, attitudes, or identities. It is not between individuals. Rather, it is the foundation of power that cradles the dialectical interaction of human agency and social structure within the racial state. Below I describe my theoretical framework of legitimized racism, which builds on color-blind racism, systemic racism, internalized oppression, and tribal critical race theory.[87]

I conceptualize legitimized racism with particular assumptions and definitions. I provide common racial frames or racial stories to illustrate each point. First, racism is present, of course. Racism rationalizes that all the members of a racialized group have the same inherent abilities, characteristics, morals, and qualities. For example, a common myth is that Indians cannot metabolize liquor like other races. Therefore, if they drink, they will become alcoholics. This assumes inherent biological differences between racialized groups rather than critically assessing how historical trauma and socioeconomic deprivation might affect rates of alcoholism for Indigenous Peoples. Systemic racism is also present. Systemic racism is an ideology that attaches common meanings, representations, and racial stories to groups that become embedded within social institutions that serve to justify the superordination of white people and the subordination of nonwhite people.[88] Color-blind racism exists in phrases like "to the victor goes the spoils." This phrase is seemingly nonracial, but in the context of the Western invasion of North America, it positions Europeans and white Americans as strategic or lucky. It avoids the acknowledgment of the othering of Indigenous Peoples and their subsequent murder, rape, and abuse at the hands of white people.

To legitimize is to make something seem right or reasonable. Accordingly, racist actions, discourses, or institutions often seem ordinary and without malice. Dressing up to play Indian with "war paint" for Halloween is harmless. Sports teams with racist names and mascots are honoring Indians. Culturally appropriating sacred objects like tipis and headdresses is all in good fun. Legitimized racism is so common that it is accepted as the norm, as just part of the American landscape. Any attempt to change it meets excessive resistance. Empathy is not easily forthcoming, even from other marginalized groups, because they also participate in it. Individuals who protest are accused of being too sensitive or simply silly. Groups who protest are charged with being subversive and acting in their own interests and not for the good of society.[89]

The contemporary consequences of legitimized racism stem from the historically racist discourse (established within the context of imperialism, white supremacy, and colonization) that perpetuates the mythical righteousness of the murder, rape, and enslavement of Indigenous Peoples.[90] My conversations with participants reveal persistent legitimized racism in four thematic bundles: (1) lazy, drunk, casino-rich Indians, (2) dirty squaw or sexy maiden, (3) playing Indian, and (4) celebrating genocide. I include narratives from conversations with participants, and to balance respect and reciprocity, I add my own perspective and share my reflections. It is within these four themes that we can recognize the pervasiveness of legitimized racism.

Lazy, Drunk, Casino-Rich Indians

Natives constantly battle negative conceptions of their culture in entertainment, the media, and sports teams' mascots that are often combined with words that serve to create inferiority (e.g., redskins, savages, squaw, etc.). Misconceptions about Indigenous Peoples are created, produced, and reproduced in stereotypes and racial bias.[91] During every conversation, participants and I discussed typical stereotypes about Natives. Participants described three specific tropes they experience constantly: the lazy Indian, the drunk Indian, and the casino-rich Indian. Through public discourse, these distorted images of Natives have become ingrained, accepted, and legitimized to such a degree that society maintains and reproduces them without question. Tom, a forty-year-old Penobscot man, discusses how people openly disparage Indians, even at his job with the state of Maine.

> I hear things like: "Show me an Indian, I'll show you a drunk Indian." "Indians are lazy." We won't get jobs because we get everything for free. They think we all get casino money and government entitlements. But I still have to work, and I can't even drink a beer without people throwing stereotypes around. I don't feel bad at all getting in someone's face when they wanna make fun of my heritage and stuff. Even today, some people I work with at the State will say stuff. For some reason, they think it's acceptable to run down Native people. But they wouldn't dare say anything about African American people. That's something I wish would change. [They should realize] that hey, Natives are just like everybody else, so we should be respected just like everybody else. I remember a colleague talking about how his neighbors are trashy people because they ain't nothing but no-good Indians. And that upset me. I told that person, "Look, there's a lot of no-good white people too."

For more than five years, Tom worked at a prison before taking his current position as a parole officer. He shared with me that prisoners commonly called him "chief" and "Geronimo" because "those guys tried to get to everybody." Whereas he had no expectations for social politeness from the inmates, Tom was very disappointed by his colleagues. Tom emphasized how easily non-Native people repeated derogatory statements about Indigenous people in his presence, even after he transferred to a different job, but he felt that he must speak up. Tom disrupted the cycle of stereotype reproduction by confronting the assumptions.

Brayboy explains that white supremacy provides the basis for the inherent racism of common discourses by non-Natives that all Indians get entitlements from the federal government (e.g., free money, houses, and college educations).[93] Contrary to popular belief, especially among non-Natives, American Indians did not simply relinquish their rights to lands, waters, and other natural resources. The federal government pledged through laws and treaties to compensate for land exchanges accomplished through the forced removal of tribal nations from their original homelands. Unfortunately, recompense is commonly expressed as "benefits." This term—benefits—implies giving assistance, subsidy, or even charity rather than deserved reimbursement. Few understand the complexity of federal Indian policy eras, which included forced assimilation and required federally defined authenticity measures for individuals and tribes, boarding schools, and scientific racism.[94] But by framing the obligatory and promised compensation by the US government as merely "benefits" perpetuates the idea of Native dependency rather than tribal sovereignty, resulting in internalized oppression.[95]

White supremacy also undergirds the common portrayal of Indians as lazy drunks who have never had to work for anything. [One respondent] willingly admitted that alcoholism and poverty plague Native people but expresses exasperation that other people think that the circumstances of poverty on reservations speak for all Indians. Indeed, he and others exercise their agency by presenting a counterdiscourse that Indians are "just ordinary people." . . . In addition to the lazy, drunk, casino-rich Indian tropes, Indigenous women also contend with the binary construct of sexy Indian maiden or dirty Indian squaw.

Dirty Squaw or Sexy Maiden

Birthed through the correspondence of Columbus and his shipmates, the racial stereotype of Indigenous women as naïve or childlike but also savage and sexually deviant is alive and well today.[96] Sixteen women participants discussed their experiences of being sexualized and exoticized by non-Native boys and men. Almost all of them experienced it as early as the first stages of puberty. Maggie, a middle-aged Maliseet woman, discusses the trauma of puberty as a Native girl:

> As I got into puberty, white boys seemed to have some kind of idea that I was "wild" and would be more willing to have sex with them. . . . Boys would grab me and say stuff and call me "Pocahontas." They didn't treat other [white] girls on their street that way.

Maggie understood early that she was considered different from the other girls by the boys in her neighborhood. She bore the stigma of the sexualized Indian maiden in the personification of Matoaka (Pocahontas), the daughter of Algonquin chief Powhatan.[97] Much is made of her relationship with Captain John Smith. However, at the time of Smith's capture by Powhatan's men, Matoaka would have been eleven years old. The treatment of young Native girls bears great resemblance to the sexualized historical myth of Pocahontas—the idea that Indigenous women are highly sexualized, act wild, like to be held captive, and become sexually active at earlier ages than other racial groups of women. Conversely, Native women who do not fit the ideal of the sexualized "Pocahontas" then fall into the category of the dirty squaw.

The squaw trope is an example of what Johnson describes as "savagism discourses," which perpetuate an anti-Indian rhetoric and an anti-Indian sentiment in contemporary society.[98] From its origins as an Iroquois word, *otsiskwa*, "squaw" means vagina or female sexual parts.[99] For some Native women, squaw might imply dirty woman; for others, whore; and for even others, squaw might imply both. Debra Merskin, who argues that only non-Indians find neutrality in the word "squaw," provides a list of the different meanings for numerous tribes, none good.[100] For some tribes, it means prostitute, whore, or dirty woman. As a child and teenager, Eva remembers experiencing extreme prejudice numerous times:

> My dad grew up on a reservation in [the Northwest]. And we would visit every summer. When I was little I remember that there was a lot of racism around there. So there would be a lot of, you know, white kids who I think would just model the behavior that their parents taught them. I remember being pushed in the pool before, called squaw or dirty squaw. But I also remember [hanging out] with a close friend of mine and her friend once, and because I was darker skinned I was accused of being dirty. Because when you're darker, obviously on your elbows and your knees you have darker skin and she's like, "Why are you so dirty? Why don't you clean yourself?" Or whatever, and I was like, "Whoa, this is the way I was made and this is me or whatever."

Cornel D. Pewewardy argues that children "develop racial awareness at an early age, perhaps as early as three or four years old," and non-Indian children perpetuate negative stereotypes and derogatory images toward Indian children.[101] These children have been prevented from developing authentic, healthy attitudes about Indians. In this case, Eva experienced being stereotyped as a "dirty" squaw by way of being female. Pewewardy warns that Native children exposed to constant stereotyping and belittling of their cultures "grow into adults who feel and act inferior to other people."[102]

Even the knowledge about the meaning of squaw can become a weapon by which to inflict emotional and mental violence against Indigenous women. Indeed, the common use of the word "squaw" results in low self-esteem and vulnerability to symbolic and physical violence for Native women.[103]

According to Mikhail Bakhtin, particular words and phrases spoken are a "two-sided" act that lacks neutrality and indeed works to "articulate an individual's beliefs operating as a form of disclosure."[106] Both the motivation and the message are constructed between the sender and the receiver. Once the source of power is identified in any social interaction, we can work to disrupt it. Rather than remain voiceless, we [can speak] out against the oppressiveness of the language.

Playing Indian

In addition to denigrating stereotypes, legitimized racism masks the demeaning and harmful savage discourses and acts of playing Indian. Curt, a Seminole man who works in Washington, DC, takes issue with savage discourse, stating, "Too many use written words attributed to Natives, like scalp, massacre, tomahawk, etc. This contributes to the developing knowledge of children and adult readers, which continues the acceptance of the repression of Native cultures and values. And it denigrates all Natives." Curt's solution to the perpetuation of racist stereotypes and the subsequent racism is simple: we must stop writing these words out of context. I argue that we must also stop playing Indian.

Every participant indicated that they recognize the prevalent savage discourse in today's society. A middle-aged Pawnee city worker, Kent, confided to me almost in a whisper that "our cultures" have been distorted through the media:

> Lot of people don't see us as we are. Hollywood has damned us all. Speaking a certain kind of language, walking a certain way, dressing a certain way. You know, we got to

> have long black hair, and big bridged noses, and carry a tomahawk and a knife. *Wantin' to scalp every white man and rape every white woman.* You know, that's what they got to portray. And there's no truth in none of that. I don't wanna watch that mess, but I'd have to stop watchin' TV or movies to stay away from it. It's everywhere.

Kent ignores distorted media representations of indigeneity in order to watch the same entertainment as the rest of society. Kent's admission about Hollywood stereotypes seemed obvious to me. But I recognized that he may be just coming into this realization. Not all Native (or non-Native) people are consciously aware of the prevalence of bias against Indigenous Peoples.[107] Changes in consciousness do not occur in a linear fashion but rather through dialogic interactions and understanding the struggle to take back our humanity.[108] For example, several participants mentioned that they dislike mascots but admit buying products that appropriate culture, often unknowingly. Natalie, a thirty-year-old Otoe woman, confessed that she has bought products that stereotype Natives and had to rethink that "hundred-dollar Coach purse with the chevron pattern" because she's learning what it means to live fully by Indigenous principles. I think back to the early 1990s and the first car I bought, a used red Jeep Cherokee. I confess to Natalie. We commiserate about our situational internalized oppression but finish with the affirmation that decolonization is a process.

All the participants express the understanding that we are all interconnected; therefore, the oppression of any group creates an imbalance in the social world. Sadly, playing Indian is still as popular as ever in marketing imagery and popular culture.[109] We see this in the surge of "cowboy and Indian" parties on college campuses, Columbus Day celebrations, Halloween costume parties, and Thanksgiving Day plays and parades. Playing Indian is also fashionable, with actors, models, musicians, and other entertainers donning headdresses or other costumes without consequence to their careers.[110] After all, if Indians no longer exist, then no harm comes from creating exaggerated imitations of clothing and ceremonial regalia. Natalie finds the pervasiveness of cultural appropriation despicable, telling me:

> I see this all the time on campus. Groups of girls with hipster fashion, you know, with fringe on skirts and boots and braids in their hair. It sexualizes Native women so much, like we just dress provocatively on purpose. We have to sit back and watch them make fun of us. It's shameful. It's hurtful. I'm disgusted. I almost want this craze to be over, this trend of Indian designs. It sounds mean, but I wish they'd go pick on another culture.

As the passage indicates, Natalie believes that society is inherently racist. If not her culture, another culture will be the target. She describes the immense pain she feels just by walking onto the college campus. Natalie recognizes that these items do not replicate her culture, but that seems to make it worse for her. But Natalie expresses real hope, saying, "Social media is helping out. It's getting the word out that it's not right. It's also helped me understand what it means to be Indian and the responsibility that goes with it."

I agree with Natalie about social media. In the last few years, Indigenous forums like Beyond Buckskin and Native Appropriations are responsible for shining light on blatantly overt acts of racism.[111] They certainly brought Paul Frank Industries' (a children's clothing line sold by multiple retailers such as Target and Macy's) recent "Dream Catchin' pow wow" party to national attention. On September 5, 2012, Disney and Nickelodeon stars and hundreds of young guests, many of color, were encouraged to don glow-in-the-dark war paint and feather headbands, hold plastic bows and arrows and tomahawks, and let out "war whoops" to play Indian. Julius the Monkey, Paul Frank's popular character, was pictured wearing a headdress. Even more egregious, considering the history of alcoholism in Native communities, the Paul Frank party had an open bar for adults with a sign that read: "Pow wow and have a drink now!"[112] As social, spiritual, and traditional events, powwows prohibit the consumption of alcohol; yet, alcoholic drinks named Rain Dance Refresher, Dream Catcher, and the Neon Teepee were served.[113] Paul Frank Industries ultimately issued an apology.[114]

Because of the prevalence of legitimized racism, participants express anger toward other Natives who claim to find no harm in stereotypes and playing Indian. But by recognizing that Indigenous Americans have been subjected to the same cultural ignorance of mainstream media, we can understand our internalization and resist participating in our own oppression.[115] That is the very nature of legitimized racism—it uses its power to convince Indigenous people to believe what is said about them. It underlies the ease by which other people portray Indians as stuck in the historical past, which makes us invisible today. Awareness of legitimized racism compels Native and non-Native people to break the silence that it depends upon to continue.

Celebrating Genocide

Finally, all the participants complained that Americans would rather believe that Columbus discovered America and proved that the world was not flat, even though these historical myths have been debunked.[116] Columbus's and his shipmates' atrocious record of enslavement, murder, and rape is relatively unknown to the public and scholars alike. The United States still celebrates Columbus as a hero every October amid the protests of Indigenous activists.[117] The nation's capital, Washington, the District of Columbia, was named after George Washington and Columbus. The American Indian Movement released a press statement on October 6, 2000, that compares Columbus Day to a holiday celebrating Adolf Hitler with parades in Jewish communities:

> Columbus was the beginning of the American holocaust, ethnic cleansing characterized by murder, torture, raping, pillaging, robbery, slavery, kidnapping, and forced removals of Indian people from their homelands.... We say that to celebrate the legacy of this murderer is an affront to all Indian peoples, and others who truly understand this history....

It was striking that participants complained repeatedly that Americans did not want to know the truth about Columbus. Doris, an Abenaki woman with a college degree, reflects on her frustration with America's obsession with Columbus:

DLR: What bothers you the most about Columbus Day?

DORIS: What doesn't? It's just another opportunity to remind Natives that their homelands have been basically, um, destroyed, really. I understand that people were taught lies in school, but now we know better, so why can't we teach better? Why are the grade school kids still learning lies? I mean, I was taught the same lies. The difference is that my family always told me that I can't trust white people's history books. [Laughs hard.] I don't mean any offense by that, really. It's just that what I read and what my grandmother said didn't line up. I asked questions.

Doris, like most of the other participants, recognized that holidays like Columbus Day are emotional triggers for Natives. Maria Yellow Horse Brave Heart and Lemyra M. DeBruyn argue that American Indians suffer from historical trauma and disenfranchised grief because of the massive, recurring trauma of Western colonialism, especially since "for American Indians, the United States is the perpetrator of our holocaust."[118] Indeed, no other country offered sanctuary for American Indians. Consequently, celebrating Columbus, a person who represents genocide for Natives, does not register within American consciousness as wrong or harmful. Jason Edward Black argues that America transformed "conquest into a language of care and concern, which helped form a benevolent identity concerning Native relations."[119] Because of the historical racist discourse of the myth of Columbus, the US public celebrates the myth of the discovery and development of an uninhabited place. An unwillingness to critically assess the legitimized racism of Columbus Day reproduces the trauma generation after generation. However, many participants resist through decolonizing tactics like speaking out and participating in anti–Columbus Day events. Above all, the survival of many diverse Native cultures speaks to the power of counternarratives that Indigenous Peoples deploy against legitimized racism.

Conclusion

Within this essay, I ask what accounts for the lack of attention by contemporary race theory to anti-Indian rhetoric and overt racism against Indigenous Peoples in the United States. This study shows that Natives experience legitimized racism through national holidays, racist labels and mascots for sports teams, the pervasiveness of playing Indian, and, ultimately, a lack of academic or social awareness of this continuing social injustice. I find that contemporary racist views of American Indians link directly to the colonial legacy of racist discourses that stereotyped Indians as uncivilized beasts.[120] This allows the American public to evoke false memories of European colonizers and American settlers as seekers of justice and benevolent providers. Historical myths of savagery commonly legitimized the conquest, enslavement, and mass murder of Indigenous Peoples by colonial powers in their greed for more land and all the resources therein. Robert A. Williams argues that "Indian savagery is deeply embedded in the American racial imagination."[121] John Chaney, Amanda Burke, and Edward Burkley find empirical evidence that shows that non-Native people find no distinction between mascots and actual Native Peoples.[122]

My theory of "legitimized racism" is like a clear jar (society) that contains different forms of racism (social beliefs and interactions) that are, in fact, overt but become invisible within the other contents of the jar (social norms, institutions, and systems). Therefore, individuals, communities, and academia struggle to see/understand/confront anti-Indian terminology, imagery, and behavior that have become legitimized to such a degree that other marginalized people accept them as nonracist and readily maintain and participate in them. To be sure, legitimized racism is not just about the production or maintenance of racial images, attitudes, or identities. It is not between individuals or individuals and groups. Rather, legitimized racism is the foundation of power that holds the dialectical interaction of human agency and social structure. That is, when multilayered, intersectional, and dynamic racism becomes legitimized (normalized, institutionalized, internalized, and systemic), it becomes simultaneously overt and invisible within social norms and social institutions.

Legitimized racism also explains the minimal attention non-Native mainstream race scholars have paid to the racialized discourses utilized over the last five hundred years against Indigenous Peoples in the United States. Racist practices toward Indigenous Peoples are hardly recognized publicly and even less often by non-Native academics. Furthermore, the failure to acknowledge and study the phenomenon of legitimized racism obstructs our understanding of the reproduction of racialized injustice, theoretically and empirically.

Significantly, the phenomenon of legitimized racism is not exclusive to Indigenous Peoples because it facilitates the means by which we appropriate and condense cultures, like the monolithic caricature of South Asian culture by way of "Bollywood" parties, dancing, and impersonations. Legitimized racism demonstrates the ease with which Arab Americans were vilified after 9/11—after all, we had a "legitimate" fear of Islamic extremists, correct? It mattered not that most Arab Peoples and Americans who have an Arab ancestry do not fall within that category. Legitimized racism sanctions the common public discourse that undocumented Mexicans take away American jobs or they receive copious amounts of public benefits that are paid for by "real" Americans, which is compounded by the tendency in the United States to racialize most Hispanic/Latin Peoples as Mexican.[128] Lastly, the American national identity possesses a normative whiteness that is accomplished through the public discourse of legitimized racism.[129]

Legitimized racism is so embedded within American society that it becomes invisible. By including Indigenous Peoples, we see that racism still operates as a legitimate force within American society not only for us, but for other groups. Without this understanding, social injustice grows within the invisibility of legitimized racism.

Notes

1. For a comprehensive treatment, see Eduardo Bonilla-Silva, *White Supremacy and Racism in the Post–Civil Rights Era* (Boulder CO: L. Rienner, 2001); Eduardo Bonilla-Silva, *Racism without Racists: Color-Blind Racism and the Persistence of Racial Inequality in the United States*, 2nd ed. (Lanham MD: Rowman & Littlefield, 2006); Leslie G. Carr, *"Color-Blind" Racism* (Thousand Oaks: Sage Publications, 1997); Joe R. Feagin, *Systemic Racism: A Theory of Oppression* (New York: Routledge, 2006); Feagin, *The White Racial Frame: Centuries of Racial Framing and Counter-Framing* (New York: Routledge, 2010).

2. Racist expressions by hate groups are the exception to the rule.

3. Bonilla-Silva, *White Supremacy and Racism.*

4. Bonilla-Silva, *White Supremacy and Racism*, 48.

5. Passionate debate persists in academia over the most useful term(s) to describe Indigenous Peoples of the United States. On the one hand, some find that the usage of "Indian" as an identifier reifies an inferior, racialized label; see Yellow Bird, "Cowboys and Indians: Toys of Genocide, Icons of Colonialism," 33–48. On the other hand, it is the most commonly used term among Native People in general. See the survey by Clyde Tucker, Brian Kojetin, and Roderick Harrison, "A Statistical Analysis of the CPS Supplement on Race and Ethnic Origin," Bureau of the Census, May 1995, 5, https://www.census.gov/prod/2/gen/96arc/ivatuck.pdf.

I respect the opposing views, but, having lived in Indian Country most c
and other Native folk use the term "Indian" on a daily basis. For the pu
I use the term "American Indian" because of its usage at the US Census B
"Indian" because it is the legal term used within federal Indian policy. I us
and "Indigenous" interchangeably, as my preferences. I capitalize the *P* in
throughout the article to indicate the sovereignty of different nations, pe
cultures that practiced self-determination long before imperialistic colonizat
that is not reliant on the will of modern nation-states to recognize them as [illegible]ous Peoples is equivalent to First Nations, American Indians, Native Americans, Europeans, Asians, and so on.

6. For example, see Martha Elizabeth Hodes, *Sex, Love, Race: Crossing Boundaries in North American History* (New York: New York University Press, 1999); Frederick E. Hoxie, *A Final Promise: The Campaign to Assimilate the Indians, 1880–1920* (Lincoln: University of Nebraska Press, 1984); Francis Paul Prucha, *Handbook for Research in American History: A Guide to Bibliographies and Other Reference Works*, 2nd ed. (Lincoln: University of Nebraska Press, 1994); Francis Paul Prucha, *Indian Policy in the United States: Historical Essays* (Lincoln: University of Nebraska Press, 1981).

7. Philip Joseph Deloria, *Playing Indian* (New Haven: Yale University Press, 1998).

8. Deloria, *Playing Indian.*

9. *Merriam-Webster's Collegiate Dictionary*, 11th ed. (Springfield MA: Merriam-Webster, Inc., 2003).

10. It is important to make clear what this work does not do. Natives may self-ascribe a racial identity of Indian and retain an ethnic identity through one or more tribal affiliations. Even so, they generally see themselves as members of distinct Indigenous cultural communities that possess particular cultural materials, like language, customs, and knowledge. Without strong, culturally driven explanations of Indigenous identity, this work does not address whether people who have been racialized as Indians actually see themselves as racialized objects or as sovereign beings. Rather, it assumes that racialized discourse of stereotypes and racialized appropriation of Indigenous cultures exist and deeply impact the lives of Indigenous Peoples. Therefore, this work has less to do with how Native people see themselves through the multiplicity of cultural lenses and more about how they navigate and adapt to the racial lens by which the dominant society sees and positions them.

87. Bonilla-Silva, *Racism without Racists*; Brayboy, "Toward a Tribal Critical Race Theory"; Joe R. Feagin, *Systemic Racism: A Theory of Oppression* (New York: Routledge, 2006); Paulo Freire, *Pedagogy of the Oppressed*, 30th anniversary ed. (New York: Continuum International Publishing Group, 2000).

88. Bonilla-Silva, *Racism without Racists*; Feagin, *Systemic Racism.*

89. Deloria, *We Talk, You Listen.*

90. Brayboy, "Toward a Tribal Critical Race Theory."

91. Michael K. Green, "Images of Native Americans in Advertising: Some Moral Issues," *Journal of Business Ethics* 12, no. 4 (1993): 323–30; Laurence M. Hauptman, *Tribes & Tribulations: Misconceptions about American Indians and Their Histories* (Albuquerque: University of New Mexico Press, 1995); Yellow Bird, "Cowboys and Indians."

92. Dwanna L. Robertson, "The Myth of Indian Casino Riches," *Indian Country Today Media Network*, June 23, 2012, http://indiancountrytodaymedianetwork.com/opinion/the-myth-of-indian-casino-riches-119957.

93. Brayboy, "Toward a Tribal Critical Race Theory," 432.

94. Robertson, "A Necessary Evil."

95. Internalized oppression results when people internalize the stereotypes and negative myths communicated about their group by the oppressive regime. See Freire, *Pedagogy of the Oppressed.*

96. Indigenous women do not escape from the innocent or wild discourse created during the four voyages of Columbus. Michele de Cuneo, Columbus's aristocratic shipmate, writes a passage that systematically describes the kidnapping, subsequent rape, and sexual slavery of one of the Carib Indian women. This is especially disturbing when we consider the current propensity for physical violence and sexual assault against Native women. The US Justice Department reports that more than 80 percent of rapes on Indian homelands are committed by non-Native men. Indigenous women are victims of violent crime at three and one-half times the national average, and one in three Native women will be raped in her lifetime. The Justice Department also believes these numbers are severely underreported, estimating that 70 percent of sexual assaults are never reported due to a distrust of police.

97. Alden T. Vaughn, "Pocahontas," in *The Reader's Companion to American History*, ed. Eric Foner and John A. Garraty (Boston: Houghton-Mifflin, 1991).

98. Johnson, "From the Tomahawk Chop."

99. Tom Porter, *And Grandma Said: Iroquois Teachings as Passed Down through the Oral Tradition*, ed. Lesley Forrester (Philadelphia: Xlibris, 2008), 137–39.

100. Debra Merskin, "The S-Word: Discourse, Stereotypes, and the American Indian Woman," *Howard Journal of Communications* 21, no. 4 (2010): 345–66.

101. Cornel D. Pewewardy, "Playing Indian at Halftime: The Controversy over American Indian Mascots, Logos, and Nicknames in School-Related Events," *Clearing House* 77, no. 5 (2004): 182.

102. Pewewardy, "Playing Indian at Halftime."

103. Merskin, "The S-Word."

104. The sexualized Indian maiden was popularized in literature as far back as 1893 with Karl May's novel *Winnetou* and institutionalized with the Land o' Lakes advertising mascot in 1928.

105. Merskin, "The S-Word."

106. As quoted in Merskin, "The S-Word," 349–50.

107. Lisa M. Poupart, "Silenced Voices: Patriarchy, Cultural Imperialism, and Marginalized Others" (PhD diss., Arizona State University, 1996); Lisa M. Poupart, "The Familiar Face of Genocide: Internalized Oppression among American Indians," *Hypatia* 18, no. 2 (2003): 86–100.

108. Freire, *Pedagogy of the Oppressed.*

109. Deloria, *Playing Indian*; Victoria E. Sanchez, *Buying into Racism: American Indian Product Icons in the American Marketplace* (Norman: University of Oklahoma Press, 2012), 153–68.

110. Actor Drew Barrymore, Andre Benjamin of Outkast (music group), actor/musician Jared Leto, actor Mary Kate Olsen, Gwen Stefani of No Doubt (music group), fashion designer Tom Ford, Victoria's Secret model Karlie Kloss, pop singer Ke$ha, comedian/actor Amy Poehler, and many, many others have all been photographed wearing stereotypical headdresses. Drew Barrymore was also wearing a Budweiser apron and flashing a peace sign in the photograph. Type the words "celebrity in Native headdress" or "cowboy and Indian party" into any search engine for thousands of images.

113. Images of the Paul Frank debacle can be found here: http://www.zimbio.com/pictures/cx_JBwva-Is/Paul+Frank+Fashion+s+Night+Out/browse.

114. Paul Frank Industries not only apologized but also collaborated with four Native artists from different tribes to create products that represented each person's culture. These items were offered in August 2013, with proceeds going to a yet-to-be-revealed Indigenous cause or scholarship. For more information, visit http://nativeappropriations.com/2013/06/the-paul-frank-x-native-designers-collaboration-is-here.html.

115. Devon A. Mihesuah, *Indigenous American Women: Decolonization, Empowerment, Activism* (Lincoln: University of Nebraska Press, 2003), 58.

116. Wilford, *The Mysterious History.*

117. Timothy Kubal, *Cultural Movements and Collective Memory: Christopher Columbus and the Rewriting of the National Origin Myth* (New York: Palgrave Macmillan, 2008).

118. Maria Yellow Horse Brave Heart and Lemyra M. DeBruyn, "The American Indian Holocaust: Healing Historical Unresolved Grief," *American Indian and Alaska Native Mental Health Research* 8, no. 2 (January 1998): 61.

119. Jason Edward Black, "U.S. Governmental and Native Voices in the Nineteenth Century: Rhetoric in the Removal and Allotment of American Indians" (PhD diss., University of Maryland, College Park, 2006), 87.

120. Renee Ann Cramer, "The Common Sense of Anti-Indian Racism: Reactions to Mashantucket Pequot Success in Gaming and Acknowledgment," *Law & Social Inquiry* 31, no. 2 (2006): 313–41.

121. Williams, "'The Savage as the Wolf,'" 12.

122. John Chaney, Amanda Burke, and Edward Burkley, "Do American Indian Mascots = American Indian People? Examining Implicit Bias towards American Indian People and American Indian Mascots," *American Indian and Alaska Native Mental Health Research* 18, no. 1 (2011): 42–60.

CHAPTER 10

Who Are We?*

Producing Group Identity through Everyday Practices of Conflict and Discourse

Jennifer A. Jones

Multiracials have the flexibility to opt out of ***multiracial identity****, to shift identities depending on context; they are characterized by in-group* ***diversity****. Given this fluid space, Jennifer Jones asks, "How do multiracials come to see themselves as a collective?" She describes an empirical example of collectivization processes at work. Specifically, she observed the process of collective identity building through ethnographic research in a* ***mixed-race*** *student-run organization. This case study indicates that group identity formation is a negotiated process involving strategies to achieve a sense of belonging and cohesion. She shows that over time, by using experiences of social conflict to construct shared experiences, the members of this mixed-race organization developed collective identity. In so doing, their experience underscores how collective identity development is socially constructed and how micropractices are essential components of group formation.*

Source: Adapted from Jennifer A. Jones, "Who Are We? Producing Group Identity through Everyday Practices of Conflict and Discourse," *Sociological Perspectives*, Volume 52, Issue 2, pages 139–161, SAGE Publications, Inc, 2011.

*Endnotes have been omitted. Please consult the original source.

Questions to Consider

Do you think that people who self-identify as multiracial are significantly different from those who self-identify as monoracial? Is identifying as multiracial or monoracial always up to the individual? What factors might influence an individual or group members to identify monoracially or multiracially?

In the early 1990s, advocates for mixed-race identity engaged in an effort to insert a mixed-race category into the U.S. census, resulting in the decision to include the "two or more races" option in 2000. This period was also marked by an explosion of research on multiracials, situating multiracials as distinct from other racial groups by focusing on their sense of fluidity and contextual racial identity, and explaining how this positioning impacts their individual development (Harris and Sim 2002; Renn 2004).

While this research is important and groundbreaking, few scholars of multiracial identity posit the collective as their object of analysis, and even fewer investigate group identity formation. Moreover, a sense of groupness among multiracials has either been ignored or presupposed. Thus, theories of mixed-race identity are largely based on analyses of individual identity, to the exclusion of a careful analysis of group behavior. And by focusing on individuals, scholars either naturalize or ignore the micro-practices groups engage in to construct collective identity and give identity categories meaning. As a result, despite the growth of literature in this field, we still know little about the process of group formation among multiracials.

Nevertheless, the legacy of the census movement produced a network of community multiracial organizations that are now being taken over by multiracial youth. Therefore, in the wake of achieving recognition, young multiracials face a paradox of organizing around the concept of multiraciality, without a collective sense of how the category of multiracial translates to group identity. Rather than take the category of "multiracial" for granted, this article contributes to the study of group formation and identity-based organizing by examining the micro-practices that produce collective multiracial identity.

To investigate how this process might unfold, I conducted an ethnographic case study with a student organization, University Mixed, in the aftermath of its decision to transition from a Hapa-oriented, to an inclusive mixed-raced organization. "Hapa" is a Hawaiian term that has been adopted in the mainland United States to refer to partial Asian/Pacific Islander ancestry, often specifically indicating Asian and white ancestry. This group is one of the fastest growing multiracial populations in the United States and represents a historically and socially specific biracial group (Jones and Smith 2001:8). My study documents the difficulty the group experienced in moving from what I argue is a distinct Hapa identity, to what the group perceived as the amorphous category of "mixed."

Hurdles to Collective Identity

Collective identity is formed by producing *new* meaning from an *existing* knowledge set of political, social, economic, and cultural experiences shared by multiple persons (Omi and Winant 1994). Unlike monoracial categories, which are in many ways externally imposed (Brown 1998), the literature on multiracial identity indicates that it is perceived as optional. Thus, while multiracials may achieve a sense of full racial and ethnic identity individually as a result of these characteristics, the literature suggests that this distinctive ability to opt out or switch identities depending on context is problematic for collectivization (Harris and Sim 2002; Kilson 2001; Renn 2004; Xie and Goyette 1997). Moreover, this fluid sense of racial identity results in an ambiguous sense of group boundaries, creating an obstacle to building the stable "community or category," that Polletta and Jasper (2001) see as central to collective identity, as multiracials may float in and out of such identities depending on context.

The level of diversity within multiraciality may also become problematic when we evaluate it in terms of constructing the collective. Representing a vast range of ethnic and racial combinations, multiracials frequently have difficulty ascertaining what is actually shared about their mixed-race experience. The literature on identity formation among multiracials documents fluidity across diverse racial and ethnic origins (Doyle and Kao 2004; Renn 2004; Root 1996; Williams 1996). Even in recent analyses of the one-drop rule and black/white racial identities (Daniel 1996; Davis 1991; Korgen 1999; Rockquemore, Laszloffy, and Noveske 2006), black/white multiracials frequently assert integrative, plural, and blended identities despite the apparent constraints of phenotype (Davis 1991:135–36). Due to these complications, Williams (2006:34) highlights that while individuals may embrace these characteristics, the development of a "panmultiracial" identity is unlikely, not only because monoracials lack the ability to lump together diverse multiracials but also because individual multiracials, even within the same family, can choose distinct racial identities. Likewise, the social movement literature suggests that weak shared identities cause organizations to fail. Indeed, what is distinctive about multiracials—their fluidity and diversity—also serves to simultaneously disrupt their sense of collectivity. This disconnect suggests that while perhaps salient as a category, it would produce, at best, weak shared identities.

In addition to these obstacles, multiracials encounter a pervasive, day-to-day pressure to identify with existing monoracial designations, creating an additional hurdle to group cohesion. As highlighted in Smith and Moore's (2000) work on intraracial diversity among blacks, for example, multiracials with black ancestry feel pressure to identify with the monoracial majority. In their sample, multiracials reported feeling that monoracial blacks demanded they show loyalty to their blackness in order to avoid alienation and exclusion.

Opposition to mixed identity has also come from race-based associations fearing the dilution of their political power. The National Association for the Advancement of Colored People (NAACP), The Asian American Legal Defense and Education Fund, and The National Council of La Raza (NCLR) each expressed opposition to the 2000 census proposal, viewing it as a selfish political venture that would injure existing minority communities (Moscoso 1996; Puente 1996; Schevitz 2001). Citing a desire to protect the enforcement of civil rights legislation and political representation, these organizations encouraged people to choose only one race option.

We might theorize diversity, fluidity, and opposition as obstacles to what Espiritu (1992:15) calls "conceptual groupness"—that is, how groups come to see themselves as mixed through individual behaviors and attitudes. Moreover, she notes that though they are often mutually productive processes, conceptual groupness is foundational to "organizational groupness"—that is, the institutionalization of mixed consciousness. What this study seeks to show is that the organizational dimension of groupness can emerge, even when significant barriers to conceptual groupness persist (Espiritu 1992).

Due to these complexities, though we might expect to find that mixed-race as a category may remain salient, at present, we cannot account for a sense of groupness. Nevertheless, I find that multiracial collectives can still cohere and that their significant weaknesses do not necessarily lead to organizational failure. Contrary to what we might expect from the literature, rather than collapse under the pressures of intergroup conflict and internal weakness, I found that in the case of University Mixed, intergroup conflict provided an opportunity to unite.

Group Identity Formation within the Context of Fluidity, Diversity, and Choice

As Wendy Brown (1998) theorizes, collective identity is often developed as the result of external forces and the collective's response to them. Coser (1956) first applied this analysis more comprehensively to the maintenance and formation of social groups, theorizing that group conflict (either real or perceived) produces internal cohesion. Both Coser and Brown found this to be particularly true among minority groups forged through the experience of being outsiders and under threat. In Coser's analysis, social conflict allows for group consolidation and the centralization necessary for social action. Nonetheless, Coser (1956:93) cautions that "if a group is lacking basic consensus, outside threat leads not to increased cohesion, but to general apathy, and the group is consequently threatened with disintegration."

In order to develop this basic consensus, identity-focused organizations must go through a process of creating shared meanings to build collective identity (Melucci 1989; Polletta and Jasper 2001; Schwalbe and Mason-Schrock 1996). These meanings are a foundation from which groups can define boundaries and a sense of belonging, binding individuals together and giving them the tools to engage with external threats. While little cohesion currently exists among multiracials, historically, some social movements have had success overcoming similar obstacles. Examples include panethnic groups of the 1970s and 1980s that transcended the complexity of diversity and fluidity to build social movements (Espiritu 1992; Josephy, Nagel, and Johnson 1999; Nagel 1995; 2003). Acts of violence against Chinese-Americans who were misidentified as Japanese-Americans in the 1980s were used as a point of unity against violence that threatened the entire Asian-American community (Espiritu 1992). In particular, Asian panethnic movements used conflict to cohere as a racial group, while simultaneously supporting the maintenance of individuals' national identities (Benford and Snow 2000; Espiritu 1992).

Similarly stirred by political shifts, Josephy et al. (1999) found that collective ethnic renewal among American Indians was motivated largely by demographic shifts and relocation policies that created both political and economic incentives to identify as American Indian. Inspired by surges in ethnic activism throughout the 1960s, Josephy et al. (1999) argue that the Red Power movement used basic cultural links among American Indians to forge a collective, while simultaneously positioning the federal government as the enemy. In so doing, it inspired a surge in cultural panethnicity, as well as built a renewed politics around longstanding grievances against the federal government. As theorized by Kaplan and Liu (2000), these groups were able to build an active and coherent social movement founded on a core of shared identities, experiences, and stigma, strengthened by social conflict to produce collective identity and political action. By doing so, these groups successfully engaged in a process that reconfigured diversity and fluidity into strengths that in turn created the cohesion necessary for collective identity.

Drawing from these studies, I conducted a case study of one multiracial organization, within a larger context of multiracial organizing, and its capacity for collective identity formation. I argue that the development of collective identity among members of University Mixed is facilitated by constructing and framing distinct shared experiences in order to transcend diversity and build internal consensus around group meaning and identity. Moreover, I find that social conflict is the key mechanism through which identity formation processes are facilitated and provides the basis through which even the most fragile of collectives can cohere. In this way, University Mixed was able to simultaneously produce conceptual and organizational groupness, creating a framework in which the dynamic emergence of one serves to reinforce the other.

Site and Methods

This study is based on one academic year of ethnographic fieldwork in a mixed-race student organization I call University Mixed and the regional mixed-race organization network of which it was a part. University Mixed is a campus-oriented organization that was originally a chapter of the California-based umbrella organization Hapa Focus Group, initiated in 1992. At the time of observation, beginning in 2004, the parent organization had recently disbanded and forced all of its chapters to cut ties. Founded on the same campus under study, the disbanding of Hapa Focus Group meant that this campus satellite was suddenly on its own to determine its mission and future. Initiated by some of the members of the campus Hapa Focus Group, the organization decided to change its focus to address the general multiracial population, transitioning from Hapa Focus Group to University Mixed. My entrance into the site coincided with this transition.

As Hapa Focus Group, it articulated its mission as being "dedicated to enriching the lives of Asian Pacific Islanders of mixed heritage and developing communities that value diversity." While this mission is specific and practical in stating both its target audience and its goals, University Mixed's mission was remarkably less clear. "University Mixed promotes multiculturalism and establishes unity of purpose by building community; outreach through leadership & service to the campus and greater community; promoting awareness and education through dialogue of multiethnic/multicultural issues; ultimately, fostering personal growth and development as well as empowerment." Though simultaneously vague and ambitious, the new mission pointed to a major shift in purpose, including situating members within a general multiracial context. It was during this effort that I observed the process of collective identity formation in the face of multiple challenges.

University Mixed is located at a large, public, majority–minority university in which organizing and group formation are very popular. This university is also situated in a relatively diverse metropolitan community, which is also majority–minority. At the beginning of the observation period, approximately 85 percent of the University Mixed membership was Hapa. In part, this was not surprising, given the large population of Asians in the region, as well as the important role Hapa Focus Group played in the area. Thus, in the fall semester, ten out of the eleven board members were of Asian/white ancestry, and seven out of the eleven were women. However, there were also significant numbers of other multiracials on campus, and if University Mixed were to more accurately reflect the campus population, it would have to make substantial changes. During the spring semester, seven of the nine board members were of Asian/white ancestry, and six of the nine board members were women. One had no Asian ancestry, as did only a handful of the 100 members at large, signifying a barely discernable shift over the course of the semester in group dynamics, despite the dramatic change in mission. This conflict between ideas and practice provided a rich forum to interrogate the meaning and purpose of mixed-race identification.

Who Are We? The Fall Semester

University Mixed began the academic year focused on what appeared to be an impossible task—to convert the organization into one that embraced and advocated mixed-race identity. While board members were committed to such a transition, they were also overwhelmed and uncertain as to how to make this happen. For all of them, in varying degrees, members perceived diversity and fluidity as insurmountable challenges. In an interview early on in this study, I asked one of my informants, Catherine, a board member: "Do you think it's possible for mixed people to have some sort of collective consciousness on some level?"

> "There has to be. I mean, I feel like there has to be. I of course don't really know what mixed—I can't really say what mixed-race issues are, I can't say what the goal of the mixed-race community should be concretely, but I *know* that there's this collective experience and collective understanding that needs to be addressed. That we shouldn't feel like we don't have experiences or that we don't have a reason to be collective about something, you know?"

It was clear that despite their personal understandings of mixedness, as a group, they did not know how to accommodate a fluid and diverse population, and so they began as a group without boundaries. On a weekly basis, sitting around a group member's living room, a member would suggest they talk about the group name and logo. Regularly lasting for half the meeting, this discussion would be plagued with uncertainty about whom University

Mixed represents. Eventually, this conversation had to be moved to an online discussion board because it was taking up too much time in meetings. In these conversations, the board discussed including those who have been transracially adopted, individuals who belong to multiple heritage families, as well as those who simply view themselves as multicultural. This all-encompassing view of mixedness made it extremely difficult for the board to come up with a logo and name that could represent everyone. The idea that having more than one racial heritage might be sufficient criteria for membership was never considered.

Accordingly, while it posed no problem to their personal identity development, the fluidity and diversity within mixedness often made members uncomfortable and unable to conceive of themselves as a group, despite their agreement to do so. Particularly in the first semester, members often spoke nostalgically about the use of Hapa as specific and meaningful, indicating that "multiracial" lacked any such possibility. This put many members, regardless of whether they were themselves Hapa, in the position of not knowing how to represent mixedness publicly. In an early discussion regarding a group activity, members' frustration at their inability to translate multiraciality in a useful and consistent way showed up or expressed itself. In preparation for one of the first general meetings of the semester, Catherine suggested an activity. "Let's do the ice-breaker we did last year where you go around the room and say, 'I love my Hapa who . . . ' and then everyone who that statement is true for steps into the circle. And everyone takes turns at saying something." Everyone on the board thought this was a good idea because it could get the group energy up and usually got people excited to meet each other. They hit a stumbling block, however, on how to formulate the sentence. Nobody came up with a word to replace Hapa. They spent several minutes trying to figure out how to rephrase the sentence, offering "multiracial," "mulatto," "mutt," and finally, after much back and forth, they reluctantly agreed upon the term "mixed friend."

Similar issues of articulating a name or way of representing themselves frequently resurfaced in relation to how members perceived themselves as a group. Their fear of being distanced from the name Hapa created a sense of distress for them as an organization and impeded their ability to generate meaning and cohesiveness around mixedness. For three weeks they debated what to call themselves and then moved the conversation to a group listserv because they could not agree on how to best represent themselves as a group. In a board meeting, one member, James, a senior, noted that they needed to figure out "who their audience is," followed by a discussion about whether non-mixed people would be alienated from a group that calls itself mixed and whether or not it matters. Along with the ongoing controversy regarding who it was and who it wanted to be, in that first semester, University Mixed gained few new members, only one of whom was not Hapa. Despite continuing to recruit members in the same way as in the past, board members continued to attribute the lack of growth to the loss of the Hapa Focus Group name, fearing that they lost support, recognition, and most importantly, meaning. As John, a twenty-one-year-old senior, noted:

> "I think having Hapa is really important to expressing yourself. Part of it might be living out here [on the West Coast], but I don't have to explain Hapa. People understand it, they know its meaning. It's me, and I really like having that word to describe myself. I'm a little concerned now that we are this big group and with different issues being represented."

University Mixed began its first semester as a multiracial organization unable, if not resistant, to articulate anything coherent about multiraciality as a category, perceiving the problems of diversity and fluidity as insurmountable obstacles, and feeling weak and disjointed as a group. The lack of a significant demographic change was largely irrelevant to the theoretical and definitional dilemma of making sense of mixed as a category. Nonetheless, University Mixed was ultimately able to gain traction and make considerable movement toward collective identity. The following section describes this process.

The Collectivization Process: The Spring Semester

Over the course of the year, changes began to emerge and University Mixed began to slowly shape the communal aspects of its members' multiracial experience. By constructing discourses around multiracial experiences, building collectivity in response to conflict, and drawing from existing identity-building strategies, University Mixed was able to move toward its goal of collective identity.

The leadership of University Mixed began to develop a sense of group identity by using what they felt was most resonant about their own multiracial experience to create unifying multiracial discourses within the group and across networks. These experiences included their own racial fluidity, the feeling of being exoticized, and being perceived as embodying racial utopia. While these experiences were important components of the specificity of members' sense of collective mixed-race identity, I focus on one shared experience that emerged for University Mixed—social marginalization by monoracials.

Framing Situations: Social Marginality and the Conflict with Yellowmag

Approximately one year prior to University Mixed's transition to a mixed-race club in 2003, *Yellowmag*, a well-known Asian-American campus monthly, published an antagonistic editorial about Hapa Focus Group. The article was written by Janet, an editor of Asian and white ancestry. Janet claimed to have done investigative work by attending a Hapa Focus Group potluck and professed to have felt "the hypersexual, fetishizing gaze" from other Hapas, which she understood as indicative of those who took pride in Hapa identity. Janet's article recounted her experience in the club meeting: "imagine my surprise upon meeting a bunch of Hapa people, of whom I expected to know better, at this club, at which everyone was just basically checking each other out!" Throughout the article she made the claim that Hapas generally, and the Hapa Focus Group in particular, did not have any interests beyond fetishizing each other. She used the club and its planned charity date auction fundraiser as a platform to critique what she viewed as the inherently problematic relations of interracial relationships.

Despite the group's considerable outrage and tentative plans to draft a response, only Catherine—board events chair at the time and later vice president—sent a response, and it was ignored by both the group and *Yellowmag*. The group did nothing to follow up on the issue. Instead, it cancelled the date auction as a defensive response to avoid additional scrutiny. In the framework of the Hapa Focus Group, it framed this issue as an interpersonal one. Though annoyed, its sense of groupness was unaffected by the articles.

One year later, in the midst of the transition, Janet wrote another article in *Yellowmag* critiquing the methods and motivations of University Mixed in the wake of its transition from the Hapa Focus Group to University Mixed. She concluded her piece by writing: "I still adamantly stand by my initial thoughts and reaction to this club, which I feel, as do many students and friends of mine, had relied on problematic tropes of fetishism and exoticism." University Mixed was clear that, this time, it would not allow her comments to stand. At the last board meeting of the semester, members angrily discussed both articles. The board huddled around a few copies of the issue that Catherine and Euna had brought. Catherine was so angry she appeared to be fighting back tears when she commented:

> "It was a really mean article, I was really hurt, and she never talked to us about her issues with us or anything. She just showed up one day, and then this article appeared. . . . I was hurt because it was in an Asian magazine, and it seemed like another example of rejection from the Asian community. She should have suggested a meeting, dialogue. . . ."

Catherine was the first to articulate the conflict as racialized rather than interpersonal, seeing Janet's article as a form of collusion with the monoracial "oppressor" and noting that the comments came from the self-described voice of the Asian-American community—from which they have often felt alienated—through the voice of a Hapa editor.

Although Catherine again agreed to take on the responsibility of drafting a response over the break, the timing of the article and lack of motivation on the part of many members (several of whom were retiring from their leadership positions) could have easily led to a weak response, similar to the previous year.

In the spring semester, however, the articles in *Yellowmag* remained on the University Mixed radar. At the first January board meeting of the semester, Euna noted in the meeting agenda that Catherine would be presenting her proposed letter to *Yellowmag* for the approval of the club. When the item came up for discussion, Catherine read the letter she had written aloud.

> "Dear [editor-in-chief],
>
> I am writing in response to Janet's article in the December edition of *Yellowmag*. As the co-events chair of University Mixed, and as a person who identifies as Hapa, I found her article self-serving, poorly written, and completely unprofessional. Janet clearly did no other research than reading our website. The quote she provides is from a president of a different club, with a different mission statement than our own. She never spoke with anyone in our club while writing this article, nor did she express any desire in interviewing us. This is not the first time Janet has misrepresented our club. The fact that Janet herself is Hapa does not give her the right to speak for all other Hapa people or Hapa organizations. Her article is particularly troublesome for me because it appears in an Asian-American magazine. As a mixed-race Chinese-American, I have personally faced the most discrimination from the Asian community. Although

perhaps not intentional, it seems as if *Yellowmag* is expressing its anti-Hapa sentiment through its token Hapa journalist. Please assure University Mixed and myself that this is in fact not the case by never again publishing articles that are not factual and unresearched. We find that this is an issue of journalistic integrity."

The letter was approved unanimously by the board, and the issue with *Yellowmag* remained on the agenda for every weekly board meeting for the next two months while they awaited a response. Moreover, members solicited letters of support from other student and national mixed-race organizations against anti-mixed sentiment at the annual regional mixed students' conference, which was held the weekend following the letter submission, even though the letter focused on its "anti-Hapa sentiment." Agenda items throughout the semester included reports on feedback from other groups in its network and brainstorming additional ways of publicizing the incident on campus. Rather than a smattering of individual responses, the tone shifted to a collective one. The lack of a solid base from which to draw on in response could have, theoretically, further damaged its already shaky organizational foundation. Instead, the threat members felt in this instance produced group strength. This time, *Yellowmag* did print Catherine's letter in its March issue. However, the editorial response continued to push the buttons of University Mixed by stating "I know Catherine does not represent the entirety of the University Mixed's membership. But reading through her reductive sob story of discrimination from Asians does not help your club."

While the membership of University Mixed frequently confronted similar issues of hostility within the context of their own lives, the articles in *Yellowmag* created an opportunity for them to develop discourses around these issues as a group. As a result, the articles became points of cohesion for University Mixed, providing a site for members to construct boundaries and highlight marginality. At a March board meeting, during which the members decided what to do about the printed editorial response, Catherine remarked:

"And you know this in particular is offensive after the [mixed-race student] conference thing, and we explicitly discussed the whole coalition building thing, and it's just like, great! The Asian-American magazine on campus f–ing hates us. . . . Because they printed this, it makes them seem as if they [Asians] are all cool with this."

Euna: "I know this seems like a personal attack, but this could have easily been directed at any of us. You know what I mean? . . . Yeah, I don't know, the API [Asian Pacific Islander] community is shunning us. (*Thinks for a second*) At our next general meeting, let's discuss the differences across mixed-race communities, with "Mixed-race in the Asian community, mixed-race in the black community, in the white community, in the Latino community. I think that would be good. That's something we need to do."

While the focus of the articles was relations between Hapas and Asian-Americans, members discussed the issues they raised as shared by all multiracials. Members could have easily cast this as a problem between Hapas and the Asian-American community, or even just this magazine. Instead, they connected it to the shared experiences they had been discussing all semester—experiencing mixedness as outsiders to monoracial identity. Through the process of constructing the event as emblematic of a general sense of conflict with and exclusion from monoracial groups, I argue that University Mixed used this incident as a rallying point for group formation, during which it came to see itself as a distinguishable minority group, racialized, maligned, and subject to identity-based discrimination. Moreover, the fact that this was the only real and sustained instance of conflict with other groups suggests that collectivization does not require sustained conflict from various sources. Rather, one key conflict can be sufficient in providing the elements necessary to cohere.

The group strengthened its framing of this conflict as an issue that impacted all mixed-race persons by reaching out to other mixed-race groups in its network and asking them to write letters of support in its effort to get a response from the editorial board of *Yellowmag*. The group was successful in these efforts and was able to get letters from several organizations, including two representatives from national umbrella organizations. This effort did not extend to campus monoracial groups, though they did call for a general boycott of the newspaper. This outreach provided additional support in framing itself as being maligned as a mixed-race organization, and these strategic efforts suggested a key turning point in its efforts toward collective identity formation.

As this issue carried on throughout the spring semester, it provided numerous platforms for the membership to address concerns of marginalization from monoracial communities in an increasingly clear and cohesive manner. University Mixed was able to construct an "oppressor" to galvanize its members' feelings of collectivity and to frame it as a shared oppressive experience around which all multiracial members could rally. In this way, it simultaneously achieved conceptual and organizational groupness along with some material successes. Several multiracial groups sent letters of support to University Mixed and voiced their concerns to *Yellowmag*. Despite *Yellowmag*'s refusal to take disciplinary action, Janet resigned from the staff and wrote a letter of apology to the group. While it was unable to convince the *Yellowmag* staff of its position, University Mixed was pleased with the outcome, feeling that it had been heard and that its relationships with other mixed organizations were stronger.

As the year progressed, University Mixed's members began to think and talk about themselves differently, moving toward a more collective understanding of self that made embracing diversity within the category less problematic. After a mid-spring meeting during which several of the general members and board members watched clips from *Just Black*, a documentary of interviews with multiracials of partial black ancestry, the group was able to engage in a discussion about the meaning of being mixed.

> Euna: "Is there going to come a time where *we* can just be what we are? You know what I mean? If we can just be, biracial? And where we are always just representing, being of dual heritage, you know? It sounds funny now, because this is just chapter two [of the multiracial movement], but I mean, instead of identifying with, I'm Asian now, when I'm with Asian people that will come out, or when I'm with African-Americans, that side will come out. . . . But why, when I'm with that group, can't I acknowledge that I'm still Asian, you know what I mean? Do people feel like they've reached that point, where you just are who you are, or do you kind of play the race game, or whatnot?"
>
> Michelle: "I feel like for the most part, people take in your appearance, and at some level, you are always biracial, because you can't be like oh, I'm Asian, oh I'm white, or this or that."

The members agreed with member Michelle, a junior and mixed-race Latina and Asian. While their individual multiple heritages were important, they lived not as distinct parts but as mixed-race, and that was something they shared, regardless of their different backgrounds. The emphasis on "we" (as multiracials) marks a significant shift in meaning around mixed identity for the group, moving from confusion to clarity in terms of what it means to collectively identify as mixed.

Completing the Transition

In the year following this study, there were substantive organizational changes. In follow-up interviews, University Mixed reported that it had three new board members and several new general members who were not Hapa. It incorporated new modes of outreach activities, including involvement with other non-Asian-identity-based organizations; built stronger and more extensive relationships with other mixed-race organizations; and co-sponsored a conference on mixed-race activism. It engaged in a public awareness campaign in which it invited students to participate in a photo board by posting Polaroids of themselves and writing down their racial backgrounds, as well as engage in a discussion about race. Combined with this effort was a bone marrow registration drive, in part because members learned that minorities, especially those of mixed backgrounds, are underrepresented in the registry. It worked with national mixed organizations on political campaigns around mixed-race adoption and data reporting in schools. In a brief period of time, they appeared to have fully embraced their new group identity as mixed. The leadership of University Mixed expressed that they had emerged from a difficult transition and proudly noted that the group had moved toward becoming a mixed-race organization.

Implications for Collective Identity Formation

In analyzing the case of University Mixed, the hurdles of fluidity, diversity, and hostility created a situation in which the prospect of building collective identity was not presupposed. Though many racial and ethnic organizations have found ways to cohere, even multiracial scholars have been dubious about whether multiracial individuals would develop any form of collective identity, let alone collective action. This study provides an empirical example of collective identity formation and meaning-making in process, showing that these are not necessarily impossible or protracted tasks, even when there appeared to be so little *there* there. Instead, in framing themselves as minorities and engaging in a form of consciousness-raising around their common experiences, they were able to identify a baseline of common experiences around which they could build a collective identity. In so doing, we learn from University Mixed that collective identity among multiracials can actually be realized and institutionalized in a relatively short period of time, particularly when bolstered by social conflict.

Although this study cannot speak to the politicization of multiracials generally, this group's assertion of themselves as minorities and subsequent efforts to engage more political issues suggests they understand the deeply political nature of race and reject (at least at the collective level) efforts to position them as a race buffer between minorities and whites. Indeed, in the aftermath of Ward Connerly's efforts in 2003 to pass Proposition 54, known as the Racial Privacy Initiative, University Mixed and other organizations in the West Coast Network wrote letters and participated in conference calls and discussions with the media during which they rejected persisting arguments that these types of efforts would be a pathway to a colorblind society. Decisions such as these, in which they distanced themselves from conservative activists, as well as a minority of older mixed-race organizations, highlight University Mixed's and other's organizational race politics that acknowledge race as a technology of stratification, both in terms of creating it and redressing it.

While this article examines only one case study, it suggests that, by moving from investigating identity construction among multiracials at the individual level, to theorizing about the entire social structure, as the existing literature does, we miss crucial insights into how groups construct identities and their choices for doing so. Thus, we are left ill-equipped to analyze how these efforts can shape the terrain for political mobilization. I propose that conducting more studies that focus on the micro-practices and interactions that produce racial meanings prior to the development of identity politics can help us better predict and understand the frames that make identity-based political action possible.

References

Benford, Robert and David Snow. 2000. "Framing Processes and Social Movements: An Overview and Assessment." *The Annual Review of Sociology* 26:611–39.

Brown, Wendy. 1998. "Wounded Attachments: Late Modern Oppositional Political Formations." Pp. 448–74 in *Feminism, the Public and the Private*, edited by J. B. Landes. New York: Oxford University Press.

Coser, Lewis A. 1956. *The Functions of Social Conflict*. New York: The Free Press.

Daniel, G. Reginald. 1996. "Black and White Identity in the New Millennium: Unsevering the Ties That Bind." Pp. 121–39 in *The Multiracial Experience: Racial Borders as the New Frontier*, edited by M. P. P. Root. Thousand Oaks, CA: Sage Publications.

Davis, F. James. 1991. *Who Is Black? One Nation's Definition*. University Park, PA: The Pennsylvania State University Press.

Doyle, Jamie Mihoko and Grace Kao. 2005. "'Multiracial' Today, But 'What' Tomorrow? The Malleability of Racial Identification over Time." Paper presented at the 2005 Meetings of the Population Association of America, Philadelphia, PA.

Espiritu, Yen Le. 1992. *Asian American Panethnicity: Bridging Institutions and Identities*. Philadelphia, PA: Temple University Press.

Harris, David R. and Jeremiah Sim. 2002. "Who Is Multiracial? Assessing the Complexity of Lived Race." *American Sociological Review* 67:614–27.

Jones, Nicholas and Amy S. Smith. 2001. "The Two or More Races Population: 2000," edited by U.S. Census Bureau. Washington, DC: U.S. Census Bureau.

Josephy, Alvin M., Joane Nagel, and Troy Johnson. 1999. *Red Power: The American Indian's Fight for Freedom*. Lincoln, NE: University of Nebraska Press.

Kaplan, Howard B. and Xiaoru Liu. 2000. "Social Movements as a Collective Coping with Spoiled Personal Identities: Intimations from a Panel Study of Changes in the Life Course between

Adolescence and Adulthood." Pp. 215–38 in *Self, Identity and Social Movements*, edited by S. Stryker, T. J. Owens, and R. White. Minneapolis, MN: University of Minnesota Press.

Kilson, Marion. 2001. *Claiming Place: Biracial Young Adults of the Post–Civil Rights Era.* Westport, CT: Greenwood Publishing.

Korgen, Kathleen Odell. 1999. *From Black to Biracial: Transforming Racial Identity among Americans.* Westport, CT: Praeger.

Melucci, Alberto. 1989. *Nomads of the Present: Social Movement and Identity Needs in Contemporary Society*, edited by J. Keane and P. Mier. Philadelphia, PA: Temple University Press.

Moscoso, Eunice. 1996. "Push for Multiracial Category Sparks Demonstration." *The Atlanta Journal-Constitution*, July 20, p. A10.

Nagel, Joane. 1995. "American Indian Ethnic Renewal: Politics and the Resurgence of Identity." *American Sociological Review* 60:947–65.

———. 2003. *Race, Ethnicity, and Sexuality: Intimate Intersections, Forbidden Frontiers.* New York: Oxford University Press.

Omi, Michael and Howard Winant. 1994. *Racial Formation in the United States: From the 1960s to the 1990s.* New York: Routledge.

Polletta, Francesca and James M. Jasper. 2001. "Collective Identity and Social Movements." *Annual Review of Sociology* 27:283–305.

Puente, Maria. 1996. "Multiracial Families Want Identity Respected." *USA Today*, January 2, p. A2.

Renn, Kristen A. 2004. *Mixed-Race Students in College: The Ecology of Race, Identity and Community on Campus.* Albany, NY: State University of New York Press.

Rockquemore, Kerry Ann, Tracey Laszloffy, and Julia Noveske. 2006. "It All Starts at Home: Racial Socialization in Multiracial Families." Pp. 203–16 in *Mixed Messages: Multiracial Identities in the 'Color-Blind' Era*, edited by D. L. Brunsma. Boulder, CO: Lynne Rienner Publishers.

Root, Maria P. P. 1992. *Racially Mixed People in America.* Newbury Park, CA: Sage.

———. 1996. *The Multiracial Experience: Racial Borders as the New Frontier.* Thousand Oaks, CA: Sage Publications.

Schevitz, Tanya. 2001. "Multiracial Census Form Poses Dilemma: Organizations Fear Dilution of Numbers." *The San Francisco Chronicle*, March 11, pp. A1, A7.

Schwalbe, Michael L. and Douglas Mason-Schrock. 1996. "Identity Work as Group Process." *Advances in Group Processes* 13:113–47.

Smith, Sandra and Mignon Moore. 2000. "Intraracial Diversity and Relations among African-Americans: Closeness among Black Students at a Predominantly White University." *The American Journal of Sociology* 106(1):1–39.

Williams, Kim M. 2006. *Mark One or More: Civil Rights in Multiracial America.* Ann Arbor, MI: University of Michigan Press.

Williams, Teresa Kay. 1996. "Race as a Process: Reassessing the What Are You? Encounters of Biracial Individuals." Pp. 191–210 in *The Multiracial Experience: Racial Borders as the New Frontier*, edited by M. P. P. Root. Thousand Oaks, CA: Sage Publications.

Xie, Yu and Kimberly Goyette. 1997. "The Racial Identification of Biracial Children with One Asian Parent: Evidence from the 1990 Census." *Social Forces* 76(2):547–70.

CHAPTER 11

Illegality as a Source of Solidarity and Tension in Latino Families*

Leisy J. Abrego

Despite the common assumption that immigration laws target only ***undocumented immigrants****, illegality intimately and deeply affects a larger proportion of immigrants and Latinas/os. Based on in-depth interviews and participant observation with documented and undocumented Latina/o immigrants from El Salvador, Guatemala, and Mexico in Los Angeles over a ten-year period (2001–2010), Leisy Abrego examines how* ***illegality*** *encompasses all members of a family, even when only one person or a few people are categorized as undocumented or only temporarily protected. Illegality can create tension for people whose disadvantages are heightened by structural limitations related to immigration laws. From children's sense of abandonment by parents to siblings' heightened rivalries and resentments between spouses, illegality shapes families' interactions and well-being. With extensive social networks and in a social context that provides some sense of safety, families can try to reframe illegality to experience it as a source of solidarity and strength, even when it increases barriers and burdens.*

Source: Adapted from Leisy J. Abrego. (2016). Illegality as a Source of Solidarity and Tension in Latino Families. *Journal of Latino/Latin American Studies 8* (10), pages 5–21. doi: http://dx.doi.org/10.18085/1549-9502-8.1.5

*Endnotes have been omitted. Please consult the original source.

Questions to Consider

How does being undocumented affect an individual's life chances in the United States when compared to being documented? How might class or gender complicate this comparison? What happens to individual differences between undocumented and documented people when we consider that they may belong to the same mixed-status family?

Illegality and Contemporary Latino Families in the United States

Illegality—the historically specific, socially, politically, and legally produced condition of immigrants' legal status and deportability (De Genova, 2002)—intimately and deeply impacts all immigrants. There is nothing inherent in the common understanding or practices associated with someone's undocumented status. Rather, there are historically specific conditions and cues that establish the term's meaning and its consequences in the lives of those categorized in a tenuous legal status at any given time. For example, there have been moments in this country's history when, in practical terms, undocumented status had little meaning (Ngai, 2004). Even immigrants who arrived in the 1970s in Los Angeles were able to obtain a driver's license and work without the intense fear of deportation that now permeates immigrant communities in the city (Abrego, 2014). Increasingly, over the last few decades and especially since the attacks of September 11, 2001, undocumented status, and illegality more broadly, have gained significance in the public eye (Golash-Boza, 2012; Hernández, 2008). Immigrants categorized as undocumented or temporarily protected have become the target of progressively more harsh laws and ever more hateful speech, all of which work together to criminalize and dehumanize them and their families (Menjívar & Abrego, 2012).

After 9/11, legal moves to criminalize undocumented immigrants were magnified and accelerated (Hernández, 2007, 2008). Programs, such as 287(g) and Secure Communities (see Menjívar & Kanstroom, 2013), were implemented to allow more communication between local authorities, the FBI, and Immigration and Customs Enforcement (ICE) agencies. In practice, this has meant increased numbers of detentions and deportations, in part through sweeping workplace raids, but also because even routine traffic stops can quickly lead to ICE involvement and, ultimately, to the tearing apart of hundreds of thousands of families. In fact, in recent years the Department of Homeland Security (2010) reports that they have deported over 300,000 and closer to 400,000 immigrants annually. The figures of those who are detained and deported are now, therefore, more likely to include the parents of U.S. citizen children. When parents are deported, children are often then placed in foster care with little regard for principles of family unity that presumably guide both immigration and child welfare policies (Wessler, 2011). These record numbers of deportations, moreover, are taking place alongside a wave of hateful speech and growing animosity against Latino immigrants (Chavez, 2008; Menjívar & Abrego, 2012), all of which inevitably affect families' well-being.

Mainstream media's visual representations and powerful public discourses work to dehumanize Latino immigrants—whether documented or undocumented (Chavez, 2001, 2008; McConnell, 2011). While making immigrants' contributions as workers and community members invisible, these images and discourses also make immigrants' very presence in the country hypervisible—but only through the lens of illegality. Although undocumented status has been and largely continues to be a matter of civil law, mainstream media images tend to portray undocumented immigrants as criminals. For example, one common visual used to discuss undocumented immigrants is the image of them being apprehended, handcuffed, and publicly treated in ways that presume they are dangerous criminals (Santa Ana, 2012). In a battle against official statistics that confirm the majority of deported immigrants do not have criminal records (see, for example, National Community Advisory, 2011), these repeated images are unfortunately more convincing to a broad audience. Such persistently negative representations shape the general public's view, but also affect how immigrants and their families understand and experience illegality.

In this article, I heed the call of feminist social scientists to move beyond notions of familism associated with Latino families and instead underscore the role of social structures that delimit the experiences of diverse U.S. Latino groups (Alcalde, 2010; Landale & Oropesa, 2007; Zinn & Wells, 2003). In this tradition, I examine the repercussions for Latino families as they deal with issues associated with illegality during a historical moment that criminalizes and dehumanizes them merely for seeking survival. I am guided by the following questions: In such a harsh legal and political climate, how do Latino immigrant families experience illegality in their day-to-day lives? Moreover, how do individuals negotiate illegality when trying to fulfill their family roles?

Latino Families: Transnational, Undocumented, and Mixed Status

Like other members of the working poor, Latino families dealing with various facets of illegality face notable barriers. Geographically, given undocumented workers' job prospects and legal limitations, most families relying on one or two undocumented parents end up in areas of dense poverty (Chavez, 1998). These communities are typically beset with low-performing schools, high rates of crime, and few opportunities for their residents. These realities, in turn, block families and their next generation from integrating positively and thriving in this country. How do various forms of illegality further mediate these experiences?

One experience of illegality among Latino immigrants is long-term separation as members of transnational families, in which core family members live across borders. Unable to survive in their countries—largely as a result of U.S.-funded wars and neoliberal policies, including free-trade agreements—parents opt to migrate to the United States in search of work to support their children from afar (Abrego, 2014; Dreby, 2010). The vast wage inequalities in the region make this a likely strategy. Once they arrive in the United States, however, immigration laws restrict their chances for family reunification, making for prolonged family separations—often at least a decade (Abrego, 2009). It is difficult to enumerate how many people live in these types of arrangements, but it is a notable proportion for groups from various countries throughout Latin America (Abrego, 2009; Dreby, 2010; Hondagneu-Sotelo & Avila, 1997; Pribilsky, 2004; Schmalzbauer, 2005). In El Salvador, for example, it is estimated that anywhere between 16 and 40 percent of children in various regions of the country are growing up without one or both parents due to migration (García, 2012; Martínez, 2006). For these families, illegality is likely to play out differently than for families forced apart through deportation or who live together in fear.

For Latino undocumented families, in which all or most members are undocumented, they are likely more conscious about illegality's role in their everyday life. It is estimated that there are about 500,000 undocumented children in the United States growing up in families with at least one undocumented parent (Taylor, Lopez, Passel, & Motel, 2011). An additional 4.5 million U.S. citizen children are growing up in mixed-status families in which at least one of their parents is undocumented. Significantly, this figure more than doubled between 2000 and 2011 (Taylor et al., 2011). Illegality is likely to play out in different ways for these families as well. As made clear in the introductory case of this article, U.S.-born citizens are not entirely protected from the consequences of anti-immigrant laws—particularly when their loved ones are undocumented. For mixed-status families who experience the deportation of one or more family members, illegality can mean forced separation, in very painful and difficult ways (Dreby, 2012; Human Rights Watch, 2007; Wessler, 2011). Importantly, even when they are not forced into separation through the deportation of one of their members, mixed-status and undocumented families are also likely to deal with and experience illegality in different ways (Menjívar & Abrego, 2012).

In this article, I examine the ways that illegality permeates family life for Latinos whose relatives include at least one undocumented immigrant. My point is to underscore that illegality affects not only those immigrants who are undocumented. Their families must also grapple with the impact of changing laws, their implementation, and perceptions of undocumented immigrants. The consequences of illegality can lead to various types of experiences for Latino families. Here I focus on the potential for tensions and solidarity as responses to illegality at the family level.

Undocumented Families

Illegality's consequences can create tension and add burdens for undocumented families whose members are already structurally vulnerable. Beyond the usual challenges of communicating and working together across generations, undocumented parents and children may first have to reestablish a family relationship in the likely case they were separated and reunited after years apart (Suárez-Orozco, Bang, & Kim, 2010). Indeed, several undocumented youth mentioned difficult transitions with parents after joining them in the United States. Mario, who came from Guatemala at age six, was 16 when I met him. He still dealt with painful unresolved issues with his father who had migrated when Mario was only a few months old:

> It's not a good feeling. I mean, I knew I had a father, but it was just, he wasn't there.... It's still not easy getting along with my dad. We disagree a lot.... I was just thinking too highly of my dad, because I never knew him, you know. Things are just not how I figured.... I've never been really attached to my dad because of that reason.... I guess he expected me to, you know, be like, Wow, my dad" [in dreamy tone]. But it was just like, how could I show that if he wasn't there? You know?

As Mario explains, being apart from parents over several years can lead to the development of idealized and unrealistic expectations. It is difficult to establish loving bonds and smooth communication when both parents and children expect too much from each other following a painful separation. These experiences of step-migration are especially common among families who travel and live in the United States without authorization (Suárez-Orozco et al., 2010).

Even short separations can be difficult for young children. Luis, whose parents migrated from Mexico to the United States during his early childhood spent only a few months with his grandmother before his own migration at the age of four. He was separated from his father for years, but was apart from his mother for only a few months. Still, in his late teens Luis recalls that through much of his childhood, he felt uneasy about his relationship with his mother:

> Those three months made a huge difference. I didn't remember her. It felt like she wasn't my mom. You know what I mean? It felt like she was someone else. And it was only three months. I remember like when I used to get mad at her, if I was in trouble and she was telling me what to do, in my mind I was like, What if she's not my mom? What if she's another person?" . . . Yeah, it's just hard. I mean, that's your logic at that age.

Even short separations can confuse children and make them question their parents' authority. As separations are prolonged due to immigrant parents' undocumented status, reunifications are likely to involve difficult transitions that further complicate family dynamics (Suárez-Orozco et al., 2002).

Another challenge for undocumented families is rooted in the vastly different experiences and interpretations of illegality across generations (Abrego, 2011). First-generation immigrants who are usually the parents in these families feel responsible for choosing to migrate, remember clearly the horrific details of the migration journey, and deal with exploitative working conditions on a daily basis. For this generation, illegality is mainly about exclusion from society and great fear of deportation. The 1.5 generation undocumented immigrants, who are usually the children in undocumented families, often remember less about the journey; feel they had little choice in migrating; and enjoy greater levels of membership in U.S. society where they have spent most of their lives (Abrego, 2011). As they learn more details about their status, however, they experience their own forms of exclusion (Abrego, 2008; Gonzales, 2011; Gonzales & Chavez, 2012).

The exclusion associated with illegality can mean different things for various members of undocumented families. For parents, exclusion is most prominent when they are unable to perform the tasks—often gendered—that are expected of them. Mothers often speak of their great worry over their children's well-being if they were to be deported, while fathers feel their lives are worthless if they are unable to access rights, health care, and work to provide for their families. This sense of worthlessness and the fear that pervades undocumented parents are very different from what undocumented children in these families describe as their experience of illegality.

Undocumented immigrants who grow up in the United States and are socialized through schools are more likely to experience illegality as a matter of stigma (Abrego, 2008, 2011). For example, many are embarrassed that they cannot drive a car, go out on dates, go clubbing, or travel abroad like the rest of their peers (see also Gonzales, 2011). Unlike their undocumented parents, moreover, undocumented youth have adapted socially to U.S. social norms and can more easily fit in. This allows them to participate in activities their parents consider too risky, thereby adding tensions to family dynamics when parents disapprove of their children's behavior. This can be frustrating for children because they consider such behavior would, in any other legal context, be perfectly acceptable for someone their age.

Jovani, a 16-year-old undocumented Guatemalan high school student, expressed great resentment toward his parents. His mother, who is also an undocumented immigrant, volunteers at his school and tries to keep an eye on him constantly to keep him out of trouble. Meanwhile, he just wants to get a part-time job and be able to drive like all his friends, but his mother's adamant opposition is challenging for Jovani:

> When I want to get a job, I can't. I want to drive, but I can't. . . . So, most of the time, I just don't think about it, but I mean, there's sometimes when it crosses your mind, you know, you gotta get a job, you want to work, you want to have money. . . . So yeah, it's kind of hard for me. . . . I get mad because my parents brought me. I didn't tell them to bring me, but I get punished for it, for not having the papers.

The consequences of illegality—being excluded from otherwise typical experiences for people his age—deeply frustrate Jovani. But rather than blaming the legal system that prevents him and his family from thriving, he blames his parents. Therefore, despite his mother's best efforts to keep him focused on being a successful student, Jovani rebels. When I met him, he was in danger of failing most of his classes in his second attempt at junior year in high school.

To further complicate intergenerational relations in undocumented families, illegality infused by stigma, as undocumented youth experience it, allows them to develop personal discourses that help them limit the exclusion they feel. For example, undocumented youth try to justify their presence in the country by distancing themselves from negative connotations of illegality. In doing so, they underscore that their liminal status differs from the marginalized and criminalized status of their parents' generation. Most notably, they defend themselves by emphasizing they did not actively choose to come to the United States. Stellar students are especially effective when they can draw on their educational achievements to defend their honor as good people and good citizens of this country. As Isabel states: "The fact that we're students gives us credibility and, in their [anti-immigrant activists] eyes, that's better." This strategy is not available to the more marginalized and publicly targeted undocumented workers and parents in these families and may add greater tension to family dynamics.

Exclusion leads to several other associated experiences of illegality for undocumented immigrants. As Norma, a Mexican first-generation, undocumented immigrant mother, sums it up, "We are here and we know this is not our country. They don't want us here, so you have to be careful. Always be careful." In this experience of illegality, immigrants are made to feel constantly insecure, unaware of who they can trust, and unable to rely even on institutions that should represent safety for all. In such a context, navigating social relationships can be difficult. As Agustín, a first-generation Salvadoran immigrant, shares:

> It just feels like you don't know who you can trust. I tell people that I don't have papers. I feel like I'm not doing anything wrong. I'm not a criminal. But my wife gets mad at me. She tells me to be careful because you never know who could call the migra on you. But I feel like I have nothing to hide.

Most undocumented immigrants feel deeply disconnected from descriptions of themselves as criminals. They migrated in search of work for the sake of their families' survival. But in trying to counter the criminalization of undocumented status, it is difficult to know who they can trust. In this way, illegality and the cloud of distrust around undocumented status cause tension and complicate family dynamics when relatives have different approaches to handling illegality's repercussions in their lives.

Importantly, there are also spaces to build communication and solidarity among members of undocumented families. The following exemplifies this ability to work together to make claims for inclusion in this country. Adela, the undocumented mother of undocumented students who organized a press conference to support the DREAM Act, was one of a few older adults holding signs and standing in support of the event. After 14 years of living in the United States, this was the first time she had participated in such a public and political act and she was nervous, but her children had convinced her to be there. As with undocumented immigrants generally and for various reasons, parents who arrived in the country as adults are less vocal politically than their children's generation (Abrego, 2011). These different forms of socialization have the potential to create tensions, but can also generate possibilities for communication, as evident in the notes from my conversation with Adela that day.

Adela told me she had never been involved in organizations for immigrant rights. She came from Mexico 14 years ago, but she was dedicated to working and taking care of her kids. The thought of going out to protest or draw attention to herself never crossed her mind. But as her kids got older and the oldest went on to college, she realized how much it hurt them to not have papers. When she came from Mexico, she knew she would have to put up with not having papers and it might mean she could only get hard jobs, but she didn't know it would affect her kids this way—she had no idea—and all she wants is for them to achieve their dreams. It has been painful to watch them struggle just to be able to afford college. Both of her children are great students and are now at a community college. They have been participating in marches and meetings at this organization for a few years now, since high school, and they always invite her to come, but she was always too scared. This year, she finally went to one event and liked what she heard. All she wants to do is support her kids, and now she's committed to being present for them at these rallies and events because she knows how much it means to them.

Her children's persistent requests and her own understanding of how illegality was affecting them gave Adela the courage to become politically engaged. In general, because children of immigrants adapt to U.S. society at a faster pace than their parents, it is often the case that they are socialized politically in school and other spaces and they then socialize their parents

(Bloemraad & Trost, 2008). This is becoming increasingly evident even in the immigrant rights' movement—particularly among the most vocal and visible sector at a national level (see, e.g., http://www.iyjl.org/comingout2013/). For these undocumented families, then, intergenerational communication may also lead to greater political participation.

Families that include multiple generations of undocumented immigrants experience the consequences of illegality in various ways. Many of these families are likely to have migrated in steps, thereby reuniting after some time apart. In these cases, even the negotiation of a family relationship can be difficult. And when these families overcome the challenges of reunification, the different generational experiences of illegality can also lead to tension when parents, spouses, and children disagree about how to approach their lives and their actions in this country. Finally, the shared experience of illegality, even though it plays out differently in their lives, can also lead to greater solidarity among undocumented members of families.

Mixed-Status Families

Mixed-status families include members with multiple statuses. They share many of the same challenges and experiences of illegality as undocumented families, but also have unique tensions and possibilities as a result of legal internal stratification of their members. Illegality can play out in numerous ways, partly depending on the role of the undocumented persons and their relationships to others. For example, illegality will have different repercussions in a family that includes an undocumented parent and U.S. citizen children versus a family that includes undocumented parents and siblings with various statuses.

Beginning in the late 2000s, journalists and researchers have shed light on the experiences of mixed-status families that include U.S. citizen children and their undocumented parents. One of the most compelling cases is that of Encarnación Bail Romero, a Guatemalan immigrant to the United States (Brané, 2011; Thompson, 2009). In 2007, while working at a poultry plant in Missouri, immigration officials detained Bail Romero in a workplace raid. Her son Carlos, who was then only six months old, spent some time with different caretakers, until a couple approached her about adopting him. She was adamantly against this option, but helpless to act from a detention center in another state. Her lawyer, who explained the situation to her only in English (a language she did not understand), failed to protect her. Unable to leave detention, she later learned that a judge used her absence in court for a hearing about Carlos's future as evidence of abandonment. The judge terminated her parental rights and Carlos was adopted. Although Ms. Bail spent many years fighting to regain custody of her son, the laws stood against her. As unjust and bizarre as this story may sound, it reflects an increasingly common experience today: the legal system denies undocumented immigrants the same parental rights guaranteed to other parents.

In fact, among the 4.5 million U.S. citizen children growing up in mixed-status families, the chances of undocumented parents being deported have increased considerably over the last decade. With greater communication between local law enforcement and federal immigration agencies, undocumented parents caught during a routine traffic stop, for example, can be detained and deported—for having a broken taillight or driving without a license (Hagan, Eschbach, & Rodríguez, 2008; Hagan, Rodriguez, & Castro, 2011). By 2011, among the record number of deportees, 22 percent were parents of U.S. citizen children (Wessler, 2011). Parents may be detained for simply driving between home and work or dropping off or picking up their kids at school. Such increased targeting adds great stress for families.

Indeed, this sense of insecurity spreads through entire families, whether or not all members are undocumented (Dreby, 2012; Rodriguez & Hagan, 2004; Suárez-Orozco, Yoshikawa, Teranishi, & Suárez-Orozco, 2011; Yoshikawa, 2011). This is evident in the narratives of children of immigrants who grew up with one or two undocumented parents. In Southern California, just over an hour outside of Los Angeles, 20-year-old Nayeli grew up in the outskirts of an affluent city where the majority of inhabitants are white. Throughout her childhood, Nayeli's mother, who is a documented Mexican immigrant, reminded her and her siblings about the need to keep their father's undocumented status a secret. The vocal anti-immigrant groups in the area instilled great fear in Nayeli, and she grew up painfully aware of her family's vulnerability in the face of the consequences of illegality. When asked what the hardest part of the situation had been, she described how she experiences illegality at a personal level: "The silence . . . when it comes to talking about it with people that I trust, it's hard just to even talk about it. It's hard for me to even admit that my father is undocumented. I've kept it a secret for so long, and I feel like it's my secret and I don't want to tell people about it. It's the way I internalize it. We do it to protect my dad."

Nayeli's burden was heavy and constant; her neighbors' hostility exacerbated the potential for harm against her father if her family's secret were revealed. Emotionally, this crushed Nayeli, who cried throughout the interview: "Just my dad, period, is an emotional subject for me. If he took long to get home from work, I feared that he was caught. It's a scary feeling." Her relationship with her father was damaged when the secret prevented them from having open conversations about such an important topic. And to this day, as a young adult, she has difficulty discussing anything related to her father and her childhood generally because the cloud of illegality has been so deeply hurtful.

Not all mixed-status families with undocumented parents have the same experience. In another part of Los Angeles, 20-year-old Aminta, a U.S.-born child with an undocumented Guatemalan father, explains how illegality affected her father and her family:

> I think when I was a kid I didn't really understand it. But now as an adult, I feel my dad was frustrated and tired with his job and that he wanted to give us more, but he couldn't. Sometimes my dad seemed very quiet and sad. . . . My mom was the emotional backbone, I think. She always talked about the importance of family, something we had. I'm proud of my parents. They worked hard and that has made me work hard because I know I have something many people wish they had. And one day, hopefully, I can have the money to get a lawyer that will help my dad get his citizenship status. It just hurts because my dad went almost all his life living through economic challenges.

Aminta's family experienced illegality largely as an economic barrier that limited her father's ability to provide for his family. She suggests that his inability to live up to this gendered expectation weighed heavily on him as he seemed "frustrated," "very quiet and sad," much of the time. This weight can easily extend to the rest of the family. It was her mother's ability to live up to her gendered expectation as the "emotional backbone" of the family that held the family together and allowed them to work around the effects of illegality in their lives.

Aminta's experience in a mixed-status family stands in stark contrast to that of Nayeli. Although both had one undocumented parent and both were U.S. citizens by birth, their different communities mediate how their families experience illegality. While Nayeli grew up in an anti-immigrant community, Aminta's family has lived for decades in the same working class neighborhood where mixed status and undocumented families are common enough to make them seem close to the norm. Aminta, therefore, feels comfortable talking about her experiences and discussing how illegality has shaped her family's participation in the community: "It hasn't been easy, but we feel comfortable in our community. We know we're not the only family who is going through challenges and it feels like we are supportive of each other. My family is very close. We all play an important role. We each do something and the challenges seem less that way."

In Aminta's case, illegality added extra challenges to their lives, but her community's ability to integrate mixed-status families was also helpful. Moreover, illegality and the tenuous status of her father's situation led her family to find ways to increase their solidarity with one another by sharing responsibilities and bringing the family closer together.

Beyond intergenerational challenges, mixed-status families also experience other consequences of illegality when siblings do not share the same legal status. Often there is tension and resentment when U.S. citizen children have access to more resources and opportunities than their undocumented or temporarily protected siblings. Such was the case for Mario, whose younger brother was born in the United States, making him the only member of the family with U.S. citizenship. In the following excerpt, Mario describes resentments resulting from the family's mixed statuses:

> Well, basically, I don't have medical insurance. My younger brother, whenever he's sick, they always take him to the hospital, and stuff like that, because the government pays for him. . . . My mom takes him to the dentist yearly, to the doctor, you know, but if I feel really sick, like I have to be dying to go to the hospital. But then, you know, my brother, he feels a stomachache—"let's go to the hospital."

Stratified access to health care means that parents have to provide what seems like preferential treatment for some children owing to their legal status. Despite understanding that his brother had legal access to more resources, Mario harbored resentment toward his brother and his mother for what he experienced as limited concern for his well-being.

Furthermore, because immigration laws change and people move between statuses as they become eligible, families may experience illegality differently at different stages. Andrés, a 21-year-old member of a Mexican mixed-status family, was granted legal residency only a month before high school graduation; he was completing his third year of college when I interviewed him. He reflects on how being undocumented shaped his older brother's experience:

> I feel bad for him. He worked even harder than I did in high school, and he should've been graduating from college by now. He even got better grades than me, but just because of his papers he can't go.
>
> LA: What is he doing now?
>
> He works at a warehouse, packing and unpacking things from a truck all day. It makes me feel really bad, guilty because he deserves it as much as I do, but I'm the only one who gets to go [to college].

The way that families experience illegality, therefore, also depends on when statuses shift and how these shifts affect individuals. In this case, Andrés's older brother aged out of a chance to get legal permanent residency, leaving only Andrés to benefit from the change in status. Consequently, illegality played out as guilt for Andrés, who qualified for financial aid and other privileges that continued to be out of reach for his brother.

Among mixed-status families, however, there is sometimes also the opportunity to share rights and protections of one or multiple members with those who have more tenuous legal statuses. For example, Alisa, a 19-year-old Guatemalan undocumented college student, is thankful that her entire family benefits from the privileges of her sisters who are U.S. citizens. As citizens, they are eligible for government assistance, including public housing that is more spacious than what the family (all the rest of whom are undocumented) could otherwise afford.

> We moved over here because of the twins. I have two smaller twin sisters, they were born here, but when they were five months old, they got epilepsy, both of them, so it damaged their brain. . . . Because of them we moved over here because of the housing. We used to live in a smaller apartment so they gave us a larger apartment for them, because of them, so they could have more room to walk around and stuff.

Although her younger sisters' developmental disabilities have taken a physical and emotional toll on the family, Alisa is grateful that as U.S. citizens, they have access to health care and housing. She is aware of the benefits the entire family receives as a result of the twins' legal status. In this case, the consequences of illegality for a mixed-status family are mediated by the benefits of more spacious housing accorded to the U.S. citizens in the family.

The consequences of illegality in mixed-status families are multiple and varied, depending on the status of each family member and their role in the family. When parents are undocumented, this can lead to limited parental rights and fear of accessing resources for their children, even when children have legal rights to various benefits (Menjívar, 2006; Menjívar & Abrego, 2009; Suárez-Orozco et al., 2011; Yoshikawa, 2011). Illegality, moreover, can weigh heavily on all members of these families, even those who are U.S. citizens by birth or naturalization. Particularly with internal stratification of resources, children can blame each other and develop resentment, but they may also recognize when they benefit from resources given more freely to U.S. citizens in their families. Overall, mixed-status families' experiences of illegality are further mediated by local contexts—whether communities are inclusive or exclusive of immigrants more broadly—and shifts in statuses across time and at different stages in their lives. With these changes, families learn to navigate tensions and solidarity.

Conclusion

In this article, I examine how illegality encompasses all members of a family, even when only one person is categorized as undocumented. Unsurprisingly, I find that illegality can create tension for people whose disadvantages are heightened by structural limitations related to immigration laws. On the other hand, illegality can be a source of solidarity and strength when families live in welcoming communities. Based on notions of family and solidarity, some are able to pool resources to help the undocumented member(s) of their families. When they have the right context and resources, this strengthens the family, even in the face of illegality's increased barriers and burdens.

Illegality contextualizes [family members'] day-to-day lives and long-term relationships. It limits parents' authority while adding responsibilities for parents and children. Immigrant mothers, for example, experience the violence of illegality when they are unable to care for their children as they would like and as is socially expected of them (Abrego & Menjívar, 2011), while immigrant fathers are likely to be blocked from opportunities to provide for their children. This means that children have to carry part of the burden—sometimes financially, often emotionally—to help the family survive despite the limitations. Illegality, moreover, prevents all parents from accessing social services and other resources to help their children achieve optimal well-being.

When combined, all of illegality's repercussions undermine families' efforts to move out of poverty. Like parents in other working poor families, undocumented parents often work in low-paying, unstable jobs for long periods of time. And like other children who grow up in poverty (documented and undocumented), children of undocumented immigrants also face high levels of danger and few educational opportunities. Furthermore, being undocumented also increases the likelihood that families will lack health insurance (Fortuny, Capps, & Passel, 2007) and lowers their chances of accessing bank accounts and other financial services. Their parents' undocumented status is also detrimental to children in numerous, sometimes indirect ways. For example, due to fear of deportation, such families are less likely to apply for food-stamp benefits, even though their children may be eligible. They may be afraid to go into a government agency to apply for their children's health care benefits. Children in these families are thus less likely to seek the services they need (Abrego & Menjívar, 2011). In the longer term, undocumented status keeps families in the shadows, avoiding many of the institutions that have traditionally benefited immigrant families (Menjívar, 2006).

Despite these structural and very real challenges, illegality's consequences are also mediated by the demographics and political nature of their local context. People living in communities with a concentration of undocumented immigrants and mixed-status families are more likely to develop networks and access information that can mitigate the fear and insecurity so often associated with illegality. In cases where members of mixed-status communities are able to develop solidarity, they may be able to create safety nets for children and the most vulnerable members among them. However, in communities where few undocumented immigrants are known to reside and where anti-immigration advocates feel emboldened, immigrants and their families are likely to experience illegality as extreme vulnerability that can penetrate even their most intimate relationships.

In many respects, undocumented immigrants and their families are already important members of U.S. society—even if only on the lower rungs of the economic ladder. They contribute to our economy, children are educated in our schools, and all family members envision their futures here. However, these families currently have no available structural paths out of poverty. In a cruel twist, parents' efforts to secure their families' survival by migrating are met with legal obstacles. Current policies restrict their ability to thrive in this country and, for transnational families, to pull children out of poverty in the home countries as well. Without full legal rights, these families are barred from the very mechanisms that have ensured high levels of economic and social mobility to other immigrants throughout U.S. history (Abrego, 2006; Menjívar & Abrego, 2012). Legalization, therefore, is necessary to give Latino families a chance at success in this country.

References

Abrego, L. J. (2006). "I can't go to college because I don't have papers": Incorporation patterns of Latino undocumented youth. *Latino Studies, 4,* 212–231.

Abrego, L. J. (2008). Legitimacy, social identity, and the mobilization of law: The effects of Assembly Bill 540 on undocumented students in California. *Law & Social Inquiry, 33,* 709–734.

Abrego, L. J. (2009). Economic well-being in Salvadoran transnational families: How gender affects remittance practices. *Journal of Marriage and Family, 71,* 1070–1085.

Abrego, L. J. (2011). Legal consciousness of undocumented Latinos: Fear and stigma as barriers to claims making for first and 1.5 generation immigrants. *Law & Society Review, 45,* 337–370.

Abrego, L. J. (2014). *Sacrificing families: Navigating laws, labor, and love across borders.* Stanford, CA: Stanford University Press.

Abrego, L. J., & Menjívar, C. (2011). Immigrant Latina mothers as targets of legal violence. *International Journal of Sociology of the Family, 37,* 9–26.

Alcalde, M. C. (2010). Violence across borders: Familism, hegemonic masculinity, and self-sacrificing femininity in the lives of Mexican and Peruvian migrants. *Latino Studies, 8,* 48–68. Amnesty International. (2010). *Invisible victims: Migrants on the move in Mexico.* London, UK: Amnesty International Publications. Retrieved from http://www.amnesty.org/en/news-and-updates/report/widespread-abuse-migrants-mexico-human-rights-crisis-2010-04-27

Bloemraad, I., & Trost, C. (2008). It's a family affair: Intergenerational mobilization in the Spring 2006 protests. *American Behavioral Scientist, 52,* 507–532.

Brané, M. (2011). *Delayed justice for Guatemalan mother Encarnación Bail Romero.* Retrieved from http://www.huffingtonpost.com/michelle-bran/delayed- justice-for-guate_b_817191.html

Chavez, L. R. (1998). *Shadowed lives: Undocumented immigrants in American society* (2nd ed.). Fort Worth, TX.: Harcourt Brace.

Chavez, L. R. (2001). *Covering immigration: Popular images and the politics of the nation.* Berkeley: University of California Press.

Chavez, L. R. (2008). *The Latino threat: Constructing immigrants, citizens, and the nation.* Palo Alto, CA: Stanford University Press.

De Genova, Nicholas P. (2002). Migrant "illegality" and deportability in everyday life. *Annual Review of Anthropology, 31,* 419–447.

Dreby, J. (2010). *Divided by borders: Mexican migrants and their children.* Berkeley: University of California Press.

Dreby, J. (2012). The burden of deportation on children in Mexican immigrant families. *Journal of Marriage and Family, 74,* 829–845.

Fortuny, K., Capps, R., & Passel, J. (2007). *The characteristics of unauthorized immigrants in California, Los Angeles County, and the United States.* Washington, DC: The Urban Institute.

García, J. J. (2012, January). *20th anniversary of El Salvador's peace accords and implications for transnational development and voting abroad.* Paper presented at the UCLA North American Integration and Development Center, Los Angeles, CA.

Gonzales, R. G. (2011). Learning to be illegal: Undocumented youth and shifting legal contexts in the transition to adulthood. *American Sociological Review, 76,* 602–619.

Gonzales, R. G., & Chavez, L. R. (2012). "Awakening to a nightmare": Abjectivity and illegality in the lives of undocumented 1.5 generation Latino immigrants in the United States. *Current Anthropology, 53,* 255–281.

Hagan, J., Eschbach, K., & Rodríguez, N. (2008). U.S. deportation policy, family separation, and circular migration. *International Migration Review, 42*, 64–88.

Hagan, J., Rodriguez, N., & Castro, B. (2011). Social effects of mass deportations by the United States government, 2000–10. *Ethnic and Racial Studies, 34*, 1374–1391.

Hernández, D. M. (2007). Undue process: Racial genealogies of immigrant detention. In C. B. Brettell (Ed.), *Constructing borders/crossing boundaries: Race, ethnicity, and immigration* (pp. 59–86). Lanham, MD: Lexington Books.

Hernández, D. M. (2008). Pursuant to deportation: Latinos and immigrant detention. *Latino Studies, 6*, 35–63.

Hondagneu-Sotelo, P., & Avila, E. (1997). "I'm here, but I'm there": The meanings of Latina transnational motherhood. *Gender & Society, 11*, 548–570.

Human Rights Watch. (2007). *Forced apart: Families separated and immigrants harmed by United States deportation policy*. New York, NY: Human Rights Watch.

Landale, N., & Oropesa, R. S. (2007). Hispanic families: Stability and change. *Annual Review of Sociology, 33*, 381–405.

Martínez, L. (2006, April 28). El rostro joven de las remesas, *El Diario de Hoy*. Retrieved from http://www.elsalvador.com/noticias/2006/04/28/nacional/nac13.asp

Martínez, O. (2010). *Los migrantes que no importan: En el camino con los centroamericanos indocumentados en México*. Barcelona, Spain: Icaria.

McConnell, E. D. (2011). An "incredible number of Latinos and Asians": Media representations of racial and ethnic population change in Atlanta, Georgia. *Latino Studies, 9*, 177–197.

Menjívar, C. (2006). Family reorganization in a context of legal uncertainty: Guatemalan and Salvadoran immigrants in the United States. *International Journal of Sociology of the Family, 32*, 223–245.

Menjívar, C., & Abrego, L. (2009). Parents and children across borders: Legal instability and intergenerational relations in Guatemalan and Salvadoran families. In N. Foner (Ed.), *Across generations: Immigrant families in America* (pp. 160–189). New York: New York University Press.

Menjívar, C., & Abrego, L. (2012). Legal violence: Immigration law and the lives of Central American immigrants. *American Journal of Sociology, 117*, 1380–1424.

Menjívar, C., & Kanstroom, D. (Eds.). (2013). *Constructing immigrant 'illegality': Critiques, experiences, and resistance*. Cambridge, UK: Cambridge University Press.

National Community Advisory. (2011). *Restoring community: A National Community Advisory report on ICE's failed "Secure Communities" program*. Retrieved from http://altopolimigra.com/documents/FINAL-Shadow-Report-regular-print.pdf

Ngai, M. M. (2004). *Impossible subjects: Illegal aliens and the making of modern America*. Princeton, NJ: Princeton University Press.

Passel, J., & Cohn, D. (2011). *Unauthorized immigrant population: National and state trends, 2010*. Washington, DC: Pew Hispanic Center.

Pribilsky, J. (2004). "Aprendemos a convivir": Conjugal relations, co-parenting, and family life among Ecuadorian transnational migrants in New York City and the Ecuadorian Andes. *Global Networks, 4*, 313–334.

Rodriguez, N., & Hagan, J. M. (2004). Fractured families and communities: Effects of immigration reform in Texas, Mexico, and El Salvador. *Latino Studies, 2*, 328–351.

Santa Ana, O. (2012). *Juan in a hundred: The representation of Latinos on network news*. Austin: University of Texas Press.

Schmalzbauer, L. (2005). *Striving and surviving: A daily life analysis of Honduran transnational families*. New York, NY: Routledge.

Suárez-Orozco, C., Bang, H. J., & Kim, H. Y. (2010). "I felt like my heart was staying behind": Psychological implications of family separations and reunifications for immigrant youth. *Journal of Adolescent Research, 26*, 222–257.

Suárez-Orozco, C., Todorova, I., & Louie, J. (2002). Making up for lost time: The experience of separation and reunification among immigrant families. *Family Process, 41*, 625–643.

Suárez-Orozco, C., Yoshikawa, H., Teranishi, R. T., & Suárez-Orozco, M. (2011). Growing up in the shadows: The developmental implications of unauthorized status. *Harvard Educational Review, 81*, 438–472.

Taylor, P., Lopez, M. H., Passel, J., & Motel, S. (2011). *Unauthorized immigrants: Length of residency, patterns of parenthood.* Washington, DC: Pew Hispanic Center.

Thompson, G. (2009, April 23). After losing freedom, some immigrants face loss of custody of their children. *New York Times.* Retrieved from http://www.nytimes.com/2009/04/23/us/23children.html?hpw

Wessler, S. F. (2011). *Shattered families: The perilous intersection of immigration enforcement and the child welfare system.* New York, NY: Applied Research Center.

Yoshikawa, H. (2011). *Immigrants raising citizens: Undocumented parents and their young children.* New York, NY: Russell Sage.

Zinn, M. B., & Wells, B. (2003). Diversity within Latino families: New lessons for family social science. In A. S. Skolnick & J.H. Skolnick (Eds.), *Family in transition* (12th ed., pp. 389–415). Boston, MA: Allyn and Bacon.

CHAPTER 12

Are Second-Generation Filipinos "Becoming" Asian American or Latino?*

Historical Colonialism, Culture and Panethnicity

Anthony C. Ocampo

In this article, Anthony Ocampo examines how second-generation Filipinos understand their **panethnic identity**, *given their historical connection with both Asians and Latinas/os, two of the largest panethnic groups in the United States. While previous studies show* **panethnicity** *to be a function of shared political interests or class status, he argues that the cultural residuals of historical* **colonialism** *in the Philippines, by both Spain and the United States, shape how Filipinos negotiate panethnic boundaries with Asians and Latinos, albeit in different ways. Filipinos cite the cultural remnants of US colonialism as a reason to racially demarcate themselves from Asians, and they allude to the legacies of Spanish colonialism to blur boundaries with Latinos. While the colonial history of Filipinos is unique, these findings have*

Source: Adapted from Anthony C. Ocampo, "Are Second-Generation Filipinos 'Becoming' Asian American or Latino? Historical Colonialism, Culture and Panethnicity," *Ethnic and Racial Studies*, Volume 37, Issue 3, pages 425–445. Taylor and Francis, 2014.

*Some text and accompanying endnotes have been omitted. Please consult the original source.

implications for better understanding racialization in an increasingly multiethnic society—namely, how historical legacies in sending societies interact with new racial contexts to influence panethnic identity development.

Questions to Consider

What are the competing arguments for racially identifying Filipinos in the United States as Latina/o or Asian? After reading this essay, which racial category, Asian or Latina/o, best captures this group?

Introduction

During his 2011 visit to the Philippines, Pulitzer Prize–winning Latino author Junot Díaz (Matilla 2011) had this to say to a local reporter:

> You should come to the Dominican Republic because from what I've seen so far, Filipinos would have no problem over there. You wouldn't even notice you'd left . . . We have certain strong similarities. Our countries have been colonized by both the Spanish and [American]. I feel the similarities very strongly.

Having grown up around Filipinos in New Jersey, Díaz is alluding to the history of Spanish and American colonialism shared by the Philippines and many Latin American societies. Díaz implicitly blurs the boundaries between Filipinos and Latinos by drawing from what Cornell and Hartmann (1998, p. 237) term a 'symbolic repertoire'—the stories, histories and cultural markers that bond different groups together. These historical and cultural connections between Filipinos and Latinos are echoed by scholars, historians and journalists (Pisares 2006; Morrow 2007; Guevarra 2012). However, within the US context, Filipinos are classified as Asian rather than Hispanic by including the US census. Filipinos were also involved in the establishment of the Asian American movement and continue to participate in pan-Asian organizations today (Espiritu 1992).

The links of Filipinos with both Latinos and Asians introduce an interesting question: how do second-generation Filipinos understand and negotiate their panethnic identity, given their connections to two of the largest panethnic groups in the USA? In everyday life, race involves the complex negotiation of factors beyond institutional designations, including outsiders' perceptions, cultural knowledge and ways of behaving (Jackson 2001). Racial categorizations constantly evolve, and groups may develop a panethnic consciousness that transgresses 'official' designations. To address my question, I use multiple data sources that elucidate Filipino panethnic identity patterns. I draw from in-depth interviews and surveys of 50 second-generation Filipino adults from Los Angeles, a multiethnic city and the primary destination of Filipino immigrants.

Although it was not the original intent of the study to examine how colonialism affects panethnicity, the majority of interview respondents themselves brought up both Spanish and

US colonialism in the Philippines when discussing identity. Previous research highlights colonialism as an important historical backdrop for understanding assimilation (Portes and Rumbaut 2001). As Massey and colleagues (1993) have argued, colonialism matters because it creates cultural links between members of the sending and receiving countries. However, past studies mainly consider how colonialism links immigrant groups to *mainstream* members of the host country. As such, this study focuses on the way that colonialism shapes how immigrant groups relate with *minority* members of society. Additionally, this study also examines how colonialism might affect assimilation outcomes specifically among *children of immigrants* in a multiethnic society. Although children of immigrants may not have been socialized within the colonized society, colonialism has an enduring imprint on the culture passed on to them by their parents, which in turn affects identity (Kasinitz et al. 2008). Filipinos draw on their colonially influenced culture when negotiating boundaries between themselves and other groups.

Classical assimilation models once posited that immigrants and their children would assimilate into a white middle-class mainstream (Gordon 1967), but contemporary frameworks have shown them now being incorporated into diverse segments of US society (Portes and Zhou 1993). Ongoing Latino and Asian migration is dramatically changing the US racial landscape, which in turn is reshaping immigrant assimilation processes. For example, in Los Angeles, among the top destinations for Latino and Asian immigrants, nearly half of the residents are of Latino descent, and non-Hispanic whites constitute a mere 28 per cent of the population (Census 2010). Children of immigrants living in such multiethnic contexts might find more incentive in identifying with their minority peers, rather than align themselves with groups associated with the white mainstream.

Understanding panethnic identity through a cultural lens, Filipinos cited US colonialism as a reason to demarcate themselves from Asians while alluding to the cultural legacies of Spanish colonialism to blur boundaries with Latinos. While existing scholarship has explained panethnicity as a function of shared class status or political interests (Espiritu 1992), I find that the cultural legacies of Spanish and US colonialism play a defining role for Filipinos' panethnic identity development. These findings challenge studies that suggest that children of immigrants prefer identities associated with upward mobility (in this case, Asian over Latino) and highlight the mechanisms that facilitate panethnic consciousness *across* class lines, a phenomenon less discussed in previous research. This study also considers how identity is shaped by the negotiation of cultural aspects associated with both the pre-migration society and the multiethnic landscape of contemporary US society.

Assimilation Theory and Panethnicity

Identity has long been considered a mechanism of immigrant-group assimilation. Early scholars asserted that immigrants and their children identify as unhyphenated Americans to fully assimilate into US society (Park 1950; Gordon 1964). However, contemporary reformulations of assimilation suggest that children of immigrants are incorporated into different segments of society due to a constellation of structural, economic and cultural factors, a perspective known as segmented assimilation (Portes and Zhou 1993). Notably, this framework posits that connections to *ethnic* identity allow children of immigrants to acquire social and economic resources that facilitate upward mobility (Zhou and Bankston 1998). However, studies in this tradition say relatively less about the mechanisms shaping *racial* or *panethnic* identification. Some have critiqued these studies for overemphasizing the negative aspects associated with ascribing to racial identities that are externally imposed (Neckerman, Carter and Lee 1999).

Theories of panethnicity have highlighted the social, economic and political advantages of identifying with one's racial group (Espiritu 1992). Recent studies discuss the viability of panethnic identification, highlighting how children of immigrants seamlessly switch between ethnic and panethnic labels depending on the situation (Kasinitz et al. 2008), rather than viewing them as mutually exclusive options. However, intragroup dynamics and racialized constructions in mass media often prompt individuals to develop culturally based notions of panethnicity (Dhingra 2007). When these individuals feel that they do not fit the 'rules' for panethnic 'membership', they in turn express ambivalence or resistance to being lumped into these racial categories (Kibria 1998).

Colonialism and Assimilation

Some scholars have argued that assimilation, identity and panethnicity models are implicitly US-centric and overlook the transnational nature of these processes (Espiritu 2004). Recent studies show that assimilation and identity formation of immigrant groups are influenced by US economic or military presence in the home country (Espiritu 2007; Kim 2008), transnational media (Roth 2009) and migratory flows between sending and host societies (Jiménez 2010). Focusing on colonialism can highlight how historical and contemporary relations *between* sending and receiving nations interact with immigrant experiences in the US context to shape assimilation.

The effect of colonialism on immigration and assimilation patterns is multi-layered. Colonial regimes exploit the natural resources and labor of the colonized society, and the resulting economic underdevelopment of the latter creates the impetus for members of its society to migrate in the first place. Second, colonial relationships influence policies that facilitate the socio-economic selectivity of individuals who migrate even in the post-colonial period (Choy 2003). Third, the institutional and cultural influences of colonial regimes 'prepare' members of the colonized society to migrate. Potential migrants in these societies possess cultural and institutional familiarity with the colonizing nation long before crossing international borders. This familiarity in turn facilitates the decision to migrate and the ability to assimilate into mainstream jobs, neighbourhoods and organizations (Portes and Rumbaut 2001). Such findings should not at all suggest that colonialism should be framed in any positive light. Scholars show that colonialism breeds feelings of racial inferiority among immigrant groups even after the colonial period has ended, which in turn can lead to detachment from one's co-ethnic community (David and Okazaki 2006).

While studies have examined how colonialism affects the immigrant generation, few address how it distinctly influences second-generation outcomes. As Jiménez (2010) argues, immigration scholars should be more precise about colonialism's effects across generations, rather than assume that it permanently relegates immigrants with colonial histories to second-class status. Without discounting the exploitative history of colonialism, Waters (1999) notes that European colonialism has served as a basis of panethnic consciousness among second-generation West Indians from different societies—although Waters' study is among the few that considers how colonialism creates connections with other *minority* populations.

Building on this research, this study shows how Filipino children of immigrants negotiate their colonial history when navigating panethnic boundaries with other ethnic groups. Warikoo (2011) provides a template of how this might occur. Her research shows that second-generation Indo-Caribbeans inherit South Asian cultural practices from their immigrant parents' society, but the degree to which it shapes their identity depends on the value that Indian culture carries within their racial context.

Historical Context

The Philippines became part of the Spanish Empire during the early sixteenth century, the period when Spain established *Nueva España* in modern-day Mexico. Considered an extension of its empire in Latin America, Spain established the Acapulco–Manila galleon trade, which facilitated extensive cultural exchange between Filipinos and Mexicans for three centuries (Guevarra 2012). The Spanish period ended in 1899 but left enduring imprints on modern-day Philippine society. Spanish language has had a strong influence on Tagalog, which along with English is the current lingua franca of Philippine society (see Table 1). Filipinos were also given Spanish surnames (e.g. Torres, Rodríguez, Santos) during the colonial period. And similar to Spain's Latin American colonies, the Philippines remains a

Table 1 Everyday words in English, Spanish, and Tagalog

English	***Spanish***	***Tagalog***
Household		
Table	mesa	mesa
Living room	sala	sala
Chair	silla	silya
Kinship		
Uncle	tío	tito
Aunt	tía	tita
Godfather	nino	ninong
Godmother	nina	ninang
Clothing		
Pants	pantalones	pantalon
Jacket	chaqueta	dyaket
Shoes	zapatos	sapatos
Food-related		
Fork	tenedor	tinidor
Spoon	cuchara	kutsara
Snack	merienda	meryenda
Days		
Monday	Lunes	Lunes
Tuesday	Martes	Martes
Wednesday	Miércoles	Miyerkoles

predominantly Catholic society, one of only two throughout Asia. Over 80 per cent of Filipinos living in the Philippines and abroad are Catholic (Rodríguez 2006).

Despite Filipino revolutionary efforts in 1899, the Philippines was acquired by the USA following the Spanish–American War. Under the guise of 'benevolent assimilation', the Americans used cultural imperialism to subjugate the native population, establishing US-style schools and English as the medium of instruction and national language (Choy 2003). Colonial policies granted Filipinos the status of US 'nationals', a legal status created by the US government specifically to facilitate large-scale migration of mostly male laborers to low-wage agricultural and factory work. Despite their ability to migrate, Filipino workers encountered violent resistance from white nativists, who eventually helped lobby Congress to pass the 1936 Tydings-McDuffie Act, which granted the Philippines independence and effectively halted Filipino migration (Baldoz 2011).

Ironically, the legacies of the American colonial period set the stage for a highly selective group of Filipinos to migrate when the Hart-Cellar Act reopened US borders to non-white immigrants in 1965. US-modelled schools socialized Filipinos to American ways of life and provided widespread access to higher education. Filipinos had access to health care training institutions, initially established to aid US military stationed in the Philippines (Choy 2003). After US colonialism, the Philippine economy remained underdeveloped, and unemployment was rampant, creating a surplus pool of highly educated, English-speaking Filipino workers. During the 1970s, the Philippine government implemented aggressive labour emigration policies, transforming the country into a 'labor brokerage state' (Rodríguez 2010, p. 6). Millions within the surplus labour pool were primed to fill shortages in US professional sectors, particularly within health care.

These legacies explain why Filipinos are more linguistically and residentially assimilated than their Asian counterparts. Over two-thirds of Filipino migrants speak English 'very well', in contrast to less than a third of other Asian migrants (Portes and Rumbaut 2006). In addition, there are no culturally homogenous ethnic enclaves for Filipinos that compare to Chinatown, Koreatown or Little Saigon, as they generally reside in racially integrated neighborhoods (Vergara 2009). These factors also explain why higher proportions of Filipinos enter mainstream, English-speaking occupations versus ethnic economies. Filipinos are actively recruited by US employers into health care, teaching and other professional sectors (Ong and Azores 1994). However, the language barriers and residential concentration more common among Chinese, Korean and Vietnamese mean that these groups can remain in occupational sectors that are ethnically insular (Zhou 2009).

Like their parents, Filipino children of immigrants are distinct from their second-generation Asian peers. Among second-generation Asians, Filipinos by far have the highest rates of being monolingual English speakers (Zhou and Xiong 2005). Interestingly, while Filipino migrants generally have more mainstream occupational pathways than other Asian migrants, their children fare less well in their educational outcomes than their other Asian peers. While most second-generation Filipinos pursue higher education, they are less likely than their Chinese, Korean and Vietnamese counterparts to attend four-year universities, more likely to opt for less prestigious institutions and less likely to graduate with a four-year degree (Teranishi et al. 2004; Zhou and Xiong 2005). Moreover, research by Teranishi (2002) shows that Filipinos are treated like remedial students, while their East Asian counterparts are automatically perceived as more high achieving—all part of what Espiritu and Wolf (2001, p. 157) have termed a 'paradox of assimilation'.

Espiritu (1992) argues that the cultural differences rooted in colonialism also explain why Filipinos of different generations have faced challenges in developing panethnic consciousness with other Asians. She suggests that the history of Spanish colonialism presents the possibility for Filipinos to build panethnic alliances with Latinos, or in the least can be utilized as political leverage within pan-Asian organizations (Espiritu 1992, p. 172). While Asian cultures and experiences are indeed heterogeneous, there are cultural distinctions unique to Filipinos historically rooted in their dual colonial past. This article explores how the cultural residuals of this past influence how Filipinos negotiate panethnic boundaries between themselves and other ethnic groups.

Methodology

In-Depth Interviews

This study draws from in-depth interviews [conducted in 2009 and 2010] with 50 second-generation Filipinos from two middle-class, multiethnic neighborhoods in Los Angeles: Eagle Rock and Carson. Unlike other Asian immigrants in Los Angeles, there are no ethnically homogenous Filipino neighborhoods in the region comparable to Chinatown, Koreatown and Little Saigon. Filipinos live in multiethnic neighborhoods and are often the primary Asian-origin group in the area (Census 2010). Eagle Rock and Carson are two such neighborhoods that are also well-known Filipino settlements (Gorman 2007; Ibañez and Ibañez 2009). There are Filipino restaurants, community centers and immigrant service centers, although they do not dominate the neighborhood landscape in the same fashion as other Asian ethno-burbs (Zhou 2009).

Eagle Rock and Carson are majority-minority neighborhoods that are also middle class—the median household income in both Eagle Rock and Carson is about $67,000, well above the national average (Census 2010). In both neighbourhoods, 20 per cent of residents are Filipino and over 35 per cent are Mexican. However, in Eagle Rock, the remaining population is white, whereas in Carson, it is mostly African American with a small, but visible number of Samoans (about 3 per cent).

Following each interview, respondents were asked to fill out a brief demographic survey with questions about their level of education, socio-economic status (SES), and ethnic and racial identity choices. Respondents first answered the open-ended question: 'How do you self-identify?' For a subsequent question—'What is your racial background?' respondents were asked to indicate whether they identified as white, African American, Latino, Asian or Pacific Islander.

Cultural Marginalization within Asian America

Author: Do you ever identify as Asian American?

Ronald: Not really. It's like denying what I am. It's like denying that I'm Filipino, like not really acknowledging my *culture.*

Despite its political origins, Asian panethnicity has evolved to take on cultural meanings, as Ronald's remarks indicate. When presented with the question 'What groups are Filipinos most similar to?', respondents interpreted this to mean 'Whose *culture* is most similar to that of Filipinos?'. Filipinos were generally reticent about identifying as Asian, and this had to do with cultural factors. Few felt cultural connections between themselves and other Asians, and the ones they noted were superficial at best, such as food or geography. As one respondent noted: 'Filipinos' diet is very Asian, like rice, fish, and stuff a normal American wouldn't eat.' Beyond this, most associated Asian American identity with East Asian cultural stereotypes, which they felt did not fit Filipinos. As Kevin asserted: 'The face of Asian Americans is an East Asian face, literally. Not a Filipino one.'

Respondents referred to the Americanization of Filipino culture as a reason to demarcate themselves from other Asians. Some felt different from other Asians because the latter had a 'real history and therefore, had a real culture.' Jenn noted that, in contrast to other Asians, Filipino culture was associated with hybridity because of the colonial influences throughout Philippine history:

> We're not really Asian. I feel like on a cultural level, we don't relate. The Chinese have this long history that's very established, and it's written. We've been colonized like how many times? Where's the identity in that? Are we Spanish, Muslim, Chinese, and now, are we American? Because if you go to Manila, it's practically like Los Angeles. It's so Americanized.

Echoing Jenn's remarks, others felt that this colonial history was antithetical to being Asian American because 'real' Asian culture is 'untouched by Western influences'.

Others framed the post-colonial American influence as an advantage that made Filipinos 'less foreign' than other Asians. Franky noted: 'When whites see other Asian groups, they seem them as being "fobbier" [more "fresh off the boat"]. But then they see Filipinos and we're more assimilated to American culture.' Eddie pointed to the Americanized aspects of Philippine media: 'A lot of the popular culture and styles and music are based on [America]. When you watch Filipino variety shows, what do you see? They're playing Usher, Lady Gaga, and American pop and hip hop.' Implicit in such comments is the assumption that Asian culture is inherently foreign, while Filipino culture is more westernized, and thus, *not* Asian. By contrasting up-to-date trends in Philippine culture with a 'fobbier' Asian culture, these remarks also imply that Asian identity is 'uncool', which may further explain Filipinos' aversion to pan-Asian identity.

Respondents also said that the English proficiency of Filipinos in the USA—an outgrowth of American colonialism—distinguished them from Asians. Lynette recalled an uncomfortable moment in an Asian American studies course in college when her class had a discussion about the typical Asian American experience:

> I felt like there was a difference between those who were Chinese, Korean, and those who were Filipino. It just *felt* different. I think because a lot of the "Asian American experiences" that we read about in our class talked about language. The other Asians would talk about their parents only being able to speak Mandarin or Vietnamese and having to be the mediator between two cultures—*that* was the Asian American

experience. But I felt that wasn't the case for me. I was like, "You know, my parents speak English just fine."

Ironically, while Asian American studies was created to foster a shared sense of panethnic identity among different Asian ethnicities, Lynette's experience served the opposite function—it highlighted differences between Filipinos' experiences from those of East Asians, who many felt dominated mainstream Asian American narratives.

Several noted the cultural construction of Asian panethnicity on a global level. They recounted times when others referred to Filipinos as the 'wetback Asians' or the 'Mexicans' or 'blacks' of Asia. Raymond said: '[Filipinos] do the manual labor all over the world.' Kevin, in turn, argued that when people think of Asians, they automatically refer to China, Japan and Korea, or as he noted: 'The three countries that have power.' While Raymond and Kevin grew up middle class and have professional parents, their remarks show how their sense of pan-Asian identity is influenced by the international community of Filipino laborers. Their comments illustrate that panethnicity is not entirely a US-based construction, but rather, at least in part, a transnational ideological construction (Espiritu 2004; Roth 2009).

The lack of other Asian ethnicities in their childhood neighbourhoods also explains why Filipinos expressed weak panethnic ties. Proximity facilitates opportunities for people to identify commonalities across ethnic lines and develop a panethnic consciousness.

In Eagle Rock and Carson, Filipinos had minimal opportunity to interact with other Asians. Most did not interact with Asians until their college years. As Jacob noted: 'College was the first time I really was around a bunch of Asians!' Grace described her first days at UC Irvine (where non-Filipino Asians are 40 per cent of the student body) as a 'culture shock' because 'everyone is super Asian'. Such characterizations imply how both felt that Filipinos were not part of the pan-Asian collective.

Post-Colonial Panethnicity: Filipino and Latino Cultural Connections

Even though respondents used colonialism to distance Filipinos from other Asians, they used the colonialism frame to blur boundaries with Latinos. While no respondent identified as Latino outright, many more closely associated Filipinos with Mexicans and other Latinos because of the shared history of Spanish colonialism, including some who checked 'Asian' on the post-interview survey. Lia noted the 'Latinizing' effect of this history on Filipino culture, saying that Filipinos 'have more similarities with Latin culture than other Asians'.

Some felt Filipinos 'must have Spanish blood' because both co-ethnics and Latinos commonly mistook them as Mexican due to their phenotype (e.g. they 'looked' Mexican) or their Spanish surname. Nearly half of respondents recalled being spoken to in Spanish by Latinos, and some were even mistaken as Latino by other Filipinos. In her first days working as a nurse, Adriana recalled that her Filipina co-workers spoke Tagalog to each other yet conversed with her in English. When Adriana replied in Tagalog, one co-worker expressed her surprise: 'I didn't know you were Filipina. I thought you were Hispanic!'

Respondents bonded with Latinos based on three main cultural similarities: language, surnames and Catholicism. Jon, a hotel manager, recalled being mistaken as Latino by the Mexican immigrants he worked with:

> When they see me in the hall, they speak to me in Spanish. Then I tell them, "No hablo español," and they're like, "Why don't you speak Spanish?" and then I tell them I'm Filipino. And then they insist, "Well, some Filipinos speak Spanish. You have Spanish last names, right?"

Respondents recalled efforts by Filipino and Latino immigrants to communicate with each other when interacting in the neighborhood, given the heavy overlap in everyday words in Spanish and Tagalog (see Table 1). When I asked him whether he saw Filipinos and Latinos interact much, Jayson answered:

> All the time! My mom, for example, whenever she goes to the market, she [and the Latino workers] will be like, "Hola, amigo. Hola, amiga." Because of the similarities in our language, you can communicate in [each others'] native tongue.

While language bridged Filipinos with Latinos, it created further rifts with Asians. Ronald said that interacting with other Asian immigrants was relatively more difficult 'because there's virtually no overlap between Tagalog and say, Chinese or Vietnamese.'

Catholicism was another colonial legacy that Filipinos used to liken themselves with Latinos. Diana said Filipinos were 'definitely' more similar to Latinos because:

> [My] parents have *santos* and the Virgin Mary all around the house, and that's just like Latinos. I'd go to my Guatemalan friend's house, and you'd see the same thing. There's a lot of religion intermingled with her culture and my culture.

Many Filipino and Latino ethnic practices also have a religious component. Alma noted how religion was embedded in rites of passages for Filipina and Mexican young women (debuts and *quinceañeras*, respectively). She added: 'When you hear Filipino and Latino, you think Catholic automatically. I don't think religion when I think of Asians. Or if I do, maybe I think of Buddha, but not Jesus or Mary.' Although Catholicism might not have prompted outsiders to racialize respondents as Latino, it nonetheless affected how Filipinos racially positioned themselves vis-á-vis Latinos and other Asians.

This cultural closeness became evident in situations where other Filipinos were not even present. Alex attended a private college with many East Asians and Latinos, but few Filipinos. Coming from Eagle Rock, he initially felt disconnected from his Asian classmates, yet noted a sense of closeness with his Latino peers, who also invoked the colonial frame. At a party sponsored by one of the Latino organizations, Alex recounted:

> I never felt out of place at the party, even though it was all Latinos. Funny enough. My one friend who was half-Mexican, but looked more white and was from like a bougie [rich], all-white town got flack for being there. They kept calling him "white boy." But with me, a bunch of the guys would come up to me and be like, "Oh what? You're Filipino? It's practically the same thing [as Latino]. We all got punked by Spain

anyway, right?" Most of my friends in college ended up being Latino because they were the next closest thing to Filipinos.

Alex's experience shows that the negotiation of panethnic boundaries is not determined solely by national origin—otherwise his 'white-looking' friend should have felt more at home at the predominantly Latino event. Alex's comfort stemmed from his experiences growing up with Latinos, which allowed him to fit in more than someone who was 'biologically' Mexican. Alex also noted that Latino events were 'more fun' and 'cooler' than those sponsored by other Asians, whom he and other Filipinos stereotyped as studious and bookish.

This idea that Filipinos and Latinos were 'the same thing' was echoed in conversations about interracial dating. While having dated Mexican women in the past, Nelson expressed a new-found anxiety about dating a Vietnamese woman:

Nelson: I'm kind of nervous about the girl I'm dating. She's Vietnamese, so this is the first time I'm dating someone from a different culture.

Author: Didn't you say that you dated a bunch of Mexican girls before?

Nelson (laughing): Ha, that doesn't count. Mexicans are the same as Filipinos!

For Nelson, cultural differences between Filipinos and Latinos are less salient than those between Filipinos and Asians. Such comments illustrate how the cultural boundaries of racial categories subconsciously influence Filipinos' sense of 'we-ness' with Asians and Latinos.

Respondents' identification with Latinos is interesting given that Filipinos, on the aggregate level, have a higher SES than Latinos. At the same time, Eagle Rock and Carson have a large minority middle class, including middle-class Mexican Americans. The narratives suggest that there was more class convergence between Filipinos and Mexicans in these neighbourhoods than statistical data might indicate. While nearly every respondent identified as middle class, most noted having close connections with relatives who were working class (both in the USA and abroad) or recalled having been working class earlier in life. As such, class differences did not necessarily disrupt the connections they felt with Latinos who lived in the 'less nice parts' of Eagle Rock or Carson. However, Filipino-Latino connections did weaken when negative media stereotypes of Latinos were discussed. Franky said that while he felt close with Latinos in terms of religion and culture, he did not relate to the 'stereotypical Cholo [gangster] looking ones'. In addition, Filipino-Latino connections seemed to break down in the school context. Those attending public high schools said that while teachers viewed Filipinos as high-achieving students, 'Latinos weren't seen as honors students by school officials'. These findings suggest that Filipinos' connection with Latinos might decline if the association potentially compromised their middle-class standing or mobility.

Filipino Panethnic Identity Patterns

Post-Interview Survey

Respondents filled out a brief survey that asked an open-ended question about identity and then chose a racial identity from a set of discrete options. I had the opportunity to observe respondents as they answered these questions. For the open-ended question, every respondent wrote 'Filipino' without hesitation. However, when asked to select their racial background, many vacillated between the given options. Half inquired whether they could write in 'Filipino' as their race. Respondents were also split between choosing 'Asian' and 'Pacific Islander'. There was also a clear relationship between panethnic identification and neighbourhood.

Given the racial ambivalence of Filipinos in both neighbourhoods, what explains this difference? The interviews suggest that choosing 'Pacific Islander' was a function of not wanting to choose 'Asian'. Eagle Rock respondents selected Pacific Islander, but had few concrete notions of what this identity 'meant'. When prompted about why he felt Filipinos were 'more Pacific Islander than Asian', Vince said: 'I don't know. Probably because the Philippines are islands in the Pacific?' Others displayed the same lack of investment, noting merely that it was 'better than choosing Asian'. Carson respondents had more concrete ideas of Pacific Islander identity because of their interactions with Samoans. Bryan said: 'Pacific Islander is for the Samoans. And there's no Asians in Carson besides Filipinos, so I guess we can fill that in.' Such responses illustrate that Carson Filipinos did not necessarily express strong attachments to Asian identity, even if they chose it on the form. These findings show that Filipinos' identity options depend largely on the availability and meaning of categories within their local context.

Conclusion

Despite linguistic, socio-economic and cultural differences, ethnic groups develop panethnic consciousness by organizing for political interests, emphasizing cultural commonalities or highlighting shared racial experiences. Filipinos have done all these things with both Asians and Latinos, and thus can justifiably be categorized as either. Ultimately, they are officially Asian, according to the US census. Despite this, individuals do not always ascribe to the panethnic labels imposed on them, and the unique colonial history of the Philippines has prompted Filipinos to be vocally ambivalent about their racial designation. In Espiritu's (1992, p. 107) seminal book *Asian American Panethnicity*, one Filipino despondently asserted that Filipinos were Asian because of a 'geographical accident'. Espiritu has noted the possibility of Filipinos joining Latino panethnic coalitions, but ultimately acknowledges that both the pan-Asian and pan-Latino option bring significant challenges.

If these historical and cultural connections mean that Filipinos are 'kinda Asian and kinda Latino', as one respondent put it, how did the young adults in this study negotiate panethnic identity? The term 'Asian American' was born as a politicized identity, yet it was not a lack of political engagement that prompted their ambivalence. Rather, the cultural legacies of Spanish and US colonialism in the Philippines played a more significant role in how respondents negotiated panethnic boundaries. It is worth nothing that despite the cultural links between US and Philippine societies, no respondent identified as an unhyphenated American, signalling the continued significance of race in American society.

As the narratives revealed, the cultural hybridity resulting from Spanish and US colonialism was a central part of Filipino ethnic identity. Whether talking about culture, language or religion, respondents would embed them within colonial contexts. This culturally based understanding of ethnicity extended to their negotiation of panethnicity. US colonialism created a rift between Filipinos and other Asians. Their experiences of feeling more Americanized, having English-speaking households, and being less bicultural than other Asians prompted their feelings of disconnection. This social distancing was further amplified by their internalization of the Asian 'forever foreigner' stereotype and lack of interaction with other Asians in their neighborhoods. Moreover, the surveys reflected the lukewarm resonance of Asian panethnicity for Filipinos, relative to other Asian ethnicities.

In turn, Spanish colonialism bonded them with Latinos, a sentiment that at times was mutual, as the opening quote from Junot Díaz illustrates. In their everyday lives, reminders of Spanish colonialism are present in their parents' language, surnames and religion. The presence of Latinos in their neighborhood further 'replenished' the Spanish aspects of Filipino ethnic culture (Jiménez 2010), making the Filipino–Latino link especially salient. These findings challenge previous studies that suggest that Filipinos should align themselves with Asians, a group stereotyped as upwardly mobile. Within the context of a middle-class neighborhood, colonial commonalities prompt Filipinos to blur boundaries with Latinos (except in situations where it compromised their social standing).

Are Filipino Americans a unique case? Certainly the extensive colonial history in the Philippines distinguishes them from other Asians. Nonetheless, colonialism also represents an extreme case of cultural shifts in pre-migration societies that persist today, due to US militarism, foreign policy, transnational media and migration-related cultural exchanges (Kim 2008). Cultural shifts in the pre-migration society shape the identity 'toolkit' that children of immigrants use to relate with groups in a multiethnic society (Warikoo 2011). However, the use of this toolkit is also contingent on the value of 'symbolic repertoires' that children of immigrants possess. In a 'Latinized' city like Los Angeles, there is symbolic value to aligning oneself with Latinos rather than Asians, particularly for young adults who at the time may be more concerned with social standing than economic mobility. Although a study of Los Angeles may not be generalizable to second-generation experiences across the country, the choice of research site elucidates important social phenomena bound to take place in other parts of the country affected by migration: negotiation of race beyond the black–white binary, the emergence of new panethnic categories, and the interaction of historical legacies with new racial contexts. Ultimately, the Filipino case highlights the ever-evolving process of panethnic identity construction—a process that is not US-centric in nature, but one shaped heavily by the interaction of historical legacies with the changing racial landscape of American society.

References

BALDOZ, RICK 2011 *The Third Asiatic Invasion*, New York: NYU Press

CARTER, PRUDENCE 2005 *Keepin' It Real*, New York: Oxford University Press

CENSUS BUREAU OF THE UNITED STATES. 2010. *Census of Population and Housing*. Washington, DC: Government Printing Office.

CHOY, CATHERINE 2003 *Empire of Care*, Durham, NC: Duke University Press

CORNELL, STEPHEN and HARTMANN, DOUGLAS 1998 *Ethnicity and Race*, Thousand Oaks, CA: Pine Forge

DAVID, E. and OKAZAKI, SUMIE 2006 'The colonial mentality scale for Filipino Americans', *Journal of Counseling Psychology*, vol. 53, no. 2, pp. 241–52.

DHINGRA, PAWAN 2007 *Managing Multicultural Lives*, Stanford, CA: Stanford University Press

——— 2012 *Life behind the Lobby*, Stanford, CA: Stanford University Press

ESPIRITU, YEN LE 1992 *Asian American Panethnicity*, Philadelphia, PA: Temple University Press

——— 2004 'Asian American panethnicity', in Nancy Foner and George Frederickson (eds), *Not Just Black and White*, New York: Russell Sage, pp. 217–36.

——— 2007 'Gender, Migration, and Work', in Min Zhou and James Gatewood (eds), *Contemporary Asian America*, New York: NYU Press, pp. 207–32.

ESPIRITU, YEN LE and WOLF, DIANE 2001 'The paradox of assimilation', in Ruben Rumbaut and Alejandro Portes (eds), *Ethnicities*, Berkeley, CA: University of California Press, pp. 157–86.

GORDON, MILTON 1964 *Assimilation in American Life*, New York: Oxford University Press

GORMAN, ANNA 2007 'Mall anchors thriving Filipino community', *Los Angeles Times*, 22 August. [Available from: http://articles.latimes.com/2007/aug/22/local/me-filipino22 [Accessed 11 January 2013]]

GOTTDIENER, MARK and HUTCHINSON, RAY 2010 *The New Urban Sociology*, Boulder, CO: Westview

GUEVARRA, RUDY 2012 *Becoming Mexipino: Multiethnic Communities and Identities in San Diego*, New Brunswick, NJ: Rutgers University Press

IBAÑEZ, FLORANTE and IBAÑEZ, ROSEYLN 2009 *Filipinos in Carson and the South Bay*, Mt Pleasant, SC: Arcadia

JACKSON, JOHN 2001 *Harlemworld*, Chicago, IL: University of Chicago Press

JIMÉNEZ, TOMAS 2010 *Replenished Ethnicity*, Berkeley, CA: University of California Press

KASINITZ, PHILIP *et al.* 2008 *Inheriting the City*, New York: Russell Sage

KIBRIA, NAZLI 1998 'The contested meaning of "Asian American"', *Ethnic and Racial Studies*, vol. 21, no. 5, pp. 939–58.

KIM, NADIA 2008 *Imperial Citizens*, Stanford, CA: Stanford University Press

LACY, KARYN 2008 *Blue-Chip Black*, Berkeley, CA: University of California Press

MASSEY, DOUGLAS, *et al.* 1993 'Theories of international migration', *Population and Development Review*, vol. 19, no. 3, pp. 431–66.

MATILLA, DEXTER 2011 'Pulitzer Prize–winning novelist Junot Díaz', *Philippine Daily Inquirer*, 26 December. [Available from: http://lifestyle.inquirer.net/28907/pulitzer-prize-winning-novelist-junot-diaz [Accessed 11 January 2013]]

MORROW, PAUL 2007 'Mexico is just not a town in Pampanga', *Pilipino Express*, 1 October. [Available from: http://www.pilipino-express.com/history-a-culture/in-other-words/225-mexico-is-not-just-a-town-in-pampanga.html [Accessed 11 January 2013]]

NECKERMAN, KATHERINE, CARTER, PRUDENCE and LEE, JENNIFER 1999 'Segmented assimilation and minority cultures of mobility', *Ethnic and Racial Studies*, vol. 22, no. 6, pp. 945–65.

ONG, PAUL and AZORES, TANIA 1994 'The migration and incorporation of Filipino nurses', in Paul Ong, *et al.* (eds), *New Asian Immigration in Los Angeles and Global Restructuring*, Philadelphia, PA: Temple University Press, pp. 164–95.

PARK, ROBERT 1950 *Race and Culture*, Glencoe, IL: Free Press

PISARES, ELIZABETH 2006 'Do you (mis)recognize me? in Antonio Tiongson, *et al.* (eds), *Positively No Filipinos Allowed*, Philadelphia, PA: Temple University Press, pp. 172–98.

POROS, MARITSA 2010 *Modern Migrations*, Stanford, CA: Stanford University Press

PORTES, ALEJANDRO and RUMBAUT, RUBEN 2001 *Legacies*, Berkeley, CA: University of California Press

——— 2006 *Immigrant America*, Berkeley, CA: University of California Press

PORTES, ALEJANDRO and ZHOU, MIN 1993 'The new second generation', *Annals of the American Academy of Political and Social Science*, vol. 530, no. 1, pp. 491–522.

RODRÍGUEZ, EVELYN 2006 'Primerang Bituin', *Asia Pacific Perspectives*, vol. 6, no. 1, pp. 4–12.

RODRÍGUEZ, ROBYN 2010 *Migrants for Export*, Minneapolis, MN: University of Minnesota Press

ROTH, WENDY 2009 'Latino before the world', *Ethnic and Racial Studies*, vol. 32, no. 6, pp. 927–47.

TERANISHI, ROBERT 2002 'Asian Pacific Americans and critical race theory', *Equity and Excellence in Education*, vol. 35, no. 2, pp. 144–54.

TERANISHI, ROBERT, *et al.* 2004 'The college-choice process for Asian Americans', *Review of Higher Education*, vol. 27, no. 4, pp. 527–51.

VERGARA, BENITO 2009 *Pinoy Capital*, Philadelphia, PA: Temple University Press

WARIKOO, NATASHA 2011 *Balancing Acts*, Berkeley, CA: University of California Press

WATERS, MARY 1999 *Black Identities*, Cambridge, MA: Harvard University Press

ZHOU, MIN 2009 *Contemporary Chinese America*, Philadelphia, PA: Temple University Press

ZHOU, MIN and BANKSTON, CARL 1998 *Growing Up American*, New York: Russell Sage

ZHOU, MIN and XIONG, YANG 2005 'The multifaceted American experience of children of Asian immigrants', *Ethnic and Racial Studies*, vol. 28, no. 6, pp. 1119–52.

CHAPTER 13

The Persistent Problem of Colorism

Skin Tone, Status, and Inequality

Margaret Hunter

Colorism *is a persistent problem for people of color in the United States. Colorism, or skin color stratification, is a process that privileges light-skinned people of color over dark-skinned people in areas such as income, education, housing, and the marriage market. In this essay, Margaret Hunter describes the experiences of African Americans, Latinas/os, and Asian Americans with regard to skin color. She presents research that demonstrates that light-skinned people have clear advantages in these areas, even when controlling for other background variables. However, dark-skinned people of color are typically regarded as more ethnically authentic or legitimate than light-skinned people. She explains that colorism is directly related to the larger system of racism in the United States and around the world.*

Questions to Consider

Can you think of some examples that illustrate how colorism plays out in the United States? How is colorism in the United States exported around the globe, and what does a global color complex look like? What would it take to dismantle colorism in the United States and abroad?

Source: Adapted from Margaret Hunter, "The Persistent Problem of Colorism: Skin Tone, Status, and Inequality," *Sociology Compass* Volume 1, Issue 1, pages 237–254, John Wiley and Sons Inc., 2007.

Racial discrimination is a pervasive problem in the USA. African Americans, Latinos, Asian Americans, and other people of color are routinely denied access to resources and fair competition for jobs and schooling. Despite this pattern of exclusion, people of color have made great progress in combating persistent discrimination in housing, the labor market, and education. However, hidden within the process of racial discrimination is the often overlooked issue of colorism. Colorism is the process of discrimination that privileges light-skinned people of color over their dark-skinned counterparts (Hunter 2005). Colorism is concerned with actual skin tone, as opposed to racial or ethnic identity. This is an important distinction because race is a social concept, not significantly tied to biology (Hirschman 2004). Lighter-skinned people of color enjoy substantial privileges that are still unattainable to their darker-skinned brothers and sisters. In fact, light-skinned people earn more money, complete more years of schooling, live in better neighborhoods, and marry higher-status people than darker-skinned people of the same race or ethnicity (Arce et al. 1987; Espino and Franz 2002; Hill 2000; Hughes and Hertel 1990; Hunter 1998, 2005; Keith and Herring 1991; Murguia and Telles 1996; Rondilla and Spickard 2007).

How does colorism operate? Systems of racial discrimination operate on at least two levels: race and color. The first system of discrimination is the level of racial category, (i.e. black, Asian, Latino, etc.). Regardless of physical appearance, African Americans of all skin tones are subject to certain kinds of discrimination, denigration, and second-class citizenship, simply because they are African American. Racism in this form is systemic and has both ideological and material consequences (Bonilla-Silva 2006; Feagin 2000). The second system of discrimination, what I am calling colorism, is at the level of skin tone: darker skin or lighter skin. Although all blacks experience discrimination as blacks, the intensity of that discrimination, the frequency, and the outcomes of that discrimination will differ dramatically by skin tone. Darker-skinned African Americans may earn less money that lighter-skinned African Americans, although both earn less than whites. These two systems of discrimination (race and color) work in concert. The two systems are distinct, but inextricably connected. For example, a light-skinned Mexican American may still experience racism, despite her light skin, and a dark-skinned Mexican American may experience racism and colorism simultaneously. Racism is a larger, systemic, social process and colorism is one manifestation of it.

Although many people believe that colorism is strictly a 'black or Latino problem', colorism is actually practiced by whites and people of color alike. Given the opportunity, many people will hire a light-skinned person before a dark-skinned person of the same race (Espino and Franz 2002; Hill 2000; Hughes and Hertel 1990; Mason 2004; Telles and Murguia 1990), or choose to marry a lighter-skinned woman rather than a darker-skinned woman (Hunter 1998; Rondilla and Spickard 2007; Udry et al. 1971). Many people are unaware of their preferences for lighter skin because that dominant aesthetic is so deeply ingrained in our culture. In the US, for example, we are bombarded with images of white and light skin and Anglo facial features. White beauty is the standard and the ideal (Kilbourne 1999).

Historical Origins of Colorism

Colorism has roots in the European colonial project (Jordan 1968), plantation life for enslaved African Americans (Stevenson 1996), and the early class hierarchies of Asia (Rondilla and Spickard 2007). Despite its disparate roots, today, colorism in the USA is broadly maintained by a system of white racism (Feagin et al. 2001). The maintenance of white supremacy (aesthetic, ideological, and material) is predicated on the notion that dark skin represents savagery, irrationality, ugliness, and inferiority. White skin, and, thus, whiteness itself, is defined by the opposite: civility, rationality, beauty, and superiority. These contrasting definitions are the foundation for colorism.

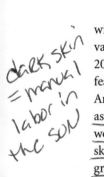

Colorism for Latinos and African Americans has its roots in European colonialism and slavery in the Americas. Both systems operated as forms of white domination that rewarded those who emulated whiteness culturally, ideologically, economically, and even aesthetically. Light-skinned people received privileges and resources that were otherwise unattainable to their darker-skinned counterparts. White elites ruling the colonies maintained white superiority and domination by enlisting the assistance of the 'colonial elite', often a small light-skinned class of colonized people (Fanon 1967). Although Mexico experienced a high degree of racial miscegenation, the color-caste system was firmly in place. Light-skinned Spaniards culled the most power and resources, while darker-skinned Indians were routinely oppressed, dispossessed of their land, and rendered powerless in the early colony. Vestiges of this history are still visible today in Mexico's color-class system.

A similar color hierarchy developed in the USA during slavery and afterward. Slave owners typically used skin tone as a dimension of hierarchy on the plantation (Horowitz 1973). White slave owners sometimes gave lighter-skinned African slaves some additional privileges, such as working in the house as opposed to the fields, the occasional opportunity to learn to read, and the rare chance for freedom (Davis 1991). During slavery, a small, but elite class of freedmen was established. These disproportionately light-skinned men and women were early business leaders, clergy, teachers, and artisans, who became economic and community leaders in the early African American community (Edwards 1959; Frazier 1957; Gatewood 1990).

Colorism for Asian Americans seems to have a more varied history. For Asian Americans with a European colonial history, like Indians, Vietnamese, or Filipinos, light skin tone is valued because of the European values enforced by the colonial regime (Karnow 1989; Rafael 2000). Europeans themselves were regarded as high status, as were white skin, Anglo facial features, and the English, French, and Spanish languages, respectively. For other Asian American groups with an indirect relationship to Western culture, light skin tone was associated with the leisure class (Jones 2004; Rondilla and Spickard 2007). Only poor or working people would be dark because they had to work outside as manual laborers. Dark skin tone is therefore associated with poverty and 'backwardness' for many Asian immigrants and Asian Americans (Rondilla and Spickard 2007).

Ronald Hall (1994, 1995, 1997) suggests that 'the bleaching syndrome' the internalization of a white aesthetic ideal, is the result of the historic legacy of slavery and colonialism around the globe. He argues that many African Americans, Latinos, and Asian Americans have internalized the colonial and slavery value systems and learned to valorize light skin tones and Anglo facial features. He understands this deeply rooted cultural value as a cause of psychological distress and socioeconomic stratification.

In many former European colonies, there remains an overt legacy of Eurocentrism and white racism in the culture (Memmi 1965). Whites or light-skinned elites continue to hold powerful positions in the economy, government, and educational sectors. Embedded in the leftover colonial structure is a strong and enduring value of white aesthetics (e.g. light hair, straight hair, light eyes, narrow noses, and light skin). This is evident in Latin American popular culture, for example, in the *telenovelas*, where almost all of the actors look white, unless they are the maids and are then light brown (Jones 2004). Movie stars and popular singers in the Philippines are often *mestizos*, half white, or extremely light-skinned with round eyes (Choy 2005; Rafael 2000). African American celebrities are typically light-skinned with Anglo features (Milkie 1999). They reinforce a beauty ideal based on white bodies (Kilbourne 1999).

Colorism is not just relevant to media images, however. A rising number of discrimination cases based on skin tone have found their way to the courts. In 2002, the EEOC sued the owners of a Mexican restaurant in San Antonio, Texas, for color-based discrimination. A white manager at the restaurant claimed that the owners directed him to hire only light-skinned staff to work in the dining room. The EEOC won the case and the restaurant was forced to pay $100,000 in fines (Valbrun 2003). Most people of color will not end up in court over color bias, but nearly all people of color have experienced or witnessed unfair treatment of others based on skin tone. Although both of these cases highlight co-ethnic perpetrators of skin-tone bias, whites are also engaged in discrimination by skin tone.

The Economics of Light Skin Privilege

The vast majority of social science research on skin-tone discrimination focuses on the employment experiences of African Americans and Latinos (Allen et al. 2000; Arce et al. 1987; Espino and Franz 2002; Gomez 2000; Hill 2000; Hughes and Hertel 1990; Hunter 2002; Keith and Herring 1991; Mason 2004; Murguia and Telles 1996; Telles and Murguia 1990). Latinos are a particularly interesting case to study because social scientists typically treat 'Latino' or 'Hispanic' as a separate category from race. Consequently there are Latinos who identify as white, black, Indian, and others. There are strong variations by national group as to which of those options Latinos choose (Mexicans are most likely to choose 'other race' and Cubans are most likely to choose 'white', for example) (Rodriguez 2000). Some researchers use the racial self-designations of Latinos as proxies for skin color when an actual skin-tone variable is not available (Alba et al. 2000).

In 2003, social science researchers found that Latinos who identified as white earned about $5000 more per year than Latinos who identified as black, and about $2500 more per year than Latinos who identified as 'some other race' (Fears 2003). A clear hierarchy is evident among Latinos with white Latinos at the top, 'others' in the middle, and black Latinos at the bottom. White Latinos also had lower unemployment rates and lower poverty rates than black Latinos (Fears 2003). Their findings are consistent with other work in this area (Montalvo 1987). Dark skin costs for Latinos, in terms of income (Telles and Murguia 1990) and occupational prestige (Espino and Franz 2002).

Other researchers found that lighter-skinned Mexican Americans and African Americans earn more money than their darker-skinned counterparts (Allen et al. 2000; Arce et al. 1987). Even when researchers account for differences in family background, occupation, and education levels, skin-color differences persist. This shows that skin-color stratification cannot be explained away with other variables such as class or family history. Keith and Herring (1991) suggest that color discrimination operates after the civil rights movement much the way it did before the movement. 'Virtually all of our findings parallel those that occurred before the civil rights movement. These facts suggest that the effects of skin tone are not only historical curiosities from a legacy of slavery and racism, but present-day mechanisms that influence who gets what in America' (Keith and Herring 1991, 777).

It can be difficult to imagine how colorism operates on a day-to-day basis. Colorism, like racism, consists of both overt and covert actions, outright acts of discrimination and subtle cues of disfavor. In employment, negotiations over salary and benefits may be tainted by colorism (Etcoff 2000; Webster and Driskell 1983). How much a new employee is 'worth' and the assessed value of her skills may be affected by her appearance (Thompson and Keith 2001). We know from research on physical attractiveness that people who are considered more attractive are also viewed as smarter and friendlier (Etcoff 2000; Hatfield and Sprecher 1986; Wade and Bielitz 2005). 'Attractiveness' is a cultural construct influenced by racial aesthetics (Hill 2002), among other things, so lighter-skinned job applicants will likely benefit from a halo effect of physical attractiveness (Dion et al. 1972; Mulford et al. 1998).

The relationship between skin color and perceptions of attractiveness may be particularly important for women on the job (Hunter 2002). Many feminist scholars have argued that beauty matters for women in much the same way that 'brains' matter for men (Freedman 1986; Lakoff and Scherr 1984; Wolf 1991). Of course, women's job-related skills are crucial for a successful career, but cultural critic Naomi Wolf (1991) has suggested that 'beauty' has become an additional, unspoken job requirement for women in many professions, even when physical attractiveness is irrelevant for job performance. If this is the case, then in 'front office appearance jobs', like restaurant hostess or office receptionist, beauty, and therefore skin color, must matter even more.

In 2002, Rodolfo Espino and Michael Franz compared the employment experiences of Mexicans, Puerto Ricans, and Cubans in the USA. They found, 'that darker-skinned Mexicans and Cubans face significantly lower occupational prestige scores than their lighter-skinned counterparts even when controlling for factors that influence performance in the labor market' (2002, 612). Mark Hill (2000), in his study of African American men, found that light-skinned black men retained a significant advantage in the labor market and that skin tone accounted for more differences in social status than family background did. Hill developed a very creative research methodology that clarified the *ongoing* nature of skin-color bias and challenged the oft-made assertion that light skin benefits are simply remnants of a historical color-caste system. In the labor market, dark skin tone is consistently penalized in terms of income (Allen et al. 2000; Keith and Herring 1991; Mason 2004), unemployment rates, and even occupational prestige (Espino and Franz 2002; Hill 2000).

Skin Color and Ethnic Identity

The economic and social advantages of light skin are clear. In societies where resources are divided by race and color, light-skinned people get a disproportionate amount of the benefits. However, light skin may be viewed as a disadvantage with regard to ethnic legitimacy or authenticity. In many ethnic communities, people view darker-skin tones as more ethnically authentic. For example, light-skinned and biracial people often report feeling left out or pushed out of co-ethnic groups. They report other people's perceptions of their racial identity as a common source of conflict or discomfort (Brunsma and Rockquemore 2001).

The task of 'proving' oneself to be a legitimate or authentic member of an ethnic community is a significant burden for the light-skinned in Latino, African American, and Asian

American communities. For some people of color, authenticity is the vehicle through which darker-skinned people take back their power from lighter-skinned people (Hunter 2005). For example, a dark-skinned African American woman remarked,

> In terms of female–female relationships, I think color affects how we treat each other. Like if you're lighter and I think you're better, and I think the guys want you, then I won't treat you nicely. I'll take every opportunity to ignore you, or not tell you something, or keep you out of my little group of friends, because really I feel threatened, so I want to punish you because you have it better than me. (Hunter 2005, 72)

In this example, the darker-skinned interviewee describes feeling 'threatened' by the high status of light-skinned African American women. She responded by using her social power and friendship networks.

Light-skinned Mexican Americans are often viewed as more assimilated and less identified with the Mexican American community (Mason 2004). Mexicans report using Spanish language ability as a way to re-establish their Mexican identity when light skin casts doubt on it (Jimenez 2004). Suggestions of not being black enough, or authentically ethnic enough, in any ethnic community, is a serious insult to many. This tactic has particular power against those lighter-skinned people who are from racially mixed backgrounds (Rockquemore 2002). It implies that they do not identify with their fellow ethnics, that they do not care about them, that they think they are better than their co-ethnics, or, in extreme cases, that they wish they were white (Bowman et al. 2004; Ono 2002; Vazquez et al. 1997).

Charges of ethnic illegitimacy were already at work in the 2008 US presidential campaign. Political commentators charged both Obama and Bill Richardson of not being 'ethnic enough'. These charges may seem inconsequential to the casual observer, but accusations of ethnic illegitimacy can be quite significant. Major media outlets, such as *Time* magazine and the *Los Angeles Times*, ran stories titled, 'Is Obama Black Enough?' (Coates 2007) and 'Obama Not "Black Enough"?' (Huston 2007). Researchers have found that voters pay close attention to racial cues and framing in election campaigns. A candidate's skin tone and ethnic identity can be crucial determinants in many elections (Caliendo and Mcilwain 2006; Terkildsen 1993).

Darker skin color, as evidenced in the above example, is associated with more race-conscious views and higher levels of perceived discrimination (Allen et al. 2000; Edwards 1973; Hughes and Hertel 1990; Ono 2002; Ransford 1970). Among Latinos, skin color is also closely associated with language, where dark skin and Spanish language ability are key identifiers of Chicano and Mexican identity (Lopez 1982). Conversely, light skin and English monolingualism are typically identified with Anglo assimilation and thus devalued by some in Mexican American communities (Ortiz and Arce 1984). Herein lies the contradiction: on one hand, dark skin is associated with being Indian or African and therefore backward, ugly, and low status. On the other hand, dark skin is evidence of being Indian or African and therefore, of being truly or authentically Mexican American or African American (Hunter 2005). This contradiction is exemplified in the previous example of Obama's presidential candidacy. His light skin tone, among other factors, is a source of trouble because it represents Anglo assimilation and ethnic illegitimacy, but his political success is also attributable in part to his light skin tone and perceived high levels of Anglo assimilation. This is the conundrum of colorism.

Research on Asian Americans revealed a similar ambivalence about skin tone (Rondilla and Spickard 2007). In one study, most Asian American respondents agreed that their communities demonstrated strong preferences for light skin, but there were notable exceptions (Rondilla and Spickard 2007). The researchers asked people to look at three different pictures of Asian American young women, one light skinned, one medium, and one dark and to create a story of each of their lives. This very creative process yielded fascinating results. Participants wrote the most positive narratives about the woman with the medium complexion. Respondents characterized the lightest-skinned woman as 'troubled', 'torn between one culture to the next', and 'she wants to shed her Oriental roots by becoming blond' (Rondilla and Spickard, 2007, 67–68). In contrast, when describing the darkest-skinned woman, respondents created stories that centered on her ethnic authenticity. They described her as a recent immigrant, close to her family, responsible for younger brothers and sisters, with limited English skills, and as the least 'American' of the three women pictured (Rondilla and Spickard 2007). The woman of medium skin tone was described as 'all-American', as a good student, good friend, smart, successful, and as an ideal choice for a daughter-in-law. Rondilla and Spickard's (2007) research reveals the complexity of skin color, status, and identity.

It is tempting to characterize the problem of colorism as equally difficult for both light-skinned people and dark. Dark-skinned people lack the social and economic capital that light skin provides, and are therefore disadvantaged in education, employment, and housing (Alba et al. 2000; Arce et al. 1987; Keith and Herring 1991). Additionally, dark skin is generally not regarded as beautiful, so dark-skinned women often lose out in the dating and marriage markets (Hunter 1998; Sahay and Piran 1997). On the other side, light-skinned men and women are typically not regarded as legitimate members of their ethnic communities. They may be excluded from, or made to feel unwelcome in, community events and organizations (Hunter 2005). At first glance, it may seem that there are equal advantages and disadvantages to both sides of the color line. Upon closer examination, this proves to be untrue. Although exclusion from some community organizations may be uncomfortable psychologically or emotionally for light-skinned people of color, it rarely has significant material effects. More specifically, emotional turmoil about ethnic identity does not have significant economic consequences. However, the systematic discrimination against dark-skinned people of color in the labor market, educational institutions, and marriage market create marked economic disadvantages (Allen et al. 2000; Hill 2000; Hughes and Hertel 1990; Mason 2004). Without minimizing the psychological trauma of exclusion from ethnic communities, it is important to clarify that the disadvantages of dark skin still far outweigh the disadvantages of light.

Gender, Beauty, and the Global Color Complex

Although colorism affects both men and women, women experience discrimination based on skin tone in particular ways. Skin tone is an important characteristic in defining beauty and beauty is an important resource for women (Hunter 2002; Wolf 1991). Beauty provides women with status that can lead to advances in employment, education, and even the marriage market (Hunter 2005). Light skin color, as an indicator of beauty, can operate as a form of social capital for women (Hunter 2002). This social capital can be transformed into other forms of capital and used to gain status in jobs, housing, schools, and social networks. Social networks can increase capital in a wide variety of ways, and one of the most important is through one's spouse. Light-skinned people of color are not more likely to be married than their darker-skinned counterparts, but light-skinned women, particularly African Americans, are likely to marry higher status spouses (Hunter 1998; Udry et al. 1971). Study after study has shown that light-skinned African American women marry spouses with higher levels of education, higher incomes, or higher levels of occupational prestige, than their darker-skinned counterparts (Hughes and Hertel 1990; Hunter 1998; Keith and Herring 1991; Udry et al. 1971). This phenomenon allows light-skinned people to 'marry up' and essentially exchange the high status of their skin tone for the high status of education, income, or occupation in their spouse (Elder 1969; Webster and Driskell 1983).

Interviews published by Rondilla and Spickard (2007) reveal this social exchange theory or 'marrying up' practice at work. A Filipina interviewee said, 'My father suggested I have children with my White ex-boyfriend so he could have mestizo grandchildren. I think years of this colonial way of thinking and all the American propaganda has made it so that my father (and most other Filipinos) think that everything "American"—White American—is superior' (Rondilla and Spickard 2007, 55). This example illustrates that marrying a lighter-skinned partner is not just a practice that gives the spouse access to more social and economic capital, but it is also a practice that could allow one's children to have a higher status by being lighter-skinned themselves.

The Philippines is a good example of the intersection of internalized colonial values and the cult of the new global beauty. Like many other former European or American colonies, the Philippines' contemporary culture valorizes American culture and white beauty (Rafael 2000). Through globalization, multinational media conglomerates export US cultural products and cultural imperialism. Part of this structure of domination is the exportation of cultural images, including images of race (Choy 2005). The USA exports images of the good life, of white beauty, white affluence, white heroes, and brown and black entertainers/criminals. As many people in other countries yearn for the 'good life' offered in the USA, they also yearn for the dominant aesthetic of the USA: light skin, blond hair, and Anglo facial features (Fraser 2003). Women in Korea, surrounded by other Koreans, pay high sums of money to have double eyelid surgery that Westernizes their eyes. 'In Asian countries like South Korea, Japan and China, double eyelid surgery is a way of life. In fact, because so many people in South Korea have undergone eyelid surgery, the country has the highest percentage of people with plastic surgery in the world' (King and Yun 2005). Women in Saudi Arabia, Uganda, and Brazil are using toxic skin bleaching creams to try and achieve a lighter complexion (Chisholm 2002; Mire 2001; Siyachitema 2002). One of the most common high school graduation presents among the elite in Mexico City is a nose job with the plastic surgeon (Taylor 2002). Each of these choices may sound extreme or pathological, but it is actually quite rational in a context of global racism and US domination. Unfortunately new eyelids, lighter skin, and new noses are likely to offer their owners better opportunities in a competitive global marketplace (Davis 1995; Kaw 1998; Morgan 1998; Sullivan 2001).

The new global racism transcends national borders and infiltrates cultures and families all over the world. It draws on historical ideologies of colonialism and internalized racism buttressed with visions of a new world order. Images associated with white America are highly valued and emulated in the global marketplace. This is part of what makes colorism and racism so hard to battle: the images supporting these systems are everywhere and the rewards for whiteness are real. In addition to wrestling with the values of their colonial pasts, many Third World nations are also contending with the onslaught of US-produced cultural images valorizing whiteness and especially white femininity (and the occasional version of light brown femininity). Television, film, Internet, and print ads all feature white women with blond hair as not only the cultural ideal, but the cultural imperative. White and light-skinned people are rewarded accordingly.

Women and men of color have ever-increasing opportunities to alter their bodies toward whiteness. They can purchase lighter-colored contact lenses for their eyes; they can straighten kinky or curly hair; they can have cosmetic surgeries on their lips, noses, or eyes. But one of the oldest traditions of this sort is skin bleaching. There are lots of old wives' tales recipes for skin bleaching, including baking soda, bleach, toothpaste, or even lye. In the USA, overt skin bleaching with the stated intention of whitening one's skin fell out of favor in many communities after the Civil Rights movements and cultural pride movements of the 1960s and 1970s. However, outside of the USA and in many postcolonial nations of the Global South, skin bleaching is reaching new heights.

Skin-bleaching creams go by many names: skin lighteners, skin whiteners, skin-toning creams, skin evening creams, skin-fading gels, etc. Essentially, they are creams regularly applied to the face or body that purport to 'lighten', 'brighten', or 'whiten' the skin. They are marketed as beauty products available to women to increase their beauty, by increasing their whiteness. The skin bleaching industry is thriving around the globe, particularly in Third World, postcolonial countries (Mire 2001). Skin lighteners are commonly used in places including Mexico, Pakistan, Saudi Arabia, Jamaica, the Philippines, Japan, India, Tanzania, Senegal, Nigeria, Uganda, Kenya, Ghana, and less so, but also USA (Charles 2003; Chisholm 2002; Easton 1998; Kovaleski 1999; Mahe et al. 2004; Schuler 1999). For many people around the world, skin bleaching seems like one of the few ways to get a piece of the pie in a highly racialized society. Skin-lightening products constitute a multibillion dollar industry. These products usually contain one of three harmful ingredients: mercury, hydroquinone, or corticosteroids (sometimes used in combination). Many skin-bleaching products are made outside of North America and Europe, in Mexico and Nigeria, but often under the auspices of larger US and European cosmetics firms (Mire 2001). The products may not be made in the USA, but US women also use them.

In fact, the pursuit of light skin color can be so important it can prove fatal. A Harvard medical school researcher found outbreaks of mercury poisoning in countries such as Saudi Arabia, Pakistan, and Tanzania. He came to learn that the mercury poisoning, found almost exclusively in women, was caused by the widespread use of skin-bleaching creams containing toxic levels of mercury (Counter 2003). Even children were suffering the effects of mercury poisoning, either from *in utero* absorption during pregnancy, or from mothers who put the bleaching cream on their children eager for them to have the benefits of light skin. These stories may seem to be only far away, but they also happen in the USA. The same team of Harvard researchers found outbreaks of mercury poisoning in the southwestern USA where thousands of Mexican American women use skin-bleaching creams to try to achieve a lighter and more valued complexion.

Skin color continues to shape our lives in powerful ways in the USA and around the globe. The cultural messages that give meaning and value to different skin tones are both deeply historical and actively contemporary. People of color with dark skin tones continue to pay a price for their color, and the light skinned continue to benefit from their association with whiteness. Only a slow dismantling of the larger system of white racism, in the USA and around the globe, will initiate a change in the color hierarchy it has created. But this is not to say it will be easy. Talking about colorism and internalized racism can be challenging. Most white Americans believe that racism is on the wane, and that any talk about racial discrimination does more harm than good (Bonilla-Silva 1999; Brown et al. 2003). This phenomenon is referred to by many social scientists as 'colorblind racism'. Colorblind racism makes racism invisible while actively perpetuating it. But white Americans are not the only ones who do not want to talk about colorism. Many African Americans feel that discussions of colorism 'air our dirty laundry' for all to see and judge (Breland 1997). Others feel that talking about colorism distracts from the larger and more significant problem of racism in the USA. Most people of color agree that colorism is an 'in house' issue, a personal one that is a tragedy within communities of color (Russell, Wilson, and Hall 1992). It is at minimum, embarrassing, and at its worst, a sign of racial self-hatred (Hall 2006).

Discussing colorism is not a 'distraction' from the important issue of racial discrimination. In fact, understanding colorism helps us better understand how racism works in our contemporary society. Colorism is one manifestation of a larger 'racial project' that communicates meaning and status about race in the USA (Omi and Winant 1994). Studies on skin-color stratification support the contention that racial discrimination is alive and well (Keith and Herring 1991; Mason 2004), and so insidious that communities of color themselves are divided into quasi-racial hierarchies (Alba et al. 2000; Hunter 2005; Seltzer and Smith 1991). As long as the structure of white racism remains intact, colorism will continue to operate.

References

Alba, Richard D., John R. Logan and Brian J. Stults 2000. 'The Changing Neighborhood Contexts of the Immigrant Metropolis.' *Social Forces* 79: 587–621.

Allen, Walter, Edward Telles and Margaret Hunter 2000. 'Skin Color, Income, and Education: A Comparison of African Americans and Mexican Americans.' *National Journal of Sociology* 12: 129–80.

Arce, Carlos, Edward Murguia and W. Parker Frisbie 1987. 'Phenotype and Life Chances Among Chicanos.' *Hispanic Journal of Behavioral Sciences* 9: 19–32.

Bonilla-Silva, Eduardo 1999. *Racism and White Supremacy in the Post–Civil Rights Era.* New York: Lynne Reiner Publishers.

Bonilla-Silva, Eduardo 2006. *Racism Without Racists.* Lanham, MD: Rowman and Littlefield.

Bowman, Phillip J., Ray Muhammad and Mosi Ifatunji 2004. 'Skin Tone, Class, and Racial Attitudes Among African Americans.' Pp. 128–58 in *Skin/Deep: How Race and Complexion Matter in the 'Color-Blind' Era*, edited by Cedric Herring, Verna M. Keith and Hayward Derrick Horton. Urbana, IL: University of Illinois Press.

Breland, Alfiee M. 1997. 'Airing Dirty Laundry: Reasons and Processes by which Skin Tone Stratification Continues to Be a Pervasive Aspect of the African American Community.' University of Wisconsin–Madison, Dissertation Abstracts International.

Brown, Michael, Martin Carnoy, Elliott Currie, Troy Duster, David Oppenheimer, Marjorie Schultz and David Wellman 2003. *White-Washing Race: The Myth of the Colorblind Society.* Berkeley, CA: University of California Press.

Brunsma, David L. and Kerry A. Rockquemore 2001. 'The New Color Complex: Appearances and Biracial Identity.' *Identity* 1: 225–46.

Caliendo, Stephen M. and Charlton D. Mcilwain 2006. 'Minority Candidates, Media Framing, and Racial Cues in the 2004 Election.' *The Harvard International Journal of Press/politics* 11: 45–69.

Charles, Christopher 2003. 'Skin Bleaching, Self-Hate, and Black Identity in Jamaica.' *Journal of Black Studies* 33: 711–28.

Chisholm, N. Jamiyla 2002. 'Fade to White: Skin Bleaching and the Rejection of Blackness.' *Village Voice* January 23–29, 2002.

Choy, Catherine 2005. 'Asian American History: Reflections on Imperialism, Immigration, and the Body.' Pp. 81–98 in *Pinay Power: Peminist Critical Theory*, edited by Melinda De Jesus. New York: Routledge.

Coates, Ta-Nehisi Paul 2007. 'Is Obama Black Enough?' *Time* February 1, 2007.

Counter, S. Allen 2003. 'Whitening Skin Can Be Deadly.' *Boston Globe* December 16, 2003.

Davis, F. James 1991. *Who Is Black? One Nation's Definition.* University Park, PA: Pennsylvania State University Press.

Davis, Kathy 1995. *Reshaping the Female Body*. New York: Routledge.

Dion, Karen, Ellen Berscheid and Elaine Walster 1972. 'What Is Beautiful Is Good.' *Journal of Personality and Social Psychology* 24: 285–90.

Easton, A. 1998. 'Women Have Deadly Desire for Paler Skin in the Philippines.' *Lancet* 352: 355.

Edwards, G. F. 1959. *The Negro Professional Class.* Glencoe, IL: The Free Press.

Edwards, Ozzie 1973. 'Skin Color as a Variable in Racial Attitudes of Black Urbanites.' *Journal of Black Studies* 3: 473–83.

Elder, Glen 1969. 'Appearance and Education in Marriage Mobility.' *American Sociological Review* 34: 519–33.

Espino, Rodolfo and Michael Franz 2002. 'Latino Phenotypic Discrimination Revisited: The Impact of Skin Color on Occupational Status.' *Social Science Quarterly* 83: 612–23.

Etcoff, Nancy 2000. *Survival of the Prettiest: The Science of Beauty*. New York: Anchor Books.

Fanon, Frantz 1967. *Black Skin White Masks.* New York: Grove Weidenfeld.

Feagin, Joe R. 2000. *Racist America: Roots, Current Realities, and Future Reparations.* New York: Routledge.

Feagin, Joe R., Hernan Vera and Pinar Batur 2001. *White Racism: The Basics*, 2nd edn. New York: Routledge.

Fears, Darryl 2003. 'Race Divides Hispanics, Report Says; Integration and Income Vary With Skin Color.' *Washington Post* July 14, 2003.

Fraser, Suzanne 2003. *Cosmetic Surgery, Gender, and Culture.* New York: Palgrave Macmillan.

Frazier, E. Franklin 1957. *Black Bourgeoisie.* New York: Collier Books.

Freedman, Rita 1986. *Beauty Bound.* Lexington, MA: Lexington Books.

Gatewood, Willard B. 1990. *Aristocrats of Color: The Black Elite 1880–1920.* Bloomington, IN: Indiana University Press.

Gomez, Christina 2000. 'The Continual Significance of Skin Color: An Exploratory Study of Latinos in the Northeast.' *Hispanic Journal of Behavioral Sciences* 22: 94–103.

Hall, Ronald E. 2006. 'The Bleaching Syndrome Among People of Color: Implications of Skin Color for Human Behavior in the Social Environment.' *Journal of Human Behavior in the Social Environment* 13: 19–31.

Hall, Ronald 1994. '"The Bleaching Syndrome": Implications of Light Skin for Hispanic American Assimilation.' *Hispanic Journal of Behavioral Sciences* 16: 307–14.

Hall, Ronald 1995. 'The Bleaching Syndrome: African Americans' Response to Cultural Domination Vis-à-vis Skin Color.' *Journal of Black Studies* 26: 172–84.

Hall, Ronald 1997. 'Eurogamy Among Asian Americans: A Note on Western Assimilation.' *The Social Science Journal* 34: 403–8.

Hatfield, Elaine and Susan Sprecher 1986. *Mirror, Mirror: The Importance of Looks in Everyday Life.* Albany, NY: State University of New York Press.

Hill, Mark E. 2000. 'Color Differences in the Socioeconomic Status of African American Men: Results of a Longitudinal Study.' *Social Forces* 78: 1437–60.

Hill, Mark E. 2002. 'Skin Color and the Perception of Attractiveness Among African Americans: Does Gender Make a Difference?' *Social Psychology Quarterly* 65: 77–91.

Hirschman, Charles 2004. 'The Origins and Demise of the Concept of Race.' *Population and Development Review* 30: 385–415.

Horowitz, Donald L. 1973. 'Color Differentiation in the American System of Slavery.' *Journal of Interdisciplinary History* 3: 509–41.

Hughes, Bradley and Michael Hertel 1990. 'The Significance of Color Remains: A Study of Life Chances, Mate Selection, and Ethnic Consciousness among Black Americans.' *Social Forces* 68: 1105–20.

Hunter, Margaret 1998. 'Colorstruck: Skin Color Stratification in the Lives of African American Women.' *Sociological Inquiry* 68: 517–35.

Hunter, Margaret 2002. '"If You're Light, You're Alright": Light Skin Color as Social Capital for Women of Color.' *Gender & Society* 16: 175–93.

Hunter, Margaret 2005. *Race, Gender, and the Politics of Skin Tone.* New York: Routledge.

Huston, Warner Todd 2007. 'Obama: Not "Black Enough"?' *Los Angeles Times* February 19, 2007.

Jimenez, Tomas R. 2004. 'Negotiating Ethnic Boundaries: Multiethnic Mexican Americans and Ethnic Identity in the United States.' *Ethnicities* 4: 75–97.

Jones, Vanessa 2004. 'Pride or Prejudice? A Formally Taboo Topic Among Asian-Americans and Latinos Comes Out Into the Open as Skin Tone Consciousness Sparks a Backlash.' *Boston Globe* August 19, 2004.

Jordan, Winthrop 1968. *White Over Black.* Chapel Hill, NC: University of North Carolina Press.

Karnow, Stanley 1989. *In Our Image: America's Empire in the Philippines.* New York: Ballantine.

Kaw, Eugenia 1998. 'Medicalization of Racial Features: Asian American Women and Cosmetic Surgery.' Pp. 167–83 in *The Politics of Women's Bodies: Sexuality, Appearance, and Behavior*, ed. Rose Weitz. New York: Oxford University Press.

Keith, Verna and Cedric Herring 1991. 'Skin Tone and Stratification in the Black Community.' *American Journal of Sociology* 97: 760–78.

Kilbourne, Jean 1999. *Deadly Persuasion: Why Women and Girls Must Fight the Addictive Power of Advertising.* New York: Free Press.

King, Elizabeth and Jinna Yun 2005. 'Plastic Surgery for Eyelids Popular Among Asian Women.' Medill News Service: Medill School of Journalism, Northwestern University, June 8.

Kovaleski, Serge 1999. 'In Jamaica, Shades of an Identity Crisis: Ignoring Health Risks, Blacks Increase use of Skin Lighteners.' *The Washington Post* August 5, 1999.

Lakoff, Robin and Racquel Scherr 1984. *Face Value: The Politics of Beauty.* Boston, MA: Routledge.

Lopez, David 1982. *Language Maintenance and Shift in the U.S. Today: The Basic Patterns and Their Implications.* Los Alamitos, CA: National Center for Bilingual Research.

Mahe, Antoine, Fatimata Ly and Ari Gounongbe 2004. 'The Cosmetic Use of Bleaching Products in Dakar, Senegal.' *Sciences Sociales et Sante* 22: 5–33.

Mason, Patrick L. 2004. 'Annual Income, Hourly Wages, and Identity Among Mexican-Americans and Other Latinos.' *Industrial Relations* 43: 817–34.

Memmi, Albert 1965. *The Colonizer and the Colonized.* Boston, MA: Beacon Press.

Milkie, Melissa 1999. 'Social Comparisons, Reflected Appraisals, and Mass Media: The Impact of Pervasive Beauty Images on White and Black Girls' Self-Concepts.' *Social Psychology Quarterly* 62: 190–210.

Mire, Amina 2001. 'Skin-Bleaching: Poison, Beauty, Power, and the Politics of the Colour Line.' *Resources for Feminist Research* 28: 13–38.

Montalvo, F. 1987. *Skin Color and Latinos: The Origins and Contemporary Patterns of Ethnoracial Ambiguity Among Mexican Americans and Puerto Ricans* (monograph). San Antonio, TX: Our Lady of the Lake University.

Morgan, Kathryn Pauly 1998. 'Women and the Knife: Cosmetic Surgery and the Colonization of Women's Bodies.' Pp. 147–66 in *The Politics of Women's Bodies: Sexuality, Appearance, and Behavior*, edited by Rose Weitz. New York: Oxford University Press.

Mulford, Matthew, John Orbell, Catherine Shatto and Jean Stockard 1998. 'Physical Attractiveness, Opportunity, and Success in Everyday Exchange.' *American Journal of Sociology* 103: 1565–92.

Murguia, Edward and Edward Telles 1996. 'Phenotype and Schooling Among Mexican Americans.' *Sociology of Education* 69: 276–89.

Ono, Hiromi 2002. 'Assimilation, Ethnic Competition, and Ethnic Identities of U.S.-Born Persons of Mexican Origin.' *The International Migration Review* 36: 726–45.

Ortiz, Vilma and Carlos Arce 1984. 'Language Orientation and Mental Health Status Among Persons of Mexican Descent.' *Hispanic Journal of Behavioral Sciences* 6: 127–43.

Rafael, Vicente 2000. *White Love and Other Events in Filipino History*. Durham, NC: Duke University Press.

Ransford, H. E. 1970. 'Skin Color, Life Chances, and Anti-White Attitude.' *Social Problems* 18: 164–78.

Robinson, Tracy L. and Janie V. Ward 1995. 'African American Adolescents and Skin Color.' *Journal of Black Psychology* 21: 256–74.

Rockquemore, Kerry A. 2002. 'Negotiating the Color Line: The Gendered Process of Racial Identity Construction Among Black/White Biracial Women.' *Gender & Society* 16: 485–503.

Rodriguez, Clara 2000. *Changing Race: Latinos, the Census, and the History of Ethnicity in the United States*. New York: NYU Press.

Rondilla, Joanne and Paul Spickard 2007. *Is Lighter Better?* Lanham, MD: Rowman & Littlefield.

Russell, Kathy, Midge Wilson and Ronald Hall 1992. *The Color Complex*. New York: Doubleday.

Sahay, Sarita and Niva Piran 1997. 'Skin-Color Preferences and Body Satisfaction Among South Asian-Canadian and European-Canadian Female University Students.' *Journal of Social Psychology* 137: 161–71.

Schuler, Corina 1999. 'Africans Look for Beauty in Western Mirror: Black Women Turn to Risky Bleaching Creams and Cosmetic Surgery.' *Christian Science Monitor* December 23, 1999.

Seltzer, Richard and Robert C. Smith 1991. 'Color Differences in the Afro-American Community and the Differences They Make.' *Journal of Black Studies* 21: 279–86.

Siyachitema, Hilary 2002. 'Health-Zimbabwe: Banned Skin Bleaching Creams Still Easy to Buy.' *Inter-press Service* April 25, 2002.

Smedley, Audrey 2007. *Race in North America*. 3rd edn. Boulder, CO: Westview.

South, Scott J., Kyle Crowder and Erick Chavez 2005. 'Migration and Spatial Assimilation Among U.S. Latinos: Classical Versus Segmented Trajectories.' *Demography* 42: 497–521.

Stevenson, Brenda 1996. *Life in Black and White: Family and Community in the Slave South*. New York: Oxford University Press.

Sullivan, Deborah A. 2001. *Cosmetic Surgery: The Cutting Edge of Commercial Medicine in America*. New Brunswick, NJ: Rutgers University Press.

Taylor, Diane 2002. 'Stitched Up: Where Plastic Surgeons Profit From Teenage Dreams.' *The Mirror* December 7, 2002.

Telles, Edward and Edward Murguia 1990. 'Phenotypic Discrimination and Income Differences among Mexican Americans.' *Social Science Quarterly* 71: 682–96.

Terkildsen, Nayda 1993. 'When White Voters Evaluate Black Candidates: The processing Implications of Candidate Skin Color, Prejudice, and Self-Monitoring.' *American Journal of Political Science* 37: 1032–53.

Thompson, Maxine S. and Verna Keith 2001. 'The Blacker the Berry: Gender, Skin Tone, Self-Esteem, and Self-Efficacy.' *Gender & Society* 15: 336–57.

Torres, Kimberly C. 2006. 'Manufacturing Blackness: Skin Color Necessary But Not Sufficient. Race Relations and Racial Identity at an Ivy League University (Pennsylvania).' Dissertation Abstracts International, University of Pennsylvania.

Udry, Richard, Karl Baumann and Charles Chase 1971. 'Skin Color, Status, and Mate Selection.' *American Journal of Sociology* 76: 722–33.

Valbrun Marjorie 2003. 'EEOC Sees Rise in Intrarace Complaints of Color Bias.' *Wall Street Journal* August 7, 2003.

Vazquez, Luis A., Enedina Garcia-Vazquez, Sheri A. Bauman and Arturo S. Sierra 1997. 'Skin Color, Acculturation, and Community Interest among Mexican American Students: A Research Note.' *Hispanic Journal of Behavioral Sciences* 19: 377–86.

Wade, T. J. and Sara Bielitz 2005. *The Differential Effect of Skin Color on Attractiveness, Personality Evaluations, and Perceived Life Success of African Americans*. Thousand Oaks, CA: Sage Publications.

Webster, Murray Jr. and James Driskell Jr. 1983. 'Beauty as Status.' *American Journal of Sociology* 89: 140–65.

Wolf, Naomi 1991. *The Beauty Myth: How Images of Beauty are Used Against Women*. New York: Doubleday Books.

CHAPTER 14

The Case for Taking White Racism *and* White Colorism More Seriously

Lance Hannon, Anna DalCortivo, and Kirstin Mohammed

Perhaps reflecting a desire to emphasize the enduring power of rigidly constructed racial categories, sociology has tended to downplay the importance of within-category variation in skin tone. Similarly, in popular media, colorism, or **discrimination** *based on skin lightness, is rarely mentioned. When colorism is discussed, it is almost exclusively framed in terms of intraracial "Black-on-Black" discrimination. In line with arguments highlighting the centrality of White racism, the present paper contends that it is important for researchers to give unique attention to* **White colorism**. *Using data from the 2012 American National Election Study, an example is presented on White interviewers' perceptions of minority respondent skin tone and intelligence. Results from a variety of statistical analyses indicate that African American and Latina/o respondents perceived to have light skin are significantly more likely to be seen by Whites as intelligent. The paper concludes that a full accounting of White hegemony requires an acknowledgment of both White racism and White colorism.*

Source: Adapted from Lance Hannon, "White Colorism," *Social Currents*, Volume 2, Issue 1, pages 13–21, SAGE Publications, Inc., 2015.

Questions to Consider

Scholars of American racism understand that racism significantly and negatively affects the life chances of racial and ethnic minorities. Left unexamined is the role of colorism in this process. How does colorism between minorities and White colorism directed at minorities complicate the life chances of racial and ethnic minorities who are perceived to have lighter or darker skin?

The term "white racism" is now an integral part of sociological discourse. Popularized by Joe Feagin, Hernan Vera, and Pinar Batur (2001), the terminology helps draw attention to the fact that not all prejudices are created equal. Historical and institutionalized power dynamics matter for the large-scale consequences of bigotry and thus it is problematic to implicitly (or explicitly) equate the racist beliefs and actions of whites with the prejudicial attitudes of other racial groups. As Feagin, Vera, and Batur (2001:3) note about this false equivalency, "Black racism would require not only a widely accepted racist ideology directed at whites, but also the power to systematically exclude whites from opportunities and rewards in major economic, cultural and political institutions."

The present paper argues that this logic should be extended to sociological analysis of discrimination based on continuous variation in skin lightness or "colorism." In the case of colorism, however, the problem is not simply the tacit suggestion that all racial and ethnic groups are equally guilty of intolerance and discrimination. The problem is much deeper, as shown by discussions of colorism in the popular press focusing almost exclusively on preferences for light skin among minority group members and framing racism as *inter-* and colorism as *intra*racial discrimination. Moreover, rarely is there any acknowledgment of the historical origin of within-race colorism or its potential role in maintaining white hegemony.

In contrast, most of the social science research on colorism provides a more complex picture by explicitly noting that skin tone discrimination within the African American community is likely an adaptation to the long history of tone-based exclusionary practices by whites (Burton, Bonilla-Silva, Ray, Buckelew, and Freeman 2010; Gans 2012; Hagiwara, Kashy and Cesario 2012; Harrison 2010; Hochschild and Weaver 2007; Hunter 2005; Keith and Herring 1991; Monroe 2013; Nakano-Glenn 2009; Vedantam 2010). In a well-cited study in this area, Keith Maddox and Stephanie Gray (2002) employed a sample of 40 African American and 42 white students from an introductory psychology class to assess the stereotypes associated with skin tone for African Americans. The results from a mixed-model [statistical] analysis indicated that for both black and white study participants, there was a significant tendency to apply more negative stereotypes to African Americans with darker skin relative to African Americans with lighter skin. Of particular relevance for the current study, darker-skinned African Americans were less likely to be seen as intelligent. Maddox and Gray (2002:257) concluded that their results "provide strong support for the hypothesis that both Black and White participants are aware of a cultural distinction between light- and dark-skinned Blacks."

Still, while social science research on colorism has frequently included whites in the overall sample, there is very little research with a dedicated focus on white prejudice regarding skin lightness. Furthermore, at the time of this writing, there are no sociological studies explicitly centered on white colorism. At one level, the lack of sociological research in this area is surprising, given sociology's general insistence on prioritizing the interrogation of white privilege and white racism. However, on another level, the general lack of attention to white colorism in sociology makes sense given (1) sociology's emphasis on racial categorization as a master status in the U.S. and (2) methodological concerns about the ability of whites to perceive differences in skin darkness among nonwhites (Hannon and DeFina 2014; Hill 2002a).

For example, consider Aaron Gullickson's (2005) hypothesis about a potential decline in the impact of skin tone on stratification outcomes in the U.S. in the post–civil rights era. Gullickson (2005:22) notes, "Integration may have been more beneficial to darker-skinned blacks because it generated new white gatekeepers of opportunity who, while not race-blind, may have been largely tone-blind." Thus, the argument is that colorism was more of an issue in an earlier era of segregation where, for example, black workers were more likely to be solely hired by black managers. Gullickson's argument further implies that white people in positions of power are guided by racial prejudices but are not significantly influenced by biases associated with skin tone because they do not differentiate between light-skinned and dark-skinned blacks.

The present paper argues that while it is certainly true that race is a master status in the U.S. and African Americans are likely better able to distinguish nuanced variation in African American skin tone than whites, neither point constitutes an acceptable justification for ignoring or downplaying white colorism.

Racism versus Colorism?

An argument can be made that discussions of colorism detract from the more central issue of racism. A key component of this argument is the notion that the effect of racial category is so strong that any influence that within-group differences in skin lightness might have would be miniscule in comparison. Discussing such weak effects for the sake of completeness might dilute the more important message regarding racism's powerful impact. Along these lines, Jennifer Hochschild (2012) notes a tension between "lumpers" and "splitters." While splitters argue for the need to examine the totality of white privilege through the lens of colorism, lumpers argue that dividing broad categories up in the name of specificity limits the ability to communicate crucial information that is more easily seen when people are grouped together. Ultimately, Hochschild (2012:4) concludes that for most of U.S. history, traditional operationalizations of race have led to appropriately broad generalizations. However, in the 21st century various demographic and cultural shifts, especially related to Latino/a immigration and multiracial identification, tip the balance of utility towards greater specificity and the need for heightened attention to colorism.

Eduardo Bonilla-Silva (2009) makes a similar argument regarding the importance of recent demographic shifts in the U.S. for an emerging racial hierarchy where variation in skin lightness plays a crucial role. Bonilla-Silva (2003:352) refers to this evolving hierarchy as the "Latin Americanization of Whiteness in the United States," and notes "preference for people who are light-skinned will become a more important factor in all kinds of social transactions."

Critics might respond that the likelihood of this new order coming into being is conditioned on the ability of non-Hispanic whites to perceive variation in skin shade among racial and ethnic minorities, and social science research has consistently demonstrated an "out-group homogeneity effect" when it comes to recognizing the unique facial features of non-group members. For example, Mark Hill (2002a) analyzed the influence of interviewer race on skin color classification in the 1992–1994 Multi-city Study of Urban Inequality and found that, relative to African American interviewers, white interviewers perceived less variation in the skin tones of African American respondents. More specifically, Hill noted that the variance associated with the skin tone measure was 12% higher for African American interviewers compared to white interviewers, a statistically significant difference. Still, it is important to recognize that Hill's study and more recent research (Hannon and DeFina 2014) does not actually report that whites are "largely tone-blind" as suggested by Gullickson (2005:22), just that assessments of skin tone exhibit somewhat less variation when the interviewer and respondent are of different races.

Moreover, as noted earlier, study after study utilizing cross-race observation of skin tone data has demonstrated statistically significant skin tone effects *despite* this methodological limitation. In addition, the results from these studies are more than just statistically significant; they are substantively significant. For example, Arthur Goldsmith, Darrick Hamilton, and Sandy Darity (2006) show that the intraracial wage gap between light- and dark-skinned African Americans is nearly the same magnitude as the interracial gap between African Americans and whites. Given that whites are far more likely to hold positions of power in the labor market, it is highly unlikely that such a significant wage penalty is solely a product of colorism in the African American community.

In sum, while it is true that the impact of race on social outcomes is powerful, and that whites have a somewhat limited ability to discern differences in nonwhite skin shade, the effects of colorism by white gatekeepers appear nonetheless very pronounced. Therefore, ignoring colorism in order to provide a more easily communicated assessment of racism can lead to a substantial underestimation of white privilege. Moreover, as Edward Telles (2012) and others have argued, recognizing that continuous variation in skin tone matters does not necessarily diminish the role of race, as the two concepts overlap both empirically and rhetorically. As Janice Inniss (2010) succinctly put it, "Given the importance of race—skin color—in the larger society, why would gradations of color *not* be important?" Colorism and racism in the U.S. are intrinsically linked in that they share the same historical roots and white hegemony is central to both.

To further illustrate the potential magnitude of white colorism's impact and to provide an example of the type of research that sociologists might concern themselves with in the future, the current study asks whether non-Hispanic white interviewers evaluate the intelligence of African American and Latino/a respondents differently depending on perception of the respondent's skin tone. The analyses make use of recent additions to the American National Election Study.

Data and Variables

One of the most widely used social science datasets, the face-to-face American National Election Study, offers a plethora of variables of interest not just to political scientists but also to sociologists, psychologists, economists, and others. There are two unique features of the survey that enable the current analysis: a measure of perceived intelligence and a measure of perceived skin tone (with a color palette guide) where interviewers were required to rate respondents at the end of the survey. Given that the American National Election Study has many questions concerning U.S. politics, it is perhaps unsurprising that interviewers were asked to assess the respondent's apparent knowledge of political matters. But, one remarkable element of the survey is that it also includes an item that directly asks interviewers to state their assessment of the respondent's intelligence. More specifically, interviewers evaluated the respondent's "apparent intelligence" on a 5-point scale, coded here as: (1) Very Low, (2) Fairly Low, (3) Average, (4) Fairly High, and (5) Very High. Although survey interviewers obviously have no distinct qualifications to evaluate an individual's overall intelligence, interviewers were not allowed to opt out by saying that they did not have enough information to judge. Thus, the question can be seen as tapping into deep prejudices, especially when factors like respondent educational attainment are held constant.

The total sample includes 240 individuals who self-identified as African American or Latino/a in the survey and were interviewed by a person identifying as Non-Hispanic white. Not surprisingly, given that a low intelligence label is a strong pejorative, most of the variation in perceived intelligence was between the average and high categories. Also, in line with previous results, respondents were perceived to cover the entire spectrum of possible skin tones (from 1 to 10) in both the African American and Latino/a samples. Complete description of the data and variables can be found at http://www.electionstudies.org.

As Villarreal (2012:500) has argued, it would be "rather naïve to assume that because interviewers are given a sheet with a color palette" skin tone assessments will be "objective." Indeed, it is important to note that the present analysis utilizes the 10-point skin tone scale (Massey and Martin 2003) not as an objective measure of respondent skin darkness but rather as a measure of interviewer *perception* of respondent complexion. Ultimately, the research question explored here is whether appraisals of respondent skin tone by white interviewers are related to their appraisals of respondent intelligence. To simplify presentation, appraised skin tone is collapsed into light (1–3), medium (4–7), and dark (8–10) and appraised intelligence is collapsed into above average (4–5) and not above average (1–3).

Results

Table 1 summarizes how perceived skin tone is related to the probability that African American and Latino respondents will be viewed as having above average intelligence by white interviewers. As can be seen, respondents deemed to be light skinned were more than twice as likely to be assessed as above average in intelligence compared to those deemed to have dark skin (55% versus 23%). While the percentages displayed in Table 1 are based on the combined sample of Latinos and African Americans, the relationship between skin lightness and intelligence appraisal could also be seen for both groups separately. For example, while 63% of African American respondents considered light skinned were rated above average in intelligence only 31% of those not viewed as light skinned were judged as particularly intelligent.

Table 2 replicates the procedure used to produce Table 1 but focuses on a subsample of African American and Latino respondents that have earned a bachelor's degree as their highest level of educational attainment. Unsurprisingly, interviewers were more likely to

Table 1 Skin Tone and the Percentage of Black and Latino Respondents Perceived by White Interviewers to Be Above Average in Intelligence

Interviewer Perception of Respondents' Skin Tone	***Respondents Seen as Intelligent***
Light (sample size = 47)	55%
Medium (sample size = 150)	34%
Dark (sample size = 43)	23%

Source: 2012 American National Election Study.

Table 2 Skin Tone and the Percentage of Black and Latino Respondents with Bachelor's Degrees Perceived by White Interviewers to Be Above Average in Intelligence

Interviewer Perception of Respondents' Skin Tone	***Respondents Seen as Intelligent***
Light (sample size = 7)	86%
Medium (sample size = 15)	67%
Dark (sample size = 4)	50%

Source: 2012 American National Election Study.

assess respondents as having high intelligence in this highly educated sample. Still, skin tone continued to influence interviewer judgments for this select group; a larger percentage of those considered light skinned were thought of as intelligent relative to those considered dark skinned (86% versus 50%). The same pattern emerged for other subsamples based on educational experience. For example, focusing exclusively on African American and Latino respondents whose highest educational credential was a high school diploma or equivalent, 47% of respondents deemed light skinned were also deemed more intelligent than average while only 21% of respondents perceived to be non-light skinned were perceived to be intelligent. That skin tone still matters after taking educational background into account suggests that the results do not simply reflect the empirical reality of skin tone stratification in educational opportunities for African Americans and Latinos. Instead, the findings tell us about an important source of that reality; white observers can look at two identically qualified minorities and assess the lighter-skinned one as more intelligent.

Future research can improve on these analyses by employing a larger and broader sample and an experimental/audit design that would allow the researcher to better discern the causal direction of the relationship between perceived skin tone and perceived intelligence. While the current study assumes that observers assess the physical characteristics of others before judging their intelligence, some recent research in psychology suggests that perceptions of intelligence can drive how we see a person's skin color (Ben-Zeev et al. 2014).

Conclusion: What Are the Consequences of Ignoring White Colorism?

The results of the present study indicated that African Americans and Latinos deemed to have lighter skin tones are significantly more likely to be seen as intelligent by white interviewers. Importantly, the effects of skin tone on intelligence assessment were independent of respondent education level, as well as vocabulary test score, political knowledge assessment and several other factors (see Hannon 2015). The findings suggest that white prejudicial attitudes related to skin tone could create substantially unequal access to economic, social, and cultural resources.

For example, if white adults have a tendency to equate lighter skin with intelligence, this may impact the level of expectations white teachers and other school authorities have for certain students. While there has been a considerable amount of research in education about a potential Pygmalion effect related to a student's race and ethnicity (Cohen et al. 2006; Rosenthal and Jacobson 1968), little attention has been directed at examining how stereotypes based on skin tone can create self-fulfilling prophecies in educational achievement and school disciplinary actions. Moreover, while educational institutions frequently keep track of racial and ethnic disproportionality in outcomes, differences by skin shade are not recorded. In this sense, colorism is the unmentioned and unmonitored "ism" (Harrison 2010).

William Pizzi, Irene Blair, and Charles Judd (2005) echo this argument in reference to colorism in the criminal justice system. As they point out, members of the (overwhelmingly white) legislature and judiciary are acutely aware of disparities between whites and African Americans and Latinos in sentencing. Because of this, steps have been taken to reduce or at least monitor discrimination based on race and ethnicity. The same is not true for discrimination based on phenotype.

More generally, lack of attention to white colorism may enable overly simplistic understandings of white racism. For example, perhaps adapting to a new era of demographic diversity in the U.S. and discussions of a "post-racial society," eugenicists like Richard Lynn (2002) have argued that "Caucasian genes" (operationalized as skin lightness) can explain the considerable variation in IQ test performance *within* the African American population. Central to Lynn's (and other's) claims is the argument that even if one was to concede that African Americans as a group are still discriminated against and this harms their test performance, darker-skinned African Americans are not singled out to receive less educational resources relative to lighter-skinned African Americans. Therefore, from this perspective, since white prejudice cannot account for any within-race significant association between skin tone and test score, genetics must be the explanation. While there are certainly other ways to address this argument, appropriate attention to white colorism would rightfully bring historical and institutionalized power dynamics back into the discussion (Hill 2002b).

The history of white colorism runs as deep as the history of white racism in U.S. society. For African Americans, the skin color hierarchy is firmly rooted in the slavery regime, where white owners gave certain work privileges to slaves with more Eurocentric features, especially those with known white heritage (Burton et al. 2010; Keith 2009). Indeed, it is telling that even during a period where racial categorization meant the difference between owner and slave, whites still discriminated based on nuanced variation in skin tone. Despite this long history, the Equal Employment Opportunity Commission (EEOC 2007) has just recently started to give significant attention to skin tone discrimination with its ERACE initiative (Eradicate Racism and Colorism from Employment).

The legal foundation of colorism claims lies with Title VII of the 1964 Civil Rights Act, which prohibits employment discrimination based on "color" (separately from "race"). However, perhaps due to the historical rigidity of racial classifications in the U.S., the general public and the courts continue to have a difficult time distinguishing the concepts of race and color, a distinction that can be important in an increasingly data-driven legal process (Nance 2005; Jones 2010). Consider, for example, a hypothetical case where a white employer discriminates against darker-skinned African Americans for customer-relations positions. Claiming racism would be insufficient; such a claim could be countered with evidence of past (lighter-skinned) African American hires.

Sociologists can play an important role in elucidating the overlapping but distinct social meanings of race and skin color. To do this, future sociological research should continue to dispel the false dichotomization of racism as *inter*- and colorism as *intra*group discrimination. Extending the reasoning behind sociology's focus on institutionalized power dynamics and "white racism," it is important for future research to give special attention to "white colorism."

References

Ben-Zeev, Avi, Dennehy, Tara C., Goodrich, Robin I., Kolarik, Branden S., and Geisler, Mark W. 2014. "When an Educated Black Man Becomes Lighter in the Mind's Eye: Evidence for a Skin Tone Memory Bias." *Sage Open*. January–March 2014: 1–9.

Bonilla-Silva, Eduardo. 2003. "New Racism," Color-blind Racism, and the Future of Whiteness in America." In Ashley Doane and Eduardo Bonilla-Silva (Ed.), *White Out: The Continuing Significance of Racism* (pp. 345–360). New York: Routledge.

Bonilla-Silva, Eduardo. 2009. *Racism without racists: Color-blind racism and the persistence of racial inequality in the United States* (2nd ed.). Boulder, CO: Rowman and Littlefield.

Burton, Linda. M., Bonilla-Silva, Eduardo, Ray, Victor, Buckelew, Rose, and Hordge Freeman, Elizabeth. 2010. Critical race theories, colorism, and the decade's research on families of color. *Journal of Marriage and Family, 72*(3), 440–459.

Cohen, Geoffrey L., Garcia, Julio, Apfel, Nancy, and Master, Allison. 2006. Reducing the racial achievement gap: a social-psychological intervention. *Science, 313*(5791), 1307–1310.

EEOC. 2007. *EEOC takes new approach to fighting racism and colorism in the 21st century workplace.* Accessed November 13, 2015: http://www.eeoc.gov/eeoc/initiatives/e-race/index.cfm

Feagin, Joe R., Vera, Hernan, and Batur, Pinar. 2001. *White Racism: The Basics.* New York: Routledge.

Gans, Herbert. J. 2012. "Whitening" and the changing American racial hierarchy. *Du Bois Review: Social Science Research on Race, 9*(2), 267–279.

Goldsmith, Arthur, Hamilton, Darrick, and Darity, Sandy. 2006. Shades of discrimination: Skin tone and wages. *American Economic Review, 96*(2), 242–245.

Gullickson, Aaron. 2005. The Significance of Color Declines: A Re-Analysis of Skin Tone Differentials in Post–Civil Rights America. *Social Forces.* 84(1), 157–180.

Hagiwara, Nao, Kashy, Deborah, and Cesario, Joseph. 2012. The independent effects of skin tone and facial features on Whites' affective reactions to Blacks. *Journal of Experimental Psychology* 48: 892–898.

Hannon, Lance. 2015. White Colorism. *Social Currents.* 2(1), 13–21.

Hannon, Lance and Robert DeFina. 2014. Just skin deep: The impact of interviewer race on the assessment of African American respondent skin tone. *Race and Social Problems,* 6(4), 356–364.

Harrison, Matthew S. 2010. Colorism: The often undiscussed "ism" in America's workforce. *The Jury Expert,* 22, 67–72.

Hochschild, Jennifer L. 2012. Lumpers or splitters: analytic and political choices in studying colour lines and colour scales. *Ethnic and Racial Studies, 35*(7), 1132–1136.

Hochschild, Jennifer L., and Weaver, Vesla. 2007. The skin color paradox and the American racial order. *Social Forces, 86*(2), 643–670.

Hill, Mark E. 2002a. Race of interviewer and perception of skin color: evidence from the multi-city study of urban inequality. *American Sociological Review,* 67(1), 99–108.

Hill, Mark E. 2002b. Skin Color and Intelligence in African Americans: A Reanalysis of Lynn's Data. *Population and Environment,* 24(2), 209–214.

Hunter, Margaret L. 2005. *Race, gender, and the politics of skin tone.* New York: Routledge.

Inniss, Janis P. 2010. Colorism: The Hierarchical nature of skin tone that makes "light alright." *Everyday Sociology Blog* Accessed May 13, 2012: http://www.everydaysociologyblog.com/2010/01

Jones, Trina. 2010. Intra-Group Preferencing: Proving Skin Color and Identity Performance Discrimination, 34 *N.Y.U. Review of Law and Social Change* 657–707.

Keith, Verna M. 2009. A colorstruck world: skin tone, achievement, and self-esteem among African American women. In E. N. Glenn (Ed.), *Shades of difference: why skin color matters* (pp. 25–39). Los Altos, CA: Stanford University Press.

Keith, Verna M., and Herring, Cedric. 1991. Skin tone stratification in the black community. *The American Journal of Sociology, 97*(3), 760–778.

Lynn, Richard. 2002. Skin color and intelligence in African Americans: a reply to Hill. *Population and Environment, 24*(20), 215–218.

Maddox, Keith B., and Stephanie A. Gray. 2002. Cognitive representations of black Americans: re-exploring the role of skin tone. *Personality and Social Psychology Bulletin, 28*(2), 250–259.

Massey, Douglas S., and Martin, Jennifer A. 2003. *The NIS skin color scale.* Princeton, NJ: Princeton University.

Monroe, Carla R. 2013. Colorizing educational research: African American life and schooling as an exemplar. *Educational Researcher, 42*(1), 9–19.

Nance, Cynthia E. 2005. "Colorable Claims: The Continuing Significance of Color Under Title VII Forty Years After Its Passage." *Berkeley Journal of Employment and Labor Law* 26: 435–474.

Nakano-Glenn, Evelyn. 2009. *Shades of Difference: Why Skin Color Matters.* Palo Alto, California: Stanford University Press.

Pizzi, William T., Blair, Irene V., and Judd, Charles M. 2005. Discrimination in sentencing on the basis of Afrocentric features. *Michigan Journal of Race and Law,* 10, 327–355.

Rosenthal, Robert, and Jacobson, Lenore. 1968. *Pygmalion in the classroom: teacher expectation and pupils' intellectual development.* New York, NY: Rinehart and Winston.

Telles, Edward E. 2012. The overlapping concepts of race and color in Latin America. *Ethnic and Racial Studies, 35*(7), 1163–1168.

Vedantam, Shankar. 2010. January 19. Shades of prejudice. *The New York Times,* pp. A31.

Villarreal, Andres. 2012. Reply to Flores and Telles: Flawed statistical reasoning and misconceptions about race and ethnicity. *American Sociological Review, 75,* 495–502.

CHAPTER 15

"I'm Watching Your Group"

Academic Profiling and Regulating Students Unequally

Gilda L. Ochoa

Drawing on in-depth interviews with Asian American and Latina/o students and observations conducted over eighteen months at a school, Gilda Ochoa provides a comparative analysis of the differential forms of control detailed by Asian American and Latina/o students across campus spaces, paying particular attention to the significance of race and class. She finds that differences by race/ethnicity, class, and academic track maintain an unequal power structure that also reinforces disparities between the predominately working-class Latinas/os and the primarily middle-class Asian American students at Southern California High School.

Questions to Consider

A common belief in America is that "education is the great equalizer." Yet, in the highly stratified American education system, not all schools treat all students the same. According to Ochoa, how is inequality by race and class reproduced in high school? Can you think of some ways to make schools more equal?

Note: Reading is original to this book.

Everything is caged in, lots of bars. It's like they don't trust us, like we're just going to run away and not come to school if there weren't any bars.

—Andrew Moreno, high school senior

I call it concentration camp, our school, 'cause we're not allowed off campus, or on campus when we're outside, we're constantly being watched; there's a security guard right there.

—Jung Kim, high school sophomore

High school students Andrew Moreno and Jung Kim feel their school is like a prison. Wrought iron gates enclose it, several security guards patrol it, and occasionally drug-sniffing dogs scour it. Security and punishment are part of what has been called a discipline regime in public schools (Kupchick, 2010; Morris, 2006). While schools have a long history as sites of restriction and control, especially for working-class and communities of color, these intensified forms of social control are a part of the movement from a welfare state to a penal state (Fleury-Steiner, 2008). Emerging in the context of "tough on crime" policies of the 1980s and fueled by a culture of fear and the demonizing of youth of color, schools often use prisonlike tactics, including zero-tolerance policies because of which students caught violating school rules face strict penalties such as suspensions, expulsions, and sometimes even police interventions (Beres & Griffith, 2001; Noguera, 2008; Nolan, 2011). Physically, the parameter of Southern California High School (SCHS) is barred. However, within the campus, not all spaces are equally restrictive, and not all students recount the same levels of constraint. Drawing on in-depth interviews and observations conducted over eighteen months at a school that I refer to as SCHS, I use a macro/meso/micro framework to detail the multiple and intersecting factors influencing disparate forms of control and their implications for maintaining inequality. Students' narratives reveal that there are variations of control—including geographically and academically—across classrooms, offices, and the school campus. These often unspoken and taken for granted differences by race/ethnicity, class, and academic track maintain an unequal power structure that also reinforces disparities between the predominately working-class Latinas/os and the primarily middle-class Asian American students at Southern California High School.[1,2]

Listening to Students at a Southern California High School as a Case Study Approach

Students' perspectives are missing from most contemporary discussions about education. New educational initiatives are instituted and marketed with the pretense that they are best. However, few speak with those affected on a daily basis by what happens in our schools. Instead, students are evaluated quantitatively as though performances on standardized tests are the most meaningful determination of all that needs to be known. Going inside our schools and listening to students is more revealing of the factors influencing their educational trajectories.

Eager to hear from students, I spent over eighteen months at SCHS. Located in Los Angeles County, SCHS has a population of nearly 2,000 students with relatively equal percentages of Asian Americans (46%) and Latinas/os (43%). The remaining student body is about 7% White, 2% African American, and 1% Native American. Over 30% of students are eligible for free and reduced lunch, and about 10% are English Language Learners. As is the case nationally, the school personnel do not reflect the racial/ethnic backgrounds of the student body. About half of the teachers and administrators are White, one-fourth are Latina/o, one-fifth are Asian American, and less than 3% are African American or Native American (California Department of Education 2008).

SCHS is a relatively well-funded public high school. In addition to honors and Advanced Placement (AP) courses, it boasts an International Baccalaureate (IB) program that provides a special counselor and courses including theory of knowledge, art history, and twentieth-century history for the 30–40 juniors and seniors in the program. SCHS is known for students' high standardized test scores and rates of college attendance. As a result, it has appeared in *Newsweek* magazine's list of the top 1,000 public schools in the nation. However, as students' testimonials reveal, not all have access to the same quality and quantity of school resources.

In May and June 2001, and again from May 2007 to December 2008, I sat in on classes and attended campus assemblies, graduations, and meetings. Working with several students from the Claremont Colleges, we interviewed over fifty teachers, counselors, administrators, and parents, but most of our time was spent listening to students. Across from tables, gathered around benches, and sitting in circles, in 50- to 70-minute interviews, we asked 139 students about their schooling, friendships, and future plans. The interview questions were broad and open-ended, allowing students to share their experiences in ways that were meaningful for them.

Students provided a range of testimonials about peer groups and high school life, some highlighting the institutional constraints in school connected to race, class, gender, and academic program. With the exception of a few of the interviews, most were audiotaped, transcribed, and then analyzed for recurring themes and patterns. The quotations appearing throughout this chapter are verbatim from the transcripts, but as is the custom in qualitative research, the names of the participants and their school have been changed. I detailed the comprehensive results of this study in *Academic Profiling: Latinos, Asian Americans and the Achievement* (2013). In a 2015 book chapter entitled "Gendered Expectation and Sexualized Policing," I centered on Latinas' experiences (Ochoa, 2015). Thus, for this chapter, I provide a comparative analysis of the differential forms of control detailed by Asian American and Latina/o students across campus spaces paying particular attention to the significance of race and class.

The Participants

On average, the students included in this study were finishing their sophomore year in high school, and they were more likely to be women than men (60% compared to 40%). Of the sixty-seven Latinas/os, most identify as Mexican, Mexican American, Latina/o, or Hispanic. Most are the children or grandchildren of Mexican immigrants, but several are from families who have been in the United States for four or five generations and a few are Central American or identify as a racial minority or multiracially. About one-quarter are from homes where at least one parent had received a college degree, but on average, their parents have high school degrees and jobs in construction, trucking, and sales. In contrast, most of the sixty-three Asian American student participants moved to the United States as children or are the children of Chinese or Korean immigrants, the majority coming from Taiwan and Hong Kong. Seventy-five percent have at least one parent who has received a college degree. On average, their parents have nearly fifteen years of education and are likely to have middle-class professions in accounting and management. However, due to racial discrimination as well as language and licensing restrictions, not all are able to work in their areas of training. Some are in working-class positions, and multiple families have construction, computer, or restaurant businesses.

Thus, based on years of education and occupation and in part because of differing immigration patterns and educational opportunities in immigrant countries, the Latina/o students are more likely than their Asian American peers to come from working-class and lower-middle-class households where they would be among the first generation in their families to attend college. Nevertheless, racial/ethnic background and class position do not always correlate. Twenty-five percent of participating Latina/o students have at least one parent with a bachelor of arts degree, and a quarter of Asian Americans interviewed do not have a parent who has completed college.

I do not claim that this research is necessarily applicable to all students and schools. Nonetheless, the power of qualitative research is in the in-depth, detailed, and nuanced understandings that interviews and case studies provide in helping to unpack the institutional and everyday dynamics that often are replicated in places beyond the location under study.

Students' Experiences behind the School Gates: Opened Doors versus Restricted Pathways

Huddled around a lunch table with two of his best friends and fellow IB students—May Lee and Billy Su—senior Mike Song beams as he rattles off the privileges he has as a student in the school's IB program. He describes how simply proclaiming, "I'm an IB student" enables him to pass unencumbered by school officials throughout campus. To illustrate his point, he boasts:

> Oh, security guards. Like, one time, I was out of class 'cause I really had to go talk to the counselor, and it was like, "Oh, you're not supposed to be here." Then I was like, "Oh, umm, I'm an IB student." And then, they're like, "Oh, okay, then you can go."

Such preferential treatment persists in the counseling office. Continuing, Mike brags, "And in the office, sometimes they stop you, 'You can't meet with your counselor unless you have an appointment.' 'Oh, I'm an IB student.' Then they're, 'Okay, *you* can come in.'" Encouraged by his IB counselor to visit any time because her "door is always open," Mike appreciates his counselor who is "really close to us [IB students]. She helps us out a lot." He explains, "We had a stress group with her, and we could tell her anything and we're really cool with her." Concurring, friend Billy Su chimes, "When you want classes that you didn't get or got to get, she'll work favors for you."

This ability to physically move across campus with few restrictions is significant for enhancing a sense of belonging at school. Likewise, given the crucial role of high school counselors in providing information, determining awards, and writing letters of recommendation, easy access to counselors enhances these students' abilities to garner coveted resources and improve their life chances.

Within the classroom, Mike and his friends describe a comparable form of freedom—one encouraging them to think creatively and expand their perspectives. As part of the required IB course Theory of Knowledge (ToK), students participate in Socratic seminars discussing and posing questions about truth, reality, and knowledge with the fifteen students in their class. As Mike describes, their other assignments encourage similar forms of exploration: "We have these presentations about homelessness, or we choose an issue that's around the world, and we present it to the juniors in the IB program." Mike is also convinced that he and his IB and AP classmates have less work than students in the school's general courses (known as college prep or CP):

> I think *they* do more work 'cause we already went through it 'cause we're taking AP classes. We should be able to do this stuff that the regular kids do. I think that's why we can skip all the hard work and go into the more deeper [work]. It's like they're covering a whole bunch of shallow stuff compared to smaller areas.

The differences in the regulation of thought between the students in the AP class versus those dubbed "regular kids" unequally prepare students for distinct life courses. As education scholar Jennie Oakes (1985) has documented, courses designated as *honors* often provide students access to higher-level thinking and decision making for managerial and professional careers.

Days after meeting middle-class Asian Americans Mike Song and his friends, I met another group of students, sophomores Maria Castillo, Becky Cruz, and Isabel Fuentes. These first-generation college-going Latinas are enrolled in CP classes, commonly referred to as "regular classes." These friends report very different schooling experiences than the ones described by Mike. The warm and supportive environment that Mike and his friends encounter from educators as they move throughout campus is a stark contrast to the chilly climate and restricted pathways Maria and Becky must navigate, especially in the counselor's office:

Maria: We talked to her [our counselor] once for summer school.

Becky: She was rude.

Interviewer Sandra Hamada: What happened?

Maria: We wanted to get into Algebra 2 for summer school and—

Becky: The class was full and we asked her if there was a different class we could do, and she told us to get out the late slip. . . . I wanted to take AP and honors classes next year; so, I went in to ask her what are the

> right classes, and she told me to talk to my teachers, and I told her I had gone to talk to the teacher already. . . . She [then] said, "I can't tell you what classes to take. You have to talk to your teachers and you have to figure out if it's right for you." I told her I already did that; so then she kept going in circles about that.

Although Maria and Becky are not explicitly barred from the counselors' office or the school's top classes, the animosity, bureaucratic regulations, and the runaround they encounter gravely impede their attempts to advance academically. They are subtly shut out.

Such confinement in CP courses leaves them and their friend, Isabel Fuentes, longing for the greater flexibility, introspection, and exploration detailed earlier by Mike and his friends. In her interview, Isabel bemoans:

> My English class sucks. . . . I really like to write, and I really like to learn new words, and I've been there [with that teacher for two years], and he doesn't make us do anything. I don't want to write about Julius Caesar and something about the tyrant. I want it to be on the more personal level—you know, that *makes* us want to write. . . . Like, give us quotes and we have to think about what the quote means.

Isabel relishes writing and learning. Thus, she wishes her courses were more open-ended, allowing students to make personal connections and encouraging them to share their own reflections rather than simply regurgitating what they have read. She recommends, "I would change the teacher methods, the way they teach. . . . All we do is copy from the book, and I'm not learning it. I'm just writing just so I can get it done." Such structured and disconnected assignments, compared to the ones asked of students in the IB program, can foster boredom and outright disengagement (Shor, 1992). To the extent that some courses focus on following orders and memorizing instead of creative thought, original perspectives, and innovation, these different academic experiences can also fuel unequal career paths and life courses (see Oakes, 1985).

The Macro/Meso/Micro Processes Influencing Unequal Student Regulation: What Do Racism and Class Difference Have to Do with It?

At first glance, these students' educational trajectories and schooling experiences may appear random, based only on merit, contingent upon students' actions or choices, or just a product of their course programs—IB and AP versus CP. In particular, it may seem that racism and the class differences of these two peer groups are irrelevant—that Mike and his friends are just more determined and worthy of the special treatment and resources they receive compared to Maria, Becky, and Isabel. Prevailing discourses that we are postracial, along with liberal views assuming that everyone has the same opportunities, reinforce these assumptions. Alternatively, students' narratives may confirm popular stereotypes assuming that Asian Americans are somehow smarter and better students than Latinas/os and therefore deserve to be in different courses. However, when students' testimonies are compared and analyzed in the context of larger processes, it is easier to discern how these experiences are not isolated incidents and that there are significant differences rooted in racism and class background.

Reflecting national trends, middle- and upper-middle-class Asian American students at SCHS are significantly *overrepresented* in IB, AP, and honors courses; meanwhile, working-class Latinas/os are *underrepresented* in these top academic programs (see Ginorio & Huston, 2001; Oakes, 1985). At SCHS, where their overall enrollment at the school is basically the same, Asian Americans constitute 86% and Latinas/os 10% of students in AP courses. At 95% and 5%, the ratio in the IB program is even more glaring. Such race and class skewing in course placement typically begins before high school and often as early as elementary school. For example, a 2015 report from the second-largest school district in the United States—Los Angeles Unified—revealed that based on their enrollment in the district, Asian Americans and Whites are *overrepresented* by 150% and 60% as gifted and talented students; in contrast, Latinas/os and African Americans are underrepresented by 15% and 30% (Galvez, 2015). The results of such racial and class skewing are that students are funneled onto distinct paths at early ages that then guide their learning, being, and opportunities. Digging deeper reveals an interlocking network of macroscopic structural factors and dominant ideologies, meso-level school practices, and everyday exchanges. These macro/meso/micro–processes intersect to disparately regulate students by race, class, and academic program.

Macro-Processes: Dominant Ideologies and the Significance of Class

The differential forms of regulation at schools such as SCHS must be understood in the context of dominant ideologies—prevailing systems of belief that maintain and reproduce racial hierarchies. Rooted in a legacy of White supremacy, these ideologies include biological and cultural deficiency perspectives epitomized in the eerily similar generalizations made in the 1930s and 2000s:

> The Mexican's basic community organization of life is not of the efficient Japanese type; neither is it of the industrial-individualistic American form. On the other hand, it differs widely from the family clan-village Chinese form of community organization. It is unorganized . . . resting on daily needs, and taking little thought of the morrow. (Bogardus, 1934)
>
> The Asians seem to be motivated and driven. The Latinos don't seem to value education in the same. (Anthony Castro, SCHS teacher, 2007)

Although seventy years separate these statements, they reflect prevailing ideologies that homogenize and pit Latinas/os and Asian Americans against each other in ways that reinforce a racial hierarchy. Mexicans, and Latinas/os more broadly, are cast as disorganized, present-time oriented, and lacking drive in comparison to Asian Americans—Japanese and

Chinese, in particular—and Americans (Whites). These larger beliefs mask the significance of class and other factors in shaping experiences.

Historically rooted, these ideologies permeate all aspects of our society, including school practices and everyday attitudes. In schools throughout the 1950s, White middle- and upper-class researchers and educators often used biological and cultural deficiency arguments to explain differences in educational outcomes (Gonzalez, 1990). For example, proponents of biological arguments believed that Mexican Americans were predisposed physically to perform agricultural labor and lacked the mental capabilities to excel in academically rigorous courses (Gonzalez, 1990). To support their claims, they often used biased intelligence (IQ) tests that were administered in English (Gonzalez, 1990). By the 1920s, as cultural deficiency perspectives became more popular, educators aimed to Americanize Mexicans and Mexican Americans who they believed came from homes and cultures that did not value education and were not future-time oriented (Gonzalez, 1990). White researchers, educators, and politicians used these theories to rationalize unequal schooling and the disparate paths gearing students toward different jobs. Since assimilation to White middle-class-ness was emphasized and White students were largely schooled for higher-paying occupations in accordance with their gender and class positions, these theories also privileged Whiteness and the status of Whites.

Today, cultural deficiency explanations persist in hegemonic representations of Asian Americans as a so-called model minority in comparison to Latinas/os. As reflected in the earlier comments by SCHS teacher Anthony Castro, these beliefs position Asian Americans and Latinas/os as polar opposites—valuing versus not valuing education. Emerging in the midst of the 1960s social justice struggles and gaining prominence in the 1980s, this model minority myth praises Asian Americans as an ideal group that has supposedly advanced in the United States because of their believed unique determination and cultural emphasis on hard work. At a time when Latinas/os and Blacks were challenging a history of racial exclusion, demanding access into dominant institutions, and engaging in mass demonstrations, the mainstream media erroneously depicted Asian Americans as good citizens who did not protest and were advancing on their own accord (Lee, 1996).

Since the 1960s, the mainstream media has promulgated the false image that if Asian Americans are succeeding, something must be wrong with Latinas/os and Blacks who are lagging behind educationally and economically (Lee, 1996). Recently, media-savvy writers have also propagated such cultural beliefs praising Asian Americans relative to other groups. Ignoring historical and class differences, these contemporary arguments root educational differences and other indicators of economic well-being to assumed cultural differences in feelings of superiority or inferiority and impulse control (see Chua & Rubenfeld, 2014).

From my initial meeting with a SCHS administrator before beginning this research to the final reflections when I shared the research results at the school, the assumption that Asian Americans possess the requisite values for educational success and Latinas/os do not permeated SCHS:

> Joe Berk remembered, "When I was applying [for this position], I said that there were two campuses at this same school—a high-performing campus, which is predominately Asian, and a low-performing one that is predominately Hispanic. . . . This is not

> a [Southern California High School] phenomena. Hispanics, in general, emphasize putting food on the table over education." (Field notes, February 2007)
>
> Asian parents push education. . . . I know that all groups value education, but Asians *really* push education. (Field notes, October 2008)

These views exist despite multiple studies indicating that Latinas/os tend to have *higher* aspirations to attend college than do students from the general population and that 94% of Latina/o parents expect their children to matriculate to college (Delgado-Gaitan, 1992; Kao, 2000; Pew Hispanic Foundation/Kaiser Family Foundation, 2004).

These myths lump together heterogeneous groups and assume that all Asian Americans are excelling and that Latinas/os and African Americans are to blame for their positions in society. By pitting Asian Americans against Latinas/os and African Americans, this myth ignores how distinct histories, including unequal U.S. immigration policies and different class positions, shape access to resources and opportunities (for more details, see Ochoa, 2013). For example, as a result of migration patterns, nearly two-thirds of Taiwanese immigrants in the United States, almost 50% of immigrants from Hong Kong, and a third of immigrants from mainland China have at least four years of college education (Zhou, 2009, p. 47). In comparison, as of 2008, about 60% of Mexican immigrants in the United States over twenty-five years of age had less than a high school degree (Brick, Challinor, & Rosenblum, 2011). These larger trends are especially important at SCHS, where the class backgrounds of students are a reflection of these differences. The higher-than-average educational backgrounds and incomes of the predominantly Taiwanese, Chinese, and Korean Asian Americans from SCHS relative to their Mexican American and Central American schoolmates enhances their educational resources and opportunities for mobility. Overall, the model minority myth and dismissing of larger factors perpetuates the ideology that we live in a meritocratic society where success is determined only by hard work. It also maintains White privilege and Whiteness, since Whites are the normative group by which all other groups are measured (Frankenberg, 1993).

As will become increasingly apparent in the next two sections, the prevalence of these dichotomized conceptions about Asian Americans and Latinas/os cannot be separated from the schooling experiences of the two peer groups introduced earlier. It is not simply IB students who are given the given the benefit of the doubt and provided with more liberties, the differential racialization of Asian Americans and Latinas/os and the overall class differences of these two panethnic groups at the school shape the unequal constraints described by students.

Meso-Level: Schools Structuring Unequal Spaces of Control

The disparate forms of control and access to college counselors described by the two friendship group at the beginning of this chapter are neither unique nor race or class neutral. The very structure of U.S. schools is premised on inequality and the socialization of students into their place in society (Bowles & Gintis, 1976). At SCHS, this is exemplified most blatantly in the practice of curriculum tracking—the differential placement of students into distinct courses—IB, AP, honors, and CP courses.

Curriculum tracking has its origins in racist and classist hierarchies and ideologies. It emerged when access to public schooling was increasing and growing numbers of poor, immigrant, and second-generation children from southern and eastern Europe were entering U.S. schools (Oakes, 1985). Characterized as the most efficient way to educate a mass citizenry, it was justified by social Darwinian assumptions about the biological superiority of White Anglo Protestants, cultural deficiency perspectives advocating Americanization programs for immigrants, and scientific management–based models of the factory (Oakes, 1985). This history of allocating students to distinct educational and career paths by race/ethnicity and class position has reproduced inequalities and maintained the capitalist system by ensuring a ready supply of laborers, managers, and owners (Bowles & Gintis, 1976; Gonzalez, 1990).

The contemporary manifestations of curriculum tracking are also exclusionary. As detailed earlier, there are significant differences in track placement by race and class. Even the criteria used to place students in courses—standardized tests and teacher and counselor recommendations—are subjective. These too often work against first-generation, Latina/o, and African American students and in favor of middle-class, English-speaking, and White students whose backgrounds, experiences, and cultural references tend to reflect those designing the tests and determining course placement (Oakes, 1985).

At SCHS, middle- and upper-middle-class students also have the economic advantage of being able to afford accelerated tutoring outside of school that enhances their ability to perform on standardized tests and excel in the most rigorous courses. The correlation between enrollment in IB courses and accelerated tutoring is dramatic at SCHS. IB senior Yi Lin estimates that "99% [of the IB] students are all going to one or the other [tutoring program] like Ivy and also Stellar." Mike Song and his friends are included in this percentage. In contrast, senior Rose Gonzalez, who is among the first in her family to graduate high school and one of the few Latina/o students to complete SCHS's IB program, is financially shut out of such spaces of academic and social support because of her working-class background. Resentfully, she explains:

> Some of them [my IB classmates], their parents buy them tutors so that they can help them to do their regular homework. It's like, "Dang, I wish I had that at my house." . . . I couldn't afford it.

Just as class resources influence course access, prevailing racial ideologies intersect with the practice of curriculum tracking to influence how students are placed into courses. Foundational research highlights that Asian Americans and Whites with similar standardized test scores as Latinas/os and Blacks are still more likely to be placed in rigorous courses. At SCHS, the myth of Asian Americans as a model minority fuels what teacher Manuel Cadena characterizes as "academic profiling"—the tendency for "teachers and counselors to place an Asian student in biology or a college prep class over a Latino student." Meanwhile, Latinas/os are profiled down—assumed that they should *not* be in the school's top courses. Tom Delgado, a ten-year member of the school staff, critiques how certain teachers' actions control who they believe belongs in honors classes:

> This one student was a female who was Hispanic; she was a freshman a couple of years ago, freshman's honors class, and the teacher asked her, "What are you doing here? You

> are in the wrong class." She said, "No, I'm in the right class." The teacher said, "This is an honors class." . . . The teacher made her feel that [because] she was Mexican, she didn't belong. . . . The student checked out of the class a week later.

Echoing the experiences of Mike Song and his IB classmates, teachers at SCHS attest that there is also an unequal distribution of resources along curriculum tracks. Since course placement in racially and class skewed, tracking can become a self-perpetuating process through which students with more class resources are likely to be in the school's valued courses where they receive the most at school—such as access to their own IB counselor, as Mike boasted—and students with the least amount of resources are given the run-around and shortchanged. Teacher John Alvarez explains, "It's almost like the honors are special classes. The AP classes are special classes. So, they are anointed. They get the blessing, and my other kids basically get whatever is left." SCHS teacher Michelle Mesa details how this self-perpetuating process reinforces racial inequality as well:

> Some of the Hispanic students come to me and ask where can they find information . . . [and I say,] "Well, your teacher should've mentioned it or the counseling department." But, they only advertise it to the AP and honors classes, and here the majority [of those students] are Asian students.

Overall, those in the top classes at SCHS—who are more likely to be middle- and upper-middle-class Asian Americans—describe easier access to counselors; more college-going information; and classes where they are assigned novels, creative homework, and papers involving critical thinking. In general, they are granted more liberty at school in their assignments. Their opinions are encouraged in classes. Through a process of what Annette Lareau (2003) describes as "concerted cultivation," they are taught to "question adults and address them as relative equals." Together, such experiences are gearing select students toward leadership and decision-making positions in high school and beyond. Access to different types of knowledge and know-how are among the factors leading to unequal forms of cultural and human capital important for excelling in school.

While not as glaring as the confinement of students behind school gates, the more hidden and taken-for-granted containment that exists between classes, with different allocations of resources and unequal amounts of academic exploration, nonetheless propels students onto distinct paths with disparate opportunities.

Micro-Level Everyday Interactions

Just as larger ideologies and school structures shape students' spatial and academic mobility, so too do school officials' everyday messages and interactions.[3] Mike and his friends observe this when they are able to bypass school security and enter their counselor's office without impediment. The free pass that Mike believes he receives because of his IB status is one that other Asian American students outside of the program also encounter in ways that no Latinas/os shared during the research.

In fact, staff member Tom Delgado, who earlier critiqued a teacher for assuming that a Latina ninth grader did not belong in an honors class, reports that the school, himself included, treats groups of Latina/o students as an "unofficial gang":

> We've always had a Hispanic group, maybe between five to ten students, that hang out together. They are a group. In my line of work, maybe four or five in a group and they give themselves a little name. To us, unofficially, that's called a gang. . . . I don't really know if they are actually gang members, but they are well on their way to it.

This assumption of Latina/o criminality emerged during a discussion with several seniors enrolled in the school's college preparatory classes—including the following three Mexican American students and one biracial Black and White student. In particular, they highlight the controlling strategies of one school administrator:

Raul Melendez: Mr. Johnson, the remarks he makes to certain students make him a dick.

Marcos Rivera: Yeah, he told me, "I'm surprised you could afford the prom."

Nick Mesa: He picks on people who look like troublemakers, like Mexicans, gang members, skinheads.

Travis Jacks: He goes after Mexicans and Blacks.

Raul: He told me and my Black and Filipino friends, "I'm watching your group."

As sociologist Victor Rios (2011) describes in his ethnographic study on the policing of Black and Latino boys, such profiling, degrading, and surveying are forms of symbolic criminalization. As such, they are part of the larger youth control complex that criminalize Black and Latino youth in an attempt to control them.

Some Asian Americans students are acutely aware of this unequal policing and how it is linked to assumptions about Latinas/os and Asian Americans. Four Asian American sophomores recount their observations from their CP courses:

Kathy Hsin: There are different kinds of teachers here, and some are racists. Some are mean, and some like picking favorites.

Interviewer Mai Thai: What do you mean that some teachers are racist?

Kathy: Some people only like Asians because they're Asians.

Mark Ku: 'Cause they're like, "They're smart."

Nat Punyawong: They think there's some difference, you know?

Mark: Like Mexicans, they're like, "Oh, he doesn't try." But they judge the book by its cover.

Nat: Yeah, like if you come late to class or something, and you tell them your PE [physical education] teacher let you out late, they'll be like, "Oh, it's okay." And then a Mexican guy comes and says that, and they're like "Oh, go to the office."

These disparate forms of monitoring and questioning versus assumptions of belonging and smartness can influence students' outlooks toward school and can become self-fulfilling (Lopez, 2003; Rios, 2011). In both cases, students may become accustomed to either being stopped, questioned, and ridiculed or welcomed with high expectations. However, the unequal messages are especially pernicious when such regulation entails excluding students from classes and learning opportunities.

Implications and Conclusions

Going into our schools and listening to students reveals how more than school gates are barring students. Behind fences, students encounter multiple constraints—geographically and academically. Analyzing and comparing students' testimonials uncovers the significance of larger ideologies, school practices, and everyday interactions on reinforcing boundaries and inequalities.

The predominately middle- and upper-middle-class Asian American students in the school's top academic programs describe more openness—less regulation of movement and of thought by educators—in their course work and as they travel around campus. In contrast, working-class students, especially Latinas/os outside of the school's top courses, encounter multiple forms of school control and punishment. Latinos in particular describe being stopped, questioned, and assumed to be troublemakers or gang members.

Along with geographical constraints, students recount academic restrictions. These, too, are racialized and tied to curriculum track. Asian American students report being held to a higher standard in their classrooms because of the racialized academic profiling that expects them to excel in school. Students in the school's less prestigious CP courses, who are often Latina/o and first-generation college-going students, tend to describe structured classroom assignments and spaces where an emphasis is placed more on order and following rules than on cultivating original ideas and critical thinking.

Such disparate forms of control influence students' educational opportunities and life chances, hindering their potentials and stunting their contributions. In general, students who are the most heavily regulated feel the repercussions of these geographic and academic constraints most severely and directly. But our schools and society suffer, too, in a self-perpetuating process. The persistence of practices such as curriculum tracking that are exclusionary in their origins, manifestations, and outcomes position our schools and educators as regulators of inequality rather than as spaces and supporters of possibilities. To the extent that exclusionary practices and the ideologies justifying them become normalized, the institutionalization of racism and classism ensures the replication of inequality for future generations.

Notes

1. Throughout this chapter, I use *racial/ethnic* and *race/ethnicity* not to conflate them or to assume that they are biological, cultural, or static categories but instead to acknowledge that they are two interrelated systems and socio/political/economic/cultural constructs that influence life chances and perspectives.

2. I use the panethnic categories *Asian American, Latina/o, White, Black,* or *African American* to be inclusive. However, most of the students interviewed at SCHS identify as Asian, Mexican, or Mexican American, and many of the Asian students are the children of Chinese and Korean immigrants.
3. For a discussion of the role of students in this process, please see Ochoa (2013).

References

Beres, L. S., & Griffith, T. D. (2001). Demonizing youth. *Loyola of Los Angeles Law Review, 34,* 747–766.

Bogardus, E. (1934). *The Mexican in the United States.* Los Angeles, CA: University of Southern California Press.

Bowles, S., & Gintis, H. (1976). *Schooling in capitalist America: Educational reform and the contradictions of economic life.* New York, NY: Basic Books.

Brick, K., Challinor, A. E., & Rosenblum, M. R. (2011, June). *Mexican and Central American immigrants in the United States.* Washington, DC: Migration Policy Institute.

California Department of Education. (2008). *Students by Ethnicity, 2006–2007* and *Teachers by Ethnicity, 2006–2007.* Sacramento, CA: Education Data Partnership. Retrieved from http://www.ed-data.k12.ca.us

Chua, A., & Rubenfeld, J. (2014). "What drives success?" *New York Times,* January 25.

Delgado-Gaitan, C. (1992). School matters in the Mexican-American home: Socializing children to education. *American Educational Research Journal, 29*(3), 495–513.

Fleury-Steiner, B. (2008). *Dying inside: The HIV/AIDS ward at Limestone Prison.* Ann Arbor: University of Michigan Press.

Frankenberg, R. (1993). *White women, race matters: The social construction of Whiteness.* Minneapolis: University of Minnesota Press.

Galvez, A. (2015). "Gifted and Talented Education Update." Curriculum, Instruction and Assessment Committee, April 28.

Ginorio, A., & Huston, M. (2001). *Sí, se puede! Yes, we can: Latinas in school.* Washington, DC: American Association of University Women Educational Foundation.

Gonzalez, G. G. (1990). *Chicano education in the era of segregation.* Philadelphia, PA: Balch Institute Press.

Kao, G. (2000). Group images and possible selves among adolescents: Linking stereotypes to expectations by race and ethnicity. *Sociological Forum, 15*(3), 407–430.

Kupchick, A. (2010). *Homeroom security: School discipline in an age of fear.* New York: New York University Press.

Lareau, A. (2003). *Unequal childhood: Class, race, and family life.* Berkeley: University of California Press.

Lee, S. (1996). *Unraveling the "model minority" stereotype: Listening to Asian American youth.* New York, NY: Teachers College.

Lopez, N. (2003). *Hopeful girls, troubled boys: Race and gender disparity in urban education.* New York, NY: Routledge.

Morris, E. (2006). *An unexpected minority: White kids in an urban school.* New Brunswick, NJ: Rutgers University Press.

Noguera, P. (2008). *The trouble with Black boys: And other reflections on race, equity, and the future of public education.* San Francisco, CA: Jossey-Bass.

Nolan, K. (2011). *Police in the hallways: Discipline in an urban high school.* Minneapolis: University of Minnesota Press.

Oakes, J. (1985). *Keeping track: How schools structure inequality.* New Haven, CT: Yale University Press.

Ochoa, G. L. (2013). *Academic profiling: Latinos, Asian Americans and the achievement gap.* Minneapolis: University of Minnesota Press.

Ochoa, G. L. (2015). Gendered expectations and sexualized policing: Latinas' experiences in a public high school. In G. Q. Conchas & M. A. Gottfried with B. M. Hinga, *Inequality, power and school success: Case studies on racial disparity and opportunity in education* (164–184). New York, NY: Routledge.

Pew Hispanic Foundation/Kaiser Family Foundation. (2004). *National survey of Latinos: Education.* Washington, DC: Authors.

Rios, V. (2011). *Punished: Policing the lives of Black and Latino boys.* New York: New York University Press.

Shor, I. (1992). *Empowering education.* Chicago, IL: University of Chicago Press.

Zhou, M. (2009). *Contemporary Chinese America: Immigration, ethnicity, and community transformation.* Philadelphia, PA: Temple University Press.

CHAPTER 16

Race, Age, and Identity Transformations in the Transition from High School to College for Black and First-Generation White Men

Amy C. Wilkins

In this essay, Amy Wilkins uses interview data with twenty-six Black and White male students attending predominantly White four-year research universities to investigate the integration experiences of Black and first-generation White men in high school and college. By ***first generation****, Wilkins is referring to students whose parents did not earn a four-year degree. Both groups of men reported having positive social experiences in high school. However, while first-generation White men were able to transport their identity strategies to college, the transition to college complicated integration and identities for Black men. These processes supported White men's collegiate goals but undermined Black men's, increasing the emotional costs of college for Black men, undermining academic support, and blocking their ability to construct satisfying pathways to adulthood. She argues that identity experiences in high school matter for identity processes in college, where identity expectations can change in*

Source: Adapted from Amy C. Wilkins, "Race, Age, and Identity Transformations in the Transition from High School to College for Black and First-Generation White Men," *Sociology of Education*, Volume 87, Number 3, pages 171–187, SAGE Publications, Inc., 2014.

unexpected ways for different groups. More attention is needed to the relationship between precollegiate and collegiate identities and to the ways ***intersectionality*** *complicates identity processes.*

Questions to Consider

This essay focused on differences between Black and first-generation White men in their transition from high school to college. How might the transition from high school to college differ among Black or first-generation White women? How might other intersectional identities beyond race, class, and gender (e.g., ableism, legal status, sexual orientation) influence the transition from high school to college? Are some identities more important than others in this period of transition?

Introduction

Social mobility through higher education involves more than academic success. It requires that students find a way to fit in, make friends, and gain the social and cultural capital needed for post-collegiate social mobility (Chambliss and Takacs 2014; Lee and Kramer 2012; Stuber 2011). At stake is not just *whether* differently situated students achieve social integration, but *how* they become integrated, as the pathways they find, the support networks they carve out, and the disruptions they face are consequential beyond whether or not they leave with a four-year degree (Armstrong and Hamilton 2013).

Race and class differences in academic and social integration matter for educational success, social mobility, and personal well-being. In this article, I investigate the integration experiences of black men and of white first-generation college men attending predominantly white, four-year, public, flagship research universities. I examine each group's accounts of high school and college.

Both groups of men reported having positive social experiences in high school. However, while the white first-generation college students were able to transport their identity strategies to college, the transition to college complicated integration and identities for black men.

Identities, Education, and Social Mobility

Research on K–12 educational settings demonstrates that identities and peer cultures shape youth experiences, practices, aspirations, and social pathways (e.g., Bettie 2003; Carter 2005; Crosnoe 2011; Eckert 1989; Fordham 1996). Students who feel academically marginalized by race or class develop contextually protective identity strategies that allow them to retain dignity but also contribute to social reproduction (Bettie 2003; Eckert 1989; Willis 1977). Some race- and class-disadvantaged students achieve upward mobility by "performing" middle-class identities, making friends with middle-class peers and adopting their practices, clothing, and orientations toward schooling (Bettie 2002). Other academically successful black and Latino students shift between "street" and "school" identities (Carter 2005). Some research finds that masculinity can be difficult to assimilate with a school orientation because it demands a tougher, more "street" kind of posturing than femininity (Carter 2005; Morris 2012). In suburban schools, however, the "coolness" associated with black masculinity can ease social integration for black boys (Holland 2012; Ispa-Landa 2013). Scholars, however, have not examined what happens after these students leave secondary educational settings.

Another stream of research examines the transition to college, showing that race and class affect college cultures and student integration. Young people from class- and race-disadvantaged backgrounds often face formidable hurdles to social integration (Aries and Seider 2005; Feagin, Vera, and Imani 1996; Lehmann 2007; Stuber 2011). At residential, flagship campuses, collegiate practices and educational goals reflect those of white, class-privileged students (Mullen 2011; Stuber 2011). Class-linked cultural knowledge and expectations shape how students participate in social aspects of college life, helping class-advantaged students make friends and stockpile social and cultural capital (Armstrong and Hamilton 2013; Stuber 2011). Student friendships are critical to student retention (Chambliss and Takacs 2014). *Who* students befriend also matters: friends are critical sources of information about the educational opportunity structure (Stuber 2011). It thus matters not just *whether* one fits in, but also *how*. Researchers have not closely examined the relationship between pre-collegiate identity strategies and collegiate identities, patterns of student integration, and experiences of college life. How do the identity strategies developed before college affect students once they enter college?

Pathways to Adulthood

Demographic transitions—such as exiting school and entering work, marriage, or parenthood—have become delayed, reversible, or untenable indicators of adulthood. In their place, subjective markers, such as autonomy and self-fulfillment, have taken on new significance (Arnett 2000; Shanahan 2000; Silva 2012). For many young adults, college is one stop on a long path of self-exploration and development (Hamilton and Armstrong 2009). Not all young people adhere to this pathway and its expectations, however, as it requires class-linked cultural expectations and economic resources (Silva 2012). Mullen (2011) finds that working-class students do not enter college focused on personal development but on acquiring job-specific skills and credentials. In Mullen's study, students' approach to college matched the goals of the lower-tier commuter institution they attended. Because adulthood is a *relational* identity, individuals do not feel like adults unless an audience confirms their adult status (Silva 2012). To what degree are differently situated students able to find confirmation for their adult orientations in the context of predominantly white, affluent, flagship universities?

This article builds on these literatures to ask: First, how do first-generation white men and black men recall the identity strategies they used in high school? Second, how do race, class, and gender constrain or facilitate first-generation white men's and black men's identity strategies in college, as they explain them, and what is the relationship between the identity strategies they used in high school and the ones they used in college? Third, what are the implications of their identity strategies for their ability to construct satisfactory pathways to adult roles?

First-Generation White Men in High School

The first-generation white men in my sample had parents who worked in service or manual labor jobs, such as waitressing or flooring. Two had parents who were self-employed, leading to unevenness in their economic stability and long working hours. Two participants lived in trailer parks. Yet, these men did not recount childhoods characterized by economic hardship—perhaps because their parents were better off than many non–college educated adults. In addition, many of these participants recalled extended family providing extra resources.

First-generation white men described their parents as warmly supportive but not proactive about their education. They all reported going to neighborhood schools in the communities they could afford. Most of these schools were mixed-class, sending a portion of students to college. As Brendan recounted, their parents neither encouraged nor discouraged college: "They always told me you know whatever you end up wanting to do, we'll support that. So it's not like they were really trying to push me in any one way or the other." Similarly, Sam recalled that his parents "wanted me to do what I thought was best."

Finding College-Bound Friends: Becoming Normal

First-generation white men developed their college aspirations in school by integrating socially with college-bound youth. They did not describe their high school experiences this way, however, but instead talked about themselves as regular, "normal" guys who did "normal" things. Although these men developed their ideas about being normal in their peer groups rather than in their homes, it is worth noting that they did *not* describe being seen as odd by their families or home communities. As Patrick said: "I have a lot of friends that say I'm just like normal. Like they just say, if they think of someone normal, it's me." Patrick described himself as "normal" 16 times in his interview, and going to college was part of being normal:

> I wasn't in a bunch of advanced classes like AP and stuff. I had one AP class, but then I had a lot of other classes *that still counted for college.* But at the same time, I wasn't like nerdy or anything. But then I wasn't like a jock or anything. (emphasis added)

To Patrick, taking classes that "counted for college" was part of what it meant to be normal. Men from a range of social positions portrayed themselves as normal, as long as they were also preparing to go to college. Danny, for example, was a jock. He positioned himself and his friends as normative when he described them as "just a bunch of guys." Matt labeled himself "a nerd." When I asked what he and his friends did for fun, he said: "Just not really anything special. Just normal things. It's not like we were looked down upon for—for like trying really hard in school, it didn't affect us like negatively." It was important to him that I understand that being nerdy did not make him stand out. "It was kind of a good thing," he added, "because we were all really competitive." Matt located himself as a regular guy—competitive, but not highly visible, doing the things you need to do to head for college.

Managing Class Differences

Being normal was not, however, precisely a strategy for becoming middle class. These men acknowledged differences between themselves and their middle-class peers. By portraying themselves as "normal," these men glossed over the work it took to fit in, masking the difficulties class disadvantages often caused them. Enzo explained that when his friends started to get cars, "you know you'd feel some like kinda some resentment towards the wealthier people." But, he added,

> I had an old truck. But at the same time you know it was like . . . we had grown up together. And we were all such good friends. And we saw each other for who we were you know. . . . And you know money was kind of in the background but it wasn't, it wasn't the biggest deal.

Participants described how they worked to minimize class-related social or emotional disruptions. Being normal was about being able to blend in without standing out.

Although these men portrayed their high school friendships as natural and "normal," these disruptions suggest that making themselves fit—that making "normal" feel normal—required slow transformations of which they may have been only dimly aware. Brendan's story is revealing. An older high school friend convinced Brendan, who had recently moved to his suburban community after his parents' divorce, to try cross-country running. He remembered that his "parents didn't really have money for all that stuff" so he had not participated in organized activities before:

> I was like I don't know. Like running a lot sounds terrible. And he's like no. You'll like it. Like all the guys are cool. . . . The longer I did it, the more I really liked it and the more I felt like it was just kind of . . . a second home. . . . I liked . . . just being in shape . . . and anything that's competitive. I like to try to be the best.

Brendan's recollection indicates he was pulled reluctantly into the middle-class activity of cross-country, which did not feel normal at first, but he learned to experience it as an emotionally and socially supportive environment—"a second home." In this way, cross-country became normal to him. It was not incidental that a competitive sport provided a way to anchor his masculinity, replacing the "mischief" that had predominated in his old community. Brendan said he worried about avoiding the trouble that had derailed his own parents, and cross-country provided a clear alternative.

Avoiding Trouble

Positioning themselves as "normal" helped first-generation white men in another important way. Unlike the parents of more affluent college-bound youth, the parents of first-generation men did not have resources to leverage if their sons got in trouble. Wealthier children also benefitted from the perception that they were just "all around good people," in Enzo's words, even when they did get in trouble. First-generation men did not have that benefit. To stay college bound, first-generation men needed to stay out of trouble on their own. Blending in was an important part of this strategy. But participants were also proactive about avoiding trouble. Cross-country provided Brendan with an alternative to "mischief." Sam remembered that when he first moved to his rural town, his friends had been the "wild kids," because they were easier to get to know, but he "realized that wasn't the type of person that I was. And I started spending time with the kids that were more focused on school, and more mature, I guess you could say." Danny told a cautionary tale about a "stoner" friend who had been headed to the state-level track competition and presumably college and then "just fell off the face of the earth." In this story, his friend's drug use simultaneously undercut his class future and his athletic (masculine) future; not smoking marijuana becomes the smarter *masculine* choice.

Given limited familial information about the process of getting to college, first-generation white men needed critical information and resources available from peers and teachers. To gain this information, they needed to be seen as college bound, which meant fitting in with other college-bound youth and being "normal"—they could not risk standing out. Participants thus minimized disruptions to their social and emotional participation while simultaneously sidestepping any troublemaking behavior that could derail their trajectories. The flatness of their stories, in which they emphasize how "normal," "unexciting," or "uninteresting" they were, is testimony to how successful they were at achieving this strategy.

White men's strategies of being "normal" within their peer groups allowed them to fit in, make friends, and benefit from behavioral norms and information sources that supported college attendance. Despite a slight disruption with the transition to college, these strategies continued to work for them in college.

First-Generation White Men in College

These first-generation white men entered college imagining adult-oriented identities. Brendan said "I was really excited to come to college, live on my own, you know. I mean I'd always been pretty independent." Patrick portrayed himself as "focused more on working" while "other people have a lot more free-time stuff. So I feel like I want to do more productive stuff in my free time." Danny prioritized school over a social life: "I obviously just kind of want to get through school," he said, dreaming about how quickly he could finish to start full-time work. First-generation men depicted themselves as hard-working, goal-oriented, and independent.

Opting Out of Partying

The transition to college was not seamless. Brendan recalled, "I mean most of the schools I went to I fit in well right away. So it was weird for me to come here and really not fit in."

Having successfully distanced themselves from trouble in high school, participants were surprised to discover that partying was an important route to college friendships. They felt excluded, describing themselves as "isolated" and "lonely." Danny said, "You know because that's like how a lot of people get connected is when they smoke or drink together, and I just didn't do that."

Not partying was a choice. These men portrayed partying as antithetical to their collegiate goals. Ben anticipated that "some kids here probably won't be here in the next couple years just 'cause like they do party a lot and they don't study as much as they should." Sam said, "Once you get started down that path [partying], it's really easy to just kind of stick with it. And I figured I might as well, I'm here to learn and do my best." Patrick recalled engineering dropouts, "'cause they partied too much I guess." First-generation men portrayed avoiding partying as a safer academic strategy, but they also described it as consistent with being "mature" and "adult."

Making Friends

Not partying temporarily destabilized the social neutrality first-generation men had achieved in high school, causing them to feel like they did not belong and disrupting established pathways for creating friendships. Nonetheless, these white men recalled finding alternative ways to make friends fairly easily, through shared academic interests and low-cost leisure activities such as hiking, Frisbee, and playing video games. Brendan recalled, "The more I was in classes that I liked and stuff, the more I found people who liked the same things."

These men used the things they had learned about "normal" guys in high school to create social integration, which in turn helped them feel normal again. Patrick recalled: "I hated coming that first semester . . . [now] it seems a lot more normal."

These men's friendships supported their collegiate goals. First-generation men all talked about the importance of getting up early, being "productive," and establishing study routines. Their friendships supported these routines. More privileged, less academically focused students at Western often participate in expensive leisure activities, such as skiing, that these men could not afford. The activities through which first-generation men made friends embedded them in networks with other academically minded students. Danny explained, "A lot of my friends . . . they just don't talk about drinking . . . they just do other stuff. They're more productive I guess." Ben's friends "are pretty intellectually stimulated. And I can like talk to them about reading and stuff." Because these men's friends shared their academic interests, they helped them focus on their goals, provided study partners, and limited social distractions while ameliorating the loneliness participants felt when they first came to college.

Relationships with Girlfriends

Relationships with hometown girlfriends anchored these strategies for many men. Five of eight participants were still dating their high school girlfriends, none of whom attended the same college. Most of the girlfriends went to lower-status regional schools, lived at home, and majored in fields like nursing that would allow geographic mobility after college. Because most participants went to college in-state, girlfriends were typically only a short drive away. Long-term, off-campus girlfriends gave these men a way to opt out of the partying culture they worried would derail them. Partying culture often entails hooking up (Hamilton and Armstrong 2009), but their girlfriends provided an explanation for not participating while also "proving" their heterosexuality. These men were experienced in using this explanation. Patrick said, "I've been dating the same girl so I'm not really interested in [hooking up]." Ben explained that he had not hooked up with anyone because, "it sounds lame what I'm going to say . . . like I care about her a lot, you know." Men typically saw their girlfriends on weekends, either traveling to see them or having them visit. These visits took place during the time when other men partied, further justifying not partying. Sam explained that he and his girlfriend spend the weekend going "on dates. Fun activities and we're going camping this weekend, and [we] do some homework. . . . I mean it's exciting to me, but most people are like bummed if they don't party hard three times in one weekend." Similar to Ben's comment that caring about his girlfriend "sounds lame," Sam's caveat recognizes that spending time with his girlfriend instead of partying misses one high-status script for collegiate masculinity, yet his relationship did explain away his non-partying.

Girlfriends bestowed critical emotional support. Hometown girlfriends provided an identity bridge, anchoring men's connections to their home communities while supporting their goals of social mobility. Participants told many stories about their girlfriends getting them through when they struggled academically or felt lonely. Patrick said, "I guess we both were having a hard time with school. Both I guess supporting each other with how bad we were doing at one point." When I asked these men what they liked about their girlfriends, they all reported that they were "nice," "caring," and "listened to them." Sam said, "Just it meant more to me I guess, to be more serious and . . . just to be with someone that cared about what you were doing and about the future, and wasn't just worried about what they were doing that weekend and, I don't know, it's difficult to explain." Participants explained that their parents were not equipped to provide them with emotional or practical support in college. Danny said: "People are like their parents are giving them advice on how to succeed in it, while my parents just say good luck." Girlfriends compensated by providing these men with empathy and encouraging them to pursue their goals. Unlike for first-generation women, whose hometown boyfriends typically undermine their educational goals (Armstrong and Hamilton 2013), gendered scripts about heterosexual relationships, in which women support men, helped sustain these men's goals.

Despite an initial bump, most first-generation white men fairly smoothly turned "being normal" into a strategy for making college friends. Through common leisure and academic interests, they found a small circle of academically minded peers who supported their focus on studying, provided them with a social life, and, for some, accommodated their relationships with their hometown girlfriends. In turn, the lives they developed made them feel and seem like "normal," if still somewhat boring, men. In multiple ways, these first-generation white men were able to draw on race, class, and gender cultural scripts about manhood that, while not as high status as the cultural scripts associated with fraternity men, were still supportive of college satisfaction, persistence, and future economic security. Indeed, being "normal" was itself one of those scripts.

Black Men in High School

Most of the black men I interviewed came from families in which one or both parents worked in professions such as electrical engineering, middle management, or education. A smaller number had parents who held labor jobs such as custodian. Many parents were upwardly mobile over the course of the participant's childhood, finishing their education and moving from urban core neighborhoods to suburban neighborhoods. Unlike the white participants, black men perceived that their parents prioritized education—they moved to new neighborhoods with better schools, found desegregation programs, or secured scholarships to prestigious private schools. As a result of parental strategies, these black men attended predominantly white schools in which almost all students matriculated to a four-year college. Most of their parents had also instilled collegiate expectations. Participants sometimes bristled at these efforts. Richard reflected: "I hated it when my mom would say, 'Black man. You're intelligent.' I know I'm intelligent, you don't have to tell this to me." Richard's comment illustrates the degree to which many black men in my sample took their college trajectory for granted.

Making Friends: Negotiating Coolness

These black men all described being well liked by both white and black peers in high school. Vincent shrugged, "Everybody wanted to be with me." These men engaged strategically with black masculine images, using them to maximize peer status without jeopardizing mobility. Taylor, for example, who attended a private school, was disgusted by the disregard for teachers displayed by some of the black youth who attended the school in his predominantly black, lower-class neighborhood: "They're like, 'Fuck you, Miss.' . . . I was different, but I mean overall I didn't really see any difference. Like I was on the basketball team and all that stuff." Taylor distanced himself from the anti-school behaviors he associated with black masculinity while simultaneously using sports to claim black masculine authenticity. Participants did not all juggle these images the same way. Some capitalized on the idea that black boys are naturally athletic; others used the presumption of black masculine cool to engage in more stereotypically feminine behaviors.

Athletes

Athletics is a route to high school popularity for boys regardless of race; it intersects with cultural meanings about black masculinity to further bolster black boys' status. Tim said, "All the black kids played basketball. We were like the cool group." For David, football was part of a package of achievement-oriented, high-status characteristics, including student body president. Nick remembered how he traded more conventionally bad boy behavior for football when he started to get into legal trouble: "I was just getting in trouble, like, I guess, legal stuff, being a kid, bein' stupid, makin' bad decisions . . . so I needed to do something . . . and I started playing football." Nick, and the adults around him, saw football as a safer way to be a black boy. Sports provide an adult-sanctioned way for boys to demonstrate masculine competitiveness, toughness, and physical prowess, without necessarily compromising academic commitment—and sports may be seen as an especially appropriate outlet for black boys.

Non-Athletes

The seven men who were not high school athletes also remembered high school fondly. Ekon was on a step team and sang in the choir—activities often seen as feminine in high schools. He reflected, "I was . . . not popular, but I knew everybody. I mean I knew *everybody*." Like other non-athlete black boys, Ekon was not conventionally "popular," but he had a large circle of friends and was socially visible and comfortable. Phillip's "friends were the drama students." He played violin, although reported being terrible at it. He tried unsuccessfully to date, and later came out as queer. He laughed, "I know nothing from sports. I'm Jewish." Yet, like Ekon, he reported that he was "fairly popular with the students and with the teachers"; at one point, he even claimed, "I was running that school." Men like Ekon and Phillip—who were not athletes; who participated in uncool activities, such as drama, choir, or peer mediation; and who did not have girlfriends or who spent far more time hanging out with girls (but not pursuing them sexually) than was considered "normal" for high school boys—were not as popular as football stars, but they were not marginalized either. These men's stories suggest they were able to trade on the image of cool black masculinity to gain space to behave in more feminine ways.

Youth culture values the characteristics associated with black masculinity: athleticism, toughness, heterosexual prowess, and cultural cool. In predominantly white schools, black masculinity makes a wide range of black boys cool enough (see also Ispa-Landa 2013). Because these schools have few black boys, black masculinity is rare and more valuable. These black men were cool because their coolness was assessed against nonblack boys; they did not have to engage in risky or "hard" behaviors to benefit from presumptions of black masculine cool (Holland 2012). Instead, coolness was protective, channeling black masculinity into adult-sanctioned activities and away from troublemaking. First-generation white participants' strategy of not standing out and black participants' strategy of standing out both facilitated pathways to college, shielding boys from class- and race-linked risks.

The presumption of coolness that extended to both athletic and unathletic black men allowed a range of black men to fit in, make friends, and stay on track to college. Unlike first-generation white men, who were able to transport their strategies to college, however, black men's strategies did not continue to work for them in college.

Black Men in College

Black men in my sample entered college with similar ideas about college as the white men. Richard explained, "My mom literally dropped me off in my dorm, gave me a kiss on the cheek, [said] 'You're a man,' and left me. I was like, 'What do I do?' But again I felt relieved. Because I was like, 'Wow, no one can control me now.'" Tim said, "It's hard, it's expensive to go to school, so when you have it, you have to take it serious. You can have fun, for sure, but you have to find that balance." Offered both a track and an academic scholarship, Tyler took the academic scholarship, majoring in engineering. "Like that's just not how life works," he said about pursuing college athletics, "so I put myself in a position to succeed in . . . other areas." Like the white first-generation men, these black men saw themselves as hard-working, goal-oriented, and independent.

Social Invisibility

These black men anticipated they would have little trouble making white friends in college, as they had many white friends in high school. Like the white first-generation men, they were surprised to discover they did not easily fit in. Some participants experienced overt marginalization: Ekon recalled being kicked out of a party. Others described more subtle forms of exclusion. Vance explained that although he used to have white friends he called "brothers," now he just has "associates," a term that evokes a much greater level of emotional distance. Lance said, "I used to run things in high school, and now nobody will look in my direction." All the participants described a change in social position that was dramatic and painful.

Black men also struggled to find socially comfortable spaces with other black students. Black students call other black students who do not play intercollegiate sports "regulars." This term is misleading: Regular black men are not seen as "regular," but are socially invisible *as black men*, even to other black students. Tim said, "The athletes don't even want to talk to the regular [men]." Nick, an athlete, admitted, a little embarrassed, "They [regular black men] *are* kind of like the invisible ones to us." He was not exaggerating. Many athletes could not name a single non-athlete black man, although they knew many black women. Craig, an athlete, mused, "I don't know what it is, but we never really had you know the best relationship with all the black guys that aren't athletes on campus." Black women were often friends with regular black men, but when I asked questions about "black men," they equated "black men" with black athletes. When I asked why, Janae answered, "Maybe they're [non-athletes] just not my image of a strong black man." Kayla, embarrassed, admitted, "I'm getting myself into trouble here, but [I don't know any black men who are not athletes]." Social invisibility does not mean regular black men had no friends or acquaintances; rather, they were not socially visible *as black men*, and their social interactions did not support *their* conceptions of who they were.

Racial hostility is common on predominantly white campuses (Feagin et al. 1996), but regular black men are not marginalized simply because they are black; they are marginalized because they do not fulfill peer expectations of youthful black masculinity. Their bodies are smaller and less muscular than athletes' bodies. They reject athletic apparel, choosing a preppier look. Indeed, these black men looked and dressed much more like the non-black men on campus. Failure to embody the norms of hip hop masculinity led to questions about their masculinity and heterosexuality, as Tim complained: "Like a lot of my friends are like 'you've gotta be gay man, you've gotta be gay.' . . . The girls, they assumed that I was gay because I dress well. I'm like how can you be gay because you dress well?" Tim's style led to questions about his heterosexuality not because he breached general rules of masculine style but because he breached campus assumptions about *black* masculine style. Regular black men's failure to conform to youthful expectations of black masculine comportment jeopardized their identities as *black men*.

Adolescent Expectations in Social Interaction

First-generation white students were able to repair their identities through everyday leisure activities with other students, in which social similarities helped forge quick social ties. But for black men, everyday leisure activities are often difficult arenas of interactions. Participants expressed frustration at interactive expectations linking them to adolescent identities they were trying to shed. Jeffrey, for example, sighed, "White people want you to be the life of the party. . . . I do not want to be that stereotype." And Phillip said:

> These are white males who say "wassup" to me. . . . Because I am black and . . . male, from some of the people I get "wassup" and this, that, the other, thinking, "Oh great, I've seen the Wayans brothers and everything else. . . . I know how to engage with you."

Phillip added, "[I'm] 22 years old. This person who's talking to you is maybe 19. You don't talk to me like that." In these examples, black men's everyday interactions tethered them to the racialized adolescent interests they rejected. Their adult self-concepts and interests were not recognized, making it difficult for them to create the same kind of easy connections as white men.

Black men also found it difficult to make connections based on shared academic interests. White students regularly doubt black men's academic credentials. While first-generation white men's class differences are hidden in college, black men's class *similarities* become invisible. The class-based affirmative action programs that supported first-generation students' entrance into Western were unseen, whereas non-black students assumed that all black students benefitted from non–merit-based admissions programs, even though most did not. Richard shrugged, "[White people] usually bring it up: 'Wow, most black people I know are here for scholarships.'" He bristled, "Why is it that I can't get the same education? Why would you not want me to get the same education? Give us a chance to show that we can do things, and you'll see." Because staff from the athletic department wait outside classrooms to mark athletes' attendance, and students do not easily differentiate between athletes and black non-athletes in the classroom, black men all suffered from the infantilizing assumption that they required more educational supervision than other students, which undercut their efforts to establish autonomous, goal-oriented academic identities. These assumptions have consequences. In classes, for example, non-black students avoided working in groups with black students. Dennis reported that peers ignored his repeated efforts to discuss engineering, instead only talking with him about football: "When I got here, my identity, it wasn't as a football player, but I was 220, 230 pounds, and I'm, black." This talk affected him, eventually pushing him to walk onto the football team.

Emotion Management

Because they had been socially successful in high school, these men were unprepared for the dilemmas they faced in college. Moreover, their aspirations to middle-class adult identities constrained their interpretations of their encounters. They did not want to be "angry black men" (Wilkins 2012b). Indeed, they prided themselves on being able to get along with white people. Jeffrey boasted, "I'm able to interact with white people in a more sincere way."

Corey proudly claimed, "I can interact with whites and blacks." Jesse similarly said, "I know how to deal with the other races . . . [and] can communicate with anybody comfortably." To avoid being angry and to sustain relationships with whites, they minimized racism. As Richard illustrated, "I just take everything with a grain of salt and flick it right off because there's no point for me to have a grudge." Managing relationships with other students required these men to manage bad feelings about their interactions (Wilkins 2012b). Unlike the white men who talked about how much they enjoyed the outdoors, black men talked frequently about how exhausted they were.

Intimate Relationships

Girlfriends provided many first-generation white men with emotional support, but most regular black men did not have girlfriends or boyfriends. Half had not had an intimate relationship since coming to college. This was unusual. In a study of 57 white, upper-middle-class white students at Western (Wilkins and Dalessandro 2013), every participant had been in multiple intimate relationships. Outsiders often assume that black college students regularly date white women, but this perception is based on stereotypes about black masculinity rather than men's actual experiences (see Wilkins 2012c). Phillip explained, "I'm not seen as something attractive." Jeffrey noted, "Among non-athletes, leave it [interracial dating] alone. It's . . . more of an athlete thing." Tyler said that white women "think black guys are hot, but they would never like date a black guy. . . . They wouldn't even sleep with one. They just like . . . to look." McClintock (2010) found that black men at Stanford hook up, but do not date, interracially; in my sample, nonathlete black men did not perceive their relationship *or* hook up options to be good.

Black men's efforts to draw on scripts about middle-class adult masculinity were not recognized by outsiders, who instead insisted they conform to scripts associated with adolescence and the black lower class. These identity struggles complicated black men's social integration, intensified their emotional dilemmas, and denied them some of the support systems the first-generation white men experienced. Their more fraught friendships and intimate relationships did not provide them with comparable emotional support to white men's; instead, these relationships often undermined how they saw themselves. Black men and first-generation white men entered college with similar expectations and goals, but only white men were allowed to perform adult-like roles consistent with school success; black men were asked to perform adolescent roles that were anti-school and counterproductive. Because other students did not recognize their view of themselves as adult men, they were limited by race, class, and gender cultural scripts about black masculinity in ways that undermined their collegiate efforts, increasing the personal, identity, and emotional costs of higher education.

Discussion

Identities and identity transitions matter for academic success, social integration, and personal well-being. Past research has not examined how identities developed in high school affect identity processes in college; how these processes are influenced by the contextual intersections of race, class, and gender; and how identity processes and social integration affect the construction of satisfying pathways to adulthood. In this study, I used the cases of first-generation white men and black men to examine these questions, focusing on continuity and changes in their identity experiences in high school and college. I now discuss each of these points further.

First, high school identity strategies matter for college identity experiences. Studies of working-class college students find that adjusting to the upper-middle-class habitus and expectations of universities, like the ones in this study, is often prolonged and painful (e.g., Aries and Seider 2005; Lee and Kramer 2012). However, the first-generation white men in this study had already begun making identity transformations in high school. The identity strategies they developed in high school eased their transitions to college, where they readily converted their high school strategies of "being normal" into adult identities. Masculinity facilitated this strategy; for example, gendered relationship scripts supported the growth of their collegiate identities.

In contrast, identity strategies that worked for black men in high school *unexpectedly* no longer worked in college, increasing the difficulty of social integration and the emotional cost of their social struggles. The strategy of "being normal"—not standing out—was never available to black men. Black men always stood out in predominantly white schools. Black men in this study, like others in predominantly white schools (Holland 2012; Ispa-Landa 2013), used the meanings of black masculinity to craft various successful high school identities. The cultural meaning of black masculinity as cool allowed them to engage in a range of behaviors and still be seen as cool enough, even when they deviated from cultural images of black masculine cool. Expectations for the performance of black masculinity became narrower in college, however, and the costs of coolness increased. Because they had so much latitude over their images in high school, they were surprised that they could no longer manipulate images of black masculinity—they had been stripped of choice over their identities. Their positive social experiences in high school left black men unprepared for the social and emotional dilemmas they faced in college. Because black women's experiences in suburban high schools are so different from black men's (Holland 2012; Ispa-Landa 2013), their transition dilemmas are likely distinct (see Wilkins 2012a), underscoring the need for more intersectional research.

Second, identity strategies are contextually constrained and facilitated by intersectional identity locations. Cultural scripts about white masculinity, including the idea of the "normal guy," constrain and enable first-generation white men, just as cultural scripts about black masculinity constrain and enable black men. The first-generation white men in my sample worked to fit the normal guy script in high school; once they accomplished this, knowing how to be a normal guy helped them make new friends and create stable lives in the context of college. For black men, in high school, being the cool black friend could mean doing almost anything they wanted, but in college, they were limited to a small set of stereotypical, adolescent behaviors. At the same time, their peers did not allow them to be anything *but* the cool black friend. The context, which was shaped in part by changing *age* expectations, altered the degree to which they could control the script. To black men's surprise, they had much more latitude over scripts about black masculinity in high school than they did in college, where the audience's expectations boxed them in in new ways.

Third, educational experiences matter for how differently situated stude pathways to adulthood. Opportunity structures create divergent gender strateg approach adulthood: according to Messner (1989), poor black boys assess the opportunity structure and continue their investment in sports, whereas middle-clas boys reinvest in education. The men in this study, however, entered college with similar but could not create equally satisfying pathways to adulthood. First-generation white men were allowed to adopt adult-oriented identities, whereas black men were not. Like other achievement-oriented black college men (Harper 2004; Ray and Rosow 2009), they claimed hardworking identities as professionally oriented college students, but their peers constantly challenged how they saw themselves, making it difficult for them to craft emotionally and academically supportive personal relationships.

Structural opportunities and personal identity preferences were not the only things that mattered: the audience's cultural expectations were also important. These expectations allowed first-generation white men to successfully tap into a class-linked script about white manhood and to find peers who confirmed and supported their views of themselves (Silva 2012). This script did not yield white men high-status peer positions in college, nor is it likely to land them the most lucrative post-collegiate careers, but it did allow them to successfully achieve identities as adult men. This path was closed to the black men in my sample, particularly if we take seriously Silva's (2012) finding that adulthood is relational, requiring outsider confirmation. This difference has real consequences for black men's experiences, affecting their ability to create supportive friendships and intimate relationships, and their sense of belonging at university.

References

Aries, Elizabeth and Maynard Seider. 2005. "The Interactive Relationships between Class Identity and the College Experience: The Case of Lower Income Students." *Qualitative Sociology* 28:419–43.

Armstrong, Elizabeth A. and Laura T. Hamilton. 2013. *Paying for the Party: How College Maintains Inequality.* Cambridge, MA: Harvard.

Arnett, Jeffrey Jensen. 2000. "Emerging Adulthood: A Theory of Development from the Late Teens through the Twenties." *American Psychologist* 55:469–80.

Bettie, Julie. 2002. "Exceptions to the Rule: Upwardly Mobile White and Mexican American High School Girls." *Gender & Society* 16: 403–22.

Bettie, Julie. 2003. *Women without Class: Girls, Race, and Identity.* Berkeley: University of California.

Carter, Prudence. 2005. *Keepin' It Real: School Success beyond Black and White.* New York: Oxford.

Chambliss, Daniel F. and Christopher G. Takacs. 2014. *How College Works.* Cambridge, MA: Harvard.

Crosnoe, Robert. 2011. *Fitting In, Standing Out: Navigating the Social Challenges of High School to Get and Education.* New York: Oxford.

Feagin, Joe R., Hernan Vera, and Nikitah Imani. 1996. *The Agony of Education: Black Students and White College and Universities.* New York: Routledge.

Fordham, Signithia. 1996. *Blacked Out: Dilemmas of Race, Identity, and Success at Capital High.* Chicago: University of Chicago Press.

Hamilton, Laura and Elizabeth Armstrong. 2009. "Gendered Sexuality in Young Adulthood: Double Binds and Flawed Options." *Gender and Society* 23: 589–616.

Harper, Shaun R. 2004. "The Measure of a Man: Conceptualizations of Masculinity among High-achieving African American Male College Students." *Berkeley Journal of Sociology* 48:89–107.

Holland, Megan M. 2012. "'Only Here for the Day"': The Social Integration of Minority Students at a Majority White High School." *Sociology of Education* 85:101–20.

Ispa-Landa, Simone. 2013. "Gender, Race, and Justifications for Group Exclusion: Urban Black Students Bussed to Affluent Suburban High Schools." *Sociology of Education* 86:218–33.

Lee, Elizabeth M. and Rory Kramer. 2012. "Out with the Old, In with the New? Habitus and Social Mobility at Selective Colleges." *Sociology of Education* 86: 18–35.

Lehmann, Wolfgang. 2007. "I Just Don't Feel Like I Fit in: The Role of Habitus in University Drop-out Decisions." *Canadian Journal of Higher Education* 37: 89–110.

McClintock, Elizabeth Aura. 2010. "When Does Race Matter? Race, Sex, and Dating at an Elite University." *Journal of Marriage and Family* 72:45–72.

Messner, Michael. 1989. "Masculinities and Athletic Careers." *Gender & Society* 3:71–88.

Morris, Edward M. 2012. *Learning the Hard Way: Masculinity, Place, and the Gender Gap in Education.* New Brunswick, NJ: Rutgers.

Mullen, Ann L. 2011. *Degrees of Inequality: Culture, Class, and Gender in American Higher Education.* Baltimore, MD: Johns Hopkins.

Ray, Rashawn and Jason Rosow. 2009. "Getting Off and Getting Intimate: How Normative Institutional Arrangements Structure Black and White Fraternity Men's Approaches toward Women." *Men and Masculinities* 10:1–24.

Shanahan, Michael J. 2000. "Pathways to Adulthood in Changing Societies: Variability and Mechanisms in Life Course Perspective." *Annual Review of Sociology* 26:667–92.

Silva, Jennifer M. 2012. "Constructing Adulthood in an Age of Uncertainty." *American Sociological Review* 77:505–22.

Stuber, Jenny M. 2011. *Inside the College Gates: How Class and Culture Matter in Higher Education.* Lanham, MD: Lexington.

Wilkins, Amy C. 2012a. "Becoming Black Women: Intimate Stories and Intersectional Identities." *Social Psychology Quarterly* 75:173–96.

Wilkins, Amy. 2012b. "'Not out to Start a Revolution': Race, Gender and Emotional Restraint among Black University Men." *Journal of Contemporary Ethnography* 41:34–65.

Wilkins, Amy C. 2012c. "Stigma and Status: Interracial Intimacy and Intersectional Identities among Black College Men." *Gender & Society* 26:165–89.

Wilkins, Amy C. and Cristen Dalessandro. 2013. "Monogamy Lite: College, Women, and Cheating." *Gender & Society* 27:728–51.

Willis, Paul. 1977. *Learning to Labor: How Working Class Kids Get Working Class Jobs.* New York: Columbia.

CHAPTER 17

Out of the Shadows and Out of the Closet

Intersectional Mobilization and the DREAM Movement

Veronica Terriquez

In this essay, Veronica Terriquez investigates the role of queer-identified youth in the DREAM movement, revealing how ***DREAMers*** *from diverse and marginalized identities—that is, a marginalized subgroup within a larger group that is also marginalized and disadvantaged—engaged in* ***intersectional mobilization*** *to successfully represent the interests of undocumented youth activists.*

Questions to Consider

Most individuals identify themselves as belonging to more than one group. For example, an individual may identify as belonging to classifications within the categories of race, class, gender, sexuality, and the like. Do some identities matter more than others at home, work, or school? Are there some identities that may matter more than others when fighting for the rights of a marginalized group?

Undocuqueer [undocumented and queer] leaders have been very visible in the immigrant rights movement in recent years. They have been at the forefront of

Note: Reading is original to this book.

many of the major protests and actions for the DREAM Act. I believe they have played a critical role in making sure that the public becomes aware of our situation and how we are fighting for our rights in this country.

—Jaime, twenty-two-year-old straight-identified undocumented youth activist from Los Angeles

Jaime's claims echo those of other participants in and observers of an early 2010s youth-led movement that was fighting for the rights of undocumented youth who lacked citizenship, legal permanent residency, and other documentation to reside legally in the United States. Jaime and many of his peers recognized the leadership of queer youth ([LGBTQ] here meaning lesbian, gay, bisexual, transgender, or other nonheterosexual). At the time, these undocumented youth activists, both queer and straight, were often referred to as the DREAMers because they had been leading the charge to gain congressional support for the federal DREAM (Development, Relief, and Education for Alien Minors) Act. The aim of this proposed legislation was to provide a pathway to citizenship for eligible undocumented youth.

Borrowing from the gay and lesbian movement's "coming out of the closet" narrative, in which individuals publicly declare their homosexuality, the DREAMers began organizing the "coming out of the shadows" campaign in 2010. As part of this effort, activists publicly came out as undocumented, declaring their undocumented legal status in order to combat the stigma associated with their precarious legal situation and humanize their experiences in the eyes of broader audiences. Among some activists, these declarations of a legal status were accompanied by the disclosure of a queer identity in online venues, public demonstrations, and mainstream media.

LGBTQ visibility in the DREAM movement was notable for several reasons. First, LGBTQ people of color and immigrants sometimes encounter many challenges to publicly disclosing a queer identity. Second, this movement's primary focus was on a pathway to citizenship for the undocumented, not on LGBTQ issues. And third, though queer individuals historically have been active in movements focused on the rights of immigrants and people of color, their LGBTQ identities have often remained invisible. These past movements often made salient a single and unifying identity; they did not attend to how multiple and overlapping—or *intersectional*—identities (Crenshaw, 1989) based on race, class, gender, sexual orientation, and legal status shaped the experiences of their members.

How, then, can movements mobilize their members in a way that accounts for their intersectional identities? How can they generate high levels of participation of members who experience multiple layers of marginalization based on their identities? To address these questions, this chapter examines the identity formation processes within the DREAM movement in California, the state with the largest undocumented immigrant youth population in the United States. It uses survey data to demonstrate high levels of representation and activism among queer-identified youth. It also draws on in-depth interviews to demonstrate that LGBTQ leadership can, in part, be attributed to the ways in which identities were expressed and acted upon in within the DREAM movement. In this grassroots effort, activists' multiple marginalized identities were recognized within the broader national social movement, within local organizations, and by individuals themselves. This led to *intersectional mobilization*—that is, high levels of activism and commitment among individuals who represent a disadvantaged subgroup within a broader marginalized constituency.

In order to explain the intersectional mobilization of undocumented DREAMers, this chapter begins with a review of the relevant literature on intersectionality, coming out, and the role of collective identity in social movements, followed by a description of the data used for this study. The chapter concludes with a discussion of how this research on the DREAMers informs sociological theory and offers insights for other efforts to promote the leadership of multiply marginalized minority groups.

Intersectionality and Barriers to the Public Display of an LGBTQ Identity

Intersectionality theories offer a useful starting point for understanding LGBTQ leadership in the DREAM movement. Intersectionality theory reminds us that each individual has multiple identities based on their race, gender, class, sexual orientation, legal status, disability status, age, and other social markers. These identities shape whether or not and how individuals experience discrimination and social inequalities (Collins, 1986; Crenshaw, 1989).

An intersectional theoretical framework suggests that nonwhite youth from low-income and undocumented backgrounds might experience a number of challenges to openly sharing a queer identity. For example, Latino and Asian immigrant youth may lack a strong identification with a larger White LGBTQ population that can sometimes hold racist attitudes toward people of color. Family ties, traditional gender roles, conservative religious values, and widespread homophobia can prevent LGBTQ individuals, including immigrants, from openly disclosing their sexual orientation. Financial dependence may prompt some LGBTQ immigrants from being too public about their sexual orientation because they do not want to risk losing their family's financial support.

Moreover, being undocumented potentially can add to the risks of coming out as a sexual minority. Undocumented immigrants often live "in the shadows," hiding the fact that they lack authorization to live in the United States (Chavez, 1998). They face the risk of deportation, must cope with the stigma of being labeled *illegal*, and frequently endure significant economic and social hardships. Because they rely heavily on family networks for support, queer undocumented immigrants may face legal consequences and challenges if their families and communities reject them because of their sexual orientation.

Intersectional Mobilization

While belonging to a minority identity group (i.e., nonwhite racial group, LGBTQ, undocumented) can result in the experience of discrimination and social marginalization, a minority identity can also function as a source of political power. Historically, social movements have empowered individuals who belong to marginalized groups by framing their identity in politicized ways. Such framing can entail making a case for injustice experienced by the group and the advantages of collective action in addressing the injustice (Polletta & Jasper, 2001).

Social movements can seek to make salient a single, shared identity among participants in order to support collective action. To this end, social movements may seek to avoid difficult discussion regarding the group's internal diversity (Lichterman, 1999).

Yet the identities of multiply marginalized individuals and their interests do, at times, receive attention. Social movements have the potential to encourage *intersectional mobilization,* meaning high levels of activism and commitment among multiply marginalized subgroups. Gamson's (1992) conceptualization of collective identity formation occurring at three interconnected layers—movementwide, organizational, and at the social location—serves as a useful framework for understanding how movements might be inclusive of diverse identities and motivate participation among individuals who experience various forms of identity-based marginalization. Specifically, intersectional mobilization can be facilitated by the recognition and activation of participants' relevant marginalized identities at the movement, organizational, and individual levels. The movement-, organizational-, and individual-level identity processes described in the sections that follow are often interconnected.

Movement-Level Collective Identity

Some social movements engaged in *identity politics* generate the public visibility of marginalized identity groups. Typically, such movements aim to improve the social standing of individuals who can be identified with a single identity group, but it is possible for such movements to feature prominently more than one identity in the course of advocating for demands (Townsend-Bell, 2011). As such, movements as a whole can publicly recognize activists' multiple identities and raise awareness of the challenges experienced by disadvantaged subgroups.

It is possible for social movements to make salient the identities and experiences of minority group members by adapting the strategies of other identity-based social movements. Facilitated in part by overlapping memberships between two movements, such social movement spillover of identity strategies may enable activists to recognize the collective identity promoted by the original movement in addition to the identity highlighted by the second movement. For example, the women's movement (an identity-based movement) strongly influenced the 1980s peace movement by increasing the leadership of women and promoting feminism within other aspects of the peace movement's activities (Meyer & Whittier, 1994).

The spillover of the LGBTQ movement's coming-out identity strategy may serve as one, but not necessarily the only, contemporary vehicle for combatting multiple stigmas and motivating action among the multiply marginalized. The gay rights movement has long used this coming-out strategy—the public disclosure of LGBTQ identities—as a means to promote acceptance by the dominant society, demand rights, and mobilize a constituency.

Organizational-Level Collective Identity

Organizations can play an important role in determining whether or not and how actors' multiple identities are articulated and mobilized. Prior research indicates that social movement organizations can engage in multi-identity work to create inclusive environments and buy-in from members who occupy different social locations (Ward, 2008). Organizations can create inclusive environments through diversity trainings, separate spaces for specific identity groups, structures that ensure diverse leaderships, cultural celebrations, and other activities. Additionally, organizations must address unequal relationships and tensions between and among groups.

Individual-Level Collective Identity

How activists understand and interpret their own identities can determine their personal investment in and the types of roles they play within a social movement (Polletta & Jasper, 2001). In this regard, movement participants can sometimes be quite cognizant of how their own race, class, gender, legal status, and/or sexual orientation affect their experience and may draw upon more than one identity to motivate their activism. For example, Pastrana's (2006, 2010) research on LGBTQ activists of color demonstrates that multiply marginalized identifiers serve as a resource in social justice organizing efforts. He shows that because activists' racial minority status and sexual orientation result in discriminatory treatment both within activists' own racial communities and in White-dominant LGBTQ spaces, they are hyperaware of oppressive social structures within a variety of settings. As such, the experience of being an outsider within (Collins, 1986) contributes to activists' consciousness of multiple forms of oppression. Such intersectional consciousness can inspire commitment to multiple subordinate groups and motivate activists to pursue a more holistic call for social justice and social change (Pastrana, 2006, 2010).

Data and Methods

This mixed-methods study relies on analysis of data from 402 Web surveys collected from undocumented youth activists and follow-up in-depth interviews with fifty activists, including twenty-five who identified as straight and twenty-five who identified as queer. Collected in 2011–2012, survey data come from young adults involved in forty-two groups affiliated with two California-based networks of undocumented youth organizations that maintained strong ties to national efforts. Survey data are used to generally assess queer representation in the DREAM movement and to explore differences in the activism of LGBTQ and straight-identified members. Meanwhile, qualitative interview data are used to examine undocumented youths' experiences of coming out as LGBTQ and to investigate the identity processes within this movement. Men and women are almost equally represented, with twenty-four individuals identifying as women, twenty-five identifying as men, and one transgender individual who did not identify along the gender binary. Forty-two respondents were born in Mexico, three in South America, two in Central America, two in the Pacific Islands, and one in Southeast Asia.

Survey Results

Descriptive Statistics

Table 1 describes the LGBTQ composition, demographics, and civic engagement of the DREAM survey sample. Results indicate significant representation of queer activists, as 13% of survey participants identified as gay, lesbian, bisexual, queer, or some other nonheterosexual identity. While we cannot determine the extent to which this sample is representative of DREAMers as a whole, this percentage appears to be high, considering that a separate 2011 representative sample survey of California young adults found that 5% of 18- to 26-year-olds (and 7% of college-educated youth) identified as LGBTQ. Survey results also indicate that women outnumbered men, and almost all respondents had enrolled in some type of postsecondary education.

Table 1 Descriptive Statistics for LGBTQ and Straight-Identified DREAMers

	LGBTQ DREAMers		***Straight DREAMers***		***Total***	
	%	***n***	**%**	***n***	**%**	***N***
Sample percentage and size	13%	55	87%	355	100%	410
Gender						
Male	64%	35	39%	137	42%	172
Female	33%	18	61%	217	58%	235
Other	4%	2	<1%	1	1%	3
Sexual Orientation						
Heterosexual or Straight	0%	0	100%	355	86%	355
Gay	40%	22	0%	0	5%	22
Lesbian	5%	3	0%	0	1%	3
Bisexual	31%	17	0%	0	4%	17
Other	23%	13	0%	0	3%	13
Race/Ethnicity						
Latino	84%	46	90%	320	89%	366
Asian/Pacific Islander	9%	5	7%	24	7%	29
White/Other	7%	4	3%	11	4%	15
Average Age	22.1	55	21.3	355	21.3	410
Ever Enrolled in Postsecondary Education	93%	51	96%	340	95%	391

	LGBTQ DREAMers		Straight DREAMers		Total	
	%	n	%	n	%	N
Civic Engagement						
Membership in organizations (average #)[a]	3	55	2.4	355**	2.5	410
Worked with others on a community issue[b]	87%	48	81%	289	82%	337
Shared social/political issue online[b]	93%	51	74%	263**	77%	314
Participated in a protest, march, or rally[b]	80%	44	65%	231*	67%	275

Source: California Young Adult Study, Immigrant Youth Survey 2011–2012.

Notes: Total percentages may not add up to 100% because of rounding error.

* p = <.05, ** p = <.01 (two-tailed test).

a. A bivariate Poisson regression was used to test differences in number of organizational memberships, a limited count dependent variable.

b. A bivariate logistic regression was used to test differences in civic engagement, as measured by dichotomous variables.

The bottom panel of Table 1 shows results for members' civic engagement. Survey results offer evidence for the intersectional mobilization of queer DREAMers, as findings suggest that LGBTQ-identified respondents were more civically engaged than their straight-identified counterparts. Specifically, queer members reported membership in more civic organizations (3.0 on average) than did straight members (2.4 on average); this difference is statistically significant. Additionally, statistically significant results indicate queer respondents were more likely than their straight peers to have shared their perspectives online and to have participated in a protest.

Semi-Structured Interview Findings

Barriers to the Public Display of an LGBTQ Identity among the Undocumented

Interview findings indicate that activists often encountered obstacles to coming out of the closet within the contexts of their families or broader immigrant communities. For most queer DREAMers in this study, coming out as LGBTQ was a painful experience, and many still struggled with being open about their sexual orientation.

With a handful of exceptions, most queer activists claimed that homophobia within their families or broader immigrant communities presented a barrier to coming out of the closet. The story of Alberto, age twenty-six, provides an illustration of the homophobia some confronted. Born in Guadalajara, Mexico, Alberto grew up in a socially conservative family. Alberto recalled an experience as a child growing up in Southern California that taught him early on that being gay was not acceptable.

> There was a boy in elementary school who was really, really feminine. I mean, he took it to the ballpark—you know, like homerun femininity. He was fabulous. But I remember my mom saying, "Oh, my God, I would be devastated if I was his mother." And that really hit me. It stuck with me.

Like several other youth, Alberto also noted that his parents' religious beliefs made coming out especially challenging. He explained:

> My dad belonged to one of the most conservative organizations within the Catholic Church, and he was very vocal about his distaste for certain things, including homosexuality. So I thought it was wrong to be gay because I grew up in that environment.

Consequently, for Alberto, coming to terms with his sexual orientation was a very painful process that created a considerable amount of family conflict, especially since his parents actively sought a "cure" for his gayness.

In addition to fear of disapproval from their families, a few interviewees experienced negative material consequences when their families learned about their sexual orientation. Most DREAMers, regardless of their sexual orientation, relied heavily on family and extended networks for their economic survival and other resources. Loss of family financial support was a real concern for some LGBTQ activists, as twenty-four-year-old Samir asserted:

> We can't [legally] have jobs, so we already have these financial issues. Once you come out to your family—and if they don't respond very well—then there is that chance of losing your bed, a place to sleep. There's a lot more you can lose because you can't really take care of yourself financially when you're undocumented.

Indeed, queer undocumented youth had to overcome significant financial vulnerabilities because their families were unaccepting. For example, after being kicked out of his family's household for being gay, one young man resorted to living in his car; lacking regular employment, some days he went hungry. Another young woman's family ceased helping her pay for college after she came out as a lesbian. She was ineligible for government financial aid at the time and was forced to withdraw from school when she ran out of funds.

Coming out to unsupportive family members could also have legal consequences. This was the case for twenty-four-year-old Nacho, who first met his estranged father as a teenager. Initially impressed by his academic achievements, his father, a U.S. citizen, introduced Nacho to his extended family and promised to fix his papers. "They were all super supportive of me," Nacho recounted. "They were going to help me pay for college. They were going to help me get my legal status." This changed, however, when he came out as gay. "They pretty much cut me off, and it felt horrible.... It was really heartbreaking. It hurt so much." His family's homophobia not only took an emotional toll on Nacho, it also cost him a potential opportunity to become a legal permanent resident.

In addition to noting family-related barriers to coming out, a few queer DREAMers also expressed concerns about disclosing their identities in the context of their community activism. The immigrant rights movement as a whole seeks to gain support from mainstream and religious audiences not always accepting of LGBTQ individuals (Yukich, 2013). For example, Zaira, a twenty-four-year-old activist, explained:

> I never say that I'm queer. I deal with a lot of religious people, whether it's in the immigrant rights movement or out in the community. If I come out as queer to them, I think they'll judge me before they see the work that I'm doing. Coming out as queer might be a hindrance to my work.

Zaira believed that the broader Latina/o immigrant community and other potential allied communities would not be as receptive to her political work if they learned she lived with a female partner. Other activists, like Zaira, reported minimizing their queer identity within what they perceived to be a homophobic broader community.

While most queer DREAMers encountered challenges to being out within their families and communities, there were several who openly shared their queer identities in almost all social settings. This minority had gained the acceptance of their families, and this familial support appeared to afford these young people a greater ability to disclose their queer identities in a wide range of social settings.

The Intersectional Mobilization of Undocuqueers within the DREAM Movement

Movement-Level Collective Identity Formation and the Spillover of the Coming-Out Strategy

Evidence suggests that the DREAM movement's "coming out of the shadows" identity strategy—initiated in 2010 by LGBTQ undocumented activists in Chicago—played an important role across the movement nationally in helping some undocumented LGBTQ activists to come out of the closet and become politicized around both their legal status and sexual orientation.

Notably, DREAMers' "coming out of the shadows" national strategy openly acknowledged the intersectional identities of activists at the outset. For example, the online "Coming Out of the Shadows—A How To Guide," posted by the national organization DreamActivist.org, states, "In the same way the LGBTQ community has historically come out, undocumented youth, some of whom are also part of the LGBTQ community, have decided to speak openly about their status." In line with this pronouncement, activists across the country used social media to publicly counter the double stigma associated with their undocumented and LGBTQ identities.

Some leaders had been out as LGBTQ in the movement prior to the "coming out of the shadows" campaign. These individuals helped widely spread the coming-out strategy. At the same time, interview findings suggest that the DREAMers' "coming out of the shadows" strategy played a significant role in contributing to the proportion of openly LGBTQ-identified youth in the movement. For example, some interviewees claimed that their involvement in their undocumented student group first helped them publicly proclaim their legal status, which in turn paved the way for sharing their sexual orientation. As Ixchel, a prominent and openly bisexual leader, explained, being open about one's legal status "is a transition that helps queer folks come out; they experience the acceptance of coming out as undocumented, so it helps people come out as queer."

Mateo's experience serves as an example of the impact of the DREAM movement's "coming out of the shadows" campaign on queer identity development and disclosure among activists. As a college freshman, Mateo became an active member of his campus organization, but he initially kept his LGBTQ identity a secret. As Mateo attested, this changed as a result of the movement's "coming out of the shadows" campaign:

> It wasn't always okay to say that you were undocumented, but I guess when I first started college, it was taboo, completely. I think now it's okay to say, "I'm undocumented." For me, I first got comfortable saying that I'm undocumented before I started saying I'm queer or I'm gay or I'm LGBTQ. I guess once you go through saying you're undocumented, it's easy to accept a queer identity and be able to talk about it with other people. Maybe it's because you already have this sense of self-empowerment based on your undocumented status, that you can use that for your queer identity.

While some activists discussed how they came out as undocumented first, a few others instead experienced a "double coming out." These young people were motivated to be open about their queer identities and legal status around the same time. For example, twenty-three-year-old Francisco explained, "In my case, both struggles have been difficult, so I think that connecting both, being comfortable with both, and being open about these identities makes life so much easier." The high degree of visibility of queer leaders made it easier for some to claim both identities, as noted by Gustavo, an "older" twenty-eight-year-old activist:

> Lately a lot of people are being very in-your-face about their queer and undocumented identities. . . . It has given other folks—it has given me—the empowerment to come out, and say, "Okay, I've got to own both things."

The evidence therefore suggests that the spillover of the coming-out identity strategy at the movement level contributed to intersectional mobilization by facilitating the widespread public declarations of two marginalized identities—undocumented and queer. Likely contributing to the significant representation of out LGBTQ members among the ranks of the DREAMers (as suggested by survey findings), this case of spillover also contributed to the LGBTQ inclusivity of DREAM organizations.

Organizational-Level Multi-Identity Work

While the movementwide coming-out strategy promoted LGBTQ visibility among activists, multi-identity work within movement organizations further acknowledged the identities and needs of queer members. Contributing to the intersectional mobilization of undocumented LGBTQ activists, organizational practices helped combat homophobia and validated the experiences of LGBTQ members.

LGBTQ and straight activists alike believed that DREAM organizations were overall very open to queer members, especially when compared to other non-LGBTQ youth organizations and the broader immigrant rights movement comprised of older activists. Undocumented activists described their DREAM organizations as "welcoming," "a safe space," "very accepting," "like family," or "very open." As one twenty-six-year-old queer leader explained, "First and foremost, the movement is a network of support—we're supporting each other through our education and personal lives, and I think we've all done a good job of supporting each other with our identities." David, a recent graduate of a four-year university, concurred: "You feel a sense of belonging because people understand what you're going through, not just as an undocumented person, but also as someone who is gay." For the LBGTQ interviewees, DREAMer organizations served as a space where they connected with other immigrant youth who also confronted challenges associated with their legal documentation status. Perhaps not surprisingly, these youth typically reported feeling more at home in their DREAM organizations than they did in queer campus or community organizations because of the lack of demographic diversity within these LGBTQ organizations.

LGBTQ identities had not always been salient in the activities of DREAM organizations. It is important to recognize that LGBTQ leaders initiated the charge to make the movement more inclusive. At the same time, some straight undocumented allies have helped promote inclusivity within DREAM organizations. For example, Cris, a transgender activist, noted feeling comfortable in the local campus organization because

> stated or unstated, the space was queer. You felt it. It was predominantly straight social females working it. Social males were in the space, but they were very conscious of their privilege because the women kept them in check. The organizing that I had done in the past didn't have that.

Cris was not the only one to acknowledge the role of straight females in combating homophobia.

Multi-identity work included workshops that exposed straight members to the experiences of the movement's queer-identified members. Held at regional events, within campus organizations, or at broader community venues, workshops often included testimonials from queer members about their LGBTQ coming-out experiences and the impact of homophobia on their lives. They humanized queer members' experiences and often drew connections between living in the shadows and living in the closet. As Samir, introduced earlier, explained, "We're in the same struggle for acceptance. I think that to be able to connect both [an undocumented and queer identity] and acknowledge both makes the movement stronger." Educational workshops, which sometimes explicitly framed the identities and experiences of queer activists as *intersectional*, tended to have an impact on straight-identified members who learned to be empathetic toward the experiences of queer members.

Organizations employed other forms of multi-identity work that explicitly recognized LGBTQ identities. At one central coast organization, leaders often announced at the beginning of membership meetings that their organization was queer inclusive. At another organization, e-mail announcements regularly stated the group was queer inclusive. A few queer leaders claimed that it was a general practice in their organizations to privately confront members who made homophobic remarks, and one mentioned that straight allies in his group would speak up in support of LGBTQ rights so that the burden of combating homophobia did not always fall on queer members.

Straight and queer activists alike maintained that queer activists were prominent at regional and national DREAMer protests and events. However, some local college- or community-based organizations had been slow to adopt multi-identity practices that acknowledge the experiences of queer members. In other words, not all DREAM organizations effectively implemented multi-identity strategies that supported queer leadership.

The Individual-Level Intersectional Consciousness of Activists

Reflecting a pattern found within the broader DREAM movement and its organizations, individual activists—queer and straight—were attuned to how people's multiple identities can affect their life chances. Yet those who identified as LGBTQ, in particular, often linked the personal challenges that they faced to their marginalized identities. As outsiders within (Collins, 1986), or a minority within a minority, these youth exhibited a hyperconsciousness of multiple oppressions. LGBTQ-identified DREAMers' intersectional consciousness, which prompted them to connect personal experiences of discrimination to larger social systems, likely contributed to their intersectional mobilization.

Without prompting, queer activists often discussed in the interviews how different dimensions of discrimination and power relations affected their lives. Although not the case for all, several interviewees developed this intersectional consciousness through their involvement in the movement. For example, Yohanna, a twenty-four-year-old community college student, described her own multiple identities: "I've learned though the movement that we're not only one thing; we're not only DREAMers. I'm a single mom, a queer. I'm undocumented. I'm a woman of color. I'm all these things." This understanding of how the "personal is political" equipped her with an inclusive vision of social justice. She explained, "If you are sensitive to an issue facing one community, to the struggle that those people go through, you need to be aware of and more accepting of all struggles." Similarly, Nacho, the Sacramento-area activist introduced earlier, believed that the multiple subordinate identities that he and fellow queer DREAMers embody can heighten an awareness of social injustices. He explained:

> Queer people have an understanding that these problems shouldn't exist. I think we feel oppressed all the time, so I think we're able to understand other sets of oppression as well. Obviously, I don't go through what a black male goes through, but I know what a brown man goes through. Sometimes the cops arrest me. But it's just the many layers that make up who I am that makes me more understanding of the bigger picture. There's just so much prejudice and racism and homophobia in this country!

Nacho and many other queer activists in this study expressed a sense of urgency about taking a stance on multiple issues that affected their lives. Because of their personal awareness of the varied ways in which oppression and discrimination systematically affect the communities of which they are a part, they felt compelled to act. Speaking prior to the *Obergefell v. Hodges* Supreme Court case that legalized gay marriage, Samir said as much in explaining LGBTQ members' commitment to the movement:

> For some reason it matters more to us. Because we [queer folks] can't get legalized through marriage or all these other avenues the straight people have. So, if you look at the events that happen or the actions that do take place, there are queer people who are prominent within those actions and events.

In addition to motivating their high levels of participation in the DREAM movement, an intersectional consciousness shaped queer activists' understanding of how to broaden the movement's scope. Some leaders were highly invested in trying to ensure that the movement proceeded with an understanding of the complexity of people's experiences. Ixchel described the work that she and others have led: "We've been trying to connect these intersecting issues. We've talked about developing curriculum that would set up tools and having these conversations."

A vibrant contemporaneous LGBTQ rights movement provided some activists the political opportunities to act on their intersectional consciousness, likely facilitating the particularly high levels of civic engagement among queer members demonstrated in survey findings. Some queer leaders, with varying levels of success, sought to forge connections between the LGBTQ and immigrant rights movements. For example, twenty-seven-year-old Roman literally went on the road to talk to both constituencies about "how undocumented and queer communities intersect." He described the rationale behind his efforts:

> Both communities face laws that treat us like we are less human. We both are very vocal about society's problems, we both are afraid for the security of our families, we both feel vulnerable and unsafe because of policies, institutions, and attitudes that keep us on the margins. We are frequently ignored, misrepresented, or made fun of by the dominant culture!

Because of parallel experiences with oppression, Roman strongly believed that the immigrant and LGBTQ rights movements should work in coalition. He was committed to forging a dialogue between the two movements, which at times had worked at cross-purposes to each other. Because of this, he and others initiated Queer Dream Summer, which placed undocumented queer youth in summer internships in LGBTQ organizations. One of the goals of this placement was to raise awareness of immigrant rights issues in LGBTQ organizations.

Overall, the intersectional consciousness of individual LGBTQ activists helped drive the intersectional mobilization of *undocuqueer youth* in the DREAM movement. Such politicized understanding of and experiences with multiple forms of identity-based oppression intensified this minority group's commitment to a vision of social change that accounted for diverse experiences. Many of these queer undocumented activists acted on opportunities to make the immigrant youth movement more inclusive of LGBTQ members by developing alliances between immigrant and LGBTQ organizations that had previously lacked a history of collaboration.

Discussion

In the latter half of 2012, many DREAM organizations shifted their focus to the implementation of DACA (Deferred Action for Childhood Arrivals), a temporary policy victory that, to a certain degree, demobilized the movement, as many activists gained access to formal employment and other benefits. This study examines the prominence of LGBTQ youth in the immigrant youth movement in California just prior to the implementation of DACA. Survey findings suggest that queer youth were, at that time, well represented among activists and that they were more civically engaged in some activities than their straight-identified peers. Yet interview findings show that many queer activists encountered challenges to coming out of the closet to their families and their communities. Evidence therefore suggests that the DREAM movement served as a gateway for individuals to become more open about their sexual orientation and provided a space for them to become highly involved in activism.

Queer youths' representation and visibility in this movement can, at least in part, be attributed to their intersectional mobilization or the recognition and activation of undocumented and queer identities in the broader movement, within DREAM organizations, and among individual activists. At the broader movement level, the "coming out of the shadows" identity strategy empowered some members to disclose publicly not only their legal status but also their sexual orientation. Meanwhile, at the organizational level, deliberate efforts to combat homophobia contributed to organizational environments in which queer members felt welcome and safe. Finally, queer activists' intersectional consciousness further intensified their own activism as they sought to address LGBTQ issues within the immigrant rights movement and build bridges with the gay rights movement.

This study contributes to sociological theory by adapting Gamson's (1992) conceptualization of layered movement identity formations to offer a new framework for examining social movement participation among multiply marginalized minority groups. The case of the DREAMers suggests that the acknowledgment and activation of participants' multiply-marginalized identities at the movement, organizational, and individual levels can deepen engagement among minority subgroup members. At each of these levels, activists' multiple identities can be addressed or suppressed. Therefore, attention to the interests, needs, and unique experiences of groups who encounter multiple identity-based hardships at these three levels not only can assist these groups in overcoming barriers to political activism but also can inspire high levels of commitment and activism.

This research also offers valuable insights into LGBTQ identity among immigrants. Findings indicate that undocumented individuals encounter additional economic and legal risks in disclosing their sexual orientation when confronted with homophobic family and community environments. The case of the DREAMers points to the importance of social movement and organizational contexts that enable young people to come to terms with this stigmatized social identity. Organizations that are not necessarily focused on gay rights but are sensitized to the experiences of sexual minorities can function as a source of support, helping young people overcome some obstacles to coming out of the closet.

Implications

Social movements, universities, government bodies, corporations, and other institutions can learn from the DREAMers about the benefits of fostering the leadership of multiply-marginalized minority-group members. Accordingly, institutions can make widespread concerted efforts to articulate and attend to the particular experiences and needs of disadvantaged subgroups. Such broad-based and structural initiatives—coupled with the adoption of organizational practices that deliberately counter classism, racism, sexism, homophobia, xenophobia, or other forms of discrimination—can enable those who experience various types of identity-based marginalization to develop and act upon an intersectional consciousness. As demonstrated by the DREAM movement, the alignment of collective identity formation processes at multiple levels can go a long way toward empowering groups and individuals to overcome and work against overlapping forms of identity-based oppression.

References

Chavez, L. R. (1998). *Shadowed lives: Undocumented immigrants in American society.* Fort Worth, TX: Harcourt Brace College.

Collins, P. H. (1986). Learning from the outsider within: The sociological significance of Black feminist thought. *Social Problems, 33,* 14–32.

Crenshaw, K. W. (1989). Demarginalizing the intersection of race and sex: A Black feminist critique of antidiscrimination doctrine, feminist theory and antiracist politics. *University of Chicago Legal Forum,* 139–168.

Gamson, W. A. (1992). *Talking politics.* Cambridge, UK: Cambridge University Press.

Lichterman, P. (1999). Talking identity in the public sphere: Broad visions and small spaces in sexual identity politics. *Theory and Society, 28,* 101–141.

Meyer, D. S., & Whittier, N. (1994). Social movement spillover. *Social Problems, 41,* 277–298.

Pastrana, A., Jr. (2006). The intersectional imagination: What do lesbian and gay leaders of color have to do with it? *Race, Gender and Class, 13,* 218–238.

Pastrana, A., Jr. (2010). Trump(et)ing identities: Racial capital and lesbian and gay organizing. *Sexuality Research and Social Policy, 7,* 93–104.

Polletta, F., & Jasper, J. M. (2001). Collective identity and social movements. *Annual Review of Sociology, 27,* 283–305.

Townsend-Bell, E. (2011). What is relevance? Defining intersectional praxis in Uruguay. *Political Research Quarterly, 64,* 187–199.

Ward, J. (2008). Diversity discourse and multi-identity work in lesbian and gay organizations. In J. Reger, D. J. Myers, & R. L. Einwohner (Eds.), *Identity work in social movements* (vol. 30, pp. 233–255). Minneapolis: University of Minnesota Press.

Yukich, G. (2013). Constructing the model immigrant: Movement strategy and immigrant deservingness in the new sanctuary movement. *Social Problems, 60,* 302–320.

CHAPTER 18

Racial Inclusion or Accommodation?

Expanding Community Boundaries among Asian American Organizations

Dina G. Okamoto and Melanie Jones Gast

In this essay, Okamoto and Gast examine how community-based organizations (CBOs) and their leaders negotiate and expand the boundaries of the communities they serve and represent. Drawing upon interviews with organizational leaders and documentary data from Asian American CBOs in the San Francisco Bay Area, they find that nearly all of the organizations in their sample engaged in **cross-racial** *work, incorporating other racial groups into their programs, campaigns, and partnerships. However, leaders varied in how they understood this work as tied to maintaining or expanding their community of focus. The majority of the leaders in their study discussed cross-racial work as a way to accommodate other racial groups while maintaining a focus on Asian Americans or Asian ethnics. Other leaders included other racial groups, mainly Latinos and African Americans, in expanded missions and goals, broadening not only resources and collective action efforts but also community boundaries through racial inclusion. They argue that pressures and incentives related to funding, shared interests, and organizational survival may encourage CBOs to engage in cross-racial work, but these factors do not necessarily sustain racial inclusion over time. Instead, how leaders identify*

Source: Adapted from Dina G. Okamoto and Melanie Jones Gast, "Racial Inclusion or Accommodation? Expanding Community Boundaries among Asian American Organizations," *DuBois Review Journal,* Volume 10, Issue 1, pages 131–153, Cambridge University Press, 2013.

*Some text and accompanying endnotes have been omitted. Please consult the original source.

and construct a sense of expanded group boundaries for the community that they serve and represent helps an organization to commit to racial inclusion.

Questions to Consider

What kinds of factors matter in determining whether a community-based organization will serve one or more ethnic or racial groups? What are the benefits and detriments of a community-based organization that serves only one ethnic or racial group in a given community, such as Korean Americans or Asian Americans? What are the benefits and detriments of a community-based organization that broadens its reach to encompass multiple ethnic or racial groups within the larger community, such as Korean and Mexican Americans or Asian and African Americans?

Introduction

Recent studies have documented the field of minority nonprofits (Cortés 1998; Cortés et al., 1999; Gleeson and Bloemraad, 2010; Hung 2007) and the role of nonprofit community-based organizations (CBOs) in immigrant adaptation and mobility processes for low-income communities (Marwell 2007; Ramakrishnan and Bloemraad, 2008; Schrover and Vermeulen, 2005). As local institutions, CBOs provide social support, services, and advocacy related to a number of issues such as health, arts, civil rights, housing, and employment for communities defined by neighborhood or other identifiable boundaries, such as racial or ethnic status (Cordero-Guzmán 2005). Past research has emphasized that CBOs contribute to the social, economic, and political incorporation of immigrant and ethnic minorities by providing spaces where co-ethnics can develop leadership, strong ties, and resources (Bloemraad 2006; Chung 2007; de Graauw 2008; Marwell 2007; Wong 2006; Zhou 2000; Zhou and Lin, 2005). However, this work does not examine how CBOs may expand and define community boundaries to share resources, build relations, and work across ethnic and racial lines. In other words, when CBOs widen their boundaries to include multiple groups that cross immigrant, ethnic, and racial lines, this has important implications for (1) social and economic mobility, as CBOs can distribute resources; (2) intergroup relations, as CBOs can help to build intergroup ties which can break down cultural barriers and lead to greater understanding among diverse groups; and (3) civic society, as CBOs can bring together disadvantaged groups to create a stronger political voice.

Yet, organizational change and the expansion of group boundaries to include others in coalition and collaborative work have proven difficult (Morris and Staggenborg, 2004; Van Dyke and McCammon, 2010). The reality of scarce resources, perceptions of intergroup competition, and risks associated with organizational change can often work against the expansion of community boundaries (McClain and Tauber, 2001; Minkoff 1999; Olzak 1992). Despite shared interests related to neighborhood safety, better public schools, or the passage of a local initiative, shifts in resources from one group to another can be viewed as threatening (Jones-Correa 2001). Expanding group boundaries can also come with compromises in regards to organizational identity, making it more difficult to retain the support of community and group members (Dalton 1994; Hathaway and Meyer, 1993; Rose 2000). Moreover, the unique needs of specific ethnic, immigrant, and racial populations may hinder organizational expansion. Given the multiple barriers CBOs may face, how do these organizations expand group boundaries? How do they serve and incorporate diverse groups in practices and programs and eventually come to assert new community boundaries?

We build upon past research by drawing upon interviews with organizational leaders and documents from Asian American CBOs in the San Francisco Bay Area. We identify the different ways that organizations participate in *cross-racial work*—the organizational practices, programs, and partnerships to include, serve, or work with people, organizations, or communities representing a different racial background. All of the organizations in our sample engaged in cross-racial work to some extent, but only a handful included other racial groups in new public identities, missions, or goals—what we identify as *racial inclusion*—and sustained this work over time. Instead, the majority engaged in *racial accommodation* by simply incorporating other racial groups in individual programs or campaigns while maintaining their focus on Asian Americans.

We argue that while external pressures such as government funding, public policies, and shared interests may encourage cross-racial work, a key element in shaping racial inclusion is how leaders perceive their organization as serving a broader community and how they take action to fulfill this vision. CBO leaders create organizational community boundaries through their interpretation of commonalities among and between groups. While race in the United States constitutes a "bright" boundary and affects the processes by which individuals build collective identities (Alba 2005), it is important to recognize that collective groupings can be based on other dimensions such as ethnicity, language, immigrant, or economic status (Jones-Correa 2007). Our case of Asian American CBOs is useful here because of the different identities and statuses upon which leaders can draw from to build a community and allocate resources. We investigate how CBO leaders view and understand group boundaries, paying attention to whether they view their constituents as immigrants or low-income populations in need of social services, as ethnics in need of a supportive co-ethnic community, or as racial groups in need of advocacy and political empowerment. We find that leaders play an important role in reinventing community boundaries and carrying out work on behalf of expanded group affiliations. Furthermore, as representatives that work on behalf of collective communities, CBO leaders shape the allocation of resources and collective action efforts based on these identified group boundaries.

Related Literature

Past literature has demonstrated that individuals construct and negotiate ethnic and racial boundaries in their everyday lives (Horowitz 1975; Nagel 1994; Waters 1999). For example, Kibria (2002) found that Chinese and Korean second-generation college students crafted their identities based on perceptions of shared experience and history. Some opted for an Asian American panethnic identity that was marked by the experience of being racially labeled and stereotyped as Asian while they were growing up, and by certain orientations and values, such as an emphasis on education, family, and work. Other students readily adopted a panethnic identity that was based on the founding goals of the Asian American movement which involved a shared racial identity united by political interests.

Organizations and group entities also negotiate ethnic and racial boundaries. Immigrant and ethnic groups—often at the behest of community leaders—may organize across ethnic lines to gain access to resources in response to public policies or funding mandates (Espiritu 1992; Nagel 1994). In particular, ethnic groups have typically expanded their boundaries and organized as a larger panethnic group to create strength in numbers when trying to gain the attention of elites or to compete for funding (Leighley 2001; Okamoto 2003). Espiritu (1992) found that social workers from various Asian ethnic groups coordinated their efforts to compete against other racial groups for access to resources (Nagel 1994; Padilla 1985). Because funders and mainstream institutions viewed distinct ethnic groups as a racial category, this encouraged organizing along panethnic lines (Shiao 1998). Studies have also found that changes in neighborhood demographics can shape whether CBOs incorporate new racial or ethnic groups, given that public funding requires provision of services and programming for the local community regardless of ethnic, immigrant, or racial background (Becker 1998). However, this literature neglects a focus on how organizational actors—in our case, CBO leaders—construct group-level affiliations and engage in efforts to expand organizational boundaries, which have important consequences for collective action and resource distribution. Moving beyond the factors shaping the expansion of group boundaries identified by past literature, we focus on how CBO leaders, as individual actors and representatives of their organizations, construct and expand boundaries when defining their organizational community and carrying out central organizational work.

Data and Methods

We selected organizations using snowball sampling methods as part of a larger project on the boundary dynamics of Asian American and Asian-ethnic CBOs in the San Francisco Bay Area. Due to our interest in capturing a diverse set of organizations, we gathered a purposive sample of thirty-seven CBOs comprised of ethnic organizations representing Japanese, Chinese, Filipino, Korean, Southeast Asian, and Asian Indian populations as well as pan-Asian organizations that served multiple Asian ethnic groups in our chosen cities. All of the organizations were founded by community members with the mission to serve a specific Asian ethnic group or the larger Asian American community; none of the organizations were originally formed to serve or represent other racial groups such as Whites, Latinos, or African Americans. These organizations differ from other non-profits and membership-based associations because they typically include cultural components in their mission, services, and programs and frequently represent or serve specific racial/ethnic or disadvantaged populations.

We conducted in-depth, face-to-face, and semi-structured interviews with forty-four existing or previous executive and program directors and presidents, which we identify as organizational "leaders," as well as one board member, from the thirty-seven CBOs in 2003–2004. The average number of years leaders worked at each CBO was about ten years. Interviews lasted from one to two hours. We focus on leaders because they can shape how group members perceive their own group interests and the interests of others, and push toward or away from cooperation and the promotion of common cultural, social and political linkages (Kaufmann 2003; Regalado 1995; Sonenshein 2001). In addition, their voices and narratives are public representations of the organizations' identities and goals.

Findings

Leader Roles in Implementing Cross-Racial Work

The organizational leaders in our sample all played prominent roles in managing staff, programs, operations, budgets and funding, and communicating with boards of directors. While each organization in our sample had a board of directors, all but six leaders had a great deal of power and autonomy to influence organizational partnerships, programs, and structures. These leaders oversaw and implemented programs, engaged in fundraising, and made organizational decisions about when the board met and which items went forward to the board for further discussion. Executive Directors (EDs) noted that they played central roles in envisioning the direction of the organization and in carrying out organizational missions and goals. Many also mentioned that the board rarely questioned or interfered with their work, and that they had control over programs and structures and were "the public face of the organization."

Given the influential role of organizational leaders in initiating and implementing organizational work, partnerships, and programs, we focus on how leaders construct and expand boundaries to define their organization's community of focus and carry out central organizational work. We find that CBO leaders play significant roles in shaping community boundaries, resources, and representation. We also discover that how leaders view the shared experiences, culture, and history of Asian Americans—either as distinctive from or similar to other racial groups—has important implications for the ways in which CBOs carry out missions, goals, and work on behalf of these identified communities. All of the leaders mentioned that they worked with or served other racial groups in programs, partnerships, coalitions, or services at one point or another—what we call cross-racial work—because of funding mandates, to generate broader impacts or organizational expansion, or because of shared interests with other organizations or groups. Yet, there were distinct variations in how leaders connected this work to an organizational identity and community boundaries.

Racial Accommodation: Solidifying Ethnic or Racial Boundaries

A majority of leaders viewed cross-racial work as a way to improve organizational funding, impacts, or capacity so that they could more effectively serve Asian communities, rather than as a way to work on behalf of broader group affiliations. For these leaders, the distinct culture and history of an Asian-ethnic or Asian American community solidified group boundaries. Furthermore, these leaders maintained the organization's overall mission and focus on serving or representing the Asian-ethnic or Asian American community, despite working with or incorporating other racial groups in individual programs or campaigns. In the end, this resulted in *racial accommodation*, when organizations engaged in cross-racial campaigns or provided services and programs across racial lines that were infrequent, short-term, and separate from the organization's overall mission and goals while maintaining a focus on Asian Americans or a specific Asian-ethnic group.

For instance, Carolyn, the director of the Korean Organization (KO) described how their job placement, citizenship, senior, and meal programs serve Korean as well as Russian immigrants and African American low-income residents; they were one of the few organizations to offer these programs in the neighborhood. At one point, a large number of Russian immigrants enrolled in the citizenship classes. She explained that there were "lines outside [the door]" because "we don't shut our doors to non-Korean groups." However, serving other racial groups did not necessarily translate to including other groups in KO's main mission and community of focus. Instead, Carolyn emphasized how KO's main purpose was to promote the unique language, food, history, art, and other aspects of Korean culture to other groups as a way to "establish an identity" for the Korean community.

Other leaders believed that the unique culture or history of Asians helped to signify boundaries, which kept them from including other racial groups in organizational missions, goals, and main communities of focus, even when working with other racial groups in long-term coalitions and partnerships. When we asked Sandy, the ED of Asian American Arts (AAA), about their partnerships and programs with other racial groups, she replied:

> It is our mission to serve the APA (Asian Pacific American) community. We have partners with other cultures such as [a Latino arts organization] . . . but we primarily serve the APA community. . . . [This partnership started] with our purpose of each serving our own community and once in a while then we'd get together . . . and try to bring awareness to other communities, so we had Latino artists show at our gallery and then we showed at their gallery.

To Sandy, partnering with a Latino organization helped AAA bring awareness about the arts and culture of "our" community, defined as Asian Pacific American, to the Latino community, which represented a "culture" distinct from that of Asian Americans. This distinction provided rationale for why the organization needed to showcase the uniqueness of Asian American culture and art. While this long-standing collaboration with Latino artists started a few decades ago during the Asian American and Civil Rights movements, it was infrequent, and Sandy viewed this work as separate from their overall mission of serving Asian Pacific Americans.

Some leaders of racially accommodating organizations focused on the shared culture and history of Asian Americans, as well as their experience of being racialized as foreigners and model minorities, which created an Asian American community that was distinct from other racial groups. Stephen, the leader of Japanese Americans Creating Action (JACA), described how the organization worked on a number of campaigns and programs with Latinos and African Americans to fight against hate crime and discrimination issues that affected all racial minorities. However, despite this work, Stephen did not place Blacks and Latinos within JACA's community of focus. Instead, he framed political or hate crime campaigns as tied to an "Asian American" identity, while ethnicity was often reserved for talking about specific community needs or issues related to culture, language, or neighborhoods. Stephen used the Vincent Chin case in the 1980s, when two unemployed auto workers in Detroit mistook a Chinese American for a Japanese national, blamed him for the economic downturn in the area, and killed him with a baseball bat, as one example of how racialization impacted Asian Americans despite differences in national origin: "For White America, there was no difference between Chinese, Japanese, Korean." To him, Asian Americans ultimately experienced unique and separate circumstances compared to Blacks and Latinos, which made it difficult for interracial coalitions and partnerships to endure after a campaign or issue ended:

> I don't know if [interracial] partnerships really work quite honestly. . . . [Foundations will] tell us that we should go work with some Black or Latino organization and do these joint projects, . . . [but] they have their problems and we have our problems; we want to work on what we want to work on. We know what our issues are and our issues are not Latino or Black issues. . . . I think the coalition concept works, when you come together on the need that there is and you work together and share together, and when the issue is resolved you go back to whatever it is you're doing.

His emphasis on "our" issues signified a clear boundary between JACA's community of focus—Japanese and Asian Americans—and other racial groups. Despite recognizing that shared interests with other minority groups help to build interracial coalitions, Stephen thought it was necessary for each organization to "go back to whatever it is you're doing" after a multiracial coalition has ended, suggesting that each racial group has its own set of problems and issues that cannot be addressed through cross-racial work.

While funding requirements, common goals, and shared immigrant or refugee status facilitated partnerships or services that incorporated other racial groups, these factors did not produce expanded community boundaries for a majority of leaders. Instead, the racialization or unique culture and history of Asians in the United States provided the justification for strictly working on behalf of Asian Americans. At the same time, racial boundaries often became reified as CBO leaders viewed "our" or "Asian American" issues as different from that of other racial groups. Past literature notes that when others impose a racial category upon different ethnic groups who are distinct in regards to culture, language, and religion, this process of racialization can affect how individuals identify with and unify as a collective group (Espiritu 1992; Trottier 1981); yet, we find that CBO leaders can also reify the racial boundaries of communities that they serve and represent. In this sense, CBO leaders may facilitate *accommodation* or cooperation with other racial groups through programs, coalitions, or campaigns, but still not view them as in-group members of the community because of the ways that leaders understand the racialization experiences of Asian Americans as unique.

Racial Inclusion: Expanding Community Boundaries

While the above leaders viewed cross-racial work as a way to better serve or represent Asian-ethnic or Asian American communities, leaders from eleven other organizations linked cross-racial efforts with working on behalf of a broader community defined by immigrant, low-income, and/or minority status. As an example, Asians for Environmental Justice

(AEJ) formed in 1993 to empower and serve low-income APA communities around issues of environmental and social justice. "Working in multiracial alliances" became a formal part of the organization's main strategies and goals in 2002. Around this time, AEJ leaders realized that they could not carry out the organization's goals of pushing for environmental justice without including other racial/ethnic minorities experiencing similar circumstances of inequality and discrimination. Aligning with other people of color would improve the conditions of all minority communities, including Asian Americans. Jeremy, AEJ's leader articulated this new goal:

> We asked ourselves, 'Can APIs [Asian Pacific Islanders] achieve systemic change by ourselves, as a community?' The answer is no, and that is why we believe that . . . only a multi-racial alliance, led by people of color, poor people, women and young people can achieve systemic change goals. We do not organize low-income API so that we can get our piece of the pie. We organize . . . to contribute to a larger multi-racial movement to better conditions for all [of these] communities.

This leader viewed the organization's main purpose as creating systemic changes on behalf of people of color and other disadvantaged groups, beyond Asian Americans. This is consistent with Emerson's (2006) study of multiracial congregations, which found that like other organizations, congregations became multiracial because such a process was consistent with their larger goals or missions.

We also find that CBO leaders can play an important role in developing, expanding, or shifting missions and goals. Chinese for Civil Rights (CCR) was founded in the early 1970s to create social change, alter systems of inequality, and advocate on behalf of Chinese Americans. In the 1990s, the organization expanded from a focus on Chinese Americans to serving and acting on behalf of Asian Americans, Blacks, and Latinos through multi-racial campaigns addressing racial inequalities experienced by broader immigrant and minority communities. The executive director during that time played a key role in this shift by working with Latino organizations on behalf of disadvantaged minority students to desegregate public schools in San Francisco. Since large Asian American populations already attended San Francisco's highly-ranked schools, this policy change was not necessarily in the best interest of Chinese and Asian Americans. However, CCR's leader ultimately decided to participate in the campaign because he felt that Latino and African American communities did not have equal opportunities to attend good public schools. Even though CCR came under attack within the Asian American community for similar campaigns that privileged the interests of Latinos and African Americans over Asian Americans, Harold, the current ED, interpreted this work as "a wonderful aspiration towards trying to give people the resources to participate civically" and as part of a process of social change. He supported CCR's move towards representing broader communities: "We tend to be probably more multi-racial than most organizations. . . . We're not out there to push just for Chinese and Asian Americans; we do it in a larger perspective."

For these organizational leaders, boundaries did not exist between Asian Americans and other racial/ethnic minorities, such as Blacks and Latinos, but between *disadvantaged and advantaged groups*—those with more resources, privileges, or power. This ideology was reinforced through interactions with mainstream, historically White organizations. Jessica, the leader of Asian American Health Initiative (AAHI), explained: "I do not feel like I can go to NARAL or National Organization of Women . . . they have so much power already; it is not worth our effort . . . they think it's a White women's issue, it's just about abortion access . . . [and] don't care how women of color have a range of things that inhibit our reproductive rights." To Jessica, although the organization primarily serves Asian American women, the work that they do is on behalf of women of color who are marginalized and experience different issues related to reproductive rights compared to White women.

Organizations with leaders that viewed people of color or broader communities as part of the organization's main work and purpose engaged in *racial inclusion*, which involved including racial minorities in expanded missions and goals and long-term, extensive programs or partnerships. One organization completely removed its Asian American focus later on by changing its name to reflect a broader constituency, and a few others changed their leadership and staff to reflect a new community identified by racial minority, immigrant, or low-income status. For instance, Asian Housing Corporation (AHC), originated as a community development nonprofit serving Asian neighborhoods, but later included Latinos and African Americans in their housing and employment programs, as well as their board, staff, mission, and goals. Sue, AHC's director, explained that their federal funding mandated the provision of services for all needy groups, but that she and the board "made a conscious decision from being [an] Asian-focused organization to openly serve other people" in order to fulfill a new mission to "take a more comprehensive approach to neighborhood revitalization."

For these leaders, broader identities related to immigrant, limited English proficiency, people of color, or low-income status took precedence over ethnic or racial boundaries, which helped them to support expanded mission statements and goals. How leaders interpreted issues and commonalities as connecting communities across racial boundaries provided legitimacy for racial inclusion. Inclusive programs and practices were not just temporary responses to meeting organizational or neighborhood needs, but fundamental components of how leaders asserted and defined their work and goals.

Leader and Organizational Characteristics: Shaping Boundary Expansion

While past research has demonstrated that funding opportunities, policy incentives, and survival in a competitive market are key components of incorporating ethnic and racial others in organizational settings, we find that these conditions and incentives may facilitate cross-racial work, but do not necessarily result in the inclusion of other racial groups as part of an organization's community and identity. While availability of funding to serve broader racial/ethnic groups and the pressure of organizational survival helped CBOs to open their program doors and services, these organizations needed leadership support to engage in racial inclusion, which often came from the leader's and organization's history, ideology, and prior work with other racial groups.

Asian Americans are both immigrants and racial minorities, coming from diverse national origins with unique language and historical backgrounds, and are also impacted by experiences of discrimination and racialization (Takagi 1998; Tuan 1998; Wong et al., 2011). Thus, leaders of Asian American CBOs had to negotiate different group boundaries—immigrant, ethnic, and racial—based on their own experiences and backgrounds, which influenced how they connected the goals and missions of their CBOs to Asian ethnics or broader affiliations based on immigrant, minority, or low-income status.

The characteristics of leaders themselves provide insights into how leaders were able to broaden community boundaries or reify racial and ethnic boundaries as firmly in place. Our data reveal that nearly all of the leaders from *racially inclusive organizations* had served on the boards of multi-racial advocacy organizations or coalitions that addressed issues such as poverty, homelessness, or employment rights, which often corresponded with their own organization's mission and goals. These leaders, who were also second or later generation, had also worked in the non-profit CBO sector on social justice and community issues for over ten years, which may have helped to solidify distinct boundaries between those with greater power and advantages and the less advantaged, allowing them to see across racial boundaries and view their work as part of broader social changes. Some had also been active in the Asian American movement and other social justice movements, where working across racial lines was a key part of social change.

In contrast, only a few leaders of *racially accommodating organizations* served on multi-racial boards or coalitions, and they viewed their involvement as a way to represent Asian Americans, rather than as a way to represent broader communities. Only a handful were active in social movements during the 1970s and beyond, and despite wanting to create broader impacts through working on political and social justice issues, they viewed their work as tied to the Asian American community, rather than other minority and disadvantaged groups affected by these social movements. Leaders of accommodating organizations were also typically of the first generation. Their experiences as newcomer immigrants in the United States may have influenced them to focus on their ethnic group's unique needs and issues or the unique issues of Asian Americans.

For CBOs engaged in racial accommodation, racial inclusion may not have been a priority because the costs were often too high. One issue that continually arose for these CBOs was the fact that they had not yet established funding streams or reputations in the field. Leaders of these organizations felt that they needed to effectively serve their own constituencies or members before they could think about expanding to advocate or serve others. That said, not all of the large, well-established organizations achieved racial inclusion. In fact, some of the civil rights organizations had engaged in racial accommodation for decades, and they were among the oldest and most established organizations. Leaders of these organizations did not view common interests or goals with other minority groups as taking priority over their ethnic or panethnic focus. Moreover, a majority of both accommodating and inclusive organizations were formed during or in the recent wake of the Asian American and Civil Rights movements, which could have propelled these organizations to be racially inclusive. Despite these historical beginnings and low costs of racial inclusion (as they likely were for the large, well-established organizations), leaders still needed to play an active role in framing and implementing cross-racial work in a way that is consistent with organizational goals to boards, staff, and members.

We also found that racial inclusion can occur even when organizations [that started out serving an Asian-ethnic or pan-Asian community] retain their Asian-ethnic or pan-Asian name. For many leaders of inclusive organizations, working on behalf of Asian Americans *and* other racial minorities was a way to maintain the original focus of the organization. Past work suggests that identities can be layered, as individuals may choose to situate or identify themselves using multiple group identities depending on the situation (Jones-Correa 2007; Okamoto 2003; Waters 1999). Our findings support this notion in that inclusive CBOs and their leaders identified with multiple communities at one time. However, what is most important is that these leaders privileged broader group affiliations, such as immigrant, racial minority, or low-income status *and* engaged in more extensive organizational changes, such as name changes or policies not solely in the best interest for Asian Americans. Therefore, we see racial inclusion as existing along a continuum, where organizations involved in racial accommodation may later move towards inclusion, but only if their leaders begin to focus on the needs of broader communities.

Broader Implications of Cross-Racial Work

The differences we find in the depth and extent of cross-racial work are important because CBOs shape resource distribution and political activities among racial and ethnic communities. While racial accommodation simply involves including other racial groups in practices and partnerships, racial inclusion may potentially provide greater economic and political benefits and impacts because it involves the inclusion of multiple racial groups within community boundaries. Leaders of inclusive CBOs talked about material gains for their respective ethnic and racial communities, but also for a broader array of minority groups. They highlighted their participation in legislative and advocacy efforts regarding city and statewide language access policies, redistricting to create racially-balanced precincts, and fights against anti-immigrant ballot initiatives, and how these efforts challenged racial and ethnic inequality.

Leaders who pushed their organizations toward racially inclusive practices did not always make decisions that benefited only Asians. They put their weight behind efforts that improved conditions for all racial minorities, and talked about how they viewed part of the organization's work as facilitating intergroup communication and relations across racial lines. As an example, Harold from CCR explained how the organization entered into a long-term partnership to teach African American and Chinese immigrant parents about their rights and how to be their own advocates within the San Francisco public school system:

> So we were trying to get basically Chinese parents and African American parents who were interested in their kids' education on the same page, do the same training with them, and then our whole goal is to start getting them to work together . . . they literally don't speak the same language. So often we have to be in the room to translate and make sure things are understood.

Here, the organization's efforts were not simply about facilitating intergroup contact within a safe and cooperative setting, but about teaching both groups that they share common interests and can achieve their goals together. And ultimately, when CBOs expanded their missions and goals to include other racial groups, this reflected an organization's commitment to a new population and often shifted some resources and services away from the original CBO constituents. Such a shift had the potential to create problems or tensions, such as dissent from the original community of focus or the risk of losing legitimacy within the community. Like many leaders, Harold of CCR addressed this issue by framing their partnership with African American parents as reflective of their original mission and goals of helping the Chinese community to be more progressive:

> One of our major roles here, I don't know if I made this clear, the founders of this organization said the organization is to educate Chinese Americans and make the community more progressive. It isn't just reaching out to African Americans, it's reaching back to Chinese immigrants giving them education on civil rights issues and helping them to understand that they live in a multicultural society . . .

Because inclusive CBOs often originated with missions and goals related to civil rights or social justice and shared a progressive philosophy of community empowerment, it may have been easier for these leaders to connect this philosophy to cross-racial work and subsequent racial inclusion. Furthermore, these CBOs often had access to resources such as large organizational and staff capacity, funding streams, established programs, and strong reputations in the field to maintain services and programs for their original Asian American community in conjunction with extensive cross-racial work. Although a handful of accommodating organizations also shared these characteristics in terms of capacity and reputation, leaders from accommodating CBOs did not connect a progressive ideology with cross-racial work.

In contrast to racially inclusive CBOs, organizations that engaged in racial accommodation primarily did so to advance the needs and interests of Asian ethnic and panethnic groups. These CBOs held fundraisers, became involved with legislative campaigns, and some even participated in collective action efforts, but the impacts that they articulated related to (1) the importance of maintaining and promoting ethnic cultural traditions such as language and other cultural practices or (2) the need for a place where ethnics could build a community and a sense of belonging. These CBOs were spaces where kids could be dropped off for programs or day care, and where people in the neighborhood could spend the day, meet their friends, and attend classes. As one organizational leader of an ethnic-specific organization explained: "We have funerals here. We have marriages here. . . . There should be a place in the community for people to rest . . . to meet their friends." Many of these leaders viewed cultural and community centers as key for building healthy identities and relationships among their fellow ethnics, including ties between the first and second generations.

While these organizations engaged in cross-racial work and provided the opportunity for people of different racial backgrounds to interact in meetings or campaigns based on shared interests or goals, leaders did not emphasize a shared identity or community with non-Asian groups. These organizations brought some awareness to their members about the cultures and histories of different ethnic and racial groups, but leaders were more focused on how CBOs could help their own ethnic communities. This focus may indeed help to strengthen Asian ethnic and Asian American communities, but does little to directly encourage positive intergroup relations and trust across racial lines, or generate support for racial integration among diverse groups (Pettigrew and Tropp, 2011).

Conclusion

This paper details how leaders of Asian American CBOs are key players in negotiating and highlighting different types of group boundaries, and ultimately in the expansion of organizational boundaries. While all leaders engaged in cross-racial work—working with or serving diverse racial groups in programs and partnerships, as well as formal political coalitions and campaigns—not all supported the expansion of community boundaries. A majority of leaders discussed cross-racial work as a way to effectively serve and meet the needs of Asian ethnics or Asian Americans—their original constituents or members. This resulted in *racial accommodation*, where organizations served and represented groups across racial lines but did not include them as part of the organization's main community of focus. In contrast, other leaders identified and constructed a sense of expanded group boundaries for the community that they serve, which facilitated a broader and deeper commitment to immigrants, low-income, and/or racial minorities as a whole. This resulted in *racial inclusion*, as leaders broadened the definition of their community and included other racial groups in the organization's broad-scale visions and goals. Leaders viewed incorporating other racial minority groups as an important way to create systemic changes and advance the needs of disadvantaged communities as a whole.

While other social factors such as funding pressures and shared interests or issues, as well as organizational factors related to capacity and reputation may have helped leaders to implement cross-racial work, we argue that these factors do not necessarily sustain cross-racial work over time nor do they lead to racial inclusion. As key decision-makers for community-based organizations, leaders play large roles in creating and carrying out organizational missions and goals and, consequently, in shaping community boundaries, resources, and representation. While our study privileges the voices of leaders who are important in determining the direction of organizations, future research should address how members and constituents view other racial groups and document their role in shaping the direction of organizations. The specific case of CBOs provides insights into the processes and mechanisms that encourage community boundary expansion.

References

Alba, Richard D. (2005). Bright vs. Blurred Boundaries: Second-Generation Assimilation and Exclusion in France, Germany, and the United States. *Ethnic and Racial Studies*, 28: 20–49.

Becker, Penny Edgell (1998). Making Inclusive Communities: Congregations and the 'Problem' Of Race. *Social Problems*, 45: 451–72.

Bloemraad, Irene (2006). *Becoming a Citizen: Incorporating Immigrants and Refugees in the United States and Canada*. Berkeley, CA: University of California Press.

Chung, Angie Y. (2001). The Powers that Bind: A Case Study of the Collective Bases of Coalition Building in Post–Civil Unrest Los Angeles. *Urban Affairs Review*, 37: 205–226.

Chung, Angie Y. (2007). *Legacies of Struggle: Conflict and Cooperation in Korean American Politics*. Stanford, CA: Stanford University Press.

Cordero-Guzmán, Hector R. (2005). Community-Based Organisations and Migration in New York City. *Journal of Ethnic and Migration Studies*, 31: 889–909.

Cortés, Michael (1998). Counting Latino Nonprofits: A New Strategy for Finding Data. *Nonprofit and Voluntary Sector Quarterly*, 27(4): 437–458.

Cortés, Michael, William A. Díaz, and Henry A. J. Ramos (1999). A Statistical Profile of Latino Nonprofit Organizations in the United States. In Diana Campoamor (Ed.), *Nuevos Senderos: Reflections on Hispanics and Philanthropy*, pp. 17–54. Houston, TX: Arte Público Press.

Dalton, Russell J. (1994). *The Green Rainbow: Environmental Groups in Western Europe.* New Haven, CT: Yale University Press.

de Graauw, Els (2008). Nonprofit Organizations: Agents of Immigrant Political Incorporation in Urban America. In S. Karthick Ramakrishnan and Irene Bloemraad (Eds.), *Civic Hopes and Political Realities: Community Organizations and Political Engagement among Immigrants in the U.S. and Abroad*, pp. 323–350. New York: Russell Sage Foundation.

Emerson, Michael (with Rodney Woo) (2006). *People of the Dream: Multiracial Congregations in the United States.* Princeton, NJ: Princeton University Press.

Espiritu, Yen Le (1992). *Asian American Panethnicity: Bridging Institutions and Identities.* Philadelphia, PA: Temple University Press.

Gleeson, Shannon and Irene Bloemraad (2010). Where Are All the Immigrant Organizations? Reassessing the Scope of Civil Society for Immigrant Communities. Working Paper Series. Berkeley, CA: Institute for Research on Labor and Employment.

Hathaway, Will and David S. Meyer (1993). Competition and Cooperation in Social Movement Coalitions: Lobbying for Peace in the 1980s. *Berkeley Journal of Sociology*, 38: 156–183.

Horowitz, Donald (1975). Ethnic Identity. In Nathan Glazer and Daniel Patrick Moynihan (Eds.), *Ethnicity: Theory and Experience*, pp. 111–140. Cambridge, MA: Harvard University Press.

Hung, Chi-Kan Richard (2007). Immigrant Nonprofit Organizations in U.S. Metropolitan Areas. *Nonprofit and Voluntary Sector Quarterly*, 36(4): 707–729.

Jones-Correa, Michael (2001). Structural Shifts and Institutional Capacity: Possibilities for Ethnic Cooperation and Conflict in Urban Settings. In Michael Jones-Correa (Ed.), *Governing American Cities: Interethnic Coalitions, Competition, and Conflict*, pp. 183–210. New York: Russell Sage Foundation.

Jones-Correa, Michael (2007). Fuzzy Distinctions and Blurred Boundaries: Transnational, Immigrant and Ethnic Politics. In Rodolfo Espino, David Leal, and Kenneth Meier (Eds.), *Latino Politics: Identity, Mobilization and Representation*, pp. 44–60. Charlottesville, VA: University of Virginia Press.

Kaufmann, Karen M. (2003). Cracks in the Rainbow: Group Commonality as a Basis for Latino and African-American Political Coalitions. *Political Research Quarterly*, 56: 199–210.

Kibria, Nazli (2002). *Becoming Asian American: Second-Generation Chinese and Korean American Identities.* Baltimore, MD: Johns Hopkins University Press.

Leighley, Jan (2001). *Strength in Numbers?: The Political Mobilization of Racial and Ethnic Minorities.* Princeton, NJ: Princeton University Press.

Marwell, Nicole (2007). *Bargaining for Brooklyn: Community Organizations in the Entrepreneurial City.* Chicago, IL: University of Chicago Press.

McCammon, Holly J. and Karen E. Campbell (2002). Allies on the Road to Victory: Coalition Formation between the Suffragists and the Woman's Christian Temperance Union. *Mobilization*, 7: 231–251.

McClain, Paula D. and Steven C. Tauber (2001). Racial Minority Group Relations in a Multiracial Society. In Michael Jones-Correa (Ed.), *Governing American Cities: Inter-Ethnic Coalitions, Competition, and Conflict*, pp. 111–136. New York: Russell Sage Foundation.

Meier, Kenneth J. and Joseph Stewart, Jr. (1991). Cooperation and Conflict in Multiracial School Districts. *Journal of Politics*, 53: 1123–1133.

Minkoff, Debra (1999). Bending with the Wind: Strategic Change and Adaptation by Women's and Racial Minority Organizations. *American Journal of Sociology*, 104: 1666–1703.

Morris, Aldon D. and Suzanne Staggenborg (2004). Leadership in Social Movements. In David A. Snow, Sarah A. Soule, and Hanspeter Kriesi (Eds.), *The Blackwell Companion to Social Movements*, pp. 171–196. Malden, MA: Blackwell Publishing.

Nagel, Joane (1994). Constructing Ethnicity: Creating and Recreating Ethnic Identity and Culture. *Social Problems*, 41: 101–126.

Okamoto, Dina G. (2003). Toward a Theory of Panethnicity: Explaining Collective Action among Asian Americans. *American Sociological Review*, 68: 811–842.

Okamoto, Dina G. and Kim Ebert (2010). Beyond the Ballot: Immigrant Collective Action in Gateways and New Destinations in the United States. *Social Problems*, 57: 529–558.

Olzak, Susan (1992). *The Dynamics of Ethnic Competition and Conflict.* Palo Alto, CA: Stanford University Press.

Padilla, Felix M. (1985). *Latino Ethnic Consciousness the Case of Mexican Americans and Puerto Ricans in Chicago.* Notre Dame, IN: University of Notre Dame Press.

Pettigrew, Thomas F. and Linda R. Tropp (2011). *When Groups Meet: The Dynamics of Intergroup Contact.* New York: Psychology Press.

Ramakrishnan, S. Karthick and Irene Bloemraad (Eds.) (2008). *Civic Hopes and Political Realities: Community Organizations and Political Engagement among Immigrants in the U.S. and Abroad.* New York: Russell Sage Foundation.

Regalado, J. (1995). Creating Multicultural Harmony? A Critical Perspective on Coalition-Building Efforts in Los Angeles. In E. Yu and E. T. Chang (Eds.), *Multiethnic Coalition Building in Los Angeles*, pp. 35–53. Los Angeles, CA: Institute for Asian American and Pacific American Studies, California State University Los Angeles.

Rose, Fred (2000). *Coalitions across the Class Divide: Lessons from the Labor, Peace, and Environmental Movements.* Ithaca, NY: Cornell University Press.

Schrover, M. and Floris Vermeulen (2005). Immigrant Organisations. *Journal of Ethnic and Migration Studies*, 31: 823–832.

Shiao, Jiannbin Lee (1998). The Nature of the Nonprofit Sector: Professionalism Versus Identity Politics in Private Policy Definitions of Asian Pacific Americans. *Asian American Policy Review*, 8: 17–43.

Sonenshein, Raphael J. (2001). When Ideologies Agree and Interests Collide, What's a Leader to Do? The Prospects for Latino-Jewish Coalition in Los Angeles. In Michael Jones-Correa (Ed.), *Governing American Cities: Inter-Ethnic Coalitions, Competition, and Conflict*, pp. 210–229. New York: Russell Sage Foundation.

Takagi, Dana (1998). *The Retreat From Race: Asian American Admissions and Racial Politics.* New Brunswick, NJ: Rutgers University Press.

Trottier, Richard W. (1981). Charters of Panethnic Identity: Indigenous American Indians and Immigrant Asian Americans. In C. F. Keyes (Ed.), *Ethnic Change*, pp. 271–305. Seattle, WA: University of Washington Press.

Tuan, Mia (1998). *Forever Foreigners or Honorary Whites?: The Asian Ethnic Experience Today.* New Brunswick, NJ: Rutgers University Press.

Van Dyke, Nella and Holly J. McCammon (Eds.) (2010). *Strategic Alliances: Coalition Building and Social Movements.* Minneapolis, MN: University of Minnesota Press.

Waters, Mary (1999). *Black Identities: West Indian Immigrant Dreams and American Realities.* New York: Russell Sage Foundation.

Wong, Janelle (2006). *Democracy's Promise: Immigrants and American Civic Institutions.* Ann Arbor, MI: University of Michigan Press.

Wong, Janelle, S. Karthick Ramakrishnan, Taeku Lee, and Jane Junn (2011). *Asian American Political Participation: Emerging Constituents and their Political Identities.* New York: Russell Sage Foundation.

Zhou, Min (2000). Social Capital in Chinatown: The Role of Community-Based Organizations and Families in the Adaptation of the Younger Generation. In M. Zhou and J. V. Gatewood (Eds.), *Contemporary Asian America: A Multidisciplinary Reader*, pp. 315–335. New York: New York University Press.

Zhou, Min and Mingang Lin (2005). Community Transformation and the Formation of Ethnic Capital: Immigrant Chinese Communities in the United States. *Journal of Chinese Overseas*, 1: 260–284.

CHAPTER 19

The Place of Race in Conservative and Far-Right Movements*

Kathleen M. Blee and Elizabeth A. Yates

In this essay, Kathleen Blee and Elizabeth Yates explore current understandings and propose new directions for research on the place of race in ***rightist social movements*** *in the contemporary United States. They examine two broad categories of rightist movements. The first is White-majority conservative movements that deny their participation in racialized politics but in which race is implicit in their ideologies and agendas, such as the Tea Party. The second is far-right movements that explicitly espouse racist ideologies and agendas, such as neo-Nazi groups. They point to productive possibilities for new research on the racial positionality of scholars of social movements, the relationship between rightist movements and larger social trends, and process-oriented and longitudinal aspects of rightist movements.*

Questions to Consider

Some far-right movements are explicitly racist while others are not. For example, the Ku Klux Klan is an explicitly racist organization whereas the Tea Party is not. Nevertheless, the authors suggest that race and racism may influence the ways in which far-right movements operate. Does race and racism shape the make-up and goals of all far-right movements or only those that are explicitly racist? Explain.

Source: Kathleen M. Blee and Elizabeth A. Yates, "The Place of Race in Conservative and Far-Right Movements," *Sociology of Race and Ethnicity*, Volume 1, Number 1, pages 127–136, SAGE Publications, Inc., 2014.

*Some text and accompanying endnote have been omitted. Please consult the original source.

Race is implicated in a range of contemporary rightist movements in the United States. This is most obvious in far-right movements that promote overtly racist agendas, but race also is salient in conservative mobilizations that disavow racial motives or consequences. In both cases, the place of race is not fully captured by examining how movements frame their intentions and agendas to their supporters and audiences. Understanding race in rightist politics requires attention to the range of factors identified in social movement studies and the sociology of race and ethnicity.

We take the opportunity in this inaugural issue to provide an overview on race in contemporary U.S. right-wing movements and suggest directions for future research. Since the literature on rightist movements is vast, we focus on two broad movements in which race is significant, but in different ways. One is conservative mobilizations whose members are mostly white and in which racial themes and agendas are largely implicit. These movements are the product of a dual political legacy, forged in the fiscal conservatism and anticommunism of the mid-twentieth century Old Right (Ribuffo 1983) and the social conservatism of the New Christian Right (Blee and Creasap 2010; Diamond 1998; McGirr 2001). . . . As an example of a primarily-white conservative mobilization, we look at the Tea Party, a large and loosely affiliated network of activists who advocate a mixture of libertarian and traditional conservative opposition to taxation and government-sponsored social welfare, participate in Republican electoral campaigns, and mobilize supporters through mass media, social networks, and direct recruiting (Skocpol and Williamson 2012).

Our second focus is far-right movements that explicitly promote racist ideologies and, for some, goals of violent racial terrorism. Their racial targets vary but generally include African Americans, Jews, Muslims, Latinos/as, and immigrants from Africa, South Asia, and Latin America. In the last decades, such movements generally have reflected the political legacies of either World War II–era German Nazism and/or American traditions of organized racism and xenophobia (Durham 2000, 2007). As such, they include groups that seek an international alliance with pro-Aryan groups around the world as well as intense nationalists who want to establish a white homeland in the United States (Blee 2002; Dobratz and Shanks-Meile 2000). Not all far-right movements are explicitly racist; for example, some radical antiabortion movements advocate violence that is not attached to a racial agenda, while vigilante, patriot, and militia groups generally disavow racism even if their anti-immigrant, anti-state, and pro-gun stances attract racist members (Rydgren 2007; Shapira 2013; Stern 1996; Zeskind 2009). As an example of a far-right movement, we look at U.S. neo-Nazis, who advocate the violent overthrow of the government because of its supposed accommodation to the interests of Jews and people of color. Unlike popular conservative movements, the neo-Nazi movement is tiny and, to minimize infiltration by the police or antiracist groups, recruits largely through direct personal contacts made in the subculture of white power music shows, parties, rallies, and gatherings.

To orient scholars of race and ethnicity to the particular issues of studying rightist movements, we begin by summarizing the theoretical trends and methodological challenges that have characterized this scholarship. Here, we draw special attention to differences in how scholars have analyzed right-wing and progressive movements and the implications for understanding the place of race on the right. Next, we explore a set of issues that have commanded considerable scholarly attention. For white-dominated conservative movements which generally insist that they are not racially defined, we show how scholars have explored the extent to *which* racial factors are operative in movement practices and the beliefs of their participants and how these movements address accusations that they are racist. For far-right movements that openly proclaim racist agendas, we show how scholars examine the complexities in *how* these movements define and enact racial agendas. We conclude with ideas for additional research on the place of race in rightist movements.

Scholarly Approaches to the Study of Rightist Movements

Scholarship on rightist movements has gone through two distinct conceptual stages. Until the 1990s, these movements were understood through the lens of psychology, even as this framework had been largely abandoned for studies of progressive social movements. Through a psychological lens, rightist movements were viewed as the product of the personality deficits, problematic familial upbringing, and stunted emotional responses of their members and supporters. By focusing on prejudices, rigidity, and scapegoating, this scholarship left race essentially unanalyzed except to the extent that rightist politics reflected the irrational racial schemas and animus of its adherents.

More recently, studies of the right have adopted the social-structural lens commonly used to study other social movements. This approach assumes that rightist movements are motivated by the rational concerns of their members, advancing beyond theories of individual irrationality to identify the social structures and dynamics that generate group interests, such as economic competition and racial domination (e.g., Cunningham 2012b; McVeigh 2009; McVeigh and Cunningham 2012; van Dyke and Soule 2002). This approach has been extended by scholars who argue that movements are not the product of the immediate and obvious interests of its adherents, but rather that participants' interests are shaped by cultural factors and moral valuations (Polletta 2006; Smith 2003).

An area of considerable attention today is the effect of rightist movements on their members. Rather than assuming that people join rightist movements because they are confused (irrationality lens) or because they regard such movements as vehicles to promote their interests (rationality-structural lens), this scholarship questions how racial beliefs and perceived self-interests are transformed in rightist politics, a question that lies at the intersection of microlevel processes of individual mobilization and mesolevel factors of group dynamics and organization. These studies have found that far-right movements typically intensify the racial commitments of their members, especially by introducing them to conspiratorial logics, such as the idea that Jews are engineering worldwide racial conflict or that the white race is on the brink of racial suicide (Barkun 1994; Blee 2010; Hughey 2012; Simi and Futrell 2010). There is less work using this approach to study race in conservative movements, although it is possible that the racial rhetoric in conservative movements may reinforce members' associations of crime, poverty, and social dysfunction with racial minorities (Hardisty 1999).

Scholars who investigate the place of race in rightist movements confront unique challenges of access that shape what can effectively be investigated. Conservative movements often are reluctant to grant unrestricted access to their organizational materials or members to university-based researchers since they suspect that these scholars will seek to elicit racist statements from members or depict the movement in a negative light. Conservative movements that are heavily funded by corporate elites or right-wing foundations or tied to politicians and elected officials are especially reluctant to disclose information that could be racially sensitive. Far-right movements pose even more profound difficulties to scholars of race. Some hide themselves from public view, fearing infiltration by antiracist activists or police informants. Others make themselves visible but attempt to threaten or intimidate researchers who are critical, as illustrated in the libel case brought against a historian by a major figure in the Holocaust-denial movement (Emory University N.d.).

In all rightist movements, the perceived racial category of the researcher has a significant effect on access to groups and members. Scholars seen as nonwhite or Jewish face the danger of personal violence at the hands of far-right racist activists who regard them as enemies, although a few scholars have effectively used their enemy status to elicit important information on these movements (Ezekiel 1996; Shapira 2013). In parts of the far-right in which the sense of racial loyalty is surprisingly elastic, even scholars perceived as white and non-Jewish may be regarded as race traitors and targeted for violence (Blee 2002, 2000; Twine and Warren 2000). The racial dynamics between researchers and participants are less studied for conservative movements, although nonwhite scholars likely would have limited access to majority-white groups, especially for studies that probe issues of race. Despite these hurdles, some scholars have been remarkably successful in gaining permission to interview and observe the internal racial dynamics of conservative and far-right movements and analyzing how such movements frame their racial ideas to the public (Adams and Roscigno 2005; Hughey 2012; Miller-Idriss 2012; Simi and Futrell 2010).

The Place of Race in Conservative Movements

The debate over race in conservative movements engages both movement spokespersons and scholars, particularly on three issues. One is whether conservative ideologies are inherently racist. A few conservative movements use explicitly racist appeals, as for instance depicting Latinos/as, Native Americans, and African Americans as lazy, satisfied to rely on the largess of government benefits, or perpetrators of voter fraud (Collins 2000). However, such open racism is increasingly stigmatized in the larger society, and most contemporary conservative movements insist that they do not engage in racial politics but simply favor equal treatment for all, including whites. This claim is a conservative twist on the widespread color-blind ideology that regards racism as relevant only in an individual, discriminatory context (Bonilla-Silva 2009). By ignoring how racial privileges and subordination are embedded in the social structures and patterns of everyday life, color-blind ideology fits conservative efforts to eliminate government policies that address structural racism or benefit racial minorities as a group, such as Affirmative Action or equal opportunity laws (Bonilla-Silva 2009; Feagin 2006). Moreover, by insisting that the cultural and moral failures of poor communities hinder the achievements of their members, conservative movements argue that their opposition to social welfare programs and guarantees of racial equity (such as same-day voting registration, equal opportunity policies, and immigration reform) is a race-neutral position (Ansell 1997).

Another issue is whether individual conservative activists are motivated by racist animus, irrespective of the stated ideology of their organization or the ideological claims they make directly (Parker and Barreto 2013). This is a contentious issue among conservatives who, like others who embrace color-blind ideologies, consider as racist only expressions of individual racial prejudice (Feagin 2006). Meanwhile, conservative movements often use cultural symbols to mobilize sympathizers based on cultural identities that are not exclusively, and likely not overtly, race-based (McVeigh 2014). Moreover, emphasizing the racism of conservative activists can obscure the pervasive nature of racism across political boundaries (Burke 2013; Hughey 2010). For example, there is some evidence that conservative movements attract those with racial grievances, particularly downwardly mobile or working and lower middle class whites who regard racial minorities as unfairly benefitting from liberal policies in competition for economic and political power (Kimmel 2013). Elite whites, however, also often support conservative movements without being cast as racists (Lassiter 2007).

A third issue is how conservative movements manage accusations of racism, through efforts that may be authentic, strategic, or both. Some conservative leaders promote the visibility of racial minority members to demonstrate that their movement is not racist as well as to present models of racial minorities who have been successful through individual effort rather than by depending on government policies and programs (Burghart and Zeskind 2010; Dillard 2001; Hardisty 1999). Other leaders address charges of racism by preventing members from making racist statements in public (Prior 2014). And many conservative movements use ideological frames borrowed from racial equality movements such as the Civil Rights Movement to present whites as victims of current social policies, arguing that whites are subject to reverse discrimination in the workplace, deprived of their rights, and accused of being racist simply for wanting equal treatment in society (Lassiter 2007; Lio, Melzer, and Reese 2008; Lowndes 2011). Such efforts have had some success, as evidenced by the conservative African American and Latino candidates who have found support among white activists at the grassroots level (Brennan and Sullivan 2011; Vozella 2013).

The Conservative Tea Party Movement

The Tea Party movement began in 2009 to oppose federal government intervention in the fiscal crisis and the federal healthcare mandate. Over time, its agenda has broadened to support strict fiscal policies and dramatically reduced government regulation and public investment. Initially organized by conservative elites, the Tea Party quickly developed a broad grassroots base, with more than 800 local groups and as many as 200,000 participants in 2011 (Skocpol and Williamson 2012); recent analysis shows its continuing strength at the grassroots level (Burghart 2014). At the national level, Tea Party–affiliated politicians, candidates, and organizations lobby Congress to maintain tax deductions for the wealthy while slashing federal funding for social services. These national leaders operate separately from local Tea Party groups, the latter of which hold regular meetings with conservative speakers, provide members with information on how to campaign for conservative candidates, educate the public on conservative issues, and lobby local and state officials on behalf of fiscally conservative policies (Yates 2014).

There is considerable debate about the racial nature of Tea Party support. On one hand, some evidence suggests that racial animosity fueled the emergence of the Tea Party immediately after the inauguration of America's first nonwhite president, Barak Obama. Indeed, analysts consistently find that Tea Party supporters and activists are overwhelmingly white, and polling data show that Tea Party supporters express greater resentment toward racial minorities than do non–Tea Party supporters, other Republicans, and whites overall. For example, a 2010 survey examining racial and political attitudes among citizens primarily in battleground electoral states found that 73% of Tea Party supporters believe that African Americans merely need to "try harder" to obtain equal status as whites, as compared with 56% of whites overall. A full 88% of Tea Party supporters said that African Americans should do so "without special favors," compared with 70% of whites (Parker and Barreto 2013; Parker and Towler 2010; see also Abramowitz 2011).

On the other hand, scholars caution against according too much importance to racial animosity in Tea Party mobilization, arguing that racial issues are complicated by anxieties about wider social changes that affect many social groups. Theda Skocpol and Vanessa Williamson (2012) found that Tea Party activists essentially differentiated between broad categories of "deserving" and "undeserving" citizens, a distinction that is often racialized but also is frequently applied to distinguish among nonracial groups, such as older and younger people. Yet as Lisa Disch (2011) emphasized, the Tea Party's valorization of hardworking, taxpaying citizens ignores the greater benefits that whites have derived from government services and benefits compared with nonwhites. In that sense, its activists draw from what Meghan Burke (2013:101) described as a "continuum of knowledge" in which racialized political beliefs are shaped by genuine economic, political, and social concerns as well as by racial ideologies promulgated by conservative media and social networks.

The Place of Race in Far-Right Movements

Unlike conservative movements, far-right groups openly advocate white and/or Aryan supremacism; some seek to harm, even exterminate, their racial enemies. Despite these extremist goals, such movements often mix mainstream and extremist frames in messages to supporters and the public, both adopting language from the Civil Rights Movement to mobilize whites as a racial interest group (White Americans) and declaring whites to be on the verge of "race suicide" (Berbrier 2000; Morris and Fleming 2014).

Far-right movements have used different understandings of race over time. Until recently, most extreme racist groups relied on essentialist definitions of race, insisting that biological differences account for racial disparities in social life. Far-right activists thus regarded policies such as equal employment laws as both objectionable and futile since they insisted that whites were biologically superior. These activists also saw race as stable and starkly dichotomous: People were purely white, descended from northern Europeans, or they were not (Durham 2007; Gardell 2003; Ignatiev 2008; Nagel 2003).

In the last few decades, far-right movements that aspire to recruit larger numbers have shifted to a cultural definition of race they consider more compatible with mainstream beliefs. These movements continue to defend white supremacy but trace it to a racial culture that values perseverance, achievement, and adherence to the rule of law. Moreover, some far-right adherents use a fluid sense of race. They regard as white only those who work toward white supremacism, so whites who do not support white superiority are considered to be essentially nonwhite. Oddly, the reverse can be true as well. People who appear nonwhite can be considered white if they support white supremacism and its activists (Blee 2002).

The groups deemed enemies of the white race vary somewhat among far-right groups. African Americans and Jews are the most commonly regarded as enemies. Yet, whether Jews or African Americans are considered to be the most pernicious group changes over time. For example, the original Ku Klux Klan (KKK) of the post–Civil War South directed its malevolence toward African Americans and the political allies of former slaves such as white supporters of the Reconstruction state (Chalmers 1987). In its next incarnation in the 1920s, the KKK attacked both African Americans and Jews, along with Catholics (Blee 1991; McVeigh 2009). Klans of the 1960s returned to a focus on African Americans as their racial enemies, drawing on the racial tensions of desegregation conflicts across the nation (Cunningham 2012a). The most recent Klans, influenced by neo-Nazi doctrines, have mainly targeted Jews as the antagonistic racial category, viewing people of color as inferior but manipulated by Jewish conspirators (Durham 2007).

The Neo-Nazi Movement

A variety of groups that espouse Nazi ideologies have emerged in recent decades, including racist skinhead gangs, the Aryan Brotherhood and related prison networks, Nazi-oriented white supremacists, and Christian Identity networks that regard Jews as the literal, biological descendants of Satan (Barkun 1994; Zeskind 2009). All neo-Nazis identify Jews as the central racial enemy, and most describe the U.S. government, especially at the federal level, as Jewish-controlled or ZOG (Zionist Occupied Government). They vary in the extent to which they express ultranationalist and xenophobic sentiments, especially toward immigrants, or seek to participate in a global project of pan-Aryanism with neo-Nazis in Europe and other regions. In the United States, neo-Nazi groups attract substantial numbers of women, especially to the younger segments of the movement such as skinheads (Blee 2002). Outside the United States, neo-Nazi groups have been disproportionately male, although this is beginning to change in European groups (Blee and Linden 2012; Miller-Idriss 2012).

Racist ideas are not necessarily what bring people into neo-Nazism. Indeed, research finds that recruits to such groups were not necessarily more racist or anti-Semitic than similarly situated others prior to joining. Rather, many learned these beliefs by participating in racist groups. In that sense, racist beliefs can be as much *effects* as *causes* of participating in neo-Nazism. One reason is that neo-Nazism exists in an intense culture of violence that can be a powerful lure to potential recruits, especially young people, by suggesting that such groups confer both protection and empowerment. Recruits enter for the violence and learn the racism. The other reason is that neo-Nazism today is highly conspiratorial. Only when recruits are brought into its "secret knowledge" about race are they given details of supposed Jewish domination, African American criminality, and immigrant depravity (Blee 2002).

In neo-Nazism there can be a substantial gap between the stated doctrines of the movement and the beliefs of even its most dedicated adherents. The propaganda and internal documents of neo-Nazi groups promote racial ideas that are little changed from those of World War II–era German Nazism. Most either applaud Hitler's attempt to exterminate European Jews as justified by the degenerate culture of Jews or claim that Holocaust accusations are false, part of an effort by contemporary Jews to extract monetary reparations from Aryan Europeans and promote the interests of the state of Israel (Blee 2002; Zeskind 2009).

Even in their daily practices, neo-Nazis make frequent reference to the twentieth-century German Nazi movement. They greet each other by signaling 88, a coded reference to the eighth letter of the alphabet, for "Heil Hitler," and display the swastika on their bodies, websites, and documents. Yet, at least some ardent neo-Nazis express quite different racial beliefs in private, even expressing skepticism about the movement's claims of Jewish atrocity or German military victories. They value the comradeship of these groups but often have a thin commitment to their racial ideals. Moreover, individual neo-Nazis often know little about the history they are dedicated to repeating. Young skinheads cannot explain why they wear brown shirts or carve "SS" or iron cross tattoos on themselves (Blee 2002).

Directions for Future Research

It is clear that race has a place in rightist movements, even in those that deny involvement in racial issues. As the preceding discussion indicates, scholars have made significant advances in understanding how race is understood in conservative and far-right activism and how racial appeals can advance rightist agendas. In this final section, we offer ideas for new scholarship on rightist movements. We begin with suggestions for studies that consider rightist movements as a whole, and then we outline different possibilities for additional scholarship on the far-right and on conservative movements.

First, there is a need for more attention to racial positionality in research on rightist movements. Race scholars have analyzed the considerable complexities introduced into scholarship by contrasting racial identities or attributed racial statuses of researchers and those they study (Hughey 2012; Twine and Warren 2000). Yet, these ideas are generally used narrowly in social movement scholarship to understand how race affects rapport and access to data. Less studied are the broader implications of racial position on research outcomes, such as how race shapes the analytic process, making some aspects noticeable and significant and others seem trivial. As an example, white scholars situated in the largely progressive milieus of universities may have limited experience with open expressions of racial hostility. Such expressions—common in many rightist movements—are likely to be understood as highly significant by scholars. These expressions may prompt scholars to assume, rather than investigate, that racial hostility is the central factor in movement mobilization or cohesion.

Second, studies of rightist movements could move beyond documenting that race matters on the political right to examine more extensively the extent to which and how it does. Studies that assess the salience of race across the temporal cycles of rightist movements might be particularly valuable, including those that assess changes across the lifetimes of groups, the length of activists' participation, and the cycles of rightist activity. Is race more likely to be strategically deployed at the onset of a movement (as a mobilizing tactic) or as the movement is in decline (as a defensive maneuver)? Contextual and comparative studies of the right are needed as well. These could assess whether the place of race varies by location, type of leadership, fluidity of membership, presence of concurrent or overlapping movements, level of repression and policing, or the social class and gender composition of the movement.

Third, scholars should continue to investigate the relationship between rightist movements and the societies in which they are embedded. Commentators frequently assert that rightist movements are prompted by the structure of racial privileges and disadvantages and that, in turn, such movements exacerbate racial divisions. Yet, there are remarkably few empirical studies on how this occurs. Scholars might trace how racial ideas and actions flow between movements and the larger society to assess, for instance, how changing societal definitions of Jews, Muslims, or South Asians as white or nonwhite affect and are affected by rightist movements. Too, scholars could examine whether racial conflicts spill over into rightist recruitment, how these movements are affected by antiracist organizing or negative media attention, and under what conditions rightist movements shape broader public dialogues on race and other issues. Additional microlevel analysis is needed on how the racial understandings of members are affected by their participation in rightist movements, including seemingly color-blind conservative movements.

Fourth, more research is needed to assess the extent and nature of connections between far-right and conservative movements. Do conservative movements prime some activists to take part in extremist racist groups, or are the ideologies and practices of these movements too different to allow this to happen? Do racial ideas circulate between far-right and conservative groups, or do these movements shape their messages and collective identities by contrasting themselves to others on the right, as well as on the left? For instance, do far-right denunciations of conservatives who accept government-promoted ideas of racial integration and tolerance, or, conversely, conservative condemnations of far-right racists as irrelevant extremists, serve to block ideological transmission across these segments of the right?

Due to the significant differences in the place of race in far-right and conservative movements, there also are distinct needs for future research in each type of movement. Below, we outline possible directions for both scholars of race in conservative movements and those that study the far-right.

Conservative Movements

More research is needed on how color-blind politics operate in conservative movements. Studies could explore in greater detail how strategies of what Ruth Frankenberg (1993) terms "color evasion" are used in conservative groups and how they affect members' racial beliefs. Do racial beliefs change over the life cycle of the movement? Do conservative movements use different strategies of color evasion for internal discussions than when they are framing messages for the public? To what extent do members reinforce the color-blind ideologies promoted by movement leaders? Do such efforts flow exclusively from the top down, or do they also move from the bottom up?

Scholarship also is needed on the relationship between racial frames (or evasion) and the organizational characteristics of conservative movements. How is race discourse affected by the presence of activists of color? Is color-blind ideology expressed differently in centralized movements, compared with those like the Tea Party that have significant local autonomy? Does it differ in conservative movements that seek to educate the public, in contrast to those focused on influencing policy makers, or in fiscal conservative groups compared with social conservatives?

Far-Right Movements

Three sets of issues are particularly urgent for future studies of the far-right. One is to hone research methods and conceptual categories to the changing shape of these movements. Ironically, as scholars of the far-right have moved away from individual-level understandings and toward the social-structural frameworks of social movement studies, far-right racist groups are dissolving into loosely connected tiny activist cells and single operatives known as "lone wolves." This transformation has rendered some of the core conceptual categories of social movement analysis less meaningful for studying the far-right. For instance, defining a "member" or a "leader" is difficult in a highly transient and fragmented movement. So is defining a "group." To understand the place of race in this changing movement, it may be useful to borrow the approach of terrorism studies and focus on brittle networks of people and information rather than durable groups and organizations.

Comparative and international work is a second area in which research on racial movements of the far-right is needed, especially in light of suggestions that some far-right leaders are engaged in an effort to create a global pan-Aryan movement. Despite some evidence that ideas, resources, and activists of these movements are exchanged across national borders, the ties and influences across these movements are understudied. Such scholarship faces difficult problems, even beyond those of limited access. As Kathleen Fallon and Julie Moreau (2012) have argued, defining the political right can be complicated outside the context of stable Western nation states. So too it can be difficult to define race and racism outside the historical and political contexts in which these were mapped onto social divisions of superiority/inferiority and oppression/privilege (Blee and Twine 2001; Frederickson 2002).

A third area of opportunity lies in the end stages of mobilization in the far-right. The preponderance of research has focused on how mobilization begins, by studying how people are recruited and radicalized and how groups and movements are established. Far less studied are the processes of demobilization, such as how activists exit and how far-right movements collapse. For racist movements, it is particularly urgent for scholars to compare the processes of demobilization and deradicalization for both movements and activists. Do racist movements that are in decline (demobilizing) become more radical by disproportionately shedding their more moderate members (della Porta 2013)? Do individual racist activists become more dangerous as they leave racist groups and operate as lone wolves?

These suggestions are presented as a starting point for extending the productive intellectual exchanges between scholars of the sociology of race and those working within the framework of social movement studies.

References

Abramowitz, Alan I. 2011. "Grand Old Tea Party: Partisan Polarization and the Rise of the Tea Party Movement." Pp. 195–211 in *Steep: The Precipitous Rise of the Tea Party*, edited by L. Rosenthal and C. Trost. Berkeley: University of California Press.

Adams, Josh and Vincent J. Roscigno. 2005. "White Supremacists, Oppositional Culture and the World Wide Web." *Social Forces* 84(2):759–78.

Allen, L. Dean II. 2000. "Promise Keepers and Racism: Frame Resonance as an Indicator of Organizational Vitality." *Sociology of Religion* 61:55–72.

Ansell, Amy Elizabeth. 1997. *New Right, New Racism: Race and Reaction in the United States and Britain.* New York: New York University Press.

Barkun, Michael. 1994. *Religion and the Racist Right: The Origins of the Christian Identity Movement.* Chapel Hill: University of North Carolina Press.

Bartkowski, John P. 2004. *The Promise Keepers: Servants, Soldiers, and Godly Men.* New Brunswick, NJ: Rutgers University Press.

Berbrier, Mitch. 2000. "The Victim Ideology of White Supremacists and White Separatists in the United States." *Sociological Focus* 33:175–91.

Blee, Kathleen M. 1991. *Women of the Klan: Racism and Gender in the 1920s.* Berkeley: University of California Press.

Blee, Kathleen M. 2000. "White on White: Interviewing Women in U.S. White Supremacist Groups." Pp. 93–110 in *Race-ing Research: Methodological and Ethical Dilemmas in Field Research*, edited by F. W. Twine and J. Warren. New York: New York University Press.

Blee, Kathleen M. 2002. *Inside Organized Racism: Women in the Hate Movement.* Berkeley: University of California Press.

Blee, Kathleen M. 2010. "Trajectories of Action and Belief in U.S. Organized Racism." Pp. 239–65 in *Identity and Participation in Culturally Diverse Societies: A Multidisciplinary Perspective*, edited by E. Azzi, X. Chryssochoou, B. Klandermans, and Simon. London: Blackwell.

Blee, Kathleen M. 2012. *Democracy in the Making: How Activist Groups Form.* New York: Oxford University Press.

Blee, Kathleen M. and Kimberly A. Creasap. 2010. "Conservative and Right-wing Movements." *Annual Review of Sociology* 36:269–86.

Blee, Kathleen M. and Annette Linden. 2012. "Women in Extremist Right Parties and Movements: A Comparison of the Netherlands and the U.S." Pp. 98–114 in *Women of the Right: Comparisons and Interplay Across Borders*, edited by K. Blee and S. Deutch. University Park, PA: Penn State University Press.

Blee, Kathleen M. and France Winddance Twine, editors. 2001. *Feminism and Anti-racism: International Struggles for Justice.* New York: New York University Press.

Bonilla-Silva, Eduardo. 2009. *Racism without Racists: Color-blind Racism and the Persistence of Racial Inequality in the United States.* 3rd ed. New York: Rowman and Littlefield.

Brennan, Kevin and Sean Sullivan. 2011. "The Tea Party's Surprise: The Conservative Movement Has Helped Elect Blacks and Hispanics Who Faced Resistance from the Republican Establishment." *National Journal Magazine*, October 22. http://www.nationaljournal.com/magazine/tea-party-fuels-surge-of-minorities-into-office-20111020. Accessed 18 October 2014.

Burghart, Devin. 2014. "Special Report: The Status of the Tea Party Movement: Part One: The Tea Party in 2013." Kansas City, MO: Institute for Research and Education on Human Rights. Retrieved April 2, 2014 (http://www.irehr.org/issue-areas/tea-party-national-ism/tea-party-news-and-analysis/item/525-status-oftea-party-part-one).

Burghart, Devin and Leonard Zeskind. 2010. "Tea Party Nationalism: A Critical Examination of the Tea Party Movement and the Size, Scope and Focus of its National Factions." Kansas City, MO: Institute for Research and Education on Human Rights. Retrieved April 2, 2014 (https://docs.google.com/gview?url=http://www.irehr.org/images/stories/pdf/TeaPartyNationalism.pdf&chrome=true).

Burke, Meghan A. 2013. "Beyond Fear and Loathing: Tea Party Organizers' Continuum of Knowledge in a Racialized Social System." *Gender, Race, and Class* 20(1):93–109.

Chalmers, David. 1987. *Hooded Americanism: The History of the Ku Klux Klan.* 3rd ed. Durham, NC: Duke University Press.

Collins, Patricia Hill. 2000. *Black Feminist Thought: Knowledge, Consciousness, and the Politics of Empowerment.* New York: Routledge Classics.

Cunningham, David. 2012a. *Klansville, U.S.A.: The Rise and Fall of the Civil Rights-era Ku Klux Klan.* New York: Oxford University Press.

Cunningham, David. 2012b. "Mobilizing Ethnic Competition." *Theory and Society* 41(5):505–25.

della Porta, Donatella. 2013. *Clandestine Political Violence.* New York: Cambridge University Press.

Diamond, Sarah. 1998. *Not by Politics Alone: The Enduring Influence of the Christian Right.* New York: Guilford.

Dillard, Angela K. 2001. *Guess Who's Coming to Dinner Now? Multicultural Conservatism in America.* New York: NYU Press.

Disch, Lisa. 2011. "The Tea Party: A White Citizenship Movement?" Pp. 133–51 in *Steep: The Precipitous Rise of the Tea Party*, edited by L. Rosenthal and C. Trost. Berkeley: University of California Press.

Dobratz, Betty A. and Stephanie Shanks-Meile. 2000. *The White Separatist Movement in the United States: White Power, White Pride!* Baltimore: The Johns Hopkins University Press.

Durham, Martin. 2000. *The Christian Right, the Far Right and the Boundaries of American Conservatism.* Manchester, UK: Manchester University Press.

Durham, Martin. 2007. *White Rage: The Extreme Right and American Politics.* New York: Taylor & Francis.

Emory University. N.d. "Holocaust Denial on Trial." (http://www.hdot.org/en/trial/index.html). Accessed 9 August 2014.

Ezekiel, Raphael S. 1996. *The Racist Mind: Portraits of American Neo-Nazis and Klansmen.* New York: Penguin.

Fallon, Kathleen M. and Julie Moreau. 2012. "Righting Africa? Contextualizing Notions of Women's Right-wing Activism in Sub-Saharan Africa." Pp. 68–80 in *Women of the Right: Comparisons and Interplay across Borders*, edited by K. Blee and S. Deutsch. University Park: Pennsylvania State University.

Feagin, Joe R. 2006. *Systemic Racism: A Theory of Oppression.* New York: Routledge.

Fleming, Crystal and Aldon Morris. 2014. "Theorizing Ethnic and Racial Movements in the Global Age: Lessons from the Civil Rights Movement." *Sociology of Race and Ethnicity* 1(1):107–128.

Frankenberg, Ruth. 1993. *White Women, Race Matters: The Social Construction of Whiteness.* Minneapolis: University of Minnesota Press.

Fredrickson, George M. 2002. *Racism: A Short History.* Princeton, NJ: Princeton University Press.

Gardell, Mattias. 2003. *Gods of the Blood: The Pagan Revival and White Separatism.* Durham, NC: Duke University Press.

Hardisty, Jean. 1999. *Mobilizing Resentment: Conservative Resurgence from the John Birch Society to the Promise Keepers.* Boston: Beacon Press.

Hughey, Matthew W. 2010. "The (Dis) Similarities of White Racial Identities: The Conceptual Framework of 'Hegemonic Whiteness.'" *Ethnic and Racial Studies* 33(8):1289–309.

Hughey, Matthew W. 2012. *White Bound: Nationalists, Antiracists and the Shared Meaning of Race.* Stanford, CA: Stanford University Press.

Ignatiev, Noel. 2008. *How the Irish Became White.* New York: Routledge.

Irvine, Janice M. 2002. *Talk about Sex: The Battles over Sex Education in the United States.* Berkeley: University of California Press.

Kimmel, Michael. 2013. *Angry White Men: American Masculinity at the End of an Era.* New York: Nation Books.

Lassiter, Matthew D. 2007. *The Silent Majority: Suburban Politics in the Sunbelt South.* Princeton, NJ: Princeton University Press.

Lewis, Angela. 2005. "Black Conservatism in America." *Journal of African American Studies* 8(4):3–13.

Lienesch, Michael. 2007. *In the Beginning: Fundamentalism, the Scopes Trial, and the Making of the Antievolution Movement.* Chapel Hill: University of North Carolina Press.

Lio, Shoon, Scott Melzer, and Ellen Reese. 2008. "Constructing Threat and Appropriating 'Civil Rights': Rhetorical Strategies of Gun Rights and English Only Leaders." *Symbolic Interaction* 31(1):5–31.

Lowndes, Joseph. 2011. "The Past and Future of Race in the Tea Party Movement." Pp. 152–70 in *Steep: The Precipitous Rise of the Tea Party*, edited by L. Rosenthal and C. Trost. Berkeley: University of California Press.

McCright, Aaron M. and Riley E. Dunlap. 2003. "Defeating Kyoto: The Conservative Movement's Impact on U.S. Climate Change Policy." *Social Problems* 50(3):348–73.

McGirr, Lisa. 2001. *Suburban Warriors: The Origins of the New American Right:* Princeton, NJ: Princeton University Press.

McVeigh, Rory. 2009. *The Rise of the Ku Klux Klan: Right-wing Movements and National Politics.* Minneapolis: University of Minnesota Press.

McVeigh, Rory. 2014. "What's New about the Tea Party Movement?" Pp. 16–34 in *Understanding the Tea Party Movement,* edited by N. Van Dyke and D. S. Meyer. Surrey, UK: Ashgate.

McVeigh, Rory and David Cunningham. 2012. "Enduring Consequences of Right-wing Extremism: Klan Mobilization and Homicides in Southern Counties." *Social Forces* 90(3):843–62.

Miller-Idriss, Cynthia. 2012. *Blood and Culture: Youth, Right-wing Extremism, and Belonging in Contemporary Germany.* Durham, NC: Duke University Press.

Nagel, Joane. 2003. *American Indian Renewal: Red Power and the Resurgence of Identity and Culture.* New York: Oxford University Press.

Parker, Christopher S. and Matt A. Barreto. 2013. *Change They Can't Believe In: The Tea Party and Reactionary Politics in America.* Princeton, NJ: Princeton University Press.

Parker, Christopher S. and Christopher C. Towler. 2010. "2010 Multi-state Survey on Race and Politics—Attitudes towards Blacks, Immigrants and Gay Rights, by Tea Party Approval." University of Washington Institute for the Study of Ethnicity, Race and Sexuality. Retrieved April 2, 2014 (https://depts.washington.edu/uwiser/mssrp_table.pdf).

Polletta, Francesca. 2005. "How Participatory Democracy Became White: Culture and Organizational Choice." *Mobilization: An International Journal* 10(2):271–88.

Polletta, Francesca. 2006. *It Was Like a Fever: Storytelling in Protest and Politics.* Chicago: University of Chicago Press.

Polletta, Francesca and James M. Jasper. 2001. "Collective Identity and Social Movements." *Annual Review of Sociology* 27:283–305.

Prior, Francis B. 2014. "Quality Controlled: An Ethnographic Account of Tea Party Messaging and Action." *Sociological Forum* 29(2):301–17.

Quadagno, Jill. 1994. *The Color of Welfare: How Racism Undermined the War on Poverty.* New York: Oxford University Press.

Ribuffo, Leo P. 1983. *The Old Christian Right: The Protestant Far Right from the Great Depression to the Cold War.* Philadelphia: Temple University Press.

Rydgren, Jens. 2007. "The Sociology of the Radical Right." *Annual Review of Sociology* 33:241–62.

Shapira, Harel. 2013. *Waiting for Jose: The Minutemen's Pursuit of America.* Princeton, NJ: Princeton University Press.

Skocpol, Theda and Vanessa Williamson. 2012. *The Tea Party and the Remaking of Republican Conservatism.* New York: Oxford University Press.

Simi, Pete and Robert Futrell. 2010. *American Swastika: Inside the White Power Movement's Hidden Spaces of Hate.* Lanham, MD: Rowman & Littlefield.

Smith, Andrea. 2008. *Native Americans and the Christian Right: The Gendered Politics of Unlikely Alliances.* Durham, NC: Duke University Press.

Smith, Christian. 2003. *Moral, Believing Animals: Human Personhood and Culture.* New York: Oxford University Press.

Stern, Kenneth. 1996. *A Force upon the Plan: The American Militia Movement and the Politics of Hate.* New York: Simon & Schuster.

Twine, France Winddance and Jonathan Warren. 2000. *Racing Research, Researching Race: Methodological Dilemmas in Critical Race Studies.* New York: New York University Press.

van Dyke, Nella and Sarah Soule. 2002. "Structural Social Change and the Mobilizing Effect of Threat: Explaining Levels of Patriot and Militia Organizing in the United States." *Social Problems* 49(4):497–520.

Vozella, Laura. 2013. "Jackson Keeps GOP Establishment at Arm's Length in VA Lieutenant Governor Campaign," *Washington Post,* September 3. http://www.washingtonpost.com/local/virginiapolitics/2013/09/03/936e7178-0f84-11e3–85b6-d274 22650fd5_story.html. Accessed 18 October 2014.

Yates, Elizabeth A. 2014. "Hosting the Tea Party: Grassroots Mobilization in a Conservative Bubble." Master's thesis, University of Pittsburgh.

Zeskind, Leonard. 2009. *Blood and Politics: The History of the White Nationalist Movement from the Margins to the Mainstream.* New York: Farrar, Straus and Giroux.

CHAPTER 20

Negotiating "The Welfare Queen" and "The Strong Black Woman"*

African American Middle-Class Mothers' Work and Family Perspectives

Dawn Marie Dow

In this essay, Dawn Marie Dow analyzes how African American middle- and upper-middle-class mothers understand their work and family decision making in relation to two **controlling images***—the Strong Black Woman (SBW) and the Welfare Queen—that they describe regularly confronting in their lives. In-depth interviews with sixty African American middle- and upper-middle-class mothers reveal the strategies they use to overcome assumptions that they are poor single mothers on welfare or, alternatively, are self-reliant and resilient caregivers who do not need help. Although most interviewees distanced themselves from the image of the Welfare Queen, they had a range of responses to the SBW: Some invested in it, some resisted it, and some rejected it. This study shows how the controlling images of the SBW and the Welfare Queen influence the meanings African American middle- and upper-middle-class mothers attach to their decisions related to work and family and create a sense of exclusion from White middle-class mothering communities.*

Source: Adapted from Dawn Marie Dow, "Negotiating 'The Welfare Queen' and 'The Strong Black Woman': African American Middle-Class Mothers' Work and Family Perspectives," *Sociological Perspectives*, Vol. 58(1), pages 36–55, SAGE Publications, Inc., 2015.

*Some text and accompanying endnotes have been omitted. Please consult the original source.

> **Questions to Consider**
> What is a controlling image, and how it is different from a stereotype? This essay discusses controlling images of African American women. Can you think of different controlling images that other groups confront?

Scholars have examined how controlling images have influenced mainstream perceptions of African American women and the formulation of government policies directly affecting the lives of poor and working-class African American mothers (Collins 2009; Hirschmann and Liebert 2001; Roschelle 2013). In the face of economic and structural constraints, these mothers have often created their own definitions of "good motherhood" (Blum and Deussen 1996). Controlling images are different from stereotypes because they guide both the behavior toward and from the members of subordinated groups (Beauboeuf-Lafontant 2009). These images constrain what people see and believe about the members of these groups and, if internalized can profoundly influence how members of marginalized groups view themselves and group members. Less is known about the impact of these images on middle- and upper-middle-class African American mothers.

African American mothers have been excluded from dominant images of motherhood [associated with middle-class white women and] that are derived from the ideologies of the cult of domesticity and the separate spheres [of home and work]. Instead, the African American middle- and upper-middle-class mothers whom I interviewed described regularly confronting the controlling images of the Welfare Queen and the [Strong Black Woman] SBW during their quotidian activities.

The mothers in my sample believed that they had to counter assumptions related to the Welfare Queen to gain access to, and acceptance in, white middle-class mothering activities such as mothers' groups, "mommy and me" activities, and extracurricular activities. These mothers' experiences complicate discussions of middle-class parenting practices (Lareau 2011) by uncovering the challenges that they believe they must overcome to meaningfully gain access to predominately white extracurricular enrichment activities. Some interviewees internalized aspects of the Welfare Queen (Pyke 2010), using them to make distinctions between themselves and poor African American mothers. Interviewees had varied responses to the SBW, at times internalizing, resisting, rejecting, or attempting to transform it. Mothers also embodied aspects of the SBW to counter assumptions they believed they encountered related to the Welfare Queen. Together these racially specific controlling images influenced the meanings these mothers attached to their family and work decisions and experiences.

Conceptual Framing

Ronald Reagan first used the term *welfare queen* during his 1976 Republican presidential campaign to describe a mythical black woman from the South Side of Chicago who was unjustly receiving aid. He said,

> There's a women in Chicago. She has eighty names, thirty addresses, twelve Social Security cards and is collecting veteran's benefits on four non-existing deceased husbands. ... She's got Medicaid, getting food stamps and she is collecting welfare under each of her names. Her tax-free cash income alone is over $150,000. (*Washington Star* 1976)

Reagan and his political strategists thus successfully mobilized opposition to welfare polices using images of unwed African American mothers raising children fathered by different men as the prototypical beneficiary (Hirschmann and Liebert 2001). In the 1990s, during the Clinton era, the image of the Welfare Queen influenced the reforms included in the Personal Responsibility and Work Act of 1996 (Gilliam 1999; Hancock 2003; Mink and Solinger 2003; Nadasen 2007). Instead of being cast as the beneficiaries of financial assistance that would enable them to do the important work of raising their children, these mothers were described as lazy, lascivious, and lacking morals. This image of the Welfare Queen continues to have power, both in the political landscape and in the imagination of Americans (Blake 2012; Stein 2013). The subtext is clear: Staying at home to raise children is not an appropriate use of African American mothers' time, and if they receive welfare benefits, they should be obligated to work.

Although African American mothers' participation in the labor force has often been necessary for their families' survival and encouraged by state policies, their employment has also been used to explain the challenges their families face. Senator Daniel Patrick Moynihan argued that the "Black Matriarch" was an emasculating figure: The fragile economic position of many African American families was attributed to African American mothers' employment and authority in the household (Massey et al. 2009; U.S. Department of Labor, Office of Policy Planning and Research 1965). In response to the degrading and controlling images of African American womanhood that have been produced and projected by mainstream society, African American women have engaged in a continual practice of self-definition and valuation (Collins 2009). Although there are a number of possible origins for the image of the SBW, it nevertheless can be viewed as an attempt to reject the pathological image of the Black Matriarch (Collins 2009; U.S. Department of Labor, Office of Policy Planning and Research 1965) and to reinterpret African American mothers' familial duties as symbols of strength and resilience (Collins 2009). Rather than viewing their labor force participation as a failure to live up to the separate spheres ideal, scholars suggest that African American women created their own standards of womanhood that incorporated paid work as a necessary component (Blum and Deussen 1996; Collins 2009; Higginbotham 2001; Landry 2000) and now take for granted they will work outside of the home (Barnes 2008; Damaske 2011; Dean 2013).

Numerous examples in both mainstream and academic discourses emphasize the strength of African American women as an important element of their distinctive experience. In a 1963 exposé "The Negro Woman," featured in *Ebony Magazine*, strength and resiliency were extolled as the core characteristics of African American womanhood (Bennett 1963). In 1939, sociologist E. Franklin Frazier wrote, "Neither economic necessity nor tradition has instilled in the [African American woman] subordination to masculine authority" (Frazier 1939:125). The image of the SBW has continued to appear in literary works (Angelou 1978; Morrison 1970; Naylor 1983; Walker 1982) and popular magazines (Edwards 1998; Randolph 1997, 1999). The image is found in popular television shows including *Julia* (1968–1971), *The Cosby Show* (1984–1992), *Grey's Anatomy* (2005–present), and *Scandal* (2012–present), and in music including Alicia Keys' "Superwoman" from the album *As I Am*, Tupac Shakur's single release "Keep Your Head Up," and Kanye West's "Hey Mama" from the album *Late*

Registration. The SBW may, in part, originate from a desire to empower African American women, but in the contemporary setting, it also functions as a controlling image that justifies their lived experience and constrains their choices (Beauboeuf-Lafontant 2009). African American feminist scholars (Collins 2009; Harris-Perry 2011; Hooks 1984; Lorde 1984) argue that controlling images are elite white male interpretations of African American womanhood and serve as powerful rationalizations for African American women's subordinate place in society and their continued oppression. Despite the criticism of these images, the SBW is often viewed positively by African Americans and internalized as an ideal to aspire.

Recent research has shown that African American women are less likely to receive emotional support from kin networks or friends, suggesting that they do not feel comfortable divulging emotional challenges or weakness to others because they have internalized the image of the SBW (Sarkisian, Gerena, and Gerstel 2007). Some research cautions that internalizing emotions related to struggles and disappointment in the name of being a SBW can have negative impacts on the bodies and minds of African American women (Beauboeuf-Lafontant 2009). With the exception of Tamara Beauboeuf-Lafontant's research (2009; 2003), largely absent from discussions of controlling images is how these images influence the meanings African American middle- and upper-middle-class mothers attach to their family and work decisions, and how these mothers respond to these images when they confront them in their daily lives.

This article adds to the nascent efforts of researchers to remedy these absences in the literature by analyzing how African American middle- and upper-middle-class mothers understand their family and work–life choices. This analysis is based on interviews with 60 African American middle- and upper-middle-class mothers who worked full-time, part-time, or stayed at home. My interviewees referenced two controlling images that they described regularly confronting and negotiating in their daily lives. In this article, special attention is paid to the images of motherhood that interviewees referred to when discussing their families and work lives. I conclude by analyzing the meanings interviewees attached to their family and work–life decisions and how the Welfare Queen and the SBW constrain and empower their decisions.

Method

The interview data were derived from a study that took place from 2009 to 2011 examining how 60 African American middle- and upper-middle-class mothers understood their work, family, and parenting decisions. Interviewees were asked about their childhood families, what their parents expected of them as adults, their paths to motherhood, and how they made their decisions about work, childcare, schools, and parenting.

Negotiating the Welfare Queen

The majority of the mothers that I interviewed believed that they had to navigate and challenge assumptions about being poor and on welfare in their daily social interactions, assumptions based in the controlling image of the Welfare Queen. In their daily interactions, stay-at-home mothers described referring to husbands to underscore that they were at home based on financial support from their husbands, not from the state. To counter the Welfare Queen image, single working mothers often referred to their jobs, and, if married and working, they too referred to their marital status and their jobs when interacting with others. Hana,[1] a married mother of two who was currently a stay-at-home mother because she had been laid off from her job, believed people assumed that she was single and on welfare when she went on outings with her children during the day. She described what she did to counter the assumptions she believed others were making:

> I think about how I am dressed, like do I have a scarf on my head today while I am taking a walk with my children. And I am always worried about that perception, wondering if people are thinking I am just another ghetto mother. If I don't have my [wedding and engagement] rings on, and I am out with my kids, I wonder if people are thinking, "Here comes another 'baby mama.'" I am very aware of that, and through the course of conversation, I will mention my husband and let it be known that I am married.

Although Hana saw white mothers and their children when she went for walks, she believed that she was interpreted differently as an African American mother. Maya, a professor who was married and the mother of four, engaged in similar strategies to underscore that she was middle class. Maya's children were the products of different relationships, and they took the last names of their respective fathers. Because she believed that her personal life matched some of the characteristics of the Welfare Queen, Maya was proactive in dispelling the assumptions she believed others were making. She said,

> In the doctor's office, I can see people start to categorize me, with all the kids, with all the last names. I make sure they know I have a PhD because there is a way that my class status supersedes my race and how they are positioning me based on my race. So, I counter it very explicitly. You know, I dress certain ways on airplanes and I talk to my children about that, and [I] say that I don't want people to think I'm some young, ignorant person. I dress like this so they know I am a professional and they have to respect me.

For these mothers, being perceived as middle class was something that they believed they (and their children) had to consistently work at. They tried to accomplish this by using social cues, such as occupation and marital status; visual cues such as dress, hairstyle, and accessories (like wedding and engagement rings); and their vernacular.

Mothers also felt that they had to counter stereotypes related to the Welfare Queen when they participated in mothering or parenting activities comprised of primarily white mothers and children. Christine, engaged to be married and a working mother of one, said in her interview, "The main thing about being a black mom that is probably important to say, is not feeling included in white motherhood society. . . . It feels like when I go to the playground there is the 'them' and there is the 'us.'" Christine believed that there is a racial divide in middle-class motherhood that is produced by white mothers treating her, and other African American middle-class mothers, differently in a myriad of child-related activities. She described,

> I have friends who have left playgroups because the white women look at us funny or like you don't exist. I had a friend who was at a [mother and child] gym class and she didn't exist to other women in the class. They were all friends and laughing and talking and not trying to be friendly with her at all, and they kind of looked at her with her kids and thought, "What are you doing with your kid; your kid is not doing it right." So, I feel that a lot. It is actually surprising that in the Bay area you would feel it so much. I have been at playgrounds, and it is not across the board, but they are looking at you funny. Like those music-together classes, [white mothers] look at you like you are not there. . . . There are certain playgrounds that I don't go to because they are not friendly to black moms. . . . They just ignore us.

Christine participated in a range of middle-class mother and child activities but she felt that she had to do additional work to be accepted by the white mothers who dominated these venues. This was work she did not always want to do, that discouraged her from engaging in these activities, and made her feel that she did not fully belong and was not accepted in these settings. These settings included parks in predominately white middle-class neighborhoods, children's museums, certain extracurricular activities, and other "mommy and me" activities. It was also work she believed that white mothers did not have to do. A white mother's standoffish demeanor, combined with what was viewed as a more cordial one to other white mothers, left a similar impression on many mothers in my sample. The mothers in my sample felt that they needed to demonstrate their class status to white mothers before these mothers would meaningfully engage with them. These mothers consciously engaged in class perception management strategies to attempt to overcome assumptions that they believed others were making, that they were poor and on welfare, and to ensure they and their children were treated well. These mothers' accounts suggest they did not have the same experiences, access, or comfort when they engaged in predominately white extracurricular activities with their children.

The image of the Welfare Queen was, at times, invoked when African American middle- and upper-middle-class mothers described the boundaries they drew or did not draw between themselves and other African American mothers that they believed were not as thoughtful about raising their children. This often explicitly came up when mothers described trying to find other African American mothers to include in their social circles. For example, Sharon, a mother of a son and a daughter who worked full-time at a major technology company described the challenges she encountered in finding a community of African American mothers that she said, "defied statistics." Her ideal group members were African American mothers who were married, professionally accomplished, middle-class, homeowners, and had children later in life. Sharon described her initial failed attempts to find such mothers before finding her current mothers' group:

> Before I found [my current] black mom's group, it was hard finding black mothers with similar values, particularly in my age group. Before, when I went to the crazy class [a new mothers' class facilitated by the hospital where her child was born]—I call it the crazy class—there was a black young mother of twins in that class. . . . I knew she was kind of lost, but I didn't realize how lost until I asked her if she wanted to go get a Jamba Juice. It was all bad. She didn't know who the [children's] father was. She didn't

> care who the father was. Everybody was trying to find out who the father was, but she wasn't telling who she thought he was. It was all this around the father of these two little girls. And I asked her about, you know, "what are they eating now that they are two?" She said, "she likes ho hos and she likes ding dongs." . . . I just couldn't find anyone who shared my values. . . . I was looking for people who would come over, and have a dinner party and bring the kids. We've got a swing set in the back yard. We'll all have a good time, but I couldn't find that type of connection and I thought I probably never would.

Sharon wanted to be a part of a community of African American mothers who were educated, financially well-off, and married. She simultaneously distanced herself from mothers who were not middle class and not in stable relationships and sought out mothers who were engaged in a middle-class lifestyle similar to hers and who shared her concerns about providing their children with the best educational and extracurricular opportunities. In describing the group that she ultimately joined, she said, "You don't join a group like this if you are not the kind of mother who cares about things like nutrition and educational development. . . . It is really a gift to have a group like this." For Sharon, these mothers not only provided socializing opportunities for her children and support about motherhood for her, but they also offered emotional and instrumental support on issues she faced in negotiating other white social spaces. . . .

In sum, the Welfare Queen—a gendered and racialized controlling image—played in the minds of mothers as they encountered and strategized around experiences of exclusion. The image of the Welfare Queen is pervasive in American popular and academic discourse and media representations (Blake 2012; Gilliam 1999; Hancock 2003; Johnson 1995; Littlefield 2008; Nadasen 2007; Stein 2013; Wagmiller 2006). To engage comfortably in white middle-class mothering domains, mothers in my study believed that they had to overcome others' automatic assumptions that they were poor, single, and on welfare. Until mothers believed that they overcame these assumptions, they felt invisible in these environments but most were unwilling to engage in this additional labor on an ongoing basis. The Welfare Queen was also internalized by some mothers and used as a guide about how they should and should not behave. This image was used to draw boundaries between themselves, as good middle-class mothers who were not "wild parents," and other African American mothers who made less thoughtful choices about their children and did not share their middle-class values. It was also used to evaluate the mothers they wanted to have in their social circles.

Negotiating the SBW

Mothers were also regularly confronted by, and sometimes invoked, the controlling image of the SBW as a way to make sense of their family and work experiences. The SBW represents extreme female self-reliance, emotional resilience, and moral propriety and was produced by and for African American women in response to negative mainstream images of African American womanhood. Farah, a married and a working mother of two, had her first child when she was in college and had recently given birth to her second child. We met in the early evening at a café near her work, where she planned to return after our interview. Farah was clear about her definition of the ideal African American mother, and it conformed to the SBW. She explained,

> [A SBW] is a strong woman, who can do all of the "Big Momma" things. She can cook like nobody else can cook, she can iron, do all that stuff like nobody else can do, but then she also does her own thing, whether that be work or some other activity . . . She is very confident of who she is and what she wants in her life. She can do it all on her own.

For Farah, the ideal mother was a SBW who cares for her children, provides financially for her family, and is active in the community. Although she did not believe she completely conformed to this image, Farah believed that her friends, her family, and the African American community at large judged her against it.

During my interview with Kristen, whose quote underscored the different cultural expectations African American middle- and upper-middle-class mothers confront in their lives, she said, "I'm a strong black woman and I am proud of it." When I asked her what it meant to be an SBW, she said,

> To know your mind, to know what you want, to not compromise your values, don't compromise who you are. . . . You have to be strong in this society because there are so many people who are trying to define you as a black woman. How you should be, what you should look like, who you should be with, how you should act.

Kristen's description of being a SBW echoes Patricia Hill Collins's (2009) depiction of the way that African American women, not just those who are middle class, engage in a continual process of self-definition and valuation as a survival strategy within a society that might not share those beliefs. Although most interviewees were critical of the SBW image, many adhered to some of its elements, which affected their work and family decision making and the kinds of support they were willing to seek out from friends and family. Like other scholars (Beauboeuf-Lafontant 2003, 2009; Collins 2009), I argue that although the SBW, in part, originates from a desire to redefine African American female strength as a value to be revered, it has become a controlling image that both empowers and constrains choices.

Investing in the SBW

Samantha was a married, working mother of one child, and was one of the few interviewees who fully embraced the SBW and drew on it also to justify the current division of responsibilities in her household. She described how the image of the SBW resonated with her:

> I would agree with being a strong black woman; my mom is kind of my role model for that . . . she had more resilience and strength than anybody. . . . I think it can have a negative connotation, but when I think of myself, I kind of think of it as being a supermom. . . . There is this idea that you are a super woman in many ways because you have two full-time jobs. When you come home from work, you are still working. And my husband totally acknowledges that the division of responsibility in terms of raising our kid is probably 70/30 percent. . . . If I need to stay up late I will to get [a project] done,

> and I think of those as being the characteristics of a strong black woman. As being a provider, nurturer, and making sure your house is in order.

The image of the SBW gave Samantha a way to normalize the unequal distribution of labor in her household. She viewed taking on the lion's share of household and childrearing duties as unproblematic and simply what was required to be a good employee, wife, and mother. The SBW supports the idea that African American women do not and should not need help, particularly from the men in their lives.

Given the SBW is strongly connected to a "do it all" ethic that includes economic independence from men, one might assume that stay-at-home mothers would be less invested in this image. My data reveal a more complicated story about the place of paid work in defining a mother's identity and experiences. Tamika, a married mother of one son, identified as a stay-at-home mother but actually worked 30 hours a week. This apparent contradiction in Tamika's self-identification as a stay-at-home mother and the amount of time she spent engaged in paid labor was connected to her commitment to being a SBW. Tamika explained:

> I have three clients that I like. It is not a heck of a lot of money, but it is enough where if I see something I want at the mall, I can buy it. If I want to buy my kid a tricycle, I don't have to say, "Honey, I need sixty bucks to get this bicycle." I don't like that, I don't do that, and I don't think my husband would be down with that, to be quite honest. I think he kind of digs that I am not the shrinking violet type.

Tamika's husband worked two full-time jobs to make her staying at home and sending their son to preschool part-time financially viable. Although her income did not pay for big household expenses, by having some income she was able to reconcile two competing cultural expectations—being self-sufficient and "not the shrinking violet type"—with her desire to be more available for their son. Surprisingly, almost half of the mothers who identified as stay-at-home mothers were employed in part-time to full-time jobs. Generally, these were not traditional 9 a.m. to 5 p.m. jobs and these mothers had some flexibility about their work schedules. Mothers worked the night shift or during the portion of the week that their child(ren) attended daycare or preschool. In addition, when these children were not in the care of their mothers, they remained in the care of another parent or family member. These mothers viewed themselves as "staying-at-home" because they were available to their children during the daylight and out-of-school hours. Because these mothers actually worked, they were protected from disapproving comments from spouses and community members.

Resisting the SBW

Vastly more common than interviewees who invested in the image of the SBW were those who were critical of this expectation, even as they believed that African American mothers had to at times be strong and resilient.

Mary, a married mother of two, was probably the most critical of the SBW image, while simultaneously conforming to many of its characteristics out of necessity. Before Mary met her husband, she created a savings account for getting married and having children. She was determined to stay at home with her future children but assumed that it was unlikely that the African American man she hoped to someday marry would make enough income to enable her do so. Mary ultimately married a man who was a high school graduate, earned less than half of her six-figure income, and paid child support for a child from a previous marriage. Despite the financial challenges it presented, when Mary became a mother she carried out her plan. She was a stay-at-home mother for 3 years, but because of shrinking savings, she decided to find a temporary, part-time evening job to increase her family's income. She had hoped that her husband would respond by finding a second job, allowing her to return to being a stay-at-home mother, but six months later, she was still working. In fact, Mary had increased her work hours and her husband was not actively looking for additional income.

Mary provided a definition of the SBW while simultaneously identifying how it created challenges in her life and the lives of African American mothers. She explained,

> One of the challenges that mothers of color face is our history of black women being the pillar in the family. . . . I think the idea that we will provide the finances, do the childrearing, do the cooking, and just do it all. If the man has married a strong black woman, he can end up not doing much of anything because the black woman is not going to let her family fail, not going to let her marriage fail. She will do what it takes to hold it together and . . . accept things from our men of color that maybe shouldn't be accepted. We have seen our parents do it and we have accepted this role, but we need to reassess it because we can't go on like that forever. I think that you can't maintain happiness and balance if you are trying to do everything.

Mary's quote underscores the origins of the SBW image—the result of African American women redefining their breadwinning roles in the family as unproblematic and, indeed, something to value. Mary interpreted both her savings for motherhood and her need to return to work as examples of her strength. She made, what turned out to be, an accurate assessment of the educational attainment and earning ability of the African American man she would marry. Nonetheless, she felt that she should not have needed to take either action. She felt trapped by the expectations she believed that the SBW image set for African American mothers and by the larger context of the labor market. In addition, based on discussions with her husband and what she perceived as his lackluster effort to find another job, Mary believed that he interpreted her decision to return to work as what she should be willing to do as an SBW. At the time of the interview, Mary was trying to negotiate a different division of household labor with her husband, but she believed that the expectations set by the SBW presented a challenge in those negotiations because she was expected to do it all.

Rejecting the SBW and Constructing Alternative Paths

A significant minority of mothers, all of whom identified as stay-at-home mothers and most of whom did not engage in paid employment, rejected the idea that African American middle-class mothers should "do it all." These mothers believed the SBW created a perception that women who are not engaged in both breadwinning and caregiving activities are less authentically African American. This rejection of the SBW, by choosing not to engage in paid employment, often created conflict in these mothers' relationships with their spouses, family, and communities. Among this group was Jessica, a self-employed, divorced, mother of one child. When she was married, her decision to stay at home with their daughter was not met by support from her husband. Like many mothers in my sample, Jessica was in a hypogamous marriage, earning more money than her husband. Choosing to stay at home cut their household income by more than half. She recounted,

> After I became pregnant, it was expected that I go back to work . . . but I didn't go back to work. I stayed home and took care of my daughter because that was what was in my heart to do. Ultimately that led to the problems that led to my divorce, because that wasn't the marriage agreement, you know.

Jessica also described resistance from her family: "Everybody thought I was absolutely crazy to leave a job like that and they thought it was laziness." After a year of staying at home with her child, Jessica enrolled in a graduate program in the hopes that her family would stop asking when she planned to return to work. Making the decision to stay at home defied both her husband's expectations for married life and her family's expectations that African American mothers, particularly those who are educated, should handle both work and family responsibilities.

Many other interviewees echoed a similar need for support from African American stay-at-home mothers' groups to offset the cultural expectation that they should work outside of the home. They sought out, created, or yearned for groups that would validate and support their decisions to opt out of careers. Indeed, in the late 1990s, African American Mothers United was founded with the specific goal of connecting stay-at-home African American mothers with each other to support their decision to reduce their commitment to paid work and to focus on raising their *own* children. The emphasis on raising one's own children is directly related to the history of African American mothers working as domestics and nannies in white middle- and working-class families' homes. African American Mothers United recognizes that African American middle-class mothers were confronted by different assumptions about how they would and should manage work and family. Acknowledging that the decision to work is often influenced by financial concerns, African American Mothers United underscored that its members often also lacked emotional and psychological support from their community when deciding to stay at home. Sarah, a mother of one, who was pregnant with her second child and occasionally worked part-time as a teacher, expressed this sentiment:

> What we all share in common is trying to maximize the time we spend with our children. Even career women stay at home for eight months, and they try to maximize their time with their children. It definitely is important to me because I . . . know a lot of women who are more career women and who don't have kids, and I don't know a lot of people who think being a stay-at-home mom is a good thing to be. I think a lot of people think, "What are you doing all day?" They don't realize you are busting your ass all day. Taking care of a child is work—that is why they are called childcare workers—because it is work. For me, for my self-esteem, it has been important to be connected to other women who believe that it is an important thing. It is okay. And, in fact, it is important to be with your child.

Sarah made it clear that by not working outside of the home, she was going against the expectations of her spouse, family, and community, but that the women in her mothers' group empowered her to interpret staying at home differently. Rather than viewing herself as lazy and not pulling her full weight in her household, Sarah saw staying at home as engaging in the important work of raising her children. It is also important to note that Sarah and the other stay-at-home mothers in my sample sought out race-specific stay-at-home mothers' groups. These mothers told me that although white mothers might share some of their motivations for staying at home, they would not understand the shifting economic and racial sands that they contend with in making that decision. By seeking support from similar African American middle-class mothers, these mothers were revisiting the strategies of self-definition and valuation that Collins (2009) identified as essential to the survival of African American women and their families. Many of the mothers in my study were, in part, choosing to stay at home to raise their children in response to the historical inability of women of color to do so in the past. These mothers considered raising their own children to be an important privilege that many African American mothers have not enjoyed and continue not to enjoy. In my study, these mothers were clearly rejecting the image of the SBW to produce an alternative image of African American motherhood that they hoped would gain greater acceptance within both African American and mainstream communities.

Conclusion

Sociological researchers are exploring how the meanings that mothers attach to their family, work, and life decision making influence how they experience motherhood (Christopher 2012; Damaske 2011; Macdonald 2011). This literature generally assumes that mothers are influenced by and evaluated by similar images of motherhood (Damaske 2011). This study adds to this body of literature by highlighting two controlling images of motherhood that African American women confront—the Welfare Queen and the SBW—and how those images affect their decisions. These distinctly racialized images of motherhood represent a form of gendered racism (Wingfield 2007, 2009) that African American middle- and upper-middle-class mothers believe they must negotiate in their daily lives. In addition, these images influence how these mothers understand their choices and the meanings they attach to their experiences.

Existing research suggests that class has a stronger influence on parenting practices than does racial identity (Lareau 2011), but these findings complicate those claims. The middle- and upper-middle-class African American mothers in this study believed that they confronted a range of challenges when they participated in predominately white enrichment activities with their children. Annette Lareau (2011) acknowledges that African American parents often place their children in extracurricular activities with children who share their racial identity, but the present findings point to the possibility that these parents feel constrained in the kinds of activities they can seek out for their children. The mothers in my sample believed they had to overcome the image of the Welfare Queen to gain acceptance within predominately white middle-class childrearing and parenting settings. They did this by asserting their middle-class status, while not calling attention to the fact that they were doing this. For some mothers in my sample, this increased their comfort in these settings but it left others feeling alienated and reluctant to return. These mothers said that being misrecognized as poor, single, and on welfare directly affected the treatment they and their children received in public when they engaged in commerce, and interacted with teachers and other white mothers and their children.

Many mothers admitted that the image of the SBW left them feeling like failures as mothers if they admitted to being overwhelmed or needing help. This image also meant that being able to do it all was simply expected of them, and this expectation became a stumbling block when they tried to chart a different course for themselves. This research demonstrates that African American middle- and upper-middle-class mothers face a curious cultural and structural predicament. On the one hand, the image of the SBW is an issue for mothers who choose to stay at home; it can lead to stigmatization because they are viewed as not pulling their weight within their families. African American middle- and upper-middle-class mothers, both employed and staying at home, must also respond to the image of the Welfare Queen because they are assumed to be on welfare by others. On the other hand, the image of the SBW who can do it all has historically been used to combat the adversity and racism these mothers face in their lives. It has removed any stigma from African American women's ongoing participation in the public sphere of work and created a cultural expectation that they will work outside of the home. In this way, it is an example of the end result of Collins' (2009) three-prong process of self-valuation and definition, understanding the interlocking nature of oppression and appreciating the importance of African American women's culture. My data complicate the meaning of this image by demonstrating that some African American middle- and upper-middle-class mothers, most notably those who stay at home, experience this ideal as oppressive and as an obstacle when negotiating changes in their household division of labor. On a larger scale, these controlling images may present challenges to enacting different versions of womanhood that are perceived as not authentically African American. To reconcile these predicaments, African American middle- and upper-middle-class mothers must constantly perform a subjectivity that is based on class and race and that varies based on context.

Note

1. All names have been changed.

References

Angelou, Maya. 1978. *And Still I Rise.* 1st ed. New York: Random House.

Barnes, Riché Jeneen Daniel. 2008. "Black Women have Always Worked: Is There a Work-Family Conflict among the Black Middle Class?" Pp. 189–210 in *The Changing Landscape of Work and Family in the American Middle Class: Reports from the Field,* edited by Elizabeth Rudd and Lara Descartes. Lanham, MD: Lexington Books.

Beauboeuf-Lafontant, Tamara. 2003. "Strong and Large Black Women? Exploring Relationships between Deviant Womanhood and Weight." *Gender & Society* 17(1):111–21.

Beauboeuf-Lafontant, Tamara. 2009. *Behind the Mask of the Strong Black Woman: Voice and the Embodiment of a Costly Performance.* Philadelphia, PA: Temple University Press.

Bennett, Lerone. 1963. "The Negro Woman." *Ebony Magazine,* September, pp. 86–94.

Blake, John. 2012. "Return of the Welfare Queen." *CNN.* Retrieved October 18, 2014 (http://www.cnn.com/2012/01/23/politics/weflare-queen/index.html).

Blum, Linda M. and Theresa Deussen. 1996. "Negotiating Independent Motherhood—Working-class African American Women Talk about Marriage and Motherhood." *Gender & Society* 10(2):199–211.

Christopher, Karen. 2012. "Extensive Mothering: Employed Mothers' Constructions of the Good Mother." *Gender & Society* 26(1):73–96.

Collins, Patricia Hill. 2009. *Black Feminist Thought: Knowledge, Consciousness, and the Politics of Empowerment.* 2nd ed. New York: Routledge Classics.

Damaske, Sarah. 2011. *For the Family?: How Class and Gender Shape Women's Work.* New York: Oxford University Press.

Dean, Paul. 2013. "Cultural Contradiction or Integration? Work–Family Schemas of Black Middle Class Mothers." *Advances in Gender Research* 17:137–58.

Edwards, Audrey. 1998. Black and White Women: What Still Divides Us? *Essence,* March, pp. 77–80, 136–140.

Frazier, Edward Franklin. 1939. *The Negro Family in the United States.* Chicago, IL: University of Chicago Press.

Gilliam, Franklin D., Jr. 1999. "The 'Welfare Queen' Experiment." *Nieman Reports* 53(2):49–52.

Hancock, Ange-Marie. 2003. "Contemporary Welfare Reform and the Public Identity of the 'Welfare Queen.'" *Race, Gender & Class* 10(1):31–59.

Harris-Perry, Melissa V. 2011. *Sister Citizen: Shame, Stereotypes, and Black Women in America.* New Haven, CT: Yale University Press.

Higginbotham, Elizabeth. 2001. *Too Much to Ask: Black Women in the Era of Integration (Gender and American Culture).* Chapel Hill, NC: University of North Carolina Press.

Hirschmann, Nancy J. and Ulrike Liebert. 2001. *Women and Welfare: Theory and Practice in the United States and Europe.* New Brunswick, NJ: Rutgers University Press.

Hooks, Bell. 1984. *Feminist Theory from Margin to Center.* Boston, MA: South End Press. Johnson, Karen. 1995. "Myth of the Welfare Queen." *Essence,* April, p. 42.

Landry, Bart. 2000. *Black Working Wives: Pioneers of the American Family Revolution.* Berkeley, CA: University of California Press.

Lareau, Annette. 2011. *Unequal Childhoods: Class, Race, and Family Life.* 2nd ed. Berkeley, CA: University of California Press.

Littlefield, Marci Bounds. 2008. "The Media as a System of Racialization: Exploring Images of African American Women and the New Racism." *American Behavioral Scientist* 51(5):675–685.

Lorde, Audre. 1984. *Sister Outsider: Essays and Speeches (Crossing Press Feminist Series).* Trumansburg, NY: Crossing Press.

Macdonald, Cameron Lynne. 2011. *Shadow Mothers: Nannies, Au Pairs, and the Micropolitics of Mothering.* Berkeley, CA: University of California Press.

Massey, Douglas S., Robert J. Sampson, Phyllis C. Kaniss, and American Academy of Political and Social Science. 2009. *The Moynihan Report Revisited: Lessons and Reflections after Four Decades.* Thousand Oaks, CA: Sage Publications.

Mink, Gwendolyn and Rickie Solinger. 2003. *Welfare: A Documentary History of U.S. Policy and Politics.* New York: New York University Press.

Morrison, Toni. 1970. *The Bluest Eye: A Novel.* 1st ed. New York: Holt, Rinehart and Winston.

Nadasen, Premilla. 2007. "From Widow to 'Welfare Queen.'" *Black Women, Gender & Families* 1(2):52–77.

Naylor, Gloria. 1983. *The Women of Brewster Place.* New York: Penguin Books.

Pyke, Karen D. 2010. "What Is Internalized Racial Oppression and Why Don't We Study It? Acknowledging Racism's Hidden Injuries." *Sociological Perspectives* 53(4):551–572.

Randolph, Laura B. 1997. "Strong Black Woman Syndrome." *Ebony*, July, p. 24.

Randolph, Laura B. 1999. "Strong Black Woman Blues." *Ebony*, July, p. 24.

Roschelle, Anne R. 2013. "Why Do You Think We Don't Get Married? Homeless Mothers in San Francisco Speak Out about Having children Outside of Marriage." *Advances in Gender Research* 17:89–111.

Sarkisian, Natalia, Mariana Gerena, and Naomi Gerstel. 2007. "Extended Family Integration among Euro and Mexican Americans: Ethnicity, Gender, and Class." *Journal of Marriage and Family* 69(1):40–54.

Stein, Gary. 2013. Where Are All the Couch Potatoes and Welfare Queens? *Huffpost Live: The Huffington Post.* Retrieved October 30, 2014 (http://www.huffingtonpost.com/gary-stein/where-are-all-the-couch-p_b_4085773.html).

U.S. Department of Labor, Office of Policy Planning and Research. 1965. *The Negro Family: The Case for National Action.* Washington, DC: The Superintendent of Documents.

Wagmiller, Robert L. 2006. "Causes and Consequences of 'Welfare Reform.'" *Contexts* (Spring) 5:64–66.

Walker, Alice. 1982. *The Color Purple: A Novel.* New York: Harcourt Brace Jovanovich.

Washington Star. 1976. "'Welfare Queen' Becomes Issue in Reagan Campaign." February 15. Retrieved October 30, 2014. (http://query.nytimes.com/mem/archivefree/pdf?res=950CE5DA123DE532A257 56C1A9649C946790D6CF).

Wingfield, Adia Harvey. 2007. "The Modern Mammy and the Angry Black Man: African American Professionals' Experiences with Gendered Racism in the Workplace." *Race, Gender & Class* 14(1–2):196–212.

Wingfield, Adia Harvey. 2009. "Racializing the Glass Escalator: Reconsidering Men's Experiences with Women's Work." *Gender & Society* 23(1):5–26.

CHAPTER 21

Nailing Race and Labor Relations*

Vietnamese Nail Salons in Majority–Minority Neighborhoods

Kimberly Kay Hoang

In this essay, Kimberly Hoang brings theories of ***immigrant entrepreneurship*** *into conversation with a broader literature on Asian American* ***racialization*** *in the United States. Drawing on four months of ethnographic field research, she sheds light on the micro-processes, routines, and everyday interactions in two Vietnamese-owned nail salons located outside of Vietnamese enclaves in majority Black and Latino neighborhoods in Northern and Southern California. She highlights a system of racialized and class-based labor relationships among owners/workers/clients that are crucial to sustaining business relationships in majority–minority neighborhoods.*

Questions to Consider

Have you ever been a client or customer in an immigrant business where the workers or owners often talk to each other in their country-of-origin language? Did you notice how the differences between you and the worker/owner across race, ethnicity, and nativity might have shaped your interaction? Do immigrant-owned businesses in minority neighborhoods provide a site where race relations among immigrants, Whites, and racial and ethnic minorities improve, worsen, or stay the same?

Source: Adapted from Kimberly Kay Hoang, "Nailing Race and Labor Relations: Vietnamese Nail Salons in Majority–Minority Neighborhoods," *Journal of Asian American Studies*, Volume 18, Number 2, pages 113–139, Johns Hopkins University Press, 2015.

*Some text and accompanying endnotes have been omitted. Please consult the original source.

Nail salons in the United States constitute a $7.5-billion industry. Nearly 80 percent of this industry is owned by Vietnamese immigrants, making it one of the fastest growing Asian immigrant-dominated businesses.[1] Vietnamese nail salons are prevalent not only in Vietnamese American enclaves but also in diverse white and nonwhite neighborhoods. They are sites of racialized encounters among multiple immigrant and ethnic groups in the United States.

Immigrant entrepreneurship is widely recognized as an important segment of the U.S. economy. A 2012 report from the Fiscal Policy Institute's Immigration Research Initiative revealed that 18 percent of all small business owners in the United States are immigrants; among these immigrant entrepreneurs, Asian Americans constitute the largest racial/ethnic group.[2]

This article brings theories of immigrant entrepreneurship into conversation with a broader literature on Asian American racialization in the United States.[4] Drawing on four months of ethnographic field research, I shed light on the micro-processes, routines, and everyday interactions in two Vietnamese-owned nail salons located outside of Vietnamese enclaves in majority black and Latino neighborhoods in Northern and Southern California. These salons were a fruitful place to observe immigrant entrepreneurship and economic incorporation, interracial relationships, and new labor processes in service work.

Previous scholarship describes the racialized relations that emerge when Asian immigrants come into contact with nonwhite Americans in urban spaces, with a special focus on Korean entrepreneurs in predominantly black neighborhoods.[5] This article turns to Vietnamese entrepreneurs [outside the ethnic enclave] to describe how race relations are intertwined with labor processes in immigrant businesses. In doing so I incorporate Claire Kim's concept of *racial triangulation*, which focuses primarily on *race* relations among immigrant entrepreneurs and their black and white patrons and Miliann Kang's concept of *body labor*, which looks at *labor* relations between workers and clients to develop the *triangular system of labor relationships* concept.[6]

More specifically, the triangular system of labor relationships concept highlights three sets of interconnected interactions on the shop floor. Interactions between the owner and clients, the owner and workers, and the workers and clients form the three legs of a triangle. Together, these interactions constitute a *system* of racialized and class-based labor relationships that were necessary for the two salons I studied to sustain business relations in non-coethnic neighborhoods that catered primarily to black and Latino clients. The owners operated at the apex of the triangle, bridging workers and clients, because they spoke English and Vietnamese, had lived in the United States longer than the workers, and were more knowledgeable about how to operate a business that catered to multiethnic clients. The workers, most of whom did not speak English, relied on the owners to help them communicate with the clients. Although clients are typically supposed to operate at the apex of triangular relations in a service economy, subtle racialized cues in these salons upheld a racial hierarchy that placed Asians (in this case Vietnamese) entrepreneurs above black and Latino clients and their coethnic workers.

This study of Vietnamese-owned nail salons located in majority black and Latino neighborhoods sheds new light on racialized labor relations among owners, coethnic workers, and clients in one niche market of immigrant businesses. Through the empirical examination of two particular instances of a triangular system of labor relations, this study demonstrates that power imbalances based in economics, labor, language, and race/ethnicity all interact within the space of immigrant small businesses.

Racialized and Class-Based Relations

This case study focuses on two nail salons that were owned and operated by ethnic Vietnamese but catered primarily to black and Latino clients.[14] By taking an empirical turn toward three aspects of shop relations between (1) owners (merchants) and clients, (2) owners and workers, and (3) workers and clients, this article shows how the *intra*ethnic and *inter*racial relations among workers, clients, and owners were embedded in a triangular system of labor relations. Together, these three legs of the triangle provide a unique window into racialized and class-based labor conditions and relations within a thriving immigrant industry.

The first leg of the triangle looks at race and labor relations between owners and clients. The Vietnamese owners I studied strategically chose to open salons in predominantly black and Latino/a neighborhoods to avoid *intraethnic* competition with coethnic Vietnamese in their respective enclaves and to avoid the feelings of racial inferiority and class degradation that other Vietnamese salon owners experienced in predominantly white neighborhoods. Yet at the same time, fears of downward assimilation inhibited them from settling in the very communities that they served, thereby reproducing the kind of racial triangulation that elevates whites and treats blacks and Latinos as inferior.

The second leg consists of relations between owners and workers. Under the system of *an chia* (split profits), workers took 60 percent and owners took 40 percent of the earnings from services they provided to the clients. On the surface, this system appeared to make workers individual entrepreneurs within a larger enterprise. However, because owners also provided nail services to the clients, a deeper ethnographic analysis reveals that owners were able to exploit workers by having them perform the least desirable tasks and lowest paying services. This economic exploitation overlapped with spheres of care in the workplace as workers depended on their coethnic owners to provide them with culturally accepting work environments. As such, coethnic employment catering to black and Latino communities blocked workers' upward mobility while providing them with some relief from racial and class degradation in predominantly white neighborhoods or businesses.

The third leg of the triangle focuses on relations between workers and clients. These relations depended a great deal on the owners' presence. Workers relied on owners to provide clients highly personalized services, while workers provided fast and efficient routinized nail services because of their limited English skills. This division of labor between owners and workers shaped the triangular system of relations among owners, workers, and clients as Vietnamese immigrants set up businesses in neighborhoods with a diverse set of clients outside of culturally protected enclaves.

By capturing the detailed micro-level processes involved in interactive and bodily service work, this study problematizes a simplistic understanding of immigrant entrepreneurship and the costs and benefits of coethnic employment. I show that labor exploitation is embedded within a broader context of racial exclusion of nonwhite clients, owners, and workers in the United States.

Vietnamese Nail Salons in the United States

From the early 1920s to the late 1960s, manicures and pedicures were a luxury service provided to the rich, mainly by black working-class women.[18] During the late 1970s and into the 1980s, the racial composition of nail services changed as Vietnamese and Korean immigrants opened an array of high-tech nail salons. These salons offered acrylics, fiberglass, paraffin, UV topcoats, silk wraps, gels, airbrushing, reflexology, and even nail painting, in which "patterns [were] sprayed and painted onto natural nails or, onto nail tips."[19] As Willet points out, "New immigrants, particularly from Vietnam and Korea, successfully courted a new working-class clientele who would embrace nail art, lengthy fake talons, and mini-massages, all of which helped transform nail salons into one of the fastest growing businesses in the late twentieth century."[20]

By the early 2000s, Vietnamese manicurists made up approximately 40 percent of the nail industry nationwide.[21] Today, the estimates are up to nearly 80 percent.[22] Of all Vietnamese workers in the United States, 5 percent are manicurists, compared to only 0.04 percent of non-Vietnamese workers.[23] Vietnamese immigrants entered the nail salon industry in large numbers during the 1990s, beginning in areas with large Vietnamese enclaves, such as Southern California, and spreading throughout the country. In California, Vietnamese constitute 60 percent of all manicurists statewide, with the largest shares in Santa Clara County and Los Angeles/Orange Counties.[24] Federman et al. argue that Vietnamese immigrants appear to have been responsible for innovations in the marketing of manicures, such as stand-alone nail salons, that have increased the demand for manicurists.[25]

Although Vietnamese manicurists are heavily concentrated in metropolitan areas with Vietnamese enclaves, in recent years many Vietnamese entrepreneurs have opted to start businesses in white and majority-black or -Latino neighborhoods.[26] Immigrants looking to start a business with lower start-up costs where they can capitalize on the economies of scale and provide minimal emotional labor tend to move into poorer urban neighborhoods and serve a diverse nonwhite clientele.[27]

The steady growth of Vietnamese nail salons outside of ethnic enclaves provides an opportunity to examine how immigrant businesses fare in a broader market. For this research, I chose to study two nail salons, one in Northern California (East Bay area) and one in Southern California (Inland Empire area). Each of these nail salons was located within an hour's drive from their respective ethnic enclaves in Orange County and San Jose, the two areas with the largest concentrations of Vietnamese immigrants in the United States.[28] Both salons were located in shopping areas frequented by black and Latino consumers. Hi-Tech Nails in California's Inland Empire was located in a complex next to a small Latino grocery store and a Mexican restaurant.[29] Fantasy Nails was situated in the East Bay beside an African American hair salon and a Mexican wedding dress shop. During the time of my observations, Hi-Tech Nails never had a white client, while Fantasy Nails did have a few.

Fostering Regular Clientele: Owner–Client Relations

Claire Kim proposes that racialized relations in the United States involve *racial triangulation*, in which Asians are simultaneously constructed as a model minority in relation to black

Americans and ostracized from white communities.[31] I apply and expand Kim's concept by explaining how Jennifer and Linda not only capitalized on racial triangulation by strategically choosing to open salons in black and Latino neighborhoods instead of in white or coethnic neighborhoods, but also created a new racial triangulation in the absence of whites that racialized Latino clients as docile and blacks as deviant.

Linda, the owner of Hi-Tech Nails in Southern California, and Jennifer, the owner of Fantasy Nails, expressed their desire to avoid feelings of racial exclusion and inferiority in relation to white clients and their distaste for opening salons in white neighborhoods. Prior to opening Hi-Tech Nails, Linda spent a few months working for "high-class white people" in Huntington Beach, California, where a good friend owned a salon. Linda said,

> I hated working in that salon. One time, a white woman came in. She sat down and started to order me around. She was like, "I want you to get up and grab that bottle of polish for me." I didn't say anything to her, but then she turned to the other clients in the store and caused a scene in the shop. I got so mad that I told her to get up and leave the store [Vietnamese translated to English]. I told her, "You pay me 100 dollar, I still no do your nail if you talk to me like that. I no need your money" [spoken in English].

Linda told me that she quit the salon in Huntington Beach because she experienced frequent racial and class degradation like the incident with the white client. In addition, Linda explained that she did not want to work for white people because to her, those clients wanted more than just a good nail job, requiring what Linda called "talking service."[32]

In Kang's study, Korean owners opened salons in predominantly minority neighborhoods primarily to avoid the extensive emotional labors required in white middle-class neighborhoods,[33] but the Vietnamese owners in this study had another reason as well: stiff competition within their respective enclaves motivated them to [leave the enclave]. When I asked Linda and Jennifer why they chose not to open salons in Orange County or San Jose, where there were large concentrations of coethnics, they told me that they did not want to work for Vietnamese clients. Linda said,

> I live in Little Saigon, but I came out here to open a business because I didn't want to work for Vietnamese people. The competition is so high that it drops the prices down very low, but then the people there expect high-class services. They are very picky. Everything has to be perfect, so you end up spending more time on a smaller number of clients. And because we speak Vietnamese, you end up having to talk to the people. I don't like talking to Vietnamese clients because they gossip a lot and they show off a lot so that people are always competing with each other about who has a nicer car or big house.[34]

Like the Korean merchants in Jennifer Lee's study, who were more likely to engage in *intra*-ethnic than *inter*ethnic competition,[35] Linda described preferring to work with black and Latino clients rather than competing with salons in her coethnic Vietnamese community.

In contrast to the discomfort she felt in predominantly white neighborhoods and the competition she felt in the ethnic enclave, Linda expressed her readiness to work in a black and Latino neighborhood because her clients were nicer and because she felt empowered to capitalize on economies of scale. When I asked her why she chose to work in a predominantly black and Latino area, Jennifer said to me (in Vietnamese),

> I work mainly for Mexican [Latino/a] and black clients because, unlike Vietnamese or white clients, they care more about the quality of the work done on their nails than the quality of service. Some of the Mexican people don't even speak English, so they just point to me what they want done and I do it. I know that I could make a lot more money if I spoke great English and catered to rich white people who care more about [servility]. But Mexican and black people don't expect me to talk to them. White people are paying higher prices for talking services whereas my clients pay for nail services.

By catering to black and Latino working-class clients, the Vietnamese immigrant owners successfully created a niche that provided clients with quick, high-quality nail work involving little servility or emotional labor. The language barrier between themselves and their clients was actually a boon in these neighborhoods because it allowed the owners to speed up service to bring in a larger number of clients.

[Outside the ethnic enclave,] Linda and Jennifer were "racially triangulated"[36] insofar as they racialized themselves (and had been racialized by others) as inferior to whites but superior to blacks and Latinos. As Kim notes in her study of racial triangulation, the "racial order does not involve a simple vertical hierarchy (A over B over C), but rather a field constructed on at least two dimensions or axes, that of superior/inferior and that of insider/ foreigner."[37] However, my conversations with these owners also revealed a more nuanced layer to the *racial order* vis-à-vis black and Latino clients.

In the physical absence of whites, Linda and Jennifer both constructed a new racial triangulation among Asians, Latinos, and blacks by separating Latinos as docile from blacks as deviant. Black marginalization guided the interactions between owners and clients such that Latino clients were preferred as less "picky." Linda said (in Vietnamese), "In this store, my clients are nice people. I love working for Mexican people. They are the sweetest. They never complain, they are not picky, they are easy going and they don't expect us to talk and talk. I like the black people who come in here too, but some are harder to deal with." In a context where whites rarely frequented her salon, Linda constructed a racial hierarchy where Mexican clients were slightly more desirable than blacks because to her they were less demanding and less likely to complain about poor service. She explained to me that when Latinos did complain they were often quiet and rarely caused a scene in front of other customers. In my own observations on the shop floor, I witnessed several of the Latino clients complaining about a poor nail job. However, when they did so, it was often a quiet interaction between the worker and the client. For example, while observing a Latino woman getting a manicure, I saw a look of disapproval on her face. When I looked down I noticed several small bubbles from the nail polish forming over her fingernail. The Vietnamese manicurist noticed it, and instead of removing the polish and starting over, she proceeded to try to fix it with more polish and then moved on to the next nail. In that moment the Latino client who spoke very little English pointed her finger to the problem area for the worker to fix. The worker nodded her head and proceeded to remove the polish to start over. Several of the Latino patrons spoke very little English and often communicated through sign language in a way that did not involve other customers in the store.

Although it was a rare occurrence for black clients to spend a long time complaining about the nail service, on the rare occasions that they did, they complained to other customers in the store. These incidents were humiliating to Linda, and she tried to avoid them. However, because both Linda and Jennifer were able to capitalize on economies of scale in neighborhoods with working-class clients of color by dropping their prices so low that clients knew they would have to pay higher prices elsewhere, they had no problem turning down picky clients because they never had a shortage of clients. Linda further explained, "I could never do that if I was catering to high-class white people. I would lose business."

The move [outside the enclave] allowed Vietnamese nail salon owners to capitalize on this racial triangulation for their *economic advancement* by escaping competition in the enclave and capitalizing on economies of scale in predominantly black and Latino neighborhoods. Moreover, this also enabled their *social mobility* as Vietnamese owners were conscious to avoid downward assimilation for their children by choosing to reside within their respective ethnic enclaves. As a result, this model of immigrant mobility and incorporation through entrepreneurship [outside the ethnic enclave] ultimately reproduced the situation of racial triangulation.

Though Linda strategically chose to establish a business in an area that catered mainly to black and Latino clients, neither Linda nor her husband expressed a desire to invest in that community by settling in a residential area with a high concentration of black and Latino families. When I asked Linda why she chose to live in the Vietnamese enclave of Orange County as opposed to the Inland Empire, where her business was located, she said that she and her husband "do not want our kids to go to school with black and Mexican kids. We want our kids to have Vietnamese friends at school who study hard and stay out of trouble. Black and Mexican kids all hang out and get in trouble. I see little girls come in here and get manicures. Vietnamese people, we know better. We save every penny and we work hard." Both Linda and Jennifer held racial stereotypes around the "deviant" lifestyles of lower-income blacks and Latinos, and they feared downward mobility in their children's assimilation.[38] Linda's conscious choice to commute forty-five minutes each way to work every day so that she could live in the Vietnamese enclave illustrates how owners capitalized on this racial triangulation for their economic and social mobility.

In her book *Civility in the City,* Jennifer Lee recognizes that racialized conflicts exist among Koreans, Jewish people, and black Americans, but she points to the ways in which Korean business owners demonstrate routine, civil, and positive interactions with multiethnic clients on a day-to-day basis.[40]

In my conversations with the clients, they often told me that they enjoyed getting their nails done in these two salons because of the *quality* of the nail job and the low prices. One client said, "I love having Jennifer do my nails even though she talks on the phone with her friends while she does them because she does a great job. These suckers [her acrylic nails] will stay on for a long time. There are other salons where I get my nails done and not only do they cost more, but they all fall off after one week." The clients were usually polite and apologetic to the owners when they had complaints. For instance, one of the workers, Vuong, finished a pedicure for a black client who was dressed in plaid pajama pants and a white T-shirt. The woman did not like the nail design and said to Linda (the owner), "I don't like this design; they don't match. Can you do another design, any design? I am sorry." Linda responded, "Yeah, I do design again for you okay." Linda went over and redid the design, and the woman tipped both Linda and Vuong saying, "I know I can be difficult sometimes," before leaving the store.

A close look at the exchanges that occurred between the owners and their clients demonstrates that their exchanges were civil, polite, and nonconfrontational. This civility was possible because the owners were able to interact politely with the client in English and then vent their frustrations to the workers in Vietnamese. However, while civility in the nail salons fostered positive surface-level interactions between the owners and their clients, Kim's concept of racial triangulation is crucial here for deepening my analysis. The implicit hierarchy that sets whites as superior to blacks and Asians makes it such that Linda avoided working with white customers so that she would have the power to reject customers whom she considered "rude" or "picky." At the same time, the inferior subject position of blacks in this racial triangulation prompted black clients to apologize for legitimate complaints to avoid reinforcing broad stereotypes of black women as "bossy" and "complaining"—stereotypes that even the owners held. This is very different from the white clients in Huntington Beach, who felt entitled to their complaints, prompting Linda to quit.

An Chia (Split Profits): Owner–Worker Relations

In her book *Doméstica*, Pierrette Hondagneu-Sotelo indicates that newer immigrants often experience economic exploitation from their more established coethnics. These new immigrants often find themselves stuck in the *worker* position and have a hard time moving up to become an *owner*.[43] The two nail salons I observed provide a critical case study of coethnic exploitation because of their pay structure: Vietnamese nail salons in California operated under the practice of *an chia* (splitting profits), where the owner does not pay the workers a wage. Instead workers and owners split the clients' payments sixty-forty.[45] This allowed owners to capitalize on a coethnic labor supply of non-English-speaking workers.[46] Linda stated that the *an chia* system "makes workers feel like they are independent entrepreneurs." When I asked her to elaborate, she said, "Vietnamese people are business people. We have an entrepreneurial spirit (*mau kinh doan*) we had to be like that in Vietnam to survive. No one wants to feel like they work for someone else. [*An chia*] makes the workers feel like they own their own business. They are just renting a stall [booth where they service clients] in a larger shop and they rent the stall for 40 percent of all services. That pays for the rent, electricity, and the bills to run this place." When I asked Jennifer about her take on the split profit system, she said, "Being an owner of a store isn't nearly as glamorous as it sounds. When you are the owner, you don't just sit and watch people work. In the nail business, my profits come from my work [*lam cong*]. The money that I get from my workers is very little. . . . The money that I make and take home comes from the nails that I do." According to Jennifer, under this system, owners and workers profit and lose money together. Both owners believed that their workers were operating as independent entrepreneurs within the space of their salons. In practice, however, the split profit system was not so straightforward. Owners and employees indeed shared the same shop floor, but owners controlled who took clients and which services they performed. When business was slow, owners were motivated to take on clients themselves to get the full payment instead of the 40 percent that they would receive if a worker performed the service. Moreover, shop owners typically took higher-paying clients who wanted acrylic nails, leaving the lower-paying clients to the workers. Even though workers were allowed to keep their own tips, these were usually smaller than the tips owners received because they worked with lower-paying clients performing services that were less artistic and/or less interactive. Attention to the distribution of labor reveals that, in effect, payments were not split sixty-forty between workers and storeowners because owners decided how services were allocated. In this way, working for a coethnic boss involved economically exploitative working conditions.

Moreover, all occupations have tasks that are undesirable or considered "dirty."[47] In studying occupational "dirty work," Everett Hughes calls attention to the study of the "arrangements and devices by which men [or women] make their work tolerable, or even glorious to themselves and others."[48] As an owner, Linda acknowledged that workers generally performed both the lowest paid and least desirable activities like pedicures, which involved cleaning and polishing the client's feet, and that owners performed the most desirable activities like nail designs. In both salons, the owner typically performed pedicures only when all of her workers were occupied with other clients. It was very common to see two different people work on the same client. For example, if the owner was doing a pedicure and another client walked in asking for a full set of acrylic nails (the most expensive service in the nail salon), rather than finishing the first client's pedicure, the owner would tell the worker to finish the pedicure and move to work on the new client. This was a typical practice when owners worked on pedicures. In addition, when two people worked on the same client, the owner and worker split the tips fifty-fifty, and then split the payment for the nail service sixty (worker) to forty (owner).

Under the split-profit system, owners made workers feel responsible for their low earnings because workers operated under the illusion that they were small entrepreneurs within a larger enterprise. However, the owners did not feel threatened by the workers' potential to open a competing establishment for two key reasons: workers' language abilities and time of migration. First, the workers' limited ability to speak English meant they depended on the owners to establish and maintain personal relations with the clients. Although owners communicated with their clients mostly in broken English, their language skills enabled them to figure out their clients' needs and translate communication between clients and workers. Jennifer, the owner of Fantasy Nails, described the triangular relationship:

> The difference between being a worker and a boss when it comes to interacting with clients is that as a boss, you have to do all of the talking with the clients. Nails are good work for women who just came over from Vietnam, especially uneducated women like Loan [an employee] because they don't have to learn English and they don't have to talk to clients. But as the owner, I have to do all of that for them. I am the one who greets the customer. I am the one who talks to them even if [the conversation] is short. These women who just came over from Vietnam, they don't know the American way to work.

In the last part of this statement, Jennifer described workers' dependence on owners as tied to language skills, time of migration, and owners' ability to assert a certain kind of superiority over workers. As an owner, Jennifer suggested that she knew more than her workers about how to do "business" with American clients, not only because she had the language skills but also because she had been in the United States longer. Owners in both salons reinforced their "American" way of doing business by using the American names Linda and Jennifer, while the workers tend to go by their Vietnamese names.[49] Whenever a client walked into the store, Linda and Jennifer were always the ones to ask, "Can I help you?" and to tell the workers what to do.

Although the workers performed the "dirty work" in both salons, it would be inaccurate to say that the workers expressed feeling exploited. When I asked the workers about their working conditions, they often talked about how their bosses offered them a comfortable working environment. It was not uncommon to witness workers eating a homemade Vietnamese lunch, taking a nap, talking on the phone, watching Vietnamese movies, or joking with their bosses. Workers said that the nail salon provided them with a comfortable, well-paying job without having to learn English or work for an American boss who would not let them have downtime in the store. Truc said, "I don't speak English, so there are very few jobs that would pay me as much as Jennifer does. When I work here, I can talk to someone in Vietnamese and eat Vietnamese foods. I am grateful to Jennifer because she picks me up from my house to go to work every morning and she drops me off in the evening [Truc did not know how to drive]. I can't imagine an American boss doing the same for me." From the workers' perspective, the flexible and easy-going environment coethnic owners provided humanized their dirty work.

Rather than creating conditions of outright exploitation, the distribution of labor and dirty work created barriers for workers' mobility. The structure of these two salons did not encourage the workers to learn to speak English or to establish a stable client base that would move with the worker if she opened her own shop. However, the owners provided workers with a culturally comfortable work environment and seemingly better working conditions than they could expect with non-Vietnamese employers. Furthermore, the owners of both salons took steps to restore their workers' sense of dignity when a client complained about a nail design. The owners also took care never to publically scold their workers because they feared that workers would leave for other Vietnamese nail salons if they did not feel supported by the owners. Jennifer, for example, said, "In San Jose, the Vietnamese are so competitive with each other. Everyone wants to be richer, more beautiful . . . than other people. Here, there are less Vietnamese people. . . . It is mostly black and Mexican so we have to stick together. I have to support them. . . . [Kimberly: Why?] Because they will leave and I will have no workers." From this perspective, ethnic businesses [outside the enclave] benefit both the worker and the owner. The ethnic business allows the owner to escape low-wage jobs in the secondary labor market and experience upward mobility, while the workers avoid joblessness or employment with owners with whom they cannot communicate.[51]

Routinized Labors: Client–Worker Relationships

In her study, Kang points out differences in the kinds of *body labors* workers provided to clients from different racial and class groups.[52] In salons that catered to white clients in upper-class neighborhoods, workers provided clients *pampering body labor*, which involved a great deal of emotional labor while simultaneously upholding the racialized and classed privileges of their white clients.[53] In lower-cost salons that catered to black and Latino clients, Kang describes a *routinized body labor*, which provided clients with low-cost and expedient services. The Vietnamese-owned nail salons I studied showed a similar division of personalized and routinized labor,[54] but this division occurred between owners and workers rather than across different salons. In both Hi-Tech and Fantasy Nails the owners provided clients with limited but personalized emotional labor, while the workers provided clients with routinized bodily labors. Interactions between workers and clients could be quite long (some services lasted up to two hours), but they mainly involved long periods of silence punctuated by occasional small talk. To develop a loyal client base, the owners added more personalized service by remembering client names and service preferences. This division of labor allowed the salon to capitalize on economies of scale that came with expedient *routinized body labors* while building client loyalty to the salon.[55]

Worker-client relationships at both Hi-Tech Nails and Fantasy Nails depended on the presence of the owner, where workers performed nail work as quickly as possible to maximize economies of scale and owners did all of the "talking work" with clients. Whenever clients wanted to communicate something to the workers, they depended on the owners to help with translation. For example, one afternoon at Fantasy Nails, Truc was painting a black woman's toenails with a tiger-stripe design in black and orange. After about fifteen minutes, the client tried to tell Truc that she did not like the pattern. Jennifer interjected and asked, "Is this okay?" The client pointed to her toes and said to Jennifer, "This looks like a bunch of dots. I want a design like that [pointing to the model nail]. What is the problem?" Jennifer quickly responded, "Okay. You no like it, I take it off." The client repeated, "I want it like that [pointing again to the design on the model nail], but with orange." Jennifer said, "Okay try again," and then turned to Truc and in Vietnamese instructed, "Do the tiger design but use the orange highlight and the silver in the middle. If the woman doesn't like it take it off and redo it. Just do it until we get it right. She is difficult [*kho*], but she is right."

In this situation the owners' presence was necessary to the client–worker interaction. Truc and the client both needed the owner to help facilitate the conversation around client requests. More importantly, the dynamic of this relationship allowed the owners to maintain a personal relationship with the customers while also maintaining distance between workers and customers to avoid worrying about losing clients should a worker decide to open a competing salon. Notably, Jennifer and Linda went by their chosen American names so that the clients would have an easier time remembering them and referring to them by name, while all of the workers went by their Vietnamese names—names that the clients rarely remembered and could hardly pronounce.

Moreover, Jennifer and Linda reinforced racial triangulation on the shop floor by providing room for their workers to talk freely about the clients in Vietnamese. While sitting in Fantasy Nails, a black woman dressed in black pants and a purple top walked into a store. She said, "I need to get one of my nails fixed—it broke." Jennifer told Truc to file the woman's nail down and begin putting on a new fake nail. The woman started to talk to Truc about how she could afford to pay only three dollars to get her nail fixed. Truc did not respond. The woman repeated, "That's all I can afford. I know you wish that I was getting more done, but I just can't afford it. I sure hate to admit it. I am broke. People look at me like I have committed a crime or something because I am broke." No one responded to her or tried to comfort her.

Jennifer said to Truc in Vietnamese, "This woman is crazy. Why does she talk so much? Who does she think you are?" The woman continued to talk to Truc, and she did not respond. After Truc finished her nails, the woman paid and walked out, saying to me, "These people in here can't even carry a decent conversation. I didn't come in here to talk to a wall." In instances like these, the workers' racial prejudices emerged on the shop floor as they complained about their clients openly in another language. The fact that workers had no problem calling a client "crazy" on numerous occasions or talking about their clients in Vietnamese on the shop floor reinforces Kim's concept of racial triangulation and the implicit racial hierarchies not just between the owners and their clients *but also* between the workers and their clients.

Importantly, the ability of the owners and workers to talk about their clients in front of their faces, albeit in Vietnamese, enabled them to take advantage of their linguistic abilities in the triangle to create a safe space that made the work more pleasant. At the same time, the worker–owner solidarity in these kinds of interactions reproduced the workers' foreignness in front of the clients, making them less threatening to owners who feared the possibility that the workers would leave and take their client base with them. This racial triangulation on the shop floor illuminates broader relations within and across minority groups in the U.S. As such, while Vietnamese entrepreneurs capitalize on racial triangulation, they are also implicated in it and harmed by it with respect to their own social integration into U.S. society.

Conclusion

Research on immigrant entrepreneurship [outside the ethnic enclave, or the "enclave export sector"[56]] overlooks the multiple relationships that shape workplace dynamics on the shop floor. This article considers entrepreneurship by Vietnamese immigrants out of their enclosed enclaves into racially diverse neighborhoods and communities. Owner, client, and worker interactions formed a triangular system of labor relations, in which workers and owners both engaged in civil interactions with their clients, but those interactions were racially coded within an implicit hierarchy. Moreover, in the absence of whites and with the presence of Latinos, a new racial triangulation emerged on the shop floor as the Vietnamese owners constructed Latinos as quiet and docile and blacks as deviant but American.

Owners who strategically opened nail salons in diverse neighborhoods catering to a predominantly black and Latino clientele escaped intraethnic competition in their respective enclaves and racial degradation in neighborhoods that cater to middle- or upper-class whites. However, as they move into these neighborhoods, their stereotypes, perceptions, and racist attitudes about the communities that they enter also come to the fore. The owners and workers in both salons chose to commute nearly forty-five minutes each way to work every day so that they could experience economic upward mobility while being careful to avoid social downward mobility for their children.

Ethnographic analysis reveals the contours of racialized and classed relations that structured the division of labor within these immigrant ethnic businesses. The distribution of emotional and bodily labors between owners and clients allowed salons to capitalize on economies of scale to serve a higher number of clientele. By employing newer immigrants who spoke very little English, owners were able to provide the clients with a more personalized service while the workers provided the routinized labors. These relationships established client loyalty with the owner and the shop rather than with individual workers who provided the nail services, thereby diminishing the threat of competition should workers eventually save enough money to open up their own salon.

This work is significant because it provides insight into one mode of immigrant entrepreneurship embedded in intersectional relations of race and class. Importantly, these salons reproduce hierarchies of race as white privilege and power is a constant backdrop for the triangular system of labor relations and as Vietnamese immigrants capitalize on a minority culture of mobility that constructs Latinos and blacks as inferior. Nail salons are not just spaces of beauty that allow clients to walk out feeling relaxed, attractive, and desirable;

rather, these are highly racialized and classed spaces that anchor new immigrants and influence their broader patterns of integration within a majority–minority context.

Notes

1. Adele Pham, *Viet Nail Teaser* (Brooklyn: Vimeo, 2013).
2. David Kallick, James Parrott, and Frank Mauro, *Immigrant Small Business Owners: A Significant and Growing Part of the Economy* (New York: Fiscal Policy Institute's Immigration Research Initiative, 2012).
4. Beginning in the 1980s, research on the economic fate of immigrants began to examine employment of various types of urban ethnic enclaves. See, for example, Kenneth Wilson and W. A. Martin, "Ethnic Enclaves: A Comparison of Cuban and Black Economies in Miami," *American Journal of Sociology* 88 (1982): 135–60; Alejandro Portes and Robert Bach, *Latin Journey: Cuban and Mexican Immigrants in the United States* (Berkeley: University of California Press, 1985); Alejandro Portes and Leif Jensen, "The Enclave and the Entrants: Patterns of Ethnic Enterprise in Miami before and after Mariel," *American Sociological Review* 54 (1989): 929–49.
5. See Claire Kim, *Bitter Fruit: The Politics of Black–Korean Conflict in New York City* (New Haven, Conn.: Yale University Press, 2003); Jennifer Lee, *Civility in the City: Blacks, Jews, and Koreans in Urban America* (Cambridge, Mass.: Harvard University Press, 2006); Pyong Gap Min, *Caught in the Middle: Korean Communities in New York and Los Angeles* (Berkeley: University of California Press, 1996); Kwang Kim, *Koreans in the Hood: Conflict with African Americans* (Baltimore: Johns Hopkins University Press, 1999).
6. Kim, *Bitter Fruit*; Miliann Kang, *The Managed Hand: Race, Gender, and the Body* (Berkeley: University of California Press, 2010).
14. Wilson and Portes, "Immigrant Enclaves."
18. Julie Willet, "Hands across the Table: A Short History of the Manicurist in the Twentieth Century," *Journal of Women's History* 17, no. 3 (2005): 59–80.
19. Margot Mifflin, "Nail Art Creates Fingertip Renaissance," *New York Times*, July 14, 1996.
20. Willet, "Hands across the Table," 8.
21. "Briefs: Vietnamese Americans Warned about Salon Product," *AsianWeek*, 2000. February 9, 2000 http://www.highbeam.com/doc/1P1-79130044.html.
22. Karen Bates, "Nailing the American Dream, with Polish," *American Dreams: Then and Now*, November 18, 2013.
23. Maya Federman, David Harrington, and Kathy Krynski, "The Impact of State Licensing Regulations on Low-Skilled Immigrants: The Case of Vietnamese Manicurists," *American Economic Review* 96, no. 2 (2006): 237–41.
24. Ibid.
25. Maya Federman, David Harrington, and Kathy Krynski, "Vietnamese Manicurists: Are Immigrants Displacing Natives or Finding New Nails to Polish?," *Industrial and Labor Relations Review* 59, no. 2 (2006): 302–18.
26. Ibid.
27. Kang, *Managed Hand.*

28. James Freeman, *Hearts of Sorrow: Vietnamese-American Lives* (Stanford: Stanford University Press, 1991).

29. All names have been changed to conceal the identity of the nail salons and the people working in them.

31. Kim, *Bitter Fruit.*

32. Arlie Hochschild, *The Managed Heart: Commercialization of Human Feeling* (Berkeley: University of California Press, 2003).

33. Kang, *Managed Hand.*

34. Little Saigon is a Vietnamese enclave in Orange County. It has the largest concentration of ethnic Vietnamese in the United States.

35. Lee, *Civility in the City.*

36. Kim, *Bitter Fruit.*

37. Ibid., 16.

38. Portes and Zhou, "New Second Generation."

40. Lee, *Civility in the City.*

43. Pierrette Hondagneu-Sotelo, *Domestica: Immigrant Workers Cleaning and Caring in the Shadows of Affluence* (Berkeley: University of California Press, 2001).

45. When a client comes in and gets his or her nails done, the worker and the boss split the payment. For example, if the client pays ten dollars for the services, the worker will receive six dollars and the owner four. The worker also usually keeps the tip.

46. Willet, "Hands across the Table."

47. Hannah Meara, "Honor in Dirty Work: The Case of American Meat Cutters and Turkish Butchers," *Work and Occupations* 1 (1974): 259–63.

48. Everett Hughes, "Work and Self," in *The Sociological Eye: Selected Papers* (Chicago: Aldine-Atherton, 1971), 342.

49. The owners Jennifer (Mai) and Linda (Hanh) went by their Vietnamese names when interacting with me and with the workers in their stores.

51. Ibid.

52. Kang, *Managed Hand.*

53. Ibid.

54. Ibid.

55. Ibid.

56. Zhou, Min (1992). *Chinatown: The Socioeconomic Potential of an Urban Enclave.* Philadelphia Temple University Press. Min Zhou divides the enclave economy into two sectors. On the one hand, the *enclave protected sector,* which has received the most scholarly attention, arises within the ethnic community and is oriented toward coethnic goods and service activities. This sector is protected from structural changes in the larger economy because it is secured by its own exclusive capital market, labor market, and consumer market. On the other hand, the *enclave export sector* is oriented toward the broader economy outside of their respective enclaves.

CHAPTER 22

Becoming a (Pan)ethnic Attorney*

How Asian American and Latino Law Students Manage Dual Identities

Yung-Yi Diana Pan

Managing professional and personal identities often is stressful to upwardly mobile racialized individuals. In this essay Yung-Yi Pan examines how Asian American and Latina/o law students negotiate ***ethnic*** *and* ***panethnic identities*** *while learning to become lawyers. She contends that managing dual identities creates a (pan)ethnic duty among Asian American and Latina/o law students. While there are many career options for law students, most, irrespective of race, pursue initial careers at law firms. What leads them there? How do racialization and expectations play a role in this career aspiration? And how do students negotiate the pressure to give back or manage the internally/externally imposed duty they feel to serve respective communities? She finds that Asian American and Latina/o law students draw on a repertoire of strategies (marginal panethnicity, tempered altruism, and instrumental ethnicity) that encompass different accounts, identities, and roles enabling creativity and elasticity for professional and personal identities. The findings suggest that* ***panethnicity*** *remains salient for upwardly mobile individuals of color, even those who do not ostensibly appear to be concerned with panethnic communities and causes.*

Source: Adapted from Yung-Yi Diana Pan, "Becoming a (Pan)ethnic Attorney: How Asian American and Latino Law Students Manage Dual Identities," *Sociological Forum*, Volume 30, Issue 1, pages 148–169. John Wiley and Sons, 2015.

*Some text and accompanying endnotes have been omitted. Please consult the original source.

Questions to Consider

How do Asian and Latina/o American law students negotiate their identities as individuals, lawyers, and members of ethnic and panethnic groups? Is there a choice in identifying as a lawyer only or are they destined to be an Asian lawyer or Latina/o lawyer in their chosen careers? Why do ethnic/panethnic identities matter for these student lawyers, even for those who say it doesn't?

Introduction

> *[N]o matter what anybody does—they can say all they want about "oh, I don't owe anything to anyone." Or, "I don't owe anything to my Asian community" or whatever community we classify them in. I don't care what they say about that because at the end of the day, you look at someone and it registers in your head. . . . People can say whatever they want to say . . . it would be great to live in their utopia where race doesn't play a role into our existence. . . . Just because I didn't have people in my family that were put in those internment camps in Southern California and in Utah, doesn't mean the Japanese struggle doesn't affect me in some way or another. (Estelle, Chinese Vietnamese)*

The United States has a mixed-race president, a Latina Supreme Court Justice, and Asian Americans make up the majority on California's Supreme Court. Ostensibly, it seems that this country is indeed "postracial" and that race no longer poses an obstacle for upwardly mobile individuals of color. However, the [quote] above illustrate[s] that race, or panethnicity, structures how nonwhite law students think about their personal and professional lives. And as I argue in this article, panethnicity also structures their career trajectory. As budding attorneys, Asian American and Latino law students must assimilate standard, legal professional practices and expectations. They also negotiate identities as nonwhite individuals entering a predominantly white profession. Estelle's comment reflects the panethnic negotiation of Asian American and Latino law students in this study, and captures how racialization is a process devoid of ethnic differences. Although she is not ethnically Japanese, historical experiences affect how she is perceived as a racialized individual in law school, and racialization further influences others' expectations of her. Susan bemoans the expectation *of* and *for* students of color to pursue public interest work. Estelle's and Susan's comments represent common sentiments that speak to the ways that Asian American and Latino law students manage simultaneous professional and (pan)ethnic identities.[1]

I examine in this article how these law students negotiate (pan)ethnic identities while learning to become lawyers. I contend that managing dual identities creates a sense of (pan) ethnic duty among Asian American and Latino law students. I focus on those with a normative career trajectory—that is, planning to work in law firms, at least initially. Professional socialization begins the moment a law student walks through the law school doors. While there are many career options for law students, most, irrespective of race, pursue initial careers at law firms. What leads them there? How do racialization and expectations play a role in this career aspiration? And how do students negotiate the pressure to give back, or manage the internally/externally imposed duty they feel to serve respective communities?

Most literature on law school omits a central focus on race, or introduces it as an afterthought. Haven't law students, regardless of race, already "made it" by preparing to join one of the most elite professions? Some immigrant adaptation literature leads one to suppose so (Alba and Nee 2003; Bean and Stevens 2003; Lee and Bean 2007). In the aggregate, Asian American and Latino professionals are successfully adapting to mainstream America. However, most scholarship on race and ethnicity cautions that race continues to matter for upwardly mobile nonwhite individuals (Feagin 1991; Tuan 1998, 1999; Wilkins 1998). Panethnic identities are political, structural, and cultural, but these labels are ascribed through external forces, such as U.S. Census forms requiring identification as Asian, black, Hispanic/Latino, or white. When nonwhite law students adopt panethnic identities, they encounter internal tensions that highlight their "otherness" in this otherwise white profession.

How do (pan)ethnic identities matter while one undergoes legal socialization? To what extent do internalized expectations affect the way students think about their careers? In other words, does (pan)ethnicity matter? If so, how? Asian American and Latino law students who intend to work at law firms do not possess outward professional allegiances to (pan)ethnic communities. Firm-bound Asian American and Latino law students seemingly focus only on acquiring practical lawyering skills without particular political leanings, which differs from their public interest–minded peers whose career interests center on (pan)ethnic issues. By all ostensible measures, (pan)ethnic causes do not seem to matter for firm-bound students. However, they do. I argue that (pan)ethnic identities invoke an internalized struggle among Asian American and Latino law students leaning toward firm work. They contend with internal and external pressures to confirm and activate a sense of duty toward co-(pan)ethnics. This negotiation then encourages these students to adopt three strategies in order to manage their identities: marginal panethnicity, tempered altruism, and instrumental ethnicity. The strategies reflect how students think about becoming successful attorneys, and vary depending on students' backgrounds, cultural fluency, and rank of law school. These factors underscore how (pan)ethnic identities and affiliations inform integration into a mainstream profession.

Literature Review

Professional and Legal Education

Prior research on professional education describes the processes by which students learn how to become doctors, lawyers, social workers, and police officers, among others (Becker et al. 1961; Costello 2005; Erlanger and Klegon 1978; Mertz 2007; Van Maanen 1975). Current literature on professional, and especially legal, education identifies how professional socialization orients individuals toward corporate America (Erlanger et al. 1996; Granfield 1992; Schleef 2006; Stover 1989). Scholars describe that most students, without regard to race, start law school with a set of altruistic ideals, but become apathetic upon graduating, and join fellow alumni at law firms. A six-figure starting salary coupled with the opportunity to work on complex, high-profile cases prove irresistible and often alter students' original career plans.

While current literature on legal education engages the mechanisms of legal socialization, we still do not know how students of color extract and apply meaning to their own experiences. As agents of their own professional indoctrination, law students alter their career goals by rationalizing a need for high-quality training, and the availability of creative and meaningful work—goals met by an initial firm trajectory. Some scholars hint that white women and nonwhite students benefit least from a language and culture that boasts elitism, masculinity, and white-Anglo-Saxon-Protestant normativity (Fischer 1996; Mertz 2007). Often, these students feel marginalized in the classroom, or are less confident speaking in class compared with their upper-middle-class, white male peers. Current sociological literature fails to adequately address how intimate, subjective identities factor into law students' educational experiences.

What is the place of race and ethnicity in law student experiences? Law has, to this point, seemingly embraced and reproduced the status quo of "bleached out" attorneys (Wilkins 1998) to the detriment of those who deviate. "Bleached out" refers to attorneys of color who focus only on acquiring practical legal skills without acknowledging their racial background. The precedence of professional socialization literature focuses on the nitty-gritty of practical skills, and for the most part, does not assess how race matters for attorneys of color.

Intersections in Law

Although differences in racial, ethnic, and cultural history remain, some scholars argue that the matter of "race" remains poorly addressed in current socio-legal literature (Gómez 2004; Haney-Lopez 2006). The assumption is that in order to overcome racism (in law, and in society at large), one must first overcome race. Gómez (2004:455) critiques, "rarely have they [socio-legal scholars] made racial inequality, racism, or racial identity the central focus of their inquiry (the dependent variable), and thus a certain lopsidedness characterizes law and society scholarship on race." In so doing, scholars possess a limited understanding of race—one that neglects social, political, and individual experiences.

Theoretical charges spurred research into the unbleached ways that individual attorneys experience the profession in both the United States and the United Kingdom. For one, scholars contend that the legal profession reproduces white male hegemony (Epstein 1970, 1993; Garth and Sterling 2009; Sommerlad and Sanderson 1998; Sommerlad et al. 2010). Legal education also propagates such expectations (Mertz 2007; Moore 2008; Schleef 2006).

But how exactly is the profession masculine and white? Earlier works on gender in law underscore the dominant male culture to which women are expected to adapt (Epstein 1970, 1992, 1993; Pierce 1995; Sommerlad and Sanderson 1998). Women must aspire to become "Rambo litigators" (Pierce 1995) while simultaneously perform as "tinkerbells" (Epstein 1992). Human capital further favors male litigators as they are "in with the lads," while women are occasionally seen as "honorary men" (Sommerlad and Sanderson 1998). The honorary status is short-lived as "the sexual objectification of women must serve ultimately to further undermine the professional status and authority of the female lawyer and to rea rm stereotyped gender identities and hence relations of domination" (Sommerlad and Sanderson 1998:181). Moreover, the actual positions held by men and women, especially at large firms, reflect gender hierarchy wherein the former are attorneys and the latter are often paralegals subject to lower pay and lower prestige (Pierce 1995).

Parallel experiences exist between white women and nonwhite attorneys who seem to benefit from the profession's tolerance and openness to diversity, yet continue to face obstacles (Garth and Sterling 2009; Wilkins 2000; Wilkins and Gulati 1996). Aside from adopting a "bleached out" orientation to fit into the profession, lawyers of color seek alternative paths to be seen as "successful." Black attorneys learn to "do good" (i.e., take part in *pro bono* or other public service assignments) in order to "do well" (i.e., excel in the profession). To succeed as attorneys, "many of today's black corporate lawyers have formed close ties with black peers outside of their organizations" (Wilkins 2004:89), so long as it permits the black attorney to gain "expertise, credibility, and clout" (Garth 2004:105).

Although the scale appears to be tipped in favor of the status quo at the expense of nonwhite and white women attorneys, other research suggests that black women in predominantly white professions can succeed if they take advantage of their unique positions. Professional black women are not seen as potential career threats or sexual distractions, thus they garner colleague support and respect (Epstein 1973:932). Further, African American women attorneys who delay childbearing do not seem to suffer wage penalty (Blair-Loy and DeHart 2003). Despite some progress, black professionals continue to experience marginalization. For instance, black engineering and math students (both men and women) have to prove their intellect in academic programs where they are numerical minorities (McGee and Martin 2011). Those who persevere manage stereotypes by working hard to be perceived as smart, and taking on mentoring roles for future generations of black math and engineering students.

These findings speak to the racial inequalities in mainstream professions and education, including law. In general, nonwhite attorneys (black, Latino, Asian American, and Native American/American Indian) experience discrimination at work, and yearn for more mentorship and training from senior colleagues (Wilder 2008). While there is variation among racialized groups, the fact remains that nonwhite lawyers are neither separate nor equal.

Native-born, Asian Americans and Latinos are becoming a part of mainstream America, which is one indication of successful immigrant integration (Gordon 1964). Discrimination and exclusion of non–Anglo-Saxon Protestants mars the history of U.S. professions in the aggregate, but law served as a gateway to the mainstream for many European immigrants (Abel 1989). As the brief discussion demonstrates, current sociological scholarship have only begun to interrogate how panethnicity matters for Asian Americans and Latinos, who are making headway into mainstream professions. Comparing experiences among and between law students, I identify how they manage the tension between (pan)ethnic identities and professional socialization. I argue that Asian American and Latino law students on the firm trajectory use strategies that reveal variations in *how* they embrace their (pan)ethnic identities, and inform *what* they consider to be important for their professional goals and commitments.

This article is guided by the following questions: How do (pan)ethnic identities inform integration into an elite mainstream profession? What strategies do Asian American and Latino law students use to manage professional and (pan)ethnic identities? Asian American and Latino law students are still racial others despite their numerical increase in the legal profession. With regard to black lawyers, Wilkins (2000:553, italics original) notes, "it is hard for these lawyers not to feel a little resentful about the extra burdens they carry simply because they are black, even if some of these burdens (such as providing service to the black community) are ones that most believe they *should* carry because of their privileged position in relation to other blacks." If a racial burden (or duty) exists for black attorneys and law students, how might this burden affect racialized Asian American and Latino law students?

Data and Methods

Data for this article derive from direct observation of panethnic student organization meetings and events, in-depth interviews with 106 law students, and diary entries completed by apprenticing law students who were interviewed prior to engaging in the exercise.

Field Sites

Research spanned between 2009 and 2012 at two separate field sites in the American West: elite Western Tier 1 (WT1) and nonelite Metro Tier 4 (MT4). I chose two divergently ranked institutions to underscore similarities within legal education more generally, and to also understand how demographic and institutional prestige may affect student experiences and career trajectories. WT1 is a nationally ranked top-20 law school nestled among trees, academic buildings, and coffee shops as a part of a larger university campus. According to data derived from the American Bar Association (ABA 2010a), over 60% of WT1's 2012 graduates went on to work for law firms—of that population, approximately 65% joined firms with over 500 employees, otherwise known as international or large law firms.

In contrast, MT4 is a tier-four law school that sits within a concrete forest of buildings filled with local and international businesses, including law firms. According to ABA (2010a) data, over 30% of MT4's graduates went on to work at law firms, with roughly 71% working in small outfits of 2–10 employees. Discrepancies in the size of the law firms where graduates from WT1 and MT4 secure employment demonstrate status inequalities. Large, national firms offer higher starting salaries, and typically recruit from highly ranked institutions compared with smaller firms that cannot match similar compensation.

Findings: Strategies for Professional and (Pan)Ethnic Identity Management

As mentioned at the outset of this article, Asian American and Latino law students use three strategies to manage their socialization: marginal panethnicity, tempered altruism, and instrumental ethnicity. These students also assert a prominent "professional" identity, prioritizing the markers of professional success, and acquiring lawyering skills. When asked what constitutes success, most respondents, regardless of race, mentioned work product, client satisfaction, and tangible legal expertise. This response resonates with answers provided by white students—otherwise understood as the baseline for "bleached out."

Unlike their white peers, these students do not stop there, and continue to convey how (pan)ethnicity matters for their professional future. Asian American and Latino law students

Table 1 Strategies of (Pan)ethnic-Professional Identity Management

	Marginal Panethnicity	***Tempered Altruism***	***Instrumental Ethnicity***
Role as (Pan)ethnic Individual	Mentorship and representation	Direct service	Cultural brokerage
Normative Obligation	Profession	Profession and disenfranchised communities	Profession within ethnic communities
Spatiality of Obligation	Law school	(Pan)ethnic and disenfranchised communities	Ethnic communities
Temporality of Obligation (focus)	Primarily law school	Law school and work	Primarily work

adopt marginal panethnicity, tempered altruism, or instrumental ethnicity as strategies to manage professional and (pan)ethnic identities. Each strategy consists of four dimensions: students' conceptualization of her/his role as (pan)ethnic individuals, students' normative obligation to (pan)ethnic communities, the spatiality of students' obligation, and the temporality, or focus, of such obligations [see Table 1].

Marginal Panethnicity

As seen in Table [1], Asian American and Latino law students who adhere to marginal panethnicity are only peripherally interested in (pan)ethnic causes, and emphasize the normative "professional identity." They focus on increasing co-(pan)ethnic representation in law school and in the legal profession—marginal and temporary engagement with (pan) ethnic communities. These students did not belong to identity groups while in college, and typically grew up in communities lacking co-ethnics or nonwhite individuals. Upon entering law school, they joined respective panethnic organizations for what they claim to be serendipitous reasons—diversity recruitment events or activity fairs on campus led them to establish immediate acquaintances. Araceli, a second-year Mexican American student who was not involved in panethnic organizations while in college, recounts visiting the Latino Law Student Organization (LLSO) booth at an orientation fair: "I think coming in, I was like this [LLSO] is going to be where I'm going to meet people that have my experience. So, that's how I started going to stuff. And then I met friends there, and that kind of kept me going." Like Araceli, common traits in panethnic organizations (e.g., culture or background) helped panethnic law students maneuver the first few days of law school. Once found, they "met friends there, and that kind of kept [them] going." Asian American and Latino law students also experience marginalization in the identity groups to which they are tracked, especially if they did not necessarily identify with respective co-panethnic before law school.

For example, Matt, a Korean American second-year student, grew up in the American South, and plans to work at a big law firm for the foreseeable future. He attended a magnet high school with mostly black and white students, but very few Asian Americans. Matt recalls that he was "kind of nerdy" in high school, and "grew up feeling pretty white." He graduated from an Ivy League undergraduate institution and was not involved in any Asian or Asian American activities or organizations. However, he joined the Asian American Student Organization (AASO) at WT1, and tells me the following about how the organization inspired him to think more about Asian American communities: "So, coming to law school I thought it would be fun to try [to join AASO] and, again I wasn't that interested in Asian American issues. But since joining AASO, I have volunteered with the immigration clinic—the Asian immigration clinic." While Matt was slightly dubious about joining AASO, he now has a new, if only slight, interest in Asian American issues because of his membership.

Law students like Matt use marginal panethnicity as a strategy to connect with panethnic communities. They volunteer at clinics, or sit on panels to recruit more Asian American or Latino law students, although they do not necessarily foresee providing direct service to Asian American or Latino communities unless such opportunities arise. These students place their focus on professional development while cognizant of the dearth of minority representation in the legal profession.

On the whole, these students rely on the prospect of *pro bono* services, or mentoring co-panethnics as their *modus operandi* to connect with respective (pan)ethnic groups. For example, Diego, a Mexican American second-year, says, "I [would] like to think that I'll get out there and find plenty of time to do *pro bono* work for all sorts of wonderful people. I don't know if that will be the case. We'll see." Diego foresees working at a firm, specializing in environmental law, and is unsure how work pressures would permit him to "do *pro bono* work for all sorts of wonderful people."

Asian American and Latino law students who subscribe to marginal panethnicity can play the part of an interested panethnic when opportunities are presented to them. The ability to peripherally invest in panethnic issues is, for these students, similar to the way that most European ethnics are able to choose and assert their ethnicities (Waters 1990). Most of the students who adopt marginal panethnicity moved to a different part of the country to attend law school, and thus feel minimal connection to the (pan)ethnic communities near their law schools. Law school tier mattered in the sense that there are fewer local students at WT1 than at MT4. In other words, MT4 students not from the geographic area also subscribe to this strategy.

Tempered Altruism

Asian American and Latino law students who adopt tempered altruism focus on providing direct service as a part of their conjoined (pan)ethnic and professional identities. Unlike marginal panethnicity, tempered altruism emphasizes professional development in conjunction with service toward disenfranchised communities. The students who subscribe to this strategy were also not involved in panethnic organizations before law school. These students' spatial obligation extends beyond law school, and into disenfranchised communities. The temporality of their obligation intertwines law school with a legal career. And these law students negotiate professional socialization by remaining committed to transformative work. Meyerson and Scully's (1995) "tempered radicals" identify with and are committed to their nonactivist employment, but are also passionately dedicated to causes, communities, or ideologies that do not resonate with their work culture. The authors define tempered radicals as, "individuals [who] must struggle continuously to handle the tension between personal and professional identities at odds with one another. This struggle may be invisible, but it is by no means rare" (Meyerson and Scully 1995:586). Likewise, Gilkes's (1982) "black rebellious professionals" maintain commitment to causes that positively connect to black communities. Asian American and Latino law students embody Gilkes's description as they negotiate becoming a part of an elite mainstream profession while "giving back" to (pan) ethnic communities. In other words, they temper their panethnic allegiances by solely subscribing to a "lawyer identity" at the office. They intend to, however, work toward transformative change in other ways.

I further separate these students into subcategories of "organic" and "cultivated." Students who adopt the *organic* form of tempered altruism were raised in or near immigrant communities, and feel a sense of urgency to contribute to their respective communities primarily, and to disenfranchised populations secondarily. For instance, Manuel, a Mexican American second-year law student, grew up in a predominantly Latino community on the West Coast. He credits his community and his family's unconditional support that motivated him to graduate from college and enroll in law school. He foresees working for a law firm specializing in business and environmental law. Manuel tells me,

> I've seen so many people in the Hispanic community just struggle—struggle for their economic rights, social rights. There's a lot of people struggling out there. And I'm very fortunate to be able to continue my education; even to have a bachelor's is special enough. But to be a lawyer is something almost unheard of! I don't know many individuals who are Hispanics who are going to law school. And yet, this is my community. So I definitely want to reach back and help the individuals. It's just the right thing to do. The community has given so much to me. It's the least I could do.

For Manuel, being an attorney requires *actively* reaching out to his community. Unlike the students we met earlier who passively speak of peripheral *pro bono* services or mentorship, Manuel and others like him intend to proactively find opportunities to help the communities that have helped them because it is "the least [they] could do." Again, unlike the law students who subscribe to marginal panethnicity, Manuel and others like him intend to proactively assist co-(pan)ethnics.

Other Asian American and Latino law students who subscribe to tempered altruism speak of concerns beyond their own communities. I describe *cultivated* tempered altruism to mean a connection to panethnic and disenfranchised communities through education or political activism. Students who align with *cultivated* tempered altruism did not necessarily grow up in immigrant communities, but feel tethered to particular causes and issues. Beatriz is one such example. A third-year law student of Salvadoran decent, she is married to an Irish immigrant, and plans to focus on employment law at a law firm. With both parents born in El Salvador, Beatriz feels an intimate connection to the country, but also proudly asserts that she is an American. She plans to balance her "day job" with work for immigrant communities: "I'd have a day job, Monday through Friday. And then if I could somehow do extra hours during the week or maybe on weekends, I wouldn't mind doing that. I wouldn't mind lending myself to that at all. Yeah, especially with the whole immigration thing I see happening now." Although Beatriz has other career interests, she intends to focus her energy on making strides, albeit small, toward immigration concerns and not dissent from these issues.

Asian American and Latino law students who adopt tempered altruism may not necessarily dedicate their careers to public interest work, but they are committed to servicing underserved populations. This contrasts from marginal panethnicity because of an *active* focus to incorporate panethnic services as a part of their professional agendas. Individuals with an *organic* interest grew up in the region where they attend law school, and are familiar with their communities, thus feel urgency to provide assistance. Like Manuel, their commitment stems from a sense of duty as upwardly mobile individuals who benefited, in one way or another, from their co-(pan)ethnic communities. Those who lean toward *cultivated* tempered altruism were not necessarily raised in the same region as the location of their law school, but they feel connected to disenfranchised communities through their education and/or political leanings. As such, most students from both WT1 and MT4 adopt this strategy. Both variations of the strategy conceptualize students' professional identities in conjunction with their altruist obligations, which qualitatively differs from the law student who subscribes to marginal panethnicity. A third strategy, instrumental ethnicity, contrasts from the two already mentioned, and prioritizes cultural brokerage between legal and ethnic communities.

Instrumental Ethnicity

Instrumental ethnicity refers to the strategic use of legal skills as a resource to service coethnic communities. Unlike marginal panethnicity or tempered altruism, instrumental ethnicity features insider cultural knowledge and proficiency, if not fluency, in the languages spoken by members of the students' respective ethnic communities. Whereas the previous two strategies emphasized panethnicity, this one is more culturally laden. Law students who lean toward instrumental ethnicity act as "cultural brokers," intending to not only bring services to their ethnic-specific communities, but to also act as a "bridge" between mainstream America and their respective immigrant groups. Cultural brokerage exists in the strategic hiring of black employees in Jewish- and Korean-owned businesses in predominantly black neighborhoods (Lee 2002); in urban classrooms where teachers' aides serve as a bridge between middle-class teachers and the impoverished students and families they serve (Weiss 1994); or termed "cultural straddlers" to describe high-achieving black high school students (Carter 2005). I extend this conversation by applying it to the experiences of law students as they consider combining service to coethnics as a part of their career plans.

The law students who adhere to instrumental ethnicity seek to become a bridge for coethnics who are not fluent English speakers and/or are not proficient with American culture. As neophytes, these students also see a community that most mainstream (i.e., white) attorneys do not direct their services. For example, Evelyn, a Filipina third-year law student who intends on a firm trajectory, says, "I think there's a big, there's like an untapped clientele I could reach in the Asian American community because most of the clientele that my boss takes care of are white people. And I know a lot of people in the Filipino community that don't have wills and don't have an estate planned. And I could reach out to them." Evelyn stumbled upon estate planning during internships, and identified elderly Filipinos' legal needs. She plans to serve as that bridge—linking together *ethnic* networks, cultural knowledge, and her newly acquired skills.

In addition to providing direct legal services to ethnic communities, instrumental ethnicity includes serving as a resource for coethnics as they adapt to American society. Consider what Andersen, a Korean American third-year law student, has to say about using his legal knowledge to work within the ethnic Korean community:

> I want to be a bridge for the Korean American community to be able to utilize the American legal system because they have these barriers: one for language, two, cultural difference. I have spoken with some Korean business owners who have been sued, and they are really . . . they want to stay away from the whole legal system, period. . . . My sense was they are really afraid of the whole legal process. So, I want to be able to be a bridge because of my language ability.

Andersen plans to work with the Korean American community by serving as a bridge between them and mainstream America. Other bilingual law students, especially those at lower-ranked MT4 with relatively limited career options, espouse a sense of duty to use their legal skills within ethnic communities. This obligation, then, partially resonates with Agius Vallejo and Lee's (2009) assertion that while middle-class Mexican Americans "give back" to their ethnic communities, their approaches vary depending on their socioeconomic upbringing. Individuals from the working class are more likely and willing to financially assist family members versus those from the middle class, who subscribe to individual meritocratic rewards.

The law students in this study, however, intend to "give back" to their communities not necessarily through monetary assistance to family or extended kin, but by becoming mentors for Asian American and Latino college students aspiring toward law (marginal panethnicity), actively assisting disenfranchised communities (tempered altruism), and providing direct legal services (instrumental ethnicity). In this way, they are unlike Agius Vallejo and Lee's respondents because their motivations do not vary by socioeconomic background. Factors that influence (pan)ethnic-professional identity management include region, community from which these students hail, issues that resonate with the students, and the ability to speak an ethnic tongue.

Discussion and Conclusion

As a conduit to the legal profession, law schools construct and perpetuate an elite social status. Law students learn that as a part of a legal professional identity, they should also strive toward a career path that demonstrates their capacity to think analytically and reason critically. A career, at least initially, working with other bright, legal minds in law firms places them on a progressive professional track. Furthermore, these students will earn substantial salaries, glean resources, receive valuable training, and have access to staff who manage mundane tasks so as not to distract them from the bottom line: getting the best results for their clients.

Within this context, Asian American and Latino law students aspiring toward firm work adopt strategies to manage their identities. While these students vary in socioeconomic background, particular racialized identities, and law school rank, they nevertheless negotiate dueling identities. Law students who adopt marginal panethnicity primarily focus on the day-to-day tasks of being an attorney, but will engage with panethnic causes peripherally if opportunities arise to provide mentorship, or participate in school-sponsored clinics that serve co-panethnics. Including panethnic causes into their professional repertoire appears to be an inconsistent extracurricular. Moreover, these students do not hail from the region where they attend law school, thus do not feel an intimate connection to respective panethnic communities.

Law students who adopt tempered altruism include direct service as an important "must do" in their careers. They have either cultivated a connection with (pan)ethnic groups, or already established organic roots within one or more ethnic communities. Evoking tempered altruism provides these students with the opportunity to connect with disenfranchised communities, including their own. This is a simultaneous priority while working in intellectual property, environmental, or real estate law.

The third strategy—instrumental ethnicity—focuses on providing legal services within ethnic communities. The Asian American and Latino students who adopt instrumental ethnicity assert a professional identity that is closely intertwined with an *ethnic* one instead of panethnic. They aim to provide legal services to ethnic communities in an altruistic manner, but also because their ethnic communities are "untapped" by mainstream, white attorneys. Additionally, they are exclusively from MT4, which could indicate one of two things: (1) their career prospects are limited due to the lower rank of their law school, and thus [they] consider opportunities within ethnic communities, or (2) they use their local ties with coethnics to strategically carve out a professional niche.

It deserves mentioning that while the strategies in the repertoire are seemingly neat, the lines differentiating them can be porous. This is particularly true for women who experience conflicting messages about assimilating into a profession traditionally inhabited by men, and also aligns with gendered expectations.

The Pitfall of Colorblindness and Multiculturalism

Colorblindness and multiculturalism are often interpreted to mean numbers in representation, and not necessarily interactional dynamics. As I demonstrate in this article, the intersection of race, ethnicity, and professional socialization remain critical to understanding the experiences of Asian American and Latino neophytes. Although a relatively small sample, we see that Asian American and Latino law students are influenced by expectations of and for individuals to advocate on behalf of co-(pan)ethnics. In these ways, (pan)ethnicity matters more significantly for some than others.

As we see with the respondents in these pages, learning to become a lawyer is messy and is an exercise in managing identities. Ostensibly, we perceive the legal profession as an avenue that provides advancement opportunities for nonwhite Americans. However, numbers alone do not capture convoluted expectations while these individuals ascend the socioeconomic ladder. As Asian Americans and Latinos are becoming a part of mainstream America, they carry with them different sociocultural baggage than their white counterparts. Specifically, we see that (pan)ethnicity matters in law school and shapes (pan)ethnic duties that affect students' thoughts about their career plans.

This racialized integration into mainstream America speaks directly to the social and cultural value of race, which complements critical race theory. Ideologies and stereotypes about race are socially transmitted with deep roots in American culture that even blind individuals "see" race (Obasogie 2010). The strategies used by Asian American and Latino law students to fulfill a sense of panethnic duty also serve as an assertion of racial ownership. If Asian American and Latino law students do not feel compelled to contribute to (pan)ethnic communities, whether ascribed or asserted, then we can ascertain that race or panethnicity, does not in fact matter. But as demonstrated in this article, panethnicity remains salient for upwardly mobile individuals of color, even for those who do not ostensibly appear to be concerned with panethnic communities and causes.

Note

1. I use (pan)ethnicity and panethnicity intentionally to represent different communities. Whereas (pan)ethnicity refers to panethnic and/or ethnic communities (e.g., Latino or Mexican American, respectively), panethnicity solely references panethnic ones (e.g., Latino or Asian American).

References

Abel, Richard. 1989. *American Lawyers.* New York: Oxford University Press.

Agius Vallejo, Jody, and Jennifer Lee. 2009. "Brown Picket Fences: The Immigrant Narrative and Patterns of 'Giving Back' Among the Mexican-Origin Middle Class." *Ethnicities* 9: 1: 5–31.

Alba, Richard, and Victor Nee. 2003. *Remaking the American Mainstream: Assimilation and Contemporary Immigration.* Cambridge, MA: Harvard University Press.

American Bar Association (ABA). 2010a. *Legal Education Statistics.* Retrieved March 2, 2011 (http://www.abanet.org/legaled/statistics/stats.html)

American Bar Association (ABA). 2010b. *Racial and Ethnic Diversity in the American Bar Association.* Prepared by the Commission on Racial and Ethnic Diversity in the Profession. Chicago, IL: ABA.

Bean, Frank D., and Gillian Stevens. 2003. *America's Newcomers and the Dynamics of Diversity.* New York: Russell Sage Foundation.

Becker, Howard S., Blanche Geer, Everett C. Hughes, and Anselm L. Strauss. 1961. *Boys in White: Student Culture in Medical School.* Chicago, IL: University of Chicago Press.

Blair-Loy, Mary, and Gretchen DeHart. 2003. "Family and Career Trajectories Among African American Female Attorneys." *Journal of Family Issues* 24: 7: 908–933.

Carter, Prudence L. 2005. *Keepin' It Real: School Success Beyond Black and White.* New York: Oxford University Press.

Costello, Carrie Yang. 2005. *Professional Identity Crisis: Race, Class, Gender, and Success at Professional Schools.* Nashville, TN: Vanderbilt University Press.

Epstein, Cynthia F. 1970. "Encountering the Male Establishment: Sex-Status Limits on Women's Careers in the Professions." *American Journal of Sociology* 75: 6: 965–982.

Epstein, Cynthia F. 1973. "Positive Effects of the Multiple Negative: Explaining the Success of Black Professional Women." *American Journal of Sociology* 78: 4: 912–935.

Epstein, Cynthia F. 1992. "Tinkerbells and Pinups: The Construction and Reconstruction of Gender Boundaries at Work." In Michèle Lamont and Marcel Fournier (eds.), *Cultivating*

Differences: Symbolic Boundaries and the Making of Inequality; pp. 232–256. Chicago, IL: University of Chicago Press.

Epstein, Cynthia F. 1993. *Women in Law*, 2nd edition. New York: Basic Books.

Erlanger, Howard S., and Douglas A. Klegon. 1978. "Socialization Effects of Professional School: The Law School Experience and Student Orientations to Public Interest Concerns." *Law and Society Review* 13: 1: 11–35.

Erlanger, Howard, Charles R. Epp, Mia Cahill, and Kathleen M. Haines. 1996. "Law Student Idealism and Job Choice: Some New Data on an Old Question." *Law and Society Review* 30: 4: 851–864.

Feagin, Joe R. 1991. "The Continuing Significance of Race: Antiblack Discrimination in Public Places." *American Sociological Review* 56: 1: 101–116.

Feagin, Joe R., and José A. Cobas. 2014. *Latinos Facing Racism: Discrimination, Resistance, and Endurance.* Boulder, CO: Paradigm.

Fischer, Judith D. 1996. "Portia Unbound: The Effects of a Supportive Law School Environment on Women and Minority Students." *UCLA Women's Law Journal* 7: 1: 1–56.

Garth, Bryant G. 2004. "Commentary: Noblesse Oblige as an Alternative Career Strategy." *Houston Law Review* 41: 1: 93–111.

Garth, Bryant G., and Joyce Sterling. 2009. "Exploring Inequality in the Corporate Law Firm Apprenticeship: Doing the Time, Finding the Love." *Georgetown Journal of Legal Ethics* 22: 4: 1361–1394.

Gilkes, Cheryl Townsend. 1982. "Successful Rebellious Professionals: The Black Woman's Professional Identity and Community Commitment." *Psychology of Women Quarterly* 6: 3: 289–311.

Gómez, Laura E. 2004. "A Tale of Two Genres: On the Real and Ideal Links Between Law and Society and Critical Race Theory." In Austin Sarat (ed.), *The Blackwell Companion to Law and Society*; pp. 453–470. Malden, MA: Blackwell.

Gordon, Milton. 1964. *Assimilation in American Life: The Role of Race, Religion, and National Origins.* New York: Oxford University Press.

Granfield, Robert. 1992. *Making Elite Lawyers: Visions of Law at Harvard and Beyond.* New York: Routledge, Chapman and Hall.

Haney-Lopez, Ian. 2006. *White by Law: The Legal Construction of Race.* New York: New York University Press.

Lee, Jennifer. 2002. *Civility in the City: Blacks, Jews, and Koreans in Urban America.* Cambridge, MA: Harvard University Press.

Lee, Jennifer, and Frank D. Bean. 2007. "Reinventing the Color Line: Immigration and America's New Racial/Ethnic Divide." *Social Forces* 86: 2: 561–586.

McGee, Ebony O., and Danny B. Martin. 2011. "'You Would Not Believe What I Have to Go Through to Prove My Intellectual Value!': Stereotype Management Among Mathematically Successful Black Mathematics and Engineering Students." *American Educational Research Journal* 48: 6: 1347–1389.

Mertz, Elizabeth. 2007. *The Language of Law School: Learning to "Think Like a Lawyer."* New York: Oxford University Press.

Meyerson, Debra E., and Maureen A. Scully. 1995. "Tempered Radicalism and the Politics of Ambivalence and Change." *Organization Science* 6: 5: 585–600.

Moore, Wendy Leo. 2008. *Reproducing Racism: White Space, Elite Law Schools, and Racial Inequality.* Boulder, CO: Rowman & Littlefield.

Obasogie, Osagie K. 2010. "Do Blind People See Race? Social, Legal and Theoretical Considerations." *Law and Society Review* 44: 3–4: 585–616.

Pierce, Jennifer L. 1995. *Gender Trials: Emotional Lives in Contemporary Law Firms.* Berkeley: University of California Press.

Schleef, Debra. 2006. *Managing Elites: Professional Socialization in Law and Business Schools.* Boulder, CO: Rowman & Littlefield.

Sommerlad, Hilary. 2007. "Researching and Theorizing the Process of Professional Identity Formation." *Journal of Law and Society* 34: 2: 190–217.

Sommerlad, Hilary, and Peter Sanderson. 1998. *Gender, Choice and Commitment: Women Solicitors in England and Wales and the Struggle for Equal Status.* Dartmouth, MA: Ashgate.

Sommerlad, Hilary, Lisa Webley, Liz Duff, Daniel Muzio, and Jennifer Tomlinson. 2010. *Diversity in the Legal Profession in England and Wales: A Qualitative Study of Barriers and Individual Choices.* London, UK: Legal Services Board, University of Westminster.

Stover, Robert V. 1989. *Making It and Breaking It: The Fate of Public Interest Commitment During Law School.* Chicago: University of Illinois Press.

Tuan, Mia. 1998. *Forever Foreigners or Honorary Whites? The Asian Ethnic Experience Today.* New Brunswick, NJ: Rutgers University Press.

Tuan, Mia. 1999. "Neither Real Americans nor Real Asians? Multigeneration Asian Ethnics Navigating the Terrain of Authenticity." *Qualitative Sociology* 22: 2: 105–125.

Van Maanen, John. 1975. "Police Socialization: A Longitudinal Examination of Job Attitudes in an Urban Police Department." *Administrative Science Quarterly* 20: 2: 207–228.

Waters, Mary C. 1990. *Ethnic Options: Choosing Identities in America.* Berkeley: University of California Press.

Weiss, Melford S. 1994. "Marginality, Cultural Brokerage, and School Aides: A Success Story in Education." *Anthropology and Education Quarterly* 25: 3: 336–346.

Wilder, Gita Z. 2008. *Race and Ethnicity in the Legal Profession: Findings From the First Wave of After the JD Study (Monograph).* Washington, DC: The National Association for Legal Career Professionals.

Wilkins, David B. 1998. "Fragmenting Professionalism: Racial Identity and the Ideology of 'Bleached Out' Lawyering." *International Journal of the Legal Profession* 5: 2–3: 141–173.

Wilkins, David B. 2000. "Rollin' on the River: Race, Elite Schools, and the Equality Paradox." *Law and Social Inquiry* 25: 2: 527–556.

Wilkins, David B. 2004. "Doing Well by Doing Good?: The Role of Public Service in the Careers of Black Corporate Lawyers." *Houston Law Review* 41: 1: 1–92.

Wilkins, David B., and Mitu Gulati. 1996. "Why Are There So Few Black Lawyers in Corporate Law Firms?: An Institutional Analysis." *California Law Review* 84: 3: 493–625.

CHAPTER 23

Miles to Go before We Sleep*

Racial Inequities in Health

David R. Williams

Large, pervasive, and persistent racial inequalities exist in the onset, courses, and outcomes of illness. A comprehensive understanding of the patterning of racial disparities indicates that ***individual racism*** *and* ***institutional racism*** *remain important determinants. There is an urgent need to build the science base that would identify how to facilitate needed societal change and to identify the optimal interventions that would confront and dismantle the societal conditions that create and sustain health inequalities. For more than 100 years, scientific research has documented that racial gaps in health exist, and the federal government provides an annual update of these disparities (National Center for Health Statistics, 2011). In this article, David Williams provides an overview of current knowledge of racial inequities in health. He describes salient patterns in the distribution of disease by race and reviews evidence of race-related aspects of social experience that matter for health. He pays particular attention to recent research on self-reported racial discrimination and health. Despite thousands of published studies, our current knowledge about the most effective strategies to reduce health inequities is limited, and there is an urgent need to develop a science base to guide* ***societal*** *interventions.*

Source: Adapted from David R. Williams, "Miles to Go before We Sleep: Racial Inequities in Health," *Journal of Health and Social Behavior,* Volume 53, Number 3, pages 279–295, SAGE Publications, Inc., 2012.

*Some text has been omitted. Please consult the original source.

Questions to Consider

This essay provides evidence that health disparities exist across many different racial and ethnic groups. What are some of the main factors that lead to racial inequality in health? How does racism contribute to illness and health disparities?

Miles to Go: Large Racial Gaps in Health Persist

Race is one of America's most important social categories. It has historically captured economic exploitation, political marginalization, and social stigmatization that has made it consequential for virtually every aspect of life. The U.S. government's Office of Management and Budget (OMB) requires federal statistical agencies to classify the U.S. population into five racial categories (white, black, American Indian or Alaskan Native, Asian, and Native Hawaiian and other Pacific Islander) and into either the Hispanic or non-Hispanic ethnic category (Office of Management and Budget 1997). Accordingly, in this article, I use "race" to refer to the OMB's racial and ethnic categories, and I use the terms "black" and "African American," "Hispanic" and "Latino," and "American Indian" and "Native American" interchangeably. These racial categories capture many traditional aspects of ethnicity, such as common geographic origins, ancestry, family patterns, language, cultural norms, and traditions, but also historic legacies of social injustice and contemporary social inequality. I use the term "ethnicity" to refer to subgroups of the OMB's categories.

Mortality data provide a glimpse of health status in the United States. In the last decade, blacks had an overall death rate that was 30 percent higher than that of whites, while the rates for all other groups were lower than that of whites. African Americans had higher death rates than did whites for 10 of the 15 leading causes of death. Hispanics and American Indians had higher death rates than whites for diabetes, liver cirrhosis, and homicide. American Indians also had elevated mortality rates for accidents and hypertension.

Earlier Onset of Disease

Minorities also get sick at younger ages and die sooner than do whites. In a classic study, Geronimus (1992) showed that national infant death rates were lower for white and Mexican American women who delayed first births to their 20s compared with those who gave birth in their teens. The opposite pattern was evident for black and Puerto Rican women, with infant mortality lower for 15- to 19-year-olds than for women who had their first baby in their 20s. Geronimus argued that this pattern was due to "weathering": early physiological deterioration due to the cumulative impact of multiple social disadvantages. Recent studies provide evidence of this earlier onset of disease or accelerated aging for minorities across multiple health status indicators. White women have a higher incidence of breast cancer than do black women, but the incidence rate under the age of 40 is higher for black than white women (Anderson et al. 2008). Similarly, a 20-year follow-up study found that incident heart failure before the age of 50 was 20 times more common in blacks than whites, with the average age of onset being 39 years for African Americans (Bibbins-Domingo et al. 2009). National data also show that cardiovascular disease develops earlier in blacks than whites, with 28 percent of cardiovascular disease deaths among blacks occurring before age 65 compared with 13 percent among whites (Jolly et al. 2010).

Geronimus et al. (2006) also showed that the early health deterioration of black adults is evident across multiple biological systems. Using a global measure of allostatic load that summed 10 indicators of clinical and subclinical status, they found that blacks were more likely than whites to score high on allostatic load (high on four or more indicators) at all ages, and the size of the black-white gap increased with age. In each age group, the average score for blacks was comparable with that of whites who were 10 years older. Moreover, blacks continued to have higher allostatic load scores even after adjustment for poverty.

Racial Differences across the Continuum of Disease

Racial inequities in health are also evident in the severity and progression of disease. For example, African Americans have a higher prevalence of chronic kidney disease (CKD) than whites, require dialysis or kidney transplantation at younger ages, and have a higher incidence of end-stage renal disease at each decade of life, and their level of CKD risk factors does not adequately account for their faster progression of CKD to end-stage renal disease (Bruce et al. 2009). Disparities in the severity and progression of illness have been documented even for outcomes that are less prevalent in blacks. Breast cancer is one example. Although black women are less likely than whites to get breast cancer, they are more likely than their white peers to have tumors that grow quickly, recur more often, are resistant to treatment, and kill more frequently (Chlebowski et al. 2005). Thus, although less likely than white women to get breast cancer in any given year, black women are more likely to die from it. Major depression is another example. African Americans have lower lifetime and current rates of depression than do whites, but depressed blacks are more likely than their white peers to have higher levels of impairment, to have more severe symptoms, to be chronically depressed, and to not receive any treatment (Williams et al. 2007a).

Racial Disparities Exist in the Effects of Some Risk Factors

Although levels of cigarette smoking are similar for blacks compared with whites, a given level of tobacco use has a more adverse impact on blacks compared with whites. Black men have higher lung cancer incidence and mortality compared with their white peers (Berger, Lund, and Brawley 2007), and analysis of nicotine metabolism reveals that compared with whites, blacks have a higher nicotine intake and cotinine level per cigarette (Perez-Stable et al. 1998). In a similar vein, despite comparable levels of alcohol consumption, alcohol-related mortality is twice as high for blacks compared with whites (Stinson, Nephew, and Dufour 1996). Research also reveals that at equivalent levels of alcohol use, blacks are more susceptible to liver damage than whites (Stranges et al. 2004) and that in contrast to a protective effect for whites, there was no beneficial effect of moderate alcohol consumption on all-cause mortality for blacks (Sempos et al. 2003), and moderate alcohol consumption was positively related to indicators of cardiovascular disease for black men (Fuchs et al. 2001, 2004; Pletcher et al. 2005). It is unclear if these patterns reflect interactions of alcohol and tobacco with other social, physical, and chemical exposures and/or biological adaptations, including gene expression changes to these exposures. Alternatively, they could also reflect misunderstanding of the associations between these health practices and health status. For example, some evidence suggests that some of the reported beneficial effects of moderate alcohol consumption are due to residual confounding with high SES and good health practices (Fillmore et al. 1998; Naimi et al. 2005).

Racial Disparities in Health Persist over Time

Life expectancy data illustrate the striking persistence of racial disparities in health over time. In 1950, blacks had a life expectancy at birth of 60.8 years, compared with 69.1 years for whites (National Center for Health Statistics 2011). Life expectancy has been improving for both groups over time, but it was not until 1990 that blacks achieved the life expectancy that whites had in 1950. And although the racial gap has narrowed, [within the last decade] there was still an almost 5-year gap in life expectancy (73.6 vs. 78.4 years). Data from the Indian Health Service (2009) also provide numerous examples of persisting and in some cases widening disparities for specific causes of death over time for American Indians compared to whites.

The pattern of racial inequities in health in the United States mirrors that in other countries and suggests the potential of common societal causes across national and cultural contexts. In race-conscious societies such as Australia, Brazil, Canada, New Zealand, South Africa, and the United Kingdom, nondominant racial groups have worse health than dominant groups (Bramley et al. 2004; Hamilton et al. 2001; Nazroo and Williams 2006). For example, analyses of health data for the New Zealand Maori, Australian Aboriginals and Torres Strait Islanders, First Nations on-reserve Canadians, and American Indians and Alaskan Natives found that indigenous people had lower life expectancy compared with the nonindigenous population in every country (Bramley et al. 2004). Instructively, three specific causes of death—diabetes, homicide, and suicide—showed a consistent pattern of elevated risk for indigenous groups across these diverse societies. Racial health inequalities are also persistent over time outside of the United States. For example, a study of mortality differences between the Maori and non-Maori populations in New Zealand from 1951 to 2006 found that health inequalities remained substantial in 2006 (Tobias et al. 2009).

Making Sense of Racial Inequalities in Health

In the late nineteenth century, W.E.B. DuBois ([1899] 1967) documented that blacks in Philadelphia had elevated rates of disease and death compared with whites. He concluded that the determinants of the poorer health for blacks compared with whites were multifactorial but primarily social. His list of contributing factors included neglect of infants, bad dwellings, poor ventilation, dampness and cold, poor food, unsanitary living conditions, inadequate outdoor life, and poor heredity. Sociologists had long noted that social class and social contextual factors play a critical role in influencing the social distribution of disease. Half a century earlier, Friedrich Engels ([1845] 1984) documented that the upper classes in Liverpool, England, had an average life expectancy of 35 years, compared with 15 years for day laborers. He argued that British society was committing "social murder" by exposing workers to living and working conditions that made it difficult to be healthy and live to an advanced age. Location in social structure reflects differential power and differential exposure to psychological, social, physical, and chemical exposures in occupational, residential, and other societal contexts. There are large racial differences in SES, and they account for a substantial part of observed racial differences in health. However, race and SES combine in complex ways to affect health. Race is a social status category that was created by larger societal processes and institutions, including institutional and individual dimensions of racism (Williams 1997). SES is not thus just a confounder of the relationship between race and health but part of the causal pathway that links race to health. That is, historical and contemporary racial discrimination created and perpetuates both racial inequities in SES and racial inequality in health status.

Race Captures More Than Socioeconomic Inequality

Recent research documents that there is an added burden of race, over and above SES, that is linked to poor health. At age 25, whites live 5 years longer than African Americans (Murphy 2000). However, for both blacks and whites, variations in life expectancy by income and education data are larger than the overall black–white difference (Braveman et al. 2010). High-income blacks and whites live 7.1 and 6.8 years longer, respectively, than their low-income counterparts. For both racial groups, as income levels rise, health improves in a stepwise manner, but there are black–white differences in life expectancy of at least three years at every level of income.

Large racial differences in health at similar levels of SES are also evident in national data on birth outcomes (Braveman et al. 2010). The expected inverse association between mother's education and infant mortality is evident for blacks, whites, and Hispanics. However, the infant mortality rate for college-educated African American women is more than two and a half times as high as that of similarly educated whites and Hispanics. Moreover, black female college graduates have a higher rate of infant mortality than Hispanic and white women

Table 1 Life Expectancy at Age 25, United States

Group	*White*	*Black*	*White–Black*
All (1998)[a]	53.4	48.4	5.0
By income (1988–1998)[b]			
poor (<FPL)	49.0	45.5	3.5
near poor (>FPL to <2 × FPL)	51.4	48.0	3.4
Middle income (>2 × FPL to <4 × FPL)	53.8	50.7	3.1
High income (>4 × FPL)	55.8	52.6	3.2
Income difference	6.8	7.1	

Note: FPL = federal poverty level.
a. Murphy (2000).
b. Braveman et al. (2010).

who have not completed high school. These patterns highlight the need to understand pathogenic race-related exposures at all SES levels.

Understanding the Added Burden of Race

Research suggests that three key factors may each contribute to the residual effect of race after SES is controlled (Williams and Mohammed 2009). First, indicators of SES are not equivalent across race. Compared with whites, blacks and Hispanics have lower earnings at comparable levels of education, less wealth at every level of income, and less purchasing power because of higher costs of goods and services in their communities (Williams and Collins 1995). Second, health is affected not only by one's current SES but by exposure to social and economic adversity over the life course. Racial-ethnic minority populations are more likely than whites to have experienced low SES in childhood and elevated levels of early life psychosocial and economic adversity that can affect health in adulthood (Colen 2011). In national data, early life SES helps explain the black–white gap in mortality for men (Warner and Hayward 2006). Another recent study linked early life adversity to multiple markers of inflammation for adult African Americans but not for whites (Slopen et al. 2010).

Third, a growing body of evidence is documenting that racism is a critical missing piece of the puzzle in understanding the patterning of racial disparities in health. Institutional racism and personal experiences of discrimination are added pathogenic factors that can affect the health of minority group members in multiple ways (Williams and Mohammed 2009): Discrimination can lead to reduced access to desirable goods and services, internalized racism (acceptance of society's negative characterization) can adversely affect health, racism can trigger increased exposure to traditional stressors (e.g., unemployment), and experiences of discrimination may be a neglected psychosocial stressor.

Arguably, the most consequential effects of racism on health are due to residential segregation by race, a mechanism of institutional racism (Williams and Collins 2001). Segregation can restrict socioeconomic attainment and lead to group differences in SES and health. It also creates pathogenic neighborhood conditions, with minorities living in markedly more health-damaging environments than whites and facing higher levels of acute and chronic stressors. Although the majority of poor persons in the United States are white, poor white families are not concentrated in contexts of economic and social disadvantage and with the absence of an infrastructure that promotes opportunity in the ways that poor blacks, Latinos, and Native Americans are. The neighborhoods where minority children live have lower incomes, education, and home ownership rates and higher rates of poverty and unemployment compared with those where white children reside. In 100 of America's largest metropolitan areas, 75 percent of all African American children and 69 percent of all Latino children are growing up in more negative residential environments than are the worst-off white children (Acevedo-Garcia et al. 2008).

Research has yet to fully document the effects that the distinctive environments created by residential segregation have on the health of stigmatized racial groups in the United States. Inadequate attention has been given in prior research to the extent to which the different residential environments of racial minorities lead to elevated exposure to environmental pollutants that can interact with other psychosocial exposures to affect health risks (Gee and Payne-Sturges 2004).

Perceived Discrimination and Health

The aspect of racism that has received the most empirical study is self-reported experiences of discrimination. Impressive evidence of the persistence of discrimination in contemporary society comes from audit studies. One study found that a white job applicant with a criminal record is more likely to be offered a job than is a black applicant with an otherwise identical resume whose record was clean (Pager 2003). Another study found that applications for white-collar jobs with distinctively white names, such as Alison, Emily, Brad, and Greg, were 50 percent more likely to get callbacks for interviews than identical resumes with distinctively black names such as Latisha, Aisha, Jamal, and Darnell (Bertrand and Mullainathan 2004).

Minority group members are aware of at least some experiences of discrimination, and these incidents can be a source of stress. Recent reviews document important progress in this area of research (Pascoe and Richman 2009; Williams and Mohammed 2009). Several longitudinal studies and other studies have found that the effects of discrimination are associated with a broad range of health conditions, ranging from violence, sexual problems, and poor sleep quality to elevated risk for increased C-reactive protein levels, high blood pressure, and coronary artery calcification, breast cancer incidence, uterine myomas (fibroids), and subclinical carotid artery disease. Discrimination has also been associated with delays in seeking treatment, lower adherence to medical regimes, and lower rates of follow-up. Importantly, studies in the United States, South Africa, and New Zealand have found that discrimination accounts, in part, for the residual racial disparities in health after controls for SES (Williams and Mohammed 2009).

Recent studies highlight important but neglected aspects of discrimination. First, some studies suggest that both exposure to discrimination and its consequences are evident early in life. A study of 5,147 fifth graders found that 7 percent of whites, 15 percent of Hispanics, and 20 percent of blacks had experienced racial discrimination, and these experiences were associated with an increased risk for depression, attention deficit hyperactivity disorder, oppositional defiant disorder and conduct disorder (Coker et al. 2009). Another study found that the majority of American adolescents are exposed to racial discrimination in online contexts, such as chat rooms and social network sites, and that online racial discrimination was positively related to mental health symptoms even after adjustment for general adolescent stress and offline discrimination (Tynes et al. 2008).

Several studies have found that although whites report lower levels of discrimination than blacks, discrimination also adversely affects their health (Williams and Mohammed 2009). Limited evidence indicates that whites understand questions about discrimination in ways similar to blacks and that their emotional reactions and reported stress responses are similar to those of African Americans (Williams et al. 2012). However, it remains unclear whether perceptions of episodic, occasional experiences of discrimination by whites are equivalent to reports of discrimination by racially stigmatized groups for whom these experiences are likely to be more systematic, insidious, and constant and may serve to reinforce their historic status characterized by social inequality and oppression. At the same time, there is much that we need to understand about social stigmatization and the conditions under which it can affect health across population groups. A recent national study of Jewish Americans, a white ethnic group with a history of structural disadvantage and stigmatization, found that Jews had higher levels of income and education than other whites, but they reported health status worse than other whites (and similar to African Americans) once the association was adjusted for SES (Pearson and Geronimus 2011).

Miles to Go: Enhancing the Science of Intervention

Future research needs to build a science base that will stimulate and inform effective societal efforts to reduce inequalities in health. Several lines of evidence suggest that efforts to reduce racial inequalities in health should be characterized by a sense of urgency. First, the economic status of disadvantaged minority groups is declining in the United States. One recent report documented that [during the recent recession], the median wealth of white households declined by 16 percent, compared with 53 percent for black and 66 percent for Hispanic households (Pew Research Center 2011b). Thus, the median wealth of whites is 20 times that of blacks and 18 times that of Hispanics. Another storm cloud for the African American population is the contraction of government employment at both the state and federal levels. Public sector employment has been a key to black upward mobility and the development of the black middle class (Wilson 2011). These challenges will be especially acute for black men. There are higher levels of college completion for women than for men in all racial groups in the United States, but the gap is largest among blacks, and the black/white earnings ratio for male college graduates, aged 25 to 29, has been declining over time, from 93 percent in 1977 to 73 percent in 1987, 83 percent in 1997, and 80 percent in 2007 (Wilson 2011).

Second, the current economic crisis in the United States is leading to spending reductions at the federal, state, and local levels. Although many of these budget cuts are outside the health sector, they weaken the social safety net for vulnerable populations and will likely lead to increased rates of illness, greater numbers of premature deaths, and increased health care costs (Woolf 2011). Government spending reductions during the early 1980s led to worsening health for low-SES populations and racial minorities (Williams and Collins 1995). Third, there is declining interest in and support for policies to address racial inequalities among whites in the United States. Both whites who voted for President Obama and those who did not indicate that there is less need to address racial inequality in the United States and that they would be less supportive of policies to address inequities (Williams et al. 2010). In striking contrast, the persistence of racial inequality and discrimination suggest that antidiscrimination programs may be crucial for ensuring racial equality. Relatedly, there has been a national shift toward a conservative or Republican ideology. Since President Obama was elected, there has been marked growth in Republican Party membership among white voters that has been particularly pronounced among the young (aged 18 to 29 years) and the low income (earning less than $30,000) (Pew Research Center 2011a). Thus, in 2011, the Republican edge (Republicans or independents leaning Republican) over Democrats among whites was 13 points (52 percent to 39 percent), compared with a 2-point edge (46 percent to 44 percent) in 2008.

Building Awareness and Political Will

Over 100 years ago, DuBois ([1899] 1967) lamented that the most difficult social problem in the matter of Negro health is the peculiar attitude of the nation toward the well-being of the race. There have . . . been few other cases in the history of civilized peoples where human suffering has been viewed with such peculiar indifference. (p. 163)

Research is needed to identify effective communication strategies that would create the conditions for change. We need to increase public knowledge of the magnitude and determinants of racial inequalities in health. A recent national survey found that fewer than half (46 percent) of all American adults were aware of health disparities between blacks and whites (Booske, Robert, and Rohan 2011). Political ideology was associated with knowledge of health disparities, with liberals being three times as likely as conservatives to be aware of racial and SES gaps in health (Booske et al. 2011). Education was also positively associated with knowledge. In addition, there was limited appreciation of the contribution of social and economic factors to health. Most Americans viewed personal health behaviors and access to care as very strong determinants of health (Robert and Booske 2011). Many fewer saw employment, education, housing quality, and community safety as important determinants of health. Individuals who were politically liberal, minority group members, older, and of low SES were more likely to endorse the importance of social factors (Robert and Booske 2011).

That minorities and low-SES persons were among the most knowledgeable about social factors suggests that experience plays an important role in providing knowledge (Robert and Booske 2011). This highlights the value of narrative approaches that enable socially advantaged individuals to envision and sympathize with the harsh realities of disadvantaged individuals and situations. The strong public endorsement of the role of individual action also suggests the necessity of simultaneous attention to personal responsibility and to social policies and initiatives to reduce the barriers that make it extremely difficult for many Americans to make healthy choices.

Research is also needed to identify how best to enhance emotional identification with racial disparities and to build empathy and support to address them. The FrameWorks Institute has done pioneering work on the dominant frames about race that are activated by the mention of racial inequalities (Davey 2009). These dominant frames include the beliefs that U.S. society has made dramatic progress on race in recent decades; changes in laws and policies have eliminated discrimination and racism, except at the level of the individual; this residual level of personal racism persists and is as common in whites as in minorities; personal responsibility (and character, values, and effort) are the drivers of success in life; discrimination does not play a role; and whites and nonwhites have separate fates because of differences in core American values.

This research has also found that several widely used framing strategies such as viewing diversity as a strength, arguing that disparities for minorities are early warning indicators (canaries in a coal mine), and claiming that disparities reflect white privilege or are structurally driven were all ineffective (Davey 2009). In each of these cases, the dominant racial framing obscures an alternative viewpoint. In contrast, framings that work are those that focused less on racial disparities and emphasized widely shared American values (such as enhancing opportunity for all and ingenuity) and that link communities in a sense of shared fate. Specifically, frames that gave primacy to effective solutions and innovation, emphasized opportunity for all, highlighted the interdependence of all communities, stressed preventing community problems before they occurred, and emphasized fairness (not between individuals but) between places all have the potential to build support for addressing disparities.

Building on Resilience and Protective Factors

The patterning of risk factors by race highlights the need to better understand the potential contribution of resilience and protective factors. For example, American Indians and whites have suicide rates that are similar to each other and two to three times as high as those of blacks, Asians, and Hispanics (Centers for Disease Control and Prevention 2011). We do not fully understand why adverse exposures are associated with elevated risks in some disadvantaged minority population but not in others. We need to better understand how the resources, resilience factors, and capacities of social groups, at the individual and area levels, can affect their responses to exposure to health risks (Ahern et al. 2008). Both exposure to protective resources and the patterns of response to potential threats can affect the levels and impact of particular exposures. For example, higher levels of religious involvement by black than white teens play a key role in the lower levels of substance use among black adolescents (Wallace et al. 2003). Communities also vary in their levels of social cohesion and other protective resources, such that community capacity can be an important resource at the local level. Community capacity refers to characteristics of communities that can affect their ability to address community problems, including the potential to develop and deploy skills, knowledge, and resources that can aid in this effort (Goodman et al. 1998). Research is needed to better understand how to find solutions to local problems by building on the strengths and capacities of community institutions (families, neighborhoods, schools, churches, businesses, and voluntary agencies) and enlisting them to be agents of change in promoting health (McLeroy et al. 2003).

Conclusion

> In spite of these spectacular strides in science and technology, and still unlimited ones to come, something basic is missing. There is a sort of poverty of spirit which stands in glaring contrast to our scientific and technological abundance. We have learned to fly the air like birds and swim the sea like fish, but we have not learned the simple art of living together as brothers. (Martin Luther King, Jr., 1964 Nobel lecture, Oslo, Norway)

Racial disparities in health are a stark symbol of the historic and ongoing racial inequalities in society. They reflect the enduring effects of the institutionalization of inequality for stigmatized social groups. They are a potent reminder of the many miles that we still need to journey to achieve equality. The evidence reviewed in this article indicates that inequalities in health are created by larger inequalities in society. Their existence reflects the successful implementation of social policies. Eliminating them requires political will and a commitment to thorough and sustained approaches to improve living and working conditions. We have many miles to go in better understanding and maximizing the levers of change, but our greatest need is to begin, with a renewed commitment, and in a comprehensive, systematic, and integrated manner, to use all of the knowledge that we have.

References

Acevedo-Garcia, Dolores, Theresa L. Osypuk, Nancy McArdle, and David R. Williams. 2008. "Toward a Policy-Relevant Analysis of Geographic and Racial/Ethnic Disparities in Child Health." *Health Affairs* 27(2):321–33.

Anderson, William F., Philip S. Rosenberg, Idan Menashe, Aya Mitani, and Ruth M. Pfeiffer. 2008. "Age-Related Crossover in Breast Cancer Incidence Rates between Black and White Ethnic Groups." *Journal of the National Cancer Institute* 100(24):1804–14.

Berger, Mitchel, Mary Jo Lund, and Otis W Brawley. 2007. "Racial Disparities in Lung Cancer." *Current Problems in Cancer* 31(3):202–10.

Bertrand, Marianne and Sendhil Mullainathan. 2004. "Are Emily and Greg More Employable Than Lakisha and Jamal? A Field Experiment on Labor Market Discrimination." *American Economic Review* 94(4):991–1013.

Bibbins-Domingo, Kirsten, Mark J. Pletcher, Feng Lin, Eric Vittinghoff, Julius M. Gardin, Alexander Arynchyn, Cora E. Lewis, O. Dale Williams, and Stephen B. Hulley. 2009. "Racial Differences in Incident Heart Failure among Young Adults." *New England Journal of Medicine* 360(12):1179–90.

Booske, Bridget C., Stephanie A. Robert, and Angela M. Rohan. 2011. "Awareness of Racial and Socioeconomic Health Disparities in the United States: The National Opinion Survey on Health and Health Disparities, 2008–2009." *Preventing Chronic Disease* 8 (4):A73:1–9.

Bramley, Dale, Paul Hebert, Rod Jackson, and Mark Chassin. 2004. "Indigenous Disparities in Disease-Specific Mortality, a Cross-Country Comparison: New Zealand, Australia, Canada, and the United States." *New Zealand Medical Journal* 117(1207):U1215.

Braveman, Paula A., Catherine Cubbin, Susan Egerter, David R. Williams, and Elsie Pamuk. 2010. "Socio-economic Disparities in Health in the United States: What the Patterns Tell Us." *American Journal of Public Health* 100(Suppl. 1):S186–96.

Bruce, Marino A., Bettina M. Beech, Mario Sims, Tony N. Brown, Sharon B. Wyatt, Herman A. Taylor, David R. Williams, and Errol Crook. 2009. "Social Environmental Stressors, Psychological Factors, and Kidney Disease." *Journal of Investigative Medicine* 57(4): 583–9.

Centers for Disease Control and Prevention. 2011. "CDC Health Disparities and Inequalities Report—United States." *Morbidity and Mortality Weekly Report* 60(Suppl.):1–116.

Chlebowski, Rowan T., Zhao Chen, Garnet L. Anderson, Thomas Rohan, Aaron Aragaki, Dorothy Lane, Nancy C. Dolan, Electra D. Paskett, Anne McTierman, F. Alan Hubbell, Lucile L. Adams-Campbell, and Ross Prentice. 2005. "Ethnicity and Breast Cancer: Factors Influencing Differences in Incidence and Outcome." *Journal of the National Cancer Institute* 97(6):439–48.

Coker, Tumaini R., Marc N. Elliott, David E. Kanouse, Jo Anne Grunbaum, David C. Schwebel, M. Janice Gilliland, Susan R. Tortolero, Melissa F. Peskin, and Mark A. Schuster. 2009. "Perceived Racial/Ethnic Discrimination among Fifth-Grade Students and Its Association with Mental Health." *American Journal of Public Health* 99(5):878–84.

Colen, Cynthia G. 2011. "Addressing Racial Disparities in Health Using Life Course Perspectives." *Du Bois Review: Social Science Research on Race* 8(1):79–94.

Davey, Lynn. 2009. "Talking About Disparities: The Effect of Frame Choices on Support for Race-Based Policies." Washington, DC: FrameWorks Institute.

DuBois, William E. B. [1899] 1967. *The Philadelphia Negro: A Social Study.* New York: Schocken.

Engels, Frederick. [1845] 1984. *The Condition of the Working Class in England.* Chicago: Academy Chicago.

Fillmore, Kaye M., Jacqueline M. Golding, Karen L. Graves, Steven Kniep, E. Victor Leino, Anders Romelsjo, Carlisle Shoemaker, Catherine R. Ager, Peter Allebeck, R., and Heidi P. Ferrer. 1998. "Alcohol Consumption and Mortality. III. Studies of Female Populations." *Addiction* 93(2):219–29.

Fuchs, Flávio D., Lloyd E. Chambless, Aaron R. Folsom, Marsha L. Eigenbrodt, Bruce B. Duncan, Adam Gilbert, and Moyses Szklo. 2004. "Association between Alcoholic Beverage Consumption and Incidence of Coronary Heart Disease in Whites and Blacks: The Atherosclerosis Risk in Communities Study." *American Journal of Epidemiology* 160(5):466–74.

Fuchs, Flávio D., Lloyd E. Chambless, Paul K. Whelton, F. Javier Nieto, and Gerardo Heiss. 2001. "Alcohol Consumption and the Incidence of Hypertension: The Atherosclerosis Risk in Communities Study." *Hypertension* 37(5):1242–50.

Gee, Gilbert C. and Devon C. Payne-Sturges. 2004. "Environmental Health Disparities: A Framework Integrating Psychosocial and Environmental Concepts." *Environmental Health Perspectives* 112(17):1645–53.

Geronimus, Arline T. 1992. "The Weathering Hypothesis and the Health of African-American Women and Infants: Evidence and Speculations." *Ethnicity and Disease* 2(3):207–21.

Geronimus, Arline T., Margaret Hicken, Danya Keene, and John Bound. 2006. "'Weathering' and Age Patterns of Allostatic Load Scores among Blacks and Whites in the United States." *American Journal of Public Health* 96(5):826–33.

Goodman, Robert M., Marjorie A. Speers, Kenneth McLeroy, Stephen Fawcett, Michelle Kegler, Edith Parker, Steven Rathgeb Smith, Terrie D. Sterling, and Nina Wallerstein. 1998. "Identifying and Defining the Dimensions of Community Capacity to Provide a Basis for Measurement." *Health Education and Behavior* 25(3):258–78.

Hamilton, Charles, Lynn Hutnley, Neville Alexander, Antonio Sergio Alfredo Guimaraes, and Wilmot James. 2001. *Beyond Racism: Race and Inequality in Brazil, South Africa and the United States.* Boulder, CO: Lynne Rienner.

Indian Health Service. 2009. "Trends in Indian Health 2002–2003." Rockville, MD: U.S. Department of Health and Human Services, Indian Health Service.

Jackson, James S., Tony N. Brown, David R. Williams, Myriam Torres, Sherill L. Sellers, and Kendrick Brown. 1996. "Racism and the Physical and Mental Health Status of African Americans: A Thirteen Year National Panel Study." *Ethnicity and Disease* 6(1–2):132–47.

Jolly, Stacey, Eric Vittinghoff, Arpita Chattopadhyay, and Kirsten Bibbins-Domingo. 2010. "Higher Cardiovascular Disease Prevalence and Mortality among Younger Blacks Compared to Whites." *American Journal of Medicine* 123(9):811–18.

Kaplan, George A., Nalini Ranjit, and Sarah Burgard. 2008. "Lifting Gates—Lengthening Lives: Did Civil Rights Policies Improve the Health of African-American Woman in the 1960s and 1970s?" Pp. 145–69 in *Making Americans Healthier: Social and Economic Policy as Health Policy*, edited by R.F. Schoeni, J.S. House, G.A. Kaplan, and H. Pollack. New York: Russell Sage.

McLeroy, Kenneth R., Barbara L. Norton, Michelle C. Kegler, James N. Burdine, and Ciro V. Sumaya. 2003. "Community-Based Interventions." *American Journal of Public Health* 93(4):529–33.

Murphy, Sherry L. 2000. "Deaths: Final Data for 1998." *National Vital Statistics Reports* 48(11):1–105.

Naimi, Timothy S., David W. Brown, Robert D. Brewer, Wayne H. Giles, George Mensah, Mary K. Serdula, Ali H. Mokdad, Daniel W. Hungerford, James Lando, Shapur Naimi, and Donna F. Stroup. 2005. "Cardiovascular Risk Factors and Confounders among Nondrinking and Moderate-Drinking U.S. Adults." *American Journal of Preventive Medicine* 28(4):369–73.

National Center for Health Statistics. 2011. "Health, United States, 2010." Hyattsville, MD: U.S. Department of Health and Human Services, Centers for Disease Control and Prevention.

Nazroo, James Y. and David R. Williams. 2006. "The Social Determination of Ethnic/Racial Inequalities in Health." Pp. 238–66 in *Social Determinants of Health*, edited by M. G. Marmot and R. G. Wilkinson. New York: Oxford University Press.

Office of Management and Budget. 1997. "Revisions to the Standards for the Classification of Federal Data on Race and Ethnicity." *Federal Register* 62:58781–90.

Pager, Devah. 2003. "The Mark of a Criminal Record." *American Journal of Sociology* 108(5):937–75.

Pascoe, Elizabeth A. and Laura S. Richman. 2009. "Perceived Discrimination and Health: A Meta-Analytic Review." *Psychological Bulletin* 135(4):531–54.

Pearson, Jay A. and Arline T. Geronimus. 2011. "Race/Ethnicity, Socioeconomic Characteristics, Coethnic Social Ties, and Health: Evidence from the National Jewish Population Survey." *American Journal of Public Health* 101(7):1314–21.

Perez-Stable, Eliseo J., Brenda Herrera, Peyton Jacob, III, and Neal L. Benowitz. 1998. "Nicotine Metabolism and Intake in Black and White Smokers." *JAMA* 280(2):152–56.

Pew Research Center. 2011a. "GOP Makes Big Gains among White Voters." Washington, DC: Pew Research Center.

Pew Research Center. 2011b. "Wealth Gaps Rise to Record Highs between Whites, Blacks and Hispanics." Washington, DC: Pew Research Center.

Pletcher, Mark J., Paul Varosy, Catarina I. Kiefe, Cora E. Lewis, Stephen Sidney, and Stephen B. Hulley. 2005. "Alcohol Consumption, Binge Drinking, and Early Coronary Calcification: Findings from the Coronary Artery Risk Development in Young Adults (CARDIA) Study." *American Journal of Epidemiology* 161(5):423–33.

Robert, Stephanie A. and Bridget C. Booske. 2011. "US Opinions on Health Determinants and Social Policy as Health Policy." *American Journal of Public Health* 101(9):1655–63.

Sempos, Christopher T., Jurgen Rehm, Tiejian Wu, Carlos J. Crespo, and Maurizio Trevisan. 2003. "Average Volume of Alcohol Consumption and All-Cause Mortality in African Americans: The NHEFS Cohort." *Alcoholism, Clinical and Experimental Research* 27(1):88–92.

Slopen, Natalie, Tené T. Lewis, Tara L. Gruenewald, Mahasin S. Mujahid, Carol D. Ryff, Michelle A. Albert, and David R. Williams. 2010. "Early Life Adversity and Inflammation in African Americans and Whites in the Midlife in the United States Survey." *Psychosomatic Medicine* 72(7):694–701.

Stinson, Frederick S., Thomas M. Nephew, and Mary C. Dufour. 1996. *U.S. Alcohol Epidemiologic Data Reference Manual.* Bethesda, MD: National Institute on Alcohol Abuse and Alcoholism.

Stranges, Saverio, Jo L. Freudenheim, Paola Muti, Eduardo Farinaro, Marcia Russell, Thomas H. Nochajski, and Maurizio Trevisan. 2004. "Greater Hepatic Vulnerability after Alcohol Intake in African Americans Compared with Caucasians: A Population-Based Study." *Journal of the National Medical Association* 96(9):1185–92.

Tavassoli, Mojgan. 2008. "Iranian Health Houses Open the Door to Primary Care." *Bulletin of the World Health Organization* 86(8):577–656.

Tobias, Martin, Tony Blakely, Don Matheson, Kumanan Rasanathan, and June Atkinson. 2009. "Changing Trends in Indigenous Inequalities in Mortality: Lessons from New Zealand." *International Journal of Epidemiology* 38(6):1711–22.

Tynes, Brendesha M., Michael T. Giang, David R. Williams, and Geneene N. Thompson. 2008. "Online Racial Discrimination and Psychological Adjustment among Adolescents." *Journal of Adolescent Health* 43(6):565–69.

Wallace, John M., Jr., Tony N. Brown, Jerald G. Bachman, and Thomas A. Laveist. 2003. "The Influence of Race and Religion on Abstinence from Alcohol, Cigarettes and Marijuana among Adolescents." *Journal of Studies on Alcohol* 64(6):843–48.

Warner, David F. and Mark D. Hayward. 2006. "Early-Life Origins of the Race Gap in Men's Mortality." *Journal of Health and Social Behavior* 47(3):209–226.

Williams, David R. 1997. "Race and Health: Basic Questions, Emerging Directions." *Annals of Epidemiology* 7(5):322–33.

Williams, David R. 2005. "The Health of U.S. Racial and Ethnic Populations." *Journals of Gerontology: Series B* 60B(Spec. No. 2):53–62.

Williams, David R. and Chiquita Collins. 1995. "U.S. Socioeconomic and Racial Differences in Health: Patterns and Explanations." *Annual Review of Sociology* 21:349–86.

Williams, David R. and Chiquita Collins. 2001. "Racial Residential Segregation: A Fundamental Cause of Racial Disparities in Health." *Public Health Reports* 116(5):404–16.

Williams, David R., Hector M. Gonzalez, Harold Neighbors, Randolph Nesse, Jamie Abelson, Julie Sweetman, and James S. Jackson. 2007a. "Prevalence and Distribution of Major Depressive Disorder in African Americans, Caribbean Blacks, and Non-Hispanic Whites: Results from the National Survey of American Life." *Archives of General Psychiatry* 64(3):305–15.

Williams, David R., Rahwa Haile, Hector M. Gonzalez, Harold Neighbors, Raymond Baser, and James S. Jackson. 2007b. "The Mental Health of Black Caribbean Immigrants: Results from the National Survey of American Life." *American Journal of Public Health* 97(1):52–59.

Williams, David R., Dolly John, Daphna Oyserman, John Sonnega, Selina A. Mohammed, and James S. Jackson. 2012. "Research on Discrimination and Health: An Exploratory Study of Unresolved Conceptual and Measurement Issues." *American Journal of Public Health* 102(5):975–78.

Williams, David R. and Selina A. Mohammed. 2009. "Discrimination and Racial Disparities in Health: Evidence and Needed Research." *Journal of Behavioral Medicine* 32(1):20–47.

Williams, David R., Selina A. Mohammed, Jacinta Leavell, and Chiquita Collins. 2010. "Race, Socioeconomic Status, and Health: Complexities, Ongoing Challenges, and Research Opportunities." *Annals of the New York Academy of Sciences* 1186:69–101.

Wilson, William Julius. 2011. "The Declining Significance of Race: Revisited & Revised." *Daedalus* 140(2):55–69.

Woolf, Steven H. 2011. "Public Health Implications of Government Spending Reductions." *JAMA* 305(18):1902–1903.

CHAPTER 24

Identity and Mental Health Status among American Indian Adolescents*

Whitney N. Laster Pirtle and Tony N. Brown

The present study extends previous work on the relationship between mental health and race. Specifically, this study focuses on the distress that arises from discrepancy between self and interviewer racial identifications. Using the National Longitudinal Study of Adolescent to Adult Health (Add Health) data, Laster Pirtle and Brown examine mental health consequences of inconsistency over time within expressed (self) and observed (interviewer) racial identifications among American Indians. Given that ***phenotype*** *signals race, they also examine whether skin color affects the relationship between racial inconsistency and mental health. Analyses show that observed racial inconsistency—and not expressed racial inconsistency—increased American Indians' depressive symptoms and suicidal ideation. That is, when interviewers labeled a respondent American Indian at one wave of data but not another, there were deleterious implications for mental health status. In addition, an interaction between observed inconsistency and skin color demonstrated that observed inconsistency tended to be harmful when respondents were observed as having light skin. They argue that observed inconsistency captures a distressing and negative mental health consequence associated with being not readily classifiable.*

Source: Adapted from Whitney N. Laster Pirtle and Tony N. Brown, "Inconsistency within Expressed and Observed Racial Identifications: Identity, Signaling, and Mental Health Status among American Indian Adolescents," *Sociological Perspectives*, SAGE Publications, Inc., first published August 29, 2015.

*Some text has been omitted. Please consult the original source.

Questions to Consider

How important is your racial identity to you? Race is often externally defined, which means that based on your phenotype, other people might make assumptions about your racial identity. What if, based on your physical traits and features, others regularly assumed you were a member of a different racial group? How do you think that would affect your sense of belonging to that racial group in particular or in American society more generally? Would it matter a little? A lot?

Racial identifications are labels signifying racial group membership, which allow individuals to claim their own or categorize others' group membership (Brown 1999; Hogg and Abrams 1988). Racial identifications are often thought of as fixed categories, and there is an assumed consistency when individuals classify their own and others' group membership. Indeed, research shows consistency is high when individuals classify blacks or whites (see Saperstein 2006), partly because phenotype signals racial group membership. However, other groups' racial identifications are far more complex. For example, Hispanics and American Indians have low rates of consistency across self- and other-reported racial identifications (e.g., Campbell and Troyer 2007; Wilkinson 2010) and approximately half of American Indians and Pacific Islanders chose a different racial identification in the 2010 U.S. Census than they did in the 2000 U.S. Census (Liebler et. al 2014:37). Regardless of whether they are *self-reported* or *interviewer-reported*, inconsistent racial identifications may signal cognitive dissonance or a disjointed identity standard, which can produce distress (Burke 1991; Campbell and Troyer 2007).

Prior research confirms negative mental health consequences due to inconsistency *between* expressed (i.e., self-reported) and observed (i.e., interviewer-reported) racial identifications (see Campbell and Troyer 2007; 2011; Cheng and Powell 2011). In the present study, we build on such work by investigating the mental health consequences of inconsistency *within* expressed and observed racial identifications. Given that phenotype signals race, we additionally examine whether skin color is related to racial inconsistency and its impact on mental health consequences.

Identities, Identifications, Inconsistency, and Skin Color

The Self and Identities

Gecas and Burke (1995:42) define the self as "composed of various identities, attitudes, beliefs, values, motives, and experiences, along with evaluative and affective components in terms of which individuals define themselves." Rosenberg (1979) further argues that the self has three regions: (a) the *expectant self* represents how an individual sees herself; (b) the *desired self* represents how an individual would like to see herself; and (c) the *presenting self* is how an individual shows herself to others. Through ongoing negotiations among the expectant, desired, and presenting regions, the full self is formed.

Racial identities are a component of the self and are also comprised of multiple regions (Cross 1991; Demo and Hughes 1990). For example, Harris and Sim (2002:615) describe three regions of racial identities. First, what an individual believes about his or her own race is *internal racial identity.* Second, words and actions that convey beliefs about an individual's race are *expressed racial identities.* Finally, what an observer believes about an individual are *external racial identities.* Furthermore, dimensions of racial identities are interdependent (Harris and Sim 2002; Rosenberg 1979). This means people often develop internal racial identities based upon external appraisals, and in turn, one's own appraisals can affect others' appraisals. The idea that identities are situational and dynamic is well established in social psychology (e.g., Cooley 1902).

Racial Identifications

Although we do not consider racial identifications equivalent to the self or identity(ies), we do argue racial identifications shape how both are experienced and encoded. As such, racial identifications provide a *proxy* for survey researchers interested in racial identities. Informed by Roth's (2010) typology of racial identifications, we consider a respondent's reply to a race question on a survey as representing an *expressed racial identification.* Similarly, an interviewer's assessment of a respondent's race during a survey represents an *observed racial identification.* Considering their situational and dynamic nature (as with identities), racial identifications can be inconsistently self-reported and even inconsistently interviewer-reported (see Saperstein and Penner 2014). Relevant to the present study, we suspect that such *within reporter variation,* whether the reporter is the self or an interviewer/other, could signal failures in the environment to confirm the desired (*racial*) self.

Inconsistent Expressed and Observed Racial Identifications

Prior research has examined conflicts *between* expressed (self) and observed (interviewer/other) racial identifications (for example, see Campbell and Troyer 2007; Roth 2010; Saperstein 2006; Vargas 2013; Veenstra 2011; Wilkinson 2010). We focus, however, on discrepancies *within* expressed and observed identifications. For example, using Add Health data, Harris and Sim (2002) found that 12% of adolescents provide inconsistent expressed racial identifications due to survey context during the same period of data collection. That is, 12% of youth reported one racial identification in the survey conducted at their school and a different racial identification in the survey conducted in their home. The authors concluded that having a family member present for an in-home interview might have affected adolescents' expressed racial identifications because it heightened salience of familial racial identifications (see also Liebler 2004).

Scholars have also studied changes in expressed racial identifications over time. Hitlin, Brown, and Elder (2006), also using Add Health data, found that 4% of adolescents reported inconsistent racial identifications over time and that multiracial youth were four times as likely to switch categories rather than self-identify consistently as multiracial. Additionally, multiracial youth with high parental socioeconomic status and ambiguous phenotype (i.e., light skin) were more likely to have inconsistency in expressed racial identifications (Doyle and Kao 2007; Hitlin et al. 2006). In a study using National Longitudinal Survey of Youth data, Saperstein and Penner (2012) examined changes in both expressed and observed racial identifications and found that 20% of respondents experienced some inconsistency over two decades. In a more recent study, Saperstein and Penner (2014) tracked both expressed and observed racial inconsistency in Add Health data to determine whether changes in racial identification over time resolved previously incongruent classifications. Moreover, they examined whether an interviewer reported a racial identification different than what the respondent reported and assessed whether the respondent then changed their racial identification in a later wave to match what the prior interviewer had reported them as. They found that incongruence between self and interviewer was not resolved through changing racial identifications over time; rather, more cases of discordance between self and interviewer were created over time than were resolved.

Inconsistent Racial Identifications among American Indians

American Indians have high rates of both inconsistent expressed and observed racial identifications (Liebler 2004; Liebler et al. 2014). In fact, comparing all racial groups, American Indians have the highest rates of expressed racial identification inconsistency over time (Doyle and Kao 2007; Harris and Sim 2002; Hitlin et al. 2006; Saperstein and Penner 2014). For instance, using Add Health data, Cheng and Powell (2011:348) reported that 80% of the self-identified American Indians at Wave 3 did not self-identify as American Indian at Wave 1. Additionally, American Indians have gone through historical shifts that shaped how they identify with their racial group (Nagel 1995). In terms of observed inconsistency, research has revealed that census enumerators routinely misclassified American Indians prior to 1960 (Snipp 1992), and further research has found that 80% of American Indians were not identified as American Indians by their own parents (Eschbach 1993). We agree with Campbell and Troyer's (2007:761) argument that American Indians are the exemplar case for investigating inconsistency because of the groups' heterogeneity, history of forced assimilation, and ambiguous phenotype.

Skin Color and Inconsistent Racial Identifications

Given the significance of phenotype in signaling racial group membership, skin color should not be neglected as a correlate of racial identification. For instance, Roth (2010) further distinguishes the category of observed racial identification in her typology and contends that it can be: (a) *appearance based*, which is imputed by physical features such as skin color, and (b) *interaction based*, which is imputed by characteristics signaled in interactions such as accent. Whereas interviewers can detect both appearance and interactions while administering a survey, skin color, a strong marker of appearance, is one indicator that is often recorded in surveys.

Research (Brebner et al. 2011; Saperstein 2012) confirms that skin color is important to how observers classify individuals. The *determinant features hypothesis* asserts that observers rely on certain physical features to distinguish between racial groups (Herman 2010). For instance, Brown and colleagues (1998) found that observers chose skin color as the most important characteristic when identifying a target's race. In a similar study, Herman (2010) found that observers classified individuals shown in photographs based primarily on targets' phenotypes.

Skin color is also important for expressed racial identification. For example, Rockquemore and Arend (2003) found that skin color constrained multiracial individuals' ability to identify as white. Those with lighter skin opted for white whereas those with darker skin could not. Not only are individuals aware of their skin color, they are aware of how others perceive their skin color (see Veenstra 2011), which has implications for choice of racial identification.

Skin Color and Inconsistent Racial Identifications among American Indians

Skin color plays a role in American Indians' racial identifications. Weaver (2013) suggests that most people view American Indians as having "medium brown skin; long, dark, straight hair; and dark eyes. The image might also include 'props' assumed to accompany an 'Indian' identity, such as horses, tepees, and—of course—feathers" (p. 287). Despite this monolithic depiction of American Indians, there is considerable skin color variation within the American Indian population (Nagel 1995; Vaughan 1982; Weaver 2013). Phenotypic divergence from an identity standard could produce racial inconsistency, especially among those with light skin, because they are ambiguous (Doyle and Kao 2007). Let's say, for instance, there are two young adults who self-identify as American Indian, express this racial identification, and have select American Indian features (e.g., thick, dark, straight hair)—except that one has darker skin tone and the other has light skin tone. Both may choose an American Indian identification, but observers may be more likely to identify them as American Indian and white, respectively (see Cheng and Powell 2011). Taking this example further, the light-skinned American Indian might recognize their ability to pass as white and change their own racial identification. In the next section, we connect identities, inconsistency, and skin color to derive hypotheses about American Indians' mental health status.

Racial Inconsistency, Skin Color, and American Indians' Mental Health Status

Although there is now ample evidence that racial inconsistency is common in some groups, psychological implications of inconsistency remains unclear. It is reasonable to hypothesize that inconsistent racial identifications would produce distress. Identity control theory suggests inconsistency creates lack of control over the self (Burke 1991). The identity standard, or a set of meanings defining oneself, is constantly adjusted from input from the environment—that is, perceptions from others and one's own reflected appraisals (Burke 1991). According to Burke (2006:83),

> error or discrepancy between the perceptions and the identity standard not only governs behavior, but also produces an emotional response. We feel distress when the discrepancy is large or increasing; we feel good when the discrepancy is small or decreasing.

Therefore, inconsistent racial identifications, representing discrepancy in identity standards and lack of control over the self, may have deleterious mental health implications.

In support of this notion, Campbell and Troyer (2007) addressed whether individuals who self-identify with one racial group but are observed by interviewers as belonging to a different racial group—what they term *misclassification*—experience poor mental health status. Using Add Health data, they found that misclassified American Indians (58%) reported increased levels of suicidal ideation and attempts and fatalism. However, Cheng and Powell (2011) identified several flaws in Campbell and Troyer's study. Of relevance here, Cheng and Powell demonstrated that most misclassified American Indians report inconsistent *expressed* identifications. That is, Cheng and Powell (2011) questioned whether misclassification was "real" because many American Indians inconsistently self-identify as such. We build upon this line of research by examining the psychological consequences of inconsistency *within* expressed racial identifications. Moreover, we reason that inconsistency within expressed racial identification indicates lack of control over the self, which could, in turn, have negative mental health consequences. Thus, we hypothesize the following:

> **Hypothesis 1**: Inconsistency across Wave 1 and Wave 3 in *expressed* racial identifications as American Indian would predict more mental health problems.

Observed racial inconsistency could also predict poor mental health status. As noted, *interviewer classification* represents how the generalized other perceives the respondent (see Campbell and Troyer 2007; Herman 2010). For instance, Saperstein and Penner (2014) contend that Add Health interviewers are representative of teachers, classmates, employers, and so on. These observers are privy to information about how the respondent looks and other racial cues (e.g., language, clothing style), all available in typical social interactions. Given variable dynamics of social interactions, observers' decisions about respondents' racial identifications could be inconsistent across observers or even over time. Further, research has shown that individuals have a sense of how observers classify them (Campbell and Troyer 2011; Stepanikova 2010; Vargas 2013). Perceptions that vary across observers likewise influence the identity standard (Burke 1991, 2006). Inconsistency in observations may manifest an individual's failure to *signal* with sufficient strength, clarity, and consistency their desire to be perceived as a certain racial identification. Thus, we examine whether inconsistency *within* observed racial identifications matters for mental health status. Moreover, we argue discrepancy among racial identifications by observers could also result in distress and hypothesize the following:

> **Hypothesis 2**: Inconsistency across Wave 1 and Wave 3 in *observed* racial identifications as American Indian would predict more mental health problems.

Finally, we address whether skin color impacts the relationship between inconsistency and mental health. Although extant literature directly connects racial misclassification to mental health status and, alternatively, skin color to mental health status, no studies to date explore the interaction between racial identification inconsistency and skin color in predicting mental health status. For instance, in separate analyses, Veenstra (2011) found that inconsistency between expressed and observed racial identifications (i.e., misclassification) predicted poor mental health outcomes *and* that dark skin also predicted poor mental health outcomes. He did not, however, examine misclassification and skin color in the same model or, more importantly, how skin color and misclassification interact to predict mental health outcomes.

Most literature that examines the relationship between skin color and mental health status reports findings consistent with Veenstra (2011): Darker skin predicts poor mental health. Such findings are consistent with the concept of colorism, which defines skin color as a system of stratification, with darker skin ranking the lowest. As a result, light skin is linked to higher economic status, preferences in dating, self-esteem, and mental health (see, for instance, Espino and Franz 2002; Hunter 2005, 2007; Russell, Wilson, and Hall 1992; Thompson and Keith 2001). However, within the racial identification literature, a colorism paradox emerges: Light skin can be viewed as a disadvantage in terms of racial authenticity (Hunter 2007). Specifically, lighter-skinned individuals are tasked with proving themselves to be an authentic member of a specific racial group.

Hunter (2005) illustrates the colorism paradox among Mexican Americans. On the one hand, dark skin among Mexicans signals Indian or African ancestry and is therefore associated with low status. On the other hand, dark skin among Mexicans is taken for evidence of having some Indian or African ancestry and is therefore associated with being authentically Mexican. Additionally, McDonough and Brunsma (2013:263) argue that, for multiracial individuals, "racial expectations are fundamentally tied to appearance." Moreover, if biracial individuals appear black but do not conform to expectations of what being black means, there might be negative repercussions for their experienced authenticity. McDonough's (2005) interviews with biracial Americans revealed that disappointment and aggravation occurred when biracial individuals' authenticity was questioned. These processes are also at work among American Indians. Weaver (2013) agrees that light skin among American Indians can lead to preferential treatment but refers to it as a double-edged sword. Moreover, Weaver (2013) argues that normative ideas about who is American Indian leads some people to discount authenticity of those whose appearance varies from expectations. She further argues that rejected authenticity harms individuals' sense of self, especially when those individuals do not fit the American Indian identity standard. Thus, light skin would amplify potential deleterious mental health effects of both expressed and observed racial inconsistency. Here, we hypothesize the following:

Hypothesis 3: The association between (expressed and observed) inconsistency and poor mental health would be more pronounced for American Indians with light skin color.

Methods

Data

We analyzed data from the National Longitudinal Study of Adolescent to Adult Health (Add Health). Add Health is a nationally representative sample of U.S. adolescents (Udry 1998, 2003). Add Health's multiple measures of racial identification (e.g., across survey context, waves, and reporter) make it an appropriate data source for the present study. The first wave of Add Health was collected in 1994 by sampling 7th to 12th graders and included a subsample of 20,745 adolescents in their homes. Wave 3 resampled 15,197 respondents, then young adults, from 2001–2002. Wave 2 was excluded from our analyses because it did not ask respondents to report their racial identification (i.e., it was "presumed" from Wave 1 data); thus we examine Waves 1 and 3.

Variables

Mental Health Status

Depressive symptoms, suicidal ideation, and use of psychological counseling measured at Wave 3 were our mental health outcome variables. A 10-item scale captured depressive symptoms. Respondents had to answer, for instance, whether they "could not shake off the blues," they "felt that people disliked [them]," and if they were "too tired to do things." All depressive symptom items were highly correlated with each other (alpha = .82). Suicidal ideation was measured as follows: "During the past 12 months, have you ever seriously thought about committing suicide?" (1 = yes; 0 = no). Finally, use of psychological counseling was measured as follows: "In the past 12 months, have you received psychological or emotional counseling?" (1 = yes; 0 = no).

Inconsistent Racial Identifications

We used two measures of inconsistent racial identifications among American Indians: *expressed* and *observed. Expressed inconsistency* captured discrepancies in self-report as American Indian across Wave 1 and Wave 3 (1 = yes; 0 = no). For instance, if a respondent self-reported as "American Indian" at Wave 1 and Wave 3, then they received a "0" (or "no") for expressed racial identification inconsistency. However, if a respondent self-reported "American Indian" at Wave 1 but did not report "American Indian" and instead only "white" at Wave 3, then they received a "1" (or "yes") on expressed racial identification inconsistency.

Observed inconsistency captured across wave discrepancies in interviewers' perceptions that the respondent was American Indian (1 = yes; 0 = no). The only difference between expressed and observed inconsistency was that interviewers reported the latter. If an interviewer identified a respondent as "American Indian" at Wave 1 and Wave 3, then they received a "0" (or "no") for observed racial identification inconsistency. However, if an interviewer identified a respondent as "American Indian" at Wave 1 but the respondent was not identified by an interviewer as "American Indian" and instead only "white" at Wave 3, then they received a "1" (or "yes") on observed racial identification inconsistency. Altogether, this means we restricted our sample to any respondent who was self- or other-identified as American Indian in either Wave 1 or Wave 3. [1]

We did include individuals who reported more than one race (i.e., multiple racial identifications) in our analyses to account for American Indians' high rates of multiple identifications. For instance, in one recent report from census data, nearly 44% of American Indians report more than one race (Liebler et al. 2014). We also agree that including multiple identifications better captures complexities of racial identifications (Saperstein and Penner 2014). Therefore, we operationalize racial inconsistency in this study as the absence of American Indian identification over time. This means that if a respondent checked "American Indian" and "white" at Wave 1 but only "American Indian" at Wave 3, then they had consistent racial identifications. [2] We include and control for American Indians with multiple racial identifications (1 = yes; 0 = no).

Skin Color

Measurement of respondents' skin color was coded as 1 = "white", 2 = "light brown", 3 = "medium brown", 4 = "dark brown", and 5 = "black." Skin color was observed and recorded by interviewers at Wave 3. The majority of the analytic sample (54%) was reported to have white skin color, 21% were reported to have light brown skin color, 13% were reported to have medium brown skin color, 7% were reported to have dark brown skin color, and 5% were reported to have black skin color.

Controls

Informed by previous work on this topic, we included several control variables. We controlled for sex (1 = male; 0 = female) and age (continuous). Add Health uses separate questions to assess race and Hispanic ethnicity: Respondents can identify as Hispanic and with any racial group. We therefore control for Hispanic ethnicity (1 = yes; 0 = no).[3] As mentioned above; multiple identifications (1 = yes; 0 = no) captures whether a respondent has checked at least one additional racial identification besides American Indian. Parental education proxies socioeconomic standing and equals the highest educational attainment of either parent (ranging from "8th grade or less" to "advanced degree"). Social support and substance abuse are key correlates of mental health status for American Indians (Middlebrook et al. 2001); thus, we controlled for closeness to parents (ranging from 1 = "not close at all" to 10 = "extremely close") and alcohol or marijuana use (1 = yes; 0 = no).

Results

For this analysis, we examined bivariate and multivariate statistical relationships using regression analysis that adjusted for Add Health's complex survey design.[4] First, Table 1 presents a cross-tabulation of *expressed* (self) identification as American Indian across waves. Rows represent self-identification at Wave 1 and columns represent self-identification at Wave 3. The tabulation shows that 176 respondents expressed consistent American Indian identifications across waves; 269 respondents self-identified as American Indian at Wave 1 but not at Wave 3; and 401 self-identified as not American Indian at Wave 1 but as American Indian at Wave 3. Also shown in Table 1 are the 31 respondents did not self-identify as American Indian at either wave, and are thus not included in the expressed inconsistency analysis (these respondents are included in the full analytic sample total because they were

Table 1 Cross-Tabulation of Expressed (Self) Racial Identifications among American Indian Respondents from Wave 1 to Wave 3, Add Health

		Wave 3		
Racial Identification		***American Indian***	***~American Indian***	
Wave 1	American Indian	176 (20%)	296 (33%)	472
	~American Indian	401 (44%)	31 (3%)	432
		577	327	904

Note: Adjusted for the complex survey design. Design-based χ^2 = 276.5512***.
Add Health = National Longitudinal Study of Adolescent to Adult Health; ~ = Not.
***$p \leq .001$, two-tailed tests.

Table 2 Cross-Tabulation of Observed (Interviewer) Racial Identifications of American Indian Respondents from Wave 1 to Wave 3, Add Health

		Wave 3		
Racial Identification		***American Indian***	***~American Indian***	
Wave 1	American Indian	81 (9%)	68 (8%)	149
	~American Indian	93 (7%)	694 (76%)	755
		154	750	904

Note: Adjusted for the complex survey design. Design-based χ^2 = 119.973***.
Add Health = National Longitudinal Study of Adolescent to Adult Health; ~ = Not.
***$p \leq .001$, two-tailed tests.

observed as American Indian). To sum, 79% of the 873 respondents represented in this sample self-identified as American Indian expressed inconsistency in their racial identifications.

Table 2 presents a cross-tabulation of *observed* (interviewer) American Indian racial identifications across waves. Rows represent interviewer observations at Wave 1 and columns represent interviewer observations at Wave 3. The tabulations show that interviewers observed 81 respondents as American Indian at both waves; 68 as American Indian at Wave 1 but not at Wave 3; and 93 were identified as not American Indian at Wave 1 but as American Indian at Wave 3. Also shown in Table 2 are the 694 respondents were never observed as American Indian and are thus not included in the observed inconsistency analysis. To sum, 77% of the 242 respondents in this sample were inconsistently observed as American Indian.[5]

To sum, rates of expressed and observed inconsistency were high in among American Indian respondents (see Tables 1 and 2). As a comparison point, rates for other racial groups in the Add Health data were remarkably lower: blacks = 2.8% expressed inconsistency, 2.9% observer inconsistency; whites = 5.7% expressed inconsistency, 3.8% observer inconsistency; Asians = 12.9% self-identified inconsistency, 16.8% observer-identified inconsistency.

Table 3 displays descriptive and bivariate statistics for study variables by type of racial identification inconsistency. Table 3 does show differences in sample characteristics within both the expressed and observed inconsistency subsamples; however, there were more differences between American Indians in the observed inconsistency sample (right panel of Table 3). Interestingly, at the bivariate level, evidence suggests that racial identification inconsistency was not related to mental health status.

Table 4 shows results from three sets of regression models. All models control for the sample characteristics (i.e., gender, age, Hispanic ethnicity, multiple identifications, parental education, closeness to parents, alcohol or marijuana use), and also Wave 1 mental health status (these variables were removed from the tables for ease of interpretation but results are available upon request). The first, or baseline, models exclude skin color. Models were then repeated to include an interaction between skin color and racial inconsistency. Depressive symptoms was the outcome for models 1a and 1b, suicidal ideation was the outcome for model 2a and 2b, and use of psychological counseling was the outcome for model 3a and 3b.

Table 3 Study Variables by Inconsistency in Expressed (Self) and Observed (Interviewer) Racial Identifications: American Indian Respondents in Add Health

	Expressed Inconsistency		***Observed Inconsistency***	
	Yes	***No***	***Yes***	***No***
Depressive Symptoms	Not significant	Not significant	Not significant	Not significant
Suicidal Ideation (1 = yes; 0 = no)	Not significant	Not significant	Not significant	Not significant
Use of Psychological Counseling (1 = yes; 0 = no)	Not significant	Not significant	Not significant	Not significant

[***Editor's note:*** Please consult the original source for statistical output. For ease of presentation, the table presents data in terms of statistical significance (significant/not significant) for variables of interest only.]

We found that expressed racial identification inconsistency had no association with depressive symptoms, suicidal ideation, or use of psychological counseling. Skin color also did not have a significant main effect. Similarly, an interaction between expressed inconsistency and skin color was statistically insignificant. Hence, we found little evidence to support Hypothesis 1 and Hypothesis 3 when considering expressed racial identification inconsistency.

In Table 5, we substituted observed racial identification inconsistency for expressed racial identification inconsistency and replicated the three sets of regression models. Model 1a shows that there was a significant and positive effect of observed inconsistency on increased depressive symptoms, such that being inconsistently identified as American Indian was linked to more depressive symptoms. In addition, the interaction between observed inconsistency and skin color was significant (Model 1b). Respondents inconsistently observed as American Indian and having light skin color reported higher levels of depressive symptoms than those inconsistently observed as American Indian and having dark skin color. That is, the deleterious impact of observed inconsistency on mental health status was amplified by light skin. The converse was true for respondents observed consistently as American. For those respondents with the darkest shades of skin color, observed inconsistency was less psychologically damaging than being consistently classified by interviewers as American Indian.

Model 2a shows that observed inconsistency was significantly associated with increased likelihood of suicidal ideation. The odds of suicidal ideation were larger for those who were inconsistently observed as American Indian compared to those with consistent observed identification. In Model 2b, the interaction between observed inconsistency and skin color was negative and significant. However, even when respondents had darker skin color, being inconsistently observed was detrimental. That is, dark skin actually increased all American Indians' likelihood of suicidal ideation. It is important to remember that there are fewer number of respondents in the darker-skin categories. Nonetheless, at "black" skin color, those consistently observed had the highest probability of suicidal ideation.

Finally, Models 3 predict psychological counseling. We found no direct effect of observed inconsistency (Model 3a) but the interaction between observed inconsistency and skin color in Model 3b was significant. The interaction reveals that American Indians who were

Table 4 Coefficients from Regressions of Mental Health Status on Inconsistency in Expressed (Self) Racial Identification: American Indian Respondents in Add Health

	Depressive Symptoms (n = 812)		***Suicidal Ideation (n = 787)***		***Use of Psychological Counseling (n = 813)***	
	Model 1a	***Model 1b***	***Model 2a***	***Model 2b***	***Model 2a***	***Model 3b***
Expressed Inconsistency (1 = yes; 0 = no)	Not Significant	Not Significant	Not Significant	Not Significant	Not Significant	Not Significant
Expressed Inconsistency x Skin color		Not Significant		Not Significant		Not Significant

[***Editor's note:*** Please consult the original source for statistical output. For ease of presentation, the table presents data in terms of statistical significance (significant/not significant) for variables of interest only.]

Table 5 Coefficients from Regressions of Mental Health Status on Inconsistency in Observed (Self) Racial Identification: American Indian Respondents in Add Health

	Depressive Symptoms (n = 229)		***Suicidal Ideation (n = 221)***		***Use of Psychological Counseling (n = 228)***	
	Model 1a	***Model 1b***	***Model 2a***	***Model 2b***	***Model 3a***	***Model 3b***
Observed Inconsistency (1 = yes; 0 = no)	Significant	Significant	Significant	Significant	Not Significant	Significant
Observed Inconsistency x Skin color		Significant		Significant		Significant

[***Editor's note:*** Please consult the original source for statistical output. For ease of presentation, the table presents data in terms of statistical significance (significant/not significant) for variables of interest only.]

observed inconsistently and observed as light skinned had the highest probability of using psychological counseling. However, for respondents with dark skin color, being consistently observed was harmful.

Contrary to null results for expressed racial identification inconsistency shown in Table 4, Table 5 showed that observed racial identification inconsistency damaged mental health status. Specifically, a direct effect of observed inconsistency was supported for depressive symptoms and suicidal ideation. In addition, the interaction between observed inconsistency and skin color revealed that those who were observed inconsistently and who were also observed as having light skin reported increased depressive symptoms and use of psychological counseling. To sum, these results provide support Hypothesis 2 and Hypothesis 3 for observed inconsistency (but not Hypothesis 1 and Hypothesis 3 for expressed inconsistency).

Discussion

Our contribution is an examination of *within reporter* (i.e., self and interviewer) *over time* racial identification inconsistency and its mental health consequences. We additionally contribute by bringing skin color into the ongoing conversation about racial identifications. Overall, we found that *expressed* (self) racial identification inconsistency across two waves of data did not have mental health consequences. However, we found that *observed* (interviewer) racial identification inconsistency harmed mental health, and this was especially true when respondents were reported having the lightest skin color.

Why was only one type of racial identification inconsistency potent and what are the implications of our results for identity theory? Cheng and Powell (2011) imply that variation within expressed racial identifications in the Add Health data may indicate confused or troubled respondents. Furthermore, identity theory proposes that a disjoint in the identity standard-feedback loop (i.e., inconsistent cues about the self) could result in cognitive dissonance and distress (Burke 1991, 2006). Our findings contradict this line of reasoning. Discrepancy in expressed racial identifications among American Indian respondents was not psychologically harmful. What then are plausible explanations for our (null) findings? Saperstein and Penner (2014) argue that most individuals who change their race (not just American Indians) do so for three main reasons (1) to follow classification norms, (2) as a means to achieve higher prestige or move away from negative connotations, and/or (3) because they have a wide range of available classifications to choose from.

We offer two related explanations for American Indians. First, identifying inconsistently as American Indian could be a strategy in service of securing material rewards allotted to this underrepresented group (Nagel 1995) or avoiding stigma associated with being a discriminated-against group (see Saperstein 2012). It might also represent a newfound familial heritage (Liebler 2004). Second, the transition to adulthood is a time of experimentation. Trying on different racial identifications may be a normal process for American Indians and for other groups wearing ambiguous racial uniforms (Doyle and Kao 2007; Hitlin et al. 2006; Rockquemore and Brunsma 2008). We conclude that inconsistency in expressed racial identification as American Indian does not appear to represent a weak or troubled sense of self but might be an exercise in agency.

In contrast, inconsistent observation as American Indian predicted elevated levels of poor mental health. [6] Although prior research establishes the more obvious result that misclassification *between* self-reported race and other-reported race can be harmful (Campbell and Troyer 2007; Stepanikova 2010; Veenstra 2011), little work attends to inconsistency *within* observed racial identifications or does so with longitudinal data. Still, we claim that identity theory provides plausible explanations for the deleterious impact of observed racial identification inconsistency. According to Burke (1991, 2006) lack of control of one's identity can be detrimental. Inconsistency in observation as American Indian may manifest the respondent's failure to *signal* with sufficient strength, clarity, and consistency their desire to be perceived as American Indian.

Racial signaling is important. For instance, MacLin and Malpass (2001) found that changing a hairstyle from one that is stereotypically Latino to stereotypically black on a racially ambiguous person meant observers were more likely to categorize the ambiguous person in the direction of the racial marker (the person would be identified as black, in this example). Without a clear signal, interviewers may have been confused about the authenticity of respondents' racial group membership. If respondents typically give off ambiguous racial cues, then it is possible that those respondents would be observed inconsistently as American Indian. Such may be the case for the nearly 90% of respondents who interviewers thought were American Indian who themselves reported a self-racial identification as American Indian. Similarly, Campbell and Troyer (2011:752) said:

> We hypothesize that young American Indians today experience added stress, not because they feel unclear about their identity, but because others routinely racially misclassify them. In other words, many young American Indians appear racially ambiguous to others, even if they do not have any internal conflict over their "true identity."

Importantly, however, we also contend that respondents (American Indian or not) may experience poor mental health because they are perceived ambiguously and identified inconsistently by those around them. Following this line of reasoning, previous research (e.g., Doyle and Kao 2007; Hitlin et al. 2006) demonstrates that inconsistency in racial identifications occurs often when an individual's phenotype is ambiguous. Indeed, significant interactions between inconsistency in observed racial identifications and skin color further support our conclusion. Specifically, respondents with light skin color who were inconsistently observed as American Indian reported higher levels of depressive symptoms and use of psychological counseling than their consistently observed counterparts with light skin. Furthermore, there were crossovers in two of the interactions such that observed racial identification inconsistency became less harmful when respondents' skin color became dark. However, caution is warranted when interpreting effects at the dark end of the skin color continuum because cell counts there were small—the majority of American Indians were observed to have "white" or "light brown" skin color.

We contend that individuals with light skin are more ambiguous and must signal their racial group membership and racial authenticity. Not only is failure to signal membership into a racial identification group problematic then, but the generalizable experience of inconsistent racial identifications by observers is problematic. We reason that individuals with light skin, who might also have ambiguous racial cues, likely encounter identity interruptions that require negotiation of others' perceptions. In other words, fielding questions about one's race—or even perceiving others to be confused about your race—causes distress. An example of a racial identity interruption could be the confrontation with the "*What are you?*" question. People with ambiguous racial features routinely report being asked this query (see Gaskins 1999; McDonough 2005; Williams 1996). For instance, multiracial respondents in Williams' (1996) study recall being asked this question by acquaintances and even strangers, who are inquisitive about their expressed racial identification. What's more, Sue's (2010) research on multiracial populations asserts that this type of racial identity interruption is a *microaggression*, a mundane but psychologically harmful stressor. We take it a step further and argue that *observed inconsistency acts as a marker for the stressful experiences associated with being not readily classifiable in a world obsessed with tidy racial classifications.*

In contrast, at the dark end of the skin-color continuum, we observe a result consistent with main effects of skin color as reported in prior studies—relatively dark-skinned racial minorities report poor mental health outcomes (e.g., Thompson and Keith 2001; Veenstra 2011). We assert that when consistency in observation as American Indian is confirmed by darker skin color, then there is little escape from identification with, and the associated sometimes stressful experiences of belonging to, a marginalized group. These results manifest the "no-win" or "double-edged sword" situation, produced by malicious nature of racism, faced by some American Indians today. On the one hand, when their phenotype dictates their observation by others as American Indian, they may be confronted with their assumed inferior placement in the racial hierarchy. On the other hand, when their phenotype allows them to be observed by others as racially ambiguous, they must work to signal their racial group membership and their authentic connection.

Our results suggest that racial identifications are socially constructed yet have critical consequence for outcomes such as mental health status. We agree with Roth's (2010) recommendation that scholars develop a *language of race* that communicates the multiplicity of social processes involved in its construction. Moreover, we must avoid the assumption that either racial self-identifications *or* others' observations are valid indicators (Cheng and Powell 2011; Saperstein and Penner 2012). It seems that now is a good time to more fully explore sociological factors that explain the lived fluidity and authenticity of racial group membership.

Notes

1. We note that response options for the self-reported and interviewer-reported racial identification questions changed between waves. Specifically, the *other* category was removed as a response option from the Wave 3 race questions. Respondents who choose only *other* at Wave 1 or who were observed as only *other* could not have consistent expressed racial identifications. Therefore, we omitted respondents who were self- or interviewer-identified as *other*. Although we removed respondents with an *other* identification from the paper, we included respondents who were self- or interviewer-identified as *other* in supplementary analyses and results were consistent with what is presented here.

2. This operationalization of multiple identifications has implications only for expressed racial inconsistency because interviewers were not allowed to check more than one race when categorizing respondents. We ran separate supplementary analyses including only monoracial American Indian respondents to determine whether incorporation of respondents with multiple identifications biased our results. Doing so substantially decreased our sample size, given the high rate of multiple-racial identifications among American Indians; however, the substantive conclusions were unchanged (results available upon request).

3. We also excluded Hispanics as a robustness check and results remained consistent.

4. Analyses were completed using Stata 12. The *-svy-* commands in Stata (see Chantala and Tabor 1999) adjusted for the Add Health's survey sampling design, including stratification and clustering, and sampling weights. We defined the American Indian subpopulation as respondents who self-identified *or* were interviewer-identified as American Indian in either wave (n = 904). This subpopulation was specified in *-svy-* commands for all analyses. Listwise detection was used for regression analyses.

5. Tables 1 and 2 represent independent samples in these analyses. For instance, respondents could be included in the expressed inconsistency sample and not the observed inconsistency subsample if they were never identified as American Indian by an interviewer. Likewise, respondents could be included in the observed inconsistency sample and not the expressed inconsistency subsample if they were identified as American Indian by an interviewer. Indeed, thirty-one cases in the bottom right cell of Table 1 represent respondents who never self-identified as American Indian (and therefore were not included in the expressed racial inconsistency subsample) but were identified as American Indian by an interviewer and were included in the observed racial inconsistency subsample. Given that those respondents never self-identified as American Indian, we ran supplementary analyses excluding them, and results were unchanged substantively. We therefore keep these respondents in our models, because expressed and observed racial identification inconsistency are separate processes. Furthermore, we believe it important to consider multiple forms of racial identification as potentially valid identifications (Campbell and Troyer 2007; Harris and Sim 2002; Roth 2010; Saperstein 2006).

6. In additional analyses (not shown), we explored the mental health significance across waves of first being observed as American Indian and then being observed as not American Indian and vice versa. Results were virtually identical to those presented above. Observed inconsistency was detrimental regardless of the sequence across waves that produced it.

References

Brebner, Joanne L., Olav Krigolson, Todd C. Handy, Susanne Quadflieg, and David J. Turk. 2011. "The Importance of Skin Color and Facial Structure in Perceiving and Remembering Others: An Electrophysiological Study." *Brain Research* 1388:123–133.

Brown, Tony N. 1999. "Predictors of Racial Label Preference in Detroit: Examining Trends from 1971 to 1992." *Sociological Spectrum* 19(4):421–442.

Brown, Terry D. Jr., Francis C. Dane, and Marcus D. Durham. 1998. "Perception of Race and Ethnicity." *Journal of Social Behavior and Personality* 13:295–307

Burke, Peter. 1991. "Identity and Social Stress." *American Sociological Review* 56(6): 836–849.

———. 2006. "Identity Change." *Social Psychology Quarterly* 69(1):81–96.

Campbell, Mary and Lisa Troyer. 2007. "The Implication of Racial Misclassification by Observers." *American Sociological Review* 72(5):750–76.

———. 2011. "Further Data on Misclassification: A Reply to Cheng and Powell". *American Sociological Review* 76(2):356–364.

Chantala, Kim and Joyce Tabor. 1999. "Strategies to Perform a Design-Based Analysis Using Add Health Data." Add Health Working Paper. Chapel Hill, NC: Carolina Population Center.

Cheng, Simon and Powell. 2011. "Misclassification by Whom?: A Comment on Campbell and Troyer." *American Sociological Review* 76(2):347–355.

Cooley, Charles H. 1902. *Human Nature and Social Order*. New York: Charles Scribner's Sons.

Cross, William. 1991. *Shades of Black*. Philadelphia, PA: Temple University Press.

Doyle, Jamie M. and Grace Kao. 2007. "Are Racial Identities of Multiracials Stable: Changing Racial Self-Identification among Single and Multiple Race Individuals." *Social Psychology Quarterly* 70(4):405–423.

Demo, David, and Michael Hughes. 199. "Socialization and Racial Identity among Black Americans." *Social Psychology Quarterly* 53(4):364–374.

Eschbach, Karl. 1993. "Changing Identifications among American-Indians and Alaska Natives." *Demography* 30(4):635–652.

Espino, Rodolfo and Michael M. Franz. 2002. "Latino Phenotypical Discrimination Revisited: The Impact of Skin Color on Occupational Status." *Social Science Quarterly* 83(2):613–23.

Gaskins, Pearl. 1999. *What Are You? Voices of Mixed-Race Young People*. New York: Holt.

Gecas, Viktor and Peter Burke. 1995. "Social Identities." Pp. 41–67 in *Sociological Perspectives on Social Psychology*, edited by K. Cook, G. Fine and J. House. Needham Heights, MA: Allyn and Bacon.

Harris, David R., and Jeremiah Sim. 2002. "Who is Multiracial? Assessing the Complexity of Lived Race." *American Sociological Review* 67(4):624–627.

Herman, Melissa. 2010. "Do You See What I Am? How Observes' Background Affect their Perceptions of Multiracial Faces." *Social Psychology Quarterly* 73(1):58–78.

Hitlin, Steven, J. Scott Brown, and Glenn H. Elder, Jr. 2006. "Racial Self-Categorization in Adolescence: Multiracial Development and Social Pathways." *Child Development* 77(5):1298–1308.

Hogg, Michael A. and Dominic Abrams. 1988. *Social Identifications: A Social Psychology of Intergroup Relations and Group Processes*. London, UK: Routledge.

Hunter, Margaret. 2005. *Race, Gender, and the Politics of Skin Tone*. New York: Routledge.

———. 2007. "The Persistent Problem of Colorism: Skin Tone, Status, and Inequality." *Sociology Compass* 1(1):237–254.

Liebler, Carolyn, A. 2004. "Ties of the Fringes of Identity." *Social Science Research* 33:702–723.

Liebler, Carolyn A., Sonya Rastogi, Leticia E. Fernandez, James M. Noon and Sharon R. Ennis. 2014. "America's Churning Races: Race and Ethnic Response Changes between Census 2000 and the 2010 Census." Working Paper #2014-09. Washington, D.C.: Center for Administrative Records Research and Applications U.S. Census Bureau.

MacLin, Otto H. and Roy S. Malpass. 2002. "Racial Categorization of Faces: The Ambiguous Race Effect." *Psychology, Public Policy, and Law* 7(1):98–118.

McDonough, Sara. 2005. *What Are You? A Sociological Study on the Racial Identity Development in Multiracial Individuals*. Undergraduate Thesis, Department of Sociology, College of William and Mary, Williamsburg, VA.

McDonough, Sara and David Brunsma. 2013. "Navigating the Color Complex: How Multiracial Individuals Narrate the Elements of Appearance and Dynamics of Color in Twenty-First-Century America." Pp. 257–272 in *The Melanin Millennium Skin Color as 21st Century International Discourse*, edited by J. Hall. New York: Springer.

Middlebrook, Denise L., Pamela L. LeMaster, Janette Beals, Douglas K. Novins, and Spero M. Manson. 2001. "Suicide Prevention in American Indian and Alaska Native Communities: A Critical Review of Programs." *Suicide and Life-Threatening Behavior* 31:132–65.

Nagel, Joane. 1995. "American Indian Ethnic Renewal: Politics and the Resurgence of Identity." *American Sociological Review* 60(6):947–965.

Rockquemore, Kerry Ann and Patricia Arend. 2003. "Opting for White: Choice, Fluidity and Racial Identity Construction in Post Civil-Rights America." *Race and Society* 5(1):49–64.

Rockquemore, Kerry A., and David L. Brunsma. 2008. *Beyond Black: Biracial Identity in America*. 2nd ed. New York: Rowman and Littlefield.

Rosenberg, Morris. 1979. *Conceiving the Self.* New York, NY: Basic Books.

Roth, Wendy. 2010. "Racial Mismatch: The Divergence Between Form and Function in Data for Monitoring Racial Discrimination of Hispanics." *Social Science Quarterly* 91(5): 1288–1311.

Russell, Kathy, Midge Wilson, and Ronald E. Hall. 1992. *The Color Complex: The Politics of Skin Color among African Americans.* New York: Random House.

Saperstein, Aliya. 2006. "Double-Checking the Race Box: Examining Inconsistency Between Survey Measures of Observed and Self-Reported Race." *Social Forces* 85(1):57–74.

———. 2012. "Capturing Complexity in the United States: Which Aspects of Race Matter and When?" *Ethnic and Racial Studies* 35(8):1484–1502.

Saperstein, Aliya and Andrew M. Penner. 2012. "Racial Fluidity and Inequality in the United States." *American Journal of Sociology* 118(3):676–727.

———. 2014. "Beyond the Looking Glass: Exploring Fluidity in Racial Self-identification and Interviewer Classification." *Sociological Perspectives* 57(2):86–207

Snipp, Matthew. 1992. "Sociological Perspectives on American Indians." *Annual Review of Sociology* 18:351–71.

Stepanikova, Irena. 2010. "Applying a Status Perspective to Racial/Ethnic Misclassification: Implications for Health." Pp. 159–83 in *Advances in Group Processes*, Vol. 27, edited by S. R. Thye and E. Lawler. Bingley, UK: Emerald Group Publishing.

Sue, Derald W. 2001. *Microagressions and Marginality: Manifestations, Dynamics and Impact.* Hoboken, NJ: John Wiley and Sons.

Thompson, Maxine S. and Verna M. Keith. 2001. "The Blacker the Berry: Gender, Skin Tone, Self-Esteem, and Self-Efficacy." *Gender and Society* 15(3):336–357.

Udry, J. Richard. 1998. *National Longitudinal Study of Adolescent [to Adult] Health (Add Health), Waves I & II, 1994–1996.* Chapel Hill, NC: Carolina Population Center.

———. 2003. *The National Longitudinal Study of Adolescent [to Adult] Health (Add Health), Wave III, 2001–2002.* Chapel Hill, NC: Carolina Population Center.

Vargas, Nicholas. 2013. "Off White: Color-blind Ideology at the Margins of Whiteness." *Ethnic and Racial Studies* 37(13):2281–2302.

Vaughan, Alden T. 1982. "From White Man to Redskin: Changing Anglo-American Perceptions of the American Indian." *The American Historical Review* 87(4):917–953.

Veenstra, Gerry. 2011. "Mismatched Racial Identities, Colourism, and Health in Toronto and Vancouver." *Social Science & Medicine* 73: 1152–1162.

Weaver, Hilary N. 2013. "What Color Is Red? Exploring the Implications of Phenotype for Native Americans." Pp. 287–300 in *The Melanin Millennium Skin Color as 21st Century International Discourse*, edited by J. Hall. New York: Springer.

Wilkinson, Lindsay. 201. "Inconsistent Latino Self-Identification in Adolescence and Academic Performance." *Race and Social Problems* 2(3):179–194.

Williams, Teresa K. 1996. "Race as a Process: Reassessing the "What Are You?" Encounters of Biracial Individuals." Pp. 191–210 in *The Multiracial Experience: Racial Borders as the New Frontier*, edited by M. P. P. Root. Thousand Oaks, CA: Sage.

CHAPTER 25

Assimilation and Emerging Health Disparities among New Generations of U.S. Children*

Erin R. Hamilton, Jodi Berger Cardoso,
Robert A. Hummer, and Yolanda C. Padilla

This essay shows that the prevalence of four common child health conditions increases across generations (from ***first-generation*** *immigrant children to* ***second-generation*** *U.S.–born children of immigrants to third- and higher-generation children) within each of four major U.S. racial/ethnic groups. In the third-plus generation, Black and Hispanic children have higher rates of nearly all conditions. Health care, socioeconomic status, parents' health, social support, and neighborhood conditions influence child health and help explain third- and higher-generation racial/ethnic disparities. However, these factors do not explain the generational pattern. The generational pattern may reflect cohort changes, selective ethnic attrition, unhealthy assimilation, or changing responses to survey questions among immigrant groups.*

Source: Adapted from Erin R. Hamilton, Jodi Berger Cardoso, Robert A. Hummer, and Yolanda C. Padilla, "Assimilation and Emerging Health Disparities among New Generations of U.S. Children," *Demographic Research*, Volume 25, Number 25, pages 783–818, Copyright Erin R. Hamilton et al. 2011. Used with permission.

*Some text has been omitted. Please consult the original source.

Questions to Consider

If the immigrant paradox suggests that immigrants are healthier than later generations born in the United States, what does this trend suggest about the relationship between health and assimilation? Thinking more broadly, does assimilation always result in improved circumstances for immigrants and their descendants?

Introduction

Children of immigrants currently make up one in four of all children in the United States, and this proportion is expected to increase to one-third by 2050 (Passel and Cohn 2008). Although children of immigrants are an ethnically and socioeconomically diverse group, on average they are more likely than children of natives to live in poverty, experience food insecurity, and live in crowded housing. Additionally, they are less likely than children of natives to receive public assistance or to have health insurance (Capps et al. 2004). Given the context of disadvantage facing this large and growing group, it is important to document and understand how children of immigrants are faring in terms of their health and development in comparison to children of native-born parents (Mendoza 2009).

In this article we provide a comprehensive picture of the health of children of immigrants in comparison to children of natives using recent, nationally representative data. Comparing immigrant generations within four race/ethnic groups, we examine the prevalence of seven common child health conditions and developmental outcomes: asthma, allergies, developmental problems, learning disabilities, ear infections, frequent headaches, and overweight. We distinguish between children of immigrants born abroad (i.e., first-generation children) and children of immigrants born in the United States (i.e., second-generation children) in comparison to U.S.-born children of U.S.-born parents (i.e., third-plus-generation children). We compare these immigrant generations within each of four major U.S. racial/ethnic groups, thereby building on work that compares Asian and Hispanic children of immigrants to black and white natives (e.g., Hernandez and Charney 1998; Mendoza and Dixon 1999; Padilla, Hamilton, and Hummer 2009). To do this, we use newly available data from the 2007 National Survey of Children's Health, the only existing national data set with samples large enough to estimate the prevalence of common child health conditions for twelve distinct race/ethnic/immigrant-generation groups: white, black, Hispanic, and Asian children in first, second, and third-plus generations.

Research on the Health of Children of Immigrants

Health Assimilation

In the immigration literature the classic theoretical model of assimilation understands assimilation as disappearing differences between groups over time (Alba and Nee 1997). A common assumption in classic assimilation theory is that disappearing differences implies disappearing disadvantage—that, over time, immigrants and their descendants move from marginal social and economic positions into the mainstream through upward mobility. The health assimilation model provides evidence of an opposite pattern. Immigrants tend to have better health than average when they arrive, and health assimilation, or disappearing differences in the health of immigrants and their descendants as compared to natives, implies worsening health over time and across generations.

In the past two decades critics of classic assimilation theory have developed a new paradigm called segmented assimilation which recognizes that immigrant groups arrive with diverse resources into diverse contexts of reception (Portes and Zhou 1993; Zhou 1997). According to the theory of segmented assimilation, this diversity may yield three patterns of assimilation—the classic version of upward mobility and declining difference over time, an ethnic retention model where immigrant groups arrive with substantial socioeconomic resources or achieve upward mobility while retaining a strong ethnic attachment, and downward mobility into the native underclass. A key factor shaping these various outcomes is race, and the three patterns of assimilation may reflect sorting into the U.S. racial stratification system: white immigrant groups are thought to generally follow the classic model, Asian immigrant groups are thought to generally follow the ethnic retention model, and black and some Hispanic immigrant groups are thought to generally follow the downward assimilation model (Portes and Rumbaut 2006). Racial identity and/or skin color may differentiate patterns among Hispanics, who share an ethnicity but are a racially diverse group (Frank, Akresh, and Lu 2010).

By examining the health of children across generations in distinct race/ethnic groups, we can assess the extent to which there is a common generational pattern across race/ethnic groups or whether race differentiates outcomes among generational groups, particularly within the third-plus generation.

Risk Factors

The first two sets of factors that are key to the immigrant paradox are access to health care and socioeconomic status. The fact that immigrants have good health despite socioeconomic disadvantage and limited access to care is why their good health is termed a paradox. Social models of racial disparities in health emphasize that racial disparities reflect societal and structural inequality (Hummer 1996; Williams and Sternthal 2010). This inequality is most clearly measured by group differences in socioeconomic status. Socioeconomic status (SES) is consistently associated with health in a graded fashion, meaning that high-SES groups live longer and healthier lives than low-SES groups (Adler et al. 1994).

Socioeconomic disadvantage and other forms of structural inequality affect health outcomes through a variety of factors, one of which is access to and quality of health care (Hummer 1996). Racial disparities in health may reflect racial disparities in health care since limited access to and poorer quality of care results in worse health outcomes (Williams and Sternthal 2010). However, in many survey data sets, including the National Survey of Children's Health (NSCH), the measurement of child health conditions is based on parental reports of doctor diagnosis (e.g., Mendoza and Dixon 1999). Thus, group differences in these reports may reflect the underdiagnosis of conditions among those with limited access to health care.

Protective Factors

Scholars have identified several factors that may protect immigrants and their children in the face of socioeconomic disadvantage and limited access to care. First, immigrants may benefit from tight-knit social networks (Guendelman 1998). Social networks are protective because they provide social support, which can serve to reduce stress and improve self-esteem (Umberson and Montez 2010), and instrumental support, including information and financial resources (Radey and Padilla 2009). For example, studies find that social support is associated with better self-reported health and can moderate the effects of discrimination (Finch and Vega 2003). One source of social support that may provide assistance to immigrants is religious institutions. Adults who attend religious services regularly have longer life expectancies than adults who attend irregularly or never attend (Hummer, Rogers, et al. 1999).

A second category of protective factors is parents' good health and health behaviors, especially among immigrant mothers. Studies have shown that maternal health behaviors are a primary protective factor for the good health of infants born to immigrant women (Reichman et al. 2008). Immigrants, particularly women, are less likely to smoke or drink than natives (Lopez-Gonzalez, Aravena, and Hummer 2005) and changes to these and other health behaviors may be a key pathway through which health assimilation occurs (Akresh 2009; Landale et al. 1999; Kimbro, Lynch, and McLanahan 2008). One central question arising from the literature on the paradox in children is whether the good health behaviors of mothers continue to protect their children past infancy (Guendelman 1998). The overall positive health selection of immigrants (Akresh and Frank 2008) may also influence better than average health among the children of immigrants.

Risk and Protective Factors at the Neighborhood Level

Beyond support available to children through their parents, other social relationships, and religious institutions, children of immigrants may benefit from social networks at the neighborhood level. Bond Huie and her colleagues (2002) found that mortality risks declined for adults in neighborhoods with large concentrations of foreign-born individuals, perhaps as a result of networks that are embedded in immigrant co-ethnic communities. Neighborhoods may also affect child health through other pathways, particularly through deleterious social and environmental conditions or through providing community resources and environments for safe outdoor play (Kimbro, Brooks-Gunn, and McLanahan 2011).

In sum, there are clear reasons to expect race/ethnic and immigrant status differences in child health. Moreover, we expect that measures of parental socioeconomic status, access to health care, health and health behavior, social support, and neighborhood resources help to explain both immigrant status differences and race/ethnic differences in child health. We now turn to an explanation of our data and methods and the summary of our study results.

Data and Methods

Data

The National Survey of Children's Health (NSCH) is a random-digit dial telephone survey designed to produce national and state estimates of the health status of U.S. children (Blumberg et al. 2009; Child and Adolescent Health Management Initiative 2007). One child was randomly selected within each household with children, and respondents were the child's parent or primary caregiver. The survey was administered in English, Spanish, and four Asian languages to 91,642 respondents.

Measures

Immigrant generation is based on the child's and their parents' place of birth. Children born outside of the United States are first generation (i.e., immigrants). Children who were born in the United States to one or two parents born abroad are second generation (i.e., children of immigrants). Children who were born in the United States and whose parents were both born in the U.S. are third-plus-generation. We were unable to distinguish between third and higher-order generations because grandparents' place of birth is not reported. Nor do we have information about the documentation, citizenship status, or timing of arrival of the first generation or of the parents of the second generation. The generational status groups were analyzed within each of four major U.S. racial/ethnic groups: non-Hispanic whites, non-Hispanic blacks, non-Hispanic Asians, and Hispanics of any race. The child's race was reported by the respondent. More specific national-origin or ethnic groups were not reported in the NSCH.

Results

Descriptive Results

Table 1 shows weighted, age-standardized percent distributions of the seven health conditions for the first, second, and third-plus generations by race/ethnicity. Figure 1 illustrates these patterns. For four common conditions—allergies, asthma, developmental problems, and learning disabilities (affecting 27.5%, 15.3%, 20.4%, and 10.6% of all children, respectively)—the data show a generally graded pattern of higher prevalence of health conditions in the second and third-plus generations. For example, the proportion of children with allergies

Table 1 Percent Distributions of Health Conditions for First-, Second-, and Third-Plus-Generation Children, by Race/Ethnicity

	White			*Hispanic*			*Black*			*Asian*			
	1st	*2nd*	*3rd+*	*1st*	*2nd*	*3rd+*	*1st*	*2nd*	*3rd+*	*1st*	*2nd*	*3rd+*	*All*
Allergies**	23.8	26.9	28.9	16.4	18.7	26.0	10.6	24.6	33.7	9.9	20.8	36.5	27.5
Asthma**	6.9	11.6	14.0	8.3	12.5	19.3	6.7	13.6	22.6	9.3	16.7	25.3	15.3
Developmental problems**	8.6	18.1	21.9	12.4	14.9	22.0	4.5	16.2	23.7	2.9	2.1	20.7	20.4
Ear infections**	2.4	3.3	4.8	5.7	6.3	4.9	7.2	5.0	4.5	0.5	0.5	3.2	4.8
Headaches**	8.0	4.8	5.4	2.3	2.1	6.8	0.1	4.2	6.0	0.0	3.7	3.8	5.2
Learning disabilities**	5.6	8.8	10.2	9.6	10.0	14.4	4.2	7.5	13.5	2.4	0.8	6.6	10.6
Overweight (>95% BMI)**	3.2	16.5	13.0	28.1	20.8	19.8	14.5	15.9	26.6	6.6	11.4	9.3	16.3
Unweighted N	558	2549	45482	937	3439	3654	157	578	6320	122	454	262	64509

Source: 2007 National Survey of Children's Health, Child and Health Measurement Initiative (CAHMI).
*p<.05, **p<.01 for differences across race/ethnicity/generation groups, on the basis of *F*-tests of equal means.

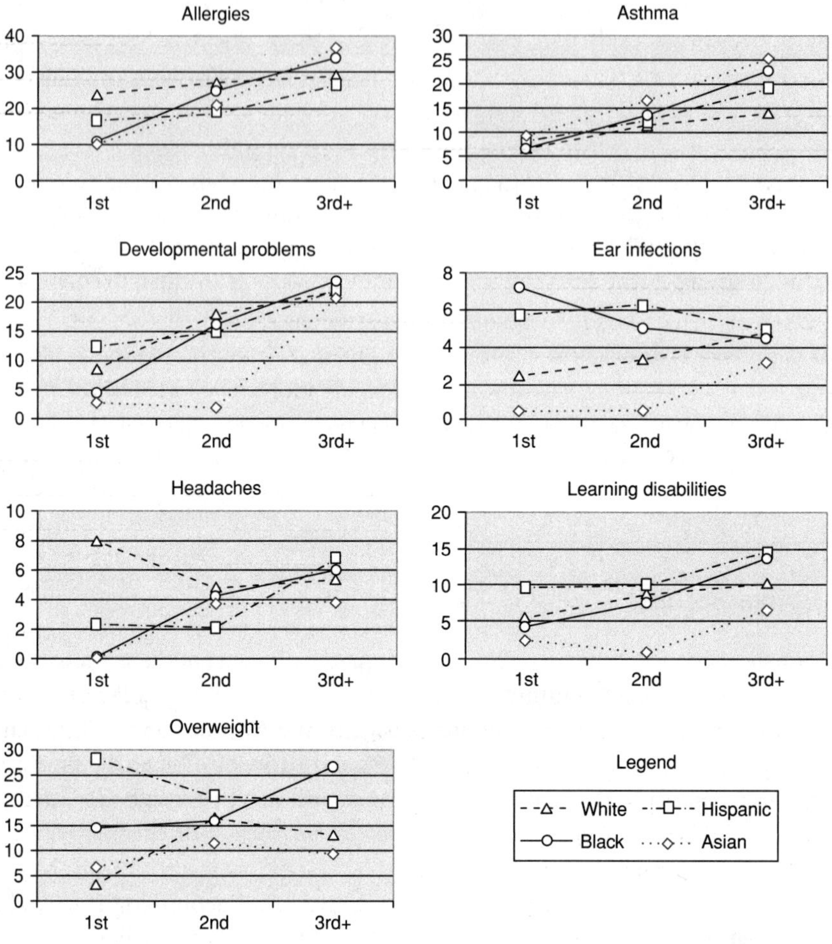

Figure 1 Prevalence of Child Health Conditions across Generations by Race/Ethnicity
Source: 2007 National Survey of Children's Health, Child and Health Measurement Initiative (CAHMI).

increases by 21% across the three generation groups for white children, by 58% for Hispanic children, and by more than 300% for black and Asian children. The prevalence of asthma more than doubles from the first to the third-plus generation for all groups. With only two exceptions (developmental problems and learning disabilities among Asians), there is a graded pattern whereby the proportion of children with these conditions increases from the first to the second generation and from the second to the third-plus.

A fourth condition, overweight, is prevalent among more than 15% of 10–17 year-olds and shows a graded pattern across the three generations for black children, but not for the other groups. For whites and Asians, the proportion of children who are overweight increases from the first to the second generation, but is lower in the third-plus generation. For Hispanic children, the pattern is reverse: the proportion of children who are overweight is highest in the first generation, lower in the second, and lowest in the third-plus generation. This outlying pattern for overweight among Hispanics is consistent with recent studies showing a higher rate of overweight among first- and second-generation Hispanic children (Buttenheim et al. 2011; Hamilton, Teitler, and Reichman 2011; Van Hook and Baker 2010).

A generational pattern is less consistent for the two remaining conditions, which affect proportionally fewer children (5.2% report frequent headaches and 4.8% report frequent ear infections). Headaches are most common among third-plus-generation Hispanic, black, and Asian children, but there is no consistent pattern between the first and second generations. Headaches are least prevalent among third-plus-generation white children, as compared to first- and second-generation white children. The prevalence of ear infections is highest in the third-plus generation of white and Asian children, but the prevalence decreases across generations for black children and exhibits no clear trend for Hispanic children.

Table 2 shows percent distributions of all of our covariates for first-, second-, and third-plus-generation children by race/ethnicity. Generational patterns in these characteristics are different across race/ethnic groups, with a general pattern of worsening conditions for white and black children across generations, as opposed to improving conditions for Hispanic and Asian children across generations, thus highlighting why it is important to [separate out] race/ethnicity and immigrant generation. For example, the proportion of white and black children living in poor households (i.e., below 100% of the federal poverty line) and the proportion of parents reporting poor general health or mental health is higher in the third-plus generation than in the first generation whereas the opposite is true for Hispanic and Asian children. The proportion of respondents with a college-level education and the proportion of children with private health insurance decreases across generations for black and white children, but increases across generations for Hispanic and Asian children. The relatively advantaged characteristics of first- and second-generation white and black children, compared to their third-plus-generation counterparts, likely reflects the higher socioeconomic status of the populations of origin (particularly of white immigrants) and a highly select pattern of migration out of origin populations (Akresh and Frank 2008; Feliciano 2005).

For the most part first-generation children are disadvantaged in terms of access to and use of care. Hispanic, black, and Asian first-generation children are less likely than their second- and third-plus-generation counterparts to have any health insurance coverage. Hispanic and black first-generation children are also less likely to have had preventive care in the past year and more likely than their later-generation counterparts to have had difficulty obtaining care in the past year. Because most of the health outcomes we analyze are parent reports of doctor-diagnoses, these patterns of less access to and use of care among first-generation children may suggest that the lower prevalence of health conditions is due to underdiagnoses, a possibility we test below.

A final pattern worth noting is the racial/ethnic inequality revealed in these data. Whereas white and Asian children are relatively advantaged, Hispanic and black (particularly black third-plus-generation) children are significantly disadvantaged. Comparing children of all generations, Hispanic first-generation children are by far the most disadvantaged group by these measures: more than half have no health insurance coverage, nearly four out of five live in poor households, and more than half of their responding adults (i.e., parent or caretaker) have less than a high school education. Comparing just third-plus-generation children, black children are the most disadvantaged in terms of poverty status, respondent education, single parent and other family types, parents' general and mental health, household smoking, emotional support, neighborhood support, and neighborhood disorder. The fact that first-generation Hispanic children are more disadvantaged than the most disadvantaged native minority group is, indeed, the reason their relatively good health noted here and in previous studies is considered paradoxical.

Table 2 Percent Distributions and Means of Demographic and Social Characteristics for First-, Second-, and Third-Plus-Generation Children, by Race/Ethnicity

	White			Hispanic			Black			Asian			
	1st	*2nd*	*3rd+*	*1st*	*2nd*	*3rd+*	*1st*	*2nd*	*3rd+*	*1st*	*2nd*	*3rd+*	*All*
Age (mean)**	11.6	10.1	10.5	11.6	9.6	10.2	13.2	10.0	10.7	11.8	9.2	10.1	10.4
Female (%)	52.4	44.6	48.2	48.0	48.0	51.4	47.0	49.9	49.5	45.5	54.8	53.8	48.7
Access to and use of health care													
Insurance coverage (%)**													
Private	86.2	83.5	76.8	19.6	31.6	57.1	40.8	57.6	38.7	61.8	81.9	95.7	64.3
Public	8.4	10.8	17.1	27.9	52.3	33.4	27.1	30.1	53.2	28.2	14.9	3.9	26.8
None	5.4	5.7	6.1	52.5	16.1	9.5	32.1	12.3	8.1	10.0	3.2	0.4	8.9
No preventive care in past year (%)**	10.2	9.8	13.9	24.5	14.1	14.9	14.1	6.2	10.0	15.2	15.9	13.9	13.5
Difficulty obtaining care in past year (%)**	4.0	5.6	6.1	11.3	7.7	9.2	12.1	10.1	9.1	3.7	1.8	6.4	7.0
Socioeconomic status and family structure													
Household income to poverty ratio (%)**													
<100	19.8	18.9	24.3	79.8	68.3	40.4	52.1	38.5	59.7	33.7	17.7	5.8	36.0
100-400%	34.5	28.3	37.7	13.6	22.7	34.2	39.3	30.4	26.1	32.4	24.7	40.6	33.1
>400%	45.7	52.8	38.0	6.6	9.0	25.4	8.6	31.1	14.2	33.9	57.6	53.6	30.9
Respondents' education (%)**													
<High school	1.6	2.7	5.8	52.4	45.9	10.9	15.0	7.2	13.0	2.2	6.9	0.1	12.8
High school or equiv	16.7	16.8	23.7	21.7	28.3	29.2	11.7	18.8	35.2	21.2	16.5	2.5	25.4
>High school	81.7	80.5	70.5	25.9	25.8	59.9	73.3	74	51.8	76.6	76.6	97.4	61.8

Family structure (%)**													
Two parent bio	81.9	79.7	72.6	68.5	72.3	50.8	43.2	62.1	30.7	78.5	94.2	81.3	65.6
Two parent step	5.6	9.6	8.7	8.3	7.7	11.2	24.9	8.4	10.1	0.9	1.3	1.7	8.9
Single parent	10.9	7.9	13.1	19.4	16.8	28.5	25.6	23.7	45.8	12.2	3.0	14.9	19.1
Other	1.6	2.8	5.6	3.8	3.2	9.5	6.3	5.8	13.4	8.4	1.5	2.1	6.4
Number of residential moves in child's life mean)**	3.1	1.7	1.8	2.5	2.4	2.4	2.1	1.7	2.4	1.7	1.4	0.9	2.0
Parents' health and behaviors													
Parent's health good/fair/poor**	21.8	23.6	27.8	62.9	57.1	39.2	44.0	37.2	47.0	48.6	31.9	25.4	35.6
Parent's mental health good/fair/poor**	13.4	22.3	23.9	51.5	44.3	31.7	38.1	25.4	37.4	34.9	28.0	11.5	29.4
Number of days parent exercises per week (mean)**	2.6	2.6	2.9	2.1	2.3	2.9	2.6	2.7	2.7	2.6	2.3	2.2	2.8
Someone in household smokes (%)**	19.8	20.6	27.7	21.8	19.3	29.5	7.5	11.4	30.2	17.7	12.8	4.9	26.1
Social support													
Respondent has emotional support (%)**	88.2	91.1	93.8	70.4	73.8	88.6	81.8	84.9	87.7	84.6	73.1	92.2	90.9
Child attends religious services regularly (%)**	51.7	47.8	54.1	56.8	60.4	51.6	75.5	65.2	61.6	53.2	43.0	51.4	55.5
Neighborhood environment													
Support scale (mean)**	3.45	3.45	3.56	3.15	3.19	3.33	3.15	3.24	3.14	3.35	3.40	3.45	3.42
Resources scale (mean)**	0.81	0.82	0.74	0.67	0.73	0.79	0.82	0.87	0.79	0.89	0.86	0.82	0.75
Disorder scale (mean)**	0.07	0.10	0.11	0.16	0.16	0.17	0.09	0.14	0.22	0.11	0.15	0.16	0.14
Unweighted sample size	558	2549	45482	937	3439	3654	157	578	6320	122	454	262	64509

Source: 2007 National Survey of Children's Health, Child and Health Measurement Initiative (CAHMI).

$^{*}p < .05$, $^{**}p < .01$ for differences across race/ethnicity/generation, on the basis of *F*-tests of equal means or chi-square tests of equal distributions.

Discussion

Patterns of Health Assimilation

This analysis extends the work that documents an immigrant health advantage at birth by investigating generational differences in seven health and development outcomes through childhood across four major U.S. racial/ethnic groups. For all groups, we find a generational status gradient in four common measures of child health: asthma, allergies, developmental problems, and learning disabilities. The prevalence of these conditions increases from the first to the second to the third-plus generation. The relative advantage of first-generation and second-generation children for these four outcomes is largely unexplained by differences across groups in access to and use of health care, socioeconomic status, family structure, parents' health and behaviors, social support, and neighborhood conditions. This advantage is paradoxical given that children of immigrants, particularly Hispanic immigrants, are socioeconomically disadvantaged compared to children of natives. Our results suggest that the immigrant paradox, which has been well documented at birth, persists into childhood for the first and second generations for some common measures of child health, but not others.

Indeed, we observed no consistent generational pattern for frequent ear infections, severe headaches, and overweight status. Among Hispanics, the pattern for overweight across generations is the reverse of that observed for allergies, asthma, developmental problems, and learning disabilities. We return to the implications of these inconsistencies below.

The process of health assimilation appears to be segmented, as by the third-plus generation there are significant racial and ethnic disparities in childhood health. As third-plus-generation whites and blacks are largely made up of higher-order generational descendants of immigrants and slaves arriving prior to or during the early 20th century, disparities between these two groups do not reflect the process of recent assimilation but rather the U.S. racial stratification system, a legacy of historic and contemporary racism. The fact that Hispanic third-plus-generation children have rates similar to black third-plus-generation children, and Asian third-plus-generation children have rates similar to white third-plus-generation children suggests that the process of health assimilation is segmented along racial lines as Asians and Hispanics are sorted into the U.S. racial stratification system. Further differentiation between immigrant groups among the third-plus generation would be helpful, but data sources that collect information about grandparents' place of birth are rare.

An important implication of these generational differences is that estimates of race/ethnic group disparities in child health may yield misleading conclusions if racial/ethnic groups are not disaggregated by immigrant generation. Because the majority of Hispanic children in the United States are first- or second-generation, the relative health disadvantage of the third-plus generation may be obscured in national data on the health of Hispanic children when generational status is not disaggregated. Grouping all black children together will lead to the opposite conclusion. Since the majority of black children are third-plus-generation, the health advantages of first- and second-generation black children may be overlooked.

Although our [descriptive statistics] were unable to explain the first- and second-generation health advantage for asthma, allergies, developmental problems, and learning disabilities, [we conducted additional, more sophisticated statistical analyses (not shown). These additional analyses did] a good job of explaining race/ethnic variation among the third-plus generation. Racial disparities in child health among native-born children to native-born parents are largely driven by the socioeconomic disadvantage of racial minorities. When we controlled for socioeconomic status and family structure in our [statistical analyses (not shown),] the elevated odds of poor health outcomes for blacks and Hispanics were substantially reduced, and in some cases reversed, meaning that, [all things being equal in terms of socioeconomic characteristics,] these groups would have similar or lower odds of the health condition compared to third-plus-generation white children. The fact that our analyses explain third-generation differences but not first- and second-generation differences is a key element of the immigrant paradox. If the social model of health disparities does not explain the generational pattern, what might?

Explanations for Health Assimilation

There are four potential explanations for the pattern of generational differences in health that we documented for asthma, allergies, developmental problems, and learning disabilities. First, the results may suggest that more recently arrived cohorts of immigrants are healthier (or have healthier children) than earlier-arriving immigrants (and their descendants).

Second, patterns of health assimilation can be influenced by patterns of racial and ethnic identification across time and generation. Race/ethnicity is a sociocultural construct: individuals (including parents and caregivers who report for children) can and do change their identification patterns over time. One recent study, for example, shows that some Mexican Americans change identity to either "Hispanic" or "white" between censuses, and that such changes depend on factors such as educational attainment, racial/ethnic intermarriage, and generational status (Alba and Islam 2009; see also Trejo 2010). Racial/ethnic fluidity may have important implications for the understanding of children's health assimilation patterns if, for example, highly educated and high income parents are less likely to identify as Hispanic and more likely to identify as white over time. Such racial/ethnic identity shifts could help partially explain the apparently worse health of third-plus-generation Hispanic children compared to their first- and second-generation counterparts.

The third [explanation suggests that there] could be deterioration in the relative health standing of children given longer (across-generation) time spent in the United States following immigration. Or, [the fourth explanation suggests that] there could be a process of changing response to and reporting of health conditions given longer (across-generation) time spent in the United States following immigration rather than actual health deterioration.

It is worth noting that these explanations are not mutually exclusive. It is possible that the generational gradient reflects health deterioration and, at the same time, a process of changing responses to and reporting of health conditions. Both are consistent with a process of assimilation—one to the U.S. health distribution and the other to U.S. norms surrounding health practices. It is possible that diverse mechanisms operate for diverse health outcomes. Whereas parents may be largely responsible for responding to asthma and allergies, school teachers and counselors play a greater role in responding to learning disabilities and developmental delays. Thus, differences across groups may also reflect the complex and diverse schooling experiences among children of immigrants and children of diverse racial/ethnic backgrounds.

The outlying patterns observed for overweight, headaches, and ear infections may help elucidate underlying processes. If, for example, headaches and ear infections are more consistently responded to and reported across immigrant generations than other conditions because their symptoms are commonly understood, then the fact that they do not reveal a pattern of worsening health may suggest that worsening health is not occurring for other conditions, such as asthma or allergies, but rather there is a process of health norming. The case of overweight is also suggestive. Overweight status is based on parental/caretaker reports of weight and height, with the problem designation made by the analyst based on the child's position within a national distribution. It would be interesting to see whether a pattern of worsening health across generations would be observed if parents were asked to evaluate whether their child's weight status was a problem; some research suggests that, indeed, these kinds of evaluations are different for recent immigrants (Evans et al. 2011). It is also important to note that the generational pattern for overweight among Hispanics may not suggest improvement over time, but instead may reflect the fact that recent cohorts of Hispanic immigrants are heavier than earlier cohorts.

Conclusions

As this discussion suggests, our analysis draws attention to the fact that measuring health in childhood is not straightforward. The absence of standard measures of population health in childhood demands that analysts inspect a variety of outcomes, which, as in our case, raises the question of whether differences in patterns observed across outcomes are substantive or based on other types of reporting and interpretation issues. Nevertheless, the generational patterns across racial and ethnic groups that we observed indicate that further research is needed to advance our overall understanding of disparities in childhood health.

In conclusion, our article reports generally worse children's health outcomes across generation groups among four major U.S. racial/ethnic groups. Such a pattern is troubling to the extent that it truly measures worsening health across generations. At the same time, it is also troubling to the extent that it measures a process of medicalization, which may detract from underlying social inequalities with real financial costs (Lantz, Lichtenstein, and Pollack 2007). Recognizing and building on the healthy beginnings of new generations of immigrant children should be a priority in the face of threats to health posed by poverty and limited access to healthcare, especially given the cumulative disadvantaged experienced by Hispanics and blacks across subsequent generations. Further work in this area should continue to closely monitor and measure the health of U.S. children in various racial/ethnic and generational status groups to help inform how social and public health policy might best be focused to address the health needs of children and disparities between them.

References

Adler, N.E., Boyce, T., Chesney, M.A., Cohen, S., Folkman, S., Kahn, R.L., and Syme, S.L. (1994). Socioeconomic status and health: The challenge of the gradient. *American Psychologist* 49(1): 15–24.

Akresh, I.R. (2009). Dietary assimilation and health among Hispanic immigrants to the United States. *Journal of Health and Social Behavior* 48(4): 404–417.

Akresh, I.R. and Frank, R. (2008). Health selection among new immigrants. *American Journal of Public Health* 98(11): 2058–2064.

Alba, R.D. and Islam, T. (2009). The case of the disappearing Mexican Americans: An ethnic-identity mystery. *Population Research and Policy Review* 28(2):109–121.

Alba, R.D. and Nee, V. (1997). Rethinking assimilation theory for a new era of immigration. *International Migration Review* 31(4): 826–874.

Angel, R. and Guarnaccia, P.J. (1989). Mind, body, and culture: Somatization among Hispanics. *Social Science and Medicine* 28(12): 1229–1238.

Antecol, H. and Bedard, K. (2006). Unhealthy assimilation: Why do immigrants converge to American health status levels? *Demography* 43(2): 337–360.

Blumberg, S.J., Foster, E.B., Frasier, A.M., Satorins, J., Skalland, B.J., Nysse-Carris, K.L., and Morrison, H.M. (2009). Design and operation of the national survey of children's health, 2007. *Vital Health Statistics* 1. (Atlanta, GA: National Center for Health Statistics).

Bond Huie, S.A., Hummer, R.A., and Rogers, R.G. (2002). Individual and contextual risks of death among race and ethnic groups in the United States. *Journal of Health and Social Behavior* 43(3): 359–381.

Buttenheim, A.M., Pebley, A., Hsih, K., and Goldman, N. (2011). *The shape of things to come: Obesity prevalence among foreign-born and U.S.-born Hispanic children in California.* Paper presented at the Population Association of America Conference, Washington D.C., March 31–April 2, 2011.

Capps, R., Fix, M., Ost, J., Reardon-Anderson, J., and Passel, J.S. (2004). *The health and well-being of young children of immigrants.* Washington, DC: The Urban Institute.

Child and Adolescent Health Measurement Initiative (CAHMI) (2007). 2007 National Survey of Children's Health. Indicator Data Set [electronic resource]. Portland, OR: Data Resource Center for Child and Adolescent Health. http://www.childhealthdata.org.

Conrad, P. (1992). Medicalization and social control. *Annual Review of Sociology* 18: 209–232.

Conrad, P. and Barker, K.K. (2010). The social construction of illness: Key insights and policy implications. *Journal of Health and Social Behavior* 51(1): S67–S79.

Evans, A., Seth, J.G., Smith, S., Harris, K.K., Loyo, J., Spaulding, C., Van Eck, M., and Gottlieb, N. (2011). Parental feeding practices and concerns related to child underweight, picky eating, and using food to calm differ according to ethnicity/race, acculturation, and income. *Maternal and Child Health Journal* 15(7): 899–909.

Feliciano, C. (2005). Educational selectivity in U.S. immigration: How do immigrants compare to those left behind? *Demography* 42(1): 131–152.

Finch, B.K., and Vega, W.A. (2003). Acculturation stress, social support, and self-rated health among Latinos in California. *Journal of Immigrant Health* 5(3): 109–117.

Frisbie, W.P. and Song, S. (2003). Hispanic pregnancy outcomes: Differentials over time and current risk factor effects. *The Policy Studies Journal* 31(2): 237–252.

Guendelman, S.P. (1998). Health and disease among Hispanics. In: Loue, S. (ed.). *Handbook of Immigrant Health.* New York: Plenum Press: 277–301.

Hamilton, E.R., Teitler, J.O., and Reichman, N.S. (2011). Mexican American birth weight and child overweight: Unraveling a possible early lifecoursehealth transition. *Journal of Health and Social Behavior* 52(3): 333–348.

Hernandez, D.J. and Charney, E. (1998). *From generation to generation: The health and well-being of children in immigrant families.* Washington, D.C.: National Academy Press.

Hernandez, D.J. and Darke, K. (1999). Socioeconomic and demographic risk factors and resources among children in immigrant and native-born families: 1910, 1960, and 1990. In: Hernandez, D.J. (ed.) *Children of immigrants: Health, adjustment, and public assistance.* Washington, D.C.: National Academy Press: 19–126.

Hummer, R.A. (1996). Black-white differences in health and mortality: A review and conceptual model. *The Sociological Quarterly* 37(1): 105–125.

Hummer, R.A., Biegler, M., De Turk, P.B., Forbes, D., Frisbie, W.P., Hong, Y., and Pullum, S.G. (1999). Race/ethnicity, nativity, and infant mortality in the United States. *Social Forces* 77(3): 1083–1117.

Hummer, R.A. and Chinn, J.J. (2011). Race/ethnicity and U.S. adult mortality: Progress, prospects, and new analysis. *Du Bois Review* 8(1): 5–24.

Hummer, R.A., Powers, D., Pullum, S., Gossman, G., and Frisbie, W.P. (2007). Paradox found (again): Infant mortality among the Mexican-origin population in the United States. *Demography* 44(3): 441–457.

Hummer, R.A., Rogers, R.G., Nam, C.B., and Ellison, C.G. (1999). Religious involvement and U.S. adult mortality. *Demography* 36(2): 273–285.

Jasso, G., Massey, D.S., Rosenzweig, M.R., and Smith, J.P. (2004). Immigrant health: Selectivity and acculturation. In: Anderson, N.B., Bulatao, R.A., and Cohen, B. (eds.). *Critical perspectives on racial and ethnic differences in health inlate life.* Washington, D.C.: The National Academies Press: 227–266.

Keeter, S., Miller, C., Kohut, A., Groves, R.M., and Presser, S. (2000). Consequences of reducing nonresponse in a national telephone survey. *Public Opinion Quarterly* 64(2): 125–148.

Kimbro, R.T., Brooks-Gunn, J., and McLanahan, S. (2011). Young children in urban areas: Links among neighborhood characteristics, weight status, outdoor play, and television-watching. *Social Science and Medicine* 72(5): 668–676.

Kimbro, R.T., Lynch, S.M., and McLanahan, S. (2008). The influence of acculturation on breastfeeding initiation and duration for Mexican Americans. *Population Research and Policy Review* 27(2): 183–199.

Landale, N.S., Oropesa, R.S., and Gorman, B.K. (2000). Migration and infant death: Assimilation or selective migration among Puerto Ricans? *American Sociological Review* 65(6): 888–909.

Landale, N.S., Oropesa, R.S., Llanes, D., and Gorman, B.K. (1999). Does Americanization have adverse effects on health? Stress, health habits, and infant health outcomes among Puerto Ricans. *Social Forces* 78(2): 613–641.

Lantz, P.M., Lichtenstein, R.L., and Pollack, H.A. (2007). Health policy approaches to population health: The limits of medicalization. *Health Affairs* 26(5): 1253–1257.

Lopez-Gonzalez, L., Aravena, V.C., and Hummer, R.A. (2005). Immigrant acculturation, gender, and health behavior: A research note. *Social Forces* 84(1): 581–593.

Mendoza, F.S. (2009). Health disparities and children in immigrant families: A research agenda. *Pediatrics* 124(Suppl): S187–S195.

Mendoza, F.S. and Dixon, L.B. (1999). The health and nutritional status of immigrant Hispanic children: Analyses of the Hispanic Health and Nutrition Examination Survey. In: Hernandez, D.J. (ed.). *Children of immigrants: Health adjustment and public assistance.* Washington, D.C.: National Academy Press: 187–244.

Padilla, Y.C., Boardman, J.D., Hummer, R.A., and Espitia, M. (2002). Is the Mexican American "epidemiologic paradox" advantage at birth maintained through early childhood? *Social Forces* 80(3): 1101–1123.

Padilla, Y.C., Hamilton, E.R., and Hummer, R.A. (2009). Beyond the epidemiological paradox: The health of Mexican American children at age 5. *Social Science Quarterly* 90(5): 1072–1088.

Palloni, A. and Arias, E. (2004). Paradox lost: Explaining the Hispanic adult mortality advantage. *Demography* 41(3): 385–415.

Passel, J.S. and Cohn, D. (2008). U.S. population projections: 2005–2050. Pew Research Center Social and Demographic Trends. Washington, D.C.: Pew Hispanic Center.

Portes, A. and Rumbaut, R. (2006). *Immigrant America: A portrait.* Berkeley, California: University of California Press.

Portes, A. and Zhou, M. (1993). The new second generation: Segmented assimilation and its variants. *Annals of the American Academy of Political and Social Science* 530(1): 74–96.

Radey, M. and Padilla, Y.C. (2009). Kin financial support: Receipt and provision among unmarried mothers. *Journal of Social Service Research* 35(4): 336–351.

Reichman, N.E., Hamilton, E.R., Hummer, R.A., and Padilla, Y.C. (2008). Racial and ethnic disparities in low birthweight among urban unmarried mothers. *Maternal and Child Health Journal* 12(2): 204–215.

Scribner, R. (1996). Editorial: Paradox as paradigm—The health outcomes of Mexican Americans. *American Journal of Public Health* 86(3): 303–305.

Trejo, S.J. (2010). On the intergenerational mobility of U.S. Hispanics. In: Landale, N.S., McHale, S., and Booth, A. (eds.). *Growing up Hispanic: Health and development of children of immigrants.* Washington, DC: Urban Institute Press: 73–85.

U.S. Department of Health and Human Services (2011). Federal poverty guidelines [electronic resource]. Washington, D.C.: U.S. Department of Health and Human Services. http://aspe.hhs.gov/poverty/07poverty.shtml.

Umberson, D. and Montez, J.K. (2010). Social relationships and health: A flashpoint for health policy. *Journal of Health and Social Behavior* 51(S): S54–S66.

Van Hook, J. and Baker, E. (2010). Big boys and little girls: Gender, acculturation, and weight among young children of immigrants. *Journal of Health and Social Behavior* 51(2): 200–214.

Williams, D.R. and Sternthal, M. (2010). Understanding racial-ethnic disparities in health: Sociological contributions. *Journal of Health and Social Behavior* 51(S): S15–S27.

Zhou, M. (1997). Segmented assimilation: Issues, controversies, and recent research on the new second generation. *International Migration Review* 31(4): 975–1008.

Zola, I.K. (1966). Culture and symptoms—Analysis of patients' presenting complaints. *American Sociological Review* 31(5): 615–630.

CHAPTER 26

The Racialization of Crime and Punishment*

Criminal Justice, Color-Blind Racism, and the Political Economy of the Prison Industrial Complex

Rose M. Brewer and Nancy A. Heitzeg

The current explosion in criminalization and ***mass incarceration*** *is unprecedented in size, scope, and negative consequences—both direct and collateral—for communities of color. These macro-systems exist in relation to the micro-dynamics of living in the midst of police scrutiny, economic marginalization, and political disenfranchisement. In this essay, Rose M. Brewer and Nancy A. Heitzeg use* ***critical race theory*** *(CRT) to understand the racist and classist foundations of current micro and macro injustices. Using Supreme Court opinions and the voices of political prisoner/prisoners of conscience as evidence of the dominant text and the dissent, this essay explores the following issues: the roots of U.S. law, criminal justice, and* ***mass imprisonment*** *in classism and racism; the political economy of the criminal justice system and the* ***prison industrial complex****; the intersectionality of injustices rooted in micro and macro systems; and the role of prisoners of conscience/political prisoners in inspiring resistance to micro and macro injustice.*

Source: Adapted from Rose M. Brewer and Nancy A. Heitzeg, "The Racialization of Crime and Punishment: Criminal Justice, Color-Blind Racism, and the Political Economy of the Prison Industrial Complex," *American Behavioral Scientist,* Volume 51, Issue 5, pages 625–644, SAGE Publications, Inc., 2008.

*Some text has been omitted. Please consult the original source.

Questions to Consider

Most Americans believe that prisoners are incarcerated because of their individual acts—that they alone are responsible for the actions that put them in prison. Brewer and Heitzeg suggest that, beyond individual acts, there are other social and structural forces that have led to mass incarceration in the present era. What are these factors and how do they support the current mass incarceration regime?

Current Situation of Criminal Injustice

There is no dispute as to the extent of the dramatic escalation in criminalization and incarceration in the United States that has occurred during the past 35 years. Much of this increase can be traced to the war on drugs and the rise of mandatory minimum sentences for drug crimes and some other felonies. More than 47 million Americans (or 25% of the adult population) have state or federal criminal records. An estimated 13 million Americans—6% of the adult population—are either currently serving a sentence for a felony conviction or have been convicted of a felony in the past (Mauer & Chesney-Lind, 2002, p. 51). Approximately 7 million adults are currently under some sort of correctional supervision in the United States. More than 4 million are under some sort of community correctional supervision such as probation and parole; another 2 million are incarcerated in prisons and jails. More than 3,500 of these are awaiting execution, some for federal crimes and most for capital offenses in 1 of the 38 states that still allow for capital punishment. For every 100,000 Americans, there are 699 in prison—this is the highest incarceration rate in the world (Bureau of Justice Statistics, 2004).

There is also no dispute that the poor and people of color, particularly African Americans, are dramatically overrepresented in these statistics at every phase of the criminal justice system. The overwhelming majority of those in prisons and jails were unemployed or employed in the minimum wage service sector at the time of their commitment offense (Bureau of Justice Statistics, 2004). More than three quarters of a million Black men are now behind bars, and 2 million are under some form of correctional supervision. One in every 8 Black men between the ages of 25 and 34 is in prison or jail. One in 3 African American men and 1 in 10 Latinos between the ages of 20 and 29 are under some sort of correctional supervision (Mauer & Chesney-Lind, 2002). Approximately 50% of all prisoners are Black, 30% are White, and 17% Hispanic. Whereas the adult male prison population has tripled in the past 20 years, the number of women incarcerated has increased tenfold during the same time span. Women represent the fastest growing sector of the prison population. More than 90,000 prisoners are women, and they are overwhelmingly women of color. African American women are 3 times more likely than Latinas and 6 times more likely than White women to be in prison. More than 60% of women who are in prison are serving time for nonviolent offense, especially for drugs (Bureau of Justice Statistics, 2004).

And there is no dispute as to the devastating impact of these policies and practices on communities of color. In addition to the direct impact of mass criminalization and incarceration, there is a plethora of what Mauer and Chesney-Lind (2002) refer to as "invisible punishments." These additional collateral consequences further decimate communities of color politically, economically, and socially. The current expansion of criminalization and mass incarceration is accompanied by legislation that further limits the political and economic opportunities of convicted felons and former inmates. Felony disenfranchisement is permanent in 14 states. Forty-eight states do not permit prison inmates to vote, 32 states disenfranchise felons on parole, and 28 states prohibit probationers from voting. Nationally, 40 million felons are disenfranchised; 2% of the nation on average cannot vote as a result of a felony conviction. Of African American males, 13% are disenfranchised; in 7 states, 1 in 4 are permanently barred from voting. In Florida alone, nearly one third of all Black men are permanently disenfranchised (Mauer & Chesney-Lind, 2002). Twenty-five states bar felons from ever holding public office, 33 states place a lifetime ban on gun ownership for convicted felons, and all states require driver's license suspension for convicted drug felons. States have also increased the occupational bans for convicted felons, prohibiting them from teaching, child care work, related work with children, or law enforcement. This is accompanied by eased access to criminal records, an increase in all employers' checking criminal backgrounds, and new technology, which facilitates quick checks.

Research indicates that the explosion in incarceration is negatively correlated with Black male employment rates (Travis, 2002). Drug felons are permanently barred from receiving public assistance such as Temporary Assistance for Needy Families, Medicaid, food stamps, or Supplemental Security Income. Drug use, possession, or sales are the only offenses other than welfare fraud that result in a ban on federal assistance. The welfare fraud ban is limited to 10 years. Probation or parole violations also result in the temporary suspension of federal assistance. Drug felons are also permanently prohibited from receiving federal financial aid for education. Those convicted of drug felonies "or violent criminal activity or other criminal activity which would adversely affect the health, safety, or right to peaceful enjoyment of the premises by others" (Rubenstein & Mukamal, 2002) are permanently barred from public housing or Section 8. A growing number of private rental properties also screen for convicted felons. More than 20,000 persons each year are denied federal housing assistance due to a felony conviction (Rubenstein & Mukamal, 2002; Travis, 2002). A felony conviction by anyone in the household is grounds for eviction from public housing. Recent legislation also creates barriers for families and has particularly devastating consequences for women. Certain convicted felons are prevented from being approved as adoptive or foster parents. Congress has accelerated the termination of parental rights for children who have been in foster care for 15 of the most recent 22 months. Nineteen states regard felony conviction as grounds for parental termination; 29 states identify felony conviction as grounds for divorce (Chesney-Lind, 2002; Ritchie, 2002). And finally, the conditions of incarceration contribute to physical illnesses (e.g., Hepatitis B and C, HIV/AIDS, tuberculosis, general lack of adequate medical care), injuries (e.g., physical and sexual assaults from correctional officers and other inmates), and mental disorders that continue to plague former inmates, families, and their communities on release (Fellner, 2004).

The reasons for this unprecedented explosion in criminalization and incarceration, however, are in dispute. The rhetoric of color-blind racism would have us believe that this situation is the unfortunate result of disproportionate Black and Latino participation in crime. These so-called "racial realists" (Brown et al., 2005) argue that racism is over, successfully eradicated by civil rights legislation, and that if racial inequality persists, it is "the problem of the people who fail to take responsibility for their own lives" (Brown et al., 2005, p. vii).

This adherence to the ideology of color-blindness (a co-optation and subversion of the dream of Dr. King) pervades conservative political and intellectual discourse, the corporate media, and the minds of the public. Racism is widely held to be an individual problem, rather than structural and systemic, an integral feature of what Bonilla-Silva (2001) referred to as "racialized social systems" (p. 57). From this vantage point, the issue then is crime, not race, and certainly not racism.

On the contrary, many contest this color-blind interpretation of contemporary racial arrangements as well as its specific application to criminal justice (Bonilla-Silva, 2001, 2006; Brown et al., 2005; Feagin, 2000; Mauer & Chesney-Lind, 2002; Walker, Spohn, & DeLone, 2004). The scale, scope, and extremes of negative consequences—both direct and collateral—for communities of color are new, especially for women, but the role of criminal justice in policing, prosecuting, imprisoning, and executing people of color has deep historical roots. What is not new is the racist and classist economic and political agenda that is foundational. The paradigms shift from essentialist to color-blind and the practices of oppression are refined and renamed, but the resulting inequality remains much the same. The law and its attendant machinery were, and still are, enforcers of both White supremacy and capitalist interests.

The Past Is the Present

It is well established that our Constitution was written with a narrowly construed view of citizenship that at the time included only White, property-holding men. This property included both wives and children, but the most lucrative property of all—indeed that property that made any economic survival, let alone prosperity, possible—was slaves. By the time of the Constitutional Convention of 1787, the racial lines defining slave and free had already been rigidly drawn—White was free, and Black was slave. The Three Fifths Clause, the restriction on future bans of the slave trade, and limits on the possibility of emancipation through escape were all clear indications of the significance of slavery to the founders. Any doubt as to the centrality of White supremacy was erased a few decades later in the case of *Scott v. Sandford* (1857), where a majority of the Supreme Court denied the citizenship claims of Dred Scott and went further to declare that the Missouri Compromise requirement of balance between free and slave states in the expanding United States was a violation of the due process rights of slaveholders. Referring to the legal status of African Americans, Justice Taney's opinion for the majority makes it painfully clear:

> They are not included, and were not intended to be included, under the word "citizens" in the Constitution, and can therefore claim none of the rights and privileges which that instrument provides for and secures to citizens of the United States. On the contrary, they were at that time considered as a subordinate and inferior class of beings, who had been subjugated by the dominant race, and, whether emancipated or not, yet remained subject to their authority, and had no rights or privileges but such as those who held the power and the Government might choose to grant them.

The growing abolition movement could not overcome this legal bar with debates, written appeals, or legislative action. The economic and political interests of the slave states were too dependent on the rising trade in slaves and cotton. It took the armed resistance of slaves and radical abolitionists—of Vesey and Prosser, of Tubman, Turner, and finally Brown—to push the question into conflict. Frederick Douglass (1881, cited in Zinn, 2004, pp. 18–19) observed,

> If John Brown did not end the war that ended slavery, he did at least begin the war that ended slavery. . . . Until this blow was struck, the prospect for freedom was dim, shadowy and uncertain. The irrepressible conflict was one of words, votes and compromises. When John Brown stretched forth his arm, the sky was cleared. The time for compromises was gone.

The abolition of slavery did not result in the abolition of essentialist racism in the law; it merely called for new methods of legally upholding the property interests of Whiteness. In the presence of now freed Black labor, the vote was now offered to unpropertied White men, and, as Du Bois and others have argued, Whiteness played a central role in the reduction of class tensions. The "wages of whiteness" for the working class were material as well as social; "whiteness produced—and was reproduced by the social advantage that accompanied it" (Harris, 1993, p. 116).

Postslavery, White supremacy in the law was accomplished by the introduction of a series of segregationist Jim Crow laws, a new model for an essentialist racial paradigm that was now legitimated by so-called biology; the laws did not mandate that Blacks be accorded equality under the law because nature—not man, not power, not violence—has determined their degraded status (Harris, 1993, p. 118). The courts were complicit and explicit in their support for the purity and attendant property rights of Whiteness. This is made most dramatically clear in *Plessy v. Ferguson* (1896). In a challenge to the legalized segregation of public transportation in the state of Louisiana, Plessy argued that these laws denied him equality before the law. The majority disagreed and set forth the principle of separate but equal. Justice Brown wrote for the majority:

> It is claimed by the plaintiff in error that, in a mixed community, the reputation of belonging to the dominant race, in this instance the white race, is "property," in the same sense that a right of action or of inheritance is property. . . . We are unable to see how this statute deprives him of, or in any way affects his right to, such property. If he be a white man, and assigned to a colored coach, he may have his action for damages against the company for being deprived of his so-called "property." Upon the other hand, if he be a colored man, and be so assigned, he has been deprived of no property, since he is not lawfully entitled to the reputation of being a white man.

The sole dissenter in *Plessy* sets up the juxtaposition of Jim Crow and color-blindness that frames the contemporary debate on race today. Justice Harlan, while acknowledging the reality of White supremacy, decries its support with the law:

> The white race deems itself to be the dominant race in this country. And so it is, in prestige, in achievements, in education, in wealth, and in power. So, I doubt not, it will continue to be for all time, if it remains true to its great heritage, and holds fast to the principles of constitutional liberty. But in view of the constitution, in the eye of the

> law, there is in this country no superior, dominant, ruling class of citizens. There is no caste here. *Our constitution is color-blind, and neither knows nor tolerates classes among citizens. In respect of civil rights, all citizens are equal before the law.*

The corollary to the enhanced promotion of Whiteness was—and still is—the ongoing devaluation of Blackness. The criminal justice system begins to play a new and crucial role here. Angela Y. Davis (2003), in *Are Prisons Obsolete?* traced the initial rise of the penitentiary system to the abolition of slavery; "in the immediate aftermath of slavery, the southern states hastened to develop a criminal justice system that could legally restrict the possibilities of freedom for the newly released slaves" (p. 29). There was a subsequent transformation of the Slave Codes into the Black Codes and the plantations into prisons. Laws were quickly passed that echoed the restrictions associated with slavery and criminalized a range of activities if the perpetrator was Black. The newly acquired 15th Amendment right to vote was curtailed by the tailoring of felony disenfranchisement laws to include crimes that were supposedly more frequently committed by Blacks (Human Rights Watch, 1998). And the liberatory promise of the 13th Amendment—"Neither slavery nor involuntary servitude shall exist in the United States"—contained a dangerous loophole: "except as a punishment for crime." This allowed for the conversion of the old plantations to penitentiaries, and this, with the introduction of the convict lease system, permitted the South to continue to economically benefit from the unpaid labor of Blacks. As Davis (2003) noted, "the expansion of the convict lease system and the county chain gang meant that the antebellum criminal justice system, defined criminal justice largely as a means for controlling black labor" (p. 31).

After decades of resistance via legal challenges, grassroots organizing, boycotts, *Letters from the Birmingham Jail,* sit-ins, jail-ins, marches, and mass protest, legalized segregation began to come undone. Indeed, part of its undoing was the role that activists played in exposing the official and extralegal violence that had previously been cloaked in the legitimacy of the law. Emmett Till, Birmingham, Bloody Sunday, and more bared the lie. In the historic 1954 *Brown v. Board of Education* decision, *Plessy* was overturned; the essentialist racist paradigm was no longer codified in law. This was complete with the passage of the Civil Rights Act of 1964, the Voting Rights Act of 1965, and the passage of the 24th Amendment to the Constitution. Whereas there was once hope that the law itself could be pressed into the service of racial equality, those victories now seem bittersweet. Judge Robert L. Carter (1980), one of the attorneys who argued *Brown,* noted, "The fundamental vice was not legally enforced racial segregation itself; this was a mere by-product, a symptom of the greater and more pernicious disease—white supremacy" (pp. 23–24). Legally supported essentialist racism was about to be replaced with a more insidious counterpart—the paradigm of color-blindness.

Following the end of legalized racial discrimination, there was an especially concerted effort to escalate the control of African Americans via the criminal justice system. Marable (1983) made this point: "White racists began to rely almost exclusively on the state apparatus to carry out the battle for white supremacy. . . . The criminal justice system became, in short, a modern instrument to perpetuate white hegemony" (pp. 120–121). These practices gain primacy during the post–civil rights years as the essentialist racist paradigm gives way to the new color-blind racism where race and racism are ostensibly absent from the law and all aspects of its enforcement. The criminal justice system provides a convenient vehicle for physically maintaining the old legally enforced color lines as African Americans are disproportionately policed, prosecuted, convicted, disenfranchised, and imprisoned. The criminal justice system and its culmination in the prison industrial complex also continues to guarantee the perpetual profits from the forced labor of inmates, now justifying their slavery as punishment for crime. Finally, the reliance on the criminal system provides the color-blind racist regime the perfect set of codes to describe racialized patterns of alleged crime and actual punishment without ever referring to race. As Davis (1998a) observed, "crime is one of the masquerades behind which 'race', with all its menacing ideological complexity, mobilizes old public ears and creates new ones" (p. 62). There is no discussion of race and racism; there is only public discourse about crime, criminals, gangs, and drug-infested neighborhoods. This color-bind conflagration of crime with race is, in addition, insidious in its dishonesty and indirect effects; as Justice Powell, writing for the Supreme Court, noted, "discrimination within the judicial system is most pernicious because it is 'a stimulant to that race prejudice which is an impediment to securing to [Black citizens] that equal justice which the law aims to secure to all others'" (quoting *Strauder v. West Virginia*, 1880, in *Batson v. Kentucky*, 1986).

There were early warnings about the potentially devastating interconnections between race, crime, and the law in the era of late capitalism. The mid-20th-century criticism of the criminal justice system as foundationally racist initially emanated from the Black Power Movement's critique of institutionalized racism and police brutality in communities of color. The writings of political prisoners (e.g., Angela Davis, Huey P. Newton, Assate Shakur) and prisoners of conscience (e.g., Malcolm X and George Jackson) brought racism and its intimate connection with the penitentiary to light. The 10 Point Program of the Black Panther Party began to make the connections between capitalist exploitation of the Black community and the criminal justice system. Their demands provided the foundations for the contemporary critiques of the role of criminal justice in upholding both capitalism and White supremacy.

> We want an immediate end to **police brutality** and **murder** of black people. We want freedom for all black men held in federal, state, county and city prisons and jails. We want all black people when brought to trial to be tried in court by a jury of their peer group or people from their black communities, as defined by the Constitution of the United States. (Foner, 1970, pp. 3–5)

These warnings went unheeded; indeed, they were too often violently suppressed. The conflation of race and crime and the resultant rise of the criminal and prison industrial complexes did and does find support in judicial decisions that legitimate the central tenets of color-blind racism. The color-blind Constitution foreshadowed in Harlan's dissent has now become the voice of the Supreme Court's majority. Color-blindness as the new legal doctrine begins to emerge—despite judicial dissent—in cases involving affirmative action and other remedies to centuries of racial inequality. The Supreme Court adopts the color-blind model in *Regents of the University of California v. Bakke* (1978), where the ruling is in favor of a White student who claimed racial discrimination in his denial of admission to medical school. If the Constitution is to be color-blind, race can only be considered with strict scrutiny, even as a remedy for past discrimination. Justices Brennan and Marshall, in separate dissents, pointed out the flaws of this approach. Brennan observed,

> Claims that law must be "color-blind" or that the datum of race is no longer relevant to public policy must be seen as aspiration rather than as description of reality . . . for reality rebukes us that race has too often been used by those who would stigmatize and oppress minorities. Yet we cannot . . . let color blindness become myopia which masks the reality that many "created equal" have been treated within our lifetimes as inferior both by the law and by their fellow citizens.

Justice Marshall's dissent is even more prescient:

> For it must be remembered that, during most of the past 200 years, the Constitution as interpreted by this Court did not prohibit the most ingenious and pervasive forms of discrimination against the Negro. Now, when a state acts to remedy the effects of that legacy of discrimination, I cannot believe that this same Constitution stands as a barrier.

As a series of subsequent cases from *Bakke* to *Gratz v. Bollinger* (2003) have shown, that same Constitution has indeed erected a legal barrier with claims of color-blindness (Bell, 2000; Brown et al., 2005).

Perhaps the most significant barrier to the pursuit of equality before the law comes in the case of *McCleskey v. Kemp* (1987). After a series of death penalty cases wherein the court decried racial discrimination in the application of the criminal laws' ultimate penalty, it is here that the Supreme Court, in a 5 to 4 decision, clearly defined discrimination as individual, not institutionalized. Citing statistical evidence from the now famous Baldus study, McCleskey argued that the application of the death penalty in Georgia was fraught with racism. Defendants charged with killing White victims were more likely to receive the death penalty, and in fact, cases involving Black defendants and White victims were more likely to result in a sentence of death than cases involving any other racial combination. The majority did not dispute the statistical evidence but feared the consequences. If the court were to accept McCleskey's claim, then the Equal Protection Clause of the 14th Amendment would apply to patterns of discrimination, to institutionalized racism and sexism, and to questions of structured inequality. These fears are expressed in Powell's opinion for the majority:

> First, McCleskey's claim, taken to its logical conclusion, [481 U.S. 279, 315] throws into serious question the principles that underlie our entire criminal justice system. The Eighth Amendment is not limited in application to capital punishment, but applies to all penalties. Solem v. Helm, 463 U.S. 277, 289–290 (1983); see Rummel v. Estelle, 445 U.S. 263, 293 (1980) (POWELL, J., dissenting). Thus, if we accepted McCleskey's claim that racial bias has impermissibly tainted the capital sentencing decision, we could soon be faced with similar claims as to other types of penalty. Moreover, the claim that his sentence [481 U.S. 279, 316] rests on the irrelevant factor of race easily could be extended to apply to claims based on unexplained discrepancies that correlate to membership in other minority groups, and [481 U.S. 279, 317] even to gender.

Justice Brennan's impassioned dissent makes clear the implications of this decision:

> Yet it has been scarcely a generation since this Court's first decision striking down racial segregation, and barely two decades since the legislative prohibition of racial

> discrimination in major domains of national life. These have been honorable steps, but we cannot pretend that in three decades we have completely escaped the grip of a historical legacy spanning centuries. Warren McCleskey's evidence confronts us with the subtle and persistent influence of the past. His message is a disturbing one to a society that has formally repudiated racism, and a frustrating one to a Nation accustomed to regarding its destiny as the product of its own will. Nonetheless, *we ignore him at our peril, for we remain imprisoned by the past as long as we deny its influence in the present.*

Color-blind racism, with its call to ignore race and its treatment of any residual racism as individual and intentional, was now ensconced. Equal protection of the law was for individuals, not oppressed groups, and discrimination must be intentional and similarly individual. *McCleskey* closed off the last avenue for remedying structural inequality with the law and left us imprisoned by the past, imprisoned with the present.

Intersections: Criminal Injustice, Race, and Political Economy

The legal entrenchment of color-blind racism allowed White supremacist political and economic advantage to be pursued—unchecked by either law or public discourse—under the guise of criminal justice. Davis (1998b) noted,

> When the structural character of racism is ignored in discussions of crime and the rising population of incarcerated people, the racial imbalance in jails and prisons is treated as a contingency. . . . The high proportion of black people in the criminal justice system is this normalized and neither the state nor the general public is required to talk or act on the meaning of this imbalance. . . . By relying on the alleged "race-blindness" of the law, black people are scrumptiously constructed as racial subjects, thus manipulated, exploited, and abused, while the structural persistence of racism—albeit in changed forms—is ignored. (p. 62)

As before, this newest political and legal construction of White supremacy is intimately interconnected with capitalist economic interests. The extreme racialization of criminal justice and the rise of the prison industrial complex are directly tied to the expansion of global economy, the decline of the industry and rise of the minimum wage service sector in the United States, and the growth of privatization of public services. The internationalization of the labor force and the turn to robotics, computers, and hi-tech are having a profound impact on labor in the United States and globally. The prison industrial complex is an expression and re-articulation of the political economy of late capitalism. The intense concentration and privatization of wealth in a few hands continues unchecked in this country. Indeed, the unparalleled growth of corporate power is at the heart of the economic inequality African Americans and all working people are confronting.

Angela Davis (2003) again becomes important in interpreting the multiple intersections of race, economy, and the prison industrial complex. She traced the historical links between current practices and the policies that emerged during the post–civil war era:

> Vast amounts of black labor became increasingly available for use by private agents through the convict lease system and related systems such as debt peonage. *This transition set the historical stage for the easy acceptance of disproportionately black prison populations today*. . . . We are approaching the proportion of black prisoners to white, during the era of the southern convict lease and country chain gang systems. Whether this human raw material is used for purposes of labor or for the consumption of commodities provided by a rising number of corporations directly implicated in the prison industrial complex, it is clear that black bodies are considered dispensable within the "free world," but as a source of profit in the prison world. (p. 95)

This quest for dispensable labor increasingly includes women of color who, in light of globalization, deindustrialization, and the dismantling of social services, are propelled by state economic interests into the slave labor markets of the prison industrial complex.

> The prison industrial complex is not a conspiracy, but a confluence of special interests that include politicians who exploit crime to win votes, private companies that make millions by running or supplying prisons and small town officials who have turned to prisons as a method of economic development. (Silverstein, 1997)

This complex now includes more than 3,300 jails, more than 1,500 state prisons, and 100 federal prisons in the United States. Nearly 300 of these are private prisons. More than 30 of these institutions are super-maximum facilities, not including the super-maximum units located in most other prisons. The prison industrial complex consumes vast amounts of tax dollars at the expense of education and other social programs. Each year, the United States spends more than $146 billion dollars on the criminal justice system, including police, the judiciary and court systems, and corrections. More than $50 billion of this is spent directly on corrections, with the majority of those expenditures going toward incarceration and executions—the two most expensive sentencing options (Bureau of Justice Statistics, 2004). The quest for profit has led to international U.S. expansion of the prison industrial complex in the United States. Both private companies and the U.S. military industrial complex rely on the global proliferation of both U.S. prisons and their internal practices at Basra, Abu Ghraib, Guantanamo Bay, and untold other locations.

In essence, the prison industrial complex is a self-perpetuating machine where the vast profits (e.g., cheap labor, private and public supply and construction contracts, job creation, continued media profits from exaggerated crime reporting, and crime/punishment as entertainment) and perceived political benefits (e.g., reduced unemployment rates, "get tough on crime" and public safety rhetoric, funding increases for police, and criminal justice system agencies and professionals) lead to policies that are additionally designed to ensure an endless supply of "clients" for the criminal justice system (e.g., enhanced police presence in poor neighborhoods and communities of color; racial profiling; decreased funding for public education combined with zero-tolerance policies and increased rates of expulsion for students of color; increased rates of adult certification for juvenile offenders; mandatory minimum and three-strikes sentencing; draconian conditions of incarceration and a reduction of prison services that contribute to the likelihood of recidivism; collateral consequences—such as felony disenfranchisement, prohibitions on welfare receipt, public housing, gun ownership, voting and political participation, and employment—that nearly guarantee continued participation in crime and return to the prison industrial complex following initial release). As Donzinger (1996) aptly noted,

> Companies that service the criminal justice system need sufficient quantities of raw materials to guarantee long term growth *in the criminal justice field, the raw material is prisoners*. . . . The industry will do what it must to guarantee a steady supply. For the supply of prisoners to grow, criminal justice policies must insure a sufficient number of incarcerated Americans whether crime is rising or the incarceration is necessary. (p. 87)

In sum, Black workers, men and women, are at the center of this prison industrial process. They are used again as exploited labor and as consumers—of products produced by prison labor. African Americans and other working people are less needed in the free labor market under current conditions of globalization. Highly exploited global workers match cheap prison labor. So the processes of deindustrialization and economic restructuring contribute to the process of accumulation for capital and the increasing immiseration of the Black poor, and this is true because many of the decisions are explicitly racial in form. Corporate actors choose to move out of Black communities on racial grounds (Brewer, 1983). Thus, private prisons play a key role in the political economy of transnational capital. But so do public prisons. These prisons are equally tied to the corporate economy "and constitute an ever growing source of capitalist growth" (Davis, 2003, p. 96).

This exploitation of Black labor continues, made permissible, indeed possible, with the law. Although the names and legal legitimations have changed, there is little to distinguish the plantation from the penitentiary. Nevertheless, in the United States, Blacks have been a central political force in checking unabashed profit realization. Historically, this occurs through political struggle. We contend that it is only through organized political struggle and radical pedagogies for change that the current situation will be transformed for social justice.

Transparency, Political Struggle, and Radical Pedagogies for Social Justice

The call for social justice is "an implicit call for solutions, a call for remedies, a call for action" (Coates, 2004, p. 850). As we have seen, the call for social justice cannot rely on civil justice or macro-level remedies alone; law has been the handmaiden of what hooks (1992) has termed "the white supremacist capitalist patriarchy" in the ever-evolving political and economic exploitation of persons of color. To paraphrase Bell (1992), the 14th Amendment cannot save us. The call for social justice requires more.

As the latest project in racialization, criminal justice and the prison industrial complex have fundamentally racist and classist roots that must be exposed and abolished. Reform is insufficient; "there can be no compromise with capitalism. There can be no compromise with racism, patriarchy, homophobia and imperialism" (Marable, 2002, p. 59). The work of justice must begin at the micro level; it must emerge from the grass roots. Drawing links between the movements to abolish slavery and segregation, Davis (2003) asked us to imagine the abolition of prisons and the creation of alternatives to mass incarceration with all its racist and classist corollaries. Davis (1998b) identified three key dimensions of this work—public policy, community organizing, and academic research:

> In order to be successful, this project must build bridges between academic work, legislative and other policy interventions, and grassroots campaigns calling, for example for the decriminalization of drugs and prostitution, and for the reversal of the present proliferation of prisons and jails. (pp. 71–72)

Much of this work is in progress. Organizations such as The Sentencing Project (http://www.sentencingproject.org/), the Prison Moratorium Project (http://www.nomoreprisons.org), Critical Resistance (http://www.criticalresistance.org), Families Against Mandatory Minimum Sentencing, Amnesty International, Human Rights Watch, and the Prison Activist Resource Center (http://www.prisonactivist.org) have successfully linked a large and growing body of research with a critique of current practices and a call for legislative and policy change.

But this latest abolition movement faces a unique challenge. The paradigm of color-blind racism must be exposed before the deep connections between race, crime, and political economy become transparent. Hegemonic media coverage and misrepresentations about the reality of crime and criminal justice must be countered by multiple voices (Davis, 2003; Entman & Rojecki, 2000; Sussman, 2002). As long as the public course centers on crime—not race, class, or gendered racism—the true role of criminal justice and the prison industrial complex in preserving White supremacy in the context of advanced capitalism remains invisible. Davis (1998a) warns us,

> The real human beings, designated by these numbers in a seemingly race neutral way, are deemed fetishtically exchangeable with the crimes they have committed. . . . The real impact of imprisonment on their lives need never be examined. The inevitable part played by the punishment industry in the reproduction of crime need never be discussed. The dangerous and indeed fascist trend toward progressively greater numbers of hidden, incarcerated human populations is itself rendered invisible. (p. 63)

The true underpinnings of criminal justice and the prison industrial complex must become transparent. They must be surfaced by micro-level social justice projects. They must be surfaced via radical and relentless pedagogies of resistance; they must be surfaced in the stories, the narratives, of political prisoners and prisoners of conscience; they must be surfaced through the research, writing, and teaching of those whom Mumia Abu-Jamal (2005) called "radical intellectuals" and ultimately through the coalitions between the two that bridge the lines of difference between freedom and incarceration, as well as those of race, class, and gender.

As noted earlier, the writings of political prisoners and prisoners of conscience sounded the early warning about the role of the police, the courts, and prisons in economic and political repression of people of color. These works publicly clarified the extent to which there were political prisoners in the United States and served to raise the consciousness of what, in 1970, were the 200,000 mostly Black and Brown inmates in prisons and jails. Just as the writings of George Jackson, Assata Shakur, Huey P. Newton, and the early Angela Davis inspired an earlier generation of activists, so too do new voices rise in dissent from our prisons and jails. Leonard Peltier, Sanykia Shakur, Paul Wright's *Prison Legal News* (http://www.prisonlegalnews.org), Marilyn Buck, and the prolific Mumia Abu-Jamal have given voice to the more than 2 million who are now incarcerated in increasingly harsh and isolated conditions. They have made the invisible horrors of the prison industrial complex visible and again sparked the call for resistance. They offer both an insider's view and a deep critique of the law. Abu-Jamal (1995) wrote of Pennsylvania's death row,

> From daybreak to dusk black voices resound in exchanges of daily dramas that mark time in the dead zone. Echoes of *Dred Scott* ring in *McCleskey's* opinion, again noting the paucity of black rights in the land of the free. Chief Justice Taney sits again, reincarnate in the Rehnquist Court of the Modern Age. . . . One hundred and thirty three years after *Scott,* and still unequal in life, as in death. (pp. 92–93)

The writings of many political prisoners might have remained suppressed were it not for the efforts of scholars to bring them forward. This coalition between "organic and radical intellectuals" (Abu-Jamal, 2005) is crucial to the uncovering of the deep structural connections between race, political economy, and crime. The work of Angela Davis and Joy James is exemplary here. Their extensive writings on these matters and their careful attendance to connecting with those inside prison walls serve as a model for future work. In *Imprisoned Intellectuals,* James (2003) gave voice to the range of political prisoners and traced the common thread of resistance across generations, nationalities, racial/ethnic differences, genders, sexual orientations, and political causes. She hopes that writing and reading will force a transformative encounter "between those in the so-called free world seeking personal and collective freedoms and those in captivity seeking liberation from economic, military, racial/sexual systems" (James, 2003, p. 4).

The call to social justice, especially when addressing complex and cloaked systems of racialization, requires critical and systematic documentation, the surfacing of deep political and economic structures, and bold confrontation. It requires the analytical tools and methods of multiple disciplines, as we have attempted to offer here. The dismantling of the White supremacist and capitalist machinery of criminal justice requires coalitions between intellectuals of all sorts. In the words of Mumia Abu-Jamal (2005),

> Yet this world and life itself, is broader than the ivory towers of academia. Make external connections. Build bridges to the larger, nonacademic community. Build social, political and communal networks. . . . The word "radical" means from the roots—so, build roots! Touch base with real folks, and work for the only real source of liberty—life! (p. 179–184)

Ultimately, the realization of social justice will require still broader coalitions. Criminal justice and the prison industrial complex represent particular manifestations of the entanglements of racialization, the law, and the global economy in late capitalism. Truly challenging this project in racialization calls for coalitions with those who are addressing different aspects of these foundation dilemmas. Audre Lorde (1984) reminded us that much of Western European history conditions us to see human differences in simplistic opposition to each other: dominant/subordinate, good/bad, up/down, superior/inferior. In a society where the good is defined in terms of profit rather than in terms of human need, there must always be some group of people who, through systematized oppression, can be made to feel surplus, to occupy the place of the dehumanized inferior. Within this society, that group is made up of Black and Third World people, working-class people, older people, women, gays/lesbians, and physically different and physically challenged people. Lorde went on to say,

> Institutionalized rejection of difference is an absolute necessity in a profit economy which needs outsiders as surplus people. As members of such an economy, we have all been programmed to respond to the human differences among us with fear and loathing and to handle that difference in one of three ways: ignore it, and if that is not possible, copy it if we think it is dominant, or destroy it if we think is subordinate. But we have no patterns for relating across our human differences as equals. As a result, those differences have been misnamed and misused in the service of separation and confusion. (p. 115)

Most important, we must organize, continuing the legacy of struggle. We must come together across boundaries of national identity, gender, race, class, and ethnicity. We must work in alliance to realize the vision that another world is possible.

References

Abu-Jamal, M. (1995). *Live from death row.* New York: Seven Stories Press.

Abu-Jamal, M. (2005). Intellectuals and the gallows. In J. James (Ed.), *Imprisoned intellectuals: America's political prisoners write on life, liberation and rebellion* (p. 179). New York: Rowman and Littlefield.

Amnesty International. (1998). *United States of America: Rights for all.* London: Author.

Batson v. Kentucky, 476 U.S. 79, 87–88 (1986).

Bell, D. (1992). *Faces at the bottom of the well: The permanence of racism.* New York: Basic Books.

Bell, D. (2000). After we're gone: Prudent speculations on America in a post-racial epoch. In R. Delgado & J. Stefancic (Eds.), *Critical race theory: The cutting edge* (2nd ed., pp. 2–8). Philadelphia: Temple University Press.

Bonilla-Silva, E. (2001). *White supremacy and racism in the post–civil rights era.* Boulder, CO: Lynne Rienner.

Bonilla-Silva, E. (2006). *Racism without racist: Color-blind racism and the persistence of racial inequality in the United States.* New York: Rowman and Littlefield.

Brewer, R. (1983). Black workers and corporate flight. *Third World Socialists,* 1, 9–13.

Brown v. Board of Educ., 347 U.S. 483 (1954).

Brown, M. K., Carnoy, M., Currie, E., Duster, T., Oppenheimer, D. B., Schultz, M. K., et al. (2005). *White-washing race: The myth of a color-blind society.* Berkeley: University of California Press.

Bureau of Justice Statistics. (2004). *Sourcebook of criminal justice statistics.* Washington, DC: Government Printing Office.

Carter, R. L. (1980). A reassessment of Brown v Board. In D. Bell (Ed.), *Studies of* Brown*: New perspectives on school de-segregation.* New York: Teacher's College Columbia University.

Chesney-Lind, M. (2002). Imprisoning women: The unintended victims of mass incarceration. In M. Mauer & M. Chesney-Lind (Eds.), *Invisible punishment: The collateral consequences of mass imprisonment* (pp. 79–94). New York: New Press.

Coates, R. (2004). If a tree falls in the wilderness: Reparations, academic silences, and social justice. *Social Forces*, 83(2), 841–864.

Davis, A. (1998a). Race and criminalization: Black Americans and the punishment industry. In J. James (Ed.), *The Angela Y. Davis reader* (pp. 61–73). New York: Blackwell.

Davis, A. (1998b). Racialized punishment and prison abolition. In J. James (Ed.), *The Angela Y. Davis reader* (pp. 96–110). New York: Blackwell.

Davis, A. (2003). *Are prisons obsolete?* New York: Seven Stories Press.

Delgado, R., & Stefancic, J. (Eds.). (2000). *Critical race theory: The cutting edge* (2nd ed.). Philadelphia: Temple University Press.

Donzinger, S. (1996). *The real war on crime: Report of the National Criminal Justice Commission.* New York: Perennial.

Ehrenreich, B., & English, D. (1973). *Complaints and disorders: The sexual politics of sickness.* New York: Feminist Press.

Eisner, A. (2004). *Gates of injustice: The crisis in America's prisons.* New York: Pearson.

Entman, R. M., & Rojecki, A. (2000). *The Black image White mind: Media and race in America.* Chicago: University of Chicago Press.

Feagin, J. R. (2000). *Racist America: Roots, realities, and future reparations.* New York: Routledge.

Fellner, James Esq. (2004). *Prisoner abuse: How different are U.S. prisons?* New York: Human Rights Watch.

Foner, P. S. (Ed.). (1955). *The life and writings of Frederick Douglass: Vol. 4. Reconstruction and after.* New York: International.

Foner, P. S. (Ed.). (1970). *The Black Panthers speak.* Philadelphia: J. B. Lippincott.

Gratz v. Bollinger, 02–516 (2003).

Harris, C. (1993). Whiteness as property. In D. R. Roediger (Ed.), *Black on White* (pp. 103–118). New York: Schocken.

hooks, b. (1992). *Black looks.* Boston: South End.

Human Rights Watch. (1998*). Losing the vote: The impact of felony disenfranchisement laws in the U.S.* New York: Author.

Human Rights Watch. (2000). *Out of sight: Super-maximum security confinement in the United States.* NY: Author.

Human Rights Watch. (2003). *Ill-Equipped: U.S. Prisons and Offenders in the United States.* NY: Author.

James, J. (Ed.). (2003). *Imprisoned intellectuals: America's political prisoners write on life, liberation and rebellion.* New York: Rowman and Littlefield.

Johnson v. California, 03-636 543 U.S. 499 (2005).

Lorde, A. (1984). *Sister outsider: Essays and speeches.* Freedom, CA: Crossing Press.

Marable, M. (1983). *How capitalism underdeveloped Black America.* Boston: South End.

Marable, M. (2002). Black radicalism and an economy of incarceration. In J. James (Ed.), *States of confinement: Policing, detention and prisons* (p. 59). New York: Palgrave.

Mauer, M., & Chesney-Lind, M. (Eds.). (2002). *Invisible punishment: The collateral consequences of mass imprisonment.* New York: New Press.

McCleskey v. Kemp, 482 U.S. 279 (1987).

Plessy v. Ferguson, 163 U.S. 537 (1896).

Regents of the University of California v. Bakke, 438 U.S. 265 (1978).

Ritchie, B. (2002). The social impact of the mass incarceration of women. In M. Mauer & M. Chesney-Lind (Eds.), *Invisible punishment: The collateral consequences of mass imprisonment* (pp. 136–149). New York: New Press.

Roberts, D. (1997). *Killing the Black body: Race, reproduction and the meaning of liberty.* New York: Vintage.

Rubenstein, G., & Mukamal, D. (2002). Welfare and housing—Denial of benefits to drug offenders. In M. Mauer & M. Chesney-Lind (Eds.), *Invisible punishment: The collateral consequences of mass imprisonment* (pp. 37–50). New York: New Press.

Scott v. Sandford, 60 U.S. 393 (1857).

Silverstein, K. (1997, June). America's private gulag. *Prison Legal News.*

Sussman, P. Y. (2002). Media on prisons: Censorship and stereotypes. In M. Mauer & M. Chesney-Lind (Eds.), *Invisible punishment: The collateral consequences of mass imprisonment* (pp. 258–278). New York: New Press.

Travis, J. (2002). Invisible punishment: An instrument of social exclusion. In M. Mauer & M. Chesney-Lind (Eds.), *Invisible punishment: The collateral consequences of mass imprisonment* (pp. 15–36). New York: New Press.

Walker, S., Spohn, C., & DeLone, M. (2004). *The color of justice: Race, ethnicity and crime in America* (3rd ed.). Belmont, CA: Wadsworth.

Zinn, H. (2004). *Let the people speak.* New York: Perennial.

CHAPTER 27

Mass Deportation at the Turn of the Twenty-First Century

Tanya Golash-Boza

The United States currently is deporting more people than ever before: 4 million people have been deported since 1997—twice as many as all people deported prior to 1996. There is a disturbing pattern in the population deported: 97% of deportees are sent to Latin America or the Caribbean, and 88% are men, many of whom were originally detained through the U.S. criminal justice system. In this essay, Tanya Golash-Boza explains the factors that have led to the ***mass deportation*** *of native-born Blacks and Latinos in the contemporary period.*

Questions to Consider

What factors have led to this era of mass deportation? Are there just more undocumented immigrants in the United States today than in the past, or are other factors at play?

In Fiscal Year (FY) 2013, deportations reached an all-time high: an average of 1,200 people were removed from the United States every day that year. *Removal* is "the compulsory and confirmed movement of an inadmissible or deportable alien out of the United States based on an order of removal" (Simanski, 2014, p. 2) and is commonly understood as a deportation.

The number of deportations today is far more than it has been historically. In 1892, the first year removals were recorded, 2,801 immigrants were removed from the United States.

Note: Reading is original to this book.

The number of removals ebbed and flowed for the next century, never surpassing 40,000 removals a year. The average number of removals between 1900 and 1990 was 18,275 per year. In the 1990s, however, the number of removals began to escalate. Between 1990 and 1999, there were a total of 788,078 removals, an average of 78,000 per year that decade.

The major reason for the escalation in removals during the 1990s was the passage of restrictive laws in 1996. In 1997, the first year these laws were in effect, there were 114,432 removals. This number went up to 174,813 the following year. President Bill Clinton signed these bills into law at the beginning of his second term. By the end of his presidency, there had been 869,646 removals. President George W. Bush surpassed this figure, with just over two million removals during his two terms in office. By the time President Barack Obama finished his fifth year in office, he had already surpassed two million removals.

1996 Laws

The slow and steady rise from less than 100,000 to more than 400,000 removals a year is largely due to two bills President Clinton signed into law in 1996: the Antiterrorism and Effective Death Penalty Act (AEDPA), and the Illegal Immigration Reform and Immigrant Responsibility Act (IIRAIRA). AEDPA and IIRAIRA expanded the grounds on which people could be deported. They also narrowed the grounds on which people could appeal a deportation, thereby making large numbers of immigrants deportable.

IIRIRA and AEDPA eliminated judicial review of some deportation orders, required mandatory detention for some noncitizens, and introduced the potential for the use of secret evidence in certain cases. Six years prior, the Immigration Act of 1990 had expanded the definition of who could be deported for engaging in criminal activity and made many immigrants deportable for having committed "aggravated felonies" (Fragomen & Bell, 2007). The 1996 laws further expanded the definition of an aggravated felony and made deportation mandatory. Under IIRAIRA, aggravated felonies include any felony or misdemeanor for which the person is sentenced to at least one year in prison, regardless of whether the sentence is served or suspended. These crimes can be relatively minor, such as shoplifting, or the combination of two minor illegal drug possessions. These cases do not require judicial review, meaning people do not have the right for a judge to take into account the specifics of the case or the ties that person has to the United States. In addition, Congress appropriated more funds to immigration law enforcement, thereby ensuring the laws would be enforced. As a consequence, deportations nearly quadrupled, from 50,024 in 1995 to 188,467 in 2000.

The second substantial rise in deportations is connected to the creation of the Department of Homeland Security (DHS) in 2002, discussed in the next section.

Follow the Money

Deportations have continued to escalate, and the number of deportations that take place each year is directly related to the amount of money invested in immigration law enforcement. Each year, the DHS requests billions of dollars from Congress to enforce immigration laws. The FY 2011 budget for DHS was $56 billion. To put this $56 billion in perspective, the Department of Education FY 2011 budget was $77.8 billion, and the Department of Justice $29.2 billion. The rise in deportations over the past decade primarily stems from Executive Branch decisions to expand immigration law enforcement as part of the broader project of the War on Terror.

A recent report by the Migration Policy Institute found that the U.S. government spends more on federal immigration enforcement than on all other principal federal criminal law enforcement agencies combined. My calculations confirm this: Immigration enforcement spending heavily outweighs domestic law enforcement spending. In FY 2011, the U.S. government spent $27 billion on Immigration and Customs Enforcement (ICE), Customs and Border Protection (CBP), and the U.S. Coast Guard. In contrast, the U.S. government spent a total of $13.7 billion on domestic law enforcement, including the Federal Bureau of Investigation (FBI), the Drug Enforcement Administration (DEA), the Secret Service, the U.S. Marshals Service, and Alcohol, Firearms, and Tobacco (AFT). These budgetary details are important because Barack Obama, as president, is in charge of the Executive Branch's budget. Moreover, President Obama appointed Janet Napolitano to head the DHS, knowing that immigration policy enforcement had long been one of her priorities. Notably, the DHS is charged with keeping the nation safe from terrorism, and it is thus far from obvious why they dedicate half of their budget to immigration law enforcement.

Deportations have been able to escalate each year because DHS has requested money from Congress to achieve a higher number of deportations, and Congress has honored these budget requests. Alongside the increase in deportations, we have seen a significant rise in detentions. Immigrant detention increased from a daily average of 5,532 in 1994 up to 34,000 in 2011 (Golash-Boza 2012). The number of detainees has remained steady since 2011, in part due to what is known as the *detention bed mandate.*

In 2009, then-Senator Robert Byrd added a line to the DHS Appropriations bill that says that the DHS is required to "maintain a level of not less than 34,000 detention beds." This "detention bed mandate" requires immigration detention facilities to fill 34,000 beds each day with noncitizens who are either awaiting deportation or awaiting an immigration hearing. This mandate has played a significant role in the continued escalation of deportations. And, it has been included in the annual appropriations bill ever since. In 2015, the appropriations bill stated, "Funding made available under this heading shall maintain a level of not less than 34,000 detention beds through September 30, 2015."[1]

This mandate has been profitable for private corporations, particularly Corrections Corporation of America and the GEO Group. In 2015, 62% of ICE immigration detention beds were in for-profit facilities, up from 49% in 2009.

Border versus Interior Removals

Obama has been called "Deporter-in-Chief" for overseeing the most expansive removal program in history. But who is counted in the two million deportations is the subject of widespread debate. Conservative pundits claim that the U.S. ICE is counting *border removals* toward the annual 400,000 deportations quota to show that Obama has been tough on deportation. Immigrant rights activists claim the administration is enhancing *interior removals*, tearing immigrant families and communities apart.

The distinction is important. For example, catching migrants at the border and returning them to their home countries (as is typical of border removals) is different from arresting long-term U.S. residents in their home, in front of their children, and sending them back to countries they left long ago (as is typical of interior removals). Nevertheless, the distinctions between these types of removals are imprecise—7% of border removals between 2004 and 2013 involved people who had lived in the United States for more than one year and 11% of interior removals during that time period involved people who had been in the United States for less than two weeks. For the most part, however, when an undocumented immigrant living in the United States is removed, this counts as an interior removal. A border removal, in contrast, usually involves a person who crossed the border less than two weeks prior to being apprehended.

So far much of the debate over Obama's deportation policy has occurred in the absence of comprehensive data. A new report by the Migration Policy Institute, a Washington, D.C.-based global think tank that studies the movement of people, offers detailed data on interior and border removals. The report reveals that Obama is on track not only to carry out far more removals than any of his predecessors but is also poised to oversee more interior removals than any U.S. president.

For context, there were 30,000 annual interior removals in 2003 when President Bush created the DHS. By 2008, Bush's last year in office, this number rose to 140,000 interior removals per year. It is clear that Bush initiated an immigration law enforcement program targeting interior removals. The Obama administration continued Bush's legacy by further enhancing the focus on interior enforcement. The report shows that interior removals reached a peak (188,000 annual deportations) in 2011—two years *after* Obama took office.

In 2012, perhaps in response to widespread criticism from Latinas/os, Obama reversed course. As a result, interior removals fell to 131,000 in 2013, a sharp drop but still far higher than the number of interior removals under the Bush administration, except for 2008. Overall, during Obama's first term alone, there were nearly three-quarters of a million interior removals. That is far more interior removals than all of Bush's eight years in office.

Beyond the evidence on interior versus border removals, the report also details the number of years deportees lived in the United States prior to being apprehended. According to the Migration Policy Institute, from 2003 to 2013, there were 1.3 million interior removals. Nearly half of them (47%) had lived in the United States for at least three years. And one in six, or 216,000 of them, had lived in the United States for at least 10 years. The deportations of long-term U.S. residents are often the most harmful to families and communities in the United States, as they are the most likely to lead to family separation.

In a nutshell, the two million deportations during Obama's first five years of office do not necessarily mean that two million families were separated. But this program of mass deportation has meant that least 216,000 people who had likely intended to settle permanently in this country have been torn from their homes over the past decade. That amounts to the city of Rochester, New York, slowly being depleted of its population over the course of ten years. Or perhaps more accurately, imagine every father in San Francisco being removed from this country.

Felons Not Families?

President Obama claims, "If we're going to go after folks who are here illegally, we should do it smartly, and go after folks who are criminals, gangbangers, people who are hurting the community—not after students. Not after folks who are here just because they're trying to figure out how to feed their families." His policies, however, tell a different story.

The American Civil Liberties Union (ACLU) uncovered documents that revealed that ICE agents targeted undocumented immigrants convicted of minor traffic crimes to meet their criminal deportation quotas. Because of policies like these, under Obama, we have seen not only a rise in deportations generally, but specifically in deportations that involve immigrants who have lived in the United States for long periods of time. These deportations have happened primarily through cooperation between local law enforcement and immigration law enforcement agents. President Obama has supported this cooperation and pushed for immigration law enforcement to focus on criminal aliens.

The Obama administration insists the focus on interior enforcement is making our communities safer. However, the numbers belie Obama's claim that he is focused on deporting criminals. To be sure, the percentage of criminal removals under the Obama administration (46%) *is* higher than under the Bush administration (36%). By 2013, fully 87% of interior removals involved people with criminal convictions. However, the details paint a different story. For example, in 2013, immigration offenses accounted for 30% of the total 200,000 removals on criminal grounds. The vast majority of these crimes are illegal entry or illegal reentry. The difference between a noncriminal, undocumented immigrant and a criminal alien convicted of illegal entry or reentry is entirely a matter of prosecutorial discretion. Ultimately, it is difficult to substantiate the official claim that a higher percentage of criminal removals means that deportations are enhancing public safety. Overall, the data reveals that people with fairly minor convictions account for the majority of criminal removals in 2013. About 14,000 people were deported for drug possession, 28,000 for traffic crimes, and nearly 5,000 for nuisance offenses such as trespassing and vandalism.

On April 6, 2014, the *New York Times* reported that nearly two-thirds of the two million deportations since Obama took office have involved either people with no criminal records or those convicted of minor crimes. Just two days later, TRAC (Transactional Records Access Clearinghouse) Immigration issued an even more detailed, and more damning, report. The report, which looks at deportations carried out by ICE, found that 57% of ICE deportations in 2013 were of people who had criminal convictions. However, this statistic hides the fact that most of these convictions are minor. The authors write:

> ICE currently uses an exceedingly broad definition of criminal behavior: even very minor infractions are included. For example, anyone with a traffic ticket for exceeding the speed limit on the Baltimore-Washington Parkway who sends in their check to pay their fine has just entered ICE's "convicted criminal" category. If the same definitions were applied to every citizen. . . . Evidence suggests that the majority of U.S. citizens would be considered convicted criminals.

In other words, not only have nearly half of all deportations involved people with no criminal record whatsoever, large numbers of "criminal" deportations involve people with traffic offenses. According to the TRAC report, each year of the Obama administration, the percentage of deportations that involve a criminal conviction has increased.

However, most of these convictions were minor. Some of these convictions would only be considered criminal in a very broad definition of the term. For example, about a quarter of the criminal convictions involved the immigration crime of illegal entry. The difference between a person deported on noncriminal grounds for being undocumented and one deported on criminal grounds for illegal entry is almost entirely a question of prosecutorial decisions. In other words, these 47,000 people deported for illegal entry were converted into criminals for reporting purposes.

The next-largest category is traffic offenses—the majority driving under the influence or speeding—which account for nearly another quarter of all criminal deportations. Although safe driving is valued in this country, in common parlance in the United States, we do not generally refer to people with traffic convictions as *criminals.*

The third-largest category is drug offenses. Notably, the most common offense in this category was marijuana possession, which has been decriminalized in Washington, Colorado, and other locations.

The TRAC analysis renders it clear that the increase in the number of noncitizens who have been deported on criminal grounds under the Obama administration is mostly a consequence of an increase in the deportation of noncitizens with immigration and traffic violations—convictions that are only considered criminal in a very broad definition of the term. In fact, based on ICE's own definition of a serious or "Level 1" offense, only 12% of all deportations in 2013 were of people convicted of such offenses.

Although President Obama claims to have focused immigration law enforcement priorities on criminals, the TRAC report reveals that this is simply not true. Instead, the evidence is conclusive that deportation policy has put thousands of kids in foster care, deported hundreds of thousands of parents of U.S. citizens, and created a massive "Latino problem" for the Democratic Party.

DHS policy under Obama has been to focus on criminal aliens, achieve a quota of at least 400,000 deportations a year, and strengthen the U.S.-Mexico border. Meanwhile, fewer people are trying to cross the U.S.-Mexico border. These policies have thus translated into increasing numbers of people being deported who have lived in this country for years and who have children who are U.S. citizens. There has been an increase in the number of deportees who have family ties in the United States. Between July 1, 2010, and September 30, 2012, nearly a quarter of all deportations—or 204,810 deportations—involved parents with U.S. citizen children. This is remarkable, as a previous report found that DHS deported about 100,000 people who had U.S. citizen children in the ten years spanning 1997 and 2006.

Focusing on criminals sounds like a smart plan. However, few people deported on criminal grounds are serious criminals. In 2011, 86,000 people were prosecuted by the Department of Justice for immigration crimes—nearly all for illegal entry or illegal reentry. The difference between a person who is deported on noncriminal grounds and one who is deported on criminal grounds for illegal entry is nominal. About a quarter of people deported on criminal grounds are deported for immigration crimes. Another 50% are deported for drug or traffic crimes. Again, these are crimes only if you prosecute them. An undocumented immigrant can be processed civilly for Entry without Inspection or criminally for illegal entry—although the action—crossing the border—is the same. A person found with marijuana can be prosecuted criminally for a drug offense, fined, or simply let go. When your goal is to enhance the numbers of criminal deportees, it makes sense to prosecute these offenses criminally and claim you are deporting criminals.

In light of the facts that (1) deportation rates are higher than they ever have been in history; (2) deportation laws are draconian; and (3) the federal government spends more money on immigration law enforcement than all other federal law enforcement agencies combined, it is worthwhile to consider who is targeted by immigration law enforcement.

Most Deportees Are Men

In the data publicly available on the Office of Immigration Statistics (OIS) website, the sex of deportees is not provided. The annual reports issued by OIS have not mentioned gender since the late 1990s. Scholarly studies of deportation rarely mention gender (Brotherton & Barrios, 2011; Coutin, 2000; Golash-Boza, 2012; Hagan, Eschbach, & Rodriguez, 2008; Hernandez, 2008; Kanstroom, 2012; King, Massoglia, & Uggen, 2012; Kretsedemas, 2012). Yet, in 2011, 89% of all removals involved men. Moreover, the rise in removals since 1998 almost exclusively affected male noncitizens while the number of females deported has remained stable.[2] In 2011, 53% of undocumented immigrants in the United States were men (Hoefer, Rytina, & Baker, 2012).

Whereas there were 44,029 deportations of women in 1999, there were 43,781 deportations of women in 2011. In contrast, the number of male deportations rose from 138,231 in 1998 to 347,947 in 2011—a 250% increase. The sex ratio of removals between 1998 and 2011 is displayed in Figure 1 below. This figure renders it evident that the 1996 policy changes as well as those changes brought about by the War on Terror have led to increased deportations of men, but not of women.

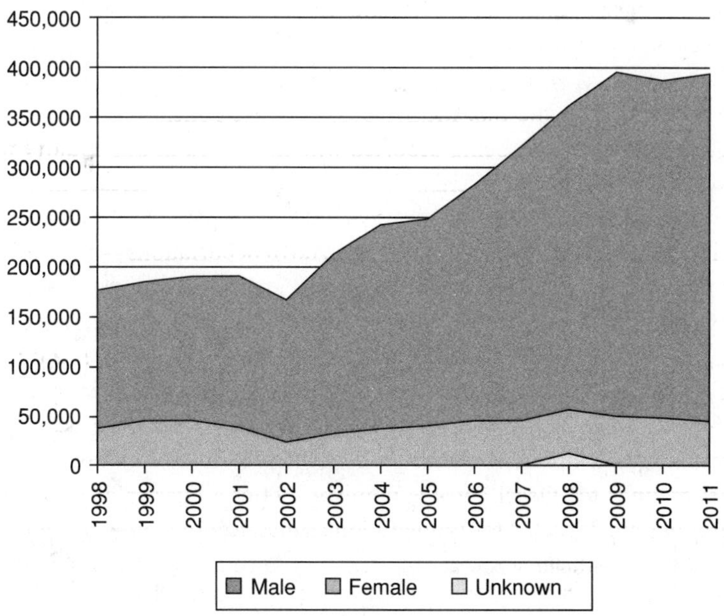

Figure 1 DHS Removals by Sex: Fiscal Years 1998–2011

Source: Department of Homeland Security, ENFORCE Alien Removal Module (EARM), January 2012, Enforcement Integrated Database (EID) December 2011.

Deporting Latin Americans

The tremendous rise in deportations has also affected some national origin groups more than others. Nearly all of the increase in removals since 1998 is due to an increase in the number of Mexican and Central American immigrants removed (see Figure 2).

The total increase in deportations from 1998 to 2011 was from 173,146 to 391,953—an overall increase of 227%. Mexican immigrants experienced the largest increase in absolute numbers. Proportionately speaking, however, the only group to experience a larger-than-average increase between 1998 and 2011 was Central American immigrants: 4.34 times as many Central Americans were deported in 2011 as in 1998. Notably, the number of European, Asian, Caribbean, and African deportations remained flat. These data render it clear that the law and policy changes in 1996 and 2003 have not affected all national origin groups equally.

Overall, deportees disproportionately go to the Western Hemisphere. In 2011, 97.5% of all deportees were sent to the Americas, with only 2.5% going to Europe, Asia, and Africa. In contrast, in 2011, 84% of unauthorized immigrants in the United States were from the Western Hemisphere (Hoefer et al., 2012). These numbers reveal that deportation rates are not reflective of the country of origins of noncitizens in the United States, as Latin American immigrants are the most vulnerable to deportation.

I have not yet seen a study that fully explains the gendered and racialized dynamics of mass deportation. However, my qualitative research with deportees reveals that nearly all people deported from the interior of the United States are deported after an encounter with local law enforcement. The first step into the deportation dragnet is nearly always a

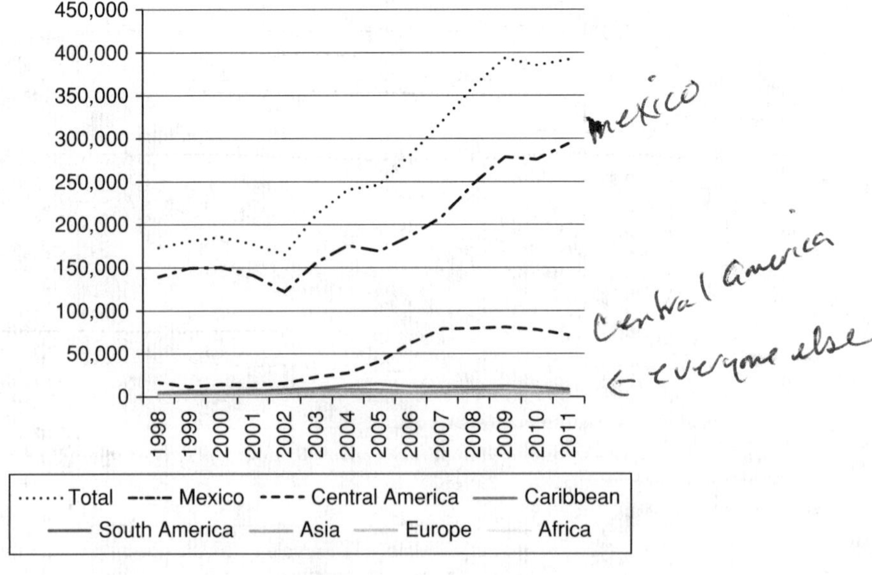

Figure 2 Total Removals and Removals by Region, 1998–2011

Source: Department of Homeland Security, Office of Immigration Statistics.

consequence of an interaction with local police. It is highly likely that this fact explains why Latin American men are the primary targets of deportation insofar as Latinos are often racially profiled for "driving while brown." Nevertheless, further research and more data are needed in order to understand more fully how this program of mass deportation is being executed.

Notes

1. https://www.congress.gov/bill/114th-congress/house-bill/240/text.
2. The Office of Immigration Statistics provided me with removal data by sex between 1998 and 2011. I requested data going back to 1982 and am still waiting to hear if I am able to obtain more historical data.

References

Brotherton, D. C., & Barrios, L. (2011). *Banished to the homeland: Dominican deportees and their stories of exile.* New York, NY: Columbia University Press.

Coutin, S. (2000). *Legalizing moves: Salvadoran immigrants struggling for U.S. residency.* Ann Arbor: University of Michigan.

Fragomen, A. T., & Bell, S. (2007). Entry of aliens to the United States: The basic structure. *Immigration fundamentals: A guide to law and practice.* New York, NY: Practising Law Institute.

Golash-Boza, T. (2012). *Immigration nation: Raids, detentions, and deportations in post–9/11 America.* Boulder, CO: Paradigm.

Hagan, J., Eschbach, K., & Rodriguez, N. (2008). U.S. deportation policy, family separation, and circular migration. *International Migration Review, 42*(1), 64–88.

Hernandez, D. (2008). Pursuant to deportation: Latinas/os and immigrant detention. *Latino Studies, 6*(1–2), 35–63.

Hoefer, M., Rytina, N., & Baker, B. (2012). Estimates of the unauthorized immigrant population residing in the United States: January 2011. Office of Immigration Statistics of the US Department of Homeland Security. Retrieved from https://www.dhs.gov/sites/default/files/publications/ois_ill_pe_2011.pdf

Kanstroom, D. (2012). *Aftermath: Deportation law and the new American diaspora.* New York, NY: Oxford University Press.

King, R. D., Massoglia, M., & Uggen, C. (2012). Employment and exile: U.S. criminal deportations, 1908–2005. *American Journal of Sociology, 117*(6), 1786–1825.

Kretsedemas, P. (2012). *The immigration crucible: Transforming race, nation, and the limits of the law.* New York, NY: Columbia University Press.

Simanski, J. F. (2014). *Immigration Enforcement Actions: 2013.* Washington, DC: DHS Office of Immigration Statistics.

CHAPTER 28

The Hyper-Criminalization of Black and Latino Male Youth in the Era of Mass Incarceration*

Victor M. Rios

In this essay, Victor Rios discusses how Black and Latino youth labeled **deviant** *are affected by criminalization after coming in contact with the juvenile justice system. Using data from ethnographic interviews he conducted in the San Francisco Bay Area from 2002 to 2005, he argues that Black and Latino youth are further stigmatized and hyper-criminalized upon entering the juvenile justice system, even when the majority are arrested for nonviolent offenses. Nonviolent juvenile offenders thus experience the full force of direct and indirect punishment and criminalization traditionally aimed at violent offenders. Furthermore, at a time when punitive crime control measures have drastically increased, youth of color not only experience this* **hyper-criminalization** *from criminal justice institutions but also from noncriminal justice structures traditionally intended to nurture: the school, the family, and the community center. Ultimately, in the era of mass incarceration, Rios observes the development of a youth control complex, a network of racialized criminalization and punishment created by various institutions of control and socialization to manage, control, and incapacitate Black and Latino youth.*

Source: Adapted from Victor M. Rios, "The Hyper-Criminalization of Black and Latino Male Youth in the Era of Mass Incarceration," *Souls Journal*, Volume 8, Issue 2, Taylor and Francis, 2006.

*Some text and accompanying endnotes have been omitted. Please consult the original source.

Questions to Consider

Rios makes an argument about the hyper-criminalization of Black and Latino male youth in an era of mass incarceration. Missing from his analysis are other racial groups and female youth. What are some reasons that White and Asian American male youth might avoid being targeted in the same way? Do you think Black and Latina female youth share similar experiences to their Black and Latino male counterparts?

In its function, the power to punish is not essentially different from that of curing or educating. (Foucault 1995, 303)

Carceralization as a Youth of Color Phenomenon

In the era of mass incarceration, Black and Latino youth face a coming of age crisis determined by criminalization and carceralization. The majority of Black and Latino inmates are youth; almost three quarters of all Black and Latino jail and prison inmates in the U.S. are between the ages of 20–39. As of 2003 12% of all Black males in their 20s were in prison or jail; almost 4% of Latinos and only 1.5% of whites in their 20s were incarcerated (Harrison, 2003). One in three African American youth ages 20–29 are incarcerated or on probation or parole (Harrison, 2003).

While Latino youth do not match the outrageous incarceration rates that Black youth contend with, they too are disproportionately confined, especially in areas with large Latino populations. For example, as of 2002, in California, Latino youth represented 36% of the state's youth population, however, they made up close to 60% of the state's juvenile detainees (Villaruel & Walker, 2002); Black youth made up roughly 7.8% of the state's population, yet they comprised almost 30% of juvenile detainees (Males & Macallair, 2000).

In Black and Latino communities, mass incarceration has become a youth phenomenon. In California, youth of color are 2.5 times more likely than white kids to be tried as adults and 8.3 times more likely to be incarcerated by adult courts. Ninety-five percent of all juveniles sent to adult court are youth of color. In Los Angeles a stunning 91% of all cases in the adult criminal court involve youth (Males & Macallair, 2000). Recent punitive expansion and the material effects of mass incarceration have come to affect some of the youngest populations in Black and Latino communities. The trajectory of this article is to account for the social effects of mass incarceration and criminalization on young males of color, those populations most affected by these systems that generate and exacerbate social misery.

These young adult deviants do not become so on their 18th birthday, rather they are systematically constructed as criminals and face the wrath of the penal state and criminalization as early as 8 years of age (see for example Ferguson, 2000). Scholars have argued that in the contemporary historical bloc punishment and carceralization are at the center of racial inequality and social misery (Davis, 2003; Castells, 1997; Parenti, 2000; Wacquant, 2002). Expanding on this argument, this article will demonstrate that spillover from the ever-expanding power and punitiveness of criminal justice policies and practices affect every member of poor racialized communities in multiple ways, especially urban youth of color. Some scholars have begun to analyze this structure of punishment that extends its tentacles beyond the offender and systematically damages the transgressor's family, friends, and community. Scholars have termed this spillover effect the "collateral consequences of mass imprisonment" (Chesney-Lind & Mauer, 2004). These scholars have argued that punishment not only affects the confined individual but rather expands itself to family members and the inmate's community. Building on this argument I demonstrate how the punitive expansion of the state has created a new system of social relations that stigmatize and criminalize poor youth of color at an everyday level.

Mass imprisonment and the cultural, political, and economic arrangements that accompany it have had a devastating social impact on young male adolescents in the inner city, specifically Black and Latino male youth. Furthermore, the lives of Black and Latino youth who are labeled "deviant" are enforced by institutional entities that treat them as serious criminal threats ready to commit savage acts of violence even if they have only been arrested for drug possession or status offenses. This collateral consequence of mass imprisonment has brought about a network of criminalization, surveillance, and punishment that serves as a main socializing and control agent for Black and Latino youth who have been labeled "deviant."

The Research Context: Studying Criminalized Experiences

The article is based on 40 in-depth, semi-structured "ethnographic interviews" (Spradley, 1979) I conducted in Oakland, San Francisco, and Berkeley, California with Black and Latino youth ages 14 to 18. Each of these cities has unique social, cultural, economic, and political landscapes. However, they are part of a larger metropolis—the San Francisco Bay Area—where extreme racial disparities in family incomes, disproportionate incarceration rates by race, and major disparities in educational, housing, transportation, and employment between communities of color and white communities exist.

Half of the youth I interviewed was Black (20) while the other half was Latino (20). I wanted to contrast and compare the experiences of both racialized groups. Were their experiences different even though they lived and grew up in similar environments? If the youth I observed and interviewed, Black or Latino, lived in the same neighborhoods and attended the same schools, were they criminalized in similar ways? Did they commit similar crimes? Did they have the same attitudes about the criminal justice system?

I recruited a "control group" of 10 youth who had never been arrested but lived in the same area and associated with the juveniles who had been arrested. Although these youth were "at-risk" and often participated in negative behaviors, they were considered to be "good kids" by their peers. This control group would show the difference in criminalization between those arrested and those who had not been arrested but had been identified in the community as risks.

Six (out of 30) of the arrested youth were arrested between the ages of 12 and 14; 17 were arrested at age 15; and 7 had been arrested between the ages of 16 and 17. For most (28 out of 30), all arrests happened for non-violent acts such as vandalism, petty theft, and burglary. Out of the snowball sample of youth that I recruited only two arrests had taken place for violent crimes against other youth. A limitation to this study was that I did not recruit many violent offenders. However, the sample seems representative of juvenile delinquency in the inner city: most youth are arrested for non-violent offenses but are managed as a serious criminal risk despite their status. Of the two violent offenders that I studied, Tyrone had stabbed another youth and Jose had hit another youth in the head with a baseball bat. Their initial arrests and experiences were similar to the youth who had not committed acts of violence. The violent youth were arrested multiple times for non-violent offenses prior to their first violent offense. Both Tyrone and Jose ended up incarcerated for long periods of time after I conducted my interviews with them. Jose would later get arrested for shooting another youth in the leg. As of the fall of 2005 he was on trial facing five to twenty years in prison. Tyrone ended up arrested for assaulting a police officer. He was sentenced to fourteen months at the county jail.

For the 28 youth who were arrested for non-violent crimes, their experiences with the justice system were similar: they went to juvenile hall from 1–60 days; they were released on a monitoring device and/or on probation; and they were given specific conditions of probation—to go directly from school to home, not to associate with their former peers, and not to hang out on the streets. Ten of them ended up with a monitoring device shackled to their ankle that would beep and alert the probation department if the youth [wandered] away from their home.

Governed as Criminals

If social structures are visible and identifiable through the everyday "common sense" expressions and interactions that individuals in society have with one another (Garfinkel, 1967), then, the "youth control complex" became visible to me as I interviewed and observed my subjects in their everyday interactions and conversations about criminalization. However, beyond simply examining my subjects as agents whose behavioral patterns I could observe in order to understand larger social structures, I took seriously the experience and thinking that youth brought to the table. Taking the voice of youth seriously allowed me to conduct my research "from the ground up." From this perspective, I followed the logic and structure of the social worlds they inhabited. This approach led me to understand how the interactions that youth had with individuals who criminalized them were used to make sense of their social world.

The findings show that youth not only felt the direct effects of incarceration and police repression but they also experience what Jonathan Simon (1997) calls "governance through crime." That is, the everyday impact that citizens experience from encounters with a society obsessed with surveillance, security, and punitive penal practices. For Simon, in a society that over the past 30 years has increased its prison population over five-fold and that continues to generate draconian punitive sentencing, it is not only the criminal that suffers from the hyper-punitiveness but also the everyday law-abiding citizen. He argues that in today's society, politicians have heavily "governed through crime." For Simon, crime has become the central tool for governing the everyday citizen, even if they have never committed crime. Crime and punishment have been prioritized in the U.S. to influence the actions of the everyday citizen. It is not that the U.S. has a crisis of crime in its inner cities but rather, it is a crisis of "governance," both in the public and private sphere. This crisis of governance stems not from an increase in crime but from the failure of traditional institutions of governance like the welfare state, labor market, and the education system and from the states inability to provide social and economic security (Simon, 1997).

The youth in this study are youth that have been affected by the decline of the welfare state and the expansion of the criminal justice system. As the youth attempted to deal with this social dislocation—this disorientation, where they could not expect any help or support from the government, where the government had become an abusive step-parent figure, beating its children, throwing them in a room with no windows nor doors—they began to lose hope in the government and in themselves. The youth felt that on an everyday level, their lives were being defined and controlled through discourses and practices of crime and policies related to crime even when they were not committing crime. As I continued to interview and observe them I realized that even if they did not want to commit crime, be seen as delinquent, or act like "thugs," they were already rendered as suspects by many in the community. Because of this, they developed identities that they often wished they could renounce. They began to resist and as they resisted they began to embrace their own criminalization.

Multi-Spatial Criminalization

Many of the youth in the study talked about being criminalized in multidimensional layers and in multiple social settings. Beyond the criminal justice system and its bureaucrats they experienced the effects of criminalization in other significant spaces: the street, school, businesses, and even their home. They compared encounters with police, probation, and prosecutors with interactions they had with school administrators and teachers who placed them in detention rooms, community centers that attempted to exorcise their criminality, and even parents who felt ashamed or dishonored and relinquished their relationship with their own children all together. For the youth, their experience in each of these institutional settings had one thing in common: being treated as a criminal.

While there are many institutions that criminalize inner city youth, I observed the ones that youth themselves suggested. On the criminal justice side I studied how the youth interacted with probation officers. On the youth development side I examined the family and the community center. I chose to look at these institutions because preliminary interviews informed me that community centers and families were a central concern for youth in terms of being criminalized. In addition, these two institutions have traditionally been settings where nurturing has taken place. In their own accounts, it was these institutions that held a firm grip on their life chances. Often their choices were limited by the attitudes and policies that the institutions had towards them. While it was not surprising to hear that probation officers had participated in criminalizing youth in damaging ways—what I call hyper-criminalization—it was shocking to discover that youth felt criminalized in damaging ways by community centers and even their own families. It seemed, in the accounts of the youth, that these three aforementioned institutions were collaborating to form a system that degraded and dishonored them at an everyday level. To understand this process of hyper-criminalization, the lives of the youth I studied had to be examined. What follows are in-depth accounts of youth who represent the experiences of most of the youth I studied.

Growing Up a Criminal

Jose

Jose is a 17-year-old gang-involved youth from Berkeley that I have worked with since he was 13. He has been in and out of trouble since 6th grade and has been to juvenile hall four times. From an early age Jose has experienced policing and surveillance from both criminal justice and non-criminal justice institutions. Over time, Jose has come to understand this combined effect of being criminalized from multiple directions as a single system out to dehumanize him. He explains,

> Man, it's like everyday teachers gotta' sweat me, police gotta pocket check me, mom's gotta' trip on me, and my P.O.'s gotta stress me . . .
>
> It's like having a zookeeper watching us at all times. We walk home and we see them [probation officers and police], we shoot some hoops and we see them, we take a shit at school, and we see them.

Jose is describing an all too common phenomenon where penal practices, traditionally carried on by probation and police officers, have entered other social and private spaces including recreation (community centers), schools, and even the family.

Jose comes from a poor, single-mother household. He has a vivid memory of deviance he saw committed around him and that he committed as early as age 9. He remembers seeing fights on the way from school to home at least once a week. When asked how many crimes, of all types, he remembers seeing on a daily basis, he responds:

> Shit! I can't even count. Crime, I see it everyday, all day. It's like if you try to hide from it, it will find you anyway . . .

Jose remembers his first act of deviance:

> The first time I was in third grade. I had set the bathroom garbage can on fire. We ran away, and they caught us and handcuffed us. . . . I was just trying to do something funny. Police came and arrested me and my friends. They only had a pair of handcuffs and they handcuffed me and my friend together. This is the first time I got arrested. I also flunked that year.

Jose and 26 out of 30 previously arrested youth I interviewed report that teachers at school have direct contact with the school officer and his probation officer. After school, when Jose attends the local youth development community center to participate in leisure activities, he meets with his probation officer who is also stationed at the community center. His mother is forced to deal with the probation officer since he maintains direct contact with her and begins to influence the way she parents. Jose explains:

> My moms started trippin' on me like never before, you feel me? She started telling me to not wear baggy pants and to stop talking the way I did. I asked her who told her

> these things since she never tripped before and she told me that my probation officer had told her to tell me this stuff. . . . I got mad and I left and went to kick it at BYA [the community center]. When I got there my PO was there hanging out. I was mad at him so I left. I went to the park and the police were there trying to fuck with me too.

For Jose and most of the other youth, their experience of being watched, managed, and treated as a criminal began at a young age and became exacerbated after their first offense, in most cases a misdemeanor. Their minor transgression had branded them with a seal that would make their one-time criminal act into a permanent criminal identity. For example, a few weeks after his first arrest for carrying a $10 bag of marijuana, Jose began to realize that everyone in the community knew about his arrest and probation. Beginning at home and ending at the local community program, adults now treated him differently. Jose began to feel watched, police began to randomly stop and search him, his teachers would threaten him with calling his probation officer if he disobeyed at school, his mother constantly reminded him that he would end up in jail if he misbehaved.

After their first offense, most of the youth in the study were labeled and treated as criminals not only by police, courts, and probation but also by teachers, community centers, and even parents. The permanent "criminal" signifier began when the youth was assigned a probation officer. The officer served the role of informing the entire community that the youth had permutated into a risk. He was now to be monitored and controlled by an authority figure assigned by the state: the probation officer.

Probation

The probation officer served the purpose of punishing the youth by branding him a criminal in front of the rest of the community and marking his territory in all settings in which the youth was a participant. Community centers made office space available for probation officers to manage youth from a closer location to their home. Parents were constantly interacting with and often being chastised and influenced by probation officers. Teachers had direct contact with probation officers to inform them when the youth had misbehaved.

At the end of their initial arrest, all youth were given some sort of surveillance program. Most youth (24 out of 30) received a probation officer that they had to meet with once a week to once a month, the rest were given probation without a formal relationship. The meetings would often take place at neighborhood community centers located near the youth's homes. Out of 24 youth that had a probation officer, 18 of them met with them at local community centers or at school. The 18 youth that met with probation officers in their local community demonstrated a feeling that others perceived them differently than those youth who checked in with probation officers at the county probation office. Youth spoke of feeling humiliated because everyone in the community knew that they were on probation. They felt like "criminals" even if they were trying to improve their lives. However, probation did keep a lot of the youth from committing further crime.

From the perspective of juvenile probation and many of the school authorities, the point of the probation officer being present at community centers and schools was to make sure that the youth who were on probation followed all the rules and did not commit another crime. For the most part, this goal seemed to work well with the youth that I interviewed; however, after the youth were released from probation, their chances of being rearrested increased drastically.

The youth believed that one of the biggest changes they faced after being released was the overwhelming presence of their probation officers. Youth went from having little direct supervision and control for most of their lives to having a disruptive control force in their lives waiting for them to, as one of the youth put it, "fuck up." In being present in all aspects of the youths' lives, probation officers could potentially have a positive impact in the youth's rehabilitation and reintegration into society. Often, the youth did follow the strict orders of the probation officer but only in the direct presence of the officer. In the accounts of the youth, at first probation officers helped them "stay in line" but later would become hindrances in their recovery. The probation officer served as a direct threat and locus of control for the youth only while the youth maintained direct contact with him or her.

As soon as youth were taken off their intensive probation program like Electronic Monitoring, weekly meetings, and home arrest, they began to commit acts that further criminalized them and often led to a second arrest. Youth often expressed that being contained, monitored, and threatened for so long to function normally made them unable to control themselves and operate normally in society when the direct authoritative treatment was removed. Youth were being taught to live normally in society under forceful supervision and sanctions from the state. When the absolute force was removed, so was the positive behavior of the youth.

Ronny

Ronny's day-to-day experience provides a deeper insight to processes of hyper-criminalization experienced by youth. Ronny is a 16-year-old African-American male from Berkeley, California. He is currently on probation and is mandated to attend an "anger management" program at Berkeley Youth Alternatives for defying his probation officer. For school he is attending Independent Study, a program where students complete courses at their own pace without attending class. On a typical day, Ronny wakes up at about 10:00 or 11:00 A.M. and walks to Berkeley High School, arriving there at lunch time. Since Berkeley High School is an open campus, students fill up the local shops and restaurants in the main avenue, Shattuck. During 11:45 and 12:45 P.M., swarms of youth travel the streets surrounding the school. For Ronny, this is a time to catch up with friends and foes as they walk from the school to the street. Ronny usually hangs out at a corner near the main avenue and waits for his friends to meet him there. When they arrive he either stands there with them or catches up on events that have occurred in school or the community. If Ronny sees one of his many rivals, he confronts them and sometimes engages in them in a fist fight. It is during this time of day that Ronny is very likely to get arrested. Twice he has been booked by police during the lunch hour for fighting.

After the lunch hour adventure at Berkeley High School, Ronny walks to the Independent Study Office where he turns in work and receives a new packet. Sometimes Ronny goes to this office even if he has not done any work to turn in or does not have an appointment for that day. He explains that he is usually bored by the afternoon and wants a place to hang out. He figures that the teachers might take him in and help him with his assignments; however, most of the time the teachers are not there or are busy with other youth. Ronny walks toward BYA (the community center) and waits outside of the center until 3:30 P.M. when they open the doors to youth. There he plays basketball with friends and takes his anger management class; meets with his probation officer; or talks with a center staff or counselor about his progress. He reports that, like his teachers, the community center staff often report him to his probation officer if he misbehaves at the center.

The center closes at 8:00 P.M. This is when Ronny walks to the park that sits adjacent to the community center. Often his friends meet there to play more basketball; smoke and drink; and talk about their lives until about 10:00 P.M. This is when most youth go home but Ronny walks home, checks in with his grandmother and walks out and sits on his front steps with a few friends who stay out late as well. Most of the time, Ronny's evenings are fairly mundane. But occasionally it is after the end of the program that Ronny and friends fight with rivals; conduct drug deals; and/or break into cars. Two of Ronny's arrests have taken place after 8:00 P.M.

A few weeks after starting his probation program, Ronny began to realize that even his own family had begun to question his innocence. Ronny explains:

> My grandma keeps asking me about when I'm gonna' get arrested again. She thinks just 'cause I went in before, I will go in again . . . at school my teachers talk about calling the cop again to take me away . . . cop keeps checking up on me. He's always at the park making sure I don't get in trouble again . . . my P.O. [probation officer] is always knocking on my door trying to talk shit to me . . . even at BYA [the local youth development organization] the staff treat me like I'm a fuck up again . . .

Over time, Ronny and other youth I interviewed normalize being treated as criminals by most adult members in their community. They see it as an everyday way of life that they have to cope with and learn to navigate. Like Pierre Bourdieou's *Symbolic Violence* (1992) where the subject internalizes and perpetuates his own oppression, the youth internalize their criminalization and respond by "acting bad." Both resistance and expectations of negative encounters with school and justice authorities become normalized as routine features of the environments in which these youth live and navigate. In order for the state to succeed in criminalizing youth it has to make the youth believe that surveillance, brutality, crime, and criminalization is part of everyday life; it has to convince the subject that he indeed is a criminal, or in the words of the youth, a "thug." In this way, the dominated group accepts as legitimate its own condition of domination (Bourdieu & Wacquant, 1992). The "bad kids" internalize their criminalization as a normal part of their everyday lives; hence, youth who are criminalized react to criminalization through criminality. Ronny concludes:

> Shit don't change. It doesn't matter where I go, I'm seen as a criminal. I just say, if you are gonna treat me as a criminal than I'm gonna treat you like I am one you, feel me? I'm gonna make you shake so that you can say that there is a reason for calling me a criminal . . . I grew up knowing that I had to show these fools [adults who criminalize youth] that I wasn't going to take their shit [*sic*] I started to act like a thug even if I wasn't one . . . part of it was me trying to be hard, the other part was them treating me like a criminal.

At an early age Ronny developed an identity that made him act aggressively towards other youth. He talks about being forced to learn to interact with peers by "acting hard" around them. When I asked him what he remembered most about growing up around peers who were involved in delinquent behavior, he said that he had to pretend to be bad in order to get respect, even if he did not want to be bad. Ronny was, as Elijah Anderson (1994) has explained, learning to "code switch." In order to survive the order of the streets and, as I explain, in order to resist the order of hyper-criminalization, Ronny was acting "bad" even if deep inside he simply wanted to do good. The youth have developed strategies of survival in order to cope with the violence of the state and other institutions that criminalize and punish them. However, as Paul Willis (1977) has demonstrated, in resisting their oppression, working class youth often dig themselves deeper into a hole, perpetuating their subordinate status in society. This was the case with the youth in this study.

Jr.

This theme continued to play out with many of the youth I interviewed. The youth knew they wanted to improve their lives and follow their probation program, however they were often influenced in other directions. Jr., a 15-year-old Latino from San Francisco, asked his probation officer for guidance when he came to the conclusion that he wanted to change this negative behavior and follow his instinct:

> I just wanted to start doing better so I told my probation officer to help me. He said that it's easy I had to stay away from all those crazy kids I hung around with. He also told me that if I got caught with them I would go back to jail. He told me to tell them that I would go to jail if I talked to them but they didn't believe me . . . he told me "its common sense" but he's not the one that has to walk on the street.

Besides facing pressure from peers, the youth had to contend with the pressure of adults who were cynical about their ability to do well. Youth often reported that instead of finding ways to support them through rehabilitation and academic and community support, adults from various institutions in the community managed the youth as risks rather than creating a support program.

Jr. reported that teachers at his school had direct contact with the school officer and his probation officer. When Jr. got in trouble in the classroom his teacher filled out a card from the school's police officer. The police officer would check in with the teacher every afternoon and if Jr. had a mark on his card the officer would come and make threats, handcuff him, and/or throw him in the back seat of the police car for long periods of time in front of his peers at the school. The constant surveillance and threats imposed by the police officer at his school made him feel that he was "doing time" in jail while at school. For Jr., school was like jail in the sense that the minute he stepped into it he was under strict supervision and faced the threat of severe punishment with every move he made.

After school Jr. would walk to the local community center to "hang out" and meet with his probation officer who was stationed at the community center. Jr. would walk into the center, greet the staff, check out a basketball and play with some of his friends. At seven o'clock he would drop the ball and walk a few offices past the gym to meet with his probation officer. His probation officer was stationed at the community center due to a grant that the community center received from the county juvenile justice department. The purpose of the grant was to provide services at the community center to juvenile delinquents. The condition was that the center was to provide a probation officer an office space to meet with clients. The result was a combining of social services with state surveillance in one location. As the study went on I realized that the punitive arm of the state, the criminal justice enterprise, had percolated itself into traditionally nurturing institutions like the family and the community center. This created a contradiction since the philosophy and practice of these two very different institutions have traditionally diverged: the criminal justice system, while at times attempting to reform, is primarily concerned with managing crime and imposing sanctions on transgressors; the community center, a social service institution, is concerned with providing emotional, physical, and academic support to its clients, unconditionally, with the intention of developing individuals into healthy, independent, and responsible citizens. What happens then when the punishing arm of the state imposes itself physically and procedurally onto nurturing institutions?

When the punitive arm of the state crosses into traditionally nurturing institutions, delinquent kids become labeled and treated as criminals not only by police, courts, and probation, but also by teachers, community centers, and even parents. This is a problem when the latter institutions are meant to make productive citizens out of youth, not to render them as criminals risking that the youth internalize this criminalization and become ticking time bombs. Stanley Cohen (1972) calls this process "deviance amplification," where parents participate in labeling their kids as criminals and in the process end up alienating themselves from their children. In his classic study, Cohen (1972) illustrates how youth can fall into a spiral of deviance when, as an act of resistance to authority figures (i.e., police) they commit more and more intense acts of deviance. Rather than break away from hyper-criminalization, Black and Latino youth are unfortunately conforming and internalizing their oppression. However, beyond Bourdieu's pessimistic symbolic violence, the youth also demonstrate their ability to change their own internalized oppression. While the youth often internalize and naturalize their criminalization, they often do it as a form of resistance, as a strategy to defy the very same process of criminalization. They embrace the label of "thug" or criminal in order to navigate their social world. However, once given opportunities to embrace a less violent and more nurturing environment they abandon the negative attitude fairly quickly. For example, when I took the youth I interviewed to community events and college functions to provide them exposure to positive settings, their "presentation of self" (Goffman, 1959) became positive; they began to express their desire to be change their lives, they expressed their hopes and dreams and began to ask, as Ronny put it, "How can I change my life? I mean I know I got a lotta' shit going on but I been through the worse already. How can I make it better?"

Hyper-Criminalization as Social Displacement

From a young age, poor urban Black and Latino male youth face stigmatizing and punitive interactions in various settings in their communities. As often well intentioned probation officers, teachers, community center workers, and police officers attempt to grapple with the deviance and risks that youth have, they adopt ideas and practices that further render young males of color suspicious and criminal. This in turn contributes to youth committing more deviance and crime. While most adults in the community attempt to support youth they have little programmatic or financial resources to provide deviant youth successful alternatives that might allow them to reform. However, reform and rehabilitation programs have continued to decline and instead, at the end of the 20th century and the beginning of the 21st century, the public and politicians continue to call for punitive policies that treat juveniles as adults. In a time when crime control seems to calm anxiety in the public, a punitive carceral system of managing the poor has developed (see, for example, Castells, 1997; Parenti, 2000; Wacquant, 2001). This system is inexpensive, easy to implement, and at first appearance successful—it is a system of all-encompassing criminalization that manages youth as criminal risks in order to calm adult anxieties in the community. Non-violent youth offenders, the majority of deviant youth, are criminalized and managed as if they were serious criminal risks.

In the era of mass incarceration solidarity in society has formed around the notion that young adults who commit small acts of deviance will inevitably return and commit a severe maybe even violent act. This leads many community members including teachers, youth development workers, and probation officers to treat all deviant youth as criminal suspects. Even some parents have demonstrated this ideology. A mother of a sixteen-year-old Latino youth I interviewed explained her perspective:

> Right now they are getting him [her son] for whatever little thing like marijuana and for stealing at the store but one day they are going to get him for robbing or shooting someone. This child is out of control . . . I think they need to incarcerate him for some time . . . until he learns to be good.

Even those adults in the community who are well-meaning seem to, often unintentionally, align themselves with racist ideologues and politicians who continue to systematically call for containment and "incapacitation" of youth of color.

While most of the adults in the community care about the youth they interact with, most are uncritical of how their epistemology shapes the way in which they treat and criminalize the youth they are attempting to support. I observed mothers asking their kids when they would be arrested again, teachers calling police officers to report spit ball incidents, and community center staff actively collaborating with probation departments. It was not only the field of the dejure policing and surveillance that affected these youth but also the field of de facto criminalization at school, home, and community centers that impacted them at an everyday level.

As the penal state expands to control and manage poor racialized bodies, a new unintended system of interconnected institutions has formed to brand, further degrade, and contain youth of color. This youth control complex, as an ecology of interlinked institutional arrangements that manages and controls the everyday lives of inner city youth of color, has taken a devastating grip on the lives of many male youth of color in the inner city. Youth experience and explain this massive structure that surrounds them as a unified and uniform criminalizing system whether in school, at home, or on the street. If we are to support poor youth of color in the era of mass incarceration and the decline of the welfare state, adult allies should be critical of their interactions with criminalized youth. Otherwise, we may be perpetuating the very force we are attempting to dismantle—the hyper-criminalization of our youth.

A New Era, a New Paradigm

In a new era where poor racialized bodies are managed as criminal risks instead of provided with social services to recuperate from social misery, youth of color face a coming of age crisis. Historically facing a coming of age crisis for youth of color in the midst of racial violence is nothing new. A little over twenty years after the Emancipation Proclamation, as a student at Fisk College (1885–1888), W.E.B. DuBois marched into the "hills of Tennessee" to teach Black children. He noticed that Black children played a different role in the new post-slavery social landscape. While, in the legal discourse, they were no longer violently forced to labor the land for no compensation, their role was undefined in post-Emancipation America. Black youth remained in a state of limbo. DuBois observed that the youth did not expect to work for nothing but that they had few alternatives. They lived in a state of identity crisis. What should their role be in this new society?

> The mass of those to whom slavery was a dim recollection of childhood found the world a puzzling thing: it asked little of them, and they answered with little, and yet it ridiculed their offering. Such a paradox they could not understand, and therefore sank into listless indifference, or shiftlessness, or reckless bravado. . . . Ill could they be content, born without and beyond the World. And their weak wings beat against their barriers,—barriers of caste, of youth, of life; at last, in dangerous moments, against everything that opposed even a whim. (1899: 101)

Today's urban Black and Latino youth live in "dangerous moments." Their role in the post-industrial mass-incarceration era is undefined. And in this limbo the punitive society is finding a place for poor youth of color: hyper-criminalization and mass incarceration.

Notes

1. As of 2003 out of a total of 832,400 incarcerated Black males 577, 300 were 20–39 years old. For "Hispanics" 270,600 out of a total of 363,900 were 20–39 years old (Harrison, 2003).
2. Association of Bay Area Governments, http://www.abag.ca.gov
3. http://www.frbsf.org Federal Reserve bank of San Francisco.
4. In the community youth who have been arrested or who have been labeled deviant or criminal by police, schools, or other adults are referred to as "criminalized" youth. I use the term in the same manner.

Works Cited

Anderson, E. 1994. *Code of the Streets: Decency, Violence, and the Moral Life of the Inner City*. New York: W. W. Norton & Company.

——— 1990. *Streetwise: Race, Class, and Change in an Urban Community*. Chicago: University of Chicago Press.

Bourdieu, P., & Wacquant, L. 1992. *An Invitation to Reflexive Sociology.* Chicago, IL: Chicago University Press.

Castells, M. 1997. *The Information Age: Economy, Society and Culture.* Cambridge, MA: Blackwell.

Chesney-Lind, M. and Mauer, M. 2004. *Invisible Punishment: The Collateral Consequences of Mass Imprisonment.* New York: New Press.

Cohen, S. 1972. *Folk Devils and Moral Panics.* London: Macgibbon & Kee.

Du Bois, W. E. B. 1899. "A Negro Schoolmaster in The New South." *Atlantic Monthly,* January, 99–104.

Ferguson, A. 2000. *Bad Boys: Public Schools in the Making of Black Masculinity.* Ann Arbor: University of Michigan Press.

Foucault, M. 1995. *Discipline and Punish: The Birth of the Prison.* New York: Random House.

——— 1988. "The Dangerous Individual." In *Michel Foucault: Politics, Philosophy, Culture: Interviews and Other Writings 1977–1984,* edited by L. D. Kritzman. New York: Routledge.

——— 1980. "Prison Talk." In *Power/Knowledge: Selected Interviews and Other Writings, 1972–77,* edited by C. Gordon. New York: Pantheon Books.

Garfinkel, H. 1956. "Conditions of Successful Degradation Ceremonies." *American Journal of Sociology,* 61, 420–24.

——— 1967. *Studies in Ethnomethodology.* Englewood Cliffs, NJ: Prentice Hall.

Goffman, E. 1959. *The Presentation of Self in Everyday Life.* Garden City, NJ: Doubleday.

Males, M., & Macallier, D. 2000. *The Color of Justice: An Analysis of Juvenile Adult Court Transfers in California.* Washington DC: Youth Law Center, Building Blocks for Youth. http://www.buildingblocksforyouth.org/colorofjustice/cojpr.html

Parenti, C. 2000. *Lockdown in America: Police and Prisons in the Age of Crisis.* London: Verso.

Simon, J. 1997. "Governing Through Crime." In *The Crime Conundrum: Essays on Criminal Justice.* Lawrence Friedman and George Fisher, eds. Boulder, CO: Westview.

Villaruel F., and Walker N. 2002. *¿Dónde Está la Justicia? A Call to Action on behalf of Latino and Latino Youth in the U.S. Justice System* [online]. Washington, D.C.: Youth Law Center, Building Blocks for Youth, Research, July 2002 [cited May 19, 2005]. Available at http://www.buildingblocksforyouth.org/Latino_rpt/pr_english.html.

Wacquant, L. 2004. "Decivilizing and Demonzing: Remaking the Black American Ghetto." In *The Sociology of Norbert Elias,* Steven Loyal and Stephen Quilley, eds. New York: Cambridge University Press, pp. 95–121.

——— 2002. *From Slavery to Mass Incarceration.* New Left Review, 13, 41–60.

——— 2001. "Deadly Symbiosis: When Ghetto and Prison Meet and Mesh." In *Mass Imprisonment: Social Causes and Consequences,* D. Garland, ed. London: Sage.

Wacquant, L. J. D., & Wilson, W. J. 1989. "Poverty, Joblessness, and the Social Transformation of the Inner City." In *Welfare Policy for the 1990s,* P. H. Cottingham and D. T. Ellwood, eds. Cambridge, MA: Harvard University Press.

Willis, P. 1977. *Learning to Labor: How Working Class Kids Get Working Class Jobs.* New York: Columbia University Press, 1977.

Wilson, W. J. 1980. *The Declining Significance of Race: Blacks and Changing American Institutions.* Chicago: University of Chicago Press.

——— *The Truly Disadvantaged: The Inner City, the Underclass, and Public Policy.* Chicago: University of Chicago Press, 1987.

——— 1996. *When Work Disappears: The World of the New Urban Poor.* New York: Vintage Books.

CHAPTER 29

"Nomas Cásate"/ "Just Get Married"

How a Legalization Pathway Shapes Mixed-Status Relationships

Laura E. Enriquez

*While most young adults are concerned about finding a compatible partner, **undocumented immigrant** young adults are forced to consider how their legal status and future legalization opportunities will be affected by their partner choice and whether their partner will be able to provide a pathway to legalization. Using ninety-two interviews with undocumented Latina/o young adults, Laura E. Enriquez contends that undocumented young adults develop a "marriage myth" that suggests that marriage may provide an easier pathway toward legalization and that most if not all undocumented young adults seek to legalize their status through marriage. She concludes that legal status complicates undocumented young adults' dating and marriage patterns in marked ways when compared to their citizen counterparts.*

Questions to Consider

Being undocumented affects many aspects of an immigrant's life, including their intimate relationships and their conception of marriage. How does the "marriage myth" influence immigrants' idea of marriage, and why does this myth persist?

Note: Reading is original to this book.

U.S. immigration law allows U.S. citizens and legal permanent residents to petition for the legalization of their undocumented immigrant spouses. This legal reality has generated a popular narrative about legalization through marriage, so it is common to get and give one piece of advice—"nomas cásate" or "just get married." Despite its widespread belief—both within the undocumented community and society at large—this narrative is in fact a myth. The legal reality is much more complicated. While most young adults are concerned about finding a compatible partner, undocumented young adults are forced to consider how their legal status and future legalization opportunities will be affected by their partner choice and whether their partner will be able to provide a pathway to legalization. This article addresses two specific questions: (1) *What are the cultural narratives surrounding marriage as a pathway to legalization?* and (2) *What are the consequences of these narratives for undocumented young adults' dating and marriage experiences?* Specifically, I find that undocumented young adults' awareness of their legal status is heightened as they receive messages in line with a two-part cultural narrative that I call the *marriage myth*. This myth suggests that (1) it is easy to legalize one's status via marriage and (2) all undocumented young adults are motivated to legalize their status through marriage to a citizen partner. I argue that popular opinions about marriage as a pathway to legalization significantly affect undocumented young adults' experience of the family formation process.

Data and Methodology

I draw on ninety-two in-depth interviews with undocumented, Latina/o young adults. Interviews were conducted from November 2011 to August 2012. All respondents are 1.5-generation young adults who entered the United States before the age of 16 and were within the ages of 20 to 35 at the time of their interviews. The vast majority of participants are of Mexican origin, with three from Guatemala. I purposefully sampled to include equal numbers of men and women from a wide range of education levels, including equal numbers of individuals who did not complete high school, graduated from high school, did not complete community college, are currently enrolled in community college or a university, and are university graduates. In addition, my analysis is informed by five years of participant observation in undocumented student organizations and the undocumented community conducted from 2007 to 2013.

At the time of the interview, 49 individuals were single (nine of which were previously married), 20 were dating someone with relationship length ranging from months to years, five were cohabitating, 18 were married or in a marriage-like relationship where they considered themselves married and would be legally married if they were in different circumstances. Of those in a relationship, 25 were with U.S. citizens, 14 with undocumented individuals, and four with legal permanent residents. All but two of the 43 individuals in a relationship were partnered with a Latina/o and only 17 of the 92 participants had previously dated a non-Latina/o.

All research was conducted in the greater Los Angeles area of California. As one of the most popular immigrant destinations, Los Angeles County hosts the highest number of undocumented residents nationally; approximately one in ten residents are undocumented (Fortuny, Capps, & Passel, 2007). Nearby Orange and San Bernardino counties, from which I also drew respondents, are also in the top ten metropolitan areas with large undocumented populations. I recruited interview respondents from the extensive networks I built within the undocumented community over the past four years. To initiate snowball sampling, I selected twelve individuals from separate social networks and who had varying levels of education and social participation. I used a dual-incentive snowball sampling technique whereby respondents received an incentive for participating in the interview and an additional incentive for referring potential respondents. Respondents tended to refer extended family members, neighbors, former classmates, coworkers, and friends.

Interviews were directed by a semi-structured interview guide and included questions about their past and present experiences as well as their expectations for the future. For this article, I draw most from their discussions of family formation, where I asked questions about their dating experiences, marriage experiences and/or expectations, and parenthood experiences and/or expectations. Interviews ranged in length from one to six hours and lasted an average of two. I analyzed interview transcripts using open coding techniques to identify the range of potential experiences and feelings about family formation. I then assessed the frequency of these codes within and across interviews in order to identify common themes.

The Marriage Myth: Media Messages and Popular Understandings of Legalization Pathways

In addition to the various negative images of undocumented immigrants as illegal aliens and workers stealing citizen's jobs (Chavez, 2001, 2008), an increasingly popular image is that of the undocumented immigrant who legalizes his or her status through marriage. Through media representations, this concept of "getting married for papers" is made to look relatively easy and appealing. This reflects, and contributes to, a larger societal trope that undocumented immigrants can easily legalize their status through marriage. As a result, most of my respondents reported being proposed to on the whim of friends or romantic partners. Raul Robles and Teri Balboa explain their reaction to these proposals and the idea of marriage for legalization purposes:

Raul Robles: My friend is like, "You should marry me. We should get married." I was like, "I don't know what you're talking about. It's not like those movies that they show you, that you just get married." I blame *The Proposal* for that. It's not like you're just gonna get your papers right away. It goes more complex. . . . You have to be at the level of confidence to be able to go through that. Cause if you get caught with a fake marriage, it's even worse.

Teri Balboa: We were just watching *The Proposal* [and my friend was] just like, "Why are you watching that? Are you considering [it]? I'm like, you know there's sometimes that you're so desperate when you actually think about it. And it's just not right. It's not right. You have to think about not just for you [but] for the other person.

Raul and Teri specifically cite the role of the media and the blockbuster hit *The Proposal* featuring Sandra Bullock as a Canadian business executive who forces her assistant to marry her so that she can keep her job and remain in the United States. Although they are almost caught in their lie by immigration officials, they end up falling in love and getting married. As Raul notes, this portrayal, among others, suggests to many (including his friend) that getting married is a viable and easy option that most undocumented young adults can use to legalize their status. Additionally, Teri suggests that simply viewing these images encourages her friends to believe that she is considering this as a strategy. These media images contribute to the spread of this trope, which I refer to as the *marriage myth.*

Although marriage to a citizen does provide a pathway to legalization, the reality of this process is complicated by laws that require undocumented immigrants who entered *without inspection* (i.e., without a visa) to return to their country of origin and face a ten-year bar to their return. Though they can petition against this bar by citing the strain it would put on their citizen petitioners (i.e., their spouses or children), there is no guarantee that this reprieve will be granted and they risk being separated from their family for ten years. As a result, legalization through marriage is a risky process for the majority of Mexican undocumented immigrants due to the limited numbers of visas, which forces them to cross the border without inspection. Alternatively, those who enter with a visa enjoy a relatively streamlined and risk-free process and can remain in the United States throughout the process. In either case, a "fake marriage," or one in which you are not in love and intending to remain with your partner, is a federal offense. These complications are largely ignored by these media representations; this contributes to the maintenance of the marriage myth.

Although the reality of legalizing one's status through marriage is complicated, the marriage myth encourages the development of opinions and messages that condemn undocumented young adults for the legal status of their partners. Daniela Sanchez summarizes these messages:

> If you're dating somebody that has papers they think "Oh you're dating him because he has papers." If you're dating somebody that doesn't have papers they're like, "Are you stupid? What's wrong? Go and date somebody that does have papers?" So sometimes it's like you feel like you're sick and somebody has the antidote. You feel like people are judging you because they think they that all you want to get is that antidote because you're sick.

Having dated both undocumented and citizen partners, Daniela expertly summarizes the messages that all of my respondents reported receiving. Specially, undocumented young adults experience both internal and external community judgment in which undocumented community members criticize undocumented young adults for not dating a citizen who can legalize them and citizens criticize them for dating a citizen in search of legal status. Daniela then compares her legal status to a sickness and legalization to an antidote. Though this is a dramatic comparison, it drives home her point that people assume that all undocumented young adults' life decisions are based on acquiring legal status. The marriage myth contributes to this assumption and forces undocumented young adults to view their dating choices and the legal status of their partners in relation to their legal status and the external and internal community judgment they face. No matter the legal status of their partners, all of my interviewees reported being judged by others and/or having a negative experience in which they or a partner were questioned about their legal status.

In a society where marriage decisions are driven by images of romance and love, the marriage myth has forced undocumented young adults to think of marriage in terms of papers. In this way, their legal status shades not only their approaches to who they can date but also their thoughts about marriage. As a result, their love lives are lived in reaction to narratives about their legal status and legalization opportunities.

Whom Do You Date? The Combined Impact of Educational Level and Marginalization Experiences

Though there is variation in immigration status-based preferences, I find that college-educated respondents—those who are currently attending community college or a four-year university or hold a bachelor's degree—are more likely to state a preference for and/or have a tendency to date citizens. In addition to being influenced by the potential dating pool they are exposed to, these preferences are shaped by the marriage myth's messages and the extent to which individuals have experienced legal barriers associated with their immigration status. Specifically, those individuals who pursue higher education are more likely to experience explicit immigration status-based roadblocks and so develop a fiercer desire to legalize their status, buy into the marriage myth's messages, and develop preferences for and/or primarily date citizens.

Twenty-six of the thirty-seven individuals[1] with higher education experience expressed a preference for or have only dated citizen individuals. Many clearly internalized the marriage myth messages and explicitly limited their dating options to citizen individuals. Abel Leon, a college graduate, explains his strict position to not date undocumented women:

> One of my friends . . . called me [and] said, "Hey [Abel], I have two girls, can you help me with one of these girls?" I'm like, "Sure, but are they AB-540[2] [or undocumented]?" He's like, "Yeah man." I'm like, "No, . . . I don't even want to waste my time. I don't want to waste my money. I don't even want to try. I don't care if they're cute. . . . I'm sorry dude, call somebody else. I don't go out with AB-540 girls."

Unapologetic, Abel clearly states that citizenship is one of his requirements for selecting potential partners. Yet, others use more tempered language that dating a citizen is simply an added benefit. For example, Sofia Gonzalez notes that the immigration status of potential partners is a secondary characteristic that she considers:

> I think about their schooling. And then maybe status. . . . It'll be probably on the list [of dating criteria], but it wouldn't be a priority. If it comes down to it, it was not gonna matter [his status] if we fall in love. But I would rather him be born here, you know, have a cool status.

Although Sofia states a preference for citizen partners because of the opportunities for legalization and upward mobility, she and others leave room for the possibility that they will fall in love with an undocumented peer. Yet, in most cases, these respondents only leave hypothetical room to date an undocumented person and have not actually dated another undocumented person.

Alternatively, those respondents who did not pursue higher education or discontinued their community college career are significantly less likely to state immigration status–based preferences. For example, Carolina Sandoval, a high school graduate, explains that "[immigration status] doesn't have to do with being in a relationship with somebody. If you like the person, you wanna be with the person, that has nothing to do with it." Indeed, Carolina directly confronted and rejected marriage myth expectations that she should be with a citizen partner when her mother told her to break up with her boyfriend, now husband, because of his undocumented status. Similarly, most respondents in this educational category said that they did not care about their partner's status. In reality, this lack of preference appears to play out as these 45 respondents were currently partnered with almost equal numbers of undocumented and citizen individuals—15 with undocumented partners, 13 with citizen partners.

On the surface, differences in marriage myth-inspired partner preferences appear to be tied to an individual's level of education. However, digging deeper into the examples of Abel and Carolina reveals that their differing levels of belief in the marriage myth are tied to their exposure to marginalization, not strictly their education levels. Compare their perceptions about the significance of legalizing their status:

Abel: I feel like I can't do anything. I do a lot of stuff. But still, it's hard. I feel like I'm waiting for somebody else to make it happen. [For lawmakers to say,] "Okay let's give them the opportunity. All these people to give them legal status." I feel that someone is holding me back.

Carolina: I'm living my life. Like I do want it [legalization] to happen. It would be so cool, but I don't [wait], I'm just living my life.

While Abel explains that legalization is critical for his future success, Carolina de-emphasizes its significance. This suggests that those in higher education, like Abel, place a higher priority in achieving legalization because they believe that their status is holding them back from reaching their goals. Those not in higher education, like Carolina, tend to believe that they will be able to navigate the limitations of their status and so are living their lives rather than waiting for legalization. Further, many of the respondents without higher education experience formed their current partnerships at a young age in high school, prior to realizing the significance of their immigration status (Gonzales, 2011) and hearing the urgency of the marriage myth. This suggests that immigration status–based roadblocks, which are more common among those undocumented young adults with higher education, create a desperate sense of urgency for legalization and sets the stage for internalizing the marriage myth's messages.

Moving Forward or Breaking Up: Thinking about Future Opportunities

In addition to affecting the selection of potential partners, the marriage myth affects relationship outcomes so that undocumented young adults are forced to think about their legal status when making decisions to about the future of their relationship—specifically breaking up and getting married.

Although deciding to break up with a long-term partner is always a complex decision, undocumented young adults in long-term, mixed-status relationships are forced to consider the potential legalization opportunities on which they are turning their backs. Lili Moreno speaks about her recent decision to end a five-year relationship with her partner who was about to acquire citizenship status and would be able to petition for her:

> I was hoping that things would work out with this person and that we would marry. But they're not. It was difficult because I was thinking how I'm losing an opportunity to get married with someone and legalize my status. When I was trying to decide to

> break up with him or not, this issue came up. If I want to get married and fix my papers, I'm gonna have to start over again and to get to that comfort level where you're sure you want to get married to this person. I had to let that go for the sake of my well-being.

Although all individuals, regardless of legal status, struggle with ending long-term relationships, the marriage myth gives undocumented young adults an extra factor to weigh when making these decisions. In Lili's case, the marriage myth produced a desire to legalize her status through her soon-to-be citizen partner. Without these expectations, she would have had an easier time ending a relationship that she knew to be unhealthy.

Although the opposite of breaking up, decisions to move a relationship forward and get married are also received by others in relation to the marriage myth. Antonio Mendez recalls questions he gets about his five-year relationship with his citizen girlfriend:

> I think that's something that people always ask, [are we together for papers]. I don't know where they got it from; I guess just movies and stuff like that. But yeah I mean we've had that question. . . . It's like, "Are you guys for real or is it just for papers and everything?" But I mean right now we've together five years so it's like how can someone be with someone else for papers if we've been together for this long?

Despite the length of their relationship, Antonio notes that he still receives questions from friends about the veracity of his relationship. Though bewildered by these questions given the length of their relationship and the fact that they have not applied to legalize his status, he attributes these suspicions to the media and the marriage myths it projects. My fieldwork has also demonstrated that mixed-status partners' decisions to get married are viewed with even more skepticism if the relationship was particularly short. Both Carol Castro and Arturo Molina legalized their status through citizen partners whom they had been dating for less than a year. They both explained that they got married out of love for their partners and did not apply for legalization for months after their marriages. Despite these assertions, their friends still questioned their relationships. Carol remembers, "At my wedding shower, a friend of mine said, 'Cut the bullshit. Just tell us the truth. Are you getting married to fix your papers?' She was disinvited from my wedding that night." In addition to direct questions like these, my fieldwork among their circles of friends at the time revealed that the legitimacy of their relationships was a source of gossip. Mixed-status marriages are continually subject to suspicion that they are fake marriages for papers. As a result, these newlyweds are forced to prove to their friends that they love each other.

Given the marriage myth's ability to raise expectations that all mixed-status marriages are the result of attempts to legalize one's status, some undocumented young adults purposely delay marriage. Vanessa Molina explains:

> In the beginning, he was like, "Oh, I'm gonna marry you, bla, bla, bla." . . . Over the years we have thought about it; we wanna wait. . . . I don't want him to feel that I'm just with him because the, because of my status or something like that. I want him to really feel like it's real love. You know? I have had people like tell me, "Oh, you're just with him because of your situation." I'm like, "No, it has been five years. If I was really with him for that I would've married him already."

In addition to combating the suspicions of her friends, Vanessa is determined to delay marriage so that her partner also knows that she actually loves him and is not with him for papers. Though Vanessa also cites her desire to finish college before getting married, she views this as secondary to her desire to prove her love for her partner. As a result, marriage decisions appear to be clearly shaped by the desire to combat the external community judgment created by the marriage myth.

In the case of respondents who were in relationships with undocumented members, a few sought to delay marriage because they knew that they would not be able to legalize through marriage. In these cases, the only hope for legalization was through a family member, which requires that adult children not be married in order to be legalized. Janet Godinez explains this decision to not get married with her undocumented partner:

> We found out that if you're married, you will not be able to fix your situation sometimes. So he tells me, "No we're not gonna get married to see if your sister will fix you guys, or your mom will ask for you." Cause my sister has to fix my mom's first, and then my mom will ask for me and my brother. So if we're married it's like totally different, you're out from the case.

Despite the strategic decision to not get married, Janet expresses frustration with her unmarried status and desire to be married, especially when their children ask her why she is not married. Although her experience differs from her peers in mixed-status relationships, her decision to get married is similarly shaped by her legal status and a desire to preserve the opportunity to legalize her status.

Marriage Decisions: For Love and/or Legal Status

In addition to facing the marriage myth, my respondents were steeped in a social context that values love as the expected rationale for marriage. As a result, my respondents suggest that undocumented young adults are subjected to competing rationales in which marriage is framed as celebration of love but is also presented as an opportunistic contract. Comparing the reasoning of my married respondents, I find that these competing narratives align with the two types of reasons for getting married—for love and to access opportunities. Regardless of which reason was given, legal status was featured as one of the main factors in these decisions.

Although the marriage myth dominated discussions of marriage, love presented a means for countering this narrative. In attempts to refute the community judgment and suspicions that came with getting married, respondents drew on popular narratives of being in love in order to justify their marriages. Celia Alvarez explains why she married her citizen husband:

> I got married because I was very ready. . . . My mentality [is] like, [legalization] it's never gonna happen. . . . [The] things that I do, I don't do them in mind [of that]. . . . When we got married, we got married 'cause I loved him.

Though she and others relied on love to justify their marriages, they still do this in reference to their legalization opportunities and the marriage myth. Aside from justifying "real" marriages, love was also used as a means to justify not entering into a "fake" marriage and responding to internal community judgment. Edith Sandoval explains her reasons for not entering into an opportunistic marriage:

> I'm a sentimental schmuck. So I think I would be giving up on that. I would be giving up on finding someone. I mean, who's gonna say, "Okay, I'll be with you [but] marry that guy." So I don't think so.

Despite the pressure and desire to legalize her status, she argues that legalizing through a fake marriage would prevent her from finding true love in the future. In fact, the women I interviewed who had engaged in an opportunistic marriage to legalize their status reported having a difficult time dating during their application process and the years of conditional legal status. By relying on these narratives of love, Edith is able to justify to herself and others why she is unwilling to succumb to the marriage myth and put her romantic life on hold for approximately five years.

Alternatively to marrying for love, some respondents reported that they saw marriage as a means of securing opportunities and resources. For example, Josue Contreras explains that he married his wife because her undocumented status did not allow her to access the healthcare services she needed: "I was gonna get insurance from my work. So I'm like, 'Okay, we'll go through the whole marriage thing. That way you can have my insurance . . . so we can start treatment.'" He explains that though they were in a real relationship, they decided to get married before they were sure of their commitment to each other because of the health benefits it would afford his partner. Similarly, Carolina Sandoval explains that she moved in with her now husband at the age of sixteen because she was looking for an opportunity to leave her house because "I was having a lot of problems at home. And at that time, my dad had just walked out on us . . . and then my mom was blaming me for the reason that my dad had left." Soon after, she got pregnant, and they got married as soon as they were old enough. In Carolina's case, cohabitation and marriage were a means to secure resources outside of her natal family, where she could have a stable living environment for herself and, later, for her son. For other teenage moms like Carolina, marriage was an expected reaction to pregnancy and a way of building a family unit for the child. While these marriages happened within the context of romantic relationships, marriage was not discussed in relation to love but rather to opportunities and resources.

Building on this opportunistic view of marriage, some respondents found it easier to buy into the marriage myth and enter into fake marriages in order to legalize their status. Interviews with five individuals who legalized their status by entering into fake marriages revealed that marriage was seen a means of securing opportunities. Lena Gomez explains:

> I was undocumented for all of my undergrad career and I was undocumented for most of my graduate career, too. . . . I got married because I was like, "I'm gonna graduate with a master's and I'm not gonna be able to have my career take off unless I leave [for a job outside the United States]. . . . I was like, "I can't continue to work as a nanny—taking the bus two hours every day just to get to work, two hours and a half back to get home when I have these degrees." So I decided to get married to legalize my status.

In light of the limitations her legal status was putting on her life, the marriage myth seemed to be Lena's only opportunity, and it trumped the popular romantic love narrative that was attached to marriage. For the other four individuals, decisions to legalize through marriage were also made at critical points when they were starting to feel the limitations of their legal status—frustration with job opportunities or completion of an educational degree.

Conclusion

Although there are drawbacks to the hyper-romantic notions of love that have come to define dating and marriage in our current social context, it is the most popular way of framing marriage decisions. Undocumented young adults simply strive to be able to frame their own romantic lives in the same way that their citizen peers do. Yet, the marriage myth forces them to experience dating and marriage in reaction to their legal status and limits their ability to proclaim romantic love for others. This suggests that undocumented immigration status has wide-reaching effects on multiple aspects of the lives of undocumented immigrants and, likely, their U.S. citizen partners.

Notes

1. Although I interviewed forty-seven individuals in this category, I do not have data on the explicit preferences of ten individuals.
2. *AB-540* is a term commonly used in California to refer to undocumented students (Abrego, 2008). California Assembly Bill 540 (AB-540) allows any individual who attended high school in California, regardless of their immigration status, to pay in-state tuition. Although not explicitly serving undocumented students, the bill made higher education more affordable for undocumented young adults and increased the number of undocumented college students.

References

Abrego, L. J. (2008). Legitimacy, social identity, and the mobilization of law: The effects of Assembly Bill 540 on undocumented students in California. *Law & Social Inquiry, 33*(3), 709–734.

Chavez, L. (2001). *Covering immigration: Popular images and the politics of the nation.* Berkeley: University of California Press.

Chavez, L. (2008). *The Latino threat: Constructing immigrants, citizens, and the nation.* Stanford, CA: Stanford University Press.

Fortuny, K., Capps, R., & Passel, J. S. (2007). *The characteristics of unauthorized immigrants in California, Los Angeles County, and the United States.* Washington, DC: The Urban Institute.

Gonzales, R. G. (2011). Learning to be illegal: Undocumented youth and shifting legal contexts in the transition to adulthood. *American Sociological Review, 76*(4), 602–619.

CHAPTER 30

I Wouldn't, but You Can*

Attitudes toward Interracial Relationships

Melissa R. Herman and Mary E. Campbell

In this essay, Melissa R. Herman and Mary E. Campbell study Whites' attitudes toward dating, cohabiting with, marrying, and having children with African Americans and Asian Americans. First, they find that almost one in three White respondents reject all types of relationships with both groups or endorse all types. Second, Whites are somewhat less willing to marry and bear children interracially than to date interracially. Finally, they find that White women are likely to approve of ***interracial relationships*** *for others but not for themselves, while White men express more willingness to engage in such relationships personally, particularly with Asians. However, neither White men nor White women are very likely to actually engage in interracial relationships. The authors conclude that widely accepted and positive global attitudes toward interracial relationships do not seem to translate into high rates of actual* ***interracial marriage*** *or interracial cohabitation.*

Source: Adapted from Melissa R. Herman and Mary E. Campbell, "I Wouldn't, but You Can: Attitudes toward Interracial Relationships," *Social Science Research*, Volume 41, Number 2, pages 343–358, Elsevier, 2012.

*Some text and accompanying endnotes have been omitted. Please consult the original source.

Questions to Consider

Many of us want to believe that we are color-blind when picking a partner. Yet, Herman and Campbell suggest that our choices, attitudes, and behaviors aren't always in sync. Why might someone be more supportive of a friend's interracial relationship but may not consider in engaging in an interracial relationship of their own?

Introduction

Studying interracial relationship formation is complex because it involves examining both *attitudes* toward relationships and actual *behaviors*. Furthermore, both attitudes and behaviors are complex: People do not always report their attitudes truthfully about a topic like interracial relationships, and their attitudes can vary based on whether they are asked about their personal feelings or their feelings about the topic more generally. Similarly, behaviors are complex because relationships necessarily involve another person's choices. Even if I am open to an interracial relationship, I might not find an interested partner. In this article, we disentangle these issues, examining the attitudes of White men and women toward dating, cohabiting and marital relationships with African Americans and Asian Americans.

Most of the existing literature on attitudes toward interracial relationships has been unable to separate *global* attitudes about the behavior of others from *personal* attitudes about one's own behavior. In fact, much of what we know about interracial dating, cohabitation and marriage is based on behavior (rather than attitudes). When we do look at attitudes, we find a curious gender gap that flies in the face of many other public opinion gender gaps: White women are less likely to approve of interracial marriage than White men, but they are more liberal in most other racial attitudes (Schuman, Steeh, Bobo, and Krysan 1997). Why does this reverse gender gap exist with respect to interracial marriage? Do women and men have different standards for judging their own personal behavior than they do for judging the behaviors of others? And do White women and men have different attitudes toward different types of interracial relationships, based on the level of commitment in that type of relationship?

Our paper examines these types of questions, distinguishing personal from global attitudes about dating, cohabiting, and marital relationships. In doing so, we test whether White men and women differ in their personal and global attitudes, and how these attitudes differ by the type of relationship and by characteristics of the individual.

Interracial Relationships: Dating, Cohabitation, and Marriage

For many years, surveys of racial attitudes have asked respondents whether they approve of intermarriage as a way to measure social distance between race groups. The classic scale of social distance asks respondents what degree of intimacy they would accept with each ethnic group, using marriage as the highest level of intimacy possible. Acceptance of a wide range of racial groups has increased over time (Knox, Zusman, Buffington, and Hemphill 2000). Some studies have shown, however, that many White survey respondents espouse the *principle* of decreased social distance for abstract others or for close family members while still expressing *personal* preferences that limit their own contact with racial minorities (Charles 2006; Farley, Schuman, Bianchi, Colasanto, and Hatchett 1978).

There is less survey evidence about Whites' attitudes toward dating, cohabiting, or marrying members of specific racial groups. Although survey items about interracial marriage are fairly prevalent (Schuman, Steeh, Bobo, and Krysan 1997), attitudinal items about the other relationship types are not common. This is important because attitudes may well differ for less serious relationships, just as actual involvement in less serious interracial relationships is greater. One explanation for the persistently low rates of intermarriage even in the face of rising interracial friendships and dating is that perhaps people have stricter criteria for selecting marriage partners (Blackwell and Lichter 2000) because they see marriage as a permanent relationship with "family and racial identity ramifications" (Yancey 2007:915), while dating and friendship are less serious. This is called the *winnowing hypothesis* (Blackwell and Lichter 2004), the idea that people apply more restrictive criteria to their field of potential partners as the relationship gets more serious.

Still, interracial dating, cohabitation, and marriage are all connected in important ways. For example, King and Bratter (2007) show that selecting a cross-race partner for the first sexual relationship is an important predictor of selecting a cross-race spouse when getting married. We generally select our more committed relationships (such as marriages) from the pool of our less committed ones (such as dates). Dating, cohabiting and marital relationships all have similar patterns of racial homogamy, although levels of homogamy increase somewhat for more serious relationships (Blackwell and Lichter 2004). We will discuss each relationship type in turn, but it is important to remember that they influence each other.

Interracial Dating: Behavior and Attitudes

Interracial dating has become more common in the most recent cohorts of young adults (Joyner and Kao 2005), and these rates are significantly influenced by proximity to individuals from other racial groups. Using nationally representative data, Carver, Joyner and Udry (2003) found that 7th–12th graders who attend more racially diverse schools report higher rates of interracial dating. For example, in schools that are less than 20% White, 46% of Whites' relationships were interracial, but in schools with more than 80% Whites, only 6% of Whites' relationships were interracial. Of all the groups in schools with few same-race peers, Latino and Asian American adolescents were most likely to have dated interracially, and Black adolescents were least likely to have dated interracially. (Using a nationwide sample of *adults*, however, Yancey (2002) found that Whites were the least likely to have dated interracially, suggesting that there may be significant age group differences in interracial dating rates.)

Interracial dating remains associated with growing up in a more diverse community or attending more diverse schools (Yancey 2002), even in comparisons of adults who currently live in a diverse community. This suggests that having a diverse peer group at a young age continues to affect individuals' later preferences for romantic partners as well (Fujino 1997). Males are also more likely to have dated interracially, as are non-Catholics, people who are more politically liberal, better educated, and younger (Yancey 2002).

There are important racial patterns in who is perceived as an appropriate interracial dating partner. Surveys of undergraduates have shown a clear hierarchy in dating patterns that corresponds to the history of racism in the United States. For example, White students who dated interracially were most likely to choose Latinos, followed by Asians and Blacks, while Latinos were most likely to choose Whites, followed by Blacks and Asians (Fiebert, Karamol, and Kasdan 2000). Fujino (1997) found that White, Chinese, and Japanese American undergraduates were mostly likely to form significant, long-term dating relationships with members of their own group, but those who dated outside their group were least likely to date Blacks and most likely to date Whites or other Asians, followed by Latinos.

Research on interracial dating has investigated another important indicator of behavior and attitudes: the stated preferences of individuals seeking dates through online personal advertisements. This is a creative way to measure behavior in a real-world setting that is unconstrained by the availability of partners, yet has real consequences for who will contact the respondent as a potential date (creating a powerful incentive for honest responses). The conclusions from these studies are limited to the population of individuals who use online personal advertisements, but Yancey (2007) argues that this population is very similar to the larger population of Internet users. White women are more likely to restrict their dating to same-race partners than White men, although the patterns differ, with White men more likely to exclude Black women and White women more likely to exclude Asian men from their pool of potential dates (Feliciano, Robnett, and Komaie 2009). Those who are younger, live in large cities, and live in the West are less likely to restrict their dating to same-race partners, while those who are more politically conservative and attend church frequently are more likely to do so (Yancey 2007).

Interracial relationships are often still accompanied by stigma, even for young people. Adolescents who are dating interracially, for example, are less likely to tell their families and friends about their relationships than adolescents who are dating a same-race partner (Wang, Kao, and Joyner 2006) and less likely to be publicly affectionate (Vaquera and Kao 2005). Whites who engage in interracial relationships are often treated in racist ways that undermine their established understandings of fairness and equal treatment (Dalmage 2000).

Interracial Cohabitation: Behavior and Attitudes

Cohabitation is rapidly growing and is increasingly important for understanding transitions to marriage. Blacks and Latinos are especially likely to be in cohabiting households and are less likely to make the transition from cohabitation to marriage (Smock and Manning 2002). Generally, cohabitating relationships are more likely to be interracial than marital relationships in the U.S. (Blackwell and Lichter 2004; Sassler and McNally 2003), but Whites are an exception to this overall pattern: Same-race relationships among Whites are actually higher for cohabiting relationships than for dating or marriage. Cross-sectional data on cohabitation and marriage suggest, however, that although cohabiting relationships are more interracial than marital relationships (Simmons and O'Connell 2003), selection processes are not as different across cohabitation and marriage as the behavioral differences might suggest (Blackwell and Lichter 2004).

Interracial Marriage: Behavior and Attitudes

Interracial marriage has been studied more than any other type of interracial relationship. For example, surveys have repeatedly asked respondents how they feel about laws against intermarriage, even after the (1967) *Loving v. Virginia* U.S. Supreme Court decision struck down all laws forbidding intermarriage. Opposition to such laws has increased steadily since the 1960s, becoming close to universal today (Schuman, Steeh, Bobo, and Krysan 1997).

However, a much lower percentage responds positively to a question asking whether they "approve" of intermarriage, though that percentage has consistently increased: less than 10% of Whites approved in 1958 while more than 76% approved in 2004 (Krysan 2008; Schuman, Steeh, Bobo, and Krysan 1997). Still, 16% of Whites "strongly disapprove" of racial intermarriage and dating (Bobo 2004). This disapproval is even greater when respondents *know* that their anonymity is protected, such as when they vote. In 1998, South Carolina voted to remove the (unenforceable, and therefore solely symbolic) ban on racial intermarriage from the state constitution, but 38% of voters opposed the removal (Yancey and Emerson 2001). A similar Alabama vote in 2000 received opposition votes from an estimated 49% of White voters (and 8% of other voters) (Altman and Klinkner 2006).

Although actual intermarriage rates are far lower than approval rates, they too have been steadily increasing since the 1960s (Qian 1997); the Census Bureau estimated that 8% of currently married women in their first marriage in 2009 were interracially married[1] (Kreider and Ellis 2011). Of course, willingness to intermarry varies by both the racial group of the individual and the racial group of the potential spouse. For example, Whites are more opposed to a close family member marrying a Black person than marrying an Asian person (Golebiowska 2007). In general, Whites express more positive stereotypes of Asians than Blacks (or Latinos), and both Whites and Asians reported feeling relatively little social distance between their groups (and much greater social distance from Blacks and Latinos) (Charles 2006). This finding shows that the large group size of Latinos is driving the higher rates of dating between Whites and Latinos that we mentioned above. Marriage patterns confirm the same racial hierarchy we see in these measures of social distance: The marriage patterns between Whites and Blacks or Mexican Americans strongly suggest a racial stratification hierarchy, while marriages between Whites and Japanese Americans do not, suggesting that racial boundaries are less salient for Asian/White pairings (Fu 2001). Intermarriage is also more accepted among people with higher education levels, higher income, and those who live in the West and outside the South (Schuman, Steeh, Bobo, and Krysan 1997; Tucker and Mitchell-Kernan 1990; Yancey and Emerson 2001). Controlling for their much smaller group size, Blacks are much more likely than Whites to marry a same-race spouse (Blackwell and Lichter 2004) and self-identified biracial individuals have higher out-marriage rates than all types of single-race individuals (Qian and Lichter 2011).

Gender and Attitudes toward Interracial Relationships

White women are slightly more likely than White men to believe that racial inequality is caused by structural factors like discrimination rather than factors under their control like ability and motivation, and they are more likely to support government interventions on behalf of minorities (Hughes and Tuch 2003; Schuman, Steeh, Bobo, and Krysan 1997). But several studies have pointed to an important exception to this generalization: White women are less willing than White men to have close social relationships with members of other racial groups. For example, Schuman et al. (1997) find that White women are less willing to send their children to schools where a majority of the students are Black and are less likely to approve of intermarriage than White men. Perhaps this is in part because White women anticipate more family disapproval than White men do; minority males dating White females indicate greater family disapproval from their partner's White family than other interracial pairings (Miller, Olson, and Fazio 2004).

There are a few studies that contradict this gendered pattern. Using a national sample of high school seniors, Johnson and Marini (1998) found that White and Black women were *more* positive about close interracial contact than men when they used a measure of social distance that was more abstract than the measures described above.

Interestingly, there is also a well-established gender imbalance in Black/White and Asian/White marriages, with more of the Black/White marriages made up of White women and Black men, and more of the Asian/White marriages made up of White men and Asian women (e.g., Qian and Lichter 2007). These behavioral patterns suggest that the intersection of racialized and sexualized images have important implications for the study of these interracial relationships (Census Bureau 2011). Feliciano et al. (2009) point out that stereotypes of Black men and Black women are hyper-masculinized, and stereotypes of Asian men and Asian women are hyper-feminized, influencing the pattern these researchers found among Internet daters, who were significantly more likely to exclude Asian men and Black women from their dating pool than their same-race counterparts (Robnett and Feliciano 2011).

The current article compares Whites' attitudes and behavior across these three relationship types, using questions that separate global attitudes toward the interracial relationships of others from personal attitudes toward engaging in an interracial relationship. We explore the gendered nature of these patterns, considering whether White men and women have different attitudes toward engaging in interracial relationships with African Americans and Asian Americans. We focus on these two groups because these two groups were historically the focus of antimiscegenation legislation and because the gendered patterns of intermarriage with Whites are most pronounced with these two groups (Feliciano, Robnett, and Komaie 2009).

Method

Data

The nationally representative 2008 Cooperative Congressional Election Survey (CCES) was a cooperative survey with over 30 colleges and universities involved in survey question design (Vavreck and Rivers 2008). In brief, a private firm (Polimetrix) matched people who had agreed to take Internet surveys with a random sample of the adult American population drawn from the 2004 American Community Survey (ACS), a national survey conducted by the US Bureau of the Census. Thus, Polimetrix was able to create a representative sample of US adults to answer our survey questions. Our respondents included $N = 246$ racial/ethnic minorities and $N = 754$ White respondents. Our analyses are weighted to approximate the national adult population using weights created from the 2006 American Community Survey.

Variables

Figure 1 shows the survey format for the questions about interracial relationships, our dependent variables.

Some people would consider a romance with someone from a different race. Others would prefer to "stick to their own kind."

What do YOU think? Please check the statement that you agree with for each behavior:

	It's not a good idea	*I would not, but it's okay for others*	*I would do this*	*I have done this*
Date an [African American/ Asian American]				
Live with an [African American/Asian American]				
Marry an [African American/Asian American]				

Figure 1 Survey item on attitudes towards interracial relationships

We created these questions to measure two things not commonly measured in studies of attitudes toward interracial relationships: first, the distinction that respondents make between their own actions and what they find acceptable for others, and second, their attitudes toward a range of different relationship types. The category "I would not, but it's okay for others" is crucial to understanding the low rate of interracial relationships because it allows us to separate a general acceptance of interracial relationships from a personal willingness to engage in such relationships. (We also tested whether social desirability bias overstates positive attitudes toward interracial relationships but found no such evidence in our sample; see Herman and Campbell forthcoming).

In our analyses, we controlled for characteristics of the respondent that were related to racial attitudes, such as *gender* and *age*, which ranged from 18 to 87. We also included two measures of social class: *annual family income* in thousands of dollars and *education*, measured as whether or not the respondent has at least a college degree. We also included variables to control for several marital statuses: *single* (never married), currently *married or in a domestic partnership*, and the reference category, those who were divorced, separated, or widowed.

We expected attitudes toward interracial relationships to be strongly related to positive feelings toward Blacks and Asians. We used "feeling thermometer" data to construct these measures. Feeling thermometers have long been used as a measure of a respondent's warmth toward particular racial groups (Bruneau and Saxe 2010; Payne, Burkley, and Stokes 2008). The text of our thermometer question read:

> We'd like to get your honest feelings about some groups in American society. Please rate each group with what we call a feeling thermometer. Ratings between 50 and 100 degrees mean that you feel favorably toward the group; ratings between 0 and 50 degrees mean that you don't feel favorably towards the group. If you don't have any particular feelings toward a group you would rate them at 50 degrees.

We collected thermometer data for five racial and ethnic groups: Whites, Blacks, Asians, and multiracial Black-Whites and Asian-Whites. On average, White ratings of the racial/

ethnic groups ranged from a low of 71 for Blacks to a high of 82 for Whites, indicating that Whites feel slightly warmer toward other Whites than toward Blacks. We subtracted the score that each White respondent assigned to her/his *own* racial group (Whites) from the scores that she/he assigned to Blacks and Asians, creating a measure of *relative warmth toward Blacks* and *relative warmth toward Asians.* Thus, positive scores represent feeling greater warmth toward another group than one's own racial group, and negative scores represent less warmth toward the other group than one's own group.

Because conservative political beliefs are associated with "traditional" attitudes toward cohabitation and negative attitudes toward racial minorities (Lye and Waldron 1997), we included a measure of *political conservatism*, using the respondent's party identification (a 7-point scale from "strongly Republican" to "strongly Democrat," coded so that larger positive numbers indicate stronger Republican party affiliations, while more negative numbers indicate stronger Democratic party affiliations). We also included a measure of religiosity, because other research has found an inverse relationship between religiosity and willingness to date interracially (Yancey 2007). Our religiosity scale was constructed from three items: "How important is religion to you?" "How frequently do you attend religious services?" and "How frequently do you pray?" Finally, we included a dummy variable for *South*, given the importance of regional differences in studies of racial attitudes (Schuman, Steeh, Bobo, and Krysan 1997) and historical differences in the sanctioning of interracial relationships.[2] Descriptive statistics for all of these variables can be found in Appendix Table 1.

Results

Descriptive Results

Table 1 shows that White men respond differently to questions about relationships with Blacks than about relationships with Asians. Less than 14% of White men report having had an interracial relationship of any type, but those who have are equally likely to report having had one with a Black person as with an Asian person. However, those respondents who have *not* personally had an interracial relationship express significantly less willingness to have a relationship with a Black person than with an Asian person and are significantly more likely than those who haven't had an interracial relationship to say that relationships with Blacks are "not a good idea." Almost three-quarters (73%) of White men report either having dated or being willing to date Asians, while only 57% report having dated or being willing to date Blacks.

In contrast to White men, Table 1 shows that White *women* are more likely to have actually *had* an interracial relationship with a Black person. White women are also more likely than White men to say they would not personally have an interracial relationship (but it's okay for others). The details of White women's attitudes are race-specific: White women are significantly more likely to report having had an interracial relationship with Blacks than with Asians, suggesting either greater openness to relationships with Blacks or the greater availability of those relationships. But they are also significantly more likely to report that relationships with Blacks are "not a good idea" than relationships with Asians. So, while

Table 1 White Attitudes towards Types of Interracial Relationships, Weighted, by Gender

	White Males, Relationships with Blacks (N=330)			White Females, Relationships with Blacks (N=298)		
	Date	Live with	Marry	Date	Live with	Marry
Not a good idea	0.14	0.17	0.15	0.14	0.17	0.15
I wouldn't, but okay for others	0.29	0.28	0.36	0.43	0.40	0.46
Not a good idea + I wouldn't	0.43	0.45	0.51	0.57	0.57	0.61
I would	0.45	0.50	0.48	0.28	0.37	0.35
I have	0.12	0.05	0.01	0.15	0.06	0.03
I would + I have	0.57	0.55	0.49	0.43	0.43	0.38
	White Males, Relationships with Asians (N=327)			**White Females, Relationships with Asians (N=296)**		
Not a good idea	0.08	0.12	0.10	0.08	0.12	0.10
I wouldn't, but okay for others	0.19	0.18	0.25	0.46	0.44	0.46
Not a good idea + I wouldn't	0.27	0.30	0.34	0.55	0.56	0.57
I would	0.60	0.64	0.63	0.41	0.43	0.43
I have	0.13	0.06	0.02	0.05	0.01	0.00
I would + I have	0.73	0.70	0.66	0.46	0.44	0.43

Source: CCES 2008 survey data.

White women appear to have similar reactions to interracial relationships with Blacks and Asians when we combined "not a good idea" with "I would not," in fact their global rejection ("not a good idea") of relationships with Blacks is a bit higher than their global rejection of relationships with Asians, just as we find for White men. This finding demonstrates that White women's reactions to relationships with Blacks are more polarized than their reactions to relationships with Asians.

Another important pattern apparent in Table 1 concerns the two largest categories ("I wouldn't but it's okay for others" vs. "I would"). We find that White women are quite a bit more likely than White men to choose the category "I wouldn't, but it's okay for others," and they are more likely than White men to express overall higher levels of disapproval of either type of interracial relationships. However, both genders are more likely to say interracial relationships are fine for other people than to say "it's not a good idea" for anyone. This finding signifies the importance of asking a set of questions that distinguish personal attitudes from attitudes about how others should behave. A question that does not separate the personal from the global in this way runs the risk of having individuals who would never interracially date say that they approve of interracial relationships. Because of the intimacy of these relationships, this distinction has important substantive meaning. Table 1 shows that White women are much more likely than White men to say they would not engage in interracial relationships but they approve of others engaging in them. This distinction suggests an explanation for why White women express lower approval of intermarriage than White men on surveys that ask about personal willingness to intermarry. Nonetheless, Table 1 also shows that White men and women are about equally likely to have actually *engaged in* interracial relationships with Blacks (although not with Asians).

Table 1 also shows that attitudes regarding interracial relationships become slightly less positive as the relationship becomes more serious, but these differences are small, undermining the winnowing hypothesis in terms of attitudes. However, White men and women are much more likely to have experienced an interracial dating relationship than any of the more serious kinds of interracial relationships and are more likely to have cohabited interracially than married interracially. This is not surprising, given that most people date more people than they marry. Further probing the relationship between dating behavior and attitudes toward interracial marriage, we found that of the 13% of White respondents who have actually dated Blacks, 90% say they would be open to marrying a Black person. Similarly, of the 9% of Whites who have actually dated Asians, 96% would be open to marrying an Asian person. Thus, approval rates among this self-selected population are extremely high compared to approval rates overall.

Table 2 further investigates the question of whether White respondents are consistent across different relationship types when they endorse or reject an interracial relationship with Blacks or Asians. The table is ordered in columns of increasing commitment, and it combines the "I would have" and "I have had" this type of relationship into a "Yes" response and the "I wouldn't" and "it's not a good idea" into a "No" response for each type of relationship. For example, 43% of White males say they would not date a Black individual. Breaking down that 43% by their responses to the cohabitation question shows that most (39% of all White males) also reject cohabitation. The next column shows the 39% of White men who say that they would not interracially date, cohabit with, or marry a Black person (shown in the first row) and the 46% who said yes to interracial dating, cohabiting, and marriage with Blacks (the bottom number in the upper left quadrant).

Comparing consistency in the responses across the questions, we find that there is a core group of White men who express willingness to engage in any of the relationship types. Forty-six percent express willingness to engage in all relationship types with a Black partner, and 62% express willingness to engage in all of the relationships with an Asian partner. The numbers are much lower for White women, only 35% of whom are willing to engage in all relationship types with a Black partner, and 39% of whom would engage in all relationship types with an Asian partner. Similarly, there is a consistent group who personally reject all relationships with a Black partner (39% of White men and 50% of White women) and personally reject all relationships with an Asian partner (26% of White males and 49% of White females). Note that these numbers are much greater than the number (on other surveys) who simply "strongly disapprove" when asked global items about intermarriage and interracial dating—personal unwillingness to engage in such relationships is far higher. Combining White men and women together, we find that 29% of all Whites reject all interracial relationships with *both* Black partners and Asian partners, and 31% are willing to engage in all of the interracial relationships with both groups. Overall, then, our findings do

Table 2 Weighted descriptives of willingness to engage in interracial relationships, by relationship type

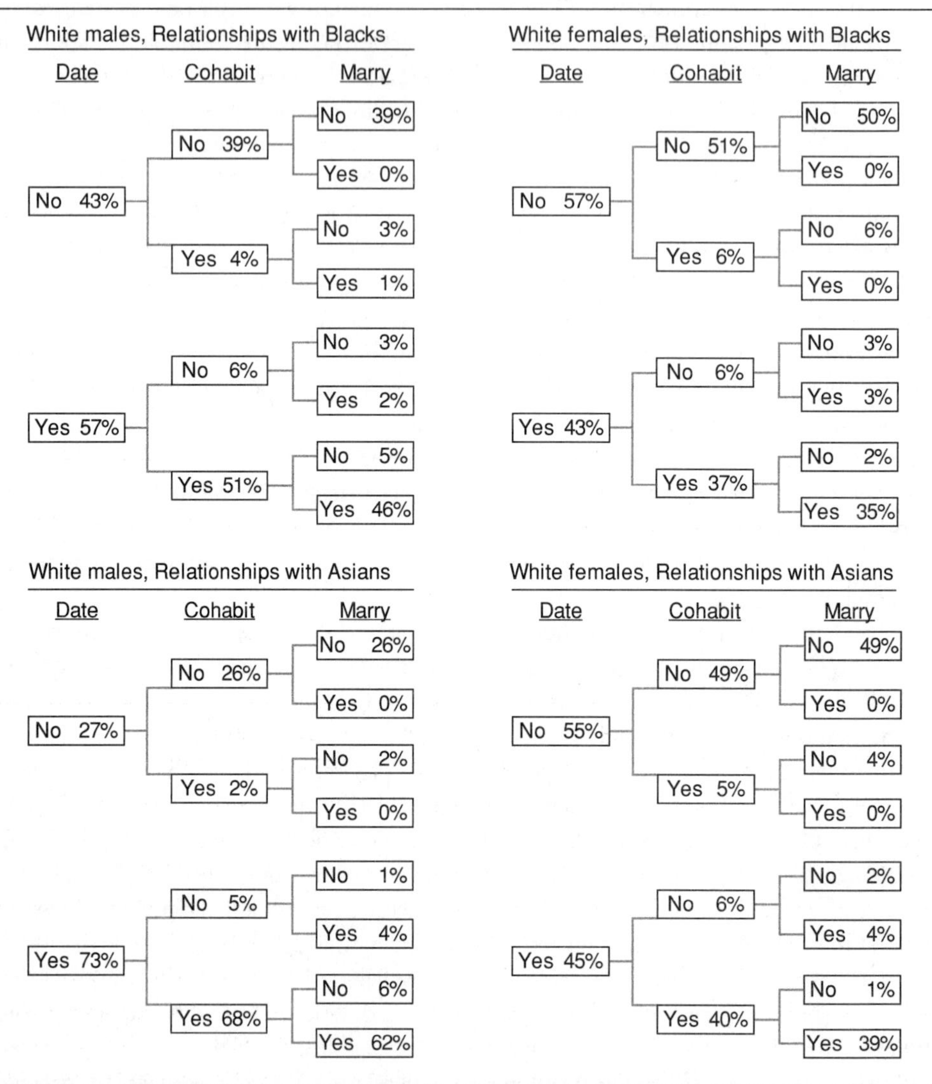

Totals do not always add to 100 percent because of rounding.

not support the winnowing hypothesis because one-third of the Whites in the sample universally reject interracial partnerships and one-third universally express willingness, leaving about one-third of the respondents whose responses vary depending on the type of relationship and the specific racial group being considered.

Multinomial Regression Results

We used multinomial logit models to estimate people's willingness to cross racial boundaries in intimate relationships, allowing us to estimate the probability that a person with a given set of characteristics will choose each response category. The models (not presented here) show a significant gender difference, with females more likely to reject interracial relationships with Blacks (for themselves, although not for others). We also found that older individuals are more likely to reject interracial relationships than younger people, but people with a college education are more likely to support all relationships with Blacks than people without a college degree. It is important to note that higher education reduces *global* rejection ("not a good idea"), not *personal* rejection. Current relationship status is not significantly related to these attitudes.

People's warmth toward Blacks is strongly related to supporting all types of relationships, with those who feel more warmly about Blacks less likely to oppose interracial relationships with Blacks globally and less likely to reject personal engagement in relationships with Blacks. Political conservatism is positively and significantly associated with personally rejecting relationships with Blacks. Religiosity is positively related to global rejection of dating and cohabitation with Blacks, but not marriage, suggesting that religiosity affects attitudes toward cohabitation more than interracial cohabitation. Finally, Southerners are more likely to reject interracial dating and cohabitation globally.

We estimated these same models for Whites' attitudes toward relationships with Asian Americans, and the findings are similar to those for African Americans, except for minor differences. Most interesting is that political conservatism has little association with attitudes toward interracial relationships with Asians.

Discussion

These results help clarify why many Whites express racial tolerance and openness to interracial interaction but few actually marry a partner of another race. Many people articulate tolerance for racial boundary crossing even while acknowledging that they would not personally engage in the behavior, and many of the respondents who say they are willing to have interracial relationships have never engaged in interracial dating, which might be considered a prerequisite to the more serious forms of interracial intimacy. Whether this is because of perceived lack of opportunity, because of unstated (and perhaps unconscious) resistance to interracial dating, or because openness may coexist with—and be trumped by—a preference for homogamous relationships is not something we can answer with this survey. But it is important to keep in mind that forming a relationship involves three stages, any of which can change the potential for an interracial relationship: *finding* a partner, *choosing* a partner, and *being chosen by* a partner.

The first issue in understanding the attitude–behavior gap is that of *finding* a partner. Lack of opportunity might help explain why White women express more willingness to have relationships with Asian men but actually engage more frequently in relationships with Black men. There are more Black men than Asian men in the U.S. Furthermore, because Blacks are geographically distributed more widely than Asians, more White women may have regular interracial contact with Black men, despite the greater integration between Whites and Asians in the specific local contexts with sizable Asian populations. The second issue is *choosing* a partner. Preference for homogamous relationships may trump willingness to try heterogamous ones. The third issue is *being chosen.* One may have access to and preference for a partner of a different race but be unable to find a willing companion. For example, higher rates of Black male–White female pairings than Black female–White male pairings could be driven by the behavior of Whites, or by higher proportions of Black males preferring and seeking out White women, or by lower proportions of Black women seeking White men. Indeed, Black men are significantly more likely than Black women to prefer heterogamous dating (Robnett and Feliciano 2011). Similarly, the higher rates of White male–Asian female pairings may be driven by the dating behavior of Whites, or Asian women's greater preferences for White men than Asian men have for White women.

Overall, then, the puzzle is if White women are more reluctant to intermarry than White men, why are there so many more Black male–White female unions than White male–Black female unions? As noted above, part of the explanation could a result of both "demand" and "supply"—if more Black males are willing to intermarry than Black females, this could also mean that the (fewer) White women who were willing to form interracial relationships with Black men would be more likely to successfully find a willing partner than the (more) White men who were willing to form a relationship with Black women. (Among Asians, this gender disparity is reversed.)

Another potential cause is the difference in how Black men are perceived. As Hill (2002) demonstrated, darker-skinned Black women are perceived by interviewers as less attractive than lighter-skinned Black women, but this relationship was weak and inconsistent for Black men. This gender difference in the reaction to dark skin could create a significant gendered difference in the dating and marriage opportunities of Black women and men and affect other groups like Latinos, who have a wide range of skin tones.

Our results clarify the gender difference in willingness to cross-racial boundaries in intimate relationships, showing that women are more likely than men to draw a distinction between what they are personally willing to do and what they condone for others. Thus it is not true that White women are more conservative about interracial relationships in a global sense (applying more conservative criteria to these relationships for *everyone*) but instead that they apply a more racially conservative set of criteria to their own personal relationships. The paradoxical finding that White women (who are usually more racially liberal than White men) oppose interracial marriage more than White men can be explained by this divide between global attitudes (those applied to others) and private attitudes (those that apply to one's own behavior). Recall that White women anticipate more family disapproval if they engage in interracial relationships than White men do, and the double standard of acceptable romantic/sexual behavior means that women expect their relationship choices to receive more scrutiny (Miller, Olson, and Fazio 2004). In contrast, the social dominance of White men raises fewer questions about their manhood or their life chances when they choose to ignore racial purity norms (Spickard 1989).

Intermarriage, therefore, is best tested by asking respondents about multiple levels of relationship, specifying the race of potential partners, and allowing a distinction between personal relationship attitudes and global attitudes toward other people's behavior. It is essential to be clear about the reference group when asking about racial attitudes, because respondents will answer differently if they believe the question is asking whether they find the behavior personally desirable versus whether it is acceptable for others.

We suspect that the increasingly positive *attitudes* toward interracial relationships will not necessarily lead to a global shift in *personal engagement* in interracial relationships (Qian and Lichter 2007; Wang, Kao, and Joyner 2006) because even individuals who engage in

Appendix Table 1 Weighted variable descriptive statistics, White respondents, $N = 634$

Independent variables	***Mean/Prop.***	***Std. Dev.***	***Range***
Male	0.50		(0/1)
Age	48.5	15.3	(18 to 87)
Family income in thousands	60.8	40.6	(5 to 160)
Bachelor's degree or more	0.28		(0/1)
Single	0.19		(0/1)
Married or partnered	0.63		(0/1)
Relative warmth toward Blacks	–10.8	20.3	(–99 to 45)
Relative warmth toward Asians	–8.5	18.3	(95 to 62)
Religiosity scale	–0.13	0.90	(–1.7 to 1.3)
Political conservatism	–0.03	0.94	(–3.0 to 3.0)
South	0.33		(0/1)

Source: CCES 2008 survey data.

interracial dating have very low rates of interracial marriage. Although attitudes can be an important precursor to social change, it is important to consider the intersection between attitudes and behavior in order to predict future social interaction. With interracial relationships, this intersection is especially important, because while tolerance for interracial unions has clearly increased over time, we still have strong evidence of preference for homogamous unions.

Note

1. "Interracially married" here includes both couples who are married across racial lines, as defined by the Census, and couples who marry across ethnic lines such non-Latino/Latino couples.

References

Altman, Micah and Philip A. Klinkner. 2006. "Measuring the Difference between White Voting and Polling on Interracial Marriage." *Du Bois Review* 3:229–315.

Blackwell, Debra L. and Daniel T. Lichter. 2000. "Mate Selection among Married and Unmarried Couples." *Journal of Family Issues* 21:215–302.

Blackwell, Debra L. and Daniel T. Lichter. 2004. "Homogamy among Dating, Cohabiting, and Married Couples." *The Sociological Quarterly* 45:719–737.

Bobo, Lawrence. 2004. "Inequalities that Endure?: Racial Ideology, American Politics, and the Peculiar Role of the Social Sciences." In *The Changing Terrain of Race and Ethnicity*, edited by M. Krysan and A. E. Lewis. New York: Russell Sage.

Bruneau, Emile G. and Rebecca Saxe. 2010. "Attitudes towards the Outgroup Are Predicted by Activity in the Precuneus in Arabs and Israelis." *NeuroImage* 52:1704–1711.

Carver, Karen, Kara Joyner, and J. Richard Udry. 2003. "National estimates of adolescent romantic relationships." Pp. 23–56 in *Adolescent romantic relations and sexual behavior: Theory, research, and practical implications*, edited by P. Florsheim. Mahwah, NJ: Erlbaum.

Census Bureau, U.S. 2011. "Statistical Abstract of the United States: 2011." Washington, DC. http://www.census.gov/compendia/statab/2011/tables/11s0060.pdf.

Charles, Camille Zubrinsky. 2006. *Won't You Be My Neighbor?: Race, Class, and Residence in Los Angeles.* New York: Russell Sage.

Dalmage, Heather. 2000. *Tripping on the Color Line.* New Brunswick, NJ: Rutgers University Press.

Farley, Reynolds, Howard Schuman, Suzanne Bianchi, Diane Colasanto, and Shirley Hatchett. 1978. "'Chocolate City, Vanilla Suburbs': Will the Trend toward Racially Separate Communities Continue." *Social Science Research* 7:319–344.

Feliciano, Cynthia, Belinda Robnett, and Golnaz Komaie. 2009. "Gendered Racial Exclusion among White Internet Daters." *Social Science Research* 39:39–54.

Fiebert, Martin S., Holly Karamol, and Margo Kasdan. 2000. "Interracial Dating: Attitudes and Experience Among American College Students in California." *Psychological Reports* 87:1059–1064.

Fu, Vincent Kang. 2001. "Racial Intermarriage Pairings." *Demography* 38:147–159.

Fujino, Diane C. 1997. "The Rates, Patterns and Reasons for Forming Heterosexual Interracial Dating Relationships among Asian Americans." *Journal of Social and Personal Relationships* 14:809–828.

Golebiowska, Ewa. 2007. "The Contours and Etiology of Whites' Attitudes toward Black–White Interracial Marriage." *Journal of Black Studies* 38:268–287.

Hill, Mark E. 2002. "Race of the Interviewer and Perception of Skin Color: Evidence from the Multi-City Study of Urban Equality." *American Sociological Review* 67:99–108.

Hughes, Michael and Steven A. Tuch. 2003. "Gender Differences in Whites' Racial Attitudes: Are Women's Attitudes Really More Favorable?" *Social Psychology Quarterly* 66:394–401.

Johnson, Monica K. and Margaret M. Marini. 1998. "Bridging the Racial Divide in the United States: The Effect of Gender." *Social Psychology Quarterly* 61:247–258.

Joyner, Kara and Grace Kao. 2005. "Interracial Relationships and the Transition to Adulthood." *American Sociological Review* 70:563–582.

King, Rosalind Berkowitz and Jenifer L. Bratter. 2007. "A Path toward Interracial Marriage: Women's First Partners and Husbands across Racial Lines." *Sociological Quarterly* 48:343–369.

Knox, David, Marty E. Zusman, Carmen Buffington, and Gloria Hemphill. 2000. "Interracial Dating and Attitudes among College Students." *College Student Journal* 34:69–71.

Kreider, Rose M. and Renee Ellis. 2011. "Number, Timing, and Duration of Marriage and Divorces: 2009." Pp. 70–125, *Current Population Reports.* Washington, DC: U.S. Census Bureau.

Krysan, Maria. 2008. "Data Update to Racial Attitudes in America." Vol. 2008. Chicago, IL.

Loving v. Virginia. 1967. Vol. 388: p. 1 U.S. Supreme Court.

Lye, Diane N. and I. Waldron. 1997. "Attitudes toward cohabitation, family, and gender roles: relationships to values and political ideology." *Sociological Perspectives* 40:199–225.

Miller, Suzanne C., Michael A. Olson, and Russell H. Fazio. 2004. "Perceived Reactions to Interracial Romantic Relationships: When Race Is Used as a Cue to Status." *Group Processes and Intergroup Relations* 7:354–369.

Payne, B. Keith, Melissa A. Burkley, and Mark B. Stokes. 2008. "Why Do Implicit and Explicit Attitude Tests Diverge? The Role of Structural Fit." *Journal of Personality and Social Psychology* 94:16–31.

Qian, Zhenchao. 1997. "Breaking the Racial Barriers: Variations in Interracial Marriage between 1980 and 1990." *Demography* 34:263–276.

Qian, Zhenchao and Daniel T. Lichter. 2007. "Social Boundaries and Marital Assimilation: Interpreting Trends in Racial and Ethnic Intermarriage." *American Sociological Review* 72:68–94.

Qian, Zhenchao and Daniel T. Lichter. 2011. "Changing Patterns of Interracial Marriage in a Multiracial Society." *Journal of Marriage and the Family* 73:1065–1048.

Robnett, Belinda and Cynthia Feliciano. 2011. "Patterns of Racial-Ethnic Exclusion by Internet Daters." *Social Forces* 89:807–828.

Sassler, Sharon and James McNally. 2003. "Cohabiting Couples' Economic Circumstances and Union Transitions: A Re-Examination Using Multiple Imputation Techniques." *Social Science Research* 32:553–578.

Schuman, Howard, Charlotte Steeh, Lawrence Bobo, and Maria Krysan. 1997. *Racial Attitudes in America: Trends and Interpretations.* Cambridge, MA: Harvard.

Simmons, Tavia and Martin O'Connell. 2003. "Married-Couple and Unmarried-Partner Households: 2000, Census 2000 Special Reports, CENSR-5." U.S. Census Bureau.

Smock, Pamela J. and Wendy D. Manning. 2002. "First Comes Cohabitation and Then Comes Marriage? A Research Note." *Journal of Family Issues* 23:1065–1087.

Spickard, Paul R. 1989. *Mixed Blood: Intermarriage and Ethnic Identity in Twentieth-Century America.* Madison, WI: Wisconsin Press.

Tucker, M. Belinda and Claudia Mitchell-Kernan. 1990. "White Attitudes toward Black American Interracial Marriage: The Social Structural Context." *Journal of Marriage and the Family* 52:209–218.

Vaquera, Elizabeth and Grace Kao. 2005. "Private and Public Displays of Affection Among Interracial and Intra-Racial Adolescent Couples." *Social Science Quarterly* 86:484–508.

Vavreck, Lynn and Douglas Rivers. 2008. "The 2006 Cooperative Congressional Election Study." *Journal of Elections, Public Opinion & Parties* 18:355–366.

Wang, Hongyu, Grace Kao, and Kara Joyner. 2006. "Stability of Interracial and Intraracial Romantic Relationships among Adolescents." *Social Science Research* 35:435–453.

Yancey, George A. 2002. "Who Interracially Dates: An Examination of the Characteristics of Those Who Have Interracially Dated." *Journal of Comparative Family Studies* 33:179–190.

Yancey, George A. 2007. "Homogamy over the Net: Using Internet Advertisements to Discover Who Interracially Dates." *Journal of Social and Personal Relationships* 24:913–930.

Yancey, George A. and Michael O. Emerson. 2001. "An Analysis of Resistance to Racial Exogamy: The 1998 South Carolina Referendum." *Journal of Black Studies* 31:635–650.

CHAPTER 31

Love Is (Color)Blind*

Asian Americans and White Institutional Space at the Elite University

Rosalind S. Chou, Kristen Lee, and Simon Ho

The literature on racism at the university level is extensive, but few studies have examined the unique position of Asian American undergraduates. Through rich qualitative data, Chou, Lee, and Ho describe how Asian American undergraduates use language to negotiate their social experiences, romantic relationships, and identity at the elite university. It documents the strategies Asian Americans use to cope with and negotiate racialized encounters. Frequent among the participants is the use of a color-blind discourse to describe such experiences. To understand the way Asian Americans practice color-blind talk, this chapter interrogates the ***intersectionality*** *of race, gender, and sexuality and the specific racialization of this minority group.*

Questions to Consider

How do Asian American undergraduates respond to racism on predominately White college campuses, what Chou and colleagues contend is a White institutional space? What strategies do Asian American undergraduates use to reproduce and resist racism? Can you think of other strategies students of color use to combat racism?

Source: Adapted from Rosalind Chou, Kristen Lee, and Simon Ho, "Love Is (Color)blind: Asian Americans and White Institutional Space at the Elite University," *Sociology of Race and Ethnicity*, Volume 1, Number 2, pages 302–316, SAGE Publications, Inc., 2015.

*Some text has been omitted. Please consult the original source.

In February 2013, more than 250 students gathered at Duke University to protest against an Asian-themed fraternity party that featured invitations with Team America Kim Jeong Il speaking in broken English and party-goers dressed as geishas and sumo wrestlers. The Kappa Sigma fraternity party, which seemed to have crossed the line between racial humor and raw insensitivity, received backlash from the university and gained national media attention. An outpouring of external support from Asian American organizations at other universities and celebrities bolstered the efforts of student activists. And yet, on campus the response was more varied. Within Duke's Asian American community, responses ranged from outrage to apathy. One student, Johnny Wei, wrote in the student newspaper:

> As an Asian-American, I was naturally disappointed in Kappa Sigma's insensitive party theme. I was equally disappointed, however, in how Asian student organizations on campus chose to respond to this crisis. . . . As Duke's largest minority group, we Asians had the opportunity to take the high road and truly break new ground in eliminating these cultural insensitivities, a problem that seems to plague Duke perennially. (Wei 2013)

The Kappa Sigma party is a prime example of the racialized social landscape that undergraduates traverse, and the varied reactions that followed demonstrate the complexity of racial ideology. Asian Americans champion education as a pathway to success that transcends race (Chou and Feagin 2008). Asian Americans occupy a unique position within university structure; while they make up only 5% of the total U.S. population, they represent up to 30% of the student population in some elite universities (Clark 2009). Even as Asian Americans become a greater proportion of the university population, little effort has been given to understanding their university experiences. In the rare instance when they are included in racial discourse on higher education, "they have been reduced to a single, stubborn persistent narrative—as a 'model minority'" (Teranishi 2010:11). A few notable articles describe Asian American experiences with physical violence and verbal harassment in high school and college (Rosenbloom and Way 2004). Fewer studies still have examined the social context and romantic relationships of Asian Americans at university.

Drawing on rich qualitative data, we place Asian American undergraduates in the driver's seat, exploring the language they use to cope, survive, and negotiate their social experience at a predominately white institution. The discourse Asian Americans use to make meaning of their racialized and sexualized relationships reveals the complicated positionality of Asian Americans as a "racial middle." On one hand, they are seen as "forever foreigners"; on the other hand, being stereotyped as a "model minority" or "honorary white" may encourage the use of color-blind racist discourse to explain their positions on campus and legitimize racist hierarchy (Tuan 1999). Stereotyping as either "forever foreign" or "model minorities" differentiates Asian Americans from white college students. To understand the meaning behind these practices, we interrogate the intersectionality of race, gender, and sexuality and the particular racialization of this group. We argue that elite campus culture, as white institutionalized space, leads Asian Americans socialized in this environment to both adopt and resist racialized messages.

Theoretical Framework

Twenty-First Century Racism

The overt Jim Crow racism that ruled through segregation, derogatory language, and violence has in many ways been replaced by the subtleties of contemporary racism (Bonilla-Silva 2002). Today, racism still operates as a system based on an ideology of inferiority that allocates societal resources by racial hierarchy (Bonilla-Silva 1997). However, the "new" racism is more covert, more likely to dance around inferiority and inequality in the hidden language of "differences" (Bonilla-Silva 2002). Although the literature has chronicled various forms of this post–Civil Rights era racism, in the context of this article we focus on what Bonilla-Silva referred to as "color-blind racism." A type of "racism without racists," color-blind racism is a racial ideology that allows whites to defend their racial interests while maintaining invisibility of whiteness and white privilege. Color-blindness refuses to examine racism within a social and historical context. It reduces race problems to matters of isolated individual prejudice and negates the existence of a larger socioeconomic racial structure with real economic, social, and political consequences for people of color (Prashad 2001). Common elements of color-blind racism are *(1)* discussing racial matters in the abstract, *(2)* attributing racially inferior standings in education and economy to cultural differences over biological explanations, *(3)* framing racial residential and school segregation as "natural," and *(4)* claiming that discrimination is a thing of the past (Bonilla-Silva 2002). To the color-blind, the problem is never race or racism. Through various denial strategies, color-blind racism obfuscates the problem of racial inequality, thus making it difficult to dismantle the white ruling class. We demonstrate that color-blind discourse is used by Asian Americans at HWCUs as well as by their white peers.

The Role of Discourse in Color-Blind Racism

Color-blind racism principally operates through the expression of conversations, media, and other forms of communication. There are numerous ways of communicating color-blind racism, but for the purpose of this paper we highlight three of its discursive practices: *(1)* the use of certain semantics to express racial views, *(2)* the almost complete incoherence when it comes to certain issues of race, and *(3)* the minimization of concerns about racial inequality (Bonilla-Silva 2002).

To adapt to the shift from Jim Crow racism to post–Civil Rights era realities where openly racist statements were no longer socially acceptable, color-blind discourse opted for specific language to express racial views. For example, one might couch a racist statement by emphasizing that it is not a racist comment. One might also use descriptors that are tacitly racialized, such as describing a neighborhood as a "ghetto" when one means to say that it is a minority community. The incoherence regarding certain issues of race is sometimes characterized by long pauses and "I don't know" statements when themes of race make difficult the identification and resolution of racist incidents. The minimization of concerns about racial inequality is fostered in color-blind racism by not only denying racial structure but also silencing those who raise the issue. For example, individuals might call Asian Americans outraged by racial discrimination "too sensitive" or "overreacting," in essence minimizing racism as an emotional problem. Embedded in the subtleties of talk, color-blind discourse may appear benign compared with the system of fear and violence that Jim Crow racism used. However, color-blind discourse could be more powerful for its tacit hegemony, moving through the minds of the majority and minority alike (van Dijk 2000).

Subordinated minorities are not immune to adopting and internalizing parts of color-blind racism. Claire Kim (1999) is one of the seminal critical race scholars to offer a structural framework to expand beyond black and white and consider the racial position of Asian Americans. She criticizes racial hierarchy for its one-dimensionality, which assigns status and privilege to whites at the top, blacks at the bottom, and other minorities like Asian Americans in the middle. Kim instead maps out white racial hierarchy on two axes: an axis of racial superiority–inferiority and an axis of insider–foreigner. In a position of "near whiteness," Asian Americans might be more likely to identify and promote white interests than other people of color. Effectively the racial triangulation of Asian Americans drives a wedge between themselves and other minorities. However, we argue that the two axes are not enough. When one conducts an analysis through an intersectional lens, including systems of gender, sexuality, and class complicates the simplified racial order that Kim outlined. Bonilla-Silva (2004) theorized a "tri-racial" model that includes class as a marker in determining racial superiority and inferiority but also fails to address the racial shuffling that occurs when including stereotypes of gender and sexuality. The common thread throughout these racial theories is that whiteness goes uninterrogated. Groups of color are compared against the standard of whiteness, and whiteness is not constructed as pathological. Kim and Bonilla-Silva offered a critical analysis. Our work extends Kim's map of racial hierarchy and Bonilla-Silva's tri-racial modeling toward a more intersectional approach, suggesting gender–sexuality as an additional axis to understand Asian American racial discourse.

Asian American Sexual Politics

Current Asian American racial formation and identity theories are inadequate. Racial analysis of Asian Americans is incomplete without consideration of gender and sexuality constructions. Connell and Messerschmidt (2005) coined the term "hegemonic masculinity" to describe the ideology of male dominance. White hegemonic masculinity constructs the white heterosexual male as the version of normalized manhood, whereas men of color are cast into weaker "subordinated masculinities." Subordinated masculinities are racially specific. For example, Asian American men face a particular placement on a gendered hierarchy and deal with battles against normalized constructions of masculinity that operate differently than those of their Latino or African American male counterparts (Chou 2012; Eng 2001). Racial stereotypes can and do change over time, but they continue to maintain the racial status quo. The stereotyping of early male Chinese immigrants was very similar to past and current constructions of African American men as hypersexual, aggressive, and dangerous (Takaki 2001). However, over time, stereotypes of Asian American men have changed, and now they are portrayed as hyposexual, impotent, and weak (Espiritu 2008). Hegemonic femininity works in similar fashion, promoting white women over women of color, although both are still subordinate to white men. White hegemonic ideology shapes not only our understanding of masculinity and femininity but also our romantic and sexual preferences.

We contend that Asian American sexuality is formed in ways that perpetuate white privilege, particularly for white men. Media and literature represent Asian and Asian American women in a dichotomous fashion, as either the mysterious "Dragon Lady" or a servile "Lotus Blossom" (Tong 1994). Both of these depictions erotize Asian and Asian American women, while Asian and Asian American men are simultaneously "castrated" or denied manhood. These representations exacerbate the "oriental fetishism" that Asian and Asian American women face (Prasso 2006). "Controlling images" of both Asian American men and women exist "to define the white man's virility and the white man's superiority" (Kim 1999:69). Again, at the core of these Asian portrayals is the strength of white hegemonic masculinity. Defining white male virility and superiority through the demeaning representations of Asian Americans is essential to retain the existing racial structure. Further, the principal distributor of these stereotypes is discourse. More specifically, public forms of discourse such as media, politics, and education are the most powerful modes to transmit these depictions. It is no accident that these forms of public discourse are predominately controlled by white elites.

Racialized Love

Higher education is a particular space where Asian Americans undergo racial identity management while exploring their romantic preferences (Chou 2012). Dating and romantic relationships are widely recognized as important parts of college life (Armstrong 2006). Asian American out-dating has been increasing rapidly while Asian American out-marriage is declining (Sassler and Joyner 2011). The racially exploratory nature of dating, especially in regard to Asian Americans, has been suggested as the reason behind this trend. This makes dating in an elite university, itself an exploratory space, an excellent setting to investigate the role of race in romantic interactions.

Patricia Hill Collins (2004:6) defined sexual politics as "a set of ideas and social practices shaped by gender, race, and sexuality that frame all men and women's treatment of one another, as well as how individual men and women are perceived and treated by others." Moreover, the manner in which these social experiences and ideas are talked about offers an intimate analysis of how love and relationships are built. What we argue is that Asian Americans' social experiences and ideas at HWCUs are shaped by white habitus, the white racial frame, and white institutional space. The relationships between Asian Americans and their non–Asian American peers are shaped by the campus climate, which is part of the larger racialized society. However, the elite college campus, such as at HWCUs, is often touted by Asian American families as a site in which merit is valued over all things. Our data suggest that race is still a factor in the social experiences of Asian American students.

Our research interrogates the intersectionality of race, gender, and sexuality and the unique position of Asian Americans at HWCUs. Although our data allude to a problematic white university culture in which whites engage in sexualized racism with little consequence, we find equally worrisome the emotional management that Asian Americans must perform to deal with such racism. We document how Asian Americans use language to negotiate the realities of sexualized racism and racialized romantic preferences. Finally, we detail the Asian American responses to racism, which range from resistance to racial resignation.

Results

At the university, a persistent stereotype of Asian Americans is that they are "quiet and content with the status quo" (Tatum 1997:161). In the *Myth of the Model Minority*, Chou and Feagin (2008) described individuals who have internalized this stereotype and deal with racism by ignoring it quietly. Our research documents Asian American undergraduates resorting to a color-blind discourse that prevents them from articulating the racialized nature of certain social experiences. The discursive strategy also at times leaves them unprepared to deal with and process racism. This ultimately creates a harmful positive feedback loop in which non-Asian Americans make racist remarks, Asian Americans in a color-blind discursive do not actively resist or address racism, and non-Asian Americans continue to make racist comments without fear of backlash.

Asian American Females as the Eroticized Other

Racist comments that rely on so-called "good stereotypes" such as the model minority assumptions should not be prematurely dismissed as complimentary; their nature is far more complicated. Asian females can exploit racial sexualized stereotypes and racialized sexual desires to gain access to white privilege, but such a privilege can have associated costs of objectification and eroticized "othering." "Good" Asian American stereotypes have consequences that far exceed their welcome. Furthermore, when Asian Americans are faced with overt sexualized racism, a lack of a collective narrative on racism often prevents them from even identifying racist situations (Chou and Feagin 2008). For example, when asked about the transition to Elite University from a largely Asian American West Coast community, Jenny, a first-year Taiwanese American female, responded that the move had not been difficult but then followed up her answer by relating a story in which she was approached by a group of white and black males in her dormitory common room who made overtly racist and sexist comments to her:

> The football players approached me, "Oh little Asian girl I would definitely love to bang you." And I said Oh my god, where am I? [Uncomfortable laugh] It was very uncomfortable [it happened] in my dorm these boys were not drunk. It was 2 pm. I said, "I'm sorry, I have a boyfriend" and left but I don't know what I don't know if they were just trying to like I don't know what they were doing because they're freshmen. It's O-Week [orientation] I don't know how it is with upperclassmen but . . .

Whereas racial teasing in high school usually concludes at the end of the school day, Jenny experienced this clearly inappropriate comment in her dormitory. Thus, the male student's comment turned Jenny's home into a hostile racialized and sexualized space.

Instead of inserting a form of resistance in response, Jenny incorporated her answer within the frame of a color-blind discourse. Jenny was almost at a loss for words. She said, "I don't know" four times and, in line with color-blindness, offered two alternative reasons besides racism in trying to explain the racialized experience. Furthermore, note the language the male chose in his comments. Using the words "little" and "girl" infantilized Jenny. To him she was an objectified sexual object to be "banged." The male student's word choice suggests that he has consumed and internalized media representations and pornographic imagery and culture of Asian and Asian American females. The words "bang" and "little Asian girl" are reminiscent of Asian American female pornography titles like *Bang That Asian Pussy* and *Cute Asian Girl Getting F***ed* ("Asian Sex Movies" n.d.). In constructing Jenny as a subordinate sexual being, the male student reaffirmed his masculinity and sexuality, a key element to hegemonic masculinity and white racial framing. The situation described ended with Jenny apologizing ("I'm sorry, I have a boyfriend") to the male who made an overtly hostile, racist sexual comment. It is quite possible the male will repeat his comments to another Asian woman, being no worse for the wear. The football player felt comfortable enough to approach Jenny without fear of retaliation, and Jenny, hampered by the model minority mentality and color-blind discourse, remained quiet and unequipped to deal with the face of overt racism.

However, Jenny and other survey respondents described the emotional work they had to perform in order to deal with these comments. Lindsay, a Chinese American female first-year, said:

> People who say things like I'm a "sexy Asian" or something. I guess I am shallowly complimented, and then I get annoyed because there shouldn't be this discrepancy between "sexy" and "sexy Asian."

Lindsay raised the point that the "compliment" to her said something more specific about her race. For example, she is sexy *because* she is Asian or *in spite of* it. In this example, what may seem like "positive stereotyping" of an Asian American woman is another demarcation of racial difference. Susan, a Chinese American female senior, explained the psychological toll of sexualized racist comments: "It made me feel violated and that they are only looking at me from a sexual and very primitive point of view." Susan keyed into the way the male gaze has the power to control; using the adjective "violated" to describe how she felt in response to the male gaze, Susan suggested a trauma or almost an emotional violence. We argue that this sexualized and gendered trauma is racialized in the white institutional space of the elite university. Numerous universities across the country are making headlines because of their "rape tolerant" cultures (Heldman and Dirks 2014). This culture is a result of white institutional space being protective of white men, and we suggest that analysis of this campus culture include race.

The males who make these sexualized racist comments restore their hegemonic masculinity by objectifying the Asian American female in a raced way. They also play on racial imagery of Asian females as hypersexual, exotic creatures to be rescued by or entangled with white males. Embedded in a color-blind world of racism without racists, non-Asian male commenters might see these sexualized racist comments as "compliments." However, these examples of sexualized racism work purposefully to establish the hegemonic masculinity of the commenters, subordinate Asian American females, and leave an emotional toll.

The Exoticized Other in Romance and Relationships

Sexualized racism becomes more complicated in the context of relationships and romantic love. Our data document the ambivalence and emotional guesswork that our respondents negotiate in their interracial relationships, particularly in regard to "yellow fever." Yellow fever is a phenomenon in which white men prefer Asian or Asian American women because of preconceived notions about their exoticized sexuality, subservience, and submissiveness (Kim 2011). The constant negotiation of preconceived notions of Asian American exoticized sexuality in romantic relationships was particularly problematic in the respondents' partner selection. Mary, a survey respondent, said,

> I feel fairly conflicted about the relationship between my race and my sexuality. At [Elite University], "yellow fever" is fairly prevalent and many people openly admit to this. The stereotypes applied to Asian women in particular are not necessarily positive—e.g., freaky girls who want to rebel against their traditional parents or girls who want to let loose after being repressed for so long. Although I'm fine with both my sexuality and my Asian identity, I'm always sensitive to the possible stereotypes that others might be applying to me. For example, if I get hit on at a bar and the person makes reference to my racial identity, I tend to be put on guard.

This respondent highlighted the frequency of yellow fever and the acceptability for "people to openly admit" to yellow fever. Yet, she also spoke with a weariness of being targeted as an Asian female stereotype and a tendency to "be put on guard." At first glance, the prevalence of this exoticized Asian female stereotype seems to advantage Asian American females.

When asked whether being called exotic bothered her, Kai, a Pacific Islander American female sophomore, said, "No, I like it. I eat it up." Throughout her interview, Kai asserted her pride in her Pacific Islander heritage. Her positive reaction to being called exotic could stem from her pride in her racial identity. However, Kai went on to make clear how being exoticized by her romantic partner led her to end the relationship:

> I mean the fact that I was [a Pacific Islander] came up all the time . . . this one guy I was seeing I swear to God I mean this is kind of why I left him I swear to God he just loved me because I was the [Pacific Islander] chick and he could just tote me around as his. I tend to take it in stride. I'm like okay yeah maybe I am [Pacific Islander]. If that makes me oh so much more desirable to you great for you but you would have to know me more than that. I don't know. I mean it's not. . . . Like you know like you know when guys go on vacation and they get to hook-up with that exotic girl and they talk about it all the time. I'm pretty sure he did that. I'm not positive but I have a pretty good idea that he did.

Kai ended her relationship with her partner because he treated her as an exoticized Pacific Islander and not as Kai, the person. Herein lies the problematic nature of yellow fever: The high sexual desirability placed on Asian American and Pacific Islander women may appear positive in terms of social position, but it also can give way to sexual objectification and racialized sexual desire. It facilitates relationships in which the Asian American females are drawn as sexual caricatures rather than people.

Asian American Male Double Consciousness

Continuous media and public discourse depicting Asian Americans in subordinate stereotypical roles may also contribute to the internalization and even belief in harmful stigmas associated with being Asian American. Asian American individuals who have internalized hegemonic masculinity begin to reflect negative feelings toward their minority group and oppress themselves through feelings of negative self-worth. This is extremely harmful, because it can lead to problems with double consciousness—perceiving Asian American characteristics as abnormal or inferior while also recognizing one's own Asian American identity (DuBois 1903). After being exposed to racialized mocking and stereotypical images of Asian American men on television, Daniel—a gay second-generation Taiwanese American senior—recounted his uncertainty and his dislike for his race:

> I tended to think that Asian guys are not really that attractive, to other people—to other guys. And, I think that Asian guys in media too, are portrayed as more effeminate unless, you look at martial arts or whatnot, in a lot of cases not in all cases, but in a lot of cases. So I struggled with that a lot, and I would say that I still struggle with that in terms of my own attractiveness to other people. And I think there's always been some kind of jokes, or stereotypes about Asian guys and cock size, things like that. But, I did struggle with that a little, because I did look kind of like the stereotype that was placed on us, and one that I thought would possibly be true, and not having a comparison, besides porn, where everyone had huge cocks, you know, you're not really sure.

Daniel's experiences are not uncommon compared with other responses given by Asian American men interviewed. All of the men interviewed mentioned that they were unsatisfied with the way Asian American men were portrayed in the media, and all mentioned that they had to negotiate the stereotype that Asian men have small genitalia. Although they tended to play down the impact of this stereotype, the fact that every single participant mentioned it makes it worthwhile to investigate, especially as sexualized insults are central to the making of contemporary adolescent masculinity (Pascoe 2007).

If there are widespread conceptions that Asian American men have small penises, and there is no easy mode of comparison of phallic size, these respondents may buy into problematic phallic-centric masculinity. Being surrounded by such controlling images and connecting the Asian American faces in the media to one's own can cause serious problems regarding self-worth. Daniel mentioned that he had "struggled a lot" with the portrayals of Asian American men as "not attractive" and "effeminate" and that he still struggled with those internalizations. Asian Americans are constantly faced with the crisis of understanding and being aware of the negative implications of their race while simultaneously identifying with their race. This double consciousness places a constant emotional burden on Asian Americans and cumulatively takes a large psychological toll (Moore 2008).

Racial Romantic Tastes

All of the interviewed Asian Americans said they were interested in finding romantic partners in college but also seemed to recognize certain racial limitations and boundaries in their love lives. For Wade, a Chinese American male first-year, his internalization of these implicit regulations had gone so far that he had begun blaming himself for social pressures and racialized oppression out of his own control:

> If you are an Asian guy, girls you can pretty much go for are Asian girls. Going for other ethnicities is definitely much harder. Especially if you don't live in a large

> metropolitan area, then it's just difficult. It's just not widely accepted, and girls don't consider Asian guys. I think it's just self-imposed. I think I have, I'm going to be self-deprecating here but I think to some extent my standards are too high.

While Wade did not explicitly mention what criteria he meant by "amount of different girls," he later mentioned that Asian men can only be romantic with Asian women, much in the way black women found themselves limited to dating only black men (Hill Collins 2004). Although Wade started out suggesting that his problems were largely a consequence of social and geographic factors (interracial dating was not "widely accepted" for Asian men or was difficult outside of a metropolitan area), he then blamed himself for his standards.

Wade said that his "standards are too high" in regard to romance and, with that, suggested the internalization of a racial hierarchy that puts whites above Asian Americans. This is most likely the case, for when asked whether race was a factor in the "obstacles" he faced as part of his romantic life, Wade responded that the only time race would be an obstacle would be "only if the girl were to be white" and that "if a girl was white and I was interested in her that would definitely play an obstacle. A lot of times white girls just aren't interested." Being an Asian, and not on the top of the racial hierarchy, he felt that attempting to have a romantic relationship with someone above his racial tier would be too difficult and would present obstacles. We contend that this type of internalized messaging is a result of white habitus and white institutionalized space. This is extremely problematic, as following seemingly racialized perceptions of beauty and attractiveness leads to internalization of the racial hierarchy.

This racial hierarchy was articulated indirectly through our Asian female respondents' racial preferences. Diana, a Chinese American female senior, said this:

> I look for predominantly white males as partners, specifically those who are over 5′10″ in height, with similar education level, and are career ambitious. I prefer white men because they are more independent and don't have a tendency to be as needy as Asian men in relationships. Also, my mom has somewhat encouraged me to seek white men because she believes they are more likely to take on equal child-rearing responsibilities. My mom has always complained about how my father did very little to raise me and my brothers. But in general, I prefer white men because they're more aggressive in all aspects of life, more independent, and are more readily seen as successful. I also feel more attractive when I'm dating someone white though it's hard to explain why. I guess in a way, I'm more proud to show off my white boyfriend than my Asian boyfriend. I just feel slightly more judged when I'm dating someone Asian and feel more prized when I'm dating someone white.

Diana used two frames to reason her preference for white males as romantic partners. The first frame of reasoning relies on seeming cultural differences; she described her mother's warning about the archetypal chauvinistic Asian male, unwilling to take responsibility for domestic and family responsibilities. The second frame stems from hegemonic masculinity. White men are "more aggressive" and "more independent," essentially more masculine, whereas Asian males are "needy" and subordinated.

Moreover, Diana said that white males "are more readily seen as successful." This implies a white maleness as "normal" and "ideal." She was perhaps alluding to the bamboo ceiling that impedes Asian males from moving up the corporate ladder because they are stereotyped as weak, quiet, and unable to lead. The economic racial mobility she mentioned is translated into romantic preferences. This respondent admitted that she "feels more attractive dating someone white." Although she said "it's hard to explain why," she went on to say that she feels "more prized when I'm dating someone white." In essence, she benefits from white privilege and power in having a white partner. By association with whites, she as an Asian female becomes "more attractive" and "more prized." In preferring white males, the respondent participates in the subordination of Asian males while she herself moves up the racial hierarchy by dating white males.

Resistance vs. Resignation

Asian Americans in college seem to suffer from many racialized social experiences that shape how they live and navigate their daily lives. As elucidated above, these experiences often are intersectional, gendered, and raced. Many problems are complex and involve various social and personal pressures. Asian American students are faced with how to react to these problems on a daily basis. While there are many different ways Asian Americans have chosen to respond to these problems, navigating the white-dominated space of college universities requires significant emotional management on the part of its students of color, regardless of how they choose to react. To illustrate a dichotomy in responses, the way they deal with these problems has been grouped into two strands: resistance and resignation.

Resistance

To resist the white racial frame, whites and people of color use "counter frames" to resist the oppressive racial ideologies (Chou 2012; Feagin 2010). Many Asian Americans who came to Elite University from a more racially heterogeneous area were surprised to find that the university's social scenes were much divided along racial lines despite an undergraduate program full of intelligent students, of whom about 40 percent were people of color. The socialization process at college, which we argue is "white habitus," informs students' romantic, social, and racialized life.

For many Asian Americans and other students of color, the historically white Greek system seems to be the heart of the university nightlife. As Tim mentions, "it's hard to not be affected by it on some level." Asian Americans who respond via resistance recognize the difficulties of being Asian American in a white-dominated space. Their responses are directed at creating space that is safe for them and acknowledging the Asian American identity as worthy.

Many Asian Americans interviewed said that they had close Asian American friends. Generally, Asian Americans chose other Asian Americans to befriend because they had lived through common racial experiences. Having Asian American friends appears important to coping with and resisting racialized experiences.

Resignation

Resistance and resignation are not mutually exclusive responses to racism. Asian Americans responding via resignation direct their behavior and responses toward fitting into white space in an attempt to make it a safe space for them. Asian Americans using resignation affirm notions of Asian Americans as irregular and whites as normal.

When asked about how Asian Americans interact in social spaces, Kate, a Korean American female senior, said:

> So if someone takes [Asian American stereotypes] to heart, which they definitely can, it will make them less confident socially and more self-aware, more socially awkward, maybe less willing to engage with those different from them so maybe that would lead to them being more secluded and more self-segregated like hanging out with only Asians.

Kate, in using the term "self-segregation," internalized the language of white privilege and colorblindness. Use of the term "self-segregation" to accuse people of color of being exclusionary and to stigmatize minority social spaces is characteristic of color-blind discourse used by whites. Kate failed to articulate how having Asian American friends and being part of a racial minority group could be protective against the difficulties of white-dominant university spaces and stereotyping. Despite the best efforts at resistance, color-blindness and hegemonic ideology can still seep into the Asian American perspective.

From the interview responses, it seems that Asian American undergraduates are divided between resistance and resignation as their principal strategies for coping with racism. In both resistance and resignation, Asian Americans must perform emotional work to cope with these racialized experiences at a HWCU.

Counter-narratives

Another tool to combat hegemonic ideologies is the use of counter-narratives. The white racial frame is a concept that racial ideology is held consciously and unconsciously by most white Americans and many people of color. Elements of the frame include racial imagery, emotions, and narratives that shape their understanding of race and also shape their behavior (Feagin 2010). Creating a different racial perspective has been paramount for the development of African American support for racialized experiences. Asian Americans also have begun to develop a different "frame," through understanding how race shapes interactions in America from their perspective. This different frame, or counter-frame, aids people of color by helping them notice and make sense of their racialized experiences. Wade, a Chinese American first-year, described how his parents explained to him the merits of academic achievement. In his family, as in some other Asian American families, there is a fear that affirmative action works to the detriment of Asian Americans and unfairly rewards other people of color:

> [My parents] kept highlighting the fact that because you're Asian, it's more difficult for you to get into schools, so you need to do better. Also because my school was majority Asian, they were like, "you can already compare yourself with your peers, because your school is simply Asian, and because you're Asian yourself, you will be judged by higher standards, so you'll have to work harder."

This kind of conversation seems common among Asian American students, as affirmative action seems to be a racialized concept that is present in many middle-class Asian American homes. Noticing and recognizing that one will be treated differently based on race is an essential part of a successful counter-frame. It is unfortunate that the topic of affirmative action as part of the Asian American counter-frame may breed competition and seeds of distrust among the members of the Asian American community; however, it is still a valuable common perspective that brings the community somewhat closer together in terms of a collective racial conscious.

Another critically important aspect of a racial counter-frame is identifying the way in which society's structure favors whites and working against that structure as a person of color. In response to the question, "For Asian Americans struggling with racism and their identity, what advice would you give them?" Beth, a Chinese American female sophomore, said, "Don't give a shit about what white people think you are supposed to do. Asians are not "supposed" to do anything . . ." This respondent recognized and rejected Asian American racial boundaries that white ideology has created and attempted to remove expectations about sexualized racism and beauty. This counter-narrative attempts to free Asian Americans from subordination to whites by recognizing that Asian Americans' rights, emotions, and desires have value.

Conclusion

Contemporary discussion surrounding Asian Americans and college is fixated on admission rates. For Asian Americans themselves, the end goal may seem to be a ticket to an elite university (Yang 2011). Yet while Asian Americans may be ready to engage in the academic rigors of university, our data suggest that they are less prepared to navigate the white institutional social space of the ivory tower and the white racial framing that is entrenched in these HWCUs. Whether they choose to acknowledge it or not, the double consciousness of being Asian American and existing in a white-dominated space takes a psychological toll on the emotional well-being of Asian American students at a college or university. Through resistance, resignation, and counter-narratives, Asian Americans as individuals perform emotional work in either challenging or maintaining the white-dominated university spaces.

Overall, Asian Americans faced the emotional challenges of resisting and resigning to sexualized and everyday racism. We argue that the elite college campus is a white institutionalized space where Asian American females are confronted with a white masculine hegemonic structure through racialized dating preferences and where Asian American males internalize the hierarchy of racial preferences and experience psychological costs. In this study we found that even the most educated Asian Americans are not immune to the pervasive racism and sexism found in the American educational system and its social spaces. We demonstrated the intersectional nature of racism, particularly how it is sexualized and gendered. With this in mind, universities must move away from their complacency about Asian Americans and understand that the social culture is in want of reconstruction, beginning with the ways in which ideas, beliefs, and experiences are expressed.

References

"Asian Sex Movies." *Redtube*. Retrieved May 5, 2011 (http://www.redtube.com/).

Armstrong, Elizabeth A. 2006. "Sexual Assault on Campus: A Multi-level Integrative Approach to Party Rape." *Social Problems* 53(4):483–99.

Bonilla-Silva, Eduardo. 1997. "Rethinking Racism: Toward a Structural Interpretation." *American Sociological Review* 62(3):465–80.

Bonilla-Silva, Eduardo. 2002. "The Linguistics of Color Blind Racism: How to Talk Nasty about Blacks without Sounding 'Racist.'" *Critical Sociology* 28(1):41–64.

Bonilla-Silva, Eduardo. 2004. "From Bi-racial to Tri-racial: Towards a New System of Racial Stratification in the USA." *Ethnic and Racial Studies* 27(6):931–50.

Chou, Rosalind S. 2012. *Asian American Sexual Politics: The Construction of Race, Gender, and Sexuality.* Lanham, MD: Rowman & Littlefield.

Chou, Rosalind S. and Joe R. Feagin. 2008. *The Myth of the Model Minority.* Boulder, CO: Paradigm.

Clark, Kim. 2009. "Do Elite Private Colleges Discriminate against Asian Students?" *US News & World Report.* Retrieved July 8, 2013 (http://www.usnews.com/education/articles/2009/10/07/do-elite-privatecolleges-discriminate-against-asian-students).

Connell, R. W. and James W. Messerschmidt. 2005. "Hegemonic Masculinity: Rethinking the Concept." *Gender & Society* 19(6):845–54.

Denzin, Norman K. and Yvonna S. Lincoln, eds. 2005. *The SAGE Handbook of Qualitative Research.* 3rd ed. Thousand Oaks, CA: Sage Publications.

Du Bois, W. E. B. 1903. *The Souls of Black Folks.* Chicago: A. C. McClurg.

Eng, David. 2001. *Racial Castration: Managing Masculinity in Asian America.* Durham, NC: Duke University Press.

Espiritu, Yen Le. 2008. *Asian American Women and Men: Labor, Laws, and Love.* Lanham, MD: Rowman & Littlefield.

Feagin, Joe R. 2010. *White Racial Frame.* New York: Routledge.

Heldman, Caroline and Danielle Dirks. 2014."Blowingthe Whistle on Campus Rape." *Ms. Magazine,* February 18 (http://msmagazine.com/blog/2014/02/18/blowing-the-whistle-on-campus-rape).

Hill Collins, Patricia. 2004. *Black Sexual Politics.* New York: Routledge.

Kim, Bitna. 2011. "Asian Female and Caucasian Male Couples: Exploring the Attraction." *Pastoral Psychology* 60(2):233–44.

Kim, Claire J. 1999. "The Racial Triangulation of Asian Americans." *Politics and Society* 27(1):105–38.

Moore, Wendy L. 2008. *Reproducing Racism: White Space, Elite Law Schools, and Racial Inequality.* Lanham, MD: Rowman & Littlefield.

Pascoe, C. J. 2007. *Dude, You're a Fag: Masculinity and Sexuality in High School.* Los Angeles: University of California Press.

Prashad, Vijay. 2001. "Genteel Racism." *Ameriasia Journal* 26(3):21–33.

Prasso, Sheridan. 2006. *The Asian Mystique: Dragon Ladies, Geisha Girls & Our Fantasies of the Exotic Orient.* Cambridge, MA: Public Affairs Books.

Rosenbloom, Susan R. and Niobe Way. 2004. "Experiences of Discrimination among African American, Asian American, and Latino Adolescents in an Urban High School." *Youth and Society* 35(4):420–45.

Sassler, Sharon and Kara Joyner 2011. "Social Exchange and the Progression of Sexual Relationships in Emerging Adulthood." *Social Forces* 90(1):223–45.

Takaki, Ronald. 2001. *Strangers from a Different Shore: A History of Asian Americans.* New York: Little, Brown.

Tatum, Beverly D. 1997. *"Why Are All the Black Kids Sitting Together in the Cafeteria?" and Other Conversations about Race.* New York: Basic Books.

Teranishi, Robert. 2010. *Asians in the Ivory Tower: Dilemmas of Racial Inequality in American Higher Education.* New York: Columbia University.

Tong, Benson. 1994. *Unsubmissive Women: Chinese Prostitutes in Nineteenth-Century San Francisco.* Norman: University of Oklahoma Press.

Tuan, Mia. 1999. *Forever Foreigners or Honorary Whites? The Asian Ethnic Experience.* New Brunswick, NJ: Rutgers University Press.

van Dijk, Teun. 2000. "New(s) Racism: A Discourse Analytical Approach." Pp. 33–49 in *Ethnic Minorities and the Media,* edited by S. Cottle. Milton Keynes, UK: Open University Press.

Wei, Johnny. 2013. An Asian American Response to the Backlash against Kappa Sigma. *Chronicle.* Retrieved July 1, 2013 (http://www.dukechronicle.com/articles/2013/02/07/asian-americans-response-backlash-against-kappa-sigma).

CHAPTER 32

A Postracial Society or a Diversity Paradox?*

Race, Immigration, and Multiraciality in the Twenty-First Century

Jennifer Lee and Frank D. Bean

At the beginning of the twentieth century, southern states decreed that one drop of African American blood made a multiracial individual Black, and even today, multiracial Blacks are typically perceived as being Black only, underscoring the enduring legacy and entrenchment of the one-drop rule of hypodescent. But how are Asians and Latinos with mixed ancestry perceived? Based on analyses of census data and in-depth interviews with interracial couples with children and multiracial adults, Jennifer Lee and Frank Bean find that the children of Asian-White and Latino-White couples are much less constrained by strict racial categories, leading to a theory that these children are living in a ***postracial*** *society. Racial identification often shifts according to situation, and individuals can choose to identify along ethnic lines as White or as American. Like their Irish and Italian immigrant forerunners, the Asian and Latino ethnicities of these multiracial Americans are adopting the symbolic character of European White ethnicity. The authors argue that the United States is entering a new era of race relations in which the boundaries of Whiteness are beginning to expand to include new nonwhite groups such*

Source: Adapted from Jennifer Lee and Frank D. Bean, "A Postracial Society or a Diversity Paradox? Race, Immigration, and Multiraciality in the Twenty-First Century," *Du Bois Review Social Science Research on Race*, Volume 9, Number 2, pages 419–437, Cambridge University Press, 2012.

*Some text has been omitted. Please consult the original source.

as Asians and Latinos, with multiracial identities or mixed-race identities among Asians and Latinos at the head of the queue. However, even amidst the new racial and ethnic diversity, these processes continue to shut out African Americans, illustrating a pattern of Black exceptionalism and the emergence of a Black–nonblack divide in the twenty-first century.

Questions to Consider

The authors argue that Asian-White and Latino-White multiracials enjoy more options in choosing their racial identity. In contrast, multiracial Blacks are more likely to be perceived as being Black only. Does this mean that Black multiracials choose to identify as Black? Or is having the option or choice to choose one's racial identity limited to certain groups?

Introduction

Race and immigration have become so inextricably linked in the United States that one can no longer understand the complexities of race without considering immigration. Correlatively, one cannot fully grasp the debates in immigration without considering the role of race in U.S. society. Further complicating our ideas about race are rising rates in intermarriage and a growing multiracial population; along with immigration, these trends have contributed to unprecedented diversity. But exactly how are trends in immigration, intermarriage, and multiracial identification changing our ideas about race, group boundaries, and the color line in the twenty-first century?

Most obviously, today's immigrants have changed the United States from a largely Black and White nation to one composed of multiple racial and ethnic groups. Immigrants and their children account for about 23% of the U.S. population, of which 85% originate from Latin America and Asia, creating a society that is more racially and ethnically diverse than at any point in history. In 1970, Latinos and Asians made up only 5% and 1% of the nation's population, respectively, but by 2010, their populations more than tripled to 16% and 5%. Latinos have grown so rapidly that they have surpassed Blacks as the largest minority group, and while smaller in size, the Asian population is the fastest growing group in the country. Demographers project that these populations will continue to grow so that by 2050, Latinos will make up nearly one-quarter of the nation's population at 24%, and Asians close to one-tenth, at 8%.

Because the majority of contemporary immigrants are neither Black nor White, they have forced the scholarly debate about race and racial divides to move beyond the traditional Black–White binary (Alba 2009; Lee 2011; Lee and Bean, 2010). Consequently, social scientists have raised the question of whether today's new non-White immigrants and their children are following the assimilation trajectory of their European predecessors, or whether their experiences with race are more akin to those of African Americans (Foner 2005; Glazer 1997; Haney-Lopez 1996; Patterson 1997; Rodriguez 2007; Sears et al., 2003). Moreover, given that the Black–White color line no longer reflects America's racial reality, scholars have raised the question of what type of color line is taking its place.

In this paper, we assess how the color line is changing by examining trends in intermarriage and multiracial identification. More specifically, [we] examine how interracial couples identify their children. When parents share the same racial background, there is little discrepancy about how they will choose to identify their children, but when parents come from different backgrounds, the choice is less obvious. Will they prioritize one racial identity over the other, or will parents choose to combine both racial backgrounds and identify their children multiracially? These questions are especially relevant given the rising rates of intermarriage in the United States (Kalmijn 1998; Perlmann and Waters, 2004; Qian and Lichter, 2007). In 1960, less than 1% of U.S. marriages were interracial, but by 2008, this figure rose to 7.6%, meaning that one out of every thirteen U.S. marriages was interracial (Jacoby 2001; Lee and Edmonston, 2005; Ruggles et al., 2009). Among new marriages that took place in 2008, the intermarriage figure rises to 14.6%, translating to one out of every seven American marriages (Passel et al., 2010).

The rising trend in intermarriage has resulted in a growing multiracial population, which became highly visible in 2000 when, for the first time in history, the U.S. Census provided Americans the option to "mark one or more" races to identify themselves or members of their households (Fig. 1). In 2000, 2.4% of Americans identified multiracially; in 2010, the figure increased by 32% to 2.9% of the U.S. population (Humes et al., 2011). Among Americans under the age of eighteen, the increase in the multiracial population was even greater, at 46%, making multiracial children the fastest growing youth group in the country. Demographers project that the multiracial population will continue to grow so that by 2050, one in five Americans could claim a multiracial background, and by 2100, the ratio could soar to one in three (Farley 2004; Edmonston et al., 2002; Lee and Bean, 2010; Lee and Edmonston, 2005).

While social scientists view intermarriage as a sign of decreased social distance between groups and as a measure of assimilation, they have paid relatively little attention to whether

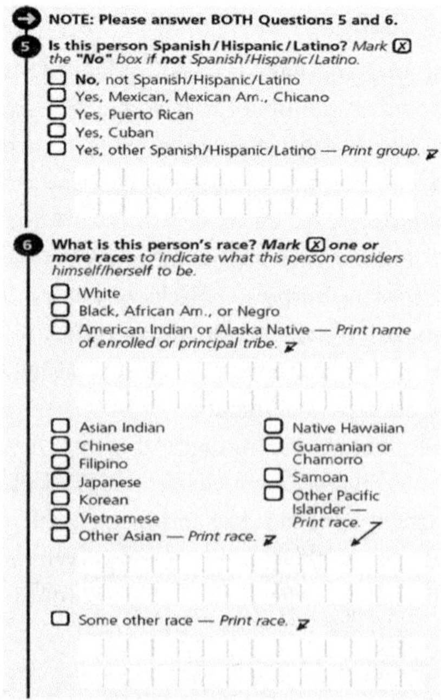

NOTE: Please answer BOTH Questions 5 and 6.

5 Is this person Spanish/Hispanic/Latino? *Mark* ☒ *the* "No" *box if* not *Spanish/Hispanic/Latino.*

- ☐ No, not Spanish/Hispanic/Latino
- ☐ Yes, Mexican, Mexican Am., Chicano
- ☐ Yes, Puerto Rican
- ☐ Yes, Cuban
- ☐ Yes, other Spanish/Hispanic/Latino — *Print group.*

6 What is this person's race? *Mark* ☒ *one or more races to indicate what this person considers himself/herself to be.*

- ☐ White
- ☐ Black, African Am., or Negro
- ☐ American Indian or Alaska Native — *Print name of enrolled or principal tribe.*
- ☐ Asian Indian
- ☐ Chinese
- ☐ Filipino
- ☐ Japanese
- ☐ Korean
- ☐ Vietnamese
- ☐ Other Asian — *Print race.*
- ☐ Native Hawaiian
- ☐ Guamanian or Chamorro
- ☐ Samoan
- ☐ Other Pacific Islander — *Print race.*
- ☐ Some other race — *Print race.*

Figure 1 U.S. Census Racial Background Questions

the assimilative power of intermarriage works in the same manner for all groups (Moran 2001). In other words, does intermarriage lead to a more rapid process of assimilation for all non-White groups? And, as a result, are group boundaries changing at the same pace for all groups through intermarriage, thereby contributing to a "postracial" America?

At first glance, trends in intermarriage and multiracial identification appear to portend that we are indeed moving into a cosmopolitan, "postracial" era, in which race is declining in significance for all Americans. The election of Barack Obama as President seemed to confirm this sentiment, as some journalists proclaimed that we have finally moved beyond race. A *New York Times* article by Nagourney (2008) which appeared the day after Obama's election focused on the collapse of the racial barrier, with a bold headline that read, "Obama Elected President as Racial Barrier Falls." That Barack Obama is multiracial seemed irrelevant, as pundits openly cheered that having elected an African American to the highest office signified that race was no longer a barrier to opportunity and mobility. However, pointing to an exception as the rule is a specious argument, as is overlooking the vast intergroup differences in intermarriage and multiracial identification.

About 30% of Asian and Latino marriages are interracial, but the corresponding figure for Blacks is only 17%. However, if we include only U.S.-born Asians and Latinos in the analyses, we find that intermarriage rates are much higher: nearly three-quarters (72%) of married, U.S.-born Asians, and over half (52%) of U.S.-born Latinos are interracially married, and most often, intermarriage is with a White partner. While the intermarriage rate for Blacks has risen steadily in the past five decades, it is still far below that of Asians and Latinos, especially those born in the United States (Lee and Bean, 2010; Ruggles et al., 2009).

Second, the pattern of multiracial identification is similar to that of intermarriage: Asians and Latinos report much higher rates of multiracial identification than Blacks. In 2010, 15% of Asians and 12% of Latinos reported a multiracial identification. The corresponding figure for Blacks is only 7%. Although the rate of multiracial reporting among Blacks has risen since 2000, it increased from a very small base of only 4.2% (Humes et al., 2011).

What remains perplexing is that given the history of racial mixing, the Census Bureau estimates that about 75–90% of Black Americans are ancestrally multiracial, yet even today, only 7% choose to identify as such (Davis, 2001; Lee and Bean, 2010). Clearly, genealogy alone does not dictate racial identification. Given that the "one-drop rule" of hypodescent is no longer legally codified, why does the rate of multiracial reporting among Blacks remain relatively low? I aim to answer this question by providing a portrait of America's multiracial youth population, and then drawing on eighty-two in-depth interviews (forty-six with multiracial adults and thirty-six with interracial couples with children) to understand how interracial couples identify their children and how multiracial adults identify themselves.

America's Multiracial Youth

In 2000, when the U.S. Census allowed Americans to mark "one or more races" to identify themselves and members of their households, 40% of interracial couples with children under the age of eighteen chose this option and checked more than one racial category. For instance, 49% of Black–White couples, 52% of Asian–White couples, and 25% of Latino–White couples identified their children multiracially (Tafoya et al., 2005). However, when interracial couples were asked to choose only one racial category to identify their multiracial children, stark differences emerged; most Black–White couples choose Black, whereas most Asian–White and Latino–White couples choose White rather than Asian and Latino, respectively (Tafoya et al., 2005). These findings mirror those reported by Harris and Sim (2002), who analyzed Add Health Data and found that when multiracial adolescents were asked about the single best race to describe themselves, 75% of Black-White multiracials chose Black, whereas 52% of Asian-White multiracials chose Asian (Farley 2004; Saenz et al., 1995; Xie and Goyette, 1997).

In California—the state with the largest multiracial population—1.6 million people identified multiracially, accounting for 4.7% of its population, or one in every twenty-one Californians. Among Californians under the age of eighteen, the ratio rises to one in every fourteen, or 7.3% of young Californians. The greater proportion of young multiracials in California is, in part, a product of the rise in interracial marriages, especially among the young Asian and Latino populations, resulting in a growing multiracial population (Lee and Bean, 2010). California has a high rate of intermarriage; at 18.1%, the intermarriage rate is two and a half times the national average, and second only to Hawaii. To help put the growth of multiracial Californians into perspective, the number of multiracial births already exceeds the number of Black and Asian births in the state (Tafoya et al., 2005). In fact, so visible is the growth of California's young multiracial population that demographers Sharon Lee and Barry Edmonston (2005) note that "it would not be surprising if the average person were to conclude that intermarriage and multiracial and multiethnic children are the norm" (p. 33).

While California may be in the vanguard of social change, it is not unique with respect to the young age of its multiracial population; Americans under the age of eighteen account for 42% of the multiracial population, and this population is rapidly growing. Among American children, the multiracial population increased by 46% since 2000 (to 4.2 million), making multiracial children the fastest growing youth group in the country (Humes et al., 2011).

Given the young age of the multiracial population, the parents are choosing their children's racial identification on official documents like the census form, so I turn to the interviews with the parents to ask how they identify their children and why they make the decisions they do. By interviewing interracial couples and multiracial adults in California, we get a preview of where the color line is changing most rapidly in the United States. The responses provide insight into the assimilative power of intermarriage, boundary change, and the placement of the color line in twenty-first century America.

Asian–White and Latino–White Couples and Their Children

When I interviewed the interracial couples, I provided them with a copy of the 2000 Census form and asked how they would identify themselves and their children (Fig. 1). I found that while the vast majority of parents acknowledged their children's multiracial or multiethnic backgrounds, the meaning of multiraciality differed remarkably for the children of Asian–White and Latino–White couples on the one hand, and the children of Black–White couples on the other. For most Asian–White and Latino–White couples, the assimilative power of intermarriage is so strong that while they recognize their children's multiracial and multiethnic backgrounds, and may go to great lengths to instill this identity in their children, they believe (and in some cases, fear) that their children will soon identify as simply "American" or "White."

These couples often used these terms interchangeably, consequently inflating a national origin identity with a racial identity and denoting that from their perspective, American equals White.

Because the Asian–White and Latino–White children in the sample were born in the United States, are strongly influenced by American culture, and speak only English, the Asian and Latino interracial couples maintain that their children "act White." These parents explain that regardless of how hard they try to instill a strong sense of their Asian or Latino ethnic ancestries, they have resigned themselves to the fact that their children will identify with the majority host culture—that is, as White or as American. For example, a second-generation Asian Indian woman married to a White man, in an interview with the author, agrees that their children will probably identify as White because "They were born here, and it's not like they're going to India." Her husband then added, "I get the feeling that they'll probably identify themselves as White mostly because they probably won't speak Hindi. Plus, all of their friends are White, and you know, that will probably be the way they identify themselves."

The Asian–White couples acknowledge that because their children are born in the United States, are English monolingual, and have little direct, sustained contact with the Asian parents' ethnic culture, they feel that their children will simply identify as White as they grow older. These patterns of identification are consistent with previous research that has shown that English monolingualism and little exposure to the minority parent's culture increases the likelihood that Asian-White and Latino-White children will adopt a White identity rather than an Asian or Latino one (Eschbach and Gomez, 1998; Harris and Sim, 2002; Korgen 1998; Saenz et al., 1995; Stephan and Stephan, 1989; Xie and Goyette, 1997).

The pattern of racial identification among the children of Latino–White couples mirrors that of Asian–White couples. For example, a White woman married to a first-generation Mexican man explains, "I would always identify them [her children] as White. I always considered them to be White. And to me, what does White mean? Caucasian is probably more specific." Others relayed that outsiders identify their children and the family as White, which in turn shapes the way they see their children and their family unit. When I asked a Latino–White couple how outsiders react to them when they are together with their son, the second-generation Mexican husband added, "Just a regular American family." When I asked how people identify their son, he responded simply, "White, Caucasian," again revealing the interchangeable use of American, White, and Caucasian.

Because outsiders' ascription powerfully affects one's choice of racial identities, the Asian–White and Latino–White couples recognize that outsiders who identify their children as White strongly influence the way their children choose to identify. As sociologists have long noted, identity formation is a dialectical process—one that involves both internal and external opinions, processes, and constraints (Eschbach and Gomez, 1998; Lee and Zhou, 2004; Loewen 1971; Loveman and Muniz, 2007; Nagel 1994; Rodríguez and Cordero-Guzman, 1992; Waters 1999). These couples have nearly resigned themselves to the seemingly inevitable fact that their children will most likely identify as simply White or American, regardless of how hard they try to maintain the distinctive elements of their Asian or Latino ethnic cultural backgrounds. The findings point to the robust strength of the assimilative power of intermarriage for Asians and Latinos when they choose White partners.

Furthermore, some of the Asian–White and Latino–White couples consider their children's Asian and Latino racial and ethnic identities as symbolic and situational. In these cases, the parents will choose to identify their children as Asian or Latino when they believe that a racial minority status will accrue benefits. A Mexican–White couple underscored this point when they debated how they should identify their daughter, Ana, on the 2000 census form. The exchange between the White wife and the first-generation Mexican husband was recorded on tape, as the wife began deliberating:

Wife:	I don't know for Ana. Would you say that Ana is Hispanic? I would say no, not Spanish.
Husband:	I would say no, she's not Spanish, but it depends. If this was a college—
Wife:	I would say she has a Spanish, Hispanic parent, but I don't think she is.
Husband:	But would that make her Hispanic or not?
Wife:	No.
Husband:	But how are you defining Hispanic? Based on birth, yeah, because that's how I'm defining it. But if this was a college application we'd say yeah.
Wife:	Oh yeah, we'd say yeah.
Interviewer:	Why would you say yes if it was a college application?
Husband:	Because she'd get into a better school because of it.
Interviewer:	Why?
Husband:	Because she's a minority. It would do more for her getting into a better college. I mean, opportunities.

While both the Mexican husband and White wife agree that their daughter is not Hispanic and choose not to mark her as such on the census form, they quickly note that they would identify her as Hispanic on a college application, where they believe she would benefit from her minority status. As they justify, by identifying their daughter as Hispanic, they are maximizing the opportunities that are available to her, even if they do not identify her as Hispanic in everyday life. They recognize and take full advantage of their daughter's multiracial background, which provides the option of privileging one identity over another depending on the context and the benefits associated with that choice. In essence, the parents' decision to shift their daughter's identity from White to Hispanic becomes a strategic and adaptive response to a specific situation (Okamura 1981; Saenz and Aguirre, 1991).

The optional and situational nature of Latino and Asian identities for multiracial Americans is also reflected in a Vietnamese White woman's response about her Asian ethnic background, which she claims to forget about entirely most of the time, as she explained:

> Say we're in a room full of all White people and I'm like the only Asian, I almost always forget that I'm Asian, or half Asian. I consider myself White. I act very White as far as I'm concerned because that's all I know. So I don't have very much Vietnamese culture in me.
>
> I don't like Asian food, I have no Asian traditions, and I know absolutely no Vietnamese. The only thing Asian about me is the fact that my mother is Vietnamese. Everything about me is White, except for my car; it's a Honda! *[she laughs]*

For this woman, her Vietnamese ethnicity is so nonconstraining that she forgets about it altogether, revealing its optional nature. However, when asked how she identifies on forms, she indicates that she marks both White and Vietnamese, or whatever identification will benefit her most at that time. For example, she explained that when she applied for a position as a flight attendant, she asked the human resources manager how she should mark her racial identification on the employment form. The manager confided that she should mark Vietnamese since there are relatively few Asians who work in the American airline industry, and therefore, an Asian ethnic identity would work to her advantage in the hiring queue. When I asked when she would identify as White, she explained that were she to apply to the University of California, Irvine (where over 50% of its undergraduate student body is Asian), she would mark White since she believes that her Vietnamese ethnicity would serve as a disadvantage in this case.

Both the Vietnamese White woman and the Mexican White couple reveal that they can turn their non-White ethnicities on and off whenever they choose; they can be ethnic when they wish to take advantage of race-based programs targeted for disadvantaged minorities, but then turn off their non-White ethnicities in their everyday lives. Critical to underscore is that their choices are *not* contested by others.

Black Interracial Couples and Their Children

Unlike the Asian–White and Latino–White couples, none of the Black–White couples identified their children as simply White or American, nor did they claim that their children identify as such. While Black–White couples recognize and celebrate the racial mixture of their children's backgrounds, they tend to identify their children as Black rather than as White, non-Black, or American, which mirrors the way that outsiders view them. Furthermore, for the children of Black interracial couples, their Black identities are not voluntary, symbolic, or costless.

For example, when I spoke to a Black multiracial male whose mother is White and whose father is Black, he admitted that he identifies as "Black American—home grown, 100%." His wife is White; together, they have two sons, and when asked how he chooses to identify them, he explains, "I would say that they're half and half on the purest level, but still, for some reason, I just look at them as Black." Here, he notes that not only does he identify as Black, but he also identifies his children as Black, even though he could claim a multiracial identification for himself and his children. When asked whether he ever identifies his children as White or something other than Black, he candidly admits, "You know I've never had an occasion to do that. Maybe it's just the eyes that I'm looking through. I just haven't at all, and that's probably not a good thing." When probed further, he and the other Black–White couples underscored the point that nobody would take them seriously if they tried to identify their children as White, reflecting the power of external ascription in determining how interracial couples choose to identify their children, and their belief that a non-Black identity would be contested by others.

The Black–White couples further explain that others' reactions (both subtle and not-so-subtle) to their unions and their multiracial families are palpable cues of other people's ambivalent feelings about their multiracial unions. For example, interracial Black couples explained that they often receive perplexed reactions from service workers in restaurants and stores who consistently assume that they are not together, and often ask to help one person before asking the other. Moreover, Black multiracial respondents described their friends' and strangers' puzzlement when they see them with their non-Black parent, as a twenty-six-year-old Black multiracial male explains:

> I remember being with my Dad, even if we were standing in a line together, people would help him and then ask if I was next. They couldn't connect that we were

> together. It got to the point where I would almost not want to go with my Dad. I mean I got to deal with this—people looking at us funny? What's this White guy doing with this Black kid? I think a lot of the time people have no idea that my Dad is my Dad, and that did kind of bother me when I was younger. People would say, "Oh, who's that?" And I would say, "Oh, that's my Dad)"

Because people often fail to recognize an older, White man and younger, Black multiracial man as father and son, the multiracial Black male admits that he reached a point where he felt uncomfortable going out with his father altogether. When I asked whether he received similar reactions when he went out with his Black mother, he initially looked puzzled, as if the answer was so obvious that he did not understand why I had bothered to ask, but then simply answered, "No, not at all."

From a parent's perspective, a Black parent of a multiracial child normally does not have to contend with the racial split between his/her child (regardless of how fair-skinned the child may be), but the same does not hold for a White parent of a multiracial Black child (Funderburg 1994; Romano 2003; Tizard and Phoenix, 1993; Wilson 1981). This is because historically the children born to Black–White unions stayed with the Black parent (usually the Black mother), so even today, while interracial marriage is on the rise for all groups (including Blacks), many Americans still find the pairing of White parents and multiracial Black children unusual and perplexing.

However, it is not simply Black and White pairings that cause confusion, but Black and non-Black pairings more generally. For example, a Black Chinese male notes that when he is with his Chinese grandfather, people often assume that he is doing some type of service work. He relays, "When I'm with my grandpa, especially now that he's older, people will ask if I'm doing some kind of community service. People always ask me, 'Wow, are you doing some kind of community service?' And I'm like, 'No, that's my grandpa.'" He then added that when he is with his Black grandfather or father, "people don't say anything."

The bewildered reactions, stares, and questions that Black interracial couples and Black multiracial families receive illustrate that for others, seeing certain racial combinations together is foreign, unfamiliar, and seemingly illogical, especially in the most intimate of relationships, pointing to what we refer to as "a racial disconnect." From an outsider's perspective, there is a racial disconnect between Black and non-Black. Given the confused reactions they receive when they venture out with non-Black family members, the children of Black interracial unions have concluded that choosing a non-Black identity is a difficult option since it would generate confusion, questions, and challenges.

The History and Consequences of the "One-Drop Rule"

The different patterns of identification between Asian and Latino interracial couples on the one hand and the Black interracial couples on the other, stem, in part, from the relative newness of the Asian and Latino multiracial populations, combined with the lack of historical rules that govern their choice of identities. Unlike Blacks, Asians and Latinos were not legally subject to the "one-drop rule" of hypodescent, which continues to constrain the racial options for Blacks in unique ways, despite its loss of legal legitimacy.

To give a brief history of the one-drop rule: it was first implemented during the era of slavery so that any children born to a White male slaver owner and a Black female slave would be legally identified as Black, and, as a result, have no rights to property and other wealth holdings of their White father. After the United States abolished slavery, Southern states including Tennessee and Louisiana legalized the rule of hypodescent in 1910, and other states soon followed suit. By 1925, nearly every state in the country had institutionalized the practice into law.

The U.S. Census soon followed suit, and in 1930 made a fateful decision that had an enduring impact on the way that Americans define Blackness. Prior to 1930, the U.S. Census acknowledged the racial mixture in the Black population, and counted mixed race Blacks as "mulattos," "quadroons," and "octoroons," depending on the extent of racial mixture with Whites (Nobles 2000). While this practice stemmed from the desire to track racial mixing and police the Black–White color line, at the very least, the U.S. government recognized the multiraciality of the Black population. However, in 1930, census enumerators were instructed to classify all mixed-race Black individuals as "Negro," with specific directions that read:

> A person of mixed white and Negro blood should be returned to Negro, no matter how small the percentage of Negro blood. Both black and mulatto persons are to be returned as Negroes, without distinction (cited in Nobles 2000, p. 188).

The sheer paradox of the one-drop rule is self-evident: it is not a two-way street. One can be seven-eighths White (as Homer Plessy was, of *Plessy v. Ferguson* 1896), and not be White. But any trace of "Black blood" makes one Black. By adopting the one-drop rule of hypodescent, the United States refused to acknowledge the mixed racial backgrounds of Black Americans by legally assigning them a Black racial identity. It was not until 1967, in the case *Loving v. Virginia* when the U.S. Supreme Court overturned the final ban on interracial marriage, that the one-drop rule lost its legitimacy. While the rule is no longer legally enforced, its legacy remains culturally intact, and explains why 75–90% of Black Americans are ancestrally multiracial, yet only 7% choose to identify as such. The legacy of the "one-drop rule" has had enduring and fateful consequences in the way that Americans view race, and explains why we are so attuned to identifying Black ancestry in a way that we are not similarly attuned to identifying and constraining Asian and Latino ancestries (Lee and Bean, 2010).

While Black interracial couples feel more constrained than their Asian and Latino counterparts in how they identify their children, it is also critical to underscore that Black racial identification also reflects agency and choice on the part of these couples and their children. Given the legacy behind the one-drop rule, and the meaning and consequences behind the historical practice of "passing as White," choosing to identify one's children as White may not only signify a rejection of the Black community, but also a desire to be accepted by a group that has legally excluded and oppressed them in the past (DaCosta 2007; Davis 2001; Kennedy 2003; Romano 2003).

Furthermore, none of the Black–White couples choose to identify their children as simply American because as native-born Americans, they feel that the American label is already an implicit part of their and their children's identity. While the children of Asian–White and Latino–White unions in the sample are also native-born, because many of the Asian and Latino parents are either immigrants or the children of immigrants, the American label has not become as implicit a part of their identity, as it has for native-born Whites and Blacks (Lee and Zhou, 2004; Zhou and Lee, 2007). Unlike the Asian–White and Latino–White couples who equated American with White, the Black–White couples did not; for Black–White couples, American also equals Black. For all of these reasons, intermarried Black couples are less likely to identify their children as exclusively White or American. The findings indicate that the cultural persistence of the "one-drop rule" of hypodescent still strongly operates to keep the practice of identifying Americans with any trace of Black ancestry as racially Black (DaCosta 2007; Davis 2001; Hollinger 2003; Lee and Bean, 2004, 2007; Roth 2005).

Conclusions and Discussion

The multiracial population is young and rapidly growing, and may soon account for one-fifth of the U.S. population by the year 2050, and one-third of the country's population by 2100. Because the multiracial population is overwhelmingly young, the parents choose their children's racial identification on official documents like the Census form, and also help to shape the way that multiracial youth see and identify themselves. Based on the in-depth interviews, we find that while Asian–White and Latino–White couples recognize and identify their children as multiracial or multiethnic, they feel that their children will soon adopt a White or American identity, regardless of how hard they may try to instill a multiracial or multiethnic culture and identity. Black intermarried couples, however, feel differently. While interracial Black couples also recognize the multiracial backgrounds of their children, they are more likely to identify their children as Black—in part, they claim, because others identify them as such.

The divergent patterns of racial identification among these couples indicate that the assimilative power of intermarriage operates differently for Blacks than it does for Asians or Latinos. The assimilative power of intermarriage operates so strongly for the children of Asian–White and Latino–White couples that most identify and are identified by others as White and/or American. By contrast, the children of Black interracial couples are much more likely to adopt a Black racial identity, suggesting that these couples appear to be traversing a different pathway, and more specifically, incorporating into a racialized, minority status. The interviews illustrate that when marrying across the color line, interracial Black couples are the least likely, least able, and/or least willing to transfer a non-Black identity and status to their children.

In addition, the Asian and Latino multiracials articulate that their racial and ethnic status holds little consequence in their daily lives, and stress the symbolic and expressive nature of their Asian and Latino ethnicities. They celebrate their ethnicities through occasional cultural practices such as eating ethnic foods including tamales, rice cakes, and sushi, and enjoying the specific cultural traditions associated with ethnic holidays such as using chopsticks and breaking open piñatas. Like European, White ethnics, these multiracials can feel ethnic without being ethnic, reflecting the voluntary and situational character of their Asian and Latino ancestries. In many respects, Asian-White and Latino-White multiracials are similar to American Indian multiracials whose racial status exemplify racial fluidity and choice (Eschbach 1995; Eschbach et al., 1998), and also resemble White ethnic Americans in the way that they express and celebrate their ethnic identities (Alba 1990; Gans 1979; Waters 1990). Hence, based on these findings, Asian and Latino multiracials are much closer to Whites than to Blacks at this point in time, pointing to a pattern of Black exceptionalism in race relations.

Why does Black exceptionalism persist, even amidst the country's new racial and ethnic diversity? It persists because the legacy of slavery and the legacy of immigration are two competing (and strangely symbiotic) mythologies on which the United States was founded. If immigration represents the optimistic side of the country's past and future, slavery and its aftermath is an indelible stain in our nation's collective memory. Moreover, the desire to overlook the legacy of slavery becomes a reason to reinforce the country's immigrant origins. That Asians and Latinos are largely immigrants or the children of immigrants means that their understanding of race and the color line are born out of an entirely different experience and narrative from that of African Americans.

Hence, despite the increased diversity, race is not declining in significance, nor is the color line disappearing. However, diversity *is* helping to erode group boundaries. States that are more racially diverse—including California, New York, New Jersey, Illinois, Texas, and Florida (plus the District of Columbia)—exhibit the highest rates of intermarriage and multiracial reporting, revealing the positive effects of diversity on breaking down racial barriers, especially for Asians and Latinos (Lee and Bean, 2010).

However, what is disheartening is that even in these new diversity states, patterns of Black exceptionalism continue to persist. So while diversity helps to break down some color lines, it does not break down all, and despite the increase in intermarriage and multiracial identification among Blacks, individual boundary crossing does not lead to boundary change at the group level, as it does for Asians and Latinos. That we continue to find a pattern of Black exceptionalism and the emergence of a Black–non-Black color line—even in the most racially and ethnically diverse parts of the country—indicates that we are far from a "post-racial" society and instead points to the paradox of diversity in the twenty-first century.

References

Alba, Richard (1990). *Ethnic Identity: The Transformation of White America.* New Haven, CT: Yale University Press.

Alba, Richard (2009). *Blurring the Color Line: The New Chance for a More Integrated America.* Cambridge, MA: Harvard University Press.

Bean, Frank D. and Gillian Stevens (2003). *America's Newcomers and the Dynamics of Diversity.* New York: Russell Sage Foundation.

DaCosta, Kimberly McClain (2007). *Making Multiracials: State, Family, and Market in the Redrawing of the Color Line.* Stanford, CA: Stanford University Press.

Davis, F. James (1991/2001). *Who Is Black? One Nation's Definition.* University Park, PA: The Pennsylvania State University Press.

Davis, Kingsley (1941). Intermarriage in Caste Societies. *American Anthropologist,* 43(3): 376–396.

Edmonston, Barry, Sharon M. Lee, and Jeffrey S. Passel (2002). Recent Trends in Intermarriage and Immigration and their Effects on the Future Racial Composition of the U.S. Population. In J. Perlmann and M. C. Waters (Eds.), *The New Race Question: How the Census Counts Multiracial Individuals,* pp. 227–255. New York: Russell Sage Foundation.

Eschbach, Karl (1995). The Enduring and Vanishing American Indian: American Indian Population Growth and Intermarriage in 1990. *Ethnic and Racial Studies,* 18(1): 89–108.

Eschbach, Karl and Christina Gomez (1998). Choosing Hispanic Identity: Ethnic Identity Switching among Respondents to High School and Beyond. *Social Science Quarterly,* 79(1): 74–90.

Eschbach, Karl, Khalil Supple, and Matthew Snipp (1998). Changes in Racial Identification and the Educational Attainment of American Indians, 1970–1990. *Demography,* 35(1): 35–43.

Farley, Reynolds (2004). Identifying with Multiple Races: A Social Movement That Succeeded but Failed? In Maria Krysan and Amanda E. Lewis (Eds.), *The Changing Terrain of Race and Ethnicity,* pp. 123–148. New York: Russell Sage Foundation.

Foner, Nancy (2005). *In A New Land: A Comparative View of Immigration.* New York: New York University Press.

Foner, Nancy and George M. Fredrickson (2004). *Not Just Black and White: Historical and Contemporary Perspectives on Immigration, Race, and Ethnicity in the United States.* New York: Russell Sage Foundation.

Funderburg, Lise (1994). *Black, White, Other: Biracial Americans Talk About Race and Identity.* New York: William Morrow and Company.

Gans, Herbert J. (1979). Symbolic Ethnicity: The Future of Ethnic Groups and Cultures in America. *Ethnic and Racial Studies,* 2(1): 1–20.

Gans, Herbert J. (1999). The Possibility of a New Racial Hierarchy in the Twenty-First Century United States. In Michele Lamont (Ed.), *The Cultural Territories of Race: Black and White Boundaries,* pp. 371–390. Chicago, IL and New York: University of Chicago Press and Russell Sage Foundation.

Glazer, Nathan (1997). *We Are All Multiculturalists Now.* Cambridge, MA: Harvard University Press.

Haney-Lopez, Ian (1996). *White by Law: The Legal Construction of Race.* New York: New York University Press.

Harris, David and Jeremiah Sim (2002). Who is Multiracial? Assessing the Complexity of Lived Race. *American Sociological Review,* 67(4): 614–627.

Hollinger, David A. (2003). Amalgamation and Hypodescent: The Question of Ethnoracial Mixture in the History of the United States. *American Historical Review,* 108(5): 1363–1390.

Hollinger, David A. (2008). Obama, The Instability of Color Lines, and the Promise of a Postethnic Future. *Callaloo,* 31(4): 1033–1037.

Humes, Karen R., Nicolas A. Jones, and Roberto R. Ramirez (2011). *Overview of Race and Hispanic Origin: 2010.* U.S. Department of Commerce Economics and Statistics Administration: U.S. Census Bureau.

Jacoby, Tamar (2001). An End to Counting Race? *Commentary,* 111, 6(June): 37–40.

Jiménez, Tomás (2010). *Replenished Ethnicity: Mexican Americans, Immigration, and Identity.* Berkeley, CA: University of California Press.

Kalmijn, Matthijs (1998). Intermarriage and Homogamy: Causes, Patterns, Trends. *Annual Review of Sociology,* 23: 395–421.

Kennedy, Randall (2003). *Interracial Intimacies: Sex, Marriage, Identity, and Adoption.* New York: Pantheon Books.

Kennedy, Randall (2011). *The Persistence of the Color Line: Racial Politics and the Obama Presidency.* New York: Pantheon.

Korgen, Kathleen O. (1998). *From Black to Biracial: Transforming Racial Identity Among Americans.* Westport, CT: Praeger.

Lee, Jennifer and Frank D. Bean (2004). America's Changing Color Lines: Immigration, Race/Ethnicity, and Multiracial Identification. *Annual Review of Sociology,* 30: 221–242.

Lee, Jennifer and Frank D. Bean (2007). Reinventing the Color Line: Immigration and America's New Racial/Ethnic Divide. *Social Forces,* 86(2): 561–586.

Lee, Jennifer and Frank D. Bean (2010). *The Diversity Paradox: Immigration and the Color Line in 21st Century America.* New York: Russell Sage Foundation.

Lee, Jennifer and Min Zhou (2004). *Asian American Youth: Culture, Identity, and Ethnicity.* New York: Routledge.

Lee, Sharon M. and Barry Edmonston (2005). New Marriages, New Families: U.S. Racial and Hispanic Intermarriage. *Population Bulletin,* 60(2): 1–36.

Lee, Taeku (2011). Post-Racial and Pan-Racial Politics. *Daedalus,* 140(2): 136–150.

Loewen, James (1971). *The Mississippi Chinese: Between Black and White.* Cambridge, MA: Harvard University Press.

Loveman, Mara and Jeronimo O. Muniz (2007). How Puerto Rico Became White: Boundary Dynamics and Inter-Census Reclassification. *American Sociological Review,* 72: 915–939.

Loving v. Virginia (1967). 388 U.S. 1.

Moran, Rachel F. (2001). *Interracial Intimacy: The Regulation of Race and Romance.* Chicago, IL: University of Chicago Press.

Nagel, Joane (1994). Constructing Ethnicity: Creating and Recreating Ethnic Identity and Culture. *Social Problems*, 41(1): 152–176.

Nagourney, Adam (2008). Obama Elected President as Racial Barrier Falls. *New York Times*, November 5. http://www.nytimes.com/2008/11/05/us/politics/05elect.html?pagewanted=all& (accessed November 8, 2011).

Nobles, Melissa (2000). *Shades of Citizenship: Race and the Census in Modern Politics.* Palo Alto, CA: Stanford University Press.

Okamura, Jonathan (1981). Situational Ethnicity. *Ethnic and Racial Studies*, 4: 452–465.

Passel, Jeffrey, S., Wendy Wang, and Paul Taylor (2010). *Marrying Out: One-in-Seven New U.S. Marriages Is Interracial or Interethnic.* Pew Research Center: A Social and Democratic Trends Report.

Patterson, Orlando (1997). *The Ordeal of Integration: Progress and Resentment in America's "Racial" Crises.* Washington, DC: Counterpoint Press.

Perlmann, Joel and Mary C. Waters (2004). Intermarriage Then and Now: Race, Generation, and the Changing Meaning of Marriage. In N. Foner and G. M. Fredrickson (Eds.), *Not Just Black and White: Historical and Contemporary Perspectives on Immigration, Race, and Ethnicity in the United States*, pp. 262–277. New York: Russell Sage Foundation.

Plessy v. Ferguson (1896). 163 U.S. 537.

Qian, Zhenchao and Daniel T. Lichter (2007). Social Boundaries and Marital Assimilation: Interpreting Trends in Racial and Ethnic Intermarriage. *American Sociological Review*, 72(1): 68–94.

Rodríguez, Clara E. and Hector Cordero-Guzman (1992). Placing Race in Context. *Ethnic and Racial Studies*, 15(4): 523–542.

Rodriguez, Gregory (2007). *Mongrels, Bastards, Orphans, and Vagabonds: Mexican Immigration and the Future of Race in America.* New York: Pantheon Books.

Romano, Renee (2003). *Race Mixing: Black–White Marriage in Postwar America.* Cambridge, MA: Harvard University Press.

Roth, Wendy D. (2005). The End of the One-Drop Rule? Labeling of Multiracial Children in Black Intermarriages. *Sociological Forum*, 20(1): 35–67.

Ruggles, Steven, Matthew Sobek, Trent Alexander, Catherine A. Fitch, Ronald Goeken, Patricia Kelly Hall, Miriam King, and Chad Ronnander (2009). Integrated Public Use Microdata Series: Version 4.0 @machine-readable database#. Minneapolis, MN: Minnesota Population Center @producer and distributor#.

Saenz, Rogelio and Benigno E. Aguirre (1991). The Dynamics of Mexican Ethnic Identity. *Ethnic Groups*, 9: 17–32.

Saenz, Rogelio, Sean-Shong Hwang, Benigno E. Aguirre, and Robert N. Anderson (1995). Persistence and Change in Asian Identity Among Children of Intermarried Couples. *Sociological Perspectives*, 38(2): 175–194.

Sears, David O., Mingying Fu, P. J. Henry, and Kerra Bui (2003). The Origins and Persistence of Ethnic Identity among the 'New Immigrant' Groups. *Social Psychology Quarterly*, 66(4): 419–437.

Stephan, Cookie White and Walter G. Stephan (1989). After Intermarriage: Ethnic Identity Among Mixed-Heritage Japanese-Americans and Hispanics. *Journal of Marriage and the Family*, 51: 507–519.

Tafoya, Sonya M., Hans Johnson, and Laura E. Hill (2005). Who Chooses to Choose Two? In R. Farley and J. Haaga (Eds.), *The American People: Census 2000*, pp. 332–351. New York: Russell Sage Foundation.

Tizard, Barbara and Ann Phoenix (1993). *Black, White or Mixed Race? Race and Racism in the Lives of Young People of Mixed Parentage.* New York: Routledge.

Waters, Mary C. (1990). *Ethnic Options: Choosing Identities in America.* Berkeley, CA: University of California Press.

Waters, Mary C. (1999). *Black Identities: West Indian Immigrant Dreams and American Realities.* New York and Cambridge, MA: Russell Sage Foundation; Harvard University Press.

Wilson, Anne (1981). In Between: The Mother in the Interracial Family. *New Community*, 9: 208–215.

Xie, Yu and Kimberly Goyette (1997). The Racial Identification of Biracial Children with One Asian Parent: Evidence from the 1990 Census. *Social Forces*, 76(2): 547–570.

Zhou, Min and Jennifer Lee (2007). Becoming Ethnic or Becoming American? Reflecting on the Divergent Pathways to Social Mobility and Assimilation among the New Second Generation. *Du Bois Review: Social Science Research on Race*, 4(1): 189–205.

Glossary

Acculturation: The process of cultural adaptation that takes place after the arrival of immigrants to a host country as immigrants learn and reproduce the cultural traits and characteristics that are typical of the host society

Assimilation: The gradual process of incorporation whereby immigrants and their descendants adopt the cultural and social practices of the host country over time and generations

Colonialism: The establishment of a colony of settlers in a country by a political power from another country for the conquest, exploitation, and control of land and goods from that occupied territory

Color-blind racism: The dominant ideology, discourse, and practice of race relations in the contemporary United States. It explains and justifies persistent racial inequality and racism as the consequence of factors other than racism or racial oppression. For example, there is substantial evidence that racial residential segregation exists due to the persistence of racist patterns and practices by realtors, home owners, banks and lenders; yet, a widely held color-blind explanation rests on the notion that racial residential segregation exists because members of different racial groups prefer or choose to live with their own kind.

Colorism: A system of skin-tone stratification and discrimination usually practiced by members of a racial or ethnic minority group whereby light-skinned members gain unjust rewards in income, education, housing, interpersonal relationships and the like over their dark-skinned counterparts

Controlling images: Stereotypical representations of subordinate groups held by the mainstream or dominant group that justify or explain oppression and inequality (e.g., the welfare queen)

Critical race theory: A theoretical framework or paradigm that is often used in disciplinary areas of law, education, and social sciences that centers race as an organizing principle and system of power and domination in society vis-à-vis racism

Cross-racial: Inter-group process or activity that occurs between individuals, groups, or organizations that represent the interests of two or more racial groups

Deviant: A behavior or practice that disrupts and violates social norms, such as engaging in a criminal act

Discrimination: Unfair treatment directed at members of a racial/ethnic minority group based on their race/ethnicity

Diversity: A concept capturing different groupings of people along the lines of race, class, gender, sexual orientation, often acknowledging the value of tolerating, respecting, or celebrating those differences

DREAMers: Unauthorized immigrants who meet certain conditions, including time of arrival, age, and residency requirements, that allow them to qualify for the Development, Relief, and Education for Alien Minors (DREAM) Act

Ethnic identity: A socially constructed identity that signals participation and belonging to a particular ethnic group

Ethnicity: A socially constructed grouping of individuals who share in common certain cultural characteristics and features associated with that group, including language, religion, food, national origin, and ancestry

First generation (education): A college student who is the first member in the family to attend a college or a university

First generation (immigrant): A group of people who migrate from one country to settle in another country; the foreign-born, immigrant generation

Hyper-criminalization: The expansion of the criminal justice system into mainstream institutions in the public and private spheres that labels or perceives Black and Latina/o youth as criminals or prone to criminality

Illegality: The feelings of fear and shame undocumented immigrants experience as they navigate the physical and social terrain of exclusion associated with being undocumented

Immigrant entrepreneurship: An economic activity comprising immigrants, often ethnic minorities, who engage in self-employment or small business ownership in the receiving/host country

Indigenous people: Nondominant groups in a society that retain a historical continuity with precolonial/pre-settler societies associated with a specific territory. Indigenous people possess distinct social, economic, and political systems as well as distinct languages, cultures, and beliefs.

Individual racism: The beliefs, practices, and structures that lead people to treat individuals differently based on race

Institutional racism: Racism as a structural force that takes place at the macro level and conditions unequal treatment based on race (academic tracking in schools, predatory lending in banking, redlining in housing, etc.)

Interracial marriage; interracial relationships: Intimate relationships, like dating or marriage, involving two people who belong to different racial groups. Interracial marriage was legalized across the entire United States as of 1967

Intersectional mobilization: Individuals who identify with multiple, marginalized subgroups and who engage in high levels of activism and commitment based on those identities

Intersectionality: A concept that captures the ways in which multiple dimensions of identity and collectivity, such as race, class, and gender, are rooted in larger systems of privilege and oppression and shape social and economic outcomes

Legitimized racism: Racist actions, discourses, or institutions that are not deemed racist, but rather, seem right, reasonable, ordinary and/or without malice (e.g., sports teams with racist names or mascots)

Mass deportation: The extreme rate and rapid expansion of the forced removals of undocumented immigrants, especially Black and Latina/o migrants, from the United States and returning them to their country of origin

Mass imprisonment; mass incarceration: The extreme rate and rapid expansion of the prison population in the contemporary United States

Minority culture of mobility: A toolkit of cultural elements that middle-class minorities employ to mediate interracial conflicts that they are more likely to confront due to their presence in predominately White spaces and interclass conflicts with their working-class or poor minority counterparts

Mixed-race: A socially constructed group of individuals recognized as sharing a similar background or ancestry of two or more races

Multiracial identity: A socially constructed individual or group identity made up of two or more races

Panethnic identity; panethnicity: A social group classification or identity comprised of multiple ethnic subgroups that collectively are perceived to share certain characteristics and features. *Panethnicity* is sometimes used in place of or interchangeably with *race*, especially in research that connects its emergence or salience with political action or mobilization.

Phenotype: Observed physical characteristics of an individual that are rooted in ancestry, such as eye color, hair texture, or skin color

Postracial: An uncritical understanding of U.S. race relations that emerged in the post–civil rights period that embraces the notion that racism no longer exists (e.g., Barack Obama, the first Black president of the United States, could only be elected in a postracial era)

Prison industrial complex: The nexus of government and industry that coincides with the current state of mass incarceration to foster the development of prison-related businesses and agencies, including the construction of prisons

Race as a social construct; social construction: The social construction of race captures the notion that the concept of *race*, or a given society's understanding or meaning of race (i.e., as a social category made up of certain biological or hereditary traits and features that shape individual identity and group belonging), is created and reproduced by society

Race: The socially constructed idea that humans can be divided into hierarchically organized groups based on perceived innate superior and inferior biological and cultural traits and features

Racial formation: The social and historical process that shapes what race means, how it is reproduced, and how its meaning can change over time and place

Racial hierarchy: An unequal system of stratification that organizes racial groups vertically based on perceived notions of superiority and inferiority, with the superior group at the top, the inferior group at the bottom, and other groups positioned in between. In the United States, the racial hierarchy is often described as Whites on top, Blacks on the bottom, and Asians, Latinas/os, and other non-White/non-Black racial groups in between.

Racialization: A process that ascribes meaning, behaviors, practices, and relationships to individuals or groups based on socially constructed racial or ethnic identities, with consequential and unequal social and economic outcomes

Racialized science; scientific racism: The use of scientific methods and techniques—including empirical, observable, and measureable evidence—to lend the veneer of credibility and reason to explain and justify White supremacy, racial inequality, and racism

Racialized social system: A society in which social, economic, political, and cultural positions and outcomes are partially structured by the hierarchical placement of individuals or groupings of individuals into racial categories or races; the totality of racialized social relations and practices that constitute the racial structure of a society

Racism: The beliefs, practices, and structures that lead to individual, group, and structural differences in treatment based on race

Rightist social movements: A group-based collective action by individuals or organizations focused on ultraconservative political or social issues rooted in far-right ideologies (e.g., extreme nationalism)

Second generation: This category of identity and belonging refers to the U.S.-born children of immigrants who arrived to the United States post-1965, after immigration policy reforms increased the numbers of immigrants arriving from Africa, Asia, the Caribbean, and Latin America

Segmented assimilation: Segmented assimilation theory refers to a contemporary assimilation framework that captures three different trajectories of incorporation among post-1965 immigrants and their descendants: Anglo conformity, ethnic cohesion or delayed assimilation, and downward assimilation

Stereotype; stereotyping: A preconceived, oversimplified, and prejudicial image or belief about members of a racial or ethnic group that is widespread and often generalized to all members of that group

Undocumented immigrant: A foreign-born person who migrates from one country to another in violation of that receiving country's immigration laws (and so does not have a legal right to be or remain in that country)

White colorism: Colorism that is practiced by Whites against racial or ethnic minority group members